Whatever you do,
don't try to overthrow
the "System"
all alone.

I have always tried to do
the little that I could
to advance Freedom's Banner
a little closer to its goal.

Don't waste any time
mourning—Organize!

Carlos Cortez: Joe Hill poster (linocut, 1973)

JOE HILL

The IWW & the Making of a Revolutionary Workingclass Counterculture

Second Edition

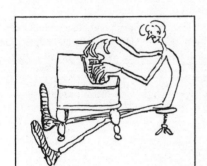

Franklin Rosemont
Introduction by David Roediger

Charles H. Kerr Library

PM Press

BTL

2015

Joe Hill: The IWW & the Making of a Revolutionary Workingclass Counterculture, Second Edition
Franklin Rosemont

© PM Press 2015

Introduction © David Roediger 2015

PM Press	C.H. Kerr Company
PO Box 23912	1726 Jarvis Avenue
Oakland, CA 94623	Chicago, IL 60626
www.pmpress.org	www.charleshkerr.com

Cover design by Josh MacPhee

ISBN: 978-1-62963-119-6 • Library of Congress Control Number: 2015930903

This edition first published in Canada in 2015 by Between the Lines
401 Richmond Street West, Studio 277, Toronto, Ontario, M5V 3A8, Canada
1-800-718-7201
www.btlbooks.com

Every reasonable effort has been made to identify copyright holders. Between the Lines would be pleased to have any errors or omissions brought to its attention.

Library and Archives Canada Cataloguing in Publication

Rosemont, Franklin, author
    Joe Hill : the IWW & the making of a revolutionary working class counterculture / Franklin Rosemont.

Co-published by: PM Press.
Reprint. Originally published: Chicago, Il. : C.H. Kerr Pub., 2003, c2002.
Includes bibliographical references and index.
Issued in print and electronic formats.
ISBN 978-1-77113-233-6 (paperback).--ISBN 978-1-77113-234-3 (epub).—
ISBN 978-1-77113-235-0 (pdf)

    1. Hill, Joe, 1879-1915. 2. Industrial Workers of the World--History.
3. Working class--United States--History. 4. Labor movement--United
States--History. I. Title.

HD8073.H55R68 2015	331.88'60973	C2015-903801-4
		C2015-903802-2

ISBN 978-1-77113-233-6	Between the Lines paperback
ISBN 978-1-77113-234-3	Between the Lines epub
ISBN 978-1-77113-235-0	Between the Lines pdf

10 9 8 7 6 5 4 3 2 1

Printed in the USA by the Employee Owners of Thomson-Shore in Dexter, Michigan.
www.thomsonshore.com

To
ARCHIE GREEN,
the Shakespeare & Hegel of
laborlore,

and to the memory of
Joe Hill's friends:

WILLIAM CHANCE,
ALEXANDER MACKAY,
LOUIS MOREAU,
& SAM MURRAY,
Wobblies true-blue.

"Human emancipation
remains the only cause
worth serving."
—André Breton—

All for One & One for All!

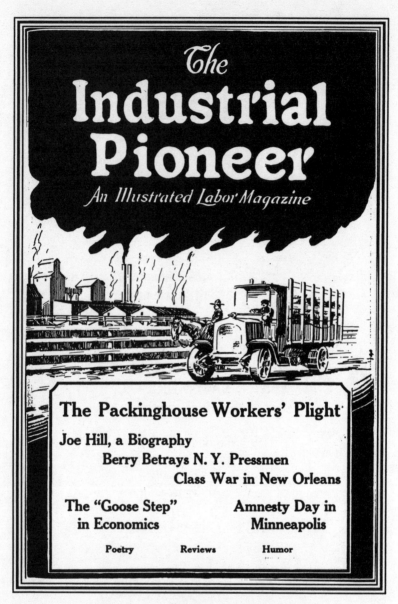

The Industrial Pioneer

An Illustrated Labor Magazine

The Packinghouse Workers' Plight

Joe Hill, a Biography

Berry Betrays N. Y. Pressmen

Class War in New Orleans

The "Goose Step"
in Economics

Amnesty Day in
Minneapolis

Poetry   Reviews   Humor

The first biography of Joe Hill, by Ralph Chaplin,
appeared in this 1923 IWW magazine

TABLE OF CONTENTS

JOE HILL'S ARTWORK
(in order of appearance in this book)

1 (p. 62). Cover of *IWW Songs* (Los Angeles edition, 1912), probably designed and lettered by Joe Hill, who edited the volume.
2 (83). "How the Memory Doth Linger" (sketch of Sam Murray) (1915).
3 (94). Cover design, sheet music for "A Trip to Honolulu" (1915).
4 (159). "Cataract." Oil painting (pre-1902).
5 (161). "I've Got a Mission to Fill" (self-portrait).Hand-drawn postcard (29 April 1911).
6 (164). "As It Was, As It Is." *One Big Union Monthly* (November 1919).
7 (166). "Class War News: IWW Submarines Are Annoying the Enemy Everywhere." *Industrial Solidarity* (24 October 1914).
8 (168). "Oh you Hoboing." Hand-drawn postcard (2 September 1911).
9 (169). "Mr and Mrs Highbrow." *One Big Union Monthly* (November 1919).
10 (195). "Constitutional Guarantee." *Industrial Worker* (24 April 1913).
11 (197). "Doings of Våran Kalle." Hand-drawn postcard (24 January 1911).
12 (258). "Aerogram—'Help! Help! We've Hit Something!'" Cartoon for *IWW Songs* (Los Angeles edition, 1912).
13 (272). Cover art, sheet music for "The Rebel Girl" (1915).
14 (292). Cover art, sheet music for "Workers of the World, Awaken!" (1915).
15 (305). "Merry Xmas and Then Some." Hand-drawn and colored postcard (18 December 1911).

A NOTE ON THE NOTES

Rather than clutter an already ample volume with another hundred-plus pages of notes, I have used throughout a variant method of citation. Basic references —citing author, year of publication, and page numbers—are included in the text itself, often but not always in brackets. Further details (*e.g.*, title and publisher) can be found in the Bibliography in the back of the book. Thus the bracketed notation [Adamic 1932, 247-249] refers the reader to the exact page of a book or article by Adamic published in 1932. In many cases author, title, year of publication are all supplied in the actual text, and only the page numbers are in brackets; for example: "In the modern labor movement," as Pat Read noted in the July 1937 *One Big Union Monthly*, "the IWW alone has made a systematic attempt to popularize the songs of the struggle" [21].

Two exceptions should be noted. It seemed confusing, when quoting Joe Hill's own letters, to cite Foner, editor of a volume of these letters; I have therefore simply cited the source as *Letters*, followed by page numbers. Similarly, the volume of printed proceedings of the IWW's Founding Convention, which has neither author nor editor, is cited as *Proceedings 1905*, followed by page numbers.

In quoting letters or interviews, names of the writer and addressee, or interviewer and interviewee, as well as the date (when known) are provided in the text; a corresponding sub-section of the Bibliography notes the libraries or private collections in which these letters and interviews are housed. The few actual endnotes—at the end of chapters—are mostly elaborations of points made in the text.

Introduction to the 2015 Edition

For me, the three greatest works in workingclass history to appear since E.P. Thompson's *The Making of the English Working Class* are Walter Rodney's *The History of the Guyanese Working People*, Peter Linebaugh and Marcus Rediker's *The Many-Headed Hydra*, and Franklin Rosemont's *Joe Hill*. They share a sense of their own creation that makes it clear that each is a collective work, drawing on the energies and expertise of other scholars and the breakthroughs generated by social movements. As Rodney wrote in the preface to another of his classic works, *How Europe Underdeveloped Africa*, "I will not add that 'all mistakes and shortcomings are entirely my responsibility.' That is sheer bourgeois subjectivism. Responsibility in matters of these sorts is always collective, especially with regard to the remedying of shortcomings." Or as Franklin put it in closing this book, "A couple hundred people, in many and varied ways, kept offering good ideas and information, and helped me to write [*Joe Hill*]."

Picked up in the dark, *Joe Hill* would feel about like *The Making of the English Working Class* or, to take an even more monumental example, W.E.B. Du Bois's *Black Reconstruction*. Nearing seven hundred pages, even with the notes streamlined, it has to be long to make room for poetry, the form in which both Du Bois and Rosemont close their masterworks. There needs to be wide room for art too, not just the Joe Hill cartoons here published together for the first time but also the beautiful further illustrations that establish their context and suggest their legacies. Nowhere else has Hill's music been explored from so many angles, as in the extended discussion of the phrase "pie in the sky" in Franklin's section on Hill's song "The Preacher and the Slave." The book needs space for Sweden, Mexico, the United States, Canada, and even Hill's short stint working in Hawaii. Franklin had given sustained advice to J. Anthony Lukas, the prizewinning journalist, during the writing of *Big Trouble* (1997), a story of the IWW and the law in Idaho, pitched nearly as broadly as *Joe Hill*. So there was a precedent.

When Franklin raised the possibility of this book, I was on the Charles H. Kerr editorial collective and he projected it at about a hundred pages, including the fifteen cartoons and other Hill artworks that were to be its focus. In a striking example of what the novelist Ishmael Reed called the "Jes Grew" virus, it multiplied by adding everything fascinating that abutted, extended, and succeeded its topic. Franklin's own passionate interest in the Earth First!/IWW alliance, his anti-racist and anti-apartheid activism over many decades, and his exposure to a whole new group of women surrealists after the 1998 publication of Penelope Rosemont's *Surrealist Women* informed grounded, wandering, and unexpected explorations regarding Hill and wilderness, white supremacy, and feminism. Franklin's surrealism informed every line, but especially the keen interest in Hill's humor.

Given his appreciation of how exemplary Hill's life was, it is remarkable how careful the book is not to claim too much. Franklin faced a problem not too different from the one I faced in the same years as I was writing about the IWW poet Covington Hall. If Hall were not, as literary friends endlessly pointed out to me, a great poet, Hill's artwork was also, well . . . artless. Franklin cheerfully acknowledged as much, helped by surrealism's longstanding refusals to canonize and rank creative works or to denounce or romanticize "naive" styles. Hill's scribbling—Franklin was also very much a scribbler, often drawing during meetings—could be taken for what it was, another chance to, in Hill's own words, "live like an artist." Drawing was part of thinking poetically in the broadest surrealist sense, one encompassing creativity and revolt in general. Franklin's observation that Hill approached songwriting with a cartoonist's perspective is especially arresting in this regard, calling to mind C.L.R. James's high praises for Herman Melville's *Moby Dick* as a classic whose scenes could easily become a comic strip.

Joe Hill likewise refuses to make its subject great, in the sense of towering, supermanish, and sainted, where life and labor politics were concerned. Franklin insists, for example, that Hill was not a riveting soapbox speaker. He speaks instead to Hill's stature as the embodying greatness of the rank-and-filer, the fellow worker. In the same way that the real is not denied but surpassed in surrealist thought and practice, the extraordinary figure of Joe Hill proceeds from his still being an ordinary worker, made new but not perfected by the movements that he helped to build.

Perhaps the areas of the book on which Franklin most sought my feedback were the sections on racism. Both of us identified with a line from Paul Buhle that Franklin quotes in closing the book—namely that those seeking to finding new ways of solidarity "inevitably return" to the IWW. In showing why that is so, *Joe Hill* recapitulates stories of Wobblies of color, of refusals to accept color bars, of the ways Hill and fellow workers supported and were inspired by the Mexican Revolution, and of the union's lonely stance against Chinese exclusion. But beyond formal stances and initiatives Franklin suggests what it meant to develop a dissenting world view, able to challenge hierarchies of race as well as class.

As in much of his work, questions of Native American examples for settler radicals are much emphasized. The concrete examples of IWW/native solidarity in the book are important but so too are the ways in which IWWs realized that they lived in the presence of dispossession and of indigenous rejection of forms of capitalist property. The brilliant chapter raising the question "Where and how did Hill learn the art of Chinese cooking?" is perhaps the most challenging in the book, forcing us to think beyond formal declarations in deciding what counts as a break from racism.

In *Joe Hill*, Franklin saw no need to think of even the best of the workers' movement as perfect where race was concerned. Especially in his discussion of racist language—albeit from the mouth of a character who was a reprobate—in the Hill song "Scissor Bill" and the absence of African American and anti-racist music in the numberless editions of the IWW's *Little Red*

Song Book, Franklin argues for the fullest disclosure of what the IWW did and perhaps could not do. Indeed the whole book is both a carefully measured and wildly enthusiastic praise song and a testimony to how much is left for us to do. It is just what we need.

David Roediger

JOE HILL

The IWW & the Making of a Revolutionary Workingclass Counterculture

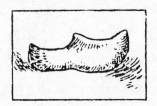

Joe Hill (photograph, 1914)

INTRODUCTION

TROUBADOUR OF DISCONTENT

Illuminate the past by the future.
—**Jean François Paul de Gondi,**
Cardinal de Retz—

Joe Hill is one of the most admired, best hated, and least known figures in U.S. history. His name is familiar to millions, but the story of his life is largely lost in mist and shadow. Now you see him, now you don't. Phantomlike, he eludes all attempts to get a firm grip on him. Questions about Hill outnumber answers a thousand to one.

By all accounts shy, quiet and modest, he rarely talked or wrote about himself. Even when he was the most publicized political prisoner in the country he airily dismissed a request for biographical information by saying that he was "born on a planet called the Earth" and considered himself a "citizen of the world" [*Letters*, 59].

For historians and biographers, Joe Hill is the Invisible Man. Next to him, B. Traven and Thomas Pynchon are as public as talk-show hosts and rock stars. Whole years of Hill's biography are completely blank. Of other years, all we know is that X says he saw him in Seattle, or Y received a card from him, postmarked Cleveland. As with other hoboes before and since, his comings and goings went largely unnoticed, and that's the way he wanted it. Our chance of tracing them today is slim indeed.

And yet, as laborlorist Archie Green observed as long ago as 1960: "More has been written about Joe Hill—novel, drama, poem, essay—than about any other labor hero" [210]. Novels, plays, poems and essays about Hill have continued to multiply since then, along with films, videos, slide-shows, internet appearances, and recordings galore, not to mention posters, postcards, postage stamps, paperweights, bumper-stickers, calendars, t-shirts, and an impressive array of accoutrements, from buttons and badges to book-bags and belt-buckles.

Such publicity is impressive, but Hill remains stubbornly with the well-known unknowns. In this odd combination of obscurity and fame, he is comparable to many other figures in U.S. history, from the pirate Jean Lafitte to bluesman Robert Johnson, whose

1

conflicting myths vastly outweigh the scanty verifiable data about them. Disagreements about Hill, however, were fierce from the start, and have maintained a remarkably high intensity ever since. This intensity, suggesting that the life and death of Joe Hill the individual involve larger life-and-death social issues that remain unresolved, has also served to keep him at a distance, and in semi-darkness. Shrouded in legends concocted by worshipful admirers and venomous detractors, Hill is one of those who simply "cannot be reached." All but a few facts about his life are hotly disputed. Like other workingclass heroes, long before his death he was automatically declared a villain by upholders of the system of inequality known as capitalism. After his arrest and frame-up in Salt Lake City in 1914, Utah newspapers reviled him as a "brute": "callous," "hardened," and "inflammatory." Eugene V. Debs, however—the most beloved and celebrated socialist in U.S. history—openly admired Hill's "poetic temperament" along with his "tender, sympathetic, and generous nature" [Debs 1990, 184].

The abundance of such irreconcilable testimony, aggravated by a shortage of ascertainable facts, has helped shape the literature on Hill. Novels about him usually stress what their authors regard as his "ambiguity": the "half crook, half saint" portrayed by James Stevens in *Big Jim Turner* (1948), and carried to excess—on the "crook" side—by Wallace Stegner in *The Preacher and the Slave* (1950). Lack of documentation always makes it easier for rumor, gossip, fiction, and cynicism to fill the gaps.

The "official," or "mainstream," or "ruling class" view of Hill is itself an example of ambiguity. For conservatives, following the lead of the Salt Lake City press, Hill remains a thorough scoundrel and arch-criminal, justly convicted by a jury of his peers. The corporate liberal view tends to acknowledge that Hill's trial was far from fair, and was indeed hideously biased, but that Hill was "probably guilty" anyway. Such are the extremes of opinion one may expect to encounter in the *New York Times*, *The New Republic*, *The Nation*, and academic journals, as well as on "public" radio and TV. With rare exceptions, those who consider themselves "molders of public opinion" have never cared a lot for Joe Hill.

The popular image of Hill is radically different, and a good illustration of the abyss that separates rulers from ruled in the Land of the Dollar. As is the case with many other personalities and incidents having to do with workers' struggles, it owes a lot to oral tradition, passed down from one generation to the next via the immemorial "grapevine" of song and story. Like the "official" image, the popular one is largely made up of legend, but here the legend is clearly a highly magnified and colorfully embroidered version of the view of Hill set forth by his friends and fellow workers.

And so it came to pass that Joe Hill entered mass consciousness—as a "real" historic figure, but even more as a folk hero and *symbol*: a multi-faceted symbol of the downtrodden rising in revolt. In the light of poet Jean Toomer's observation (1931) that "A symbol is as useful to the spirit as a tool is to the hand," it is clear that Hill's symbolic life has been unusually salutary in this respect. Like freedom and solidarity, Joe Hill is one and indivisible, but as a symbol, dynamic and protean, he has represented many different elements in humankind's long, hard struggle against Leviathan. In the popular imagination he continues to exemplify the ill-treated immigrant, the homeless poor, the wandering hobo, the worker who dares to resist tyranny, the brave nonconformist, the persecuted social outcast, the political prisoner, the wage-slave in revolt against the master class, the frame-up victim wrongfully convicted and put to death, and hence, a martyr to the Cause of Labor. Many know him above all as the author of the great rallying cry of the dispossessed: "Don't mourn, organize!"

As the IWW poet/artist Carlos Cortez observed some years ago, the "folk" who keep the memory of folk heroes alive do so because they feel strong bonds of sympathy with the lives of these heroes; they *identify* with them and regard them almost as family, with real and undying affection. Fortunately, however, like his mysterious contemporary, the French alchemist Fulcanelli—whose biography has also proved impossible to reconstruct—Hill survives not only as legend and symbol, but also in his *living works*. For Joe Hill is above all the workingclass poet and vagabond songster—the writer of songs to rouse the slaves, deflate the boss, and sound the tocsin of social revolution. His wonderful parodies of musty old hymns and platitudinous pop tunes are his greatest legacy; continuously in print for several generations, and translated into many languages, they are still sung today by working people everywhere, and by many others who share the hope that inequality and oppression will yet be overcome. The author of "Workers of the World, Awaken!" is not only a first-class American folk hero, but also a world-class international folk hero.

Many decades after a Utah firing squad ended his life, Joe Hill

3

remains a figure of heated controversy. The Cause for which he lived and died—*workingclass emancipation*, also known as the *abolition of wage-slavery*—is still the *sine qua non* of a free and egalitarian society. The class war continues, more intensely than ever, and as long as it lasts people will argue for and against Joe Hill and the principles he courageously upheld to the end.

To pretend to write "objectively" about Hill, therefore, is already to take sides against him. For my part, I readily avow myself Hill's partisan. The splendid dream he sought to realize—the creation of a truly free society, without classes, exploitation, government, cops, jails, or other violence and misery—is my dream, too.

It seems to me, however, that the best way to defend Joe Hill is to seek the truth about him, to question the many legends, and to *resist* the legends that appear to have no foundation. In exploring subjects of real complexity, oversimplification is always a dead end. Opening up new knowledge about Hill clearly requires re-examining what we already know about him from new perspectives, and looking more closely at seeming "trifles" that have thus far been overlooked.

This book is intended as a fresh look at America's most renowned workingclass poet and the revolutionary union he came to symbolize. It is by no means a "complete" life of Hill—a sheer impossibility, on the face of it—but I have re-examined the essential elements of his biography, fragmented and full of gaps though they are, and I hope to have clarified at least a few of the foggier episodes in the story. Besides bringing to light certain details of his life not heretofore recorded, or recorded only in publications so obscure that other commentators have missed them, I have put new emphasis on other details previously noted in the literature only in passing—such as Hill's adventures beyond the borders of the U.S. (in Mexico, Canada, and Hawaii), and his association with the group around the Charles H. Kerr Company and its journal, the *International Socialist Review*.

In a more speculative vein, I have explored Hill's attitude toward race, gender, law, crime, religion, the arts, and nature. I am concerned with the many facets of the Wobbly bard's life and deeds—as social critic and dreamer, as a man of ideas and imagination, as artist and humorist, as revolutionary and man of action, and as an active influence on several generations of labor activists and revolutionists. For despite the persistent "homespun" and "cracker barrel" characterization of Hill, he was in fact a workingclass intellectual—a wage-slave, yes, but also a thinker.

I have also examined the many contradictory legends that have grown up around the little that is really known about Hill's life, attempting to find the nuggets of truth that have lain buried deep in the tall tales. More particularly, I have challenged much of the "conventional wisdom" regarding Hill, and rejected some long-cherished but unfounded presumptions.

Similarly, in the light of new evidence, I have attempted to reassess Hill's influence—on the Industrial Workers of the World in particular and on American radicalism more generally, as well as his and the union's ongoing influence in the realm of culture: in poetry, fiction, and the arts. Inevitably, this is also very much a book on the IWW—Joe Hill's union—and the extraordinary counterculture it created. The concluding chapter discusses the provocative presence of Joe Hill and his union in the life of our own time, and—with that presence still very much in mind—considers the role of poetry, creativity, and humor in renewing the dream and reality of social revolution today.

Two features of this book distinguish it from all other writings on Hill. First, to a much greater degree than has hitherto been the case with Hill researchers, I have drawn on reminiscences and comments by Hill's friends and fellow workers—and to some extent friends of his friends. Particularly valuable in this regard have been the scattered letters and other writings and interviews, published and unpublished, of Alexander MacKay and Sam Murray, who knew Hill in his San Pedro years; Louis Moreau, who knew him in British Columbia during the Fraser River Strike; and Richard Brazier, who was writing IWW songs several years before Joe Hill appeared on the scene, and who, though he never actually met Hill, knew many fellow workers who knew him well.

I first heard these names—MacKay, Murray, Moreau, and Brazier—years ago, in my teens, from Chicago IWW Branch old-timers who invariably spoke of them with the greatest respect, and it has been a singular pleasure to get to know them better by reading their published writings and unpublished correspondence. Other researchers have used some of these sources and occasionally paraphrased or quoted from them. In addition to drawing on them far more extensively, I have also preferred to quote them in their own words, sometimes at length. It seems to me that this is as close as any of us are going to get to hearing the actual voices of Joe Hill's friends.

Second, I have introduced an important but heretofore ignored dimension of Hill's life: his work as a *cartoonist*—a drawer of pictures to make workers laugh and think and act. Several writers have mentioned his cartoons, but few have done more than mention them, and no one has ever discussed them in detail, or speculated on their relation to his other activities. It seems to me a strange oversight. The fact that Hill was a creator not only in words and music, but also in the visual arts—drawing, painting, watercolor, and lettering—adds new and vital substance to our all-too-shadowy image of the man. Like his songs, Joe Hill's cartoons spark the laughter of revolt and freedom. They also expand our awareness of the critical role of humor in his overall outlook as a hobo and revolutionary.

Collected here for the first time, these cartoons offer us a whole new approach to the man and his work. Of course there is much in these drawings to remind us of the songs and letters: the same biting sarcasm, flair for juxtaposition, and uproarious scorn for "things-as-they-are." But there is also much that is new: a lighter, gently ironic tone in some, a blacker mood in others, a delightful self-portrait playing the piano, a sketch from memory of a friend from the Mexican Revolution, and even a hand-drawn Christmas card—a joyous celebration of music and dancing.

For those who have never seen them, Joe Hill's cartoons and other artwork will prove to be a real revelation.

My insistence on the importance of Hill's cartooning, and my efforts to relate this slighted aspect of his work to the many other facets of his life, reflect the larger purpose behind this book: to present a truer, fuller portrayal of "The Man Who Never Died" and his living, growing legacy.

With the guidance of Hill's old friends, I have tried to get beyond the competing superficial caricatures fostered by malicious novelists, badly informed journalists, complacent historians, and naive hero-worshipers. I have attempted instead, with what success the reader will judge, to see Joe Hill as those who knew him best saw him: neither as hard-hearted hoodlum nor as candidate for sainthood, but as poet, songwriter, artist, hobo, revolutionist, dreamer, thinker, humorist, highly respected friend, fellow worker, and exemplar of a workingclass counterculture that continues to embody our greatest hopes for the future.

Chicago, Bastille Day, 2002

I
JOE HILL & HIS UNION

1. THE ABC OF THE IWW:
REVOLUTIONARY INDUSTRIAL UNIONISM

*In everything we do we must begin by creating an image
of what society must one day make a reality.*
—Piet Mondrian—

lthough Joe Hill was a member of the Industrial Workers of
the World (IWW) only for the last five or six years of his
life, those years happen to be—precisely—the years in
which a young and undistinguished Swedish immigrant hobo
became the man we know as Joe Hill. All that Joe Hill was honored for in his own time, and all that he is honored for today,
appears under the sign of those three red letters: IWW. If, then, as
the old saying goes, one can judge a man by the company he keeps,
it is essential to understand this union to which Joe Hill not only
belonged, but which, in effect, made him who he was and is.

Every student of U.S. labor history knows that the Industrial
Workers of the World (commonly called Wobblies) has a character, and even a kind of aura, all its own. Mainstream trade union
history tends to focus on collective bargaining, negotiations, contracts, arbitration, scales of prices, pension plans and other so-called benefits, but Wobbly history is so different that whole volumes have been devoted to it without even mentioning such mundane topics. From the start, the IWW refused to sign contracts with
employers, and scorned pensions, insurance, and death benefits as
pitiable concessions to a decaying social order. In writing about the
IWW the key words are always freedom, solidarity, democracy,
direct action, revolution, rank-and-file control, humor, imagination,
and "An Injury to One Is An Injury to All!"

Founded in Chicago in 1905, the IWW concentrated on organizing workers that the American Federation of Labor (AFL) considered "unorganizable" or undesirable—the unskilled, immigrants, people of color, and migratory workers in agriculture, lumber, and construction. As William "Big Bill" Haywood put it at the
founding convention, "We are going down into the gutter to get at
the mass of workers and bring them up to a decent plane of living"
[*Proceedings* 1905, 575]. With high enthusiasm and low dues, the

IWW set about its work and accomplished marvels.

The great IWW strikes were not merely routine work-stop-pages, and were not settled by a handful of union officials with their lawyers sitting across the table from a handful of bosses and more lawyers. Like the union's no less celebrated free-speech fights, Wobbly strikes were small-scale revolutions, exciting class-war dramas involving whole communities, massive social confron-tations between the repressive machinery of an old society based on exploitation and a new, truly free society that required the active, creative participation of everyone. Asked "Who is your leader?" striking Wobs characteristically replied: "We're *all* lead-ers!" Asked for their demands, they were known to answer: "We demand *everything*!"

The famous IWW Preamble—beginning with the sun-clear statement that "The working class and the employing class have nothing in common"—distilled the complete works of Karl Marx to their revolutionary essence. To my mind that 306-word mani-festo sets forth what is still the soundest basis for the creation of what Wobblies themselves liked to call "a better world." Many IWW members also belonged to the Socialist Party—especially prior to 1912, when the party's conservative leadership expelled Bill Haywood over the question of "sabotage"—and their respect and love for Gene Debs (minor disagreements notwithstanding) held steady over the years. The SP's large left wing was in fact made up almost entirely of IWWs and supporters of the IWW; it distinguished itself from the Party's right and center by its empha-sis on direct action and revolution rather than reform.

Clearly, however, Wobbly theory and practice also had "noth-ing in common" with the cold, harsh, bureaucratic "lay-down-the-law" monotone adopted by so many of those who then as now proclaim themselves revolutionary socialists or Marxists. The "One Big Union" always spoke in many voices. If the Preamble is raw, unadulterated Marx—some of it direct quotation—the Wob-bly idea also owes a lot to the pre-Civil-War Abolitionist move-ment, and to the extravagant utopian imagination of Edward Bel-lamy, not only the Bellamy of *Looking Backward*, but also its anarchist, feminist, ecology- and animal-rights-oriented sequel, *Equality* [Rosemont 1988, in Patai 1988]. Poets such as Shelley and William Morris and Walt Whitman also influenced IWW thinking. Similarly, the union's genial and creative praxis owes much to the boisterous "let's-do-it-now" spontaneity of Coxey's Army, and even more to the Haymarket anarchists' broad-based proto-syndicalism—the "Chicago Idea" [Salerno 1989]. Like Marx, Wendell Phillips, Bellamy, Morris, and the Haymarket Eight, the IWW looked forward to a future without slavery, exploitation, bosses, armies, navies, prisons, or other institutions of inequality, coercion, and violence.

Above all, however, the IWW's basic ideas and its conception of the free society were developed in the course of its founders' own widely varied experience as wage-slaves in a rapidly industrializing North America as well as in Europe and other lands, for a large portion of the union's membership, from the very beginning, were immigrants.

Their experience of old-line craft unionism and its obvious failure to adapt to the new industrial conditions was especially compelling. As U.S. capitalist production grew larger, more complex, and more centralized, workers of many distinct trades were reduced to tiny cogs in a huge industrial machine. Divided into myriad craft unions, each bargaining separately with a single employer, and often in competition with other unions, workers found it more and more difficult to practice class solidarity. When workers of one AFL union went on strike, members of dozens of other AFL unions in the same plant customarily crossed the picket-line and remained on the job, in deference to the contracts their officers had negotiated with the employer. More often than not this meant breaking the strike. In the eyes of the IWW, the traditional problem of "scabs"—unorganized workers willing to work for less than union scale—shrank to insignificance compared to the new problem of *union* scabs who put contracts and craft-union privileges above loyalty to the working class. And that is why in Wobbly discourse the AFL was commonly called the American *Separation* of Labor. Vincent St John, the best-loved official in IWW history—he was known throughout the union as The Saint—summed up the problem of the union scab in his pamphlet, *Industrial Unionism*: "Division on the economic field for the worker spells defeat and degradation" [n.d., 6].

This radical critique of archaic, business-as-usual craft unionism led directly to the key IWW theory of "revolutionary industrial unionism," as summarized in the Preamble. Between the working class and the employing class, the Preamble explains, a struggle must go on until the workers of the world organize as a class, take possession of the earth and the machinery of production, and abolish the wage system.

We find that the centering of management in industries into fewer and fewer hands makes the trade unions unable to cope with the ever growing power of the employing class. The trade unions foster a state of affairs which allows one set of workers to be pitted against another set of workers in the same industry, thereby helping defeat one another in wage wars. . . .

These conditions can be changed and the interest of the working class upheld only by an organization formed in such a way that all its members in any one industry, or in all industries if necessary, cease work whenever a strike or lockout is on in any department thereof. . . .

By organizing industrially we are forming the structure of the new society within the shell of the old.

Clearly a workingclass response to the various middle-class versions of Marxism, socialism and anarchism that held sway in left-wing and trade-union circles in those years, revolutionary industrial unionism was the IWW's practical answer to the question: How can we, the workers, free ourselves from wage-slavery and begin to enjoy the wealth that we have created? Dozens of IWW books and pamphlets were devoted to explaining, defending, and elaborating this bold, new, emancipatory unionism. One of the most popular of all IWW pamphlets, Vincent St John's *The IWW: Its History, Structure and Methods*, stressed the no-compromise character of the class war:

The IWW holds that, regardless of the bravery and spirit the workers may show, if they are compelled to fight with old methods and out of date forms of organization against the modern organization of the employing class, there can be but one outcome to any struggle waged under these conditions—defeat.

The IWW recognizes the need of working class solidarity. To achieve this it proposes the recognition of the Class Struggle as the basic principle of the organization. . . . In its basic principle the IWW calls forth that spirit of revolt and resistance that is so necessary a part of the equipment of any organization of the workers in their struggle for economic independence. In a word, its basic principle makes the IWW a fighting organization. It commits the union to an unceasing struggle against the private ownership and control of industry.

There is but one bargain that the IWW will make with the employing class—COMPLETE SURRENDER OF ALL CONTROL OF INDUSTRY TO THE ORGANIZED WORK-ERS. [revised edition, 1919, 12]

From a perspective that combined evolution and revolution, James P. Thompson, one of the IWW's top organizers and orators, put the accent on the development of *workers' power*:

the old society is pregnant with the new. The powers that rule the world today will never surrender to a weaker power. Clearly the thing to do is to build the power of organized labor. . . . Reformers try to patch up capitalism. Reactionaries try to roll back the wheels of history. Revolutionists build the new within the shell of the old.

Capitalism is rapidly spreading over the Earth, but the coming of the modern world is the coming of the proletariat. . . When the organized power of the proletariat becomes greater than the organized power of other classes, then will come the revolution! [1930, 11-12]

And there we have the guiding idea of revolutionary industrial unionism: to give Labor a form of organization that would make it invincible in the struggle against Capital.

The One Big Union was not, however, built in a day, although expectations ran high. The delegates who founded the union in 1905, and the many tens of thousands who rallied to its scarlet banner straight through to the early '20s, were convinced that it would not take long—surely no more than ten or fifteen years. Well within their own lifetime, the first generation of IWWs were certain, the workers of the world would be sufficiently organized to wrest the industries from the usurping capitalists, and thus to usher in the earthly paradise.

This sense, or mood, of revolutionary anticipation—grounded in the wildly voluntarist conviction that revolutionary industrial unionism made the New Society more or less immediately real-izable—was an important element in the IWW movement. Naively or sneeringly, many critics of the union have concluded that IWWism is a form of millenarianism, and it is not hard to see how they arrived at such a view. If so, however, it was a decidedly materialistic and anti-religious millenarianism.

The organization of industrial unions proceeded slowly, but the

IWW continued to grow anyway. Prior to the First World War, most of the membership belonged to the "Mixed Locals"—*i.e.*, locals without ties to any particular shop or industry [Salerno 1989, 7-8]. The Mixed Local was not part of the original industrial union structure adopted at the Founding Convention, but was introduced at the second convention (1906) to accommodate workers who were eager to join despite the fact that they were unemployed, or insufficiently numerous to form an industrial union. The Mixed Locals brought together employed men, women, and children, as well as unemployed and migratory workers. Their form of organization and activities differed widely from place to place, but always allowed for a maximum of rank-and-file initiative and improvisation. Although they did not function as labor unions, they played a vital role in the union's early history, supplying all manner of footloose rebels, agitators, and other reinforcements to IWW struggles everywhere. The militants who filled the streets and then the jails during the union's celebrated Free-Speech Fights, and who flocked to Lawrence, Massachusetts in 1912 just to lend a hand, were members of Mixed Locals. These locals were also a crucial factor in every IWW defense campaign.

From 1915 to 1923, actual industrial unions came to predominate in the IWW, and showed the world how powerful wage-slaves could be when organized front door to back on industrial lines. Wobbly industrial unions, however, were a real power only in a few industries (above all agriculture, lumber, metal mining, and marine transport, and to a lesser extent construction, railroads, and hotel/restaurant work); only in a few areas of the country; and, with some notable exceptions, only for a short time. In the '20s, the Mixed Local made a comeback under the name General Recruiting Union, and once again became the basic unit of the IWW.

In Joe Hill's time, the One Big Union consisted primarily of small Mixed Locals. These informal groups of rebel workers had little or no job power and little or no money. All they had were songs, poems, imagination, determination, solidarity, a revolutionary vision of the world, and a remarkable ability to organize and make their presence known all out of proportion to their numbers.

2. CONFLICTING VIEWS OF IWW HISTORY

I sing these songs for a damn good reason.
I sing them because they give me a history of our people
that I never got in school.
—Utah Phillips—

T he IWW's theory and practice—its revolutionary industrial unionism, its direct-action and "point of production" orientation, its efforts to organize "One Big Union of All Workers," its wide-open Mixed Locals, and its diverse and manysided oppositional culture—have generally been viewed with condescension as well as incomprehension by academic historians, many of whom have merely echoed the hostility of the union's early political critics and opponents. History by and large is written by the victors, and few will dispute the sad fact that so far the capitalist class has proved victorious in the class war. It therefore comes as no surprise that the most readily available histories of the finest labor organization in U.S. history have been written by people openly unsympathetic to its aims and principles.

Nearly a century after its formation, the IWW remains as controversial as ever. Critics often dismiss or damn the union for its unequivocally revolutionary stance, its "dual unionism," its non-participation in electoral politics, or its alleged inability to establish permanent job-control in major industries. Others damn it with faint praise as a rustic avant-courier of the 1930s Congress of Industrial Organizations (CIO), or for having added a few songs to the folk-music repertory. Literature on the union—historical, sociological, cultural, polemical, and fictional—is not at all in short supply, but it is as bloated with contradictions, disagreements, and divergent interpretations as the literature on Christianity, or Atlantis, or Marilyn Monroe. The serious student in search of the truth about the IWW is guaranteed not to have an easy time of it.

Amazingly, after all these years, there is still nothing even faintly resembling a comprehensive and reliable history of the union. The book most frequently misidentified as such, Melvyn Dubofsky's 575-page *We Shall Be All: A History of the IWW*, is probably the single most cited work in subsequent writings on the union. Published in 1969, it is a readable narrative survey of the IWW's early years; a second edition appeared in 1974, and a new abridged version in 2000. Unfortunately, it is so woefully wrongheaded that it would take a book twice as long to set it right. In a full-page review in the *Industrial Worker* for November 1969, Fred Thompson, for reasons of space, had to limit himself to noting only thirty-seven of what he termed Dubofsky's most "horrendous errors" of commission and omission. In one howler that Thompson didn't mention, Dubofsky refers to "Marxist-Leninist" influence in the IWW as early as 1914, before the term had even gained currency in Russia [352]. Elsewhere he attributes the concluding lines of Shelley's famous poem "The Mask of Anarchy" to IWW organizer Edward F. Doree [153].

Aside from Dubofsky's careless disregard for facts, the book also suffers from a bewildering clutter of middle-class prejudices and pretentious academic conceits. For example: By borrowing Oscar M. Lewis's dubious concept of the "culture of poverty" as one of his "main organizing themes," Dubofsky added nothing but useless fat to what was already an ideologically overweight tome. Amusingly, less than four years after the book appeared, Dubofsky himself came to recognize how hopelessly inept Lewis's notion was, and felt obliged to repudiate it formally in the preface to the 1974 paperback edition [v-vi].

Worse yet is Dubofsky's contention (one of the "two lessons" he hoped to put over in his book) that by shortening the workday, raising wages, and improving job conditions, the IWW only pushed back the "prospect for revolution," and thus in effect defeated its own aims. In his *Industrial Worker* review, Fred Thompson roundly denounced this odious bit of anti-workingclass obfuscation.

Worst of all, Dubofsky ends his history in 1918, thereby obscuring the crucial fact that, despite the corporation-inspired U.S. government terrorism against it, the IWW continued to grow—and to grow mightily—throughout the next five years (the union reached its all-time peak membership in 1923-24). How, then, did Dubofsky arrive at the arbitrary year of 1918 as his cut-off date? My guess is that, like many bourgeois historians before and after him, he simply accepted at face-value the Communist Party's tendentious perspective in this regard. Since the early 1920s, CP propagandists, in book after book and pamphlet after pamphlet, have smugly pretended that, once the Party was in the field, the IWW's heyday was automatically over.

The legend that the IWW "collapsed" or was "crushed" during or immediately after World War I persists to this day in bourgeois as well as Communist-Party-oriented histories. The best refutations of this ideologically motivated misconception can be found in abundance throughout the press of the IWW's competitors of those days—critics who saw the union forging ahead despite the persecution. The *Butte Daily Bulletin*, for example—owned jointly by the Electrical Workers, Blacksmiths, and Typographical Unions— was frequently antagonistic toward the IWW, but nonetheless had to admit, in 1920, that

> The IWW organization does not die. It is stronger today in the great lumber woods behind Centralia than it ever was before. Throughout the whole northwest the tragedy here strengthened the Wobbly movement; it revealed to the multitude of casual workers how bitter the feeling was against their solidarity. [17 Apr]

As if to drive the point home, the same paper three weeks later reported that 15,000 lumberjacks attended an IWW picnic in Seattle [6 May]. Does that sound like the group Dubofsky describes as "unable to maintain a vital role in American radicalism" [467]?

In its overall grasp of the issues as well as in matters of fact, Fred Thompson's in-house history, *The IWW: Its First Fifty Years* (1955; reissued with supplements in 1976 as *The IWW: Its First Seventy Years*), is much superior to Dubofsky's study. Unfortunately, as Fellow Worker Thompson himself conceded, his book is much "too cramped" to do justice to its subject. In its 200 pages, many major strikes, free-speech fights, and defense campaigns are treated in a line or two; many more are not mentioned at all. Thompson's book confirms what should be obvious: The epic story of the IWW cannot be told well in a short work. It needs lots of space—not only for background, development, and the big picture, but also for the multitude of indispensable details, asides, and digressions which alone can give a historical narrative the spark of life and a vibrant actuality.

Predictably, academic historians have mostly followed Dubofsky rather than Thompson, with the result that we now have a shelf of books and journal articles that repeat each other's mistakes; echo *ad nauseam* the mossgrown criticisms of the IWW made ages ago by such jaundiced enemies as Sam Gompers, Daniel DeLeon and William Z. Foster; and conclude with sickeningly similar sermons to the effect that the IWW was "too revolutionary" for the U.S. and thus a "failure"—colorful, no doubt, and not without a certain charm, but most definitely a failure.

It is only fair to add that there have always been exceptions—historians who, indifferent to academic fads, have found the IWW an attractive subject, researched it with open minds, and gone on not only to make splendid discoveries, but also to affirm the union's contemporary relevance. William Preston, Jr's *Aliens and Dissenters: Federal Suppression of Radicals, 1903-1933* (1963)—focused on the IWW and the U.S. government's war against it—is a true classic: essential reading for anyone interested in the union.

Also unreservedly recommended is Joyce M. Kornbluh's *Rebel Voices: An IWW Anthology* (first published in 1964): a rich collection of Wobbly writings and art—manifestoes, songs, poems, short stories, plays, polemics, and cartoons—with an excellent running historical commentary. No book before or since has captured the "flavor" of the IWW better than *Rebel Voices*. Revised and expanded in 1988, with a new Introduction by Fred Thompson, an essay on IWW cartoons and cartoonists by the present writer, and some three dozen new cartoons and drawings, Kornbluh's anthology remains after nearly forty years the single best book on the subject.

Solidarity Forever: An Oral History of the IWW (1985), edited by Stewart Bird, Dan Georgakas, and Deborah Shaffer, is a volume in much the same vein, with a useful historical introduction and chapter headnotes by Georgakas. Despite some errors in transcribing the tape-recorded interviews, it is an exceptionally valuable source-book: Wobbly history as told by Wobblies.

Yet another important exception among historians is Mark Leier, who, in his admirable study of the IWW in British Columbia, *Where the Fraser River Flows* (1990), subjects the ideological biases of several leading historians of the IWW to a brief but withering critique, and argues that revolutionary industrial unionism was not an "aberration," but rather a "realistic historical alternative" to business unionism, welfare-statism, social democracy, and the many varieties of Marxism-Leninism.

Luckily for us all, historians have not been the only students of IWW history. As a sociologist, Salvatore Salerno, in his *Red November, Black November: Culture and Community in the IWW* (1989), has illuminated many misunderstood aspects of the union's past. In addition to refuting the popular myth that the IWW was "primarily" a product of the American West, he has convincingly shown that the IWW's roots in "Chicago Idea" anarchism were deeper than earlier researchers had supposed, and that immigrants, along with the syndicalist ideas and tactics they brought with them from abroad, were major factors in shaping the union from the start. Salerno also shows that Wobbly cultural politics—its special mix of art, song, humor, and a revolutionary social-economic program, along with the many innovative ways in which the IWW interacted with the larger workingclass community—were not in any sense "peripheral" but rather *central* to the union's activity and goals.

A first-rate, truly comprehensive history of the IWW is yet to be written. It will have to be a multi-volume work, and will require the collaboration of many writers, including several who are fluent in languages other than English. (The neglect of the union's foreign-language locals and publications, as well as IWW activity in other countries, are major defects of most of the existing liter-ature.) Until such a work is compiled, the student has no choice but to make the best of what already exists—good, bad, and indif-ferent. And in that perspective, all contributions to IWW history are welcome, and all are worth reading. Even John S. Gambs's superficial study, *The Decline of the IWW* (1932), right-wing bias and all, includes information not easily accessible elsewhere.

The sensitive reader, however, cannot help but deplore the ignorance, conservatism, lack of imagination, and above all *lack of sympathy for the subject* shown by so many writers of IWW history. Several of them have also revealed a sense of proportion so poor, and a pettiness so pronounced, that one wonders what their real motives could have been. Joseph Conlin, for example, in a skimpy, 165-page sketch of IWW history titled *Bread and Roses Too: Studies of the Wobblies* (1969), oddly felt called upon to devote two and a half pages to a puerile and contumelious account of the Chicago IWW Branch's Solidarity Bookshop and the young workingclass volunteers that kept it going in the mid- and late 1960s [137-39]. As indicated by his chapter title ("It's Not the Same IWW"), Conlin clearly wanted to show that the "old" Wob-blies had no use for the union's younger generation. Dubofsky, too, filled up a couple of pages with similar tripe [1969, 471-472]. Just for the record, here is what Fred Thompson—the most active of all the old-timers in Chicago—had to say at the time on that very subject in an interview with Studs Terkel:

The thing that gives me the most cheer are the young people today. . . . They're the least bookish radicals I've ever known, but the most literate. . . . These . . . kids use books simply for insights. They don't have a dogma. They're far more flexible, far more open-minded, far more feeling. . . . [1970, 330]

Would that one could say the same for academic historians!

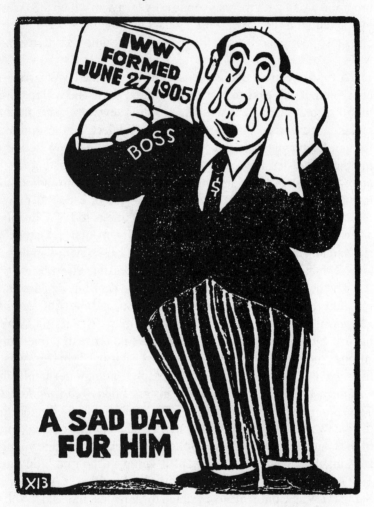

To save the union the expense of photoengraving drawings, Wobbly cartoonist Charles E. Setzer (X13) pioneered in the art of the linoleum block, or linocut—a medium later taken up by the well-known IWW artist Carlos Cortez.

3. THE HOBO CONTRIBUTION
TO CRITICAL THEORY & THE ORIGINS OF THE
WOBBLY COUNTERCULTURE

Without knowing it,
I had opened a window on something else.
—**Marcel Duchamp**—

Rarely did IWWs bother about "isms" and ideological labels: The names "IWW" and (starting around 1913) "Wobbly" were good enough for them. Their response to the notorious hair-splitting of so many sectarian "Marxists" was the rousing song, "Karl Marx's Whiskers Were Sixteen Inches Long." It is a fact, however, that the most inspired and prolific IWW thinkers and pamphleteers—Thomas J. Hagerty, Vincent St John, William Trautmann, Mary E. Marcy, Ben H. Williams, Walker C. Smith, William D. Haywood, Covington Hall, James P. Thompson, J. T. "Red" Doran, Elizabeth Gurley Flynn, E. W. Latchem, Sam Murray, Justus Ebert, J. A. MacDonald, Ralph Chaplin, T-Bone Slim (Matt Valentine Huhta), and a little later, Fred Thompson —were much better Marxists, more rigorous, more radical, and more imaginative than the great majority of the pedantic ideologues who promulgated the dry-as-dust and frequently reactionary platitudes that passed for "theory" in the U.S. Socialist and Communist parties.

Noting that "various sects and parties . . . speak of Marx far more reverently than do the members of the IWW, [and even] make a saint and seer of the man, and a Bible of his writings," Fred Thompson insisted that "you can't put things into practice by making them sacred," and that the "radical politicians" who made Marx a god were not really Marxists at all. Calling the IWW "Marxism in overalls," Thompson concluded boldly that "The only practicing Marxists in America are the IWW" [n.d., c. 1930s, 1].

Sadly, studies and anthologies of American Marxism have tended to ignore IWW Marxism altogether, or to skim over it lightly.[1] Paul Buhle's *Marxism in the U.S.A.*(1987) is something of an exception in this regard. Buhle affirms that IWW Marxism "came the closest to 'pure' Marxism of any American movement" [102]; that revolutionary industrial unionism was "the most internationally recognized theoretical or strategic perspective developed [by Marxists] in the U.S.A." and that it was "also the first American doctrine to win *political* adherents in virtually every large-scale industrial center" [100]. Recognizing the IWW as "a vehicle of the outsiders . . . [of] America's excluded—the foreign-born, un-skilled, Blacks, Asians, the 'timber-beasts,' 'bindle-stiffs' [and] romantics of every ethnic stripe," he goes on to praise Wobbly Marxism's "sophistication" and stresses that the IWW's "zest for worker self-education [was] exceeded by none" [101]. At the same time, Buhle argues that the IWW also "highlighted (made possible really) the awakening of the radical intelligentsia to *its* twentieth-century mission" (103), and credits the union with nothing less than the "formation of a counterculture" (101). The only problem with these sharp-witted and insightful remarks is that they are all too brief, scattered, and undeveloped. Whole chapters of Buhle's book are devoted to the Socialist Party, the Communists, and the New Left; surely the Wobblies merited no less.

By leaving the Wobbly Marxists out, or treating them too sum-marily, and meanwhile exaggerating the role of Communist Party propagandists, historians of U. S. Marxism have unwittingly rein-forced the prevailing anti-Marxist view that Marxism is inherently boring, authoritarian, and statist. Of the major currents in Marxism in this country, only the IWW consistently emphasized freedom, democracy, creativity, self-activity, and self-emancipation.

Despite ample evidence of Wobbly astuteness on the theoret-ical plane, most academic students of the union have perpetuated the Communists' absurd charge that the IWW was "indifferent to theory." The Wobblies' indifference clearly was not to theory, but rather to dogmatic ideological tongue-twisting and hollow, jargon-istic "theorizing" that had no other purpose than to justify bur-eaucracy, opportunism, and class-collaboration.

In the IWW, theory meant a critical examination of social reality, and was basically a way of getting at the truth in order to develop effective strategies and tactics to abolish wage-slavery and to create a free society. For social-democrats, however, and even more so for their Stalinist successors, theory tended to be little more than the manipulation of abstractions and therefore a substi-tute for truth—in other words, a lie, designed to preserve and pro-tect capitalism and the state by "reforming" them. Many individual Communists were of course sincere and courageous workingclass militants, and now and then a few made real contributions to the world of ideas: Louis Fraina and Cyril Briggs, for example, in the early period, and Mary Inman and Claudia Jones in later years. For the most part, however, these heavily bureaucratized political parties inhibited their members' original thought, suppressed their revolutionary impulses, and redirected them to non-revolutionary ends. The Communists' notorious "Popular Front"—a complete capitulation to capitalist politics—is only one glaring example of the ways in which so-called "radicals" have allowed themselves to be used to prop up the existing social order. From such pseudo-Marxists, the working class could learn nothing except how *not* to build a revolutionary movement.

One reason why IWWs were among the finest and most creative Marxists of their time is because they actually read and studied Marx. In hierarchical and multi-class organizations such as the Socialist and Communist parties—divided into "leadership," "intellectuals," and "rank and file"—reading Marx's *Capital* was largely reserved for the upper echelons; the rank and file were supposed to sell the party's paper, attend big rallies, pass out leaflets, and otherwise follow orders. In the egalitarian and rigorously workingclass IWW, education was a high priority for all, and many a workingstiff who did not get past fifth grade in grammar school worked his way through Marx's *magnum opus*—or at least the first volume.

Ironically, Wobbly wisecracks aimed at intellectual phonies may have contributed to the delusion that IWW members had no use for theory. That song about "Karl Marx's Whiskers" could easily be so construed. Charles M. O'Brien, a Canadian member of the Western Federation of Miners who later became a prominent figure in the Proletarian Party, recalls in an unpublished autobiography that his old friend Bill Haywood was fond of saying "I do not know much about Marx's *Capital*, but I carry with me the marks of Capital"—referring to the loss of his right eye in an accident [O'Brien n.d., 95]. Haywood in fact knew his way around in the world of Marxist ideas far better than most of the Socialist Party bigwigs in New York, as is plain to anyone who has taken the trouble to read his articles in the IWW press and the *International Socialist Review*.

And the same is true of many other Wobblies. Writing in October 1902—that is, nearly three years before he helped get the IWW started—Thomas J. Hagerty remarked that he had chanced upon a copy of Marx's *Das Kapital* as far back as 1892:

[and] I read, with illuminating swiftness, the complete answer to the questions which I had partially solved, I thought, by advocating a world-wide, aggressive Labor Union to demand more of the product of the workers. [7]

Fred Thompson, at the age of nineteen in 1919, was giving study classes in Marx's *Capital* to workers in Halifax, Nova Scotia [Thompson 1993, 28-29]. Several years later, confined to San Quentin for the crime of "criminal syndicalism" (*i.e.*, IWW organizing) he reread all three volumes, made summaries of each chapter, and corresponded with the publishers (Charles H. Kerr and Company) about some seeming discrepancies in the second and third volumes [*ibid.*, 76]. More than a few Wobblies learned Marxist theory while serving long prison sentences for such terrible crimes as passing out leaflets or practicing free speech.

From 1928 to 1941 Fellow Worker Thompson taught classes in Marxism at the union's Work People's College in Duluth [*ibid.*, 90]. One of his students there was a young woman of Finnish descent, Jenny Lahti, who joined the IWW in the 1930s, married Fellow Worker Charles Velsek, and became active in the union's Chicago Branch as well as a longtime member of the *Industrial Worker* Expansion Committee. (Around 1960 retiring editor C. E. "Stumpy" Payne urged her to take over the editorship, but she modestly declined.) Interviewed in 1987, Jenny Velsek reminisced about her youthful experience in learning Marxism:

At Work People's College I heard some smart-aleck boys talking about the "point of production" and what happened there. I didn't know what that meant, and I was worried. Then Fred Thompson taught a class on Marxist economics and soon I knew what the "point of production" was—along with the "accumulation of capital" and "commodities" and all the rest.

At first I found Karl Marx much more difficult than physics. When they told me that the value of a commodity was determined by the quantity of labor necessary to produce it, I thought, well, that seems right, but why do we have to get that technical about it? Pretty soon I was getting used to it, though, and after a while I began to think: What a wonderful guy Karl Marx was! And it changed my life—my relations with friends and everything else. [FR interview, 31 Mar]

Another Work People's College student, Jack Parnack, offers

a more detailed view of how the economics class was taught. The students started with Mary Marcy's *Shop Talks on Economics*, and then, after a few weeks, they were

> introduced to the text of Marx's *Capital*. Paragraph by paragraph, chapter by chapter, from "Commodities" to "Modern Theory of Colonization," the first volume of *Capital* was read and digested. At first, by reading in class; then by direct instruction and questions; finally, the whole volume was reviewed, step by step, by interpretive lectures on the text with blackboard demonstrations. [*Industrial Worker*, 15 October 1927]

All over the country, in IWW study classes, open forums, and around the soapbox, Jenny Velsek's and Jack Parnack's experiences were replicated again and again by many thousands of knowledge-seeking Wobblies.

The strongest evidence of the Wobblies' pre-eminence in U.S. Marxist theory is of course to be found in their published writings. The IWW's early pamphlet literature is far and away the finest in the history of the U.S. labor movement, unmatched for its original ideas, forceful criticism, and humor. Interestingly, in this regard, nearly all of the union's outstanding thinkers and pamphleteers were also part of the far left Marxist current centered around Charles H. Kerr's Chicago-based publishing co-op, which from around 1905 through the mid-1920s was the largest publisher of revolutionary literature in the English-speaking world. And like Joe Hill himself, these Wobblies were active collaborators on the Kerr Company's *International Socialist Review*, the leading journal of Marxist theory in the U.S.

Internationally, this Wobbly Marxism, like the Kerr Company's, had marked affinities with the libertarian Marxist Left, often called "ultra-left" by its more conservative critics. In addition to the works of Marx, Engels, and Antonio Labriola, IWWs were particularly attentive to the writings of Marx's genial son-in-law Paul Lafargue, one of revolutionary socialism's greatest humorists and, as Richard Reuss observed years ago, "perhaps the only early Marxist who wrote extensively on folklore topics—especially on songs" [Reuss 1971, 260]. Like the Kerr Company's most original thinkers—Austin Lewis, Mary Marcy, Robert Rives LaMonte, and Charles H. Kerr himself—IWWs were especially close to the Dutch "council communist" current led by poet Herman Gorter and astronomer Anton Pannekoek, and their co-thinkers in Germany: Rosa Luxemburg, Otto Rühle, Karl Korsch, Paul Mattick and others. In the 1920s Mattick came to the U.S. and was for several years active in the IWW and contributed extensively to the union's publications.

Highly critical of what they regarded as bourgeois trade-union-ism and parliamentary politics, this anti-authoritarian Marxism differed significantly from the later and better known Socialist, Communist, Trotskyist and other orthodoxies, not only in its overall heterodoxy and free-spirited open-endedness, but above all in its vastly greater breadth of vision.

Its core principle was *workers' autonomy*—an insistence on maintaining at all times the independence of the working class from the trade-union bureaucracy, electoral politics, and the state. As a union, the IWW scrupulously avoided the sordid "politicking" and vote-hunting that inevitably compromise and corrupt even the sincerest revolutionary party. One of the union's principal co-founders, Thomas J. Hagerty, sounded an anti-parliamentary note at the founding convention:

> The ballot box is simply a capitalist concession. Dropping pieces of paper in a hole in a box never did achieve emancipation for the working class, and to my mind never will. [*Proceedings* 1905, 152]

Similarly, the IWW's solidly workingclass membership, its insistence on low salaries for officials, and its implacably anti-hierarchical, rank-and-file way of doing things, helped shield it from the maneuvers of middle- and upper-class intellectuals, those "condescending saviors" who so easily insinuated themselves into the leadership of all but a few would-be Marxist groups.

Just how different the Wobblies' Marxism was from all other contenders is strikingly evident in their many periodicals. Social-ists, Communists, and Trotskyists published papers *for* work-ers—some of them admittedly of high quality. The IWW, how-ever, always published *workers' papers*: of and by as well as for. They took very seriously Marx's guiding principle, that the eman-cipation of the working class is the task of the workers them-selves.

Credit is due here to the union's mainstays: the migratory workers, better known as hoboes, and not least the hobo intellectuals: those self-taught geniuses who had been everywhere and seen everything, and who were rightly considered the brainiest characters in the whole U. S. labor movement. For sheer grounded-ness in the reality and diversity of workingclass life, these inspired nomads were unsurpassed, and probably for that very reason they also tended to be the movement's most far-sighted visionaries. Most of them were exceptionally well-read in history and the sciences; many were also devoted students of such poets as Blake, Burns, Shelley, Whitman, and William Morris; more than a few were poets themselves.

These learned 'boes often worked jobs that involved far more than the usual amount of creativity—some were tramp printers, for example, or itinerant sign-painters, or circus folk—and tended to have odd skills. Fred Thompson recalled a Wob orator at Bughouse Square who was also an accomplished sword-swallower. And Thompson himself boasted of having been an adept of what he called "the lost art of whistling"; accompanied by a percussionist and/or comb-player, he provided a lively evening's entertainment at many a hobo jungle.

Omnivorous multilingual readers, critical thinkers, highly skilled humorists, and often practicing poets, the Wobbly hoboes elaborated a Marxism that was closer than most to Marx's own —and they knew it, too. In the IWW press, "old Karl" was fre-quently hailed with a hearty familiarity, like a fellow 'bo on the main stem.

Wobbly Marxism was, in short, romantic through and through, and the colorful panorama of ideas that flourished around the union's invariable first principles is reminiscent of Novalis's dream of "the true philosophy" consisting of "freedom and infini-tude, or . . . lack of system brought under a system" [Neubauer 1980, 25].

It was hoboes rather than homeguards who generally served as editors of the IWW's many newspapers and magazines, usually for stints of a year or two between tours of the country, from one Mixed Local to another, via "side-door Pullman" (i.e., boxcar). Most of these brilliant 'boes were also first-class soapboxers, and held forth regularly at strike rallies and street meetings as well as open forums such as Ben Reitman's Hobo College and the Dil Pickle Club in Chicago.

One of the tasks of Wobbly editors was to keep the papers strictly workingclass, and therefore to keep partisan politicking out. The hobo scholars were especially good at this, for most of them—perhaps in part because their wandering ways excluded them from the electoral process—openly *despised* everything having to do with "politicians." Few Wobs, however, thought of themselves as anarchists. Indeed, more than a few—St John, Haywood, Joe Ettor, and Justus Ebert among them—tended to write off anarchists as "freaks" who did more harm than good to the workingclass movement. And yet, Marxists and anarchists alike have always recognized a strong anarchist element in IWW theory and practice: not only because of the union's indifference to bourgeois electioneering, and its hostility toward the machinery of state, but also because of the Wobblies' passionate insistence that "forming the new society" is not a project for the distant morrow, to be postponed until "after the Revolution," but rather a project already in motion, and to be steadfastly pursued, non-stop, right now.

All but a few Wobblies also disavowed the "syndicalist" label. Syndicalist organizations in other countries differed substantially from each other, as well as from the IWW; most, for example, were based on craft rather than industrial unionism. In the 1910s the IWW was closely associated for a time with Tom Mann and the *Industrial Syndicalist* group in England [Brown 1974], and even longer with the French group around *La Vie Ouvrière* (Workers' Life), whose central figures included Pierre Monatte and Alfred Rosmer [Portis 1985, 79]. Later, especially during the 1936-37 Spanish Revolution, the IWW was also close to the Spanish CNT (Confederación naciónal de los trabajadores), largely via Wobblies such as Pat Read and Raymond Galstad who fought in Spain as volunteers in the workers' militia, but also through the CNT's official U.S. representative, the Chicago-based Maximiliano Olay, a frequent contributor to the *One Big Union Monthly*.[2] However, the union's relationship with the CNT's parent body, the anarcho-syndicalist International Workers' Association (IWA), was frequently rancorous, and never close.[3] Almost all syndicalists respected and even admired the IWW, but many also agreed with Rudolf Rocker's assessment that the Wobblies were too Marxist [1989, 137]. Communists, on the other hand, considered them too anarchist.

At bottom, what set Wobs apart from the various isms was not reducible to ideology or structure. Fundamentally anti-authoritarian, open-ended, and focused on revolutionary creativity, the IWW differed not only theoretically and organizationally from other radical and would-be radical groups: Its whole *sensibility* was different. The Socialist Party, Socialist Labor Party, and later the Communist Party were so hierarchical and bureaucratic that individual initiative was largely stifled. U.S. anarchist groups, despite their many virtues, tended to be small, isolated, and ineffective —unable to put large-scale programs into practice. The IWW, on the contrary, was truly informal, wide open, constantly rejuvenated by new energies from the rank and file, and had proved itself time and again capable of mobilizing many thousands of workers in united action.

With its magnificent record of achievements, the extraordinary diversity of views that flourished among its members, and the high place it always accorded to spontaneity, poetry, and humor, the IWW was unique in the history of the labor movement. Much has been made of the union's intricate organizational charts and diagrams, but as a functioning organization it was actually very loose and always receptive to new people and new ideas—more so than any U.S. radical movement until the direct action civil rights movement of the 1960s.

On the local level, especially—that is, in the Mixed Locals —the Wobblies had very little in common with traditional revolutionary parties or trade unions, but in many respects resembled the "free associations" of artists, poets, musicians, and other creative dreamers. Surrealist poet Jehan Mayoux, who was brought up in a prominent anarcho-syndicalist family in France and was himself an active revolutionist throughout his life, left us an organizational profile of the French Surrealist Group that applies equally well to the old-time IWW. The organization he describes is based neither on "belief" nor on "doctrine," but is rather "an open road" [Mayoux 1979,V:202]. It is a group "in which affective links play an important role," but which is "never an aggregation of disciples repeating the words of their masters"; on the contrary, it is "a thinking collectivity in which each individual, according to his/her own means and energies, participates in full equality in the common life of the group" [*ibid.*, 208].[4]

Like many Marxists, some IWWs—Joe Hill included, in his song "Workers of the World, Awaken!"—quoted the old Jesuitical phrase: "the end justifies the means." However, with their unwavering emphasis on workers' *self*-organization, direct action, and point-of-production democracy, Wobblies clearly rejected the militaristic and amoral implications of that notion, and tended to agree with such anarchists as Gustav Landauer and Camillo Berneri, as well as surrealists André Breton and Jehan Mayoux, that a movement's sought-for ends are, to a great degree, shaped by the very strategies and tactics employed to reach them. As Fred Thompson put it in Wobbly terms:

> The good world of tomorrow can only be the elaboration of the means used to bring it about. Developing these means is not merely the goal of the new unionism; it *is* the new unionism. [1969, 21]

This "utopian," "romantic" or "idealistic" dimension, as many "Marxists" have variously derided it, is in truth a basic and vital element in every revolutionary mass movement, and the IWW was not ashamed of it.

In bright contrast to the AFL unions, which were glad to settle for "a Fair Day's Wage for a Fair Day's Work," Wobblies developed a critique not only of the work-ethic, but also of work itself. They recognized that a large part of the work under capitalism —the manufacture of war materials, for example, and the building of new prisons—was stupid, worthless, and even harmful; that the purpose of many jobs was not to serve real human needs but only to make profits or otherwise to increase the power of Capital and the State. While AFL unions and their Socialist (and later Communist) allies were begging the bourgeois politicians for "More Jobs"—any jobs at all—IWWs unrelentingly upheld the old Bellamyist watchword, "Production for Use, Not for Profit," along with Marx's demand for "Abolition of the Wage System."

For the Wobblies, abolishing wage-slavery was always paramount. This does not mean that they rejected ameliorative demands; on the contrary, they were far more aggressive than the so-called "bread and butter" unions in demanding and winning higher pay, shorter hours, and better job conditions. The IWW recognized, however, that real freedom and a good life for all could be attained only by doing away with the inherently exploitative system that robs working people of the wealth they produce. Their focus on this issue is doubtless one reason why so few Wobblies succumbed to the temptations of Stalinism. Numerous tortuous and convoluted arguments flowed from the pens of Communist Party theoreticians to "prove" that the USSR was in fact "communist" or at least "socialist," but Wobblies knew their Marx well enough to know that a system that pays wages and forbids strikes is by definition *capitalist*.

In the IWW view, abolishing wage-slavery meant organizing the work that needed to be done in such a way that it would in essence no longer be work. Once "profits" and "management" —and therefore exploitation—are out of the picture, workers are free to decide what they want to do and how they want to do it. The IWW vision of life in the new society involved the supersession of "work" as we know it. Such views accord well with those of Marx in his brightest moments, but they are much closer to Charles Fourier's theory of "Passional Attraction," and to surrealism, than to any of the leading brands of Marxism. The IWW, in Fred Thompson's words, could be considered

> forerunners of a future in which work and leisure are indis-
> tinguishable purposeful activities, far from inane, self-directed,
> freed from all taint of commodity culture because we work for
> the fun of it and get what we want for free. [1989, 113]

Wobblies knew too much about work to be "workerist." Their constant emphasis on shortening the hours of labor; their defense of "The Right to Be Lazy" (the title of a popular pamphlet by Marx's son-in-law, Paul Lafargue, translated and published by Charles H. Kerr); and even their advocacy of "sabotage," in the original sense of the word—signifying slowdowns on the job and other forms of workplace malingering—suffice to distinguish them from the middle-class Socialist and Communist intellectuals who so often glorified the misery known as work. Compare the depressing Stalinist fantasy of the "happy worker," proudly wearing his Stakhanovite Medal of Honor for working overtime in the torpedo factory, with these joyfully irreverent "Recipes for Health" by the IWW philosopher, T-Bone Slim:

> Do only such work as you like to do—if you don't like your job,
> quit. . . . Do not remain standing too long at a stretch—a tired
> body multiplies weariness. Sit down frequently. . . . Do not work
> too hard. . . . Hurry is unnatural—a form of insanity. . . . Never
> tire yourself out—weariness is the body's protest against over-
> exertion. [1992, 59]

Dreamers with "a new world in their minds," in Federico Arcos's charming phrase, Wobblies were all the better prepared to invent and discover untried ways of making it a reality: the sit-down strike, free-speech fight, every member an organizer, the thousand-mile picketline, organizing the unemployed, etc. [Arcos 1971]. "The way the Wobblies always [found] some new tactic for a new condition," as Walter Rogers put it, was truly a marvel [1945, 85].[5] In Seattle 1919, in the wake of the General Strike, IWW members conceived and carried out an unheard-of kind of street demonstration on the occasion of President Woodrow Wilson's visit to that city. Wilson had arrogantly refused to meet with an IWW delegation regarding the plight of the many hundreds of members who had been imprisoned during and after the war. Aware that the police would fire upon any noisy or disruptive demonstrators, IWWs planned a wholly silent protest. The Presi-dent's procession started with a troop of motorcycle cops and a brass band that played as the nation's chief executive stood up in his open car, smiling and waving at the crowd. For the first mile or so he received loud cheers from the local Democratic machine and the usual crop of gawkers, scissorbills, and pickpockets. And then, as a co-organizer and participant tells it, came the Wobblies and their supporters:

> a block where everything was quiet. Hundreds of grimy working men [and] women stood still and silent on both sides of the street. Not a cheer, not a sound, not a move. Most . . . didn't even look at [Wilson] . . . Only a couple of kids were pushing and yelling here and there, which made the Wobblies' silence and immobility even more terrible. [Wilson] smiled as he came to our block. Then the smile went off his face. . . . He knew that we were IWWs . . . but didn't know what to make of it. He looked flabbergasted. Back there the mob had cheered him till you couldn't hear the music; here these dirty bums didn't even move, but stood like statues, and among them were dozens of ex-soldiers. . . .
>
> [Wilson] continued to stand in the car, but it was obvious that he wanted to sit down. . . . His face looked old and saggy. . . . The car moved on—slowly. Then there was another block of still, silent Wobblies in denim overalls, their arms crossed on their chests, printed hatbands ["Release Political Prisoners!"] on their hats and caps, most of them not looking at Wilson, but straight ahead, past him. Thousands of them. Block after block [for] five blocks. . . .
>
> Afterward we heard that the newspaper men . . . were asked not to play up the demonstration. . . . The *New York Times* saw

30

fit to print only that the IWWs had been "undemonstrative". . .
[Adamic 1932, 247-249]

This sensational demonstration may have been inspired by Shelley's poem, *The Mask of Anarchy*, written exactly a hundred years earlier, in 1819, to protest the massacre of trade unionists in Manchester, England; a stanza near the end of the poem urges

Stand ye calm and resolute,
Like a forest close and mute,
With folded arms and looks which are
Weapons of unvanquished war.
[1961, 344]

The Seattle demonstration is typical of Wobbly audacity and imagination—the union's ability to transcend the "usual" way of doing things by doing something radically different. Think of the IWW as a group that was capable, again and again, of transforming the routine and mundane (a demonstration, a strike, a defense of free speech) into something scandalously new, effective, and unforgettable. In his introduction to the expanded 1988 edition of Joyce Kornbluh's *Rebel Voices*, Fred Thompson pointed out that "Flexibility and innovation have always been the hallmarks of this union" [vii]. In the IWW during its best years, dream and action were a vital dialectical unity.

From such a perspective, no aspect of life could be closed off. The IWW press and its sister publication, the *International Socialist Review*, took up an incredible range of issues that social-democrats and the self-styled American "Bolsheviki" generally considered "peripheral," "trivial," "irrelevant," or worse: birth control, for example, as well as forest preservation, and the problems of air-pollution and urban noise. The Wobblies' receptivity to so many "new tremors" in the intellectual atmosphere of their time, from psychoanalysis to Gandhian Satyagraha,[6] affords a refreshing contrast to the party-line narrowness of its would-be "Marxist" critics. John Lawson's experimental play "Processional" (1925) was denounced by the Communist *Daily Worker* as "Dadaist," but the IWW's *Industrial Pioneer* found it "most certainly worth seeing" [Robbins 1925, 25].

Like the Haymarket anarchists who preceded them, but on a much larger scale, the Wobblies embodied not only a social and

economic revolution but also a revolution in *culture*. Indeed, the
IWW is one of the most important and influential cultural movements in U.S. history. It is no accident that the saga of the One Big
Union is told best in its songs, poetry, plays, soapbox oratory,
diatribes, jokes, cartoons, and other art. As one of the union's earliest songwriters, Richard Brazier, told Archie Green in a 1960
interview:

> In addition to searching for the job, we were also searching for
> something to satisfy our emotional desire for grandeur and
> beauty. After all, we have a concept of beauty too, although we
> were only migratory workers. [42].

In Austin Lewis's brilliant study, *The Militant Proletariat*
(1911)—the first detailed work of Marxist theory directly inspired
by the experience of the IWW—proletarian revolution itself is
viewed as a "means of expression," muffled in the inherently
restrictive framework of the craft union, but eagerly developed in
the new unionism of the IWW.[7]

Far more than any other revolutionary group in the U.S. in the
1910s and '20s, Wobblies *lived* the revolution they dreamed about.
And that is doubtless why they never bothered themselves with
scholastic and jargon-cluttered dogmas regarding the "correct"
relationship between "base" and "superstructure," and why its
many artists and writers were bored or disgusted by the Stalinists'
bureaucratic rubbish known as "socialist realism." In a 1970s essay
on the life and work of IWW poet/organizer Covington Hall,
James Stodder reflected insightfully on the breadth and scope of
the Wobbly counterculture:

> The IWW press . . . is especially impressive for its vitality when
> compared to the artificial, consciously designed culture of the
> Communist Party press in the '30s. In the Wobbly press we find
> poems and polemics by innumerable unknown proletarian
> authors; freewheeling, humorous, and often savage debate on
> every aspect of revolutionary values in the broadest sense; . . .
> individual styles ranging from hard-boiled prole-talk [and]
> lyrical utopianism to surprisingly modernist forms of "insanity"
> suggesting expressionism or surrealism. . . .
>   When one places the record of this luxurious growth beside
> the pre-digested pap of the *Daily Worker*, one knows the
> difference between art and propaganda, freedom and adminis-

tered culture. The brutalized style of Socialist Realism, nearly indistinguishable aesthetically from Nazi art, can best be described as middle-class radicals talking the way they think workers talk and saying what they think workers want to hear. Here art is subjected to the "reason" of the Party, which is the conscious element in history, guiding the masses [who are] presumed incapable of thought. . . .

In the IWW . . . the dichotomy between intellectuals and workers . . . was at least partially healed, not by intellectuals pretending to be workers, but by the attempts of workers to become intellectuals, that is, independent critical thinkers. [n. d., c. 1970s, 18]

The nerve-centers of this IWW counterculture were the hundreds of Wobbly halls all over the U.S. and Canada. Meetingplace, reading room, and hangout—a place to relax without having to eat, drink, or buy anything—every IWW hall was a cultural center in the best sense: the union's revolutionary alternative to such conservative institutions as church, tavern, gambling parlor, race-track, and men's club. In the Wobbly halls Fellow Workers planned new organizing drives and walkouts; wrote poems, songs, leaflets, pamphlets, and articles for the *Industrial Worker*; talked about ideas, books, poetry, history, and problems of the day; and almost every evening, enjoyed good entertainment: music, plays, poetry readings, songfests, and dancing.

The hobo "jungles"—campgrounds, usually in a wooded area close to a railroad water-tank—served a similar function for this floating community. The "jungle," the crowded boxcar *en route* to the harvest, and—best of all—the IWW hall, were all subversive social spaces in which the most down-and-out wage-slaves could express themselves openly, and thus were able to savor a bit of the freedom and dignity denied them in the workplace and Starvation Army soup-kitchen.

Reminiscing about the early 1920s, Fellow Worker Nick Steelink emphasized the role of the halls in workers' education:

The IWW Hall was not a place for telling shady stories, or for relating what some congressman or senator was going to do for the poor, or what a benefactor the successful businessman was, or how bad things would soon get better—none of all that. You talked union, and how to improve yourself to serve the Cause. [n. d., c. 1970s, 230]

Joe Hill

For a good Wobbly, "to improve yourself" meant reading Marx, Kropotkin, and other revolutionary writers; attending IWW lectures and study-classes; participating actively in meetings; discussing the contents of IWW publications; asking questions of better-informed Fellow Workers; and sharing what one has learned with others.

Harvard-educated John Reed was one of many observers who were profoundly affected by the Wobbly halls and the culture that flourished in and around them. Writing in the socialist magazine *Liberator* in September 1918 he noted that

> wherever . . . there is an IWW local, you will find an intellectual center—a place where men read philosophy, economics, the latest plays, novels; where art and poetry are discussed, and international politics. In my native place, Portland, Oregon, the IWW hall was the livest intellectual center in town. [Reed 1972, 217]

Floyd Dell was similarly moved by his visit to an IWW hall in New York City, where

> the history of American labor struggle [could be] learned in many a tale from veterans old and young. . . . Where else but in the "Wobbly" halls could [one] hear talk that was not the talk of money and the things money will buy? [1926a, 162]

Dell goes on to mention a fellow worker at the New York hall "who knew the poetry of Shelley and Blake by heart."

Most of today's academic historians tend to underestimate the IWW as a creative intellectual community, but perceptive observers at the time clearly recognized it at once, and also realized that it was not confined to large urban centers. In 1922, a *St Louis Post-Dispatch* reporter in southern Illinois coal country interviewed Wobbly Ed Wieck and his companion Agnes, "the Mother Jones of Illinois" [Wieck 1992, 79]. Deeply impressed by the "young woman of culture" and her coal miner husband, known to neighbors as the local H. D. Thoreau, the reporter went on to reflect that

> if anybody imagines that a coal miner's family is just that and nothing else, a visit to the Wiecks of Belleville should go a long way toward disproving that notion. Both Mr and Mrs Wieck can "talk" literature and philosophy, and even the modernly popular science of psychology, with a knowledge and insight calculated

to put to shame the cultural pretensions of many persons who live in fine houses and drive the latest models of high-priced cars [*ibid.*].

Workingclass critical thought and creativity were always the heart and soul of this "rebel band of labor." A multicultural and countercultural movement generations before such terms were invented, the IWW distrusted the bourgeois ideology of the "melting pot" and took fierce pride in international proletarian cultural diversity. It is not at all surprising that this One Big Union —which was so much more than a union—attracted, inspired, and nurtured so many poets, artists and musicians.

One of these poets, artists, and musicians was an immigrant hobo named Joel Hägglund, better known as Joe Hill.

---

1. To mention just a few: Mills (1962) focuses exclusively on "world" figures (Marx, Engels, Lenin, Kautsky, Luxemburg, Stalin, Mao, Guevara and others), and notes that "for reasons of convenience and limitation of space" he "deliberately omitted any consideration of anarchism and syndicalism" which "are not now of immediate political significance" (17). Mills's failure to include the IWW is particularly surprising in view of the fact that he is known to have admired the union, and to have referred to his most radical friends as "good Wobblies."

Herreshoff (1967) discusses the IWW only in connection with DeLeon; his brief mentions of Haywood are devoid of substance. Wohlforth (1968) pretends that IWW theory was limited to the Preamble, demonstrating that Trotskyist criticism of the IWW can be as superficial as that of the Stalinists.

2. Many of Olay's articles appeared under pseudonyms: Onofre Dallas, Emilio, Juan Escoto, R. Lamenard, and others. See the biographical sketch in the memorial volume: Olay n. d., *c.*1941, 25-26.

3. See the exchange of letters between the IWA and the IWW in the IWW Archives at Wayne State University Library in Detroit (Box 22, Folder 22).

4. Jehan Mayoux, the son of Marie and François Mayoux, was active as poet, critic, and theorist in the Surrealist Group in France from 1932 until 1967. His *Oeuvres complètes* (five volumes) were published in 1976-79. His best known political essay is probably the preface to the pamphlet co-authored by his friends Benjamin Péret and Grandizo Munis, *Les Syndicats contre la révolution* (Unions Against Revolution), published by Le Terrain vague, Paris 1968).

5. "Walter Rogers" may well be a pseudonym, but the two books published under that name (written in collaboration with Elizabeth Rogers) are autobiographical accounts of a one-time IWW who later joined the Communist Party.

6. See, for example, "Psycho-Analysis in the Revolutionary Movement" by Card No. 747818, *Industrial Worker* (15 January 1921). Sympathetic IWW articles on Gandhi include "Nationalism and Direct Action in India," by "A Hindoo Nationalist" (*Industrial Pioneer*, Aug 1921, 48), and "Mohandas Ghandi [sic] and Soul Force" by "P. D. E." in the October issue of the same publication.

7. Charles H. Kerr called Lewis's book "the most valuable American contribution to the literature of Socialism thus far produced." Typically ignored or mentioned only in passing in U.S. books on the IWW, Lewis has long been recognized as an important Marxist theorist by researchers in Germany, the original home of Marxist theory; see, for example, Bock 1976.

Ralph Chaplin: Portrait of Joe Hill (water-color, 1915)

4. JOE HILL: THE PROBLEM OF BIOGRAPHY

All we know is still infinitely less
than what still remains unknown.
—William Harvey—

More than any other member of the IWW, or for that matter, of the U.S. labor movement, Joe Hill has entered the broader American popular culture, and even world popular culture. Millions who could not name another Wobbly know at least something of the legend of the IWW troubadour, the poet/martyr, "The Man Who Never Died."

As with all true hoboes, however, biographical data on Hill is discouragingly skimpy. A tendency to anonymity and aloofness are common traits of those who live largely "on the road." Richard Brazier—like Hill, an immigrant, Wobbly, hobo, songwriter, and poet—remarked in a 1963 letter to Joyce Kornbluh:

> We Wobblies were very restless men and, as we were mostly migratory workers, were on the move continually. . . . Most of us were only concerned with the present, and our origins and pasts were seldom talked about. We did not inquire into one and another's antecedents. Not that there was anything shameful about them, but it was just that we were more concerned with the things of the moment, the conditions of the day, and how best to confront and change them if we could. [8 Nov]

Every historian of the IWW has had to confront this difficulty. In the course of researching his important 1947 M.A. thesis on "The IWW in California, 1905-1931," Hyman Weintraub interviewed many old-timers, including songwriter Mary Gallagher. In his thesis Weintraub comments:

> In the many interviews I had with [her], she did not once tell me anything of her personal life. Whatever I learned, I gathered either indirectly from what she said or from what others told me. It seemed to be a custom among the IWW not to pry into the personal affairs of the members, and I made no attempt to break this tradition. [284-285]

That Joe Hill belonged to this tradition hardly needs to be stressed. As his good friend Alexander MacKay put it in a letter to the editor of the *Industrial Worker*, Hill was "a most reticent cuss. To drag anything biographical out of Joe was a man-size job" [27 Nov 1947].

A few weeks before he faced the firing squad, when a Swedish friend asked about his life, Hill replied:

> Biography do you say? No! We shall not ruin the fine letter paper in writing such trash. The only time that exists for me is the present. I am a "citizen of the world" and I was born on a planet called the Earth. On which side or edge of this planet I first saw light means so little that it is not worth talking about. . . . I do not have much to say about my own person. I shall only say that I have always tried to do the little that I could to advance Freedom's Banner a little closer to its goal [*Letters*, 59].

Is it possible to write the "biography" of such a person? To even think of doing so, one must dispense with the notion of a "full" biography: the day-by-day, month-by-month, year-by-year chronicle of an individual's life and interaction with many other lives. The "records"of a hobo's life rarely amount to more than a slippery fistful of disjointed fragments.

In Hill's case, of course, exceptional factors intervened, and the fragments are far more numerous than usual. Hill did, after all, have friends and relatives as well as a large number of fellow workers: men who hoboed with him around the country, and/or worked with him on one or more jobs. As he became better and better known—first as IWW poet, and then as IWW poet and class-war prisoner, and finally as IWW poet and class-war martyr—more and more people talked about him, wondered about him, and asked about him, and those who had known him or at least met him came forward with their anecdotes and reminiscences. All in all, he is probably the best-known hobo in U.S. history.

Still, in view of his popularity as a songwriter during his lifetime, and his worldwide posthumous renown, it is puzzling how little solid information about him has come to light. The biographical data we have is small and, for the most part, not very revealing. As an acquaintance of his remarked in 1950:

> [Joe Hill] was front-page news all over the country for more than a year. Any newspaperman in America could have knocked off a nice piece of change by producing an employer who could say, "This man was once on my payroll," or a landlord who could say, "This man slept under my roof," or a woman who could say,

"This man was my lover." [But nothing of the kind ever happened.] You can rest assured that every police record and mugbook in the U.S. was ransacked for anything on Joe Hill [but to no avail]. . . . The Salt Lake City jailers went through his correspondence with microscopes and fine-toothed combs—and found never a line that would give them a lead on his life or activities. [McClintock to Fred Thompson, 9 July 1950]

The first to attempt a biography of Hill was a fellow Wobbly, poet, songwriter, and cartoonist: Ralph Chaplin. His "Joe Hill: A Biography," in the November 1923 issue of the *Industrial Pioneer*, provided the basis for virtually every subsequent sketch until the early 1950s, when a wealth of new information—mostly on Hill's early life—was brought to light by Ture Nerman and other Swedish researchers. Chaplin, admitting that he had "never set eyes on Joe Hill alive," nonetheless was profoundly interested in the "young rebel songwriter," and tried to learn all that he could about him. Convinced that "the saga of an itinerant laborer whose songs were sung all over the world was something worth recording," he "talked with dozens of IWW boys who had shipped out with Joe Hill for various construction jobs around San Pedro" [1948, 184]. Even before Hill's execution, Chaplin "wanted to get that story down on paper" and in print in *Solidarity* and the *International Socialist Review* [*ibid.*].

Information proved scarce, however, until a Wob lake seaman took him to a "little saloon" in Cleveland (a place where "we used to stop for beer and sandwiches after taking *Solidarity* over to the post office") to meet another seaman, who called himself John Holland, and who said he was Joe Hill's cousin [*ibid.*, 184]. This man turned out to be an exceedingly well-informed source on the IWW bard, and Chaplin "got the story" out of him "word by word, drink by drink, and wrote it down in [his] notebook" [*ibid.*, 185].

Chaplin's 1923 biographical sketch was largely based on his interview with John Holland, though it also drew on his talks with other Wobs. Despite its brevity—the article took up only three and a half pages in the *Pioneer*—it remains to this day a key document in the Hill story. During the Cold War years, however, the text was subjected to harsh criticism by two writers who shared an intense dislike for the IWW in general and for Joe Hill in particular: Stanford University English Professor and novelist Wallace Stegner, and folk-music critic John Greenway. Although these critics' allegations were refuted long ago, the dispute itself merits brief re-examination here because it sheds some additional light on the problems of hobo biography.

Stegner, in an article on Hill in the *New Republic*[1]—described by knowledgeable old-timers as "misinformed" (Fred Thompson), "outright falsehood" (George W. Cook), and "careless with the truth" (Meyer Friedkin)[2]—belittled Chaplin's account primarily on the specious grounds that his chief informant was "drunk" [Stegner 1948, 21]. Chaplin had described Holland as "somewhat inebriated," but Stegner preferred the stronger, more emotionally charged term. In his reply—published in the *Industrial Worker* after the *New Republic* suppressed it—Chaplin did not deign to argue at length against such a silly charge, but simply pointed out that

> Holland wasn't drunk in spite of the few drinks we had together in that little Cleveland saloon. How little Stegner knows about seamen to confuse their capacity for convivial libation with that of the modern cocktail drinker. [1948a]

The great bulk of Stegner's other objections could qualify as "Classics of Nitpicking."[3] Here, as a typical example, is his comment on Holland's recollection that Hill had been shot in the leg during the Mexican Revolution:

> the examination made of him at the Utah State penitentiary . . . found scars on neck, face, nose, chest, shoulder, forearm, hand, but no bullet scars on the legs. [Stegner 1947, 186]

Such trivial complaints notwithstanding, Stegner did reluctantly admit that—"subject to some correction in detail"—"we must accept Holland's documentation except where it conflicts with the known facts" [Stegner 1948, 21]. Later we shall examine just what Stegner meant by "known facts."

Greenway, for his part, relied heavily on Stegner, but his concluding comment on Chaplin's biography was even more belligerent:

> That [Chaplin's] fragmentary biography, based on the testimony of an unreliable informant whose alleged relationship was unsubstantiated . . . should have been accepted as not only the truth but the whole truth is incredible. [1953,191]

Unfortunately for Greenway, it so happens that Joe Hill's sister Ester Dahl, when she encountered Chaplin's account for the first time in Sweden in the 1950s, immediately recognized that John Holland was in fact her (and Hill's) older brother Paul. Unruffled by the few superficial mistakes it contained, Ester Dahl had no trouble perceiving the genuineness of the interview. Thus Hill's sister confirmed Chaplin's own view, as expressed in his "Open Letter to the *New Republic*," that "Holland's story will stand for the record for the simple reason that it is true, authentic, and disinterested" [1948a].

Subsequent research on Hill has substantiated the larger part of Chaplin's biography.[4] Anyone who has ever had anything to do with "oral history" will appreciate the remarkable degree of accuracy in Chaplin's text, even in small details.

Significantly, neither Stegner nor Greenway, in their blustering attacks on Chaplin, introduced a single new piece of verifiable information on Hill. The gossip, rumors, and innuendo they offered instead have not withstood critical examination.

This in turn highlights another significant fact: Over the years, with a few notable exceptions, the really crucial new discoveries about Hill's life in the U.S., and the correction of errors made by earlier researchers, have been made not by academics, but by Wobblies—some of whom never completed grade school. A month after Chaplin's pioneering biography appeared in the *Industrial Pioneer*, that magazine published "The Last Letters of Joe Hill" —his letters to Sam Murray from the Salt Lake City jail—with a brief introduction and notes by Fellow Worker Murray. As later chapters of this book will show, Fellow Workers Richard Brazier, Alexander MacKay, Louis Moreau, and Fred Thompson also added immeasurably to our knowledge of the Wobbly bard. This should come as no surprise. After all, in seeking the truth about Joe Hill, knowing the IWW and the art of hoboing *from within* has to be considered a real advantage.

1. The 1948 *New Republic* that slandered Joe Hill passed for a "liberal" publication, as it had—rather briefly—in its first years. The magazine, however, supported U.S. entry into World War I, welcomed the Espionage and Sedition Acts, and hailed the 1918 conviction of 101 Wobblies on charges of conspiracy to obstruct the war effort as an expression of the "national will to pull the country together" [Abrahams 1988, 80-81]. Today's *NR* is openly neoconservative.

2. These critical assessments appeared in a special letters-to-the-editor section (titled "Correspondence: Joe Hill") in the *New Republic*, 9 February 1948, 38-39.

3. In an earlier article in a more obscure publication [Stegner 1947], the novelist had already made many of the same weak arguments.

4. Chaplin did make a few assertions that subsequent investigation has disproved.

For example, Hill most certainly did not produce the first IWW Song Book, and there is no evidence that he worked "on the boats between Sweden and England" before coming to the U.S., or that he was active in the Fresno or San Diego free speech fights, or that he was doing IWW organizational work in Bingham Canyon prior to his arrest.

L. S. Chumley: "Joe Hill: IWW Poet and Song Writer"
(charcoal, 1915)

5. "BORN ON A PLANET CALLED THE EARTH": A SKETCH OF THE LIFE OF A FOOTLOOSE WOBBLY

To forget who I was, and to know who I am.
—**Fabre d'Olivet**—

In their later years, Joe Hill's best friends—all Wobblies—tended to regret that they had not learned more about his life. They *knew* the man: worked with him, talked with him, listened to his music, sang his songs, laughed at his cartoons, ate meals with him, hoboed with him, went on strike with him, and hung out with him. And they knew Hill's *character*, the kind of man he was: his devotion to the IWW Cause, his spirit of solidarity, his sense of humor, his courage and modesty and basic goodness. To a man they vouched for Hill's honesty and integrity, his utter incapacity for any sort of crookedness, and his innocence of the spurious charges leveled against him in 1914 by the "authorities of the State of Utah" on behalf of the Utah copper bosses.

These friends of the Wobbly bard—and I am referring to Sam Murray, Alexander MacKay, Louis Moreau, William Chance, Ed Rowan, Meyer Friedkin, Sam Scarlett, and a few others who are known to have actually spent a few weeks or months or years in Hill's company—knew Joe Hill, but they never got around to getting his life story.

Bill Chance, for example, retained strong memories of his old friend in their San Pedro years: He remembered Hill playing piano, banjo, and violin at IWW affairs, and recalled that they often went fishing together. Their talk, however, was Wobbly talk: It was all about organizing, union matters, job conditions, abolishing capitalism, the latest issue of *Solidarity*—not about biography [Smith, 43].

Old-timers interviewed by researcher Aubrey Haan in the late 1940s agreed that Hill was "passionately interested in the IWW and seldom talked of anything else" [letter to Fred Thompson, 18 Jan 1948, 2]. And so it was with Hill's other friends. As Alexander MacKay complained in a 1960 letter to Archie Green, who had inquired about some details of Hill's life:

> Oh, if only some of us who knew Joe Hill had then had the least intimation that he would be the hero of a *cause célèbre* we

would not now have to rely on our memories. When I think of all the now-famous revolutionary relics I once knew and had the opportunity of taking notes about, I could turn around and kick myself clear through my picture window and into the manure pile—but, even then, it would not have entered my fat head to have included Joe Hill among them. He was the least likely saint among them all. [11 June]

Hill's friends, however, went on to make invaluable contributions to our knowledge of his life. They may have failed to get his biography—as he no doubt failed to get theirs—but they knew him well enough to recognize mistakes made by others: fellow workers, journalists, historians, biographers. And when they noticed such mistakes, they set out at once to correct them. It was Hill's friends who first pointed out the errors in Chaplin's biography. It was they who nailed the lies in Wallace Stegner's character assassination of Hill in the *New Republic* in 1948. It was they who first called attention to the mistakes and discrepancies in the later studies by Barrie Stavis and Philip Foner. And along the way they filled in important gaps, remembered "small" details that turned out to have big consequences, shed light on many little-known episodes, added countless crucial insights and fascinating sidelights, and, more generally, held out for the truth against a legion of rumor-mongers and mythmakers. Surely these were admirable ways to honor the memory of an old friend!

Here, then, is a digest of the known facts about the IWW's most celebrated Fellow Worker.

Joe Hill was born Joel Emmanuel Hägglund on 7 October 1879 in the seaport town of Gävle, Sweden (160 kilometers north of Stockholm) of Swedish Lutheran parents. As members of the orthodox Waldenströmmare sect, the family belonged to the Bethlehem Church in Gävle, and young Joel was a faithful attender of its Sunday School. It is amusing to note that the future author of "The Preacher and the Slave" and other parodies of hymns also attended Salvation Army meetings as a youngster [Smith 1969, 44].

Of Hill's nine brothers and sisters, six lived to maturity. His father was a poorly-paid conductor on the Gävle-Dala railroad. Years later Hill's younger sister Ester recalled their childhood: "There were no political discussions. . . . We were taught to be obedient to God and the King and to submit to all authority"

[Takman 1956, 26]. Their father, injured in a work-accident, died in 1887, leaving the family in poverty. Still a child, Joel went to work in a rope factory and later on a steam-powered crane. As a teenager he was hospitalized for skin and joint tuberculosis in Stockholm.

In January 1902 Mrs Hägglund died after a long illness. The family broke up, sold their house, and went their separate ways. In the Fall Joel emigrated to the U.S. on the Cunard Lines "Saxonia" with his older brother Paul. (The two had already studied English in Sweden.) Hill's oldest brother, Olof Efraim, worked on the Gävle-Dala railroad for several years, but later moved to Gothenberg and became a metal worker. He died in 1949 [Söderstrom, letter to FR, 8 Feb 2002].

In 1904 Hill's younger sisters, Judit and Ester, were sent to live with a family far to the north of Gävle, in the mountains [*ibid.*, 5 Feb & 19 Mar 2002]. Judit married a man name Halvarsson and became a schoolteacher; she died in 1932. Hill's brother Ruben moved to Stockholm around 1906 and worked mainly as a long-shoreman; he died in 1936 [*ibid.*].

Apart from Paul, who, as "John Holland," communicated important biographical details on Hill to Ralph Chaplin, the only other member of Hill's family who shared information with re-searchers was his youngest sister, Ester. Her appreciable contri-butions to our knowledge of the IWW poet are discussed in the next chapter. After his meeting with Chaplin, Paul dropped out of sight; his later life and date of death are unknown. Joel Hägglund's other siblings—Judit, Ruben, and Olof Efraim—never learned that their brother in the far-off U.S.A. had become a celebrated song-writer and workingclass hero.

When he reached New York at the age of twenty-two, the man we know as Joe Hill was six feet tall, slim, with deep blue eyes and dark brown hair. A handful of mostly undated photos show him as a handsome, intelligent, serious, and thoughtful young man, bold and unafraid; more hobo than poet, perhaps, but with a strong sense of humor and a dreamer's twinkle in his eye—the opposite, one might say, of a TV anchorman or an insurance executive.

For the years 1902-1912 hard facts about Hill are harder to find than a good employer. All we know for sure is that he made his way across the country working at various odd jobs. He lived in New York for a year, eking out a living "rattling the music box" (playing the piano) and cleaning spittoons in a Bowery saloon. He is also known to have spent at least some time in Philadelphia, Pittsburgh, Cleveland, Chicago, the Dakotas, Spokane, Seattle, Portland, Los Angeles, San Pedro, Fresno, Mexico, British Columbia, and probably Alaska and Hawaii. In 1906 he sent an eyewitness account of the San Francisco earthquake and fire to the hometown newspaper in Gävle, which published it.[1] In 1911 he swelled the ranks of the Wobbly contingent in the Mexican Revolution in Baja California. A year later he turned up in Canada during a major IWW strike.

At some point he changed his name to Joseph Hillstrom, and later shortened it to Joe Hill. He probably derived the name from Hille, a village just north of Gävle, where his father was born. In the Hägglund family, Hill's grandmother was commonly called "Hille Kajsa" (Kate from Hille).

Exactly when and where Joe Hill joined the IWW cannot be specified with certainty, thanks to the U.S. government, which seized the union's records in 1917 and later destroyed them. However, Hill's friend and fellow Wobbly, Alexander MacKay, felt "pretty damn positive" that Hill "lined up" in 1910, and other scattered bits of evidence—including a letter in the 27 August 1910 issue of the *Industrial Worker,* signed Joe Hill—tend to confirm it. The place was probably San Pedro, California, where Hill lived for several years, mostly working longshore, and where he served for a time as secretary of the IWW local. According to some accounts, including Chaplin's, Hill was signed up by one of the local's co-founders, Fellow Worker Miller.[2]

Some of Hill's friends—as well as his brother Paul, in his interview with Chaplin—left brief, casual reminiscences which add a little color, depth and detail to his very sketchy biography. The old-timers interviewed by Aubrey Haan, for example, pointed out that Hill was usually quiet at union meetings, but enjoyed "listening to the more philosophical discussions" [letter to Fred Thompson, 18 Jan 1948, 2].

Hill was a non-smoker, and like many Wobs, he didn't drink.[3] According to his Swedish friend and fellow worker, Edward Mattson, Hill "considered hard liquor a capitalist scheme to poison the working class" [Nerman 1979, 37]. A few years later the union popularized the adage, "you can't fight the boss and the booze at the same time" [Doran 1918, 110]. Was this saying, or something similar, already circulating in Hill's time?

Nothing is known of Hill's love life. He seems to have been

popular with women, but none of his friends could recall that he ever had a "steady girl." As Chaplin puts it, Hill was "always courteous to girls and women" but definitely "not a ladies' man" [1923, 25].

Unlike most hoboes, Hill is said to have completely avoided whorehouses. Friends would invite him to"have a good time," but Hill—according to his brother Paul—never went. To Charles Rudberg, however (an old friend from Sweden with whom he had renewed contact in San Francisco) he sent a hand-drawn postcard of a shapely burlesque dancer [see page 197], suggesting that the society of sex workers may not have been entirely alien to him.

Paul also told Chaplin that he often found his younger brother "scribbling verse" late at night, "twisting the hair on his forehead with his finger as he figured out the rhymes" [Chaplin 1948, 186]. Even on the job poetry was frequently uppermost in his mind. "During the rest hour," for example, Hill "would dream away for a little while and then jot down his inspiration in lines and verses as they came to him" [Chaplin 1923, 25].

Joe Hill loved Chinese food and enjoyed cooking it. His brother Paul told Chaplin that Hill was "an adept in the art of Oriental cookery and could prepare Chinese dishes to delight the most exacting visitor" [*ibid.,* 24]. He used chopsticks "like a native." Edward Mattson also mentions Hill's skill in the art of Chinese cuisine [Nerman 1979, 37].

An acquaintance recalled Hill as "always well-dressed—in inconspicuous blue serge, white shirt, and black tie." He also "preferred a cap to a hat" [McClintock to Fred Thompson, 9 July 150].

Hill's friends and acquaintances considered him remarkably unselfish. It was said that "he would give away to a passing stranger the last mouthful of rice in [his] little shack" in San Pedro [Chaplin 1923, 24].

He worked as a "mechanic" (which can mean almost anything), as machinist and longshoreman, in lumber and construction camps, in the wheatfields, and at numerous other jobs. From time to time he also found employment as a musician. He had grown up in a musical family; his father played the organ at church, and built another at home, which Hill learned to play. Singing at home was a family tradition. His sister Ester recalled that he also learned to play the piano, the accordion, and the guitar, but he always preferred the fiddle [Takman 1956, 25]. His friend Charles Rudberg, the only childhood chum with whom Hill remained in touch in the

U.S., said that Hill "could play the violin so beautifully it made men weep" [letter from Frances Horn to FR, 15 Apr 1985]. Paul Hägglund recalled that Hill "could play almost any kind of musical instrument" and that he was familiar with "all the music in the world" [Chaplin 1948, 185; 1923, 24]. In 1956 his sister Ester told an interviewer that Hill began composing music at the age of eighteen or nineteen—that is, in the late 1890s [Takman, 26]. His death certificate lists "musician" as his occupation.

In his teens in Sweden Hill had played piano in a local cafe, as he did years later, on occasion, at the Sailors' Mission at 331 Beacon Street in San Pedro, and more frequently at Wobbly affairs in the same city. Edward Mattson, who knew him in Seattle and in the San Pedro days, quotes an immigrant Finn as saying: "No one who heard Joe Hill sing or play could easily forget him" [Nerman, 1979, 36].

An armful of solid facts, some strong probabilities, and a bedraggled suitcase of educated guesses and plausible suppositions: Such is the stuff of Joe Hill's biography. Like the smoke and fog in the paintings of Monet, this man's life story dazzles us with color while remaining impenetrably dense.

---

1. A translation of this text was published in Smith 1969, 49-50.

2. Neither Chaplin nor anyone else ever gave the first name of the Fellow Worker who signed up Joe Hill. Of the many Millers in the union in the 1910s, the French-born Francis was the best known, but he does not appear to have worked anywhere in the west.

3. Despite the union's strong stand against drinking—a point that was even conceded by the prosecution in the 1918 Chicago IWW trial—many Wobs did enjoy a bit of liquor now and then. Some qualified as "serious" drinkers; a few were alcoholics. Robert "Blackie" Vaughan, for many years secretary of the Houston, Texas, IWW Branch, and by all accounts a first-rate Wobbly, was in his later years a bartender with a drinking problem. According to his friend, Fellow Worker Gilbert Mers, Vaughan's favorite whisky was I. W. Harper, which he always called I. W. W. Harper.

An IWW "Silent Agitator" sticker

6. ESTER DAHL: JOE HILL'S SISTER

The wonderful work . . . began in children's laughter
. . . We shall not forget that yesterday. . . .
—Arthur Rimbaud—

Ester Hägglund was only fifteen when her brothers Paul and Joel emigrated to the U.S., and she never saw either of them again. Although she received a few letters and Christmas cards from her brothers, she knew very little about their lives in the New World. The news of Joel Hägglund's execution reached her long after the fact. Not until many years later did she learn about Joe Hill, the IWW poet and songwriter.

In her later years, however, Ester Dahl (she married Ingebrikt Dahl in 1908) proved to be an invaluable aide to historians eager to learn about Joe Hill's childhood and adolescence in Sweden. It is no exaggeration to say that Hill's youngest sister was the source of most of what we know about the Wobbly bard's youth.

Oddly enough, the first person to interview Ester—or at least the first to publish the results—was an American journalist, Ray Bearse, whose article appeared in the May Day 1949 issue of the magazine *Folket i bild* (The People Illustrated). Bearse did not, however, pursue his researches in this area. His article was never published in English and his various books are on subjects far removed from labor history.[1]

Ture Nerman, the poet/socialist who translated Hill's songs into Swedish and later became his first Swedish biographer, was the first labor historian to draw on Ester's vivid and conscientious memory. In addition to sharing her own reminiscences with him, Ester directed Nerman to family friends who also recalled incidents in the life of young "Julle." Nerman's 1951 book, *Joe Hill: Mördare eller Martyr?* (Joe Hill, Murderer or Martyr?), gave the world its first account of Hill's family—his mother Margareta Caterina Wennman and father Olof, and the five surviving siblings. With Ester's help, Nerman also provided information on Hill's early passion for music, his religious upbringing and education, the first years of his working life, and even something of his medical history.

In 1956, a few years after she retired from many decades' service as director of the telephone station in Högvålen, Ester Dahl was interviewed by journalist John Takman. She was then sixty-eight years old. Takman found her warm, quiet, thoughtful, "full of memories" yet "youthfully alive" [1956, 30]. During their four-day interview she patiently answered his numerous questions and shared many memories—of her mother, for example, who "sang very beautifully in a soft and clear soprano voice," and her father, who was "very handy,"

> so when he had any free time he made the furniture himself. He built a mangle and that became mother's means for earning a living after his death. [*ibid.*, 24]

Ester explained that she and Joel, and all the other children, began to play the organ "as soon as we could reach the keys." She also told Takman about the "teasing songs" that Joel wrote and sang about her and her slightly older sister Judit, and about the letters he, still in his teens, wrote home after he found work in Stockholm —letters which "sparkled with love of life." She remembered, too, a letter Paul had sent from overseas, saying that he and Joel had led " a dog's life . . . during [their] first year in America" [*ibid.*, 28].

She even offered her reflections on the origins of Hill's well-known independence of mind:

> His chronological place in the family had given him a unique position. . . . His older brothers had their common interests and Joel was on the outside. We sisters were younger so that he had no share of our interests either. He kept much to himself and had his own interest and that was mostly music. [*ibid.*, 5]

In addition to sharing her memories—which Takman found "clear and rich in detail"—Ester showed him some cherished mementoes, including an album of family photographs and a couple of Christmas cards. There was also a letter from Paul, on the stationery of the "Saxonia," with a curious postscript by Joel:

> Agree with former speaker on all points.
> Your brother, James Brown

—which Ester considered a good example of Joel's "special humor" [*ibid.*, 29].

In the course of her interview with Takman, Ester was careful to point out mistakes that had appeared in some Swedish articles on Hill. She denied, for instance, the rumor that Hill had gone to sea several years before he left for the U.S.

Barrie Stavis also benefitted from Ester's correspondence in the 1950s and '60s. Most importantly, she told him that Hill "would go to the Salvation Army, take one of their melodies and write a song of his own" [Stavis 1964, I:4]. The IWW's outstanding parodist evidently got off to an early start.

In the years 1965-67, Ester exchanged several letters with Gibbs Smith, who was then a graduate student at the University of Utah, researching the doctoral dissertation that later appeared as the first full-length biography of Joe Hill in English. As in her conversations with Ture Nerman and her interview with John Takman, Ester once more responded to particular questions, and helped clarify a number of details regarding Hill's family background, childhood, and other matters, including the Hägglund family's street address in Gävle: 28 Nedra Bergsgatan.

Ingvar Söderstrom, Ture Nerman's successor as foremost Hill scholar in Sweden, did not know Ester Dahl personally, but some of his friends interviewed her in the 1960s, and he too has drawn appreciably from her recollections [letter to FR, 19 March 2002]. Ester Dahl's readiness to share her knowledge with historians shows that John Takman was right on the mark when he noted that she not only "remembered her remarkable brother with . . . much admiration and love," but also was "happy that her brother's memory is honored all over the world, and proud of the contribution he made to the cause of the labor movement" [Takman 1956, 30]. Though far from being an agitator herself, she also shared something of her brother's hopes "for a better world," to quote the salutation used by many old-time Wobblies to close their letters.

In November 1955, *Labor's Daily*—the short-lived national cooperative labor newspaper started by the International Typographical Union and other unions in the U.S.—devoted a special feature to the fortieth anniversary of the judicial murder of Joe Hill. Along with other illustrations and texts it included a photograph of Ester Dahl, the only living member of Joe Hill's family, and a special greeting she wrote for the occasion. This material was reprinted or excerpted in other labor papers, including *The Voice of 212*, organ of Detroit Local 212 of the United Auto Workers, CIO.

In Chicago, under the heading "Joe Hill's Sister Hopes Youth Today Spreads His Ideas," the *Industrial Worker* also reprinted Ester Dahl's bright message:

On the nineteenth of November, I wish to send you a greeting and a heartfelt thanks to all who have offered their time and work for the research that has proved that my brother was innocent of the crime for which he was executed.

That his memory be cleared, bright and beautiful, and that you honor him in the fortieth year after his execution brings happiness to me, his youngest sister.

As his ashes were strewn all over the world, so also do I hope that his ideas, his strong belief for a peaceful, creative and healthy world should also inspire the present generation to follow with renewed strength in his footsteps. [23 Jan 1956, 2]

To the end, according to Ingvar Söderstrom, the leading authority on Hill in Sweden today, Ester Dahl was "a very appreciated person in her neighborhood" [Söderstrom to FR, 5 Feb 2002]. The gracious, thoughtful sister of U.S. labor's most world-renowned martyr died in 1969 at the age of eighty-two.

---

1. Bearse's books include *The Canoe Camper's Handbook* (1974), *Sporting Arms of the World* (1976), and guidebooks to Maine, Massachusetts, and Vermont.

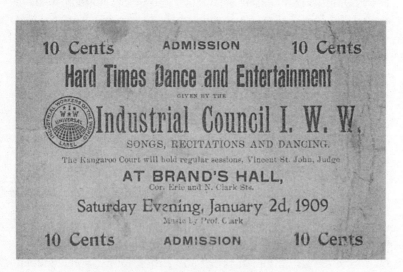

IWW Song Card & Invitation (Chicago, 1909)
On the reverse are the words for an anonymous hobo song
from the early 1890s, "Hallelujah, I'm a Bum,"
which became a Wobbly favorite.

II

THE WOBBLY BARD

1. SONGS TO WISE UP THE SLAVES

When freedom becomes reality, poetry becomes life.
—**Karel Teige**—

In his own lifetime Joe Hill was known above all for his poetry and song, and that is how he is best remembered today. He was and is the uncontested "star" of the IWW's famous *Little Red Song Book*—American labor's all-time best-seller. As a writer of popular U.S. labor songs Joe Hill has never been surpassed.

He cannot, however, be credited with "making the IWW a singing union," as Ralph Chaplin believed, for it was already a singing union when Hill joined it. This too-little-known facet of the union's history was brought out many years ago by Richard Brazier, who was himself an important IWW poet and songwriter, and one of the *Song Book*'s originators. In his fine little memoir on the history of the *Little Red Song Book*, published in the journal *Labor History* in 1968, Fellow Worker Brazier recalled that "what first attracted [him] to the IWW was its songs and the gusto with which its members sang them," and that he had heard these songs even before he first came to Spokane in 1907 (that is, two or three years before Hill is known to have joined the union):

> Such singing, I thought, was good propaganda, since it had originally attracted me and many others as well; and also useful, since it held the crowd for Wobbly speakers who followed. [91-92]

Prior to the IWW *Song Book*, America labor radicals had relied largely on Charles H. Kerr's *Socialist Songs with Music* (1901), which in turn drew heavily on William Morris's *Chants for Labour* (1888).[1] The *Little Red Song Book*, in contrast, was made up of mostly new and original lyrics written by IWW members.

The *Song Book*—the One Big Union's single most effective piece of propaganda, and by far its most popular publication— brought the IWW's songs to an ever-increasing audience. Many unions had songbooks, but they were nothing like the little red one. What made the IWW *Song Book* so different was its passionate anti-capitalism, its free-wheeling humor, and the vision it projected of a new society without exploitation, bosses, cops or jails.

After he became the best known writer of IWW songs, Hill was sometimes identified—wrongly—as the instigator or compiler of the first *Little Red Song Book*. The truth is he had nothing to do with starting or editing the *Song Book* in 1908, and no song of his appeared in its pages until three years later.

As Dick Brazier tells it, the *Little Red Song Book* as an official publication of the IWW owed a lot to the popular Spokane-based IWW National Organizer and soapboxer J. H. Walsh—renowned in the annals of the union as the ringleader of the "Overalls Brigade" which caused such a sensation at the 1908 IWW convention in Chicago. Dressed in blue denim overalls, black shirts and flaming red ties, the "Brigade" had hopped freights across the country, stopping at numerous points on the way for highly successful song-filled IWW street meetings [Kornbluh 1964, 40-42].

At the convention, these twenty delegates from the Far West sided with IWW General Secretary-Treasurer Vincent St John in ousting Socialist Labor Party boss Daniel DeLeon from the union. For the rest of his life DeLeon excoriated these unemployed migrant workers, and the entire IWW, as "rabble" and "the bummery" (the "Brigade" had sung "Hallelujah, I'm a Bum" at the convention). DeLeon seems to have been especially offended by the fact that the western delegates failed to register at respectable hotels, and actually had the temerity to sleep "on benches on the Lake Front" [*ibid.*, 6]. His slanderous attacks on the union were widely echoed in the capitalist press, and used by prosecuting attorneys to help send IWWs to jail. Most Wobs considered DeLeon power-hungry and psychologically sick. My old friend Sam Dolgoff, anarchist and Wobbly, summed him up as an "insufferable Marxist bigot" [1980, 63].

Fellow Worker Walsh was a man of altogether different caliber. Along with his organizing genius and deep dedication to the Cause of One Big Union, he clearly had a flair for attention-getting stunts. It was Walsh who initiated the practice of singing IWW parodies of Salvation Army hymns to draw crowds away from the "Sallies" and toward IWW speakers nearby. It was Walsh, too, who formed the first IWW band.

IWW street-singing in competition with the Salvation Army proved even more effective than the Spokane IWWs had hoped. As a Fellow Worker observed at the time:

> It is really surprising how soon a crowd will form in the street to hear a song in the interest of the working class, familiar as they are with the maudlin sentimental music of the various religionists. [Wilson 1908, 1]

In a letter to Fred Thompson, Dick Brazier explained J. H. Walsh's role in the development of the Song Book:

> The IWW understood the power of song long before J. H. Walsh came to Spokane and the IWW had been printing and selling a little brochure that contained several songs and sold for five cents a copy. . . . The little card brochure was the foundation of the Song Book. We had the idea of the Song Book before J. H. Walsh ever came to Spokane but could never get enough support to put it over [nationally]. Where J. H. Walsh came in was his strong support of the idea [throughout the union] and the strength he built up by his continual presentation of the idea ... before the membership. . . . In that sense J. H. Walsh might be called the father of the *Little Red Song Book*. [7 Jan 1967, 3]

The first edition of the pocket-sized volume titled *IWW Songs* —better known as the *Little Red Song Book*—appeared in 1908. Joe Hill's first song to appear in this collection of "Songs to Fan the Flames of Discontent" was "The Preacher and the Slave" (often called "Long-Haired Preachers" and "Pie in the Sky"), which was included in the third edition (Spokane, 1911). Sung to the tune of the then-popular hymn, "In the Sweet Bye and Bye," it is Hill's most popular and most-reprinted song:[2]

Long-haired preachers come out every night
Try to tell you what's wrong and what's right;
But when asked how 'bout something to eat
They will answer in voices so sweet:

    Chorus:
You will eat, bye and bye,
In that glorious land above the sky;
Work and pray, live on hay,
You'll get pie in the sky when you die.

The starvation army they play,

They sing and they clap and they pray
'Till they get all your coin on the drum,
Then they'll tell you when you're on the bum.

The fourth edition of the *Little Red Song Book* (1912) featured five new Joe Hill songs, including a powerful attack on the "union scab"—*i.e.*, the craft-unionist who remains at work when fellow workers in other crafts go on strike. "Casey Jones, the Union Scab" is another IWW favorite:

The Workers on the S.P. line to strike sent out a call;
But Casey Jones, the engineer, he wouldn't strike at all;
His boiler it was leaking, and its drivers on the bum,
And his engine and its bearings, they were all out of plumb.

    Chorus
Casey Jones kept his junkpile running;
Casey Jones was working double time;
Casey Jones got a wooden medal,
For being good and faithful on the S.P. line.

"Everybody's Joining It" was Hill's Wobbly take-off on Irving Berlin's hit "Turkey Trot" dance song, "Everybody's Doin' It Now":

Fellow workers, can't you hear,
There is something in the air.
Everywhere you walk everybody talks
'Bout the IWW.
They have a way to strike
That the master doesn't like—
Everybody sticks. That's the only trick. . . .

    Chorus
Everybody's joining it, joining what? Joining it!
Joining in this union grand,
Boys and girls of every land;
All the workers hand in hand–
Everybody's joining it now.

The Boss is feeling mighty blue,
He don't know just what to do.
. . .

Join IWW.
Don't let bosses trouble you

(The last two lines quoted here are of special interest in that they indicate that Hill, like most of the old-timers I have known, pronounced the union's initials as "I-double-double-U.")

The fifth edition of the *Song Book*, published in March 1913, added nine more Joe Hill songs. "Mr Block" was inspired by Ernest Riebe's prankish IWW comic strip of that name,[3] featuring a blockheaded worker who believed the boss was always right:

Please give me your attention, I'll introduce to you
A man that is a credit to "Our Red, White and Blue";
His head is made of lumber, and solid as a rock;
He is a common worker and his name is Mr Block.

Chorus
Oh Mr Block, you were born by mistake,
You take the cake,
You make me ache.
Tie a rock on your block and then jump in the lake.
Kindly do that for Liberty's sake.

One of Hill's most popular songs was "There Is Power in a Union" (to the tune of the gospel song, "There Is Power in the Blood"):

Would you have freedom from wage slavery,
Then join in the grand Industrial Band;
Would you from mis'ry and hunger be free,
Then come! Do your share, like a man.

Chorus
There is pow'r, there is pow'r
In a band of workingmen,
When they stand hand in hand,
That's a pow'r, that's a pow'r
That must rule in every land—
One Industrial Union Grand.

Another favorite was "The Tramp," printed here in full:

If you all will shut your trap,

Joe Hill

I will tell you 'bout a chap,
That was broke and up against it, too, for fair;
He was not the kind that shirk,
He was looking hard for work,
But he heard the same old story everywhere.

Chorus
Tramp, tramp, tramp, keep on a-tramping,
Nothing doing here for you;
If I catch you 'round again,
You will wear the ball and chain,
Keep on tramping, that's the best thing you can do.

He walked up and down the street,
'Til the shoes fell off his feet.
In a house he spied a lady cooking stew.
And he said, "How do you do,
May I chop some wood for you?"
What the lady told him made him feel so blue.

'Cross the street a sign he read,
"Work for Jesus," so it said,
And he said "Here is my chance, I'll surely try."
And he kneeled upon the floor,
'Till his knees got rather sore,
But at eating-time he heard the preacher cry---

Down the street he met a cop,
and the copper made him stop,
And he asked him, "When did you blow into town?
Come with me up to the judge."
But the judge he said, "Oh fudge,
Bums that have no money needn't come around."

Finally came that happy day
When his life did pass away.
He was sure he'd go to heaven when he died.
When he reached the pearly gate,
Santa Peter, mean old skate,
Slammed the gate right in his face and loudly cried:

In despair he went to Hell,
With the Devil for to dwell,
For the reason he'd no other place to go.
And he said, "I'm full of sin,

So for Christ's sake, let me in!"
But the Devil said, "Oh, beat it, you're a 'bo."

A sixth edition of the *Song Book* appeared in August 1913, only six months after the fifth, with four additional Joe Hill songs. "Down in the Old Dark Mill" (to the tune of "Down by the Old Mill Stream"), tells the all-too-frequent tragedy of love among the oppressed:

How well do I remember
    That mill along the way,
Where she and I were working
    For fifty cents a day.
She was my little sweetheart;
    I met her in the mill—
It's a long time since I saw her.
    But I love her still.

We had agreed to marry
    When she'd be sweet sixteen.
But then—one day I crushed it—
    My arm in the machine.
I lost my job forever—
    I am a tramp disgraced.
My sweetheart still is slaving
    In the same old place.

"Nearer My Job to Thee" (to the tune of the hymn, "Nearer My God to Me") is a dry, laconic, and yet piercing attack on "employment sharks." It is printed here in its entirety:

Nearer my job to thee,
Nearer with glee.
Three plunks for the office fee,
But my fare is free.
My train is running fast,
I've got a job at last,
Nearer my job to thee,
Nearer to thee.

Arrived where my job should be,
Nothing in sight I see,
Nothing but sand, by gee,
Job went up a tree.

No place to eat or sleep,
Snakes in the sagebrush creep,
Nero a saint would be,
Shark, compared to thee.

Nearer to town each day
(Hiked all the way),
Nearer that agency,
Where I paid my fee,
And when that shark I see
You'll bet your boots that he
Nearer his god shall be.
Leave that to me.

In 1912 the Los Angeles IWW local also issued a song book —perhaps put together by Hill himself—which included *only* Joe Hill's songs (at least thirteen of them) plus Charles H. Kerr's translation of the "Internationale" and, as a special and historic bonus, Hill's first published cartoon (see page 258).[4]

Though Hill "was not around when the first *Song Book* was launched," Brazier readily acknowledged that the author of "The Preacher and the Slave" was in fact

largely responsible for [the book's] success and expansion in size. . . . Only one other Wobbly song-writer exceeded him in the number of songs in the Song Book [Brazier himself], but none exceeded him in quality. [1968, 103]

By the early 1910s Joe Hill was the all-around favorite song-writer in the union. In Wobbly halls, in hobo jungles, at street meetings, and on picketlines throughout the country Hill's songs, sparkling with his own caustic class-war humor, were immediate "hits." Many of them—"Casey Jones, the Union Scab," "The Preacher and the Slave," "There Is Power in a Union," "The Tramp," and "Mr Block"—have remained continuously popular ever since, and have long been recognized as labor and revolutionary "standards."

As the foregoing sampling demonstrates, Hill's poetry remains securely within the folk and popular traditions. Beamed not so much at the literary-minded individual as the hard-pressed crowd, his bold and vigorous verses tend to avoid the contemplative, private, and subjective, and instead tell stories, poke fun, provoke

laughter or (less often) tears, and all along the way convey fundamental Wobbly aims and principles. Even when his theme is love
or childhood or old age, the message is always *Abolish wage-
slavery!*

The simplicity of Hill's lyrics, the innocence of heart that they
communicate along with their radical defiance, their solidarity with
the oppressed, their love of freedom, and their bright vision of a
new and happier society, call to mind Friedrich Schiller's reflections on the "simple poet" and his conflict with the powers that be:

> Genuinely simple poets scarcely have a place any more in this
> artificial age [and hence] are scarcely possible in it, or at least
> they are possible only on the condition of *traversing* their age
> like *scared persons* at a *running* pace.. . . [Such poets] still
> appear sometimes at intervals, [but] rather as strangers, who
> excite wonder, or as ill-trained children of nature, who give
> offense. . . . The critics, as regular policemen of art, detest these
> poets as *disturbers of laws or of limits*. . . . They find it hard to
> maintain their laws against [the simple poet's] example. [Schil-
> ler 1910, 284]

Unlike most modern poetry, moreover—political or otherwise
—Joe Hill's songs always invite audience participation. He did not
write virtuoso pieces. The fact that many professional singers have
sung and recorded his songs does not alter the simple truth that
they were meant to be sung by working men, women, and children
in the course of a worldwide struggle for freedom and equality.

Gradually, these songs that "breathe the class struggle," as Big
Bill Haywood described them, attracted listeners (and singers) well
beyond the ranks of the union, and even beyond the far left [Hay-
wood 1929, 280]. Writers, artists, journalists started referring to
Hill as "the IWW poet." When the State of Utah took his life, the
liberal magazine *Survey* headlined the story, "Execution of the
IWW Poet," and the tag caught on all the more. A photograph in
the *Industrial Pioneer* for November 1923 shows two or three
hundred lumberjacks out west commemorating Hill's death "in the
Joe Hill spirit"—*i.e.*, "building up the organization." In the photo
are two large banners. One reads: "Joe Hillstrom was Murdered but
his Spirit Lives On in the Hearts of his Fellow Workers." The other
reads: "Joe Hill, IWW Poet" [23].

Years later, in the 1930s, Art Young—one of the greatest
American cartoonists, and the friend of many Wobs—recounted an

evening at the home of publisher Albert Boni, where Young played the piano and everyone joined in singing old songs, including "the radical burlesques of Joe Hill, the IWW poet" [1928, 153].

1. For pre-IWW labor songs in the U.S., see Foner 1975 and Halker 1991.

2. Unless otherwise specified, only *excerpts* of songs and poems appear in this book .

3. Several *Mr Block* strips were collected and issued in 1913 as a comic book—the first revolutionary comic book in the U.S. and a forerunner of the "underground comix" of the 1960s. The *Mr Block* comic book was reissued in 1984 by Charles H. Kerr.

4. The only extant copy of the Los Angeles IWW Song Book is incomplete—at least two pages are missing.

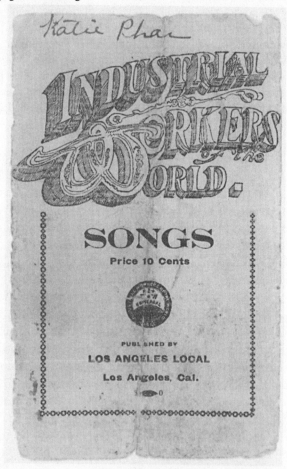

Cover of the 1912 Los Angeles edition of the Song Book, edited by Joe Hill, who probably also lettered the title.

2. A "ONE BIG UNION" OF POETS

But why are they singing?
We've never heard them sing like this before.
Something is happening that we know nothing about.
—Gaston Leroux—

The fact that Joe Hill was well known as "the IWW poet" should not obscure the far more compelling fact that there were *many* IWW poets. Worker-poets were not, in fact, unheard of before the IWW was organized. Free public education, brought about primarily through the agitation of the "land reform" labor movement in the 1830s and '40s, led to a steady increase in workingclass literacy, which in turn encouraged growing numbers of wage-earners to express themselves in writing. Meanwhile, the invention of the rotary press and improved methods of papermaking greatly lowered the cost of book-production, which resulted in the widespread availability of the world's great literature at prices workers could afford. Two generations before most of the IWW's founders were born, "Mechanics' Libraries" were a fixture of the U.S. labor movement.

As in every important change in U.S. history, immigrants played a vital role in the creation of an indigenous workingclass literature. In England, for example, the Chartist Movement had produced an impressive quantity of verse, and Welsh coal-miners had a long and enduring poetic tradition, well-documented in the many books they published. English, Welsh, Irish, and Scottish workers who came to the New World brought their literary traditions with them. In 1960, British-born IWW songwriter Richard Brazier recalled the street-singers and their printed song-sheets from his childhood in Birmingham [Green interview, 15].

Immigrants who did not know English brought literary traditions of their own. Their influence on the development of IWW poetry and song was real and important, if not always easy to pinpoint. Joe Hill was by no means the only Wobbly poet for whom English was a second language.

In this country, union printers—members of the International Typographical Union—were especially prolific writers and poets. Some of them, such as Sam K. Bangs, George C. Bowen, and Eugene Munday became well-known throughout the craft. A few—most notably Mark Twain and Charles Farrar Browne ("Artemus

Ward")—became famous throughout the world.

In many ways much closer to IWW songs were the "spirituals" of the Black slaves in the antebellum South—one of the richest currents in the entire history of workers' poetry and song. To what extent Joe Hill or other Wob songwriters had heard spirituals is impossible to say, but the fact that one of Hill's songs, "John Golden and the Lawrence Strike," was derived from a spiritual ("A Little Talk with Jesus"), and that Bill Haywood alluded to spirituals in his testimony at the biggest of all IWW trials—Chicago, 1918— indicates that at least some IWWs were familiar with them. Speaking of "the chattel slave of the Old South," whose "body was owned by his master," Haywood went on to say "but his soul was free, and that free soul gave birth to song" [George 1918, 183].

The Wobblies' well-known admiration for the nineteenth-century Abolitionist movement, as well as their own self-identification as "wage-slaves" and fighters for the "Abolition of the Wage System," would seem to have predisposed them in favor of such songs. In any event, all during the 1910s—Joe Hill's songwriting years, and the heyday of the *Little Red Song Book*— spirituals were very much "in the air." In his autobiography, Floyd Dell, a left-wing Socialist and friend of many Wobs, noted that in Chicago, 1912,

> A whole new field of aesthetic enjoyment was opened up to me . . . especially Negro spirituals, which were beginning to be reproduced on phonograph records, as sung by the Tuskegee Singers —"Go Down Moses" and that whole magnificent range of choral songs. [1933, 225]

Contrary to widespread misunderstanding, as John Lovell, Jr. pointed out long ago, spirituals are not fundamentally about religion. They are, rather, a powerful "criticism of everyday life" and "the key to [the slave's] revolutionary sentiments," reflecting an "obsession for freedom" and radical "plans for the future" [Katz 1969, 132-135]. What there is of "religion" in these songs, Lovell continues, "is chiefly an arsenal of pointed darts, a storehouse of images, a means of making shrewd observations" [*ibid*, 134]. Lovell's account of African American spirituals reads a lot like a commentary on the *Little Red Song Book*. Long before Joe Hill started making new Wobbly songs out of old Salvation Army hymns, Black slaves had shown the way by adapting Christian hymns to their own experience and needs. Writing on spirituals in his 1937 book, *Negro Poetry and Drama*, poet Sterling Brown summed up a methodology shared by many a Wobbly songster:

> The Negro singer took what he liked where he found it. And then he changed it, and, what is the important point, *made it his own*. [17]

A number of women poets also influenced the course of Wobbly poetry and song. Elizabeth Barrett Browning's "The Cry of the Children"—an impassioned condemnation of child labor—was still widely read in the 1910s and '20s. Bellamy socialist and feminist Charlotte Perkins Gilman's lyrics of industrial injustice and social transformation were especially popular in IWW circles: frequently reprinted in the union's press and constantly quoted by its soapboxers. Much admired, too, was the great poet of American anarchism, Voltairine de Cleyre, whose dark elegies to revolutionary martyrs were often recited at IWW memorial services.

Wobbly poets drew on this workingclass poetic legacy, but in no time at all it was obvious that they were adding much more to it than they were taking from it. Many earlier worker-poets were solitary craft-workers whose poems often had little to do with their working lives or their union activity, much less with class struggle or building a new society. Wobbly poets, in contrast, thought of themselves as militants in the One Big Union, and regarded their poetry and song as inseparable from their revolutionary industrial unionism. In the IWW, moreover, poetry was no longer viewed as a "light" diversion, or "sideline," but as a vital and significant feature of the union's publications and activity. "In the modern labor movement," as Pat Read noted in the July 1937 *One Big Union Monthly*, "the IWW alone has made a systematic attempt to popularize the songs of the struggle" [21].

From the start, creative self-expression was an important part of the IWW's emphasis on education, organization and emancipation. No labor union or other radical group—with the possible exception of Marcus Garvey's United Negro Improvement Association—published as much workingclass poetry as the Industrial Workers of the World [Martin 1983, 43-46].

In 1910 the union brought out a handsome little book of poems and two short stories by James Kelly Cole, who had died at 24 in a railroad accident on his way to the Spokane Free Speech Fight.

IWW poets Ralph Chaplin, Covington Hall, and Arturo Giovannitti published several collections of their poems. Much of the best Wobbly poetry—by Laura Payne Emerson, Richard Brazier, "Dublin Dan" Liston, Bert Weber, T-Bone Slim, Jim Seymour, Mary Marcy, Vera Moller, Lionel Moise, and Laura Tanne, to mention only poets active in the 1910s and '20s—remains scattered in the union's many periodicals and the *International Socialist Review*, awaiting rediscovery.

The sheer number of Wobbly poets is staggering. No one has attempted a full count, but it is a safe bet that the IWW has had more poets than most unions have members. Even more impressive, however, is the diversity and quality of the poetic work these rebellious wage-slaves produced.

At Wobbly halls, in diners, at work, in flops, on the road, in jails, and around "jungle" fires, these poets with red cards in their pockets wrote songs, odes, sonnets, free verse, ballads, limericks, jingles, ditties, and even a few haiku. Their poems range from the elegiac and narrative to the satirical and mock-heroic, from the alliterative and witty to the profoundly lyrical, with now and then a bold ascent into the blackest humor, or the truly visionary.

Much IWW poetry has been doggerel, or the work of mere rhymesters. But the union's poets have included a large number of first-rate songsmiths, several world-class parodists, and even a few true poet-seers in the great anti-traditional tradition. Further on we shall take a closer look at the work of some of these inspired and inspiring workingclass geniuses who followed in the footsteps of Fellow Worker Hill.

Not every poet who belonged to the IWW was a "Wobbly poet" in the sense that Joe Hill, Ralph Chaplin and T-Bone Slim were. Jamaican-born Claude McKay, probably the most noted poet to have carried a red card, joined the union during a short stint as a factory worker in New York in 1919, and rejoined a little later as a longshoreman, but his membership was brief and his involvement in the union slight. He did not write union songs, or poems with the IWW for a theme, and in fact does not appear to have contributed at all to the Wobbly press. (Some years later, however, the *Industrial Worker* reprinted his fine poem, "If We Must Die.")

For Joe Hill and other "Wobbly poets," poetry and unionism were inextricable. For Claude McKay, however, the two were not only distinct but widely separated fields of activity. This does not mean that he was in any way hostile or indifferent to the union:

quite the contrary. While he was at the point of production he kept his dues paid up, and in his book *The Negroes in America*, published (in Russian) in Moscow, 1923, he had nothing but the highest praise for the IWW.[1] His biographer, Wayne Cooper, sums up McKay's conclusion that

> only one American labor organization, the Industrial Workers of the World, . . . [has] truly accepted Blacks as equals in their organization and in their campaigns against American Capital. . . . [The] Communist Party . . . [has] yet to match the IWW's record. [1987, 186]

Claude McKay was a good Wobbly and an important poet, but not a "Wobbly poet." As a poet, he belonged much more to the world of literature than to the IWW.

Much the same could be said for Kenneth Rexroth, except that he seems to have identified a bit more closely with the union, maintained his membership a little longer, and—despite his 1930s collaboration on the Stalinist *New Masses* and his later conversion to the Anglican church—remained a Wob sympathizer his whole life. His so-called *Autobiographical Novel* (1991)—a bit fanciful as autobiography but in no sense a novel—includes valuable pages on the IWW in 1920s Chicago, the heyday of the celebrated Radial Bookshop, the Dil Pickle Club, and Bughouse Square.

Whatever Rexroth was writing while he was a dues-paying member of the IWW evidently did not have much to do with the union. Years later, however, echoes of his Wobbly youth turned up in several of his poems. "Again at Waldheim" invokes Voltairine de Cleyre, Rosa Luxemburg, Emma Goldman and Peter Kropotkin. "Fish Peddler and Cobbler" celebrates two great revolutionary labor martyrs:

> *No fourteen thousand foot peaks*
> *Are named Sacco and Vanzetti.*
> *Not yet.*

In "The Dragon and the Unicorn" he recalls a fund-raising party for the anarchist paper *Libertaire* in Paris:

> *An endless entertainment,*
> *All the best raconteurs and*
> *Singers of Paris donate*

Their services, the bitter
Humor and passion of the
Dispossessed. . . .
At the end, mass chants. . . .
Spain
Will Rise Again, Our Martyrs.
One by one, boys and girls step out
And sing a name. I am moved
As the foreign names ring out,
And then, unprepared, I hear,
"Parsons, Frank Little, Joe Hill,
Wesley Everest, Sacco,
Vanzetti." I weep like a baby. . . .
Along the
Beautiful rivers of France,
And in the mountains, next summer
Boys and girls will be making love,
And singing the songs of Joe Hill
In their own language.

"A Christmas Note for Geraldine Udell"—one of the loveliest poems Rexroth ever wrote—is especially evocative:

Do the prairie flowers, the huge autumn
Moons, return in season?
Debs, Berkman, Larkin, Haywood, they are dead now. . . .
Lightning storms are rare here. . . .
I, in my narrow bed,
Thought of other times, the hope filled post war years,
Exultant, disheveled
Festivals, exultant eyes, disheveled lips,
Eyes dulled now, and lips thinned. . . .
I think of you. . . .

Geraldine Udell, who at the age of eleven had been active in Joe Hill Defense agitation, helped her anarchist parents run the Radical Bookshop, one of Chicago's all-time great hangouts for IWWs, anarchists, libertarian socialists, poets, painters, and dancers. Specializing in IWW, socialist and anarchist literature as well as works by avant-garde writers and artists, the store was the scene of innumerable marvelous encounters, and even encompassed a popular "little theater"—the Studio Players—that is also evoked in Rexroth's poem (he and Geraldine appeared on stage together more than once). In his autobiography, Rexroth confirms that he

> became very fond of Geraldine Udell. . . .a quiet girl, very sure
> of herself, more secure in her position as a *revoltée* than other
> girls I knew. . . . With her I had long discussions about that
> Revolution which then seemed so near, and about Anarchism,
> Bolshevism, Syndicalism. . . . It may seem academic now and
> very far away, but it was not then; it was life and death to us in
> those days. . . . [273-274]

In Rexroth's handful of IWW-related poems, the Wobblies'
bright red love and hope and solidarity continue to sparkle, and his
poem to Geraldine Udell is a wondrous snapshot of a magic moment in the living dream of Revolution. These are fine poems by
a fine poet, but they are poems "about" the IWW, not "Wobbly
poems." Kenneth Rexroth was a poet profoundly sympathetic to
the IWW, but he too, like Claude McKay, cannot be considered
—and certainly did not ever consider himself —a Wobbly poet.

In 1965, the San Francisco Branch of the IWW—whose membership then consisted of about three dozen gainfully unemployed
youngsters, soon to be known as "hippies"—decided to form a
"Poets' Union." In a city that boasted an unusually large population of poets, recruits were not hard to find. At least one well-
known Bay Area poet, Robert Stock—a longtime anarcho-pacifist
who tended bar at the Co-Existence Bagel Shop and contributed to
the Beat magazine *Beatitude*—had lined up in the union some
years earlier, and a young poet from New York, John Ross, had
just joined. With the formation of the IWW Poets' Union, well
over a dozen prominent San Francisco Renaissance poets took out
red cards, as did a few of their out-of-town friends, including Allen
Ginsberg. After joining, however, the unionized poets seem to have
had trouble figuring out what to do next. As it turned out, the sole
activity of the Poets' Union, before disappearing from the stage of
history, was to organize one or two poetry readings—already a
crowded industry in San Francisco. In any event, Fellow Worker
Ginsberg's IWW membership does not appear to have lasted more
than two or three months at the most.

What this brief association with a small and youthful outpost
of the by-now-tiny One Big Union may have meant to the author
of *Howl* is a question I willingly leave to other researchers. As far
as I have been able to determine, the few IWW references in his

poetry occur nearly a decade *before* he filled out his membership application. "Afternoon Seattle" (in *Reality Sandwiches*, 1963) dates from 1956:

> Busride along waterfront down Yessler under street bridge
> to the old red Wobbly hall—
> One Big Union, posters of the Great Mandala of Labor,
> bleareyed dusty cardplayers dreaming behind the counter. . . .

The "mandala," of course, is "Father" Hagerty's famous diagram of industrial unionism—the so-called "Wheel of Fortune." A few lines lower Ginsberg mentions the great IWW organizer Frank Little. Another poem in the same book, also dated 1956, contains the line "I cried all over the street when I left the Seattle Wobbly Hall."

As these few quoted passages indicate, Ginsberg's social views had very little in common with those of the IWW. He was basically a liberal, although his liberalism embodied a lot of Popular Front Stalinism (inherited from his mother), as well as strong touches of Zionism and pacifism, all sorts of religious mysticism, and—during his last, highly prosperous quarter-century—a renewed faith in "Free Enterprise." Whatever his virtues, advancing the cause of revolutionary industrial unionism was not among them. At best Ginsberg was, as he himself admitted, a poet "sentimental about the IWW"—never a true Wobbly, and certainly not a Wobbly poet.

Claude McKay, Kenneth Rexroth and Allen Ginsberg have all received wide recognition as poets, and have been the subjects of a voluminous biographical and critical literature. The true "Wobbly poets," however—*as poets*—have received almost no recognition whatsoever. One and all they remain "outsiders." I do not mean that they are unknown—on the contrary, Hill's "Preacher and the Slave" and Chaplin's "Solidarity Forever" are well known to many *millions* of people. They are known as *songs*, however—not as poems, and are therefore regarded by the nation's self-appointed intellectual power-brokers as "not very important." In academia today, and throughout the entire U.S. intelligentsia, the devaluation of song is a hard, cold, anti-workingclass fact.

Within the IWW itself, songs have tended to be better known than poems, but many IWW songs started out as poems and were only later—sometimes much later—fitted to tunes. The songs are better remembered because songs are sung by groups, and in the

1910s and '20s, IWW songs were often sung by very large groups. In some strikes and free-speech fights, hundreds or even thousands would join and sing the same song.

This mass singing of revolutionary songs by men and women out on strike and in the streets was something new in the U.S. labor movement. Covering the famous IWW strike in Lawrence, Massachusetts, in 1912, muckraking journalist Ray Stannard Baker was astonished to find

> a strangely singing movement. It is the first strike I ever saw which sang. I shall not soon forget the curious lift, the strange sudden fire of the mingled nationalities at the strike meetings when they broke into the universal language of song. And not only at the meetings did they sing, but in the soup houses and in the streets. I saw one group of women strikers who were peeling potatoes at a relief station suddenly break into the "Internationale." They have a whole book of songs fitted to familiar tunes. . . . [Kornbluh 1998, 158]

A couple of years later, in an *International Socialist Review* article on migratory workers out west, Charles Ashleigh wrote:

> Certain it is that around nearly every "jungle" fire and during the evening hours on many a job in the great westland, the IWW red song book is in evidence. And the rude rebel chants are lustily sung. . . . [July 1914, 37]

In 1984, Fred Thompson recalled the importance of these songs during his own youth in the 1910s and '20s:

> When you're riding in boxcars for hours, a good way to pass the time is for everyone to join together in song. That's the way a lot of people first heard about the IWW—from fellow hoboes. [Doakes interview]

By its songs, by the number and variety of its songs, by the readiness of its members to sing, and by the enthusiasm with which they sang: For many, that is how the IWW distinguished itself from all other unions. These songs, moreover, as the Trinidadian Marxist C. L. R. James noted in 1943, "traveled all over the world" [1994, 153].

And don't forget that no IWW songs were sung more often

than Joe Hill's. The IWW may already have been "a singing union" when Hill joined up, but—as Dick Brazier would be the first to insist—Fellow Worker Hill between 1911 and 1913 did more than anyone else to make it THE Singing Union.

Empirical evidence verifies Hill's role in this regard. University of California economist Carleton Parker, in the course of his quasi-Freudian studies of "casual labor," met and interviewed hundreds of migratory workers in California in 1914. Out of some eight hundred workers "of the 'hobo' class," he noted, *half* were familiar with—and sympathetic to—the IWW program and "could also sing some of its songs" [Parker 1920, 189]. And he added: "Where a group of hoboes sit around a fire under a railroad bridge, many of the group can sing IWW songs without the book. *This was not so three years ago*" (*ibid.*, 190; emphasis added, FR).

"When you hear these songs," John Reed wrote in *The Liberator* in 1918,

> you'll know it is the American Social Revolution you are listening to. All over the country workers are singing Joe Hill's songs, "The Rebel Girl," "Don't Take My Papa Away From Me," "Workers of the World, Awaken!" Thousands can repeat his "Last Will," the three simple verses written in his cell the night before execution. I have met men carrying next their hearts, in the pocket of their working-clothes, little bottles with some of Joe Hill's ashes in them. Over Bill Haywood's desk in National headquarters is a painted portrait of Joe Hill, very moving, done with love. I know no other group of Americans which honors its singers. [Sept, 24]

It was not only Americans, however, who were singing Joe Hill's songs. They were also immensely popular in other English-speaking countries: in Australia, New Zealand, England, Scotland, and Wales. And they were also widely translated: into Swedish, Finnish, Russian, Hungarian, French, Spanish, Italian, and doubtless many more languages.

Verily, as Fellow Worker George B. Child noted in the *International Socialist Review* in June 1915, the IWW "owes as much or more to Joe Hill than to any other man or woman in it" [754].

---

1. Unfortunately, the 1979 English translation of this book by McKay was undertaken by an individual unfamiliar with the subject, and is filled with obvious errors. To cite but one typical example: William Z. Foster's Trade Union Educational League (TUEL) is cited as the "Education League of the trade unions" (33).

III
A FREE-SPIRITED INTERNATIONALIST

1. FROM SWEDISH IMMIGRANT TO CITIZEN OF THE WORLD

Surprisingly, in view of the fact that Hill is one of the most celebrated Swedes in U.S. history—right up there with Jenny Lind, the "Swedish Nightingale," "Chicago Renaissance" poet Carl Sandburg, and film-star Anita Ekberg—the Wobbly bard's involvement in the Swedish immigrant community in this country has been only lightly researched. An authoritative survey of Scandinavian-American literature has recognized him as the writer of "the only memorable poems in English by a Swedish-born immigrant" [Skårdal 1983, 256], but his interaction with fellow immigrants remains little known.

The fullest account of the subject, a short chapter in the memoirs of longtime Swedish-American socialist Henry Bengston, contains little detail and no personal memories of his own or others; indeed, his three pages on Hill do not mention a single one of Hill's Swedish friends or acquaintances in this country. Nels Hokanson, in a 1972 article on "Swedes and the IWW" in *The Swedish Pioneer Historical Quarterly*, remarks that Hill "preferred to live with Swedish families where he could enjoy Swedish food [and] talk about the old country," but provides no supporting evidence for this assertion [83]. Like Bengston, Hokanson was not personally acquainted with Hill, and does not refer to anyone else who knew him. Few of Hill's Swedish acquaintances wrote anything substantial about him. Oscar Larson, head of the Salt Lake City branch of the Verdandi—the largest Swedish organization in the U.S.—included his recollections of the Wobbly bard's last days, execution, and funeral in his book, *I främlingsland* (In a Land of Strangers), issued by the Scandinavian Workers Publishing Society in 1919. Mineworker Edward Mattson, who edited the union's Swedish-language paper *Solidaritet* in Seattle in the 1910s, and years later became president of the national miners' union in Sweden, also included some personal reminiscences in an article he wrote on Hill for the union's magazine, *Signalen*, in the 1940s [Bengston 1999, 154, 211; Söderstrom to FR, 7 Feb 2002].

The scarcity of reminiscences of Hill, or even anecdotes about him by Swedes who knew him, and of other documentation of his activities or even his presence in the U.S. Swedish community, suggests that his association with fellow Swedes in the New World was minimal. Fred Thompson, an old Wobbly widely acquainted with Swedish and other Scandinavian fellow workers, argued that the rapidity with which Hill acquired his fluency in English, and especially his grasp of American slang, confirms that the IWW poet did not spend much of his time with folks from the old country.

Hill's writings add weight to this hypothesis. Of Hill's fifty-odd surviving letters, only three were written to Swedes, and only one (to Larson) in Swedish. None contain anything that could be construed as nostalgia for his homeland. Apart from his 1906 eyewitness account of the San Francisco earthquake, he does not appear to have contributed anything to the Swedish-language press.

We do know that Hill kept in touch with at least a few Swedish friends, most notably his boyhood pal from Gävle, Charles Rudberg, who regarded the cartoon postcards he received from Hill as cherished possessions, and kept them all his life. According to Ralph Chaplin, Rudberg also received a note from Hill sometime after his arrest, which read simply: "I am not guilty" [1923, 26].

When Hill started on his ill-fated attempt to move to Chicago in 1913, he detoured briefly to Los Angeles in search of another Swedish friend, Oscar Westergren, whom he had known in the old country and later in San Francisco. In Salt Lake City he renewed his acquaintance with Otto Applequist, whom he had known in San Pedro, and both of them visited the boarding-house in Murray (a Salt Lake City suburb) run by countrymen, the Eselius brothers.

However, aside from these few names—which, moreover, are scarcely more than names, for almost nothing of substance is known about any of them—the record of Hill's Swedish friends in the U.S. is strangely silent. There are no indications that John Sandgren, director of the union's Swedish-language Joe Hill defense campaign, or John Chellman, described by Bengston as "the well-known tenor" who sang at Hill's Chicago funeral, were actually acquainted with the IWW poet, although it seems likely that they would have known other fellow workers who knew him. Neither, however, appears to have written anything on the subject.

In the absence of any evidence to the contrary, we can only conclude that Hill's involvement with the Swedish community in the U.S. was sporadic and slight.

Even slighter, however, were his contacts with his homeland. The notes and cards he sent to his sister Ester were not only few and far between, but also very brief. Aside from a single communication to his brother Efraim, letters Hill may have sent to other members of the family, and/or to friends back home, have evidently not survived.

The Swedish labor movement, however—as well as its substantial immigrant offshoot in the U.S.—have been staunch defenders of Hill's memory. A 24-page memorial pamphlet titled *Josef Hillstrom: Sångaren och rebellen som mordades av Utahs mormon-kapitalism den 19 November 1915*, by the syndicalist publisher Albert Jensen, appeared in Stockholm as early as 1916. As nothing was known about Hill in Sweden at that time, Jensen began his pamphlet with the candid admission: "Josef Hillstrom —Who was Josef Hillstrom? To be frank, I don't know" [Söderstrom to FR, 23 Feb 2002].

Many other publications followed. Augustin Souchy's pamphlet, *Anarkist maertyrena i Chicago* (Anarchist Martyrs in Chicago), published in Stockholm in 1920, focused on the Haymarket Martyrs, but also included a section on Joe Hill. According to Souchy's autobiography, *Beware! Anarchist!* (1992), this was in fact the first detailed account of the Hill case to appear in Europe. "Hill had to die because his songs against exploitation incited to rebellion. Heretofore nobody [in Europe] had tried to bring light to this dark chapter of American juggling of justice" [52-53].

In 1924, a 12-page pamphlet, *Sånger av Joe Hill* (Songs of Joe Hill), with translations by Ture Nerman, Signe Aurell, and others, was issued by the Stockholm Branch of the IWW's Marine Transport Workers Industrial Union 510. Five years later I. U. 510 also brought out an *IWW:s sång-bok*, featuring six songs and the "Last Will" by Hill, as well as songs by Ralph Chaplin and T-Bone Slim. A larger edition titled *Skandinavisk sångbok*, in the format of the *Little Red Song Book*, was published later in Seattle, and included Danish and Norwegian translations; copies were still for sale at IWW headquarters in Chicago in the late 1960s. Enn Kokk's almost complete collection, *Joe Hills sånger*, was issued by the Prisma publishing house in Stockholm as a 123-page paperback in 1969, and has been reprinted several times.

The May Day 1949 issue of the popular Swedish magazine *Folket i bild* [The People Illustrated] featured several articles on Hill, and two book-length biographies have also appeared: Ture

Nerman's pioneering study in 1951, and Ingvar Söderstrom's *Joe Hill: Diktare och agitator* (Joe Hill: Poet and Agitator) in 1970. Both have been reprinted, and Söderstrom revised and expanded his study in connection with the 2002 centennial of Hill's emigration to the United States.

Many Swedish singers, including Monica Nielsen, Mats Paulson, Fred Akerström, Hayati Kafe, Pierre Strom, Oskar Norrman, Anders Granell, and the Mora Trask group, have recorded Joe Hill's songs. In 1969 Swedish television featured a two-hour special on Hill, in color, with Tor Isedal in the starring role. As reported by Evert Anderson in the *Industrial Worker*, Isedal "got the job by reason of having sung the Joe Hill songs at union meetings so many times" [October 1969, 3].

To date, Sweden is the only country to have produced a full-length motion-picture about the Wobbly bard—Bo Widerberg's 1971 *Joe Hill*—and, in connection with the 1979 centennial of his birth, a Joe Hill commemorative postage stamp, featuring a drawing by Majvor Franzen-Mathews.

The house in which Joe Hill was born, in Gävle, serves today both as a local branch office of the Swedish syndicalist union, the SAC, and as the Joe Hill Museum, which draws 15,000 visitors a year. Joe Hill House, as the building is known, is a popular labor and community meeting-place.

A hundred years after leaving its shores for the New World, the Man Who Never Died continues to flourish in the land of his birth.

Postage stamp (Sweden,1980)
Art work by Majvor Franzen-Mathews

2. "THE PLEASURE OF FIGHTING
UNDER THE RED FLAG":
JOE HILL & THE MEXICAN REVOLUTION

*Whether they be victorious or defeated, I, for one, bow my head
to those heroic strugglers . . . who have raised the cry of Land and Liberty,
and planted the blood-red banner on the burning soil of Mexico.*
—Voltairine de Cleyre—

Published mentions of Joe Hill's doings "south of the border" tend to be dismayingly vague. Most books on Hill and the IWW either avoid the subject entirely, or dispose of it in a few lines.[1] It is certain that the author of "Workers of the World, Awaken!" took an active part in the Mexican Revolution—or more specifically, in what his friend Alexander MacKay called the "War of Liberation of Baja California" [letter to *Industrial Worker*, 27 Nov 1947]. The "paper trail," however, is sketchy and discontinuous, and practically every detail has been the subject of dispute.

For that matter, even Hill's involvement in the Revolution has been denied. Melvyn Dubofsky, for example, in his history of the IWW, categorically insists that "Hill never departed to Mexico" [1969, 309]. Other writers, equally misinformed, pretend that Hill merely "visited" Mexico at the time, without actually participating in the Revolution [Sandos 1992]. Typically, neither Dubofsky nor the others cite any sources for their arrogant assertions, which contradict Hill's own testimony and that of his closest friends.

The plain truth is that the Mexican Revolution was of vital interest to the IWW as a whole, and Joe Hill was only one of many footloose members who crossed the border at one time or another to help their Spanish-speaking fellow workers overthrow the brutal dictatorship of Porfirio Diaz. Contrary to the opinion of ignorant and cynical journalists and academics who have smugly referred to the socialist and IWW "invasion" of Mexico, the brave IWW volunteers who crossed the border to fight for Revolution exemplified the finest tradition of proletarian internationalism. The U.S. contingent itself—with the Canadian-born Native American William Stanley, the African American IWW known only as Lieutenant Roberts, a sizeable group of Italian anarchists, and at least one Swedish-born songwriter/poet/cartoonist—was a living symbol of world labor solidarity in action.

The volunteers from the U.S., moreover, were well aware that the corrupt and oppressive Diaz regime was in fact propped up primarily by U.S. capital and the U.S. capitalist state. As Charles H. Kerr pointed out in his editorial in the *International Socialist Review* in December, 1910:

> Few Americans, even American Socialists, realize the horrible conditions under which the working class is suffering in Mexico. And fewer still realize that the real slave-holders, for whose profit men, women and children are being bought and sold, starved and tortured just over our southern boundary line, are not Mexicans, but American capitalists. What is more, these capitalists are using the United States government, their government, to keep Porfirio Diaz in power, and it is Diaz that enables the slave-holders to keep their slaves in submission. But for Diaz and his soldiers, the slaves would free themselves; and without the active help of the United States Government, Diaz would soon be overthrown. [364]

John Kenneth Turner's *Barbarous Mexico*, a brilliant and influential exposé of the Diaz dictatorship published by Charles H. Kerr that same year, was read by many IWW members.

Many Mexicans, moreover, belonged to the IWW, especially in the southwestern U.S. and in Mexico itself. Historians have tended to ignore the lives and deeds of such fellow workers as Luis Rodriguez, Lazaro Guttierrez de Lara, Antonio Fuertes, J. R. Pesqueira, Francisco Martinez, Ricardo Trevino, Vicente Ortega, Jesus Rangel, Manuel Rey, and Pedro Coria, but these are all men who fought valiantly for workingclass emancipation, and deserve to be better remembered. And there were many hundreds more, few of whose names have come down to us. Between 1910 and 1918, Spanish-language IWW newspapers were published in Phoenix, Tampa, Los Angeles, and New York; a good number of these papers reached Mexican readers.

When U.S. politicians and the press began clamoring for military intervention in Mexico to protect U.S. oil and real-estate interests in that country, the IWW and the *International Socialist Review* took a strong revolutionary anti-war stand. Walker C. Smith's IWW leaflet, "War and the Workers," urged "Don't become hired murderers. Don't join the army or navy."

As one would expect, the IWW rejected the bourgeois liberalism of the wealthy landowner Francisco Madero and his party, and allied itself with the openly anarchist extreme left of the Revolution, the peculiarly named Partido Liberal de Mexico (Mexican Liberal Party), led by the brothers Flores Magon—Ricardo and Enrique—from the PLM's headquarters-in-exile in Los Angeles. Despite its name, the PLM was a thoroughly revolutionary organization, advocating direct action, and did not participate in electoral politics. Its aims were, first, to overthrow the government of dictator Porfirio Diaz, and second, to realize the PLM's slogan, later taken up by the Zapatistas: *Tierra y libertad!* (Land and Liberty!). In one of the many PLM manifestoes translated and published in the IWW press, Ricardo Flores Magon declared:

> Our salvation lies not alone in the fall of Diaz, but in the transformation of the ruling political and social system; and that transformation cannot be effected by the mere overthrow of one tyrant that another may be put in his place, but by the denial of the right of capital to appropriate to itself a portion of the toilers' product. [Thompson 1930-32, Chapter 8,16]

The Sixth Convention of the IWW in Chicago, September 1911, sent the PLM a telegram assuring the group of the IWW's "moral, financial, and physical support" [*ibid.*, 7]. For a time, the PLM shared office-space at the Wobbly hall at 219½ East 4th Street in Los Angeles.

The Mexican Revolution, then, was a high priority for the IWW in the 1910s, and its members served the Cause in many ways. In his *Labor Struggles in the Deep South*, Covington Hall noted that IWWs in Louisiana and Texas had

> many and close contacts [with Mexican revolutionists] such as the Land and Liberty Party [*i.e.*, the PLM]. We backed its great leader, Ricardo Flores Magon, to the limit of our power. [1999, 161-162]

In Chicago, Ralph Chaplin—at the request of the editors of the PLM paper, *Regeneración*—designed posters that the Magonistas used all over Mexico [Chaplin 1948, 117]. The IWW press and the *International Socialist Review* translated important Spanish-language revolutionary texts, and reported on every new development in detail. IWW branches throughout the country held forums on the Revolution, and collected money and guns to support the struggle.

The number of IWWs who went to Mexico to take part in the

Revolution is unknown, but it was almost certainly more than a hundred, and perhaps a great many more. So many members of the San Diego branch crossed the border that the branch had to disband; IWW headquarters in Chicago was informed that the reason for disbandment was not lack of interest but "Mexican Revolution" [Brissenden 1957, 366]. Fellow workers from other IWW branches in California, including Oakland, Holtville, San Pedro, and Los Angeles, also served as volunteers in the PLM's revolutionary army. An old Wobbly identified only as "Bobo," interviewed by history student Hyman Weintraub in the late 1940s, recalled "a band of eighteen or twenty" IWW members departing from L.A. to fight for Revolution in Mexico [Weintraub 1947, 273].

Initially, the prospects looked promising. In the union's first sustained account of its history—serialized in the *One Big Union Monthly*—Harold Lord Varney summed up the PLM/IWW's first major victory in Baja:

> A group of IWW men formed themselves into a secret band, bought arms and crossed the border into Lower California. . . . [T]hey were at first remarkably successful. They captured Mexicali [29 January 1911] and issued a flamboyant proclamation. But their success was short-lived. Met by regulars [Federales] . . . they were beaten and almost exterminated. . . . A few stragglers escaped across the border. [Feb 1920, 47]

Laura Payne Emerson's on-the-spot report, "A Visit to Mexico," on the PLM/IWW victory in Tijuana several weeks later was full of optimism:

> The first thing they did was to open the jail and let all the prisoners go free. . . . The wonder of the visitors and the United States soldiers on the border is that in that little town today, although a [revolutionary] army is camped there, no jail or guard house is needed. . . .
> Many of the [revolutionists] I had seen on other fields of battle, the economic field, and as I shook hands with them, while cartridge belts and guns made up a conspicuous part of their apparel, I knew it was the same old battle, only in a different form than of old. . . . [*Solidarity* No. 76, 1911, 2]

In *Regeneración* for 20 May 1911, an elated Ricardo Flores

Magon announced that "Baja California will be the principal base of our operations to carry the Social Revolution to the whole of Mexico and to the whole world" [Blaisdell 1962, 130].

Short-lived though these revolutionary successes proved to be, the IWW nonetheless attracted much favorable attention among the Mexican working class. As Fred Thompson observed in his short history of the union, in July 1911 "a number of Mexican unions confederated and adopted the IWW preamble" [1976, 50].

And what role did Joe Hill play in all this? Here, as almost everywhere else in Hill's biography, the absence of precise detail is glaring and frustrating. No one has found photographs of Hill in Mexico, or newspaper accounts of the IWW poet on the battlefield, charging the Federales. Names of several IWW volunteers in the Mexican Revolution appeared in the Mexican and U.S. press at the time, but not Hill's (it is of course possible that he used another name in Mexico). No documents regarding his brief career as a volunteer in the PLM forces have been found (the revolutionary armies of the Mexican Revolution, especially in its first phase, were not the world's greatest record-keepers).

Far worse than the lack of information, however, is the mass of *mis*information that has accumulated on the subject. Numerous are the groundless assertions glibly made by irresponsible writers and blithely repeated by others as "established fact." Quoting baseless tittle-tattle as truth is using footnotes to spread lies.

To survey the many unsubstantiated and contradictory statements regarding Hill in Mexico would run to many pages; I shall mention only a few typical examples. Wallace Stegner, the most hostile and sloppy of those who have written on Hill, stated in his 1948 *New Republic* article that "it is certain" that Hill, in Mexico, was "with the outfit of 'General' Rhys Price" [22]. However, as is generally true of Stegner's "certainties," there is in truth no evidence whatsoever that Hill had any contact at all with that dubious soldier of fortune.

Another writer offers this condescending observation:

> Celebrated Wobblies such as Joe Hill visited the Tijuana encampment and extolled its virtues, but to the popular press it looked like a scruffy, motley vagabond band. [Sandos 1992]

This one little sentence contains three crimes against simple honesty. Hill's appearance in Mexico is trivialized into a mere "visit," and we are not told where or when or to whom he "extolled" the encampment's virtues. Even more disgustingly, the "popular press" whose opinion the writer clearly respects turns out to be the Otis-and Hearst-owned Los Angeles newspapers—that is, the most viciously anti-labor publications in the country.

The credibility of still other writers on Hill in Mexico can be gauged by their references to a certain "International Workers of the World" [Taylor 1999, 4], or, in one case, to the "International Workingmen of the World" [Castillo 1970, 258, 262]. Would *you* believe anything you read on Joe Hill by an author who can't even get the union's name right?[2]

Alas, authentic testimony on this aspect of Hill's life has proved especially elusive. It would be a joy to read a Mexican Magonista's recollections of Hill at that time—I imagine he spoke at least a little Spanish (with a slight Swedish accent, of course) —but if such a memoir exists it has not yet come to light.

We do, however, have one reliable eyewitness account of Joe Hill in revolutionary Mexico. In 1955, Ethel Duffy Turner—editor (in the 1910s) of the English-language page of *Regeneracion*, and widow of John Kenneth Turner—interviewed Hill's friend Sam Murray in the Veterans' Home in Yountville, California. At 85, Fellow Worker Murray was still a militant Wobbly, lucid and active, without a trace of senility; Turner was especially impressed by his "keen memory."

"For a long time," Turner wrote, "I had been trying to run down a rumor that the great proletarian songwriter Joe Hill had fought with the Magonistas in Baja California." Her conversation with Sam Murray confirmed that the rumor was true. Although we do not have her transcription of Murray's own words, Turner published a summary of Murray's remarks in her book, *Revolution in Baja California: Ricardo Flores Magon's High Noon*, and here it is:

> Murray had been a buddy of Joe Hill in Baja California. After a talk with Ricardo Flores Magon in Los Angeles and with the wounded Jack Mosby in San Diego, Murray had crossed into the *insurrecto* camp about June 8 [1911]. Joe Hill had arrived about the first of June.

Joe Hill: "How the Memory Doth Linger" (drawing, 1914-15).
This sketch of Sam Murray as a Mexican Revolutionist
first appeared in the *Industrial Pioneer* (December 1923).

At first not much was going on. In the evenings Joe Hill used to play his violin and sing his workers' songs, the dryly ironic words mocking the bosses, the hypocrites, and the willing slaves to the system. With his warm, agreeable and yet quiet disposition he added greatly to the morale in the camp. He talked little, but he drew amusing cartoons.

On June 22 Mosby sent out a company of seventeen men under a Canadian named Sylvester. They were directed to see if they could detect the presence of [the Federales, Diaz's army]. Both Sam Murray and Joe Hill were in this group. The men all carried 30-30 rifles. About ten kilometers to the south of Tijuana they spread out along the river and over the flat terrain, taking a barn and a farmhouse.

Mosby had told them, "If you see the enemy, come back." But when the advance-guard of the [Federales] arrived, Sylvester would not retreat. His men fired on the guard and held them back until the forces under Mosby arrived. The Federales thought the barn was full of revolutionists, though no one was actually inside. They were afraid to push forward. The seventeen Liberals [*i.e.*, the PLM/IWW forces] advanced over flat ground in skirmish formation. One *insurrecto* was killed. . . .

When General Jack Mosby and his force arrived, a battle with the [Federales] broke out. It lasted about an hour. Overwhelmed by vastly superior numbers and heavy power in the form of the six machine-guns, the Liberals were forced to retreat back toward Tijuana.

That decisive defeat ended the hope of a continued large-scale struggle in Baja California. The enemy overran Tijuana. Several *insurrectos* slipped safely across the line. Joe Hill was among them. Sam Murray and many others were taken into custody by the U.S. Army and imprisoned at Fort Rosecrans, near San Diego. [Turner 1981]

In this brief account, Murray does what none of the other "mentions" of Hill in Mexico have done: He tells us when Hill went there, and where; what he did there; and when he left.

Curiously, this extraordinary interview—evidently first published in Spanish in 1960 and in English twenty-one years later—is not cited in any of the studies of Hill.

How well Hill knew the commander of his unit, General Jack Mosby, is a matter of speculation, but they were probably acquainted long before Hill left for Mexico. Hill evidently liked Mosby; he inquired about him in a letter to Murray written in the Salt Lake City jail in September 1914 [*Letters*, 13].

Along with William Stanley, who took Los Algodones, and Luis Rodriguez, who took Tecate, General John R. (Jack) Mosby was one of the major figures in the Baja California Revolution, and surely merits a full biography. He was said to be the son of one of P. T. Barnum's partners and the nephew of a Confederate guerrilla. More significantly, Mosby was a member of the Oakland, California IWW local and a deserter from the United States Marine Corps. Although considered undistinguished as a military tactician, Mosby was esteemed for his effective campfire oratory, which he probably learned as an IWW soapboxer. "His chief virtues," according to a non-radical historian, were his "kind heart" and "his loyalty to Flores Magon" [Blaisdell 1962, 110; Taft 1972].

In U.S. revolutionary circles Mosby, Fellow Worker and General, enjoyed considerable prestige, as indicated by the fact that when the June 1914 *International Socialist Review* announced Hill's forthcoming trial, the Wobbly bard was described not only as the "author of the IWW song book [and a] cartoonist," but also as "a rebel from Lower California with Jack Mosby" [763].

In addition to opening the jail, the Tijuana revolutionists under General Mosby's command burned the bullfighting ring, abolished gambling, banned liquor, and forced "soldiers of fortune" and other exploiters to leave town [Blaisdell 1962, 176]. The General's proclamation of 3 June 1911, conveys something of his revolutionary spirit:

> The Mexican Liberal Party is directing the present revolutionary movement in Mexico. . . . The fight is not being waged in the interest of . . . the American capitalists, but solely in the interest of the working class. Lower California will not be separated from the rest of Mexico, but the revolution will be carried on in all the states of Mexico until the Mexican people are freed from the present military despotism and slavery, peonage abolished, and the lands returned to the people, which have been stolen from them by the Mexican and foreign capitalists. [Martinez, 1960, 479-80]

You have to admit, that's not the language of the U.S. Marines.

Like the other officers in the PLM/IWW volunteer army in Mexico, Mosby was *elected*, not appointed. This was truly a revolutionary workers' army, and had nothing in common with the "soldiers of fortune" and filibusters who sought to "get rich quick" at the expense of the Mexican people. All through the

1910s and into the '20s the U.S. daily press denounced and ridiculed the Revolution, and journalists directed many of their worst insults at the American volunteers, especially IWWs, who were accused of being robbers, thieves, landgrabbers, and hoodlums whose sole purpose was to amass easy fortunes for themselves. This anti-IWW slander—prefiguring Hitler's "Big Lie"—was so pervasive in the mass-circulation press that it even affected some Mexican historians, who in turn used such spurious "evidence" to tarnish the Magonistas. In what is probably the best, and surely the most meticulous, study of the Baja California Revolution, historian Pablo L. Martinez—neither Magonista nor anti-Magonista, but a serious seeker of the truth—concluded that

> the taint of filibusterism that was hurled against the Liberals [*i.e.*, the PLM] was contrived by ... Harrison Gray Otis, his son-in-law Harry Chandler and William Randolph Hearst; and they spread it by means of newspapers of which they were proprietors. ... The two first-named were owners of nearly all the land in the Valley of Mexicali, and the last named had concessions of great extent in Chihuahua. [Martinez, 1960, 489-90]

In other words, the IWW's bitterest enemies spread their vicious lies, and some gullible historians believed them. Isn't that what is known as "Business as Usual"?

Over the years, other fellow workers who knew Hill, or knew people who knew Hill, added bits and pieces to the Mexican chapter of the Wobbly bard's life. In 1923 Ralph Chaplin reported that "John Holland" (*i.e.*, Hill's older brother Paul) told him that Hill, in battle in Mexico, had suffered a gunshot wound [25]. In the late 1940s, former Wob Mortimer Downing told history student Hyman Weintraub that he recalled Hill as a PLM recruiter in Los Angeles—a snippet which dovetails nicely with the statement of "Bobo" quoted above [Weintraub 1947, 282].

That Hill was personally acquainted with both of the Flores Magon brothers would seem to belong to the realm of the obvious, inasmuch as the brothers ran the PLM office in Los Angeles during the very years that Hill was active in and around that city. However, William Chance appears to have been the first to actually point it out, in a 1967 interview cited by Gibbs Smith in his Hill biography [1969, 53, 215n]. In a letter to Fred Thompson, Louis Moreau mentioned that Chance had also told him that he (Chance) "and Joe attended the Magon trial" [20 Feb 1967], but does not specify which one of Ricardo's many trials it was—probably the June 1911 trial, at which the PLM leader was convicted of infringing U.S. neutrality regulations [Avrich 1988, 210].

Especially important is Sam Murray's introduction to "The Last Letters of Joe Hill" in the *One Big Union Monthly* for December 1923, in which he stated unequivocally that he "had been with Joe in Lower California." (It was this statement that started Ethel Duffy Turner on her quest, years later, to track down Fellow Worker Murray and find out what else he had to say.) Accompanying Murray's text and Hill's letters in the *OBU Monthly* is Hill's sketch (see page 83), captioned "How the memory doth linger (Sam Murray as a Mexican Revolutionist)."

Hill's own references to Mexico, in one of his articles and in several letters to his friends, are also illuminating. In March 1913 the *Industrial Worker* published Hill's article, "The People"—a polemic against using the expression "the people," which Hill, as a good Marxist, considered demagogic, since in daily usage "the people" generally means "the middle class." By way of illustration, he evoked his experiences in the Baja Revolution:

> When the Red Flag was flying in Lower California there were not any of "the people" in the ranks of the rebels. Common working stiffs and cow-punchers were in the majority, with a little sprinkling of "outlaws," whatever that is. "The people" used to come down there on Sunday in their stinkwagons to take a look at "The Wild Men with their Red Flag" for two-bits a look. [Kornbluh 1964, 237]

A photo in Blaisdell's *Desert Revolution* [1962] shows a red flag —the *Tierra y Libertad* flag—flying over Tia Juana, with a group of revolutionists in the foreground.

Two years later, in a letter to Sam Murray written in the Salt Lake City jail on 13 February 1915, Hill refers, with more than a hint of nostalgia, to the "Tierra e [*sic*] Libertad bunch" [*Letters*, 26]. And on 30 September, expecting to be executed a few days later, he wrote Murray again: "Well, Sam, you and me had a little pleasure at one time that few rebels have had the privilege of having. . . ." [*ibid.*, 57].

To Elizabeth Gurley Flynn he was more explicit: "I had the pleasure to fight under the Red Flag once. . ." [*ibid.*, 62]. And addressing himself in Swedish to his Swedish socialist comrade, Oscar W. Larson, Hill wrote:

> I had . . . one time the great honor of struggling on the battlefield under the Red Flag and I must admit I am proud of it. . . . [*ibid.*, 59]

These words recall Hill's song, "Should I Ever Be a Soldier," which first appeared in the fifth edition of the *Little Red Song Book* in the spring of 1913. The last line of its chorus evokes his days with "the *Tierra y libertad* bunch":

> *We're spending billions every year*
> *For guns and ammunition,*
> *"Our Army" and "Our Navy" dear,*
> *To keep in good condition;*
> *While millions live in misery*
> *And millions died before us,*
> *Don't sing "My Country 'tis of thee,"*
> *But sing this little song:*

Chorus
> *Should I ever be a soldier*
> *'Neath the Red Flag I would fight. . . .*
> *Wage slaves of the world! Arouse!*
> *Do your duty for the cause,*
> *For Land and Liberty.*

---

1. Brissenden (1957 [1920]), Renshaw (1968), and Stavis (1954), contain not so much as one line about the Revolution in Mexico; Foner (1965) gives it a four-line footnote; Foner (1965a) less than two lines; Kornbluh 1998 [1964], two and a half lines; Thompson (1976), seven lines; Gibbs Smith (1969), a little over two pages.

2. Some writers name Frank Little as another IWW active in the Baja Revolution, but there seems to be no evidence of it.

Charles E. Setzer (X13)
(*Industrial Worker*, 23 January 1953)

3. THE FRASER RIVER STRIKE:
THE IWW BARD IN CANADA

A pine tree stands so lonely
In the North where the high winds blow
—Heinrich Heine—

Like his contemporary Ambrose Bierce, the Swedish-Mexican Hill seems to have disappeared in the swirling dust of historical uncertainty and disputation. Apart from passing references in his letters, brief comments by his friends, and wildly conflicting accounts by historians, all that remains of Hill's Mexican adventure are a sketch of Fellow Worker Sam Murray wearing a sombrero, and the last line of a song.

The Swedish-Canadian Hill, in contrast—although his one known trip north of the U.S.A. may have lasted as little as a month —left some tangible traces, most notably the fine song "Where the Fraser River Flows," written for Canadian Northern railroad construction workers whose strike was in fact his reason for heading north. Decades later, his Canadian sojourn was richly documented in an exceptionally detailed first-hand account of that major strike written by IWW organizer Louis Moreau, who also recalled (and recorded) fragments of three heretofore unknown Hill songs dating from his Canadian days.

Though habitually slighted by U.S. historians, the IWW in Canada spans a long and eventful history [Leier 1990, Scott 1975]. Several Canadian delegates attended the founding convention in Chicago, 1905, and thanks in part to the insistence of one of them —John Riordan—the new union adopted the name Industrial Workers of the World rather than Industrial Union of America, which had also been proposed [*Proceedings* 1905, 297-298; Leier, 36].

The IWW was especially active in British Columbia. A little over a year after the founding convention the new union had five locals in B.C., and five more were organized in the Kootenay region in 1907. Many of the best-known IWW agitators from the States—including Elizabeth Gurley Flynn, Lucy Parsons, Big Bill Haywood, Joseph Ettor and John H. Walsh—toured B.C. as speakers and/or organizers during the union's early years [Leier 1990, 43-44].

By 1912 the IWW was a vigorous presence throughout the

province: an inspiration to tens of thousands of wage-workers, and a fearsome "menace" to employers and labor contractors who, like their counterparts in the U.S., vilified the union in the press, and used the police and other machinery of state—as well as "unofficial" armed thugs—to deny IWW members such basic rights as free speech and assembly.

Repression notwithstanding, the IWW continued to grow in Canada as elsewhere. The union's reputation for "getting the goods"—wage-increases, shorter hours, and better job conditions—made the organizers' tasks easier. Indeed, once the IWW made itself known in a new town or region, workers often *organized themselves* into it. In April 1912, for example, IWW organizers in Victoria were surprised that *three hundred* street-pavers—"Greeks, Italians, Americans, Canucks, and colored men" —showed up at the union hall to take out red cards, and immediately voted to strike for a wage-increase as well as a ban on overtime. An African Canadian fellow worker was elected chairman of the strike committee [Leier 1990, 44]. Spontaneity, enthusiasm, diversity, and solidarity are the essential ingredients of IWW self-organization.

That same year, 1912, the great Canadian Northern railroad strike marked one of the largest IWW organizing efforts anywhere, involving 8000 railroad construction workers over a 400-mile area. It was this strike that gave rise to one of the IWW's outstanding tactical innovations: the "thousand-mile picketline." To prevent the hiring of scabs, IWW members and supporters picketed employment offices in Vancouver, Seattle, Tacoma, Minneapolis, and San Francisco. The slogan "Think globally, act locally" may be relatively new, but the concept goes back a long way.

Early on in this historic struggle—well known in Canada as "the Fraser River Strike"—Joe Hill showed up and started writing songs. Louis Moreau, who was there as an organizer at the request of IWW General Secretary-Treasurer Vincent St John, tells the story:

> I was a participant in the strike on the Canadian Northern railroad in B.C. in 1912. I was working before the strike with a firm of American contractors by name of Toohees Brothers with head-quarters in the little settlement of Spuzzum between Yale and Lytton on the Fraser River.
>
> Lytton was headquarters for the Construction Workers local

No. 327. Tom Whitehead was secretary. Lytton was also strike headquarters with branch No. 1, branch No. 2 at Spencer Bridge, and No. 3 at Yale. Before the strike I was camp delegate for branch No. 3 at Yale, B.C.

Joe Hill made his appearance at our strike camp at Yale a week or ten days after the strike [began]. I didn't know Joe before [that], but quite a few fellow workers knew him and [he] was very popular. Joe wrote "Where the Fraser River Flows" the first few days he was in our strike camp—it became very popular with everybody. Then he wrote "We Won't Build No More Railroads for Our Overalls and Snuff," then "Skookum Ryan, the Walking Boss," and "The Mucker's Dream."

Joe was with us until the Grand Raid by the provincial police and the mounties. I did not see Joe during or after the raid. Of course during the raid everything was in [an] uproar, but I know that Joe was not captured. The raid wasn't very success-ful as we knew it was coming—but not the date—and had prepared for it. . . .   In regards to Joe, he was well-liked by the strikers, honest, good-natured. . . . He was in Yale most of April and up to the big raid. [letter to Fred Thompson, 20 Feb 1967; last paragraph, 8 Mar 1967]

"Where the Fraser River Flows" (to the tune of the then-popular "Where the River Shannon Flows") is a robust and catchy strike song, with a soapboxer's opening and a rousing chorus:

Fellow Workers, pay attention to what I'm going to mention,
For it is the fixed intention of the workers of the world,
And I hope you'll all be ready, true-hearted, brave and steady,
To gather 'round our standard when the Red Flag is unfurled.

Chorus:
Where the Fraser River flows, every fellow worker knows,
They have bullied and oppressed us, but still our Union grows.
And we're going to find a way, boys,
*   for shorter hours and better pay, boys!*
And we're going to win the day, boys, where the Fraser River
*   flows.*

For these gunnysack contractors have all been dirty actors,
And they're not our benefactors, each fellow worker knows.
So we've got to stick together in fine or dirty weather,
And we will show no white feather, where the Fraser River
*   flows.*

"Gunnysack contractors" were the despised, low-paying subcon-tractors, assigned by the chief contractors to carry out certain aspects of the work. According to Moreau, when the chief contrac-tors agreed to a wage-increase, it was hard to get their "gunnysack" underlings to comply. "Gunnysack contractors" were also notori-ous for providing flimsy bunkhouses and other inadequate facili-ties.

A runaway hit among the strikers, "Where the Fraser River Flows" first appeared in the *Industrial Worker* on 9 May 1912. It was reprinted in the new edition of the *Little Red Song Book* later that year, and has been included in many subsequent editions. It has also been featured on LPs and CDs. Its historic value as a document of one of the union's outstanding strikes is indicated by the fact that three books on the history of the IWW in Canada have reprinted the lyrics in full [Scott 1975; Swankey 1977; Leier 1990]. Curiously, the song was omitted from the *Canadian IWW Song-book* published by the Toronto IWW Branch in 1990, which, however, did include a "Canadian version" of Hill's "Mr Block"—in which "President" was changed to "Prime Minister," and "AF of L" to "CLC"—as well as an "update" of his "There Is Power in a Union."

Hill's other Canadian songs exist only as fragments preserved in the tenacious memory of Fellow Worker Moreau, who jotted them down in 1947. Of the songs listed in Moreau's recollections, as quoted above, he remembered whole stanzas of "We Won't Build No Railroads for Overalls and Snuff" and "Skookum Ryan, the Walking Boss," but nothing of "The Mucker's Dream" except the title. Moreau also recalled a fourth song, titled "Martin Welch and Stuart"—the chief track-laying contractors for the Canadian Northern—and sung to the tune of "Wearing of the Green"):

Martin Welch is mad as hell and don't know what to do,
And all his gunnysack contractors are feeling mighty blue;
For we have tied their railroad line and scabs refuse to come,
And we will keep on striking till we put them on the bum.

This quatrain is of special interest because of Moreau's illuminat-ing commentary:

The Wobblies drove those contractors nuts. One day Martin came by our camp at Yale annex and started to talk to a bunch of

Swedes that were sitting alongside of the road. When the groaning brigade, our singing sextet, started to sing the song that Joe had made for him, Martin tore his hair and swore he'd get us. [letter to editor of *Industrial Worker*, 15 Nov 1947]

In short, thanks to Fellow Worker Moreau, we have a precious example of the on-the-job application and impact of one of Hill's songs during his own lifetime.

Like most of the great IWW battles, the Fraser River Strike was noted for the exciting and dynamic way it combined individual creativity and collective discipline. A *Vancouver Province* reporter likened the Yale strike camp to "a miniature republic run on socialistic lines," and reluctantly conceded that "so far it has been run successfully" [Leier, 1990, 49]. And thus Joe Hill, who had the pleasure and the honor of fighting under the Red Flag in the Mexican Revolution, also enjoyed a foretaste of the workers' commonwealth in a major Canadian strike.

In August, the Canadian Northern strikers were joined by 3000 more workers on the Grand Trunk Pacific line. Together, the two railway strikes are regarded as "the high-water mark of the [IWW's] activities in British Columbia" [Leier 1990, 52].

As a hobo highly skilled in the art of getting around, and a Swede familiar with colder climes, Hill may well have enjoyed other visits to the north, but his participation in the Fraser River Strike is the only Canadian episode to have entered the historical record.

As a reward for his own appreciable efforts in the strike, Louis Moreau informs us that "our uncle King George invited me to be his guest at one of his hostelries on the island of Vancouver"—*i.e.*, he was sentenced to six months in the Westminster jail [letter to Fred Thompson, 8 Mar 1967].

Joe Hill Centennial button,
Illinois Labor History Society

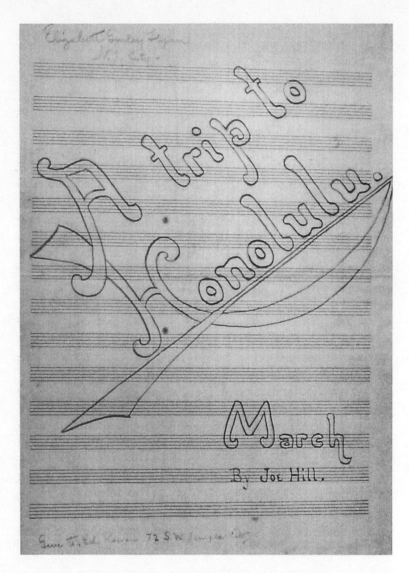

Joe Hill: Cover design for "A Trip to Honolulu" (1915).

4. MORE MYSTERIES OF A HOBO'S LIFE: FELLOW WORKER HILL ON THE HONOLULU RUN

To sit together
Drinking the blue ocean, eating the sun
Like a fruit
—Genevieve Taggard—

Reports of Joe Hill's Hawaiian sojourns come from two sources. The man who called himself Hill's cousin, "John Holland"—now known to have been his older brother Paul Hägglund—told Ralph Chaplin that Hill, during his San Pedro years, worked "freight steamers on the Honolulu run" [1948, 185]. He added that it was Hill's "association with migratory workers at sea and ashore" that originally attracted him to the IWW.

Some two decades later Harry McClintock, in a letter to Wallace Stegner, said that he, Hill and Pat Kelly shared a shack for two or three months on the beach at Hilo, employed "as longshoremen—loading raw sugar in the holds of the American-Hawaiian sugar boats" [Smith 1969, 55]. That was in the winter of 1911.

In the 1950s, in an interview with folksong collector Sam Eskin, McClintock reiterated that he had run into Hill in Hilo, Hawaii, in 1911: "We were inhabiting a shack over there, on the beach—we were working as longshoremen—and [it was] very nice going" [Folkways 1972, LP FD5272, Side 1]. In this interview, Mac fails to mention Pat Kelly.

In his short 1981 biography of McClintock, based on Mac's notes, Henry Young wrote that Mac

> heard that an old friend, Pat Kelly, an accomplished accordion
> player was very popular on the beaches of Hilo. . . . Accordingly
> he [Mac] shipped out on the steamship "Arizonan" and spent
> most of the winter at Hilo as a part-time stevedore and full-time
> beachcomber. . . . returned to San Francisco at the beginning of
> spring in 1911. [41]

Young's account contains no mention of Hill.

The image of Joe Hill as beachcomber is not without charm, and the Hawaii of those days must have been a real delight to anyone who, like Hill, was passionally attracted to the "great outdoors." It can be doubted, however, that he took up beachcombing "full-time." In 1911, Hawaii was already a beehive of

95

revolutionary activity, well-documented in the workers' press.

In the March 1911 issue of the *International Socialist Review*, for example, a feature titled "Flashes from China" by "A Socialist Sailor" tells of Comrade Lo Sun, editor of *Liberty News*, a Chinese-language socialist paper published in Honolulu. He reported that Lo Sun and another comrade, Sun Foo, were translating and publishing the *Communist Manifesto* in Chinese, along with several of the Charles H. Kerr Company's popular "Center Shot" leaflets. The author took care to relate the workers' struggle in the islands to the struggle in the U.S., pointing out that

> Millions and millions of dollars are now being spent to fortify Hawaii—for the benefit of American capitalism. They want to Americanize the island so that capitalism will have patriotic fools who will shoulder guns and fight for the masters. [518]

Noting that the Chinese consul in Honolulu had reported to the government in Peking that "all the Chinese in Hawaii [are] revolutionists," "A Socialist Sailor" concluded that the "future of revolutionary ideas" in Hawaii looked promising. [*ibid.*]

Although no documents have come to light regarding Hill's doings in Hawaii, it is a virtual certainty that he visited other representatives of the IWW while he was there. In view of what we know of his activity in other places, it does not seem unlikely that he lent a hand to the union's agitation in Hawaii. And it is not impossible that his impact there was far greater than anyone has ever dreamed. After 1911, in any case, Hawaii became a Wobbly hot spot.

Indeed, the following year the *Industrial Worker* was jubilant about the "effective work" of IWW agitation in the islands. "The little red song books," a front-page feature boasted, "are finding their way to the laborers on all the plantations." The story reported that Japanese workers are "joining in large numbers" and that the local in Honolulu had to move to a larger hall "on account of its swift growth." The article closes with a rousing call: "On with the One Big Union that takes in all wage workers, whether young or old, skilled or unskilled, white, black, yellow, brown, or red" [12 Dec 1912].

In January 1913 the paper reported that a Korean local had been formed in Hawaii, and commended organizer Albert V. Roe on his success in "bringing many new members" into the union throughout the islands. According to Roe, the union's "prime need" there was IWW literature in many languages, especially Chinese [16 Jan 1913].

A few weeks later an article titled "Doing Things in Hawaii" announced the formation of "several branches of the IWW in Honolulu, each having their own hall." These were all "foreign-language branches": Filipino, Chinese, Hawaiian, Korean and Russian. There was also a "mixed local" on Maui [6 Mar 1913].

The following month the *Industrial Worker* reported that the union was steadily growing in Hawaii, and had just rented a large house as IWW headquarters [10 Apr 1913].

The October 1913 issue of the *International Socialist Review* noted that Comrade Estelle Baker had sent in "eleven new subscriptions from Honolulu" [246]. That same month, *Solidarity* reported progress in organizing on the island of Kauai, noted that "We are enrolling slaves in all languages," and concluded with an appeal to the footloose: "All red hot rebels are invited to the 'Parasites of the Pacific'" [18 Oct 1913]. The term "Parasites" played on the tourist and real-estate agent sales-pitch that called the islands "Paradise."

Obviously, for a red-hot rebel like Hill, there was plenty to do in Hawaii besides comb the beaches. Alas, his extant letters contain nary a word on his doings there. His sole reference to Hawaii appears in a postscript to an October 1915 letter to Elizabeth Gurley Flynn:

> I made "a trip to Honolulu" the other day, and set it to music. It's a March, and what's more, "It's a Bear." Am sending you same through E. R. [Ed Rowan]." [*Letters*, 75]

"A Trip to Honolulu" was a piece of music composed by Hill. It was never published and is rarely mentioned in the literature on Hill or the IWW. Hill's original sheet music for the tune was inaccessible until 2001, when it turned up in a long lost file of Elizabeth Gurley Flynn's Hill-related documents (now part of the Flynn collection at the Research Library for Marxist Studies in New York).

Hill's Honolulu march is one of his eight surviving musical compositions, and the only one without lyrics. What inspired him to compose it, to give it that title, and to leave it wordless, are three more mysteries of a hobo's life.

In comparison, our knowledge of Hill's *other* trips to Hawaii turns out to be rather impressive.

And what became of Pat Kelly, Wobbly accordionist? An odd volume of travel literature offers a glimpse of his post-Hawaiian adventures, and incidentally lends a smattering of credibility to McClintock's story. Frederick O'Brien's *Mystic Isles of the South Seas*, published in 1921, devotes a chapter to a group of foreigners in Tahiti, who took their meals together and often sang songs afterward, accompanied by native Tahitian musicians. As O'Brien tells it:

> The heavy leads of the band were carried by an American with a two-horsepower accordion. He told me his name was Kelly. He was under thirty, a resolute, but gleesome chap, red-headed, freckled, and unrestrained by anybody or anything. . . . He had a song book of the Industrial Workers of the World . . . and in it were scores of popular airs accompanied by words of dire import to capitalists and employers. . . . [143]

He quotes Kelly as saying:

> I'm an IWW. I came here because I got tired o' bein' pinched. Every town I went to in the United States I denounced the police and the rotten government, and they throwed me in the calaboose. I never could get even unlousy. I came here six weeks ago. It's a little bit of all right. [*ibid.*]

According to O'Brien, "None of us had ever heard Kelly's songs, nor had anyone but I ever heard of his industrial organization, and I only vaguely, having lived so many years out of America. . . ." Kelly's Wobbly songs, however, were instant hits on the island, and not only among the foreigners. One song in particular was "very popular with the natives of the band," who played it repeatedly. O'Brien described it as "a crude travesty of a hymn much sung in religious camp-meetings," and recalled hearing the "proper chorus" in a Chicago mission:

> *Hallelujah! Thine the glory! Hallelujah! Amen!*

Kelly's version, of course, and the popular one among the Tahitians, went like this:

> *Oh, why don't you work, as other men do?*

How the hell can we work when there's no work to do?
Hallelujah! I'm bum! Hallelujah! Bum again!

O'Brien went on to explain that the Tahitian language did not include certain English sounds, so that the islanders' version of the Wobbly song was distinctive:

Hahrayrooyah! I'm a boom! Hahrayrooyah! Boomagay!

O'Brien's story suggests that when the Hawaiian Wobbly Trio broke up, probably in the late spring of 1911, Hill and McClintock headed back to the States, and Fellow Worker Kelly set off for Polynesia. It is not known that the redheaded Wobbly accordionist ever returned to the U.S.A.

Advertisement from an IWW pamphlet (1910s)

May Day cartoon by I. Swenson (*Industrial Worker*, 1921)

Jim Lynch: How the Capitalist
Class Treats Labor News

5. "DON'T SING 'MY COUNTRY, 'TIS OF THEE'": JOE HILL'S INTERNATIONALISM

Patriotism, which in peace is provincialism,
in war becomes stark madness.
—Fanny Bixby Spencer—

When Joe Hill declared himself a "citizen of the world" it was not a grandiloquent boast, but a simple affirmation. Like many migrant workers, he felt at home anywhere and everywhere, regarded no particular place as "his," and found the belief in a Fatherland or a Mother Country to be incomprehensible. His distance from the Swedish-American community; his unrelenting criticism of injustice in the U.S.A. (in his songs, cartoons, articles, and letters); and his revolutionary activity in Mexico, Canada, and Hawaii all point in the same direction: Joe Hill's radicalism had not even the smallest taint of patriotism. Love of country, in his view, was for Blocks and scissorbills. Recognizing the capitalist state—all states—as oppressive, he pledged his allegiance only to the revolutionary working class of all countries.

In his opposition to patriotism, nationalism, militarism, jingoism, flags, uniforms, and other forms of "My Country, Right or Wrong" claptrap, Joe Hill was the consummate Wobbly—which is to say, an intrepid proletarian internationalist—and internationalism is a recurring theme of his songs and letters. His Wobbly humor, moreover, was often directed at flag-wavers and saber-rattlers. Surely the author of "Should I Ever Be a Soldier" belongs in the distinguished company of Mark Twain, Ambrose Bierce, Eugene Debs, Jack London, Fanny Bixby Spencer, Joseph Heller, Dick Gregory, and others who have enriched the library of America's anti-militarist classics. Scorn for the very notion of "nation-states" and governments, and for those who put their faith in them, is also evident in many other of his songs. A splendid one-liner from his "John Golden and the Lawrence Strike" explains why state militias and federal troops are such ineffective strikebreakers:

Weaving cloth with bayonets is hard to do.

"Scissor Bill" nails the deluded patriotic workingstiff:

> *He'll say "this is my country," with an honest face,*
> *While all the cops they chase him out of every place.*

"Stung Right," an anti-military-recruitment song, may be a bit dated in some respects, but even after many decades it retains its sting:

> *Some time ago when Uncle Sam he had a war with Spain,*
> *And many of the boys in blue were in the battle slain.*
> *Not all were killed by bullets, though; no, not by any means,*
> *The biggest part that died were killed by Armour's Pork and*
> * Beans.*

Anti-chauvinist, anti-statist, anti-employing-class, these are songs of a rank-and-file militant in the global class war—a free spirit who refused to be duped, even for a moment, by any sort of nationalist fervor. For Hill, as for all true-blue Wobblies, internationalism was the global expression of workingclass solidarity—not an idle fancy that one could wave away whenever the political temperature changed, as was the case with so many Socialist Party members during the First World War, and Communists during the mid-1930s "Popular Front" and Second World War. (How Hill's obvious and extreme antipathy for anything that smacked of red-white-and-blue ballyhoo or other forms of state-worship eventually cost him a secure posthumous position in the pantheon of American Communism will be discussed in some detail later on.)

For the Wobbly bard, world labor solidarity was a constant, unvarying revolutionary principle, and therefore an intrinsic part of his character as a member of the IWW. His internationalism had much more to do with his basic morality, his whole self-awareness, his Wobbly sensibility—a revolutionary *class* sensibility—than with theory, program, policy, or what is usually called "politics."

An IWW "Silent Agitator" sticker

IV
A CLASSIC CASE OF FRAME-UP

1. WHY WAS JOE HILL ARRESTED?

I don't see any American dream.
I see an American nightmare.
—Malcolm X—

Joe Hill's popularity and influence as leading IWW songwriter did not go unobserved by those the Wobblies regarded as the "class enemy." In January 1914, on his way to Chicago from San Pedro, the IWW poet was arrested near Salt Lake City, Utah, and charged with murdering a local grocer, John Morrison, who had formerly been a policeman. The press described the crime as a "Revenge Killing," for the ex-cop had let it be known that he feared attack by several men he had arrested as an officer, and he had in fact been assaulted by armed gunmen on two earlier occasions, one just a few months before his death. The fact that Morrison's killers took no money further substantiates the supposition that revenge was indeed the motive.

Hill was a preposterously unlikely suspect. He had no criminal record, no connection with the victim, no motive for the killing, and made no attempt to hide or to leave town. The victim's thirteen-year-old son, Merlin, could not identify Hill as one of the two men who burst in the store shouting "We've got you now!" and started shooting. The son was sure, however, that "the men didn't mean to rob the store," and that "it must have been revenge." None of several witnesses who flocked to the scene when they heard shots identified Hill as one of two masked men leaving the store.

Indeed, not one bit of evidence was ever found linking Hill to the crime. The closest thing resembling "evidence" against him was that he, like several other men arrested that night, had a gunshot wound (we shall have more to say about this a little further on) and no verifiable alibi. However, the police chief of San Pedro, who had once held Hill for thirty days on a charge of "vagrancy" during a longshoremen's strike when Hill was secretary of the strike committee, wrote to the Salt Lake City police:

I see you have under arrest for murder one Joseph Hillstrom.

> You have the right man. . . . He is certainly an undesirable
> citizen. He is somewhat of a musician and writer of songs for the
> IWW songbook. [Fred Thompson 1979, 3]

It was for the "crime" of belonging to the IWW that Hill was tried
and condemned. The Utah police, press, governor, and judicial
system, dominated by the Copper Trust and the Mormon Church,
took their cue from the San Pedro police chief.

Utah copper country had been the site of major IWW struggles
for two years before Hill arrived on the scene. For miners and
others employed in and around mining camps, working conditions
there were among the worst in the nation. As W. G. Henry reported
in the *International Socialist Review*, the Bingham Canyon area—a
locality employing nearly 5000 men, mostly Greek immigrants—
was the site of 440 on-the-job deaths in 1911, and countless
injuries [Oct 1912, 342]. Utah Governor William Spry, pliant
stooge of the copper kings, had dutifully vetoed a bill—passed by
both houses of the legislature—that would have required a coro-
ner's investigation of miners' deaths [Foner 1965a, 16].

In Utah, as in other western mining districts, union organizing
was typically broken up by big strikebreaking agencies—veritable
armies of gunmen—whose murderous attacks on union organizers
and strikers were perpetrated with the full knowledge, and often
the active participation, of the State, local government, and police.
Such anti-labor violence was fully endorsed by Governor Spry,
who permitted the mine-owners to deputize company gunmen as
sheriffs [*ibid.*].

A 1912 Western Federation of Miners strike at Bingham introduced a new kind of strike to the West, as Justus Ebert pointed out
in his book, *The Trial of a New Society*:

> Here some 5000 men, mostly armed, seized possession of exten-
> sive mining properties. They did not leave their jobs and go
> outside of the premises to defend them against scabs, but they
> stayed on them, and compelled negotiations with them while
> thus situated. [1912, 157]

Although not an IWW strike (the WFM had withdrawn from the
IWW some years before), IWW members and sympathizers surely
took part in it.

Wobbly organizers in Utah were especially active in Park City,
Eureka, Bingham, and Tucker, where a highly successful strike in

1913 brought many new members into the union and made the IWW well known to workers throughout the state. Salt Lake City IWW Local 69 also kept up a lively agitation. Its street speakers were constantly harassed by police, and—months before Hill came to town—attempts were made to frame up at least two prominent Wobs, but the cases had been thrown out for lack of evidence [Fred Thompson 1930, 21]. When Hill arrived in the area, he found work in Park City, in the machine shop of the Silver King mine, where an acquaintance from San Pedro, a Swedish immigrant and fellow IWW named Otto Applequist, was foreman.

Prior to Hill's arrest, the major suspect in the Morrison case was a gunman and ex-convict named Frank Z. Wilson, one of the men the former policeman had helped send to prison, and who had just been released from the penitentiary. On the night of the shooting, a witness had seen a suspicious-looking man—later identified as Wilson from a police photograph—on a Salt Lake City streetcar, leaning over as if in pain, or perhaps drunk. When the police arrested Hill, they were convinced that *he* was Wilson, and so notified the press. But the real Wilson was never found. As Gibbs Smith noted in his biography of Hill, "After the police learned Hill's true identity [as IWW songwriter], their interest in Wilson as a suspect evidently faded" [1969, 76].

Four other suspects were arrested for the Morrison killing: Two were wanted for armed robbery in Arizona, another told lies to the police, and a fourth had a bullet wound in his arm (two men, he said, had held *him* up on the street). After Hill's arrest, however, they were all released and allowed to leave town.

The names of two other men who *should* have been considered suspects were never made public at the time, and have not been mentioned by name in later literature on the case. Mrs Morrison informed the police that her husband regarded the two as enemies, and had told her, "If anything ever happens to me, you may have to look them up" [Foner 1965, 19]. The police, however, chose not to pursue this lead, perhaps because the gentlemen in question were, as the *Deseret Evening News* commented on the matter, respectable citizens "in business in the neighborhood" [12-13 Jan 1914]. At the hearing, news reporter Hardy Downing, who had interviewed Morrison after an earlier armed attack, was prepared to testify in this regard, and even to name the individuals Morrison believed were out to get him. Prosecutor Leatherwood objected, however, and Judge Ritchie sustained the objection. Downing's crucial evidence was thus suppressed.

For most people unfamiliar with judicial procedure, the fact that Hill had a bullet wound may appear to be irreparably damning evidence, and that is certainly the impression fostered by the Salt Lake City police, press and prosecution in the Hill case. It should be borne in mind, however, that firearms were legal and in common use in Utah, as elsewhere in the West, and bullet wounds were no rarity. Three other men with unexplained gunshot wounds were arrested at the same time as Hill, and of course there is no way of telling how many more may have eluded the attention of the police. In any event, a bullet wound, in the absence of other evidence, can hardly be considered grounds for conviction.

In Hill's trial, it was never proved that either of Morrison's assailants was shot, or even that a gun had been fired at them. If one of them *was* shot, and the bullet lodged in the body, it could not have been Hill, who was examined by a doctor. If, however, the bullet passed through the body, a slug should have been found in the store. In either case, there would have been blood on the floor of the store, or nearby. Despite intensive searching, however, no slug was found, and no blood, except outdoors—from a dog's injured paw.

In short, Hill's bullet wound obviously had nothing to do with the Morrison murder, and should not have been considered evidence against him.

Sometime during the night of the crime, Hill's friend and fellow worker Otto Applequist disappeared without a trace. Like Hill, Applequist had no police record and there was no reason to suspect him of wrongdoing. The police, however, promoted the unfounded fiction that he was Hill's accomplice in the Morrison murder, and went so far as to offer a reward for his capture. Extensive interviews in the 1940s with people who had been involved in both sides of the Hill case led researcher Aubrey Haan the only scholar to have pursued this particular aspect of the affair—to conclude that Applequist was in fact murdered by the very police who were pretending to search for him [letter to Fred Thompson, 20 July 1948].

Haan's grim findings add yet more weight to the contention that Hill was the victim of a frame-up. As a witness who could have confirmed Hill's innocence, Applequist was clearly a menace to the framers, and had to be dealt with accordingly. The gory details are missing; even rumor is silent. What is certain is that

Otto Applequist was never seen or heard from again after the evening of 10 January 1914.

What is certain, too, is that Joe Hill was not arrested and charged because the police or anyone else thought he was guilty of any crime, for there was nothing pointing in that direction. He was arrested and charged because he was poor, homeless, an immigrant, a hobo, and above all an "undesirable citizen"—that is, an IWW and "a writer of songs for the IWW songbook."

"DON'T MOURN, ORGANIZE!"
Drawing by Pelaren (*Industrial Worker*, 19 November 1921).
A rare portrayal of Joe Hill as a ghost,
haunting a graveyard of labor (mostly IWW) martyrs.

THE GENERAL STRIKE

One of the first U.S. artists to blend photomontage and cartooning was the Russian-Jewish Wobbly known only as Sam, who clearly
regarded the demolition of capitalism's jails as one of the pleasures
of a united working class (*One Big Union Monthly*, July 1919).

Eugene Barnett's cartoon scores the hypocritical capitalists'
contempt for the U.S. Constitution and Bill of Rights.

2. RED SCARE:
WHY & HOW THE POLICE & THE PRESS
STIR UP FEAR & HATRED

How can we find out how the world is made
except by running afoul of it?
—**Mary Hunter Austin**—

For unscrupulous news-writers and their ignorant public—not to mention the prosecuting attorney, judge and jury—Hill's bullet wound was tangible evidence not only of his own criminality, but also proof that the IWW was itself a violent and criminal organization. Sensational but unfounded reports of IWW "violence" were a staple of this country's daily newspapers from the early 1910s until well into the 1930s.

The IWW program, according to which workers organized into One Big Union would take over the industries and run them in the interest of the working class rather than in the interest of a small group of exploiters, was immediately perceived as "violent" by the exploiters and their supporters. From the warped perspective of the employing class, the fact that the IWW sought to abolish capitalism automatically meant that it was an unspeakable and conspiratorial cabal of arsonists, murderers, and bombthrowers—a threat to national security, a menace to civilization, and just not nice at all!

Assisting in the campaign of vilification against the IWW were the union's political opponents, most notoriously Daniel DeLeon and his disciples in the Socialist Labor Party, who believed that any program for social transformation that was not based on electoral politics necessarily had to rely on violence.

The plain truth is that the IWW neither advocated violence nor practiced it. Few Wobblies were pacifists, but their revolutionary program is "firmly within the framework of nonviolence," as Salvatore Salerno points out in his introduction to *Direct Action and Sabotage: Three Classic IWW Pamphlets from the 1910s* [1997, 1]. Salerno further emphasizes that Wobs rejected the view, advocated by certain Marxists and anarchists, that armed insurrection, attentats, capturing state power or other forms of collective or individual violence are the only effective ways of bringing about the emancipation of the working class. Instead, the IWW consistently stressed what they regarded as the tried and true revolutionary methods: workers' solidarity, classwide collective action, and the General Strike [*ibid.*]. Staughton Lynd's *Nonviolence in America: A Documentary History* (1966), includes a long 1915 statement by Bill Haywood that harmonizes well not only with the texts of nineteenth-century Abolitionists but also with those of civil-rights and anti-war activists of the post-World-War-II years.

To the groundless charge that the IWW urged violence, the union responded with a resolution passed at its eighth annual convention in Chicago, 1913, published in the *Proceedings*, and relayed to the workers of the world in a pamphlet titled *On the Firing Line*:

> At all times it is the rulers who, being in power, are in a position to determine in great measure just how and when the struggle will be fought. . . . It is the employing class and their agencies who provoke violence and then cry out the loudest against it.... The program of the IWW offers the only possible solution of the wage question whereby violence can be avoided, or, at the very worst, reduced to a minimum. [1913, 25-26]

In August 1913, a few months before Hill's arrest, the *Salt Lake Tribune* complained that "Wherever [the IWW's] membership appears there are riots and fighting" [Smith 1969, 120]. The statement is not entirely untrue, but it ignores the decisive questions: Who *started* the violence? And *why*?

In the many cases that have been studied, researchers have found that it was always the employer, and/or the police, who initiated the violence which the press then proceeded to blame on the IWW. And why? The answer is obvious: because the IWW was organizing workers the employers and police didn't want to be organized. Time and again, when Wobbly soapboxers or organizers entered a town and began agitating for higher wages, shorter hours, healthier working conditions, free speech, and more of "the good things of life," they encountered the combined violence of the law and the lawless. The union's experiences in this regard resembled the no less brutal mistreatment of the pre-Civil-War agitators against chattel slavery, and Wobblies perceived the analogy.

The hue and cry over Wobbly "sabotage," which started around 1912, was a variant of the "violence" charge. In IWW usage, sabotage signified *a worker's withdrawal of efficiency*: a "slowdown," for example, or "working to rule" (*i.e.*, strictly following the employers' often byzantine and contradictory working rules), or other forms of passive resistance. Bill Haywood explained to the Industrial Relations Commission that sabotage was based on the principle that "the worker should refuse to be a party with the boss in robbing the public"—*i.e.*, should refuse to adulterate food, or to produce the shoddy products the profit system requires [1915, 26]. "Open mouth" sabotage simply involved telling the truth when the employer did not want the truth to be known: a store clerk, for instance, could inform a customer that the employer had diluted the milk, or added sawdust to the cereal.

The daily papers, however, in order to frighten their readers, concocted stories of a much scarier sabotage: reports of crazed Wobblies setting fires to barns and haystacks, wrecking expensive machinery, blowing up bridges, and engaging in all sorts of large-scale destruction. None of it was true, but it made "exciting" reading. Moreover, and for the press this was the main point, it hurt the IWW and sent a lot of innocent workingmen to prison. As Mary Heaton Vorse remarked in her autobiography, the "newspaper campaign of hatred" against the IWW obscured the organization "with such a haze of lies that the average citizen of this country knew less about them than about voodoo" [1935, 160].

In 1939 Johns Hopkins University published a full-length study in which the author, Eldridge Foster Dowell, made this interesting observation:

> Although there are contradictory opinions as to whether the IWW practices sabotage or not, it is interesting to note that no case of an IWW saboteur caught practicing sabotage or convicted of its practice is available. [36]

The *International Socialist Review* for December 1914 published a humorous article which, among other things, questioned the usefulness of paramilitary solutions to workingclass problems. With a wry seriousness worthy of T-Bone Slim the author calculated the cost of furnishing machine guns and automatic rifles to the miners, and wondered: "Who is going to pay for all this?" Finally he reached the conclusion that armed struggle couldn't work in the U.S. because it was *too expensive*. "Every working man and woman knows that, after the bills are paid on pay day, there is not much left to . . . buy war supplies with."

This persuasive and witty critique of the "pick up the gun" model of revolutionary change—a classic statement of the Wobbly point of view regarding violence—was written by Joe Hill.[1]

---

1. This text is reprinted in Kornbluh 1998,141-143.

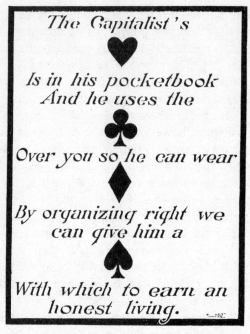

"Dust" Wallin: A quick lesson in IWWism
(*One Big Union Monthly*, July 1920)

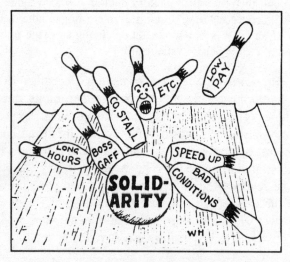

While the capitalist press fabricated lurid tales of
IWW "violence," the Wobbly press consistently
urged the practice of workingclass solidarity,
as in this cartoon by William Henkelman.

3. CONVICTING THE INNOCENT,
ENCOURAGING THE GUILTY

How strange it is, that a fool or a knave, with riches,
should be treated with more respect by the world,
than a good man, or a wise man in poverty!
—**Ann Radcliffe**—

Hill's lack of an alibi for the evening on which Morrison was killed weighed heavily against him not only at the trial, but also during the long, grueling months of "re-trial" on the front pages of the Utah press, which convicted him over and over again as he appealed for a new trial. Similarly, in his statement titled "A Few Reasons Why I Demand a New Trial," his remark that "Where or why I got that wound is nobody's business but my own" [Smith, 264] must have appeared arrogant and evasive, almost a confession of guilt, to Utah's already biased press and "public opinion." After all, aren't *good* citizens supposed to be able to account for their actions and whereabouts at all times?

As it happens, very few hoboes, or others who often travel alone—hitchhikers, for example, or the homeless—*ever* have alibis. And that is why police and prosecutors rely on them so frequently as convenient scapegoats, especially in sensational murder cases where pressure by the public (and by highly placed public officials) mandates immediate apprehension of the villain.

Hill's story of what happened that night, as reported by Frank M. McHugh, the physician who treated his wound—and who later attempted (unsuccessfully) to collect the reward for turning him in to the police—is short and straightforward:

> I got into a stew with a friend of mine who thought I had insulted his wife. I knocked him down, but he got up and pulled a gun on me and shot me. . . . Because this fellow that shot me didn't really know what he was doing, I want to have nothing said about it. If there's a chance to get over it, it will be okay with my friend. [Smith 1969, 64]

Friends and fellow workers urged him to tell more—to provide details that could be verified, and particularly to reveal the names of the other people involved, but Hill refused. He insisted that he did not want the unknown woman's name dragged into the case.

And that was that. As Fred Thompson pointed out, "Any ordinary crook . . . could have arranged with friends to set up some satisfying explanation about how he got shot—but that was not Hill's way" [1979, 20].

At no time did Hill act like a fugitive. He made no attempt to escape Salt Lake City, to disguise himself, to find a hiding-place. He gave Dr McHugh his right name and address—hardly the behavior of a desperado trying to elude the law and preparing to skip town.

Theoretically, a person on trial is presumed innocent until proved guilty. In other words, the *burden of proof* is supposed to be completely on the side of the prosecution. In trials of the poor, however, and especially in labor-related cases, and above all in cases involving revolutionaries, this principle tends to be, as the saying goes, "honored only in the breach." Gale Ahrens, the surrealist poet and prison-abolitionist agitator, points out that the rule in such cases seems to be "guilty until proven guiltier" [Sakolsky 2002, 265].

Confusion on this important matter is rife, even among people who ought to know better. It was not so many years ago that the Attorney General of the United States, Edwin Meese, made the outrageous statement, "You don't have many suspects who are innocent of a crime. . . . If a person is innocent of a crime, then he is not a suspect" [*U.S. News & World Report*, 15 Oct 1985]. Closer to home, we find Melvyn Dubofsky, author of a history of the IWW, asserting on at least two occasions that Joe Hill was "never proven innocent," as if that were somehow a terrible blot upon the man's memory [1966, 356; 1969, 312]. The truth is, a large majority of the world's population would find it difficult to "prove themselves innocent" of any number of crimes. With a hostile prosecutor and a couple of perjurers arrayed against him, Prof. Dubofsky himself might have a tough go of it.

Hill's principled attitude in this regard—his insistence that the State's "case" against him included no connection of any kind between him and the crime, no motive, no material evidence, no eyewitness testimony, no proof whatever of his guilt, and that therefore he should either be set free or given a new trial—helps explain an interesting aspect of the history of his reputation. According to Fred Thompson, the defense of Hill's innocence and overall integrity has always been strongest among either drifters or those who had spent earlier years of their life drifting and who knew what tremors run through a skid road when the local press reports the sort of crime they know requires the cops to select a skid road suspect; the content of his songs hit them, but even more his stand for the importance of the doctrine of burden of proof. The hobo is practically helpless at providing an alibi. [Smith 1969, 191]

In Hill's trial, prosecutor E.O. Leatherwood and Judge Morris L. Ritchie seem to have ignored "burden of proof" altogether, and instead concentrated solely on coaching the witnesses to say what they wanted them to say, and letting the jury know that, in a case involving such a redoubtably un-American miscreant such as Hill, only one verdict was permissible. As Hill's Appeals attorney, Orrin N. Hilton, remarked later in the *International Socialist Review*, the author of "Mr Block" and "Workers of the World, Awaken!" was condemned to die solely on the basis of "inconclusive disjointed fragments of suspicion" [Sept 1915, 172].

The gross unfairness of the trial has been fully documented elsewhere [Friends of Joe Hill, 1948; Haan 1948; Morris 1950; Foner 1965a; Smith 1969; Thompson 1979]. Judge Ritchie's efforts to prevent the selection of an impartial jury, his many biased rulings, his suppression of important testimony, and his malicious manipulation of the jury regarding the nature of circumstantial evidence; the prosecutor's constant use of inflammatory language, leading questions, and even rephrasing of testimony to conform to the State's case; the blatant incompetence of Hill's lawyers—their inept cross-examination of witnesses and their failure to introduce decisive evidence in Hill's defense: All these and many other grotesque violations of judicial procedure are part of the trial record. At one point during the proceedings Hill actually discharged his attorneys, but Judge Ritchie ruled that they remain as "friends of the court." Unfortunately, the proceedings can be reconstructed only in broad outline, with the help of newspaper accounts; many crucial details are missing, because the entire first volume of the trial transcript was mysteriously "lost" years ago by the Salt Lake County Clerk's office, and never recovered.

Hill had taken precautions to assure that a complete file of the records of his case were placed in the hands of his friends:

> I would like to have all records of the case sent to Chicago [IWW] Headquarters, to be kept on file for future reference—a copy of the preliminary records; copy of the District Court records; the two to be kept for comparison; the original of my statement. . . . In case someone, in the future, should want to learn the details of my case, from beginning to end, I would like to have it all together. [*Letters*, 78]

But these records (including the records of the preliminary hearing in January) also disappeared, seized in the Federal Government's raids on the IWW Headquarters in 1917, and supposedly later destroyed [Smith 1969, 79, 84].

Nearly all historians, and others who have studied the matter, have long since recognized the Hill case as a particularly squalid frame-up—indeed, the "classical example" of a frame-up [Adamic 1935, 173]—and one of the ignoblest travesties of justice in U.S. history. In addition to the wrongs and indecencies committed by the prosecutor and judge, there was also plenty of what Hill himself called "perjury screaming to high heaven for mercy" [*Letters*, 49].

On 27 June 1914, in an atmosphere of anti-Red hysteria, with nothing but the flimsiest of circumstantial evidence against him, the hand-picked jury convicted the "writer of songs for the IWW songbook" and the judge sentenced him to death.

Officially, this meant that the Morrison murder was "solved," but the absence of evidence and the overall sleaziness of the trial clearly indicate otherwise. That the police suddenly stopped looking for Frank Z. Wilson and ignored the pleas of Morrison's widow to investigate certain other individuals; that the court in turn suppressed important testimony in this regard; that the very men who were obviously the prime suspects were not even mentioned in the press, much less indicted or brought to trial: All this suggests that the real culprits were being protected by the authorities, probably because they were "well-connected" and knew things which, if revealed, could prove embarrassing to others in the Salt Lake City or state power structure.

Fred Thompson, one of the most thoroughgoing students of the Hill case, argued (convincingly, to my view) that convicting Hill conveniently ended a blood feud between Morrison and some gang—a feud which, had the police pursued the suspects indicated by Morrison himself to his wife and friends, might well have endangered the lives of other police officers involved in the prosecution of members of the gang. From the police standpoint, Hill's frame-up provided an easy opportunity to take care of this problem, and at the same time to get rid of an "undesirable" foreigner, hobo, and revolutionist whose songs and union they all hated anyway. Thus Hill's judicial murder was not the result of an elaborately contrived plot, but—like so many of the horrors perpetrated under capitalism—a simple matter of bureaucratic expedience. As Fellow Worker Thompson put it:

> The unjust convictions that have evoked wide indignation have usually started out, not as a conspiracy by some executive committee of the elite, but as one of the more or less routine injustices that lower authorities perpetrate, confronting those higher up with something congenial to their biases. Their superiors must go along, despite public outcry, or admit the criminal character and class bias of law enforcement. [1979, 16]

In any event, the frame-up of an innocent person is always good news for the guilty. One cannot help wondering: When the actual killers of Morrison heard the shameful and dishonest verdict, did they clink their glasses in a toast to the majesty of the Law? And how many other victims did they dispose of as the years rolled by? For that is one of the difficulties with frame-ups: They not only send innocent folks to prison or death, they also protect and therefore encourage real murderers.

Jim Lynch: When the Workers Take Things in Hand
(cover drawing, *Industrial Pioneer*, March 1926)

4. THE MYSTERY WOMAN

Someone to be watched very carefully.
—Peter Cheyney—

The English-language literature on the Hill case contains surprisingly little speculation regarding the mystery woman whose name the IWW poet refused to divulge to the police, or the court, or anyone else, including his friends. For Hill's detractors, the story was nothing more than a dramatic fabrication, and his silence on the matter a confirmation of his guilt. Hill's supporters, for their part, found the story frustrating because there was no way to verify it. In his 1923 biographical sketch, Ralph Chaplin notes that

> Arturo Giovannitti, in one of his best and least known works, a drama founded on the case of Joe Hill, brings out a very plausible theory that the IWW song writer permitted himself to be executed rather than betray the honor of a woman. [25]

Such conduct, Chaplin remarks, would have been consistent with Hill's character, but he concluded that "It is unlikely now that anyone will ever know the truth" [*ibid.*]. Three years later, in a brief tribute to Hill in the *Labor Defender*, Chaplin dismissed the "mystery woman" angle as "apocryphal" [1926, 190].

The matter surfaced again in 1948 in the "Friends of Joe Hill Committee" response to the malodorous execration of Hill written by Wallace Stegner and published in the *New Republic.* Largely written by John Beffel and published in the *Industrial Worker*, the Friends' response devoted a substantial paragraph to "The Mystery of the Woman," reprinted here in full:

> Many women involved in clandestine affairs will go to any length to avoid admitting such indiscretions, and consider their "honor" more important than anything else—even human life. But in this case there is also the possibility that the woman did not mean to let Joe be executed, that she waited through the trial hoping for an acquittal, waited for a reversal on appeal, intending as a last resort to come forward and save his life, but that she was killed by accident, died suddenly, or was slain by a jealous husband or lover to prevent her from interceding for Hill. Such a man might have murdered her far from Salt Lake City and disposed of her body, or removed all identification marks

from it. [13 November 1948, 4]

Subsequent researchers—in despair—have tended to relegate the whole topic to the domain of the unknown and the unknowable, and hence, quietly dropped it.

This raises an obvious question: Why would Hill have bothered to invent a complex and unverifiable tale when it would have been so much easier for him, and infinitely more beneficial, to devise a convincing alibi with the assistance of, say, the Eselius family and/or any number of other friends? In that perspective, the very outlandishness of Hill's story lends weight to its truth. Hill, moreover, knowing he was innocent and that therefore there could not possibly be any evidence against him, was certain that he would be acquitted. In such circumstances, what motive would he have had for inventing an unprovable story?

Clearly, in his attitude toward the U.S. "justice system"—particularly out in copper country—Joe Hill was a babe in the woods, at least prior to his conviction. Irony of ironies, his simple honesty and old-fashioned sense of honor played into the hands of the prosecution, and hastened his way to the firing squad.

The fact that the press and prosecution openly ridiculed Hill's story as a fairy tale, and that Hill's defenders—in deference to his own wishes—refused to pry further into the matter, helps explain why most later historians have preferred to forget the whole thing.

Swedish sources, however, have frequently mentioned a likely candidate for Hill's mystery woman—an immigrant from Gävle who knew Hill when they both were children. Almost all of the documents pertaining to this woman's involvement with Hill are in the Swedish language, and it is to these texts, unknown to U.S. readers, that we must now turn to illuminate this cloudy episode in the IWW poet's life.[1]

Maria Johanson was born in Gävle, and was almost the same age as Hill. According to Hill's Swedish biographer Ingvar Söderstrom, their families lived close to each other and attended the same church [Söderstrom to FR, 12 Feb 2002]. Hill's sister, Ester Dahl, recalled that Johanson had worked as a waitress at a local café [*ibid.*. 23 Feb 2002]. Like Hill, Johanson emigrated to the U.S. early in the twentieth century, but unlike Hill she came as a Mormon convert and settled in Utah. Four-fifths of the U.S. emigrants from Gävle during the period 1900-1910 were women, and most of them—including Johanson—had their travel expenses paid by Mormon missionaries, as loans [*ibid.*, 12 Feb 2002].

In December 1913 Johanson saw Hill and his friend Otto Applequist at a cafeteria in downtown Salt Lake City. She asked Hill if he was Joel Hägglund from Gävle, and he replied: "Yes, I am." They had not seen each other for twelve years. They talked a while, and Johanson invited Hill and Applequist to her home a few days later, perhaps to a party (this was during the Christmas holidays). Hill not only attended, but also played the piano there, and sang songs.

Maria Johanson was much-married and much-divorced. Her marriages were all successful—financially, at least, for each one left her more prosperous than the one before. If Maria Johanson was not fabulously rich, she was at any rate "comfortably well off"—indeed, almost the stereotype of the high-strung, self-absorbed, upward-mobile busybody.

Her meeting with Hill at the Salt Lake City cafeteria took place shortly after she divorced her third (or perhaps fourth) husband, Athana Saccoss. At Hill's trial in June of the following year, she appeared as a witness for the prosecution under the name Mrs Athana Saccoss. The name Maria Johanson does not appear to have figured in the court proceedings or in the press coverage of the trial.

At the trial, she testified that she had known Hill as a child but had not seen him since he emigrated from Sweden until their meeting at the cafeteria "just before Christmas" 1913. She also told the court that she met Hill once more, again in the company of Applequist, two days before the Morrison murder, and that she invited Hill to visit her yet again on Saturday night, the 10th—the night of the crime. Her account of Hill's reply to her invitation was deliberately sinister:

> He couldn't come, he had some excuse: he said he might and might not; if he could he would try to come. I asked him to come Sunday then, and he said he might go to California that day. [Söderstrom 1970, 134]

The prosecution, in its effort to further mislead an already prejudiced jury, interpreted Johanson's obviously hostile testimony to signify that Hill had planned the robbery/murder for that night, and intended to leave town the next day.

Ingvar Söderstrom, drawing on the researches of Hill's friend Oscar W. Larson, is convinced that Hill did indeed visit Maria

Johanson (alias Mrs Athana Saccoss) at her home that very night. Independently of Söderstrom, Joseph A. Curtis—a Salt Lake City Hill researcher who began interviewing individuals involved in the case as long ago as the 1920s—arrived at the same conclusion. Although Curtis never succeeded in publishing his findings, he did summarize his views regarding Johanson's role in a talk he gave at the big 1990 Conference on Joe Hill in Salt Lake City.[2]

What happened in the course of Hill's visit to Johanson that night, and what made Johanson conceal the truth about it in her courtroom testimony, are long lost secrets that in all probability will never be brought to light. Johanson's subsequent behavior, however, was—to say the least—highly suspect. Hill scholars, including Gibbs Smith, are "almost certain" that she was the author of an anonymous tirade against Hill published in the Swedish social-democratic paper *Arbeterbladet* (Workers' Daily) on 18 December 1915, a month after Hill's execution. An entire paragraph simply paraphrases her testimony at the trial. Wrathful and malignant throughout, the article is a grab-bag of untruths, distortions, and insinuations. A short paragraph suffices to convey the tenor of the whole:

> [Hill] seldom had any orderly work and . . . seems to have gained his livelihood in a way that could not stand police investigation. About ten years ago Morrison was police commissioner and he is supposed to have run across Hill's criminal plans, whereby H. started a deadly hate against M. [Smith 1969, 262]

When a person's life is at stake, such locutions as "seems to" and "is supposed to" are not acceptable. In Johanson's article, the prosecutorial abuses of language that helped railroad the IWW poet to his death serve only as gratuitous insults to his memory. Interestingly, the *Arbeterbladet* editor—who, as a social-democrat, cannot be considered an IWW supporter—regarded Johanson's spiteful story as "strange" and dubious. As he noted in his concluding remarks: "[I]t is clearly unbelievable that all the labor organizations in America, without exception, stood up in defense of the executed if he really was a criminal by profession. . . ." [Smith 1969, 262].

Johanson's obsessive defamation of her former childhood friend did not end with her anonymous broadside in the overseas *Arbeterbladet*. Months later, when the Chicago-based *Svenska Socialisten* ran an article on Hill by Gösta Brown, Johanson—this time under her own time—spewed forth more venom in a reply published in the next issue (17 April 1916), mostly reiterating what she had already said in court and (anonymously) in the *Arbeterbladet*.

To this day, Maria Johanson's role in the frame-up of Hill remains obscure. Oscar W. Larson and Gösta Brown had independently attempted to ascertain the details of her involvement, but with little success [Söderstrom to FR, 12 Feb 2002]. However, Swedish IWW organizer Ragnar Johanson—no relation to Maria—reported an incident that may be related. A month after Hill's death, Ragnar Johanson said that two detectives approached him in a Salt Lake City café and for some reason, in the course of their conversation, confided to him that a local Swedish woman who had written about Hill in a Swedish-language publication had in fact lied about her acquaintance with the IWW poet [*ibid.*]. Confidences from detectives are not to be depended on, but it is interesting that this unsolicited information should coincide with the view that Oscar Larson, unknown to the detectives, had already reached on his own.

For Ingvar Söderstrom, Maria Johanson was not only "deeply involved" in the Hill case, but the "key witness" in the whole story [*ibid.*]. In his view, her trial testimony was obviously truncated —she plainly "did not tell [the court] the true story" [to FR, 12 Feb 2002]. What she omitted, moreover, was so much more pertinent than what she actually said, that the omission turned her testimony into a deception. Why she failed to tell the truth at the trial, Söderstrom concedes, is a mystery, but he suggests that there may have been "a silent agreement between her and Joe" [*ibid.*]. And Söderstrom notes a striking fact: Neither Hill nor his attorneys, who freely criticized other witnesses for the prosecution, either vocally in court or in written statements afterward, made any criticism, correction, or even comment on the decidedly devious, unfriendly and damaging testimony of "Mrs Athana Saccoss."

Nothing suggests a romantic angle in her involvement with Hill. The fact that she was an incurably bourgeois snob, devoid of workingclass or revolutionary sympathies, and an active Mormon besides, would seem to preclude an affair of the heart with a revolutionary and atheistic Wobbly who was not ashamed to call himself a "wharf-rat." And yet, love notoriously respects no boundaries, desire defies all conventions, and history is full of "incompatible" couples who nonetheless lived happily ever after. Unlikely as it appears, therefore, the *possibility* of a love affair between the two immigrants from Gävle cannot be ruled out altogether.

What is certain is that *something*—quarrel, disagreement, misunderstanding—suddenly changed Maria Johanson's relationship to Hill from warm welcoming hostess to sworn enemy. If she suddenly felt rejected, insulted, or otherwise wronged by Hill and/or Applequist, would she have taken it lightly—"no hard feelings"? The egocentric vindictiveness of her court testimony and her later writing on Hill suggest otherwise. "Hell hath no fury like a woman scorned" may be a corny and sexist cliché, but it does seem to fit Maria Johanson. Most people would speak out, regardless of the threat of scandal or other embarrassment, rather than see an innocent person murdered by the State. Johanson's bitter fulminations, however, so flagrantly counter to the truth, indicate the sort of personality that would always choose "respectability" over justice.

Perhaps, at their initial Salt Lake City meetings, Hill kept his IWW activity a secret from Johanson, who took him to be the small-town, church-going Lutheran boy she had known in Gävle. Did she first learn of the Wobbly Joe Hill on the evening of the 10th, or when the newspapers reported Hill's arrest? In either case, such knowledge may well have terrified a person of her conservative disposition, and convinced her that her old friend had become a fearsome monster. Irrational upper- and middle-class fear of the IWW was rampant at the time, especially in Utah. Years later, Hill researcher Aubrey Haan learned from Utah Supreme Court Justice Straup, one of the trio who denied the Wobbly poet's appeal for a new trial, that Hill's IWW membership was enough to "crystallize his feeling that Hill was guilty" [Haan to Fred Thompson, n.d., 1948].

We shall probably never know the answers, but the questions remain: Why did Maria Johanson, a childhood friend of Hill's, who invited the poet to her home and enjoyed his singing and piano-playing so much that she wanted him to return, decide to testify against him in a trial for his life, and then to continue to defame his character after his death? Could she really have been taken in by the prosecution's patently false and flimsy "evidence"?

In the eight decades since Hill's judicial murder, no one else has been proposed as the mystery woman. There is good reason to suspect that the mystery of Hill's doings on the night of 10 January 1914 is but a brief albeit fateful interlude in the much more complex mystery of Maria Johanson.

---

1. Special thanks to Ingvar Söderstrom for providing much of the information in this chapter.
2. This information on Curtis's talk was kindly relayed to me by John Sillito, a co-organizer of the 1990 Conference.

🔲 JOE HILLSTROM 🔲
Protest Meeting!
I. W. W. HALL, 208 2d Ave., So.

Before the Board of Pardons, he said: "I don't want a pardon, or a commutation, I want a new trial or nothing. If my life will help some other workingman to a fair trial, I am ready to give it. If by living my life I can aid others to the fairness denied me, I have not lived in vain."

¶ To the press he wrote: "I am going to have a new trial or die trying. I have lived like an Artist and I shall die like an Artist."—

JOSEPH HILLSTROM

JOSEPH HILLSTROM
I. W. W. ARTIST AND POET, who is Sentenced to be Shot Nov. 19th.

"One of the chief causes of social unrest is the denial of justice in the creation, adjudication and administration of the law."
—*Commission on Industrial Relations*

¶ "I say without the slightest hesitation that the trial which resulted in Hillstrom's conviction was the most unjust, wicked and farcial travesty on justice that has ever occured in the west. To an impartial Board of Pardons I can easily demonstrate such fact without any argument. Only time would be required to read the record over once."
JUDGE O. N. HILTON

Sunday, Nov. 14th [8:00 P M.]
Speakers Representing
The A. F. of L. Socialist Party and I. W. W.
will Address the Meeting

Leaflet for a 1915 Joe Hill Protest Meeting, probably in Seattle.

5. "DO SOMETHING
TO SAVE THE LIFE OF JOE HILL":
THE DEFENSE COMMITTEE
SWINGS INTO ACTION

In the gloom of a cloudy November,
They uttered the music of May.
—**Emily Brontë**—

C onfident that his innocence was obvious and that he would
therefore soon be released, Hill at first rejected his fellow
workers' offer to organize any kind of defense on his behalf, or even to publicize his case in the IWW papers. He also felt
it was wrong for the union to use funds urgently needed for organizational work to help an individual member with what he regarded
as a personal matter.

His faith that a capitalist court would treat him fairly may seem
naive for a Wobbly, but Hill of course had no direct experience in
this area. At the 27 January 1914 preliminary hearing, however, the
judge ruled that the "evidence" warranted a trial for murder, and
Ed Rowan, a prominent figure in the Salt Lake City IWW local,
immediately organized the Joe Hill Defense Committee [Smith
1969, 90]. Rowan was its chairman, and George Child, secretary
of Salt Lake City IWW Local 69, was its treasurer. By April the
IWW press had spread the news about Fellow Worker Hill across
the country and abroad [*ibid.*].

When Hill was convicted on 27 June, the IWW defense effort
expanded and multiplied in all directions. Under the heading "Trying to Railroad a Rebel," the *International Socialist Review* reported that

> Fellow Worker J. Hill, a well-known song writer who wrote
> many of the songs in the IWW song book, which have been sung
> by thousands of strikers all over the country, was convicted of
> murder in the first degree in Salt Lake City on June 27. The
> evidence is purely circumstantial and was furnished by the
> police, who are always in touch with stools and pimps who are
> wiling to swear anything for "protection."
>
> None of the witnesses identified Fellow Worker Hill and
> steps have already been taken to appeal his case.
>
> The prosecuting attorney sprang all of the old chestnuts

about the equality of rich and poor before the law and other orthodox rot.

We all know that a poor man can buy justice if he has the price to get a good lawyer; otherwise he stands about as much chance as a snowball in hell. We trust that every reader of the *Review* will send in from a dime to a dollar or more to Comrade George Child of the Hill Defense Fund. . . . [Aug 1914, 126]

A year later, when the Utah Supreme Court upheld the decision of the district court, the defense campaign intensified even more. Bill Haywood's statement, "Sentenced to be Shot—Act Quick!" appeared in the *International Socialist Review*:

The exploiting class of Utah are determined that Joe Hill shall be executed. Our fellow worker has made himself obnoxious to them. His message of solidarity resounds in their ears. [Aug 1915, 110]

Urging all fellow workers, friends, and sympathizers to send letters and petitions to the Board of Pardons, appealing for clemency, Haywood concluded with the plea, "Do something to save the life of Joe Hill."

The same issue of the *Review* published an appeal from Ed Rowan, Phil Engle, and James Wilson of the Defense Committee:

What is needed is action—and quick action at that! Lawyers will not work for nothing. Money must be raised at once to fight the case to a finish. It's of no use to debate whether we can get justice in a capitalistic court or not. While there is life there is hope, and we can't give up while there is even one chance in a thousand to save Joe Hill's life. . . . Hold protest meetings, collect funds and give the case the widest publicity. Remember, there is no time to lose [*ibid.*, 126].

Though unsuccessful in attaining its goals—saving Hill's life, or even securing him a new trial—the Defense Committee led a dynamic and far-reaching campaign, and kept gathering momentum until the bitter end. Its influence was incalculable. Although Hill was already well-known in the IWW and the Socialist movement at the time of his arrest, the Defense Committee made his name familiar to millions more. As Hill's friend Sam Murray remarked years later in the *Industrial Pioneer*, "All the forces of both sides of the struggle were being marshaled—one to take [Hill's] life, and the other to save him" [Dec 1923, 53].

Indeed, the Joe Hill Defense Committee deserves a full-length study of its own. One of the biggest workingclass defense mobilizations since Haymarket (1886-93), the Hill defense was also a major link between that great struggle to free the Chicago Anarchists and later battles to free Tom Mooney, Sacco and Vanzetti, the Scottsboro defendants, and many more. Several radicals whose political awakening is directly traceable to Haymarket—including Emma Goldman, William D. Haywood, and Charles H. Kerr— were active in the defense of Joe Hill nearly three decades later.

Like other labor defense efforts the Hill campaign involved petitioning, street meetings, demonstrations, and mass rallies in large public halls. Trade unions as well as other organizations, and even prominent liberals and government officials were pressured to act or speak out in Hill's favor, and many did so. Among the many thousands who urged Governor Spry to re-open the case or to pardon Hill were numerous Swedish-American groups, locals of the American Federation of Labor, the Italian Socialist Federation of Detroit, the Revolutionary Laborers' Club of Philadelphia, the Russian-language Anarchist Red Cross in Chicago, and branches of the Women's Christian Temperance Union.

Above all the Defense Committee focused on mass education, primarily via the printed word in the IWW, Socialist Party, and anarchist press. Vast quantities of leaflets circulated from coast to coast. Typical of this defense literature was a statement in the socialist *Appeal to Reason*, published in Girard, Kansas—the most widely-circulated radical publication in the U.S. at the time, with a circulation in the millions. Saluting "Hill's dauntless defiance of the rotten rulers who would put a bullet in his heart as the penalty for being a class-conscious rebel against present conditions," the *Appeal* urged its readers to "Strike now for Joe Hill, for yourself and for the whole working class" [Graham 1990, 127].

A significant innovation of the Joe Hill Defense Committee was the use it made of the *Little Red Song Book*. Each copy included a leaflet explaining Hill's frame-up and urging readers to support the defense effort. Later, a special "Joe Hill Edition" of the Song Book was issued, with a printed insert on the case. Naturally, all Joe Hill Defense Meetings prominently featured his songs.

Tens of thousands—probably hundreds of thousands—took part in Hill's defense. As in other defense campaigns, Hill's attracted several figures of renown. Jane Addams, Helen Keller, veteran Jewish socialist and former Siberian political prisoner Isaac Hourwich, Socialist Presidential candidate Eugene V. Debs, and *San Francisco Bulletin* editor Fremont Older were among the celebrities of the 1910s who demanded justice for Joe Hill. Less well known nationally, but still "people in the news," California attorney Austin Lewis (who also happened to be one of America's premier Marxist theorists); anarchist editor/orator Carlo Tresca; suffragist, social worker and socialist Charlotte Anita Whitney; socialist agitator Rose Pastor Stokes; and Paul Jones, Episcopal Bishop of the state of Utah, also contributed to the Cause. *Solidarity* reported a large "Joe Hill Protest Meeting" at the Manhattan Lyceum in New York, which featured such speakers as John Reed, Anna Strunsky, and Irish freedom-fighter James Larkin [20 Nov 1915, 1].

One major player in Hill's defense, Tom Mooney, was himself framed up and convicted less than a year after Hill's execution. The Mooney case was so full of perjury and other prosecutorial chicanery that it may well have been modeled on the Hill case. A well-known labor radical and a moulder by trade, Mooney had met Hill only once, and briefly, in San Pedro, but he had long been an admirer of Hill's songs. On behalf of the fifty-three labor organizations represented by the International Workers' Defense League, of which he was the secretary, he wrote a forceful letter to Governor Spry, which said in part:

> We demand that you act [in Hill's favor]. . . . We are not going to see any workingman perish without being revenged, when we are satisfied he was not proven guilty of the crime charged. . . . [Gentry 1967, 64]

On 15 November 1915—four days before Hill was put before the firing squad—Mooney, at the thirty-fifth annual convention of the American Federation of Labor, urged adoption of a resolution instructing AFL President Sam Gompers to appeal to President Wilson, Governor Spry, and the Utah Board of Pardons to postpone the execution pending full review of the case. The resolution passed unanimously [*ibid.*, 64].

This action indicated not only Hill's popularity throughout the labor movement, but also the wide support for the IWW that existed among the AFL rank and file. (Many IWW members, of course, were also members of AFL unions.)

Mooney's own case became a *cause célèbre*, and dragged on for years. In November 1932, five thousand union members paraded in San Francisco, chanting "Free Tom Mooney!" and singing Joe Hill's songs [*ibid,*, 369]. Mooney was finally released from San Quentin in 1939, after serving twenty-three years in prison for a crime he could not possibly have committed.

In cases such as Hill's, in which a human life lies in the balance, some activists are willing to resort to desperate measures. When Mooney's friend and fellow labor agitator Warren Billings heard that Colorado miners had cached arms and ammunition in a cave during the Ludlow strike, he immediately conceived a daring plan: first, locate the hidden arsenal, and second, with a small but well-armed force, storm the Utah State Prison and free Joe Hill. The cave, however, was never found, and the quixotic scheme came to nothing. A few months later, Billings was Mooney's co-defendant, and also spent twenty-three years behind bars.

Many others, meanwhile, albeit in less sensational ways, were doing their part to liberate Hill. Widely known at the time, but not as well-remembered today as she deserves to be, was Theodora Pollok: suffragist, free-speech crusader and all-around radical social reformer. Despite serious health problems (she suffered from asthma and tuberculosis), Pollok played an exceptionally active role in the Hill defense. Although her own background was "upper class," she wholeheartedly threw in her lot with the revolutionary working class, joined the IWW, and remained particularly active in labor defense—including the "Free Mooney!" campaign—in later years [Dubofsky 1969, 435].

Another wrongfully forgotten defender of the Wobbly bard was Harmon F. Titus, who had been one of the founders of the socialist movement in Washington before getting an M.D. from Harvard. He was best known as the leading advocate of the four-hour day—a demand later taken up by the IWW. Dr Titus's letter to Governor Spry emphasized Hill the thinker and creator:

> [He] is a man valuable to society. . . . He is no low-browed villain. He is an intellectual man and a poet. . . . It will be as much a loss and disgrace to Utah to kill this man as it would have been for Scotland to kill Robert Burns. . . . I have traveled from end to end of the United States in the last three years, and everywhere I find his songs in popular use among working men. . . . [Foner 1965, 64]

A careful search through the thousands of petitions, letters, and telegrams received by Governor Spry would doubtless reveal many more notable or soon-to-be-notable writers, artists, and activists who bravely took a stand against Utah's frame-up and legal murder of the Wobbly troubadour.

In every labor defense effort, certain individuals previously known to have been quiet and uncontroversial members of the community suddenly emerge as front-line agitators. Full of energy, daring, and ideas, such figures play brief but intense and highly public roles in the struggle, only to fade back into obscurity afterward. Such was the case of Virginia Snow Stephen, one of the most fascinating personalities involved in the Hill defense.

Virginia Snow Stephen was the daughter of Mormon apostle Lorenzo Snow, who became president of the Mormon church. An artist and graduate of the University of Utah, she was for twenty years an art instructor at the university's Normal School. A contributor of articles on "Art and Nature" and other subjects to the *Utah Educational Review*, she was also an avowed socialist, though not, it seems, a member of the Socialist Party. Indeed, Stephen had decidedly anarchist leanings. An admirer of Emma Goldman, she was also active in the Salt Lake City branch of the "Modern School" movement that drew its inspiration from the martyred Spanish anarchist educator Francisco Ferrer [Sillito 1981, 231-234].

Sympathetic to the workers' movement in general and to the IWW in particular, Stephen's friends included Ed Rowan, who probably introduced her to the Hill case. She visited Hill in the Salt Lake County Jail, and was deeply impressed by his commitment to the IWW cause, as well as by his songs. Convinced of his innocence, she immediately plunged into the campaign to win his freedom. It was she who, via telegram, persuaded Judge O. N. Hilton to become Hill's chief appeals attorney.

Because she was a member of one of the most prominent Mormon families, Stephen's scandalous support for Hill received widespread press coverage. Defying the city's repressive anti-IWW atmosphere, she openly criticized the class bias of the Salt Lake City courts. Her intervention at the Utah Pardon Board hearing was characteristically vigorous:

I think the records show no true identification, only circumstantial evidence, and that leaving much room for doubt, and also no motive. I think the proceedings show prejudice—the prosecutor often referred to Hillstrom as belonging to that class that would rather kill than work—and in other ways prejudiced the jury. In my opinion certain evidence was ruled out that would have materially aided the case of the accused. [Friends of Joe Hill, *Industrial Worker*, 13 Nov 1948, 4]

In 1916 Stephen married the IWW organizer Constantino Filigno —almost certainly the man who, as C. L. Filigno, had made One Big Union history in Missoula, Spokane, San Francisco, Fresno, New Orleans, New York, Philadelphia and other places. The couple soon moved to Walnut Creek, California. Although Stephen evidently lived into her eighties or nineties—she is said to have died in the 1950s or '60s—little is known of her later life.

In Utah, Virginia Snow Stephen has been virtually expunged from the historical record; researchers have been unable to locate obituaries for her, or even to learn the date and place of her death. Her artwork seems to have completely disappeared. None of the reference-works on Utah artists mention her name.[1]

Courageous individuals such as Theodora Pollok and Virginia Snow Stephen, free spirits much in the public eye, did a lot to bring the Hill case, and the life-and-death issues involved in it—class-based "justice," frame-up, burden of proof, the rights of Labor, and the tyranny of Capital—to nationwide attention. Outspoken traitors to the oppressing class into which they were born, they were also genuinely dedicated to the workers' movement. As publicists, their contributions to the Joe Hill Defense Committee were outstanding and far-reaching.

The Committee's day-to-day sustainers, of course, were Wobblies: Rowan and Child in Salt Lake; Chaplin, Haywood, and John Sandgren at union headquarters in Chicago; Sam Murray, Emma B. Little, and C. L. Lambert out in California; E. F. Doree in East Rockport, Illinois; George Falconer in Denver; Ben Williams in Cleveland; James Rohn in Minneapolis; and Elizabeth Gurley Flynn just about everywhere. It was these and many other less-well-known workingstiffs who wrote the press releases, organized street-meetings, answered correspondence, addressed envelopes, mailed circulars, distributed petitions, soapboxed day in and day out, and kept raising the question: *What next?* Thanks to the long, hard work of such "ordinary" folks, the Joe Hill Defense Committee chalked up some extraordinary historic "firsts":

1. For the first time, a U.S. President intervened in a labor defense case on labor's side;

2. For the first time, a foreign government (Sweden), actively supported a labor defense effort;

3. For the first time, *songs* played a major role in a labor defense campaign.

The collective effort to save the life of the IWW's foremost poet fully merits the adjective *heroic*, despite the fact that it ended in failure. A union run on a shoestring, perennially broke or almost broke, and always with many fearsome battles to fight all at once, the IWW nonetheless always put the accent on *looking ahead*. Even in defeat it refused to lose sight of the shapes of things to come. In that perspective, the Joe Hill Defense Committee left us some of the most prophetic pages in the history of the U.S. labor movement.

---

1. Special thanks to John Sillito for the details in this paragraph, and for much other information on Virginia Snow Stephen.

Joe Hill: "My Last Will" (November 1915).

6. THE INTERNATIONAL DEFENSE

You have no country!
Every national flag in the world today
means protection for the employing class,
who appropriate the things produced by the workers.
It has no message for those who toil.
—**Mary E. Marcy**—

The campaign to free Joe Hill is frequently described as international, and indeed it was, but only to a very limited degree. The first World War began in August 1914, and as the workers of the various nations of Europe marched off to shoot each other at their bosses' behest, the socialist Second International ignominiously collapsed. In the suffocating atmosphere of wartime nationalist hysteria, the organized expression of international workingclass solidarity was, to put it mildly, greatly impeded.

The first international action in support of Hill seems to have been a Joe Hill Defense meeting organized by a British branch of the IWW in London on 19 December 1914. Speeches were made, songs sung, and a collection taken up for the defense fund [Foner, 1965, 53]. More impressive was the action initiated by IWW members "down under" in the form of a resolution threatening to boycott U.S.-made goods unless Hill was set free. Charles Reeve, the Australian IWW's national organizer, informed Utah Governor Spry that this resolution was endorsed not only by the IWW but also by representatives of many other large Australian unions [Modesto 1962, 8].

Other efforts on Hill's behalf—in Britain, the rest of Europe, and in most other lands—were decidedly more modest in scope. However, despite the repression that invariably accompanies war, Hill's plight continued to arouse sympathetic interest among working people. The *International Socialist Review* published a letter from Fellow Worker Charles Lahr, who was imprisoned in London for his opposition to the war, noting that he and his fellow prisoners often sang Hill's songs [Jan 1916, 442]. But I have found no mention of boycotts, demonstrations, or job actions linked to the Hill case. If meetings similar to the one in London were held elsewhere in England, or in Ireland, Scotland, or Wales—or for that matter, in Europe, South America, Africa, or Asia—they do not appear to have been recorded in the literature.

Swedish immigrants in the U.S., and second-generation

Swedish-Americans, were a large and important force in the movement to defend Hill. For reasons that are far from clear, however, and despite the intervention of the Swedish government on Hill's behalf, the case received curiously little notice in Sweden itself, even in the socialist and labor press.

If the war and the inevitable confusion and demoralization it brought with it played havoc with the international defense of Joe Hill, the bard himself had no illusions about the war. On 15 September 1914 he wrote Sam Murray:

> I guess the wholesale butchery going on in Europe is putting the kibosh on everything, even the organization work, to some extent.. . . The man who coined the phrase "War is hell" certainly knew what he was talking about. [*Letters*, 13]

In a letter to Elizabeth Gurley Flynn, on 15 July 1915, he related the war to the growing repression in the States:

> All you've got to do is look around you a little and you can plainly see that there is a movement on foot to systematically drain the resources of Organized Labor all over the country. Look at the Ford & Suhr case in Calif. The Lawson case in Colorado, etc. You've got to hand it to "Kaiser Bill." He knew what he was talking about when he said that laws and treaties are nothing but "scraps of paper." [*Letters*, 40]

On 9 September 1915, he wrote again to Sam Murray, who was then working in the shipbuilding industry:

> I see you are employed at making bait for the German "sharks." Well, war certainly shows up the capitalist system in the right light. Millions of men are employed at making ships and others are hired to sink them. Scientific management, eh wot? [*Letters*, 56]

Hill's last song, for which he also composed the music, was a protest against war. On the day before his death he sent hand-lettered copies of "Don't Take My Papa Away From Me" to several fellow workers around the country. It was included in the "Joe Hill Memorial Edition" of the *Little Red Song Book* in March 1916.

Another song Hill wrote in prison, "Workers of the World,

Awaken!"—one of his most beautiful lyrics, and certainly his most Shelleyan—resounds with internationalist and anti-war implications:

If the workers take a notion,
*   They can stop all speeding trains;*
Every ship upon the ocean
*   They can tie with mighty chains.*
Every wheel in the creation,
*   Every mine and every mill,*
Fleets and armies of the nation,
*   Will at their command stand still.*

For united we are standing,
*   But divided we will fall;*
Let this be our understanding:
*   "All for one and one for all."*

Workers of the world, awaken!
*   Rise in all your splendid might;*
Take the wealth that you are making,
*   It belongs to you by right.*

"Hill: 'Bah! The murder of my body
avails you nothing. You cannot murder ideas!'"
This cartoon by Syd Nicholls ran in the Australian IWW
paper *Direct Action* (11 December 1915). Nicholls
later became one of Australia's famous cartoonists.

Ralph Chaplin's drawing portrays Gov. Spry and
the Utah Supreme Court as Hill's murderers
(*Solidarity*, November 1915)

This plan of Hill's execution originally appeared
in the capitalist press.

7. 19 NOVEMBER 1915:
A CASE OF JUDICIAL MURDER

*The year moves toward its end
like a sound toward silence.*
—J. W. von Goethe—

Utah "justice" offers the condemned a choice between hanging and shooting. As a prisoner of the class war, Hill told the Judge, "I'll take shooting. I'm used to that. I have been shot a few times in the past and I guess I can stand it again" [Smith 1969,102].

On 19 November 1915, at sunrise, a five-man firing squad assembled at Utah State Prison. In the yard was Joe Hill, blindfolded and tied to a chair, a paper target on his chest. He had refused the prison physician's offer of a shot of morphine or a slug of whiskey. "No," said Hill, "I never have used it, and I don't intend to start taking the stuff now" [Modesto 1962, 11].

According to Utah law, a condemned person can invite friends to witness the execution, and the warden had assured Hill that he was welcome to do so. Hill invited Fellow Workers Ed Rowan, George Child, and Fred Ritter to attend. When they arrived at the prison, however, the warden turned them away with the lie that Hill did not want to see them. The blindfolded Hill was never told that his IWW friends were not present. Four times he shouted good-by to his fellow workers, and he must have been puzzled by their lack of response. Right up to the last seconds of Hill's life, the authorities of the State of Utah rigorously upheld their policy of lying, hypocrisy, and gratuitous cruelty.

The Deputy in charge called out "Ready, aim. . ."—but it was Hill, a smile on his lips, who cried "Fire!" Five men squeezed their triggers and took the life of the IWW's best loved poet. Utah State Prison Convict No. 3256 was pronounced dead at 7:42 a.m., according to the death certificate. For their services to the State of Utah, Hill's executioners received twenty dollars each.

A few weeks later the *International Socialist Review* printed this poem by John Waring:

QUESTIONED, THE EXECUTIONERS

*What did you buy with your forty pieces,
Any one of you five?*

Something to wear for child or wife?
 Release from a gambling debt?
Christmas money, perhaps
 A gaud for a sweetheart girl?
Whiskey to make you forget?
 Plenty of hire like yours,
Hiding in little tills;
 Still it's seldom one puts one's finger on it
Saying: "For this blood spills."
 This seems special, and so we ask,
Idly—a passing thought—
 What did you do with your forty pieces?
What was it that you bought?
 This we know not; but well we know,
Things that you cannot buy,
 A pillow of ease for your head at night,
A look in a straight man's eye,
 A pleasant thought when you walk alone,
Or peace when you come to die.
       [January 1916, 405]

IWW button, 1915,
probably made for
Hill's Chicago funeral.

8. RESPONSES TO THE EXECUTION

Let the voices of dead poets
Ring louder in your ears
Than the screechings mouthed
In mildewed editorials
—**Bob Kaufman**—

Response to Hill's judicial murder varied widely. When Utah Governor William Spry curtly refused President Wilson's last-minute request for a "thorough reconsideration" of the Hill case, the secretary of the Utah Copper Company sent the Governor a telegram:

> Please allow me to congratulate you most heartily on the manly and sane stand you have taken on the Hillstrom case notwithstanding the pressure brought to bear on you by those whose nerves are so easily affected by cheap sentimentality. [Smith 1969, 169]

While Hill's bullet-ridden body was still warm, Governor Spry—known to working people as "the nimble jumping-jack of the mine-owners"—held a press conference, where he announced that

> The fight has just begun. We are not going to stop until the state is entirely rid of this lawless element that now infests it. . . . Every man who is opposed to law and order—call themselves what they will—will be driven out of Utah. . . . They may talk about the throttling of free speech if they will but I am going to see that inflammatory street speaking is stopped at once. . . . [Stavis 1954, 108]

Always eager to please his masters, Spry immediately banned IWW street-meetings in Salt Lake City, and went on to outlaw the union in the State of Utah. State authorities also took retaliatory measures against individuals who had been active in Hill's defense. O. N. Hilton, for example, was disbarred in Utah, and Virginia Snow Stephen was fired from her position as art teacher at the state university [Smith 1969, 179-180].

Throughout the country, most of the big daily newspapers welcomed the execution. The Salt Lake City press gloated with special pride, as typified by this exultant bombast from the *Deseret*

Evening News:

> The law has been enforced and justice has been satisfied. For this result every good citizen should be profoundly grateful. The state by the firmness of its executive and other officials has happily escaped any reputation for weakness, sentimentality or cowardice. The integrity of the courts and the intelligence of the people have been vindicated. . . .[Smith 1969, 179]

Within the IWW, response to Hill's death respected his watchword: "Don't mourn, organize!" Wobbly speakers and the union press manifested a fierce determination not only to continue the struggle, but to redouble their efforts. Defiance marked the tone of most of these declarations, as in these lines by Ralph Chaplin:

> The murdering of martyrs has never yet made a tyrant's place secure. . . . The state of Utah has shot our songwriter into everlasting immortality and has shot itself into everlasting shame. . . . Neither Joe Hill nor the IWW will ever be found dead within the boundaries of Utah! [1915, 405]

In the same spirit, the indomitable Virginia Snow Stephen lived up to statement she had given the press the year before:

> We may be persecuted and prosecuted for doing or saying the unusual—but we will go on working for [radical change] just the same. We are not out for the honor of the hour. . . . [The] changes [we seek] will be slow in coming, they may come most unexpectedly, but they will come. [Sillito 1981, 231]

The larger radical milieu, including the Socialist Party and anarchist groups, echoed the same resolve, but shock and depression were evident as well. The government's purpose in executing radicals is obviously to discourage radicalism, and with every execution a few of the weaker ones drift away, awed into submission by such displays of merciless authoritarian violence. In others, however, the feeling of helplessness tends to be mixed with anger, or even thoughts of revenge. In the wake of Hill's death, no one expressed this combination of rage and anguish better than Margaret Anderson, the youthful editor of *The Little Review*.

Started on a shoestring in Chicago, 1912, *The Little Review* was one of the first and most audacious of America's "little magazines." Its contributors included most of the boldest and most controversial U.S. poets and writers of the time: Vachel Lindsay, Sherwood Anderson, Elsa von Freytag-Loringhoven, Eunice Tietjens, Carl Sandburg, Amy Lowell, Ben Hecht, Max Bodenheim, Gertrude Stein and many others, as well as such then-unknown Europeans as James Joyce, Marcel Duchamp, Francis Picabia, Tristan Tzara, and René Crevel. Convinced that "people who make Art are more interesting than those who don't," and "that they have a special illumination about life," Margaret Anderson insisted on living within that special "radiance," and on trying to communicate it to the world [Anderson 1953, 11].

Although she championed "Art for Art's sake"—a view radically opposed to Joe Hill's—Anderson also had what in those days was often called a "social conscience," inspired largely by her meeting with Emma Goldman. She quickly came to think of herself as something of an anarchist, and Goldman in turn admired the younger woman's "all-absorbing ardor and daring" [Goldman 1934, 532]. And when the authorities of the State of Utah sent "the IWW poet and artist" to his death, Anderson's editorial for the December 1915 issue of *The Little Review* resounded with this ingenuous, passionate, despairing cry:

> Why didn't someone shoot the Governor of Utah before he could shoot Joe Hill? For God's sake, why doesn't *someone* start the revolution? [Smith 1953, 27]

An IWW "Silent Agitator"

In Memoriam

Joseph Hillstrom

"They've filled his warrior heart with lead;
They gloat to see him safely dead. :
His voice forever hushed and still—
Our singing, fighting, brave Joe Hill."

FUNERAL EXERCISES

will be held on Thursday morning, Thanksgiving day, 1915, at 10:30, in the West Side Auditorium, 1010 South Racine Avenue (near Taylor Street). **The funeral oration will be delivered by Judge O. N. Hilton, of Denver, Colorado.** Jim Larkin and William D. Haywood will speak in English and there will be short talks by speakers in many different tongues at the Graceland Cemetery.

HIS CRIME
WORKERS OF THE WORLD, AWAKEN
By JOE HILL

"Workers of the world awaken!
  Break your chains, demand your
    rights.
All the wealth you make is taken
  By exploiting parasites.
Shall you kneel in deep submission
  From your cradles to your graves?
Is the height of your ambition
  To be good and willing slaves?

Join the union, fellow workers,
  Men and women, side by side;
We will crush the greedy shirkers
  Like a sweeping, surging tide.
For united we are standing,
  But divided we will fall—
Let this be our understanding
  'All for one and one for all.'"

"HE DIED THAT MEN MIGHT LIVE"
WORKING MEN AND WOMEN
ATTEND IN MASS—WE NEVER FORGET

Leaflet announcing Joe Hill's funeral in Chicago
on Thanksgiving Day, 1915.

9. TWO FUNERALS,
UNENDING MEMORIALS

A free man thinks of death least of all things;
and his wisdom is a meditation not of death but of life.
—Spinoza—

Today, more than eighty-five years after he was "judicially murdered by the authorities of the State of Utah," as his fellow Wobblies have traditionally referred to that infamous miscarriage of justice, Hill's position as this country's most celebrated labor martyr remains unchallenged.

His role as poet and artist, as well as labor agitator—and especially his gift as a maker of memorable phrases—helped give him the special place that he continues to hold in so many workers' hearts. As Wobbly songwriter and cartoonist—that is, as an imaginative articulator of workingclass discontent and desire for a new, non-exploitative society—he himself was an active creator of this proletarian counterculture long before his trial and martyrdom assured him a permanent high position in the pantheon of authentic labor heroes, and eventually a niche in America's popular mythology alongside John Henry, Calamity Jane, and The Shadow.

Hill's "Last Will," written in his cell on the eve of his execution, is doubtless the most widely reprinted will in history, and almost certainly the only such document that large numbers of people know by heart. It is also generally regarded as Hill's loveliest poem:

> *My will is easy to decide,*
> *For there is nothing to divide.*
> *My kin don't need to fuss and moan—*
> *"Moss does not cling to a rolling stone."*

> *My body? Ah, if I could choose,*
> *I would to ashes it reduce,*
> *And let the merry breezes blow*
> *My dust to where some flowers grow.*

> *Perhaps some fading flower then*
> *Would come to life and bloom again.*
> *This is my last and final will.*
> *Good luck to all of you.*
>
> *Joe Hill*

Hill's will, as Henry Bengston commented, "in a few short lines reveals his character in all of its gripping simplicity," and stands as "a final testament to his innocence" [1999, 78]. The will also has the added distinction of having been set to music, and more than once—most recently by Joe Uehlein of the labor rock group "Bones of Contention" [Glazer 1997, 8]. In his "Joe Hill Song Checklist," appended to Gibbs Smith's biography, Archie Green noted that Wobbly John Neuhaus sang it to the tune of "Abide with Me," a hymn composed by the nineteenth-century English composer William H. Monk.

More renowned even than the last will is the celebrated battle-cry: "Don't mourn, organize!" In its original and longer form it appeared in one of Hill's last letters, a note to Bill Haywood in which he wrote: "Don't waste any time mourning—organize!" Shortened by Haywood to the more familiar three-word version, this was the Wobbly bard's final advice to his friends and fellow workers. They are among the most famous of famous last words. For years this message of defiance and Hill's other pungent one-liners were "posted as slogans in every IWW office and hall throughout America" [Hardy 1956, 161]. Even in more recent times, Hill's "Don't mourn, organize!" has continued to inspire not only militant labor in the U.S., but oppressed people throughout the world. Page one of the *New York Times* for 11 July 1985 featured a photograph of a young Black freedom-fighter in South Africa whose t-shirt was emblazoned with those very words. In times of setback or defeat, all manner of movements for social betterment—for peace, justice, equality, environmental protection, animal rights, etc., as well as opposition to police brutality, the prison industry, and globalization—have rallied their adherents with Hill's stirring slogan.

Scattered through his letters are a number of other quips and maxims, forceful and original but practically unknown. Several are quoted elsewhere in these pages, and here are a few more:

> Whatever you do, don't try to overthrow the "system" by yourself. [*Letters*, 45]

> The idea of fighting organized capital with money is not the correct way. [*Letters*, 30]

Arguing that the union should concentrate on organizing large industrial centers rather wasting so much time on "jerkwater towns," he wrote:

> Organization is just like dripping water on a blotter—if you drip enough of it in the center it will soak through clean to the edges . . . .[letter to E. W. Vanderleith, n. d., Smith 1969, 132].[1]

He also warned against getting entangled in bureaucracy:

> Red tape is something that has to be paid for by the foot.
>   [*Letters*, 43]

On a more mordant note, after being in jail for almost a year, he wrote:

> I keep myself in good spirits by reminding myself that the worst
>   is yet to come. [*Letters*, 19]

This last is one of the rare examples of Hill's "gallows humor." Another, well known enough to be considered a classic, appears in his farewell note to Bill Haywood:

> I don't want to be found dead in Utah. [*Letters*, 84]

From a man who was about to be shot to death in Utah a few hours later, that simple little sentence is surely as striking as the inscription ("I'd rather be here than in Philadelphia") that W. C. Fields selected for his tomb.

O. N. Hilton's funeral oration for Hill preserved yet another of Hill's maxims, worthy of Vauvenargues or the *Poésies* of Isidore Ducasse:

> Duty is the principal thing. There is always some sweetness sooner or later in doing that, but without it the best things will turn to ashes and dust. [Smith 1969, 186]

As is also evident in his songs and letters, there was something of the moralist in Joe Hill—a *revolutionary* moralist, of course.

It is well to remember that these "sayings" of Hill's, in which his characteristic "no-compromise" radicalism is expressed in ways that make us smile, were written or spoken behind bars as he waited for the state's hired killers to put an end to his life. As wordsmith, humorist, and revolutionist, Joe Hill to the last stayed true to himself, his union, and his class, maintaining even at death's door his remarkable ability "to look at everything from the bright side" [*Letters,* 13].

As Ben Williams, editor of *Solidarity*, put it: "No victim of class injustice in modern times has exhibited such unswerving courage under fire. . . " [Stavis 1954, 78].

That the Joe Hill defense campaign drew such unexpectedly widespread support shows the magnitude of the popular sympathy for Hill's cause, and that profound sympathy in turn suggests that Hill's personality had struck a responsive chord in America's and the world's popular consciousness. The depth of this resonance is further indicated by Hill's funerals. The first, in Salt Lake City, was attended by "several thousand" people—a staggeringly large number in a town with a population of 50,000, especially in view of the anti-Red hysteria promoted by the "powers that be" throughout the state [Stavis 1954, 99]. Among the speakers was Utah Congressman Emil Lund, who called Hill's execution "legal murder" [Friends of Joe Hill 1948, 4].

The second funeral, on 25 November (Thanksgiving Day) in Chicago, was the city's largest since the Haymarket anarchists' funeral of 1887, and was in fact organized with the help of a younger generation of Chicago anarchists, including Russian-born Boris Yelensky. To this day Joe Hill's Chicago funeral remains the largest funeral anywhere of any individual in the U.S. labor movement. It was not its size alone, however, that distinguished it from other funerals; its whole character was different. Hill's mourners clearly took his last words to heart and thought of themselves very much as *organizers*. This least funereal of funerals was rather an immense workers' demonstration—a *singing* demonstration [Chaplin 1915].

The West Side Auditorium was filled to capacity hours before the services began, so that the great majority of the crowd had to remain outdoors. Inside, the program began with an IWW quartet singing Hill's "Workers of the World Awaken!," the audience joining in the chorus. Next came the noted soloist and IWW member Jennie Woszczynska (a student of Mary Garden), who sang Hill's "The Rebel Girl." Short addresses by Bill Haywood and Jim Larkin were followed by a longer oration by Hill's appeals attorney, O. N. Hilton. After Hilton concluded his talk, the crowd quietly marched into the streets to the strains of Chopin's Funeral March, played on the piano by IWW composer Rudolf von Liebich.

In the streets, stretched out for blocks, tens of thousands of working men and women sang Hill's own songs of proletarian humor and defiance in many languages. At Graceland Cemetery, where the body was taken by elevated train to be cremated, short speeches were made in Swedish, Russian, Hungarian, Polish, Spanish, German, Yiddish, Italian, and Lithuanian. These were followed by yet more songs—backed up by music provided by the Russian Mandolin Club and the Rockford, Illinois, IWW Band. Far into the night Hill's friends stayed on, singing his songs of workingclass revolt and revolution [Chaplin 1915, 404].

These funerals, moreover, were planned "to be continued." Hill's ashes were put in pocket-size envelopes, many of which were distributed to delegates to the union's 1916 convention. Other packets were sent to IWW locals in every state but Utah (in keeping with Hill's telegram to Haywood), and every country in South America, as well as to Africa, Asia, Australia, and New Zealand. On May Day 1916, fulfilling Hill's Last Will, his ashes were scattered to the winds all over the world, in mass meetings which again involved singing his songs [Foner 1965a, 99].

In Chicago, Hill's ashes were scattered at Waldheim Cemetery (now Forest Home), the final resting-place of the Haymarket martyrs and—as years went by—of many other labor radicals, including several who in various ways were linked to the Joe Hill story: Bill Haywood, Elizabeth Gurley Flynn, Ammon Hennacy, and Fred Thompson [Powers 1994]. In the 1990s, when the cemetery was sold, one of its new officials was quoted as saying: "We have no record of a burial or ash-scattering for anyone named Joe Hill, but we get more inquiries about him than about any other individual."[2]

In IWW locals, "In November We Remember" memorials were annual events, honoring the Haymarket anarchists, Joe Hill, Frank Little, Wesley Everest and other workingclass fighters murdered in November. Socialist and anarchist groups often held their own November memorials for Hill and others, and memorialized him in their press. The frontispiece of the December 1916 issue of the *International Socialist Review* (mailed the preceding month), featuring a photograph of Hill and his Last Will, was headed: "In Memoriam—Joe Hill—Murdered by the Capitalist Class, Novem-

ASHES

JOE HILL
MURDERED BY THE CAPITALIST CLASS
NOVEMBER 19TH, 1915
DISTRIBUTED BY R Johanson

A packet of Joe Hill's ashes.
This one originally belonged to
Swedish IWW organizer Ragnar Johanson.

ber 1915," and closed with the class-war battle-cry: "Don't mourn for me— organize."

From the 1920s through the 60s the Wobbly troubadour and his songs were also featured in countless May Day parades, rallies, and picnics. Many of these gatherings were also joined by anarchists as well as friends from the Socialist Party, Proletarian Party, Revolutionary Workers League, and other far left groups.

Some memorials were organized without any anniversary pretext. On 14 January 1917, according to the *International Socialist Review*, "services in honor of the IWW poet," co-sponsored by the IWW local and the Socialist Party, were held in San Jose, California. Nine-year-old Rita Wilson released three balloons containing Hill's ashes "which the four winds wafted over the beautiful Santa Clara Valley" [Mar 1917, 573].

In addition to IWW-initiated Joe Hill memorial events, several special "Joe Hill" issues of magazines have appeared, with his name and (in most cases) picture on the front cover: *Industrial Pioneer* (November 1925), *Sing Out!* (1954), *Talkin' Union* (1983), and *Swedish Press* (November 1990), to cite only English-language publications. And numberless other Hill-related events have taken place over the years—from picketlines and songfests to video-screenings and scholarly conferences. Most were planned to coincide with anniversaries of his birth or execution, but some arose in conjunction with new developments in the Hill saga. For the IWW poet truly has "never died" as a newsmaker. With two possible exceptions—the ever-beloved Mother Jones, who claimed to be 100 years old in 1930, the year she died, and the Teamsters' Jimmy Hoffa, whose mysterious disappearance in 1975 has provoked much speculation—no figure in U.S. labor history has excelled Joe Hill as a posthumous headline-grabber. Ironically, for a quiet guy who preferred to stay out of the limelight, and who was shot to death long ago in 1915, he keeps popping up on the front page. He is a good illustration of the old saying, "You can't keep a good man down!"

Here are just a few of the many happenings that have, at odd intervals, put Joe Hill back in the news during the past half-century:

1948: The "Friends of Joe Hill Committee" pickets the offices of the *New Republic*, which had published a disgraceful and dishonest attack on Hill by Wallace Stegner. The detailed *New York Times* coverage of the dispute was reprinted in papers throughout the country.

1955: United Auto Workers (UAW) President Walter Reuther sings the Hayes/Robinson song, "Joe Hill," at the Convention of the Congress of Industrial Unions (CIO).

1965 (fiftieth anniversary of Hill's judicial murder): Large memorial meetings are held in New York, Chicago, Detroit, and Salt Lake City.

1979 (the centennial of Hill's birth): With the assistance of Fred Thompson and other IWWs, the Illinois Labor History Society (ILHS) spearheads a massive international petition campaign to secure Hill's official exoneration. The same year, Sweden announces a Joe Hill commemorative postage stamp, issued in 1980.

1980: Thomas Babe's play about Hill, *Salt Lake City Skyline,* opens on Broadway, and later travels.

1984: Historian William Adelman, Vice-President of the ILHS, takes thousands of signed petitions to Utah to present them to the Governor who, however, refuses to see him. Both the petition campaign and the attempted presentation to the Governor are widely covered in the media, including television. One TV film-clip juxtaposes Utah Governor Matheson saying that exoneration was impossible because the Hill case was "still unclear," and Fred Thompson's response: "If the case is unclear, why was Joe Hill shot?"

1985: To commemorate the union's eightieth anniversary, IWW artist/poet Carlos Cortez organizes a big traveling exhibition titled "Wobbly: Eighty Years of Rebel Art," featuring original works by Wob artists, and copies of older works. This show, which traveled to dozens of cities throughout the U.S. and Canada over the next couple of years, marks the first public exhibition of cartoons by Joe Hill.

1988: A packet of Hill's ashes is found in the U.S. National Archives. The packet had been seized by a Chicago postmaster under the infamous "Espionage Act" during World War I, and forwarded to the Bureau of Investigation (later known as the FBI). In the news for months in '88, the packet was eventually returned to the IWW, whose members proceeded to scatter them at various Wob historic sites.

1990 (the seventy-fifth anniversary of Hill's judicial murder): The largest Joe Hill memorial meeting to date is held in Salt Lake City, featuring talks by historians, folklorists and other scholars as well as labor activists; concerts by well known musicians and vocalists; and a November 19 candlelight vigil co-sponsored by the Joe Hill Organizing Committee and Amnesty International.

1995: A three-day "Celebration of Political Song" is held in Sheffield, England, November 17-19, commemorating Hill on the eightieth anniversary of his death. The event featured folksingers, rappers, street musicians, rock bands and choirs.

1998: Ken Verdoia's 87-minute TV docudrama, "Joe Hill" (starring Robin Ljungberg), premiers on Salt Lake City's KUED and is rebroadcast on Public Broadcasting Service stations throughout the country.

1999: Swedish fascists bomb Joe Hill's birthplace, a building which also houses the local offices of the Swedish syndicalist union, the SAC.

2002: A large syndicalist May Day demonstration in Gävle commemorates the hundredth anniversary of Joel Hägglund's emigration to the U.S. A full-page story appears in Sweden's largest daily. The demonstration is followed by a gathering at the Gävle Music House, featuring Hill's songs. Further memorial events are planned for Fall.

As this sampling shows, Hill remains—after lo these many years—a hot news item worthy of page-one treatment. Meanwhile, he has also continued to receive ample coverage in other sections of the paper. For a man who never died, his ability to work his way into other people's obituaries is truly uncanny. When old-time Wob Herbert Mahler died in 1961, two paragraphs of the *New York Times* obit recalled Mahler's role as organizer of the 1948 Friends of Joe Hill Committee picketline protesting the *New Republic*'s publication of Wallace Stegner's libelous attack on the Wobbly poet [19 Aug, 17]. In 1976, many obits for Paul Robeson mentioned the "Joe Hill" song.

In other obits, Hill actually shares the headline. In 1985, when the author of the "I Dreamed I Saw Joe Hill" song died, the *Chicago Tribune*'s heading read: "Alfred Hayes, screenwriter, 'Joe Hill' poet." Six years later Earl Robinson, the song's composer, died; his hometown paper, the *Seattle Post Intelligencer*, headed the obit: "'Joe Hill' composer Robinson."

In addition to making the scene in newspaper headlines, other people's obits, and occasional features or spots on TV, our Wobbly bard also had his name in bright lights on many hundreds of theater marquees when Bo Widerberg's movie about him came out in 1971. Adding to the publicity, the film was Sweden's entry in that year's Cannes Film Festival. That it was marred by sentimentality and was otherwise disappointing in many respects is unfortunately true, but the very fact that a full-length motion-picture on Joe Hill exists at all is itself a stunning phenomenon. Like the far-from-flattering portrayals of Hill in the novels by James Stevens and Wallace Stegner, Widerberg's movie is yet another demonstration, in yet another medium, that Joe Hill has never ceased to *live* in the best-fortified of all possible hideouts: the *popular imagination*.

Let fiction-writers lie their heads off, and film-directors get their facts wrong—Fellow Worker Hill is still in the game, fanning the flames of discontent. In the blurry half-world of mass culture, as the old vaudevilleans used to say, "Every knock is a boost!"

Widerberg's movie, and the reviews it received, along with the reviews of books about Hill—especially of Gibbs Smith's 1969 biography, but also John McDermott's mass-market novel based on the film—all kept Hill's good name circulating throughout the media. And all that media attention, plus the talk and curiosity it inevitably generated, surely helped swell the crowds at subsequent Joe-Hill-related events.

Numerous artists have memorialized Hill, most notably Carlos Cortez, whose large linocut posters brighten the walls of union halls and "movement" bookstores all over the world. Many Wobbly cartoonists, including Ralph Chaplin, L. S. Chumley, and Jim Lynch, portrayed Hill, as have today's most popular labor cartoonists, Mike Konopacki and Gary Huck. Cartoonist Lisa Lyons's late 1960s "Don't Mourn, Organize!" button, picturing Hill, still turns up on picketlines today. Mike Alewitz's portable Joe Hill mural (1990), complete with a duo of Mr Blocks and a hot steaming pie in the sky, is also available as a four-color t-shirt.

Of course, in keeping the spirit of Joe Hill alive and kicking, pride of place belongs to song. Like his funerals and worldwide ash-scatterings, later memorials for Hill have always resounded with his ebullient lyrics and the loud twanging of banjoes and guitars. He was well known for his songs while he lived, and it is largely through his songs that he is even better known today. He is the most anthologized of all Wobblies; his songs have been included in numerous collections of labor songs and folk songs as well as more specialized compilations of hobo songs, socialist songs, protest songs, and revolutionary poetry.

Joe Hill's songs have been recorded by Joe Glazer, Pete Seeger, Cisco Houston, Tom Glazer, Utah Phillips, Bill Friedland, Hazel Dickens, Billy Bragg, Faith Petric, Ani DiFranco, Bucky Halker,

Si Kahn, Keith and Rusty McNeil, The Dehorn Squad, and others, as well as by many singers in Swedish and other languages. Inexplicably, Len Wallace—the "Squeezebox from Hell," and one of today's finest rebel songster/musicians in the Joe Hill tradition—has not yet recorded any of Hill's songs, but fortunately he's still young enough to rectify this oversight.

Joe Hill is one of two IWW songwriters—the other is Ralph Chaplin, author of "Solidarity Forever," long acknowledged as the anthem of the entire U.S. labor movement—whose songs have been regularly included (albeit in abridged versions) in songbooks published by AFL-CIO unions and even by the AFL-CIO itself.

Songs *about* Hill have also helped keep his name vibrant in public consciousness. The Hayes/Robinson song, "Joe Hill," as popularized by Paul Robeson, Joan Baez, Robinson himself, and many others, has had the greatest impact, although there have been many other songs about Hill, extending back to the Wobbly lyrics by Dick Brazier and T-Bone Slim in the 1910s and '20s. More recent contributions include Woody Guthrie's "Joseph Hillstrom," Phil Ochs's "Joe Hill," Si Kahn's "Joe Hill" (later retitled "Paper Heart," referring to the paper target the executioner placed on Hill's chest), Mark Levy's "Joe Hill's Ashes," and the little-known "All Hail Joe Hill" by Folke Geary Anderson, the pioneer of the 1970s/80s movement to secure Hill's official exoneration.[3]

The Hayes/Robinson song, meanwhile, has spawned its own imitations and parodies: Bob Dylan's "I Dreamed I Saw St Augustine," Billy Bragg's "I Dreamed I Saw Phil Ochs Last Night," and any number of topical and quickly forgotten versions of "I Dreamed I Saw [fill in the blank] Last Night." The Hayes/Robinson song is even mentioned in another song—Si Kahn's "We All Sang Bread and Roses," the chorus of which goes

We all sang "Bread and Roses," "Joe Hill" and "Union Maid,"
And we all joined hands together saying, We are not afraid.
"Solidarity Forever" will go rolling through the hall.
"We Shall Overcome" together, one and all.

In one of the most insightful and stimulating essays ever written on Hill and his expanding legacies, Lori Elaine Taylor (1993) reflected on the complex mutual influence and creative interaction between these various songster disciples of the Wobbly bard:

Billy Bragg, described by a *Village Voice* reporter as a cross between Joe Hill and Benny Hill, in his liner notes for . . . a Phil
Ochs recording wrote: "Everybody wants to be somebody else.
Phil Ochs wanted to be Elvis Presley. I wanted to be the Clash.
Both of us at one time or another wanted to be Bob Dylan, who
had originally wanted to be Woody Guthrie." Thus Joe Hill
begat Woody Guthrie, who with Elvis begat Phil Ochs, who with
the Clash begat Billy Bragg—there are endless ways to trace the
musical and political genealogy because it is not simply linear.
The storyteller creates his own past by choosing to emphasize or
invent certain influences, by wanting to be someone else. . . .

Joe Hill is a figure abstracted from the life of a man. Joe
Hill is a hero, a character of legend. His name, even his history
and legend are without owners, though not without heirs.

The process by which a person becomes a hero emphasizes
the teller of the tale, who gradually modifies the story according
to circumstance. Context, the ever-changing contemporary context, reveals more about the meaning of the tale than its time-
bound origins or its static texts. . . . Every person who hears the
legend [of Joe Hill] owns a version, and every teller owns the
moment. . . . Many different communities use the story of Joe
Hill to comment upon their present. [29-31]

Hill's story, of course, is indissolubly linked to dissent, poetry,
protest, the struggle for freedom and a good life for all. In their
very different ways, today's tellers of the tale are alike in at least
one respect: They are all organizing instead of mourning. At strike
rallies and other union gatherings; at anti-war, anti-racist, anti-
globalization, and radical environmentalist demonstrations; at May
Day picnics, benefit concerts for political prisoners, free-speech
events at such places as Bughouse Square, or just friendly neighborhood coffee-houses, singers customarily introduce a Joe Hill
song with a few words about the man and his union, as well as his
martyrdom. Not many songwriters are so honored. It goes to show
that there is something special about Hill and his songs, and that
those who sing them want to share that "something" with their
listeners. In that sense, every time you hear a Joe Hill song it's a
kind of memorial.

---

1. This letter to Vanderleith is one of several not included in Foner's *Letters of Joe Hill* (1965).

2. Thanks to Mark Rogovin for communicating this anecdote.

3. Singer as well as songwriter, Swedish-born Folke Geary Anderson lived for many years in Oakland, California, and began agitating for Hill's exoneration (not a mere pardon) in the early 1970s, if not before. In connection with this campaign, he carried on a prodigious correspondence with old Wobblies, Hill scholars, folk-singers, and the Charles H. Kerr Company, as well as numerous labor and public officials. Anderson wrote two songs and at least one poem about Hill.

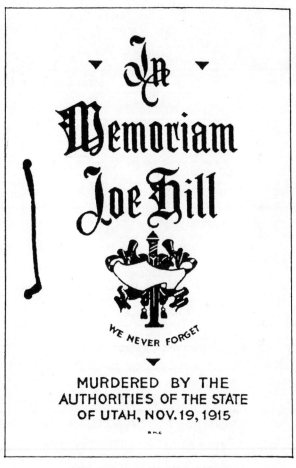

Ralph Chaplin designed the cover
for the official program of Hill's Chicago funeral.

Jim Lynch: Cover art for an IWW magazine, 1925.

V

JOE HILL & THE ARTS

1. A PAINTING BY JOE HILL

We do not know all the colors.
Each of us invents new ones.
—**Guillaume Apollinaire**—

Writing on Joe Hill has mostly focused on his role as archetypal Wobbly, folk hero, songwriter, and labor martyr. Very little has been said about his work as a visual artist. In his lifetime, however, and for more than a decade afterward, he was generally recognized in print as cartoonist and artist as well as songwriter and poet.

Taking these citations in chronological sequence, the June 1914 issue of the *International Socialist Review*— "The Fighting Magazine of the Working Class," to which Hill himself contributed on several occasions—refers to "Fellow Worker Joe Hill" as the "author of the IWW song book, cartoonist and rebel" [763]. An IWW defense leaflet (see page 124) identified him as "songwriter and artist." In his write-up of Hill's funeral in Chicago, Ralph Chaplin described him as "dreamer, poet, artist, and agitator" [1915, 405]. Five years later, an article in the November 1920 issue of the *One Big Union Monthly*, probably by the editor, John Sandgren (formerly secretary of the Swedish section of the Joe Hill Defense Committee) noted that Hill, "Besides being a writer of songs which made the workers of all countries listen... was also an amateur cartoonist" [59]. Chaplin, in his 1923 biographical sketch of Hill in the *Industrial Pioneer*, called attention to the IWW bard's "considerable talent for drawing" [24]. And in his serialized history, "The IWW Tells Its Own Story" in the *Industrial Worker* (1930-32), Fred Thompson noted that Hill was "popular among the IWW because of his numerous songs and poems as well as cartoons" [chapter 11, 20-21].

To his contemporaries, then, Joe Hill was not only a songwriter and poet, but also a visual artist, and more particularly a cartoonist. Somehow, over the years, his artwork was largely forgotten. Stavis, Foner, and Gibbs Smith neglected to include any of his cartoons in their books about Hill. Joyce Kornbluh, however, reproduced three in *Rebel Voices* (1964), and Carlos Cortez's exhibition, "Wobbly:

Eighty Years of Rebel Art," featured copies of several Hill cartoons in its long cross-country tour from 1985 through 1988.

Even if Hill's work as a visual artist lacked all intrinsic interest
—which definitely is not the case—these works would still be
important because they allow us to see him in a new light. Although his artworks are quantitatively fewer than his songs, the
mere fact that the IWW poet also happens to have been something
of an artist tells us interesting details about him that we did not
know before.

John Sandgren's reference to Hill as an "amateur" cartoonist
is true but misleading, for *all* Wobbly cartoonists were in effect
amateurs. A few, like "Dust" Wallin and Jim Lynch, may have
made a living drawing "gag"cartoons for the bourgeois press, and
Ralph Chaplin, L. S. Chumley, and Arturo (Arthur) Machia are
known to have worked as illustrators for the Charles H. Kerr
Company, but all of them freely donated their creative labors to the
One Big Union [Rosemont 1988b]. This is a remarkable phenomenon, unique in the annals of American art: The IWW in the 1910s
and '20s produced many of the first, finest and funniest cartoonists
in the history of the labor movement—Ernest Riebe, Joe Troy,
Ralph Chaplin, "Dust" Wallin, Jim Lynch, Eugene Barnett, Ern
Hansen, William Henkelman, and dozens of others—and not one
of them made a dime out of it. The same is true, of course, of the
IWW's song-writers and other contributors to the Wobbly press.
These wildly inventive characters were not really interested in
money, self-promotion, or any sort of "career." For them it was
strictly "All for One and One for All, and All for the Cause!"

Joe Hill's involvement in art preceded his IWW membership
by many years. On exhibit at the Joe Hill Museum housed in his
birthplace in Gävle is an oil painting of a waterfall on the Gävle
River that Hill did in Sweden, probably in the 1890s (see page
159). It is a study of agitated motion, rather Heraclitean in spirit,
vibrant with the restless waterway's dark, uncertain music. Its
naturalistic technique is exaggerated by a kind of "expressionist"
fervor, which in turn deepens the whole scene's disturbingly
dreamlike intensity. Although it cannot be said to have struck a
new note in the art of the time—Hill was the contemporary of
Edvard Munch, Vincent Van Gogh, Paul Gauguin, and the young
Pablo Piccasso—this painting could surely be considered an auspi-
cious beginning for a young, self-taught workingclass artist who
had time to paint only after a hard day's work at the rope factory.

Joe Hill: "Cataract" (oil painting, pre-1902)

To what extent Hill continued to paint in later years is not clear. In one of his prison letters, addressed to the editor of the *Salt Lake Telegram*, he mentions painting as one of his chief free-time pursuits:

> I have worked hard for a living and paid for everything I got, and my spare time I spend by painting pictures, writing songs and composing music. [*Letters*, 49-50]

Remarkably, "painting pictures" is first on the list. Another letter suggests that he may have doing some paintings (perhaps watercolors) in the Salt Lake City jail, but none seem to have survived [*ibid.*, 49-50]. Indeed, apart from the one early painting now in Gävle, no paintings known to have been painted by Hill, or even "attributed to" Hill, are extant.

In view of the publicity given to Hill as artist and painter, it is curious that no one—fellow workers, attorneys, members of the Joe Hill Defense Committee, reporters, or free-lance writers—ever seems to have asked to see some examples of his work. Curiously, too, in their recollections of Hill, not one of his friends ever refers to his paintings.

This would seem to suggest that, for Hill, painting was a very private matter which, unlike most of his songwriting, was not related to his IWW activity. Nowhere in the literature is there any reference to one of Hill's paintings being displayed in an IWW hall or a Socialist hall—or, for that matter, being in the possession of any of Hill's friends. The near-total disappearance of his works further suggests that his paintings did not depict workers or workers' struggles; that they were probably landscapes and seascapes (his one known painting in Sweden reinforces this supposition); that he signed them with another name; and that he sold them under that name to collectors or art dealers.

All this fits with what is known about Hill. He had changed his name at least twice in the U.S., and may have used at least one *nom de plume*—F. B. Brechler—as an IWW songwriter [Kornbluh 1964, 179; Smith 1969, 21n]. And he wrote at least three non-IWW songs—trivial, sentimental, "popular" songs—almost certainly for the sole purpose of making a little money [Smith 1969, 38-39].

My hypothesis accounts not only for his friends' seeming ignorance of his work as a painter, but also for the "disappearance" of the paintings themselves. Incidentally it provides an explanation for a statement made decades later by one of Hill's casual acquaintances, Harry McClintock—a statement, however, unsubstantiated by any other evidence—according to which Hill, at a certain period in his life, is supposed to have had "no visible means of support, though he was well dressed and had enough money" [Stegner 1948, 22].

Puzzles persist, however. Had Hill truly wanted to keep his painting a secret, why would he have mentioned "painting pictures" in his letter to the editor of the *Salt Lake Telegram*? And how did it happen that there was no trace of his work as a painter among his meager belongings? As is well known, Hill left almost no "effects" ("My will is easy to decide, For there is nothing to divide"). When he left San Pedro, did he ship all his unsold canvases, paints and brushes on to a friend in Chicago?

Another possibility, albeit unlikely in view of Hill's ready command of English, is that he never did any paintings in the U.S., but used the expression "painting pictures" to signify drawing. The only evidence pointing in this direction is that Hill, in his letters, other writings and interviews never mentions drawing or cartooning.

This much is certain: With one exception, Joe Hill's paintings are a complete mystery.

Joe Hill: "I've Got a Mission to Fill" (self-portrait).
Hand-drawn postcard to Charles Rudberg, 29 April 1911.

2. JOE HILL, IWW CARTOONIST

Our principal life
—for we lead several lives at the same time—
is the life of Imagination.
—Paschal Beverly Randolph—

Hill may never have mentioned cartooning, but he made no secret of his love for "scribbling." Commentators have taken this term to refer only to his writing, but it can just as well be applied to drawing. Cartooning with pen and ink— supremely portable, and therefore well suited to the life of a man on the road— seems to have been the visual art he preferred. If he painted to make a little money, his cartooning was a labor of love and given freely to the Cause.

That Hill "loved to draw" seems obvious from the drawings themselves, and is confirmed by Frances Horn, who heard it from her father, Charles Rudberg, a friend of Hill's since their childhood in Gävle [letter, Horn to FR, 15 Apr 1985]. Rudberg was obviously impressed by his friend's versatility in the arts: He told Frances's older sister that Hill could also "sing like an angel, play the violin like a master, and write like a fury" [Horn to Mason, 29 Jan 1980]. Alas, no examples of cartoons or other drawings Hill may have done in Sweden have come down to us. We know nothing of the artists he liked, and who may have helped shape his own art. It is a virtual certainty, however, that he was familiar with the work of his Swedish contemporary, Oskar Emil Andersson (known simply as O.A.), whose wildly imaginative strip, "The Man Who Does Whatever Comes Into His Mind," was featured in a popular Stockholm weekly [Jungmarker 1946; Maurice Horn, ed. 1976, 80]. Hill's self-portrait playing a piano (see page 161) is markedly similar to one of O.A.'s cartoons (see below).

Joe Hill was already the IWW's most popular songwriter when he made his debut as a pioneer Wobbly cartoonist in 1912 (see page 258). Labor cartooning in the U.S. was still in its infancy. In regard to content and "message," Hill found all he needed and more in the IWW press, but for visual inspiration he had to look elsewhere. Significantly, he was one of the relatively few labor cartoonists to adopt the harum-scarum style of the "funnies" instead of the more sober "editorial" cartoon. As a songwriter he favored popular tin-pan-alley tunes rather than traditional or "folk" songs; so too as a cartoonist he took his models from the daily comics page.

Oskar Andersson ("O.A."): detail from a drawing, 1899.

Thus Joe Hill joined the great tradition: Like all the cartoonists of his time, he began by imitating all the cartoonists of his time. The merest glance offers definitive proof that his art was influenced above all by the major U.S. newspaper comic-strip artists of the early 1900s: Rudolf Dirks (*Katzenjammer Kids*, which debuted in 1897)), Frederick Burr Opper (*Happy Hooligan*, 1900), Charles W. Kahles (*Hairbreadth Harry*, 1906), Bud Fisher (*Mutt and Jeff*, 1907), Thomas Aloysius ("Tad") Dorgan (*Silk Hat Harry's Divorce Suit*, 1910), George Herriman (*Krazy Kat*, 1910), and Harry Hershfield (*Desperate Desmond*, 1910). Like Hill, by the way, Dirks and Kahles were immigrants, reminding us that many of the most prominent U.S. cartoonists in the early twentieth century were foreign-born.

It is not always easy to identify specific influences on an artist. In Hill's case, the horse in his sketch of his friend, Fellow Worker Sam Murray (see page 83), is obviously a close cousin of Opper's Mule Maud. "Tad" Dorgan might have inspired—or at least reinforced—Hill's profound sense of the expressive power of slang. (Hill's song "Scissor Bill," for example, popularized that key term in the Wobbly lexicon.[1]) Cumulatively, all the aforementioned artists helped Hill develop a simpler, looser, freer way of drawing than the prevailing mode in European cartoons, along with a thoroughly "slapstick" approach to gags, with riotously crowded scenes, so evocative of the mad hurly-burly of early twentieth-century American life.

Finally, and above all, Opper, Dorgan, Herriman and the others may have convinced Hill (if he needed convincing) of the comics' capacity to say a lot and to say it noisily, in a small space—and to say it not so much with words as with the eye-grabbing art of "scribbling."

Hill left us no account of his aims as a cartoonist, but the statements he occasionally made about his songs apply just as well to his drawings. As he wrote in a letter published in the IWW paper *Solidarity* in 1914:

> If a person can put a few cold, common-sense facts into a song and dress them (the facts) up in a cloak of humor to take the dryness off of them, he will succeed in reaching a great number of workers who are too unintelligent or too indifferent to read a pamphlet or an editorial on economic science. [*Letters*, 16]

Every editor knows a picture is worth a thousand words, and a *funny* picture worth 10,000.

Joe Hill: "As It Was, As It Is." *One Big Union Monthly,* November 1919.

A comment from a letter to his friend and fellow worker Sam Murray, with whom he had fought "under the Red Flag" in the Mexican Revolution, also applies to Hill's comics:

> When I make a song I always try to picture things as they really
> are. Of course a little pepper and salt is allowed in order to bring
> out the facts more clearly. [*Letters,* 18]

Thanks to this "pepper and salt," Hill's cartoons have a felicitous "zing" of their own: a raw, uninhibited grace, and a humor that tickles the mind's eye and won't let go. Indifferent to order, balance, precision, delicacy of touch, subtlety of shading, and other graphic niceties, he was no master draftsman, but his profound sense of gags more than made up for it. Hill scribbled for laughs, and laughs are what he got, from 'boes and other workingstiffs across the land. He seems to have drawn at lightning speed, with the warmth, and energy of a crowd of strikers tearing down a jailhouse and setting the prisoners free. Each of his extant cartoons was probably completed in its first and only draft. Heeding Emile Zola's advice, that "vulgar happenings should be presented in the bluntest fashion," Hill put weighty Wobbly truths into a light comic form that could be read and enjoyed on the run.

With their playful irrationality, their animistic tendency, their defiance of mundane logic and other repressive manifestations of the "Reality Principle," Hill's cartoons provoke hilarity and therefore liberate the so-called impossible. In the very distortion and unreality of cartooning lies the secret of its delight and therefore its power. The more vividly these cartoons depicted the absurdity of capitalism and its impending demise, the more they satisfied and reassured the wage-slave readers of the Wobbly press. As with his songs, then, Hill's "scribbling" as a cartoonist served to reinforce and stimulate the IWW's community of desires and daydreams—the shared hopes, reveries, and expectations of a consciously revolutionary working class.

The fact that the IWW's most popular songwriter was also a cartoonist is fascinating, and enhances our appreciation of his amazing ability to inspire his fellow workers in so many ways. It cannot be said, however, that Hill's comic art is among the union's best. Ralph Chaplin and "Dust" Wallin are incomparably more accomplished in the art of drawing, Ernest Riebe and William Henkelman superior gag-men, and for sheer stylistic eccentricity and zaniness, Ern Hansen and a little later C. E. Setzer (who generally signed his cartoons with his initials, or with the first three numbers of his red card: X13) are in a world of their own. Hill's cartoons, however, like his songs, were effective in doing what they were supposed to do: to give wage-slaves—and especially migratory wage-slaves—something to laugh and think about.

Like the IWW itself, Fellow Worker Hill had no aptitude for being dull. Everything he drew is the opposite of static. The turbulent romanticism embodied in his early waterfall painting prefigured the frenetic action that permeates his wild and lovable drawings. Few of his "characters" are content to stand still—they prefer to run or dance or zoom up the stairs. In most of his comics, a lot of things are happening all at once. His brisk, rhythmic line gives the whole picture a vibrant sense of movement that is often unabashedly carnivalesque. *Reckless liveliness* is the hallmark of nearly every Joe Hill cartoon.

---

1. On the word Scissorbill, its origins and meanings, see the articles by Peter Tamony, Archie Green, and Patrick Huber in *Comments on Etymology* 26:3 (University of Missouri-Rolla, December 1996).

CLASS WAR NEWS

CLEVELAND, OHIO SATURDAY, OCTOBER 24, 1914.

I. W. W. Submarines Are Annoying The Enemy Everywhere

Joe Hill: "Class War News: IWW Submarines
Are Annoying the Enemy Everywhere."
(*Industrial Solidarity*, 24 October 1914)

3. A CLASS-WAR HUMORIST

Remaining serious is successful repression.
Laughter and coitus break through guilt feeling.
—Sandor Ferenczi—

Humor and spontaneity were among Hill's strongest traits. In her reminiscences decades after Hill's judicial murder, his sister, Ester Dahl, recalled his "teasing" kind of humor as a teenager, when he made up gently sarcastic songs about his younger siblings [Takman, 26]. He would also read aloud from the newspaper, "taking a line here, a line there, resulting in the strangest news events"—a procedure later discovered and developed by surrealists.[1] Edward Mattson, a fellow worker who knew Hill in Seattle and San Pedro, remembered especially Hill's incredible ability to improvise lyrics as he played. When Hill was later asked to repeat a certain song, according to Mattson, he (Hill) would invent entirely new lyrics [Nerman 1979, 36]. The man we know as the Wobbly bard was—at least within the circle of his friends and fellow workers—a stand-up improv comedian who also happened to be an accomplished musician. The fact that he had his listeners rolling in the aisles suggests that the spontaneity of his lyrics made them all the more effective. Many of his songs, including "The Preacher and the Slave," "Mr Block," "Coffee An'," and "The Tramp," are real classics—not only of IWW humor but also of American and world humor.

In most of Hill's songs, what makes us laugh are the incidents in the story, and the punch-lines at the end of each stanza. In others —such as "Casey Jones, the Union Scab," "Everybody's Joining It" and "Nearer My Job to Me"—the nervous, rattling rhythm of the lyrics heightens the humorous effect. More rarely he slips in a bit of wordplay. His little-known poem, "Let Bill Do It"—a gentle gibe at fellow workers who sit around the union hall all day and refuse to do their share—is dedicated to those who "have nothing to lose but their *chairs*" [emphasis added, FR].

The same hardhitting wit and imaginative agility that served Joe Hill so well as a writer of songs is also very much in evidence in his visual art. As it happens, the period in which most of his surviving artwork was made was the heyday of American vaudeville. Between 1910 and 1914, a comedy trio known as the Three Marx Brothers were creating havoc on stages big and little all over this land. The same decade also marks the dawn of the slapstick silent film comedies of Mack Sennett and Charlie Chaplin. Hill and other makers of the IWW counterculture took generous helpings of all that was best in the popular arts, but the end-product was always distinctively their own: not only funny but also anti-capitalist and revolutionary. The Wobbly counterculture could in fact be defined in large part as *popular culture liberated and fortified by the IWW Preamble.*

In all of Hill's cartoons the accent is on a rollicksome hobo humor, relentless in its free-for-all sarcasm and satire. His no-holds-barred class-war militancy gave pride of place to proletarian laughter. These cartoons ridicule—and expose the boundless hypocrisy of—the whole gamut of bourgeois values. One of his hand-drawn cartoon postcards is at once a refutation of the myth that "all are equal before the law" and a protest against the brutal treatment of migratory workers—*i.e.,* hoboes. From the 1910s through the '30s, cops, private detectives, railroad bulls, gangsters, and even the U.S. Army routinely pursued roving workers with pistols, rifles, and high-powered military weaponry, killing and maiming hundreds if not thousands. Many thousands more were arrested and forced to work on chain-gangs or at other unpaid labor. Hill's postcard drawing (see below) shows a 'bo (perhaps himself) being kicked off a speeding freight train, as a waiting cop, brandishing a billy-club and grinning, prepares to march the "vagrant" off to jail or workhouse. Postmarked San Pedro, 2 September 1911, and

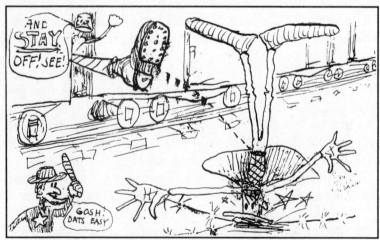

Joe Hill: "Oh you Hoboing."
Hand-drawn cartoon postcard to Charles Rudberg, 2 September 1911.

Joe Hill: "Mr and Mrs Highbrow."
(*One Big Union Monthly,* November 1919)

addressed to Charles Rudberg at the Sailors' Union Hall in San Francisco, this picture postcard also includes the artist's brief commentary, a veritable poem on the perils of a hobo's life:

> *The song of Mauser bullets*
> *may be exciting*
> *and the rattle of machine-guns*
> *may also have its thrills—*
> *but Oh you hoboing!*

Another cartoon shows us a battlefield strewn with the dead, dying, and wounded (see above). In the center, coldly oblivious to the horror and suffering around them, Mr and Mrs Highbrow are concerned only with the slight damage done to a 2000-year-old painting of "King Loco."

Interestingly, this is Hill's only cartoon directly concerned with "Art." I am sure his French contemporary Jacques Vaché, the great forerunner of surrealism, would have sensed its kinship with the subversive and protosurrealist spirit that he called Umor—humor

Jacques Vaché: "Died for the Fatherland, Acquired by the State"
(drawing, 1917)

without the h [Rosemont 1998, 95-96]. There are, moreover, strong affinities—in mood, temper, and tone—between this war cartoon of Hill's and the cartoons Vaché himself was drawing (see above) in the days of his celebrated *War Letters*. Vaché's subtle and ironic "desertion from within" reflected a sensibility quite distinct from Hill's openly proclaimed Wobbly revolutionism, but it is charming to see how similarly these two very different nonconformists expressed, in "scribbling," their absolute contempt and loathing for the first imperialist world war.

Laughing darkly, Hill also let his merciless pen reveal the utter futility and misery of petit-bourgeois "cockroach capitalism" and parliamentary "slowcialism," along with the sorry but silly efforts of self-deluded wage-slaves in pursuit of desirable but forever-elusive jobs (see page 195). Hill's humor, like the best of T-Bone Slim's—and Wobbly humor generally—tends to be *black*, never pink or baby blue. In his art and writing as in his social philosophy, he favored direct action. Hill's cartoons, as Evert Anderson wrote of his songs, were "designed to jab, to shock, to wake the American wage-slave into an awareness of his class position" [1964, 4]. The abominations of war, the brutality and injustice endured by the whole working class, the thoroughly fraudulent character of "free enterprise": Joe Hill, revolutionary industrial humorist, shows us all this and more. Wasting no time on polite euphemism, he goes straight to the point: *From top to bottom, the system stinks, and workers' solidarity is the only solution.*

As cartoonist and as songwriter, Hill never stops at mere social criticism; he is first and last a revolutionist. Always, however, he is a revolutionist with a well-developed sense of humor. He especially enjoyed creating images of capitalism being wrecked, either by its own imbecility and inertia, or by workingclass direct action. Sabotage, striking on the job, workers expropriating the bosses' stolen goods, *workers helping themselves*: These are the grand themes that warmed the cockles of his Wobbly hobo heart. His double-panel comic, "As It Was, As It Is" (see page 164), portrays literally a rebel worker helping himself to some of the "good things of life" that capitalists traditionally have reserved for themselves. Here is Joe Hill's own "Rise and Fall of Wage-Slavery" in two tableaux (reading time: six seconds).

His song lyrics pursue the same themes, and resound with the same humor. Such songs as "Casey Jones, the Union Scab," "Everybody's Joining It," "John Golden and the Lawrence Strike," and that saboteurs' marching ballad, "Ta-ra-ra Boom De-Ay" radiate the unrestrained irreverence, hilarity, audacity, and rowdiness of the wildest Felix the Cat cartoons, with IWW solidarity and direct action providing the basic plot and continuity. Albeit more subtly, Hill's eight-line poem, "The Rebel's Toast," also captures this "all-hell-can't-stop-us" rebellious spirit:

> *If Freedom's road seems rough and hard,*
> *   And strewn with rocks and thorns,*
> *Then put your wooden shoes on, pard,*
> *   And you won't hurt your corns.*
> *To organize and teach, no doubt,*
> *   Is very good—that's true,*
> *But still we can't succeed without*
> *   The Good Old Wooden Shoe.*

Joe Hill's special blend of bitterness and glee is at its explosive best in the magnificent cartoon that appeared in *Solidarity* in 1914 under the double headline: "CLASS WAR NEWS / IWW Submarines Are Annoying the Enemy Everywhere" (see page 166). An IWW wooden-shoe-shaped submarine fires a "Direct Action torpedo" at the battleship *Capitalism*, captained by a smug and corpulent capitalist—labeled "Plute" (for Plutocrat)—who, as anyone can see, is hogging "All Necessities of Life" for himself. Of course this supercilious representative of the employing class doesn't have a clue to what is going on "below." The cartoon's main action takes place under water because the work of proletarian saboteurs is clandestine and unexpected.

This single-panel drama of revenge and redemption hearkens back to David and Goliath, Robin Hood, and *The Three Musketeers*, but it also looks ahead to Tex Avery, *Little Lulu*, and a class-conscious *Calvin and Hobbes*. It is an old story that is nonetheless always new, and always worth retelling in ever-new ways: Against seemingly impossible odds, those who have been exploited, oppressed, and made to feel small and weak, band together and rise up to liberate themselves and their class. With Hill's delightful little touches—the astonished fish and sea-snake (or is it an eel?) looking on with wonder, and *five* speech-balloons, no less—this is surely his single finest cartoon, and exemplifies his knack for expressing complex revolutionary ideas simply and enticingly. Wasn't it Michelangelo who said "Trifles make a masterpiece"?

The *Little Red Song Book*, moreover, includes *many* masterpieces by Hill: songs so irresistibly funny that even hardened scissorbills often caught the drift and joined up (thereby ceasing to be scissorbills). Masterpieces though they undoubtedly are, however, these songs have been systematically excluded from studies and anthologies of American humor. From Constance Rourke (1931) and Max Eastman (1936) to the later and more comprehensive (or at least more copious) tomes of Jesse Bier (1968), Walter Blair and Hamlin Hill (1970), and Russell Baker (1993), professional students of laughter have maintained an almost religious silence regarding Joe Hill or, for that matter, any other Wobbly. This exclusion has been so alarmingly thorough that it makes one wonder whether there might not be a little-known law requiring FBI prepublication approval of all books on humor.

Discrimination along class lines is of course a well-recognized national disgrace. True, it is only one of a million or so national disgraces, including the Presidency and the prison industry and the appalling fact that shameless commercialism makes it practically impossible to hear the wonderful music of David Boykin, Hamid Drake, and Nicole Mitchell on the radio in Chicago. That is the way things happen to be at the moment, and in this degraded era of multi-billionaires and post-modern postmortems for revolutionary change, there appears to be no immediate relief in sight.

But here is a handy tip that should save you a lot of time and trouble. Next time you come across a book purporting to be about "American humor," check the Table of Contents and/or Index. If you don't find the names *Joe Hill* or *T-Bone Slim*, you have definitive proof that the book you've found is phony: It is *not* a book about American humor, but only—and at best—about American *middle-class* humor.

---

1. See Jehan Mayoux, "Correspondence," in *Le Surréalisme au service de la révolution*, No. 5 (1932), 42. "Latent News," a surrealist game similar to Hill's playful "rewriting" of the newspaper, is described (with examples) in Sakolsky (2002).

4. THE WOBBLY ART OF PARODY

Ridicule has greater power
to reform the world than sour.
—Jonathan Swift—

As a songwriter, Hill's best works are his parodies. Starting with a well-known old tune or a catchy hit of the day, he would play with the lyrics—altering them and adding new ones of his own. By following this method—"scribbling"—many stodgy old "Starvation Army" hymns and sentimental pop tunes suddenly blossomed anew as revolutionary IWW songs. Hill's gift for parody was obvious early on, and he certainly made the most of it. Measured by the enduring popularity of his compositions, he is incontestably one of the most successful song-parodists of the past century.

Hill's "Casey Jones, the Union Scab," was a parody of a popular song titled simply "Casey Jones," written by Tallifero Lawrence Sibert with music by Eddie Walter Newton, copyrighted 1909. The original portrayed a heroic locomotive engineer, but Hill showed him as a "union scab"—*i.e.*, one who remained on the job when workers from all the other Southern Pacific railroad unions had gone on strike in protest against the unsafe conditions of the trains and the track. Printed on a pocket-size card in 1911, the song was an instant hit, featured in a new edition of the *Little Red Song Book* in 1912. Hill's parody soon surpassed the original in popularity, and was part of the repertory of vaudeville singing groups for years. It remains one of the Wobbly bard's most popular lyrics to this day.

Although some critics, such as Dwight Macdonald (1960), have regarded parody as a kind of "homage" to the parodied work, this is clearly not true of Hill's and other IWW parodies, most of which are sarcastic to the point of cruelty. Anyone who believes that Sanford Fillmore Bennett, author of the pious hymn "In the Sweet Bye and Bye," would have felt honored by Hill's blasphemous and atheistic "Pie in the Sky," probably also believes in the tooth fairy. Wobbly parodists, as exemplified by Hill, sought to deflate, demolish, and replace the existing order's reactionary lyrics with their own new and explicitly anti-capitalist models.

Freud, in his *Jokes and Their Relation to the Unconscious*, noted that parody is "directed against people and objects which lay claim to authority and respect," and related it to the broader category of *unmasking* [Freud 1963, 200-201]. A mere glance at the *Little Red Song Book* suffices to show that IWW songs are inherently anti-authoritarian as well as raucously disrespectful of exploiters and apologists for exploitation, and Hill's are among the most unflinching in this regard. Tearing the hypocritical smiling masks off the ugly face of capitalism was a major Wobbly sport, and Joe Hill was its first heavyweight champion. Even before his third song made the rounds, Hill's primacy as Number One IWW parodist was conceded by his fellow songwriters. "The minute [Joe Hill] appeared with his first, and then his second song," Dick Brazier recalled, in language reminiscent of an aspiring 1960s boxer who had just witnessed his first knockout by Muhammad Ali, "we all knew he was the great one" [Stavis 1964, 43].

Like humor anthologists, however, compilers of parodies have been careful to leave Hill out. Evidently the sort of people who put together such collections don't see anything even the least bit funny about capitalism and/or the workers' struggle against it. Dwight Macdonald is an interesting case in this regard, for he probably sang Hill's songs with glee at several hundred parties, May Day rallies, and other social/political gatherings during his radical youth in the 1930s. By 1960, however, when he brought out his big compendium titled *Parodies*, he had so ingratiated himself with the "status quo" that he refused to make room for even one of those songs.

Hill's powerful parodic imagination is so obvious in his lyrics that one would expect it to be equally evident in his cartoons. With one notable exception, however, the IWW poet's surviving cartoons are not parodies. His other cartoons are all bursting with humor, satire, caricature, and ridicule, but not one is a parody of a famous painting or drawing, or another artist's cartoon, or any other pre-existing image.

The exception—probably based on a newspaper artist's sketch—appeared in the Los Angeles edition of the *Little Red Song Book* in 1912 (see page 258). A Wobbly glance at a major news-item of that year—the sinking of the *Titanic*—the cartoon stresses the vulnerability of the "invincible" as well as the hidden strength of the IWW. I shall discuss this cartoon a little further on in another connection.

In the present state of our knowledge, this cartoon seems to be the earliest of Hill's published cartoons. It is altogether possible, however, that *Solidarity*, the *Industrial Worker*, and other IWW papers contain other cartoons by Hill that have not yet been recognized as such, either because they are unsigned, or because they are signed with a pseudonym. Tracking them down should not prove too impossibly burdensome a task: All that is required is the painstaking scrutiny of the numerous cartoons published in these papers over a period of a dozen years, and their rigorous comparison with the few cartoons positively known to be Hill's.

One difficulty here is that little is known of the technical procedures used in readying cartoons for publication in the early IWW press. Were cartoons that arrived by mail simply passed on to the engravers for reproduction, or were they first copied (and refined) by another artist according to specifications provided by the engravers or IWW editors? If the latter is true, it is possible that some Hill cartoons may have been retouched by other artists. This third category of heretofore unrecognized Hill cartoons will be much harder, perhaps impossible, to recover.

Future research will also reveal just where, chronologically, Hill's *Titanic* cartoon fits in the long tradition of IWW cartoon parodies. It was certainly not the first. Though nowhere near as well known as their equivalents in song, Wobbly visual parodies have a long and impressive history, amply documented in the Wobbly press. Some examples became well known. Ralph Chaplin, for example, did a terrific parody of a World War I Liberty Bond war poster by the famous Hearst comic-strip artist Winsor McCay, who is best remembered for his *Little Nemo in Slumberland* and *Dreams of a Rarebit Fiend* (see pages 176-177). McCay's gruesomely patriotic, racist, and xenophobic poster features a towering central figure, labeled "America," standing with an upraised sword behind a large "Liberty Bond" shield, and fending off a gang of fiendish marauders labeled "Devastation," "Starvation," "War," "Pestilence," and "Death." Chaplin's parody is a brilliant exercise in what Karl Marx called "merciless criticism." He makes the central figure stand for the working class; the shield has become a big IWW emblem bearing the words "One Big Union," the upraised sword a club labeled "Organization," and the attackers are now labeled "Labor Hatred," "Hunger," "Slavery," "Slander," and "Frame-Ups." McCay had made the "War" figure a Black man lifting a sword; in Chaplin's version he is white, labeled "Slavery," and cracking a bullwhip. These significant modifications transformed McCay's authoritarian and jingoistic picture into a power-

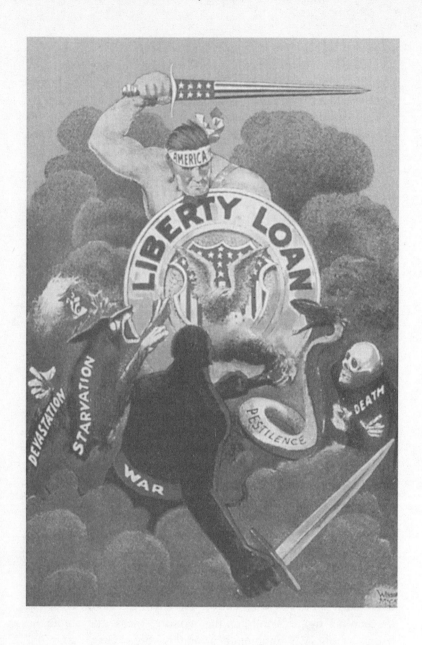

Winsor McCay: World War I Liberty Bond poster

Ralph Chaplin: IWW poster

ful image of the revolutionary IWW.

Such parodies—and the IWW excelled at them—are very much in the spirit of what André Breton later called *détourne-ment*—a way of "turning around" an image or text so that it signifies something radically *other* than the original. Radical de-mystification is their essence. William Henkelman's Wobbly paro-dies of mass-circulation magazine ads ran in the union's magazines back in the 1920s, decades before *Mad* magazine picked up the idea (see below). In 1964, when the movement against the Vietnam War was just getting started, Tor Faegre did a cover for the IWW's Chicago Branch magazine, *The Rebel Worker*, featuring the famous old recruiting poster of Uncle Sam pointing his finger at the viewer; Faegre's new caption read: "*I'm* organized, are *you*?" As recently as the 1990s, Mike Konopacki's *Wage Slave World News*—a four-page super-parody of supermarket tabloids, superan-nuated business unionism, and other superfluities—appeared for several months as a regular supplement to the *Industrial Worker*.

I doubt that all AFL-CIO unions put together have devised as many parodies as the IWW. Joe Hill, the IWW's premier parodist, left a proud legacy.

William Henkelman: IWW versions of mass media ads (1920s)

5. CARL MICHAEL BELLMAN
& JOE HILL'S FAVORITE SONG

To read means to borrow;
to create out of one's readings
is paying off one's debts.
—Georg Christoph Lichtenberg—

Hill told Oscar W. Larson, a Swedish-American socialist comrade, that his favorite among his own songs was "The Rebel Girl." "After that," he added, his favorite song in general was "Old Man Noah" [*Letters*, 59].

Hill's biographers and commentators have ignored this tantalizing detail. This neglect is all the more remarkable in that it appears to be the only instance in which the author of "Workers of the World Awaken!" indicates something of his cultural/intellectual background and interests. Indeed, it is his sole reference to a "work" that could also be considered an "influence" on his own work. Ralph Chaplin assures us that Hill was "familiar with Marxian economics" [1926, 190], and there is every reason to believe it, but no direct mention of it appears in Hill's surviving letters and other scattered writings. We know that Hill was a reader, but next to nothing is known of what he read: Swedish schoolbooks and Sunday school hymnals as a child, IWW and socialist literature as an adult, and that's about all we really know on the subject.

That is what makes the "Old Man Noah" reference so important. When a notoriously "reticent cuss" such as Hill—a man who never seems to have said a word to anyone about his favorite authors, artists, thinkers, composers, or comic-strip artists—all of a sudden decides to reveal his favorite song, it's time to sit up and take notice.

"Old Man Noah," it turns out, is one of the most popular songs of all time. It is one of many Biblical parodies written by the Swedish poet-musician Carl Michael Bellman (1740-1795).[1] Primarily a drinking song, and still popular as such today in Sweden and among Swedish-Americans, "Old Man Noah" ("Gubben Noak" in Swedish) went 'round the world, undergoing numerous permutations along the way. One reference calls it a "sea chantey," which helps account for its rapid internationalization, for seafarers long played a major role in the transmission of culture.

A parody itself, "Old Man Noah" has been parodied and repar-odied, over and over. As its popularity spread across the seas, awareness of its authorship, or even of its national origin, faded away. It is sometimes cited as a "traditional Swedish folk song," but it is likely that many Americans consider it their own. Many versions tend toward the risqué, and—as with other drinking songs—have at times been hugely popular among male college students in the U.S. But there are also pious Protestant variations, and others considered suitable for children. A doo-wop version has been posted on the Internet.

In addition to countless popular variants, "Old Man Noah" has also attracted the attention of those who prefer to be known as serious composers. For example, the most influential of the Finnish romantic composers, Oskar Merikanto (1868-1924), published in 1907 his "Old Man Noah Variations"—based on Bellman's well-known song.

Bellman himself seems to have been quite a character. Author of more than 1,700 poems and songs, he has long been recognized as one of Sweden's outstanding pre-romantics, and remains a national favorite. He had what critics have called a real "feeling for nature . . . unique in Swedish poetry," and invoked the pleasures of the "outdoor life" in many a song and poem. A large part of his work, however, portrays the good times and bad of Stockholm's hard-drinking lowlife, as he himself observed and experienced it in the city's rowdy taverns. Notable especially for his humor, his "mocking style" of satire, his lively rhythms, and the element of surprise in his work, he was highly popular in his own lifetime, when his works circulated by word of mouth and in handwritten copies as well as in printed form. Although he composed some melodies himself, he borrowed the music for most of his songs from folk tunes, minuets, marching songs and opera.

Bellman received a small stipend from King Gustav III, but it was never enough to live on, and despite his modest court connec-tions, he was no stranger to poverty. The "low" subjects of his poetry made him an outsider at court in any case. At twenty-three, deeply in debt, he fled to Norway for a time to escape his creditors. His moments of ease and prosperity appear to have been few and far between. Toward the end of his life he was jailed for writing "an evil poem," and he died of tuberculosis at fifty-five. Most of his poetry was published posthumously.

There is also a strong visual side to the Bellman story, which would also have attracted Hill. I have not ascertained that Bellman himself drew pictures, but as a celebrity of sorts—however scorned by the courtiers—he was the subject of many portraits, sketches, and caricatures. These images have been widely reproduced in the literature. Some are dramatic; some amusing—one shows Bellman playing a zither, accompanied by a howling dog. As a music-loving youngster growing up in Sweden, Joel Hägglund could hardly have missed these striking images.

That the author of Hill's favorite song was a parodist—indeed, one of the world's foremost parodists—hardly comes a big surprise, but the many similarities between the two poet-musicians *are* remarkable: their restlessness, humor, originality, and "mocking style," to say nothing of their first-hand knowledge of poverty, tuberculosis, and jail. Commentators on Hill have often likened him to Robert Burns, and his affinities with the Scots bard are by no means negligible. His kinship with Bellman, however, seems deeper and more direct.

Here, surely, is one of Hill's true intellectual ancestors—the only one he himself acknowledged, however obliquely, in his extant writings.

---

1. For most of the information on Bellman's life and work, I have relied on various Internet sites.

An IWW "Silent Agitator"

6. JOE HILL, COMPOSER

There are no wrong notes.
—Charles Mingus—

The fact that the IWW poet was also an IWW cartoonist is still not widely known. That he was also an IWW composer—one of the very few Wobs who actually composed music for some of his songs—is an even better-kept secret. Until this minute, have *you* ever read anything titled "Joe Hill, Composer"? Neither have I.

If the literature on Hill as songwriter and poet is rather small, and the literature on his work as visual artist tiny, the "literature" on his work as a composer of music can only be called microscopic. As far as I can tell, it consists of nothing more than 1) nine words by Pete Seeger from a 1954 review of Barrie Stavis's play, *The Man Who Never Died*; 2) four brief sentences by Stavis himself, from his Foreword to a pamphlet titled *The Songs of Joe Hill* (People's Artists, 1955), and 3) a few brief comments by others describing the music for "The Rebel Girl" as "awkward" or "difficult."

Seeger acknowledges that the Wobbly bard "had a real flair for lyrics," but does not specifically mention his music; he concedes that Hill "knew how to notate his songs, but little more" [1954, 22].

Here, in full, in what Stavis had to say on the subject in 1955:

> Joe Hill's talents as a composer of music in no way matches his great gifts as a writer. The fact is that he was a poor composer. Much of his original music is ordinary, some of it is banal, and some of it, alas, just doesn't play and had to be reworked by other musicians for this book. One of his compositions which was written while he was in jail, "A Trip to Honolulu," a march without words, had to be eliminated for the reason that it does not play. [6]

As criticism, these comments appear rather perfunctory and narrow-spirited, and the adjectives Stavis employed—"poor," "ordinary," and "banal"—do not really tell us very much. Their vagueness alone leads us to suspect that his judgment may not be the definitive word on the matter. Indeed, he himself went on to add some qualifying words. Invoking the "only remaining member of Joe Hill's family"—his younger sister, Ester Dahl—Stavis noted that

> In a recent letter to me, this gallant seventy-year-old lady who is proud of her great brother and his work, wrote that the most outstanding thing about him as a boy was his love of music. Had Joe Hill been able to study and have training in composition instead of having to start work at the age of ten, who knows what level of perfection he could have reached. [*ibid.*]

On this subject, as on his other creative activities, Hill himself was characteristically unassuming. To a reporter for the *Salt Lake Tribune* in 1914 he admitted that

> There are some defects in the harmony of my compositions but that is because of my lack of technical training. I am a man of little education and my modest accomplishments are due to a natural taste and some native talent in that direction. [Smith 1969, 40]

In a July 1915 letter he commented on two of the songs for which he had also written music:

> on the West Coast the . . . song "Workers of the World Awaken" is making quite a hit, they are telling me. They say "The Rebel Girl" is "a little hard to make out" and I guess it is a little more complex than the other one. The easterners have more "Kultur" than the Western roughnecks and I guess that might have something to do with it too. [*Letters*, 54]

Considering the high estimation in which Hill has long been held in folk music circles, it is surprising that no one has taken the trouble to examine his own musical compositions more closely, and to discuss them in greater detail. The raw material for such a study is ready at hand. Sheet music exists for three of his IWW songs ("Workers of the World, Awaken!," "Don't Take My Poppa Away from Me," and "The Rebel Girl"; three of his so-called "popular" songs ("Come and Take a Joy Ride in My Aeroplane," "Oh, Please Let Me Dance This Waltz with You," and "My Dreamland Girl"; and one of his last works, the apparently wordless march titled "A Trip to Honolulu."

That Hill was no Duke Ellington or Joseph Jarman is not exactly headline news, and in fact matters not at all in our estimate of his overall accomplishments. In plain truth, we are interested in Joe Hill's musical compositions because they were written by Joe Hill. Everything by and about Joe Hill is of interest, and the fact that the IWW poet/cartoonist also wrote music is of exceptional interest, for it shows him active in yet another realm of the arts. If his compositions truly are "hard to play," that too is interesting—and not necessarily damning: Much that is considered great music is also hard to play.

Here is an obviously important dimension of Joe Hill's creative work just waiting for a sympathetic and inspired inquirer.

Think of it: the author of famously simple songs writing "difficult" or even "unplayable" music. Fascinating, no?

Joe Hill: Original music for "Workers of the World, Awaken!"

7. SONGS, MUSIC & CARTOONS:
REFLECTIONS ON SCRIBBLING

On the road to Nowhere
What wild oats did you sow?
—Vachel Lindsay—

D oes Joe Hill the visual artist expand our awareness of Joe Hill the songwriter and musician? What impresses us most in this regard is the easy reciprocity between the two modes in which Hill's special humor found expression. In subverting inane bourgeois pop songs or gloomy hymns and making them into joyous revolutionary workingclass songs, Hill's "lever," so to speak, was the comics page. There is hardly a line in his humorous songs that would not work as a cartoon, hardly a stanza that would not make a good strip. As a songwriter, one could say, Hill thought like a cartoonist.

There are some interesting correspondences between Hill's songs and cartoons. The deluded worker in frantic pursuit of a job—see page 195—is the theme of the song "Nearer My Job to Thee," which appeared for the first time in an edition of the *Little Red Song Book* issued by the Seattle IWW locals in the latter part of 1913 or early '14. The "Victims of Society" cartoon, "Suggested by J. Hill" (see page 187) shows the "poor and ragged tramp [wandering] without aim along the track" who turns up again in the lyrics to Hill's "We Will Sing One Song," published in the fifth edition of the *Song Book* in March 1913. In both cases the cartoon appeared in print first; however, as the dates of composition of Hill's songs are unknown, it is impossible to draw any inferences from that fact.

His popular "Mr. Block" song was, of course, inspired by the comic strip of that name drawn by his fellow Wobbly, Ernest Riebe, which debuted in the *Industrial Worker* on 7 November 1912. The strip featured a blockheaded worker whose naive faith in capitalism, church, and state led him to one calamity after another. It ran more or less continuously in the *Industrial Worker* and then in *Solidarity* for three years, and sporadically well into the 1920s. A comic-book edition of twenty-four of the strips and an Introduction by Walker C. Smith appeared under the imprint of the Block Supply Company (almost certainly Riebe himself), in Minneapolis in 1913. The first radical comic book in the U.S., it was heavily promoted in the IWW press.

Hill's lyrics appeared in place of the strip itself in the *Industrial Worker* for 23 January 1913. It was an immediate smash hit. Wobbly soapboxers found the song especially useful in drawing crowds. Within weeks the *Industrial Worker* noted that Wobblies stranded in the desert en route to a free-speech fight in Denver passed the time singing Hill's new song. A few months later, in his report on the IWW hop-pickers' strike in Wheatland, California, Carleton Parker observed that some two thousand strikers were singing "Mr Block" when the sheriff and his deputies opened fire on the peaceful crowd [Parker 1920, 191-192].

In 1914, when *Solidarity* announced Hill's arrest in Salt Lake City, the headline described him as the "Man Who Wrote 'Mr Block'" [18 Apr].

Riebe and Hill may have known each other—one "Mr Block" strip includes the legend: "Suggested by J. Hill" (see page 188). Alas, Fellow Worker Riebe has proved even more elusive than Hill. Recent research, however, indicates that he was born and raised in Dresden, Germany, and spent his last years in China.[1]

Although historians of comics have ignored it, Hill's song about Riebe's character is one of the first songs based on a comic-strip. The fact that the song was reinforced by visual imagery doubtless hastened its rapid rise to popularity.

This constant and lively interaction between sound and sight, word and image, song and cartoon—with a little pepper and salt added for good measure—situates Joe Hill in the company of other cartoonists who also wrote songs and played music: from the shy mandolinist George Herriman, whose *Krazy Kat* includes lyrics as abundant as they are funny, to the more recent Walt Kelly, who not only wrote the crazy words and music for his *Songs of the Pogo*, but sang them, too. Hill also invites comparison with the relatively fewer composers of music who also drew cartoons: Erik Satie, for example, and John Lennon. Herriman and Kelly were undoubtedly better cartoonists than Hill, and Satie and Lennon better composers, but Hill deserves a lot of credit for being the only one of the bunch to really grasp the basic truth about class society expressed in the IWW Preamble.

Joe Hill's influence on other IWW cartoonists was considerable—but they were influenced by his songs rather than his cartoons. Riebe, for example, devoted a cartoon to Hill's song "Everybody's Joining It" (see page 187) and "Dust" Wallin portrayed

Ernest Riebe: Cartoon featuring Hill's song, "Everybody's Joining It."
(*Industrial Worker*, 9 January 1913)

Artist Unknown: "Two Victims of Society" (Suggested by Joe Hill).
Industrial Worker, 26 January 1911.

"Don't mourn, organize"
in Swedish.

Joe Hill

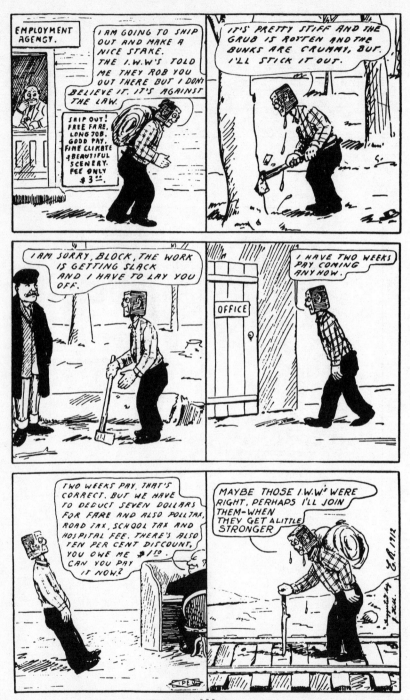

Ernest Riebe: "Mr Block—He Works in the Woods"
(*Industrial Worker*, 1912).
Note the words in the last panel: "Suggested by J. Hill."

the "long-haired preacher" from the opening line of Hill's most popular song, "The Preacher and the Slave." Hill's "Scissor Bill" was pictured by many IWW cartoonists, most effectively by Ern Hansen (see page 230). And Joe Troy, whose work as an artist for the workers' press dates back to August Spies's German-language anarchist daily *Arbeiter-Zeitung* in Haymarket days, may have been the first to draw a cartoon portraying "pie in the sky" (see below).

---

1. Thanks to David Riehle for communicating this new information on Ernest Riehle.

Joe Troy: "Those Flying Saucers Not For Us"
(*Industrial Worker*, 26 July 1947).
A later (1964) reprint of this cartoon
was titled "The President's Promises."

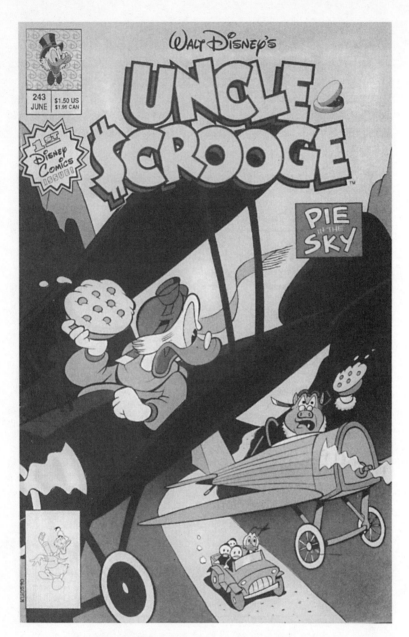

Uncle Scrooge comics (June 1990): "Pie in the Sky."

8. PIE IN THE SKY

*In the drama of life as it has been experienced
and recorded, or simply imagined,
impossibility has had a possible role.*
—Gregory Corso—

Of the hundreds of marvelous turns of phrase devised by members of the IWW over the years, "pie in the sky" early on met with the greatest success, and has proved to be the most enduring. Laborlorist Archie Green has called it "the most significant Wobbly contribution to the American vocabulary" [1960, 210]. Although there is no proof that Hill invented the expression, no one has found it in print prior to the publication of "The Preacher and the Slave" in 1911, where it appears in the refrain:

> *Work and pray, live on hay,*
> *You'll get pie in the sky when you die.*

Along with "Don't mourn, organize," "Bread and Roses," "Dump the Bosses Off Your Back," and "Direct Action Gets the Goods," Hill's famous pie-line is a classic Wobbly response to Whitman's call for a poetry full of "limber, lasting, fierce words."

Three years before "The Preacher and the Slave" was published, another IWW songwriter, Richard Brazier, published the song "Come and Get Wise" in the *Little Red Song Book*:

> *Talk about the swell way the workers don't live*
> *And the fine wages our masters don't give.*
> *Rave about the good cream that's on high above*
> *If we'll work for nothing and the boss we'll all love.*

In a 1968 letter to Fred Thompson, Brazier suggested that the line about "the good cream that's on high above" anticipates Joe Hill's "pie in the sky" [11 June, 3]. Of course he is right, and I would further suggest that Hill's supremely pithy phrase originated as a *rewriting* of Brazier's exceedingly awkward passage. By changing "the good cream" to *pie*, and "on high above" to *sky*, Hill cut eight syllables down to four and transformed a block of lacklustrous prose into a startling poetic image. Such condensation was second nature to Joel Emmanuel Hägglund, who shortened his twenty-letter name to the fifteen-letter Joseph Hillstrom and later to the seven-letter Joe Hill.

Hill's streamlining of Brazier's clunky line affords a marvelous insight into his *method* of composition. It also adds appreciable weight to the argument that it was indeed Joe Hill who gave the world the expression "pie in the sky." It seems to me a kind of poetic justice that the most famous Wobbly of them all should also be the inventor of the most famous of all Wobbly phrases.

How "pie in the sky" made its way from IWW strikes and street-meetings into the everyday speech of millions is itself a topic worthy of a special monograph. As Wobbly slang for the bourgeois "Heaven"—*i.e.*, the alleged "rewards of the afterlife"—and a double pun on "piety" as well as "sky pilot" (a Wob synonym for preacher), the phrase came to signify any pious promises premised on postponement, not only by men of the cloth but also by labor fakers and politicians (as a more recent song, "Ball of Confusion" put it: "Vote for me and I'll set you free"). Evidently people sensed a need for an expression more specific and vivid than "hot air" or "baloney," and Hill's "pie in the sky" filled the bill.

The chief task of IWW songwriters and cartoonists, as well as the union's other agitators and organizers, was to dispel the ideological mirages that misled wage-workers into misery and dead-ends: the hopeless pursuit of a "good" job, an "honest" candidate, "security," "respectability," and all the rest. Hill's 1913 *Industrial Worker* cartoon, "Constitutional Guarantee" (see page 195), features no pie, but it is nonetheless a clear warning against the foolishness and danger of pie in the sky.

"The Preacher and the Slave" is one of the most reprinted and recorded of Hill's songs, and also exists in a number of variations recorded by hillbilly stars in the 1930s. The Great Depression was the heyday of "pie in the sky." Popularized not only by soapboxers, leaflet-writers, and editors of IWW and other Left papers, but also by mass-produced recordings that could also be heard on radio, the phrase penetrated well beyond the labor and radical milieus. In 1931, a novel by Frederick Hazlitt Brennan titled *Pie in the Sky*, containing excerpts from Hill's song, was published by a big firm in New York. Some twenty years later, during the early 1950s flying saucer craze, a letter to the editor of a Philadelphia paper explained the phenomenon: "They're pieplates—left over from the pie in the sky we were promised years ago" [Modesto 1963, 2].

From the pieplate, of course, came the Frisbee—and isn't the popular sport of disc-tossing one of the more playful realizations of Hill's funny phrase? According to a historian of the sport, an early flying disc toy was in fact called "Sky Pie" [Johnson 1975, 34].

In later years, labor movement usage of the expression tended to downplay its original anti-religious intent. During the 1940s the AFL, competing with the CIO attempts to unionize Black workers in the South, issued a pamphlet titled *Pie in the Sky*, which assured the unorganized that "The AFL offers you results now—not hot-air promises of pie in the sky by and by" [Foner 1976, 281].

A 1947 canvas by the well known labor artist Ralph Fasanella —a satirical vision of the suburban *House and Garden* variety of heaven, with a tall church-spire stuck in the middle—is titled "Pie-in-the-Sky" [Watson 1973, 45]. Comic artists of all kinds— Wobblies, other labor cartoonists, and even so-called mainstream and underground cartoonists—have played a significant role in popularizing "pie in the sky." It was the title and theme, for example, of the June 1990 issue of *Uncle Scrooge* comics (see page 190). Some day someone should take the trouble to document pie-in-the-sky imagery in the popular arts.

In 1969, *Pie in the Sky* was oddly considered a suitable title for a short history of the IWW "for Young People," published by Delacorte Press. Irving Werstein's narrative, subtitled *An American Struggle: The Wobblies and Their Times*, was well-intentioned but full of ridiculous errors (the index lists the union as the *International* Workers of the World). The volume's ample misinformation begins on the flyleaf, which informs us that the IWW was "maligned by its opponents for its 'pie in the sky' philosophies."

I doubt if many kids read Werstein's confused book. A vast number, however, listened to John Lennon's songs. And it so happens that in 1970 John Lennon—a self-described "working-class hero" who, like Hill, was a singer/songwriter/musician/composer/poet/cartoonist/humorist who (ten years later) also became a martyr—recorded a song titled "I Found Out." Among Lennon's original lyrics Hill's famous phrase recurred yet again, but this time with its original anti-religious signification fully intact:

> *Old Hare Krishna got nothing on you.*
> *Just keep you crazy with nothing to do;*
> *Keep you occupied with pie in the sky,*
> *There ain't no guru who can see through your eyes.*[1]

Thus, at a time when the official labor movement and the commercial media had all but emptied Joe Hill's expression of its original force, one of the world's most popular pop singers came forth to restore it in all its irreligious soapbox glory.

The phrase also worked its way into mass-market literature. In Emil Petaja's paperback original science-fiction novel *The Time Twister* (1968), a character defends belief in a pagan god by saying that "He gives [people] something besides pie in the sky" [97].

Lia Matera is a mystery writer whose books often reflect the struggles of the 1960s, and sometimes earlier strains of U.S. radicalism. Her 1997 novel, *Star Witness*, features a mathematician who has published two books: *Simple as Pi* and *Sweet as Pi*. His forthcoming book, we are told, is—what else?—*Pi in the Sky*.

"Pie in the Sky" is also, of course, an authentically *surrealist* image, and it is interesting to find it used, with explicitly revolutionary intentions, by the American surrealist writer Paul Garon in a 1999 interview with Ron Sakolsky:

> Surrealism is not only an important method in elaborating the content of "pie in the sky," but it is only surrealism that can take the pie out of the sky and put it on the dinner table. [Sakolsky 2002, 101]

Garon's use of the phrase—fully in line with Hill's but also very much in the spirit of surrealism's poetic materialism—is a refreshing counterblast to the widespread effort to empty the expression of its critical and oppositional force. For with the passage of time, Hill's phrase has largely been drained of its radicalism. Its overtly anti-religious meaning, and by extension, the rejection of bourgeois political propaganda that the expression implied, survives today only in the small revolutionary and radical labor movement circles in which the phrase originated.

In the larger society today, it can mean almost anything. Pie in the Sky is now the name of a New Orleans pizzeria, a Toronto bakery, a bed-and-breakfast in Vermont, a gospel singing group, a race horse, a 1996 Hollywood film comedy now available in video, a more recent film about Andy Warhol, a children's book publisher, a board game, a software company, a compilation of short stories by a flying instructor, a British TV network, and a manufacturer of advertising balloons and blimps.

The phrase is by no means rare in the capitalist press. For a time it was the title of a culinary column in the *Chicago Tribune*, and now and then it turns up in news-stories. Page one of the *Tribune* for 17 May 2002 quoted the State's Attorney saying that police had hard evidence in a criminal case, not "pie in the sky."

An Internet website that purports to explain and define idioms offers these pitiably lame "synonyms" for Pie in the Sky: *unrealistic, not practical, hairbrain* [sic!], and *half baked*!

In 1870, nine years before Hill was born, Isidore Ducasse wrote in his *Poésies*: "Poetry's mission is difficult."

---

1. Lennon's song appeared on his first solo album, *Plastic Ono Band*.

Joe Hill: "Constitutional Guarantee" (*Industrial Worker,* 24 April 1913). Six months later, Covington Hall reprinted this cartoon in *The Voice of the People*, with a new caption.

9. "I HAVE LIVED LIKE AN ARTIST"

*Reversion to visual thinking
has its advantages.*
—Ella Freeman Sharpe—

It is really not so strange that commentators on the IWW, including the Wobblies themselves, have focused on Hill the bard and martyr, and slighted Hill the cartoonist. His songs and his ashes went 'round the world; his cartoons have been little known outside the union and a small band of connoisseurs. Moreover, critical appreciation of cartooning as an art has been exceedingly slow to develop. Within the IWW, cartoons were very popular but seem to have been taken for granted; the most accomplished artists were rarely praised or even mentioned in the union's publications. For that matter, studies of the classic cartoonists for the big bourgeois dailies were extremely rare until the 1960s, and even today comic criticism is a much less crowded field than, say, psychotherapy for snails. As for "serious" scholarship regarding labor and radical cartoons: Don't make me laugh. Far from being a "field," it's not even a plot of ground.

In Hill's case, discussion of his comic art is made doubly difficult by the small quantity and uneven quality of his work in this area. His surviving cartoons are very few in number—barely a dozen, hardly enough to constitute what is commonly called "a body of work." His comics, moreover, are with few exceptions fugitive efforts, made in haste. Some were dashed off solely for the amusement of friends, not at all intended for publication. They make their point, they make us laugh, but they cannot be counted among the finer examples of the cartoonist's art. Alexander MacKay recalled that Hill "beamed all over" whenever a Fellow Worker praised one of his cartoons or songs [review of Stegner 1950]. One suspects, however, that praise for the songs was more frequent and more plentiful.

This does not mean that Hill's cartoons are devoid of interest. On the contrary, they stand up much better than the work of hundreds of his less-inspired contemporaries whose humdrum strips for the bourgeois dailies are today not merely forgotten but positively unreadable. His cartoons also possess an extraordinary documentary value. Like his songs and scattered writings, they illuminate our understanding and appreciation of the emerging

IWW counterculture of those years—from the free-speech fights of 1909-10 to the founding of the Agricultural Workers' Organization five years later: the very period in which IWW members began calling themselves Wobblies [Green 1993, 97-138]. This aspect of Hill's art is just beginning to be appreciated and explored.

To attempt to evaluate Joe Hill as cartoonist may be premature, for the evidence is so slim. The wide differences of style in Hill's extant cartoons suggest that many—no one has any idea how many —have been lost. According to Chaplin, Hill "whiled away many tedious hours in prison sketching objects of his interest or his imagination" [1923, 24]. Where are these sketches now? Apart from a 1914 Christmas card, his submarine cartoon, and cover designs for sheet music, Hill's prison art has completely disappeared.

Even some of his *published* cartoons may be lost, for the files of IWW newspapers are not complete. Some of his cartoons may have been signed with other names, or not signed at all. Four previously unknown cartoons, drawn on postcards he sent to his friend Charles Rudberg, were brought to light as recently as 1984 [Mason 1984]. One of the cards to Rudberg, a two-panel comic strip titled "Doings of Våran Kalle," shows a young man eyeing a burlesque show poster and then rushing up the stairs, presumably to catch the show. Were there subsequent cards continuing the story, now lost? Or did this sketch simply recall an episode in their lives? Rudberg himself offered no explanation or commentary. As it stands, this

Joe Hill: "Doings of Våran Kalle."
Hand-drawn cartoon postcard to Charles Rudberg, 24 January 1911.

particular Joe Hill cartoon is ambiguous almost to the point of being incomprehensible.

At least one Joe Hill cartoon has never been reproduced; long in the possession of a private collector, its present location is unknown [Stavis 1954, 80]. A couple of Hill's water-colors, once deposited in libraries, now appear to have been "misplaced" (and therefore are not reproduced here). These and others may yet turn up, and if they do, our sense of the IWW bard's stature as an artist may change.

Meanwhile, Joe Hill's handful of cartoons radiate a distinctive charm that has not diminished with the passage of time. These cartoons, which he drew to lift the spirits and exercise the imaginations of his fellow wage-slaves back in the 1910s, continue to have a direct, immediate appeal even today to all who abhor injustice and seek to create a free society. And the fact that it was he—the one and only Joe Hill—who drew these cartoons is enough to make them of permanent interest. Revealing yet another facet of his personality, they help us appreciate all the more, as Frances Horn has put it, "what a talented man Joe Hill was" [letter to FR, 15 Apr 1985].

Rough and unpolished as Hill's art is, it casts a powerful light on his outlook as immigrant, hobo, social critic, and revolutionary. Happily "devoid of artistic perjury," as the great architect Frederick Kiesler once said of another untutored drawer, these fugitive pieces are, in short, an especially precious part of the rich legacy of poetry and revolt that Joe Hill left to the workers of the world [Kiesler 1942, 27].

Some weeks before he was marched to the firing squad, Joe Hill wrote that he had "lived like an artist" and would "die like an artist" [*Letters*, 50]. One of the purposes of this book is to see to it that he is also better remembered as an artist.

Bumper-sticker (1990)

VI

JOE HILL MYTHS

1. SUPERMAN, SAINT, & SAVIOR

A fact, in this country, is harder to prove than a fiction.
—**Sam Murray**—

Verifiable facts about Joe Hill's life are not easy to come by, but legends about him seem to be about as thick as politicians' lies. As if the life of a hobo and Wobbly wasn't romantic enough, he has been subjected to a veritable deluge of martyrological hyperbole. He has been likened to an incredible range of real and imaginary figures: Socrates and Che Guevara, Jesus Christ and John the Baptist, Sir Lancelot and Galahad, Wat Tyler and François Villon, Robert Burns and Shelley, John Brown and Francisco Ferrer, Abraham Lincoln and Johnny Appleseed, and lots more [Modesto 1963, 7]. He is the central figure in a long list of novels, essays, poems, plays, and even a couple of operas, and his name turns up—as a secondary character or a passing mention—in hundreds more. No figure in the history of the U.S. labor movement has been more mythologized than he. Small mistakes made by early researchers have been repeated so often and embellished so much that they are no longer small, much less recognized as mistakes. Groundless, wholly irresponsible rumors and even unabashed fictions have passed for solid fact. Joe Hill was no masked man, but numerous "interpreters"—would-be friends, declared enemies, and often the worst of all, "objective" critics —have done their best to mask him beyond recognition.

As Hill's friend Alexander MacKay warned Archie Green in 1960, researchers into the IWW poet's life "are doomed to be knee-deep in mythology" [11 June 1960].

The Alfred Hayes/Earl Robinson ballad, "Joe Hill" (a.k.a. "I Dreamed I Saw Joe Hill Last Night") has played a large role in the myth's evolution. Archie Green, in the wonderful and stimulating chapter titled "Singing Joe Hill" in his book *Wobblies, Pile Butts, and Other Heroes: Laborlore Explorations* (1993), has illuminated the song's background and popularity. Prior to the publication of Green's researches, most commentators—taking the line "'Says I, 'But Joe, You're ten years dead'" literally—dated the song 1925. Green, noting that Alfred Hayes was only fourteen that year, and was not yet familiar with the IWW, shows that the first draft of the song was in fact written "about 1932" [*ibid.*, 85]. It began simply as a poem by Hayes—significantly different from the later song —published in the *New Masses* in 1934. The song and the music date from the summer of '36, when Hayes and Robinson met at Camp Unity, a Communist Party retreat near Wingdale, New York. Collaborating on a musical skit for the camp, Hayes gave Robinson his poem, and the latter, in his own words, "simply went into a tent with my guitar and in about 45 minutes had a song. . . . I sang it that evening" [*ibid.*, 84]. A few weeks later it appeared in the *Daily Worker*.

Ironically, the song—at first only a modest example of the Communist Party's 1930s effort to integrate Joe Hill into its own cultural mythology—eventually came to serve as the principal vehicle by which the Hill legend became part of American mass culture. As a poem, its initial appearance in *New Masses* was titled "I Dreamed I Saw Joe Hill Again," and it was reprinted under the same title in an article by Alan Calmer on "The Wobbly in American Literature" in the 1935 anthology, *Proletarian Literature in the United States.* The song, titled "Joe Hill," was first recorded by Michael Loring in 1941, and popularized by the great baritone Paul Robeson, who not only recorded it, but sang it at countless concerts and strike meetings in the U.S. and abroad.

It was Robeson, in fact, more than any other individual, who brought the song—and therefore the Joe Hill legend—to worldwide attention. Many Robeson performances at which this song was sung were truly historic occasions. He sang it at a mass meeting of unemployed Welsh coal-miners in 1938 or '39; in the U.S. on a CBS radio coast-to-coast broadcast in 1939; at the University of Utah in Salt Lake City in 1947; in 1959 at Albert Hall in London, and shortly afterward at a huge "Ban the Bomb" demonstration at Trafalgar Square in the same city. In 1952, forbidden by the U.S. government to enter Canada, Robeson sang the song to an audience of 40,000 workers from the back of a flatbed truck on the U.S./Canada border in Washington. And in 1960, on his last great tour, he sang it to large gatherings of working people in Australia and New Zealand.[1]

Along with "Ol' Man River" and "Go Down Moses," "Joe Hill" was one of Robeson's signature songs, and clearly he made it his own in the deepest sense: not only by singing it many hundreds of times, but also—though this has rarely been noted—

changing it, slightly but significantly. Where the Hayes/Robinson lyric read

> *What they forgot to kill*
> *Went on to organize*

Robeson appreciably amplified the impact by singing

> *What they could never kill*

with the stress on "never." Although he changed but two words, Robeson dramatically altered the song. In the Hayes/Robinson original, "they forgot" makes Hill's survival appear as the result of an accident or oversight; in Robeson's version, Hill lives because *he* obviously had something *they* couldn't kill. "What *they* could *never* kill" was, of course, Hill's revolutionary *spirit*. And for Robeson, whose father had been born a slave, "the power of spirit" was perhaps the greatest social force of all [Robeson 1988, 100-101].

Thus, by replacing two little words with other words, Paul Robeson transformed a very good song into a splendid and extraordinarily powerful song.

In 1969, when Joan Baez sang "Joe Hill" to an audience of 500,000 at the Woodstock Festival, the song at last entered the mass-market mainstream. Baez's 1970 "Woodstock" album, which featured it, sold well over a million copies, and she has subsequently recorded it at least ten more times, most recently on the twenty-fifth anniversary "Woodstock: Three Days of Peace and Music" album in 1994.

When Earl Robinson died in July 1991, *Los Angeles Times* writer Burt Folkart noted that the song was "an unofficial anthem for the Flower Children of the '60s and '70s as it had been for their workingclass mothers and fathers" [Green 1993, 90].

Although the Hayes/Robinson song became the most popular lyric about Joe Hill, it was by no means the first. It was preceded by at least ten songs and poems by Wobblies, all published in the union's newspapers and magazines in the 1910s and early '20s. Several were also reprinted in various editions of *The Little Red Song Book*. Ralph Chaplin's "Joe Hill in Jail" appeared in 1914, when the IWW poet was still fighting for his life. Just after Hill's legal murder there appeared another Chaplin tribute, "Joe Hill"—

High head and back unbending—fearless and true,
Into the night unending: why was it you?

and Covington Hall's "A Fair Trial":

He faced the State. He was flat broke.
So too were all his friends and folk.

The State itself his scaffold built.
Its witness experts swore his guilt.
With trick on trick and lie and lie,
Its lawyers "proved" that he should die.

And all the pressmen cried aloud
The verdict's "justness" to the crowd.

Richard Brazier's "Farewell, Joe" was written at the request of Bill Haywood and first sung at the 1916 IWW Convention, where the packets of Hill's ashes were distributed to the delegates [letter to Fred Thompson, 13 Feb 1967]. Decades later, Brazier wrote two other song tributes to Hill: "The Ashes of Joe Hill," and "The Man Who Never Died." John Nordquist's "November Nineteenth" (the date of Hill's execution) and T-Bone Slim's "I Wanna Free Miss Liberty" were IWW favorites for many years. Other early Wobbly tributes to Hill include Joseph O'Carroll's "To the Governor of the Sovereign State of Utah," W. H. Lewis's "Our Martyr," Henry George Weiss's "In Memory of Joe Hill," "Joe Hill" by a Wob poet known only as "C. O. G.," and some years later, George M. Whiteside's "Wobbly Joe." Brief mentions of Hill appear in many other IWW poems, such as Robin Dunbar's "Four Heroes" (the other heroes are August Spies, Frank Little, and Wesley Everest), published in the September 1920 issue of the *One Big Union Monthly*.

The old Wobbly songs may not be well-remembered today, but in their time they were sung by many thousands of workers, just as the poems dedicated to Hill were recited to large audiences at Joe Hill Memorial Meetings, and to numerous smaller audiences in hobo jungles, small-town jails, and fast-moving boxcars. At least one Hill-related short story also appeared in the union's press during this period: "The Rosebush," by a Wobbly writer who used the pen-name Gefion, which concludes with roses blossoming from Hill's ashes [*Industrial Worker*, 6 June 1931]. Together with Ralph

Chaplin's biography in the November 1923 *Industrial Pioneer*, the fine portrait sketches drawn by Chaplin (see page 36) and L. S. Chumley (page 42)—framed in glass and displayed in every IWW hall in the country—and the IWW's popular photo-postcard (page 434), these tributes in song, poetry and story firmly established the name Joe Hill in the consciousness of the American working class: not only as the U.S.A.'s premier class-war poet and front-ranking labor martyr, but also and above all as the embodiment and symbol of all that is summed up in that magic word "Wobbly."

Many other writers, including some in the public eye, helped spread Hill's renown, but IWW members had seen to it that Joe Hill was the single best-known name in the history of the U.S. labor movement years before Upton Sinclair's play, *Singing Jailbirds* (1924), Carl Sandburg's *American Songbag* (1927), John Dos Passos's *Nineteen-Nineteen* (1931), and Kenneth Patchen's poem, "Joe Hill Listens to the Praying" (1934).

Interestingly, the moving lyrics to the Hayes/Robinson song added nothing that is really new to the Hill legend. The song's affective power derives rather from the way it brings together, in a short narrative, several pre-existing elements, all drawn from IWW sources. The famous opening line, for example, was anticipated by Wobbly song-writer T-Bone Slim in his "I Wanna Free Miss Liberty" (included in many editions of the *Little Red Song Book*), which also opens with the narrator's dream of Joe Hill. The dramatically recurring Hayes/Robinson line ("'I never died,' said he"), can be traced back as far as the eve of Hill's execution, when one of the speakers at a protest meeting said: "Something is going to happen. Joe Hill will never die. You hear it, everybody? *Joe Hill will never die!*" [Smith 1969, 171]. And finally, the lines "Joe says, 'What they forgot to kill / Went on to organize'" immediately and deliberately call to mind Hill's celebrated watchword: "Don't mourn, organize!"

Another notable feature of the song is that it is *not* (overtly, at least) a revolutionary song. Always sung solemnly and with reverence, it is indeed almost a hymn. It is not even explicitly *about* a revolutionary, but rather about a union organizer. No mention is made of Hill's anti-capitalism, or his IWW membership, or his and his fellow workers' scorn for what Wobblies often called the American Fakeration of Labor. Such distortion, tending to reduce Hill to the status of a mere liberal, conformed to American Communism's dreary mid-1930s pro-Democratic-Party "Popular Front."

Moreover, in linking themes of resurrection and immortality with labor organizing, the song expands mystification into outright mysticism, so that the IWW poet-martyr re-emerges as a miraculous figure: the Ghost of Labor Organizing Past, Present, and Future. If anyone ever starts a religion centered around Hill, this song would no doubt be the first in its hymnal.

Despite its weaknesses, however, the song—like Hill himself—lives on, and seems to be doing its work well: awakening wonder, raising questions, agitating minds. What more can you ask of a song? Above all as sung by Robeson and Baez, it has transcended time and circumstance: Its Popular Front origins, its failure to mention the IWW, and even its quasi-mystical overtones no longer matter much. With its dreamlike lyrics and haunting melody, the song has not only done much to bring the Joe Hill legend into daily life—it is itself a very active part of that legend. Archie Green has pointed out that it is "as widely known as any labor song in the country" [Green 1993, 87], and Sam Richards suggests that it is equally well known in Britain [Green 1993a, 316].

By introducing the most celebrated Wobbly of all to millions who never heard of the Wobblies before, the song in the long run served ends very different from those intended by its Communist authors.[2] Listeners who *do* know something about Hill tend to hear it as a poignant salute to an old and familiar friend. To those, however, who know nothing of Hill or the IWW, the song comes as a revelation: *Here is someone you should know about, someone you will never forget.*

Alas, its power and beauty notwithstanding, the Hayes/Robinson song has left an ambiguous legacy. Although the song has undeniably provided an awareness of Joe Hill to countless people who otherwise might never have come across the name, it has also—paradoxically—contributed to the public's *ignorance* of Joe Hill, for it prepared the way for the all-too-common misperception of the Wobbly poet as Labor's Supreme Organizer. Many later writers, most aggressively playwright Barrie Stavis, but also to a certain extent historian Philip Foner, have cast the IWW's best-loved songsmith in this improbable role. Both have written books and articles emphasizing Hill's supposedly heroic achievements as a full-time transcontinental labor agitator, organizer, and orator [Stavis 1954, 1964; Foner 1965a]. Their caricatures have in turn been caricatured by many others, so that the man we know as a modest hobo and writer of IWW songs often resembles a kind of radical labor movement version of Captain Marvel or Spiderman. Thus, in a popular history of artistic bohemianism, we find a reference to

> IWW leader Joe Hillstrom—the legendary Joe Hill who had organized the workers from San Francisco up to Maine, in every mine and mill, by teaching them to sing. [Hahn 1967, 196]

Half the just-quoted words are in fact taken direct from the Hayes/ Robinson song, but without quotation marks, thereby leading uninformed readers to accept such exaggerated claims as common knowledge.

To speak bluntly, there is no evidence to substantiate Stavis's or Foner's claims that Hill was an organizer or a strike leader, or that he took part in any of the union's free-speech fights.

All Wobs, of course, were organizers in some sense, and were counted on to do their part in bringing new members into the union. But the IWW also had what could without any exaggeration be called *professional* organizers—indeed, some of the finest labor organizers in U.S. history: St John, Haywood, Frank Little, George Speed, Ben Fletcher, Joe Ettor, James P. Thompson, Covington Hall, Jane Street, Arthur Boose, John Panzner, and Walter Nef are just a few of the best known. As one would expect, Wobbly papers as well as the capitalist press were full of news of the comings and goings and doings of these organizers. However, no contemporary witness or document suggests or even hints that Joe Hill served the Wobbly cause in this capacity.

The effort to mold Hill into some sort of proletarian superhero —the almighty organizer/strike-leader/orator who also wrote and sang songs and played piano, violin, and guitar—conflicts with all that we really know of the man. It contradicts the testimony of those who knew him best as well as the spirit communicated in his letters. One of the few things that can be said about Joe Hill with certainty is that he was unostentatious, shy, withdrawn, utterly without interest in attaining celebrity status. As he wrote to Elizabeth Gurley Flynn in January 1915:

> All the notoriety stuff is making me dizzy in the head and I am afraid I am getting more glory than I am entitled to. I put in most of the later years among the wharf-rats on the Pacific coast and

am not there with the limelight stuff at all. [*Letters*, 21]

Hill's sister Ester described him as "by nature solitary," one who "kept much to himself" [Takman 1956, 25]. Similarly, his boyhood friends and neighbors, interviewed by his Swedish biographer, Ture Nerman, recalled him as a withdrawn and serious-minded lad who made music and song his chief means of expression [29-33]. Alexander MacKay, who knew Hill in San Pedro, remembered his old buddy as "a real close-mouthed guy." And inasmuch as shy, withdrawn, close-mouthed individuals tend not to become big-time organizers and orators, it should come as no surprise that writing songs and composing music—along with cartooning—were Joe Hill's preferred means of advancing the revolutionary cause.

The Joe-Hill-as-superman legend constructed by Hayes, Robinson, Stavis, and Foner implies that the flesh-and-blood Joe Hill his fellow workers actually knew—a rather quiet drifter, dreamer, songwriter, poet, artist, and humorist, with his share of melancholy and pessimism—is somehow not good enough. It implies that the only ones who really matter in this world are the "big operators," those who are always on top, calling all the shots, formulating strategies, issuing directives, mobilizing the troops for one valiant victory after another. In a word, it reflects a notion of hierarchy and "leadership" that is wholly antithetical to the Wobbly spirit. Indeed, Stavis's book concludes with a song ludicrously titled "Joe Hill Is Our Leader"! [241]. Anyone who could conceive of Wobblies, of all people, singing such hero-worshiping folderol clearly has never learned the ABC's of the IWW. Joe Hill was nobody's leader, and surely would have laughed out loud at such an asinine proposition.

Proponents of the Hill-the-Organizer myth also assume and assert that he was a soapboxer and platform speaker accustomed to addressing large crowds. Here again the hard evidence is non-existent. As with organizers, the IWW had first-rate soapboxers and orators: Haywood, J. H. Walsh, James P. Thompson, Elizabeth Gurley Flynn, Ben Fletcher, Hubert H. Harrison, James F. Morgan, J. T. "Red" Doran, Clifford B. Ellis and many others. During Hill's active life in the union, he is never mentioned as one of them. He traveled widely, but the IWW press lists no Joe Hill Speaking Tours. He did not attend any of the union's conventions. Of the many extant posters, handbills, and notices in the IWW papers announcing Wobbly speakers at strike rallies, picnics, or other events, not one features the union's most popular songwriter.

This is not to say that Hill, like thousands of other rank-and-file Wobblies, may not have stepped up on the box from time to time to say a few words. He was, after all, a working musician, and anyone who can play a musical instrument before an audience can also speak to it. And yet, in the reminiscences of Hill by friends and acquaintances, references to soapboxing are conspicuously rare. Stavis's sole source in this regard seems to be a letter from Frank Lefferts, a charter member of Los Angeles Local 12 of the IWW in 1905, who recalled hearing Hill soapbox on at least one occasion in San Pedro in 1913 [Stavis 1964, I:49].

Another reference to Hill as speaker, which I have not found cited elsewhere, appears in the autobiography of labor activist Lucy Robins Lang, who was an active anarchist in the 1910s before becoming Samuel Gompers's secretary. She describes an IWW street meeting in Seattle in 1912, shortly after an explosion destroyed the building that housed the *Los Angeles Times*, a viciously anti-labor paper published by General Harrison Gray Otis. The Seattle IWW meeting was held to support local striking iron-workers, but because of the blood-curdling "Red Scare" headlines provoked by the L.A. explosion, the crowd that had gathered was hostile. As Lang tells it,

> Our star speaker, Joe Hill, maker of Wobbly songs and later a Wobbly martyr, was ready to charge that General Otis had dynamited the *Times* Building himself, but he couldn't make himself heard above the catcalls of the lumberjacks and long-shoremen. We stood there, our faces growing redder and redder, and at last we went home. [1948, 53]

Lang's account is not likely to boost Hill's reputation as an orator; one cannot help thinking that Haywood or Big Jim Thompson or Lucy Parsons would have found ways to make themselves heard above the din. Lang's description of Hill as "star speaker" probably signifies only that he was well known in the labor movement for his songs, not that he was an orator.

That Hill did not think of himself as anything other than a militant rank-and-filer is made plain in his letters. As he wrote to Fellow Worker E. W. Vanderleith in San Francisco in 1914: "I am just one of the rank and file—just a common Pacific Coast wharf-rat—that's all" [Smith 1969, 132]. And in a letter to Elizabeth

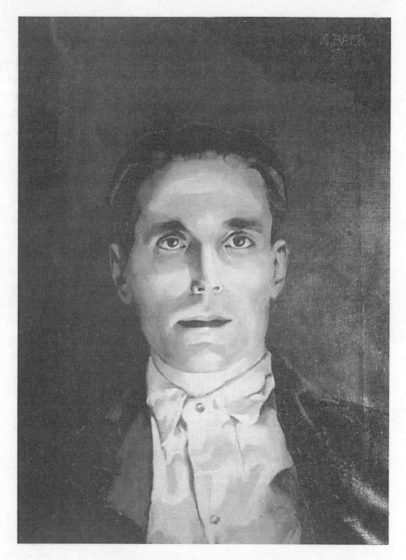

M. Baer: Joe Hill (oil painting, 1918).
This portrait was prominently displayed at IWW headquarters
in Chicago for some seven decades. It is now part
of the union's Archives at Wayne State University in Detroit.
Nothing seems to be known about the artist.

Gurley Flynn, he categorically distinguished himself from the union's organizers and orators:

> I think the organization should use all its resources to keep the "live wires" on the outside [*i.e.*, out of prison]. I mean organizers and orators. When they are locked up they are dead as far as the organization [is] concern[ed]. A fellow like myself, for instance, can do just as well in jail. I can dope out my music and "poems" in here and slip them out through the bars and the world will never know the difference. [*Letters*, 30]

The fact that Hill was no superhero does not mean he was a shrinking violet or a habitual loner. In one of the very few personal accounts of Hill in the workplace, Edward Mattson recalled that "On the job he was never afraid to stand up for his fellow workers, whenever called upon. Often he took great risks in order to help others" [Nerman 1979, 37]. Moreover, as his participation in the Mexican Revolution and the Fraser River Strike suggest, Hill liked being at the scene of workingclass rebellion. In a letter to the editor of the *Industrial Worker* in 1947, Louis Moreau—who was as far from being a mythmaker as one can be—called Hill "the stormy petrel of the IWW—where the IWW was in trouble, there you were sure to find Joe Hill" [15 Nov 1947]. The desire to be "where the action is," however, was characteristic of many Wobs—one might even say most—and definitely including Fellow Worker Moreau himself. As Walter Rogers put it, recalling his own Wobbly youth, "wherever bosses' attacks was hottest, everybody'd hop a freight to there" [1972, 96].

What is important is that Hill headed for the action not as leader, organizer or orator, but as rank-and-filer, poet and song-writer. And there we find the kernel of truth in the Hill legend: He embodied then, and still epitomizes now, the creative, devil-may-care, rank-and-file Wobbly on the move.

The Stavis/Foner "model" of Hill is, at least in part, the result of their peculiar wish-fulfilling research methodology. Naively and unquestioningly, both presumed that every mention of a "Fellow Worker Hill" in the IWW press automatically refers to the author of "Casey Jones" and "Mr Block." The trouble is, as the IWW's long-time in-house historian Fred Thompson often remarked, Hill is hardly an uncommon name. (I just checked and noted nearly a thousand listed in the Chicago telephone directory.) Without corroborative evidence, therefore, references to "Fellow Worker Hill" or "J. Hill" should not automatically be regarded as documentation of the IWW songwriter and cartoonist, but rather as *dubiosa*, pending further information.

---

1. This list of live concert performances of "Joe Hill" has been gleaned from several Paul Robeson websites.

2. Alfred Hayes left the Communist Party in the late 1930s or '40s [Green 1993, 86]. Mark Rosenzweig, librarian at the Reference Center for Marxist Studies in New York, informs me that "Earl Robinson quit the Party quietly . . . in 1957, when he was confronted with the loyalty oath necessary to join the Musicians' Union (AFM), which, by the way, the Party's attorneys advised CP members to sign"(15 May 2002).

This *Los Angeles Times* cartoon (*c.* 1919) of a vicious, drooling IWW wolf reveals that enemies of the workers' movement also tend to be enemies of wildlife.

2. REMORSELESS SCOUNDREL, DEVIL INCARNATE

Juice is stranger than friction.
—T-Bone Slim—

Idolatrous admirers are not the only manufacturers of Joe Hill legends. That the man also had voluble and hate-filled detractors is plain to anyone who takes the trouble to glance at the Salt Lake City press of 1914-15. Hill's enemies in later years have been relatively fewer, and much less shrill, but the legend they promote—that Hill was "known" to certain fellow Wobs as a thief and robber, and that therefore he was guilty of the Morrison murder (Vernon Jensen), or "probably guilty" (Wallace Stegner), or at least "never proved innocent" (Melvyn Dubofsky)—has unfortunately misled a large readership.

In a 1947 article, Stegner, a university professor and writer of fiction who also dabbled in journalism, came up with what he apparently thought was a novel idea. "It might be possible," he wrote, "if one wished to do it, to whittle the figure of Joe Hill down to the stature of a migrant yegg" [187]. Of course that's exactly what the *Salt Lake Tribune, Deseret Evening News* and other Utah papers had done many years before, and it's pretty much what Stegner did all over again in his mediocre novel, *The Preacher and the Slave*, published in 1950. Subsequently reprinted under different titles—*Joe Hill: The Man Who Chose Death*, and *Joe Hill: A Biographical Novel*—this sustained defamation of the IWW poet and martyr regrettably remains the most widely circulated and most influential book on Hill.

Agnes Inglis, the intrepid anarchist librarian, believing Stegner to be a serious and sincere inquirer into the Hill case, took pains to supply him with rare old documents from the world-famous Labadie Collection at the University of Michigan Library. Long before the novel appeared, Inglis was horrified by the malignant portrayal of Hill in Stegner's *New Republic* article. As she wrote in a letter to Fred Thompson, "I was never so disappointed in any scholar as in Mr Stegner—if you call his work the work of a 'scholar'" [25 Jan 1948].

In a clever move that seems to have deceived many readers, Stegner presented himself as a debunker—a brave David challenging a Goliath-like pro-Hill legend that he persisted in calling *the*

Hill legend. In reality, even then, at the dawn of the Cold War, *two* distinct Hill legends existed: 1) the Hill-the-martyred-saint legend, upheld by a few radicals in the labor movement along with a handful of folk-singers and other romantics outside it, and 2) the Hill-the-bad-guy legend, which was "official policy" not only in Utah but also in mainstream (conservative and liberal) opinion throughout the country. In his effort to bolster the bad-guy legend, Stegner merely added his *yea* to what was then and is still the dominant ideology, and then spruced it up a little with a few fabrications of his own.

A large part of Stegner's strategy lay in his effort to twist Hill's well-known shyness and modesty into sinister qualities, and thereby to turn the peaceful and popular Wobbly poet into a barely articulate tough guy who trusted nobody, a cold and resentful brooder: the "lone wolf" type. Irritated by this utterly false depiction of Hill as surreptitious and anti-social, skulking about by night and concealing his "real" life, Hill's friend Alexander MacKay came forth to set the record straight:

> It is all bosh to say that Joe Hill was a lone wolf; he believed profoundly in organization. Solidarity was the key-word of his thinking, writing, and living. He was not an individualist in thought or deed; on the contrary, he was a co-operator; he never traveled or batched alone, and he was a member of a militant union. [Review of Stegner 1950]

Swedish Wobbly Edward Mattson, writing in 1940—that is, long before Stegner began his campaign against Hill—recalled his friend with warmth and admiration:

> As a musician he was the most pleasant personality one could ever hope to meet. Everyone who came into contact with [Hill] liked him. Frequently he gave away his last penny to aid a friend in need. [Nerman 1979, 36, 37]

Stegner is also to blame for the insipid but oft-heard platitude that Hill secretly sought martyrdom and consequently created his own myth. The novelist's *New Republic* article gruesomely generalized that "The whole history of the IWW movement has indicated that the prime function of the Wobblies was to die, to provide the martyrs" [1948, 24]. And his novel has Joe Hill saying: "I want to die a martyr," followed by Stegner's commentary: "The words were like the striking of a light, for having said them, he knew that they were true, and had been true from the beginning" [1950, 323]. Like just about everything else that Stegner had to say about Hill, this tiresome balderdash has no foundation in truth. For Ester Dahl, "love of life" was one of her brother's characteristic traits, and surely Hill's passionate vitality, his life-affirming strength of mind, were the very substance of what Sam Murray called "that peculiar spirit which enabled Joe to bear up so well under the enormous strain" [Takman 1956, 26; Murray 1923, 53].

Stegner's vacuous notion of Hill as wannabe-martyr and designer-of-his-own-myth began as slander, fattened into a cynical cliché, and eventually evolved into a sort of myth itself. Its intent and implication, of course, is to convince us that Hill's well-known good nature—his honesty, humor, generosity, modesty, courage—and even his obvious will to live, were nothing but an egotistical neurotic's empty posturing, calculated to impress posterity. In Dick Brazier's view, however, Stegner was simply "looking for dirt to throw at the image of Joe Hill," and didn't care where he found it [letter to Fred Thompson, 21 Dec 66].

Historians who regard the IWW with hostility or condescension have eagerly echoed Stegner's slanders, and sometimes added to them. Melvyn Dubofsky, for example, in his *We Shall Be All*, not only portrays Hill as an "actor" who "played his role to the very end," but also goes so far as to argue that the real purport of Hill's prison letters was to enhance his "martyr myth" [1969, 310-11].

Stegner always liked to boast that his novel was thoroughly researched: After all, he had interviewed cops, jailers, Morrison's younger son, the sheriff who executed Hill, and an Associated Press reporter who witnessed the execution; he also pored over police and court records as well as files of the Salt Lake City dailies. In addition, he pretended to have "inside information" from former members of the IWW, although he declined to reveal their names. Of these highly questionable "sources," one is known to have degenerated into a Chamber of Commerce member by the time Stegner got to him, and another admitted to having edited the paper of the notorious "4-L's"—the Loyal Legion of Loggers and Lumbermen, an apoplectically anti-IWW company union supported by the U.S. army during World War I [Modesto 1963a, 3].

Most of Stegner's "inside information," it so happens, was supplied by a man he described as "an old Wobbly who played the

guitar in Jack Walsh's first IWW band" [1947, 186]. This loqua-
cious fellow easily persuaded Stegner that Hill was "a very tough
citizen indeed . . . who occasionally dropped hints of having 'made
a score,' and who resembled "a certain type of Western bad-
man"—the very model Stegner used in his novel [*ibid.*].

To old-time Wobblies such as Fred Thompson and Richard
Brazier, it was immediately obvious that this long-winded informant of Stegner's was Harry ("Haywire Mac") McClintock. The
identification was not in fact all that difficult, for it seems that ex-
Fellow-Worker McClintock was the *only* person claiming to have
known Hill who ever expressed such weird views about him.

In his biography of Hill, Gibbs Smith quotes a 1947 letter to
Stegner from Stewart Holbrook, author of historical potboilers,
including several dealing with the IWW (Fred Thompson called
them "slapdash compilations of other people's mistakes plus a few
of his own"). In this letter Holbrook informed Stegner that "years
ago" an unnamed Wobbly had told him that "all Wobs in the know
knew that Hill was a stick-up man, and that they [the IWW] blew
him up into a Martyr for the sake of the Cause" [Smith 1969, 59].
Here, too, as Smith himself suggests, the perceptive reader discerns
the heavy hand of "Haywire Mac."

Who was McClintock? Migrant worker, guitar-playing busker,
and songwriter, he was born in Knoxville, Tennessee, in 1882
[Young 1981]. He was briefly a member of the IWW, *circa* 1909-
16, and a delegate to the organization's eighth convention in
Chicago, 1913, where he sided with St John, George Speed, Ben
Fletcher, Joe Ettor and the other centralists [*Proceedings* 1913]. In
IWW circles McClintock is best remembered as the author of a
poem titled "Hymn of Hate," a relentless indictment of Capital and
the State [Kornbluh 1964, 29-30]. During the 1920s/30s he
recorded a number of songs on the Victor label, and was a popular
San Francisco radio comedian, teller of tall tales, and disc jockey.
In 1932 he published a songbook, *"Mac's" Songs of the Road and
Range.* He died in 1957.

Stegner seems to have sincerely believed that McClintock was
one of the three Wobs he interviewed or corresponded with who
really had known Hill well. John Greenway, whose antipathy to
Hill was even greater than Stegner's, went so far as to say that
"Probably no Wobbly knew Joe Hill better than Harry McClintock" [1953, 192]. He gives no source for that bit of misinformation, but it should not be hard to guess that the source was none

other than Harry McClintock. In truth, there is no evidence that McClintock was anything more than a slight acquaintance of Hill's, and in a 1950 letter to Fred Thompson he admitted that he knew "practically nothing" about him [9 July]. Dick Brazier even doubted that Mac knew J. H. Walsh, because "Nobody ever called him Jack, it was always J.H. or Walsh" [to Fred Thompson, 7 Jan 1967].

However, with his silly and dishonest chatter, "Haywire Mac" contributed more confusion to Hill's biography than any other individual. When he told Stegner that "I believe that he [Hill] was a crook and that he made a lot of scores" [Smith 1969, 59], Stegner —exposing his own prejudices—overlooked the word "believe" and thus took mere suspicion as established fact. Greenway, summarizing what McClintock told him, informed his readers that Hill was "thought to be a robber, but looked more like a gambler. . . . He had the reputation of being a dangerous character, yet to McClintock's knowledge, no one ever saw him get into a fight" [1953, 192]. Ignoring the uncertainty conveyed by the words "thought" and "reputation," Greenway simple-mindedly set forth McClintock's feverish imaginings as the unvarnished truth.

The passing statement that "no one ever saw him get into a fight" is the only part of Haywire Mac's "data" on Hill that coincides with the reminiscences of those who actually knew the man. Without the innuendo supplied by McClintock and exaggerated by Stegner and Greenway, these nine words confirm the prevailing Wobbly view of the IWW bard as easy-going, unaggressive, and fundamentally nonviolent.

McClintock's veracity as an informant can be gauged by the fact that he pretended to be the author of "Hallelujah, I'm a Bum," and even managed to obtain a copyright on the song in 1928. Scrupulous song researchers, however—including George Milburn, Fred Thompson, and Joyce Kornbluh, not to mention a 1930s research team from the IWW's Work People's College in Duluth —have shown that the song antedates McClintock's arrival on the scene by at least a decade [Milburn 1930; Kornbluh 1998, 71].[1] Dick Brazier recalled that Fellow Worker George Speed told him it was one of the popular marching songs of Coxey's Army during the March on Washington in 1894, when Mac was still a child [to Fred Thompson, 21 Dec 1966, 2-3].

In Fred Thompson's view, McClintock was basically a "windbag," an "egomaniac," and "the sort of ex-hobo who, as long as you keep supplying him with drinks, will tell you whatever you want to hear." Brazier's opinion of the man, based on personal acquaintance, was no higher. Recalling McClintock as a "Blow-hard," "loud talking" and "aggressive," he went on to say

> I just don't believe that McClintock was a bosom pal of Joe Hill's, for what I heard of Joe Hill's character from men who knew Joe very well—like Sam Scarlett and Meyer Friedkin—Joe and McClintock were temperamentally as far apart as the poles. Joe was a quiet chap, not much given to brag or boast, which were McClintock's characteristics. [to Fred Thompson, 21 Dec 1966]

Henry Young's 80-page biography of McClintock, based large-ly on Mac's own (unpublished) memoirs as well as interviews with his widow and "individuals who knew him," includes numerous anecdotes about Mac's acquaintances and fellow workers, inclu-ding musicians, railroad workers, Jack London, and Wobblies J. H. Walsh and Richard Brazier. Young focuses on music and songs, especially hobo songs. He devotes a couple of pages and many scattered references to the IWW, and to IWW songs, but he never mentions Joe Hill. This significant omission would seem to indicate that McClintock's own papers contained no reference to Hill, and that neither his widow nor the "individuals who knew him" recalled anything Mac had to say on the subject. If that is the case, it makes McClintock's 1940s posturing as the "expert" on Hill look more and more like a hoax. Unfortunately, the gullible Stegner and Greenway took him at his word and relayed the old hoaxer's unfounded fantasies to a broad public.

From Young's account and other sources, "Mac" appears to have been a charming, witty, versatile character, imbued with a childlike prankishness and an offbeat sense of humor. More's the pity that his irresponsible gab lined him up with the slanderers of Joe Hill.

Had Wobs "in the know" been aware of Hill's career as "stick-up man," one of them sooner or later surely would have said some-thing about it. It is absurd to believe that two or three hundred people—or even two or three dozen—could keep a secret like that for years and years. In any event, hundreds of Wobs far more "in the know" than McClintock could ever have pretended to be were unanimous in their certainty that Hill was neither stick-up man nor any other sort of criminal, that he had nothing to do with the Morrison murder, that his devotion to the IWW was absolute, and that he would never do anything that might hurt the Cause in any way. I am thinking of such fellow workers as Ralph Chaplin, Vincent St John, Bill Haywood, George Speed, Ben Fletcher, Richard Brazier, Joe Ettor, and Covington Hall: men of impeccable revolutionary integrity, tried and true fighters in the workers' struggle for equality and freedom. Surely these were Wobs "in the know"! And every one of them was certain—and said so, time and again, with not the slightest equivocation—that Hill was innocent, a frame-up victim, a loyal union man trapped in the coils of brutal class injustice. Can anyone seriously believe that such brave souls as these, exemplars of the new society of solidarity, would have devoted so much of their time and energy, not to mention so much of the union's always very limited funds, to defending the innocence of someone whom they knew to be a selfish two-bit crook and killer, and therefore an indelible blot on the great and good name of the Industrial Workers of the World?

Even as late as the Cold War years, the late 1940s and '50s, old-time Wobs such as William Chance, Meyer Friedkin, Sam Murray, Alexander MacKay and Louis Moreau—all of whom had known Joe Hill personally—were outspoken in defense of their old friend. And there were others who never met Hill, but who still qualified as Wobs "in the know": Covington Hall, Herb Edwards, C. E. "Stumpy" Payne, Matilda Robbins, Paul Pika. Still others had left the IWW long ago, but had certainly been "Wobs in the know" in the 1910s: Charles Ashleigh, James P. Cannon, Vincent R. Dunne, Carl Skoglund, Sam Scarlett, Elizabeth Gurley Flynn. Not one of them was ever known to express even the smallest doubt that Hill was an innocent class-war victim of capitalist frame-up.

In the course of researching his 1968 book, *The Wobblies*, English historian Patrick Renshaw interviewed a number of veteran Wobs, some of whom had been active in the union as far back as the 1910s. His discussion of Hill includes a footnote acknowledging that he had "found no old-timers who think Hill guilty" [153]. This was also Gibbs Smith's experience as he interviewed IWW veterans in connection with his 1969 biography of Hill [59].

Though they were far from numerous, the IWW also had turncoats—men who deserted the One Big Union for high-paying jobs with the Establishment: Harold Lord Varney, author of a history of the IWW serialized in the *One Big Union Monthly* in 1919-20, was perhaps the one who received the most publicity in the capitalist press.[2] A prominent speaker and writer for the union for a few years in the 1910s, and clearly a man "in the know" at that time, Varney in his later pro-fascist period would have been only too glad to reveal any sordid facts about the IWW's foremost martyr. He was still writing for John Birch Society publications in the 1960s, but does not appear to have said anything about Hill.

The examples of Stegner, Greenway, and Dubofsky suffice to demonstrate that Hill's detractors have also had their own wish-fulfilling methodology: an eagerness to believe the worst, and nothing but the worst, combined with a flagrant disregard for verification. As a result, mere hearsay becomes the premise and foundation of their own productions. It must be admitted, however, that in all their hostile misrepresentations, neither Stegner nor the other detractors have managed to add anything that wasn't already there in the hate-filled columns of the *Deseret Evening News*.

To maintain, without the slightest evidence, that Joe Hill was a killer or a "migrant yegg" is certainly more malicious, more harmful, and more disgusting, than naively revering him as a saint or superhero. But both extremes are sadly misguided, and highlight the fact that our knowledge of the man's life is so slight. What we *do* know about him, however—Swedish-born immigrant, hobo, IWW, musician and composer, writer of songs and a few articles, cartoonist, frame-up victim, and martyr—is solid, despite the rumor-mongers' and would-be mythmakers' efforts to embellish or demolish it.

I have always liked André Breton's maxim: "For a revolutionary, the first duty is to prefer life to legend" [Breton 1962, 284]

1. In the late 1930s, researchers at Work People's College, citing an article in the *Industrial Union Bulletin* for 4 April 1908, pointed out that the first published IWW version of the song, which appeared in that issue, was the collective production of many "singers as well as jawsmiths" who belonged to the Spokane Mixed Local. McClintock was not mentioned. See "Birth of a Song Hit," *One Big Union Monthly*, Mar 1938, 28, 31.

2. On Varney's defection from the union in 1920, see "Harold Lord Varney 'Exposes' the IWW," in the *One Big Union Monthly* (March 1920, 35-39), and the two following articles in the same issue: "One More Renegade" by George Andreytchine (40-41), and "Man Overboard" by John Sandgren (41-43).

3. ONE MAN'S JOE HILL MYTH:
JOHN MAATA RETELLS THE STORY
AS HE REMEMBERED IT

Dream is vision produced by the refraction of a ray of truth.
—Eliphas Levi—

A rich Mulligan Stew of Joe Hill legends, seasoned with a pinch of fact, appears in a little-known memoir by a Midwestern American farmer. In 1985 John Maata, the 83-year-old son of Finnish-born parents, suddenly felt compelled to record the early history of his family:

> In a hospital, seriously ill, my thoughts strayed to my youth, to the Maata family with nine children, in the community of Marengo, Wisconsin. Those years seemed to come alive. I saw my parents. Here is the story.

In ninety-two pages, *My Father's Heritage* chronicles the saga of the Maata family from the turn of the century through 1920.

Much of the story tells of everyday life: building a house, farming, fire-fighting, going to school, making a violin, encountering porcupines—but a recurring sub-theme focuses on the workers' movement. Maata's father had been a lumberjack and then a miner before taking up farming, and subscribed to several labor publications. The whole family were Socialists, and also sympathetic to the IWW, but ineligible for membership because "small farmers could not join the IWW."

Maata's memoir is notable for its passionate sincerity and lack of pretension. His purpose in writing it was clearly to record that early period of his life *as he remembered it*. He felt no need to verify what he wrote, to look up details or check sources, and that gives his book a subjective freshness often missing in autobiographies that are more carefully researched. Obviously written in a hurry, Maata's book is just what it says it is: a compendium of one man's memories of his childhood and adolescence. As is the case with everyone's memories, his were a mixture of true and false, real and imaginary—but his job, as he saw it, was simply to get them down in writing.

The short chapter titled "I Dreamed I Saw Joe Hill Last Night," though only a page and a half long, is remarkable in many ways. It blends the author's childhood recollections (he was thirteen at the time of Hill's execution); stories heard from parents, other family members, friends and neighbors; half-remembered articles from newspapers and magazines; distorted fragments from long-forgotten books; and perhaps—who knows?—scenes from old movies or even nightmares.

Here, highly abbreviated, is the gist of John Maata's own Joe Hill legend:

> Father read in the *Appeal to Reason* that IWW leader Joseph Hellstrom was tied behind a car, dragged along a road, and thrown in a ditch. Rescued by striking workers, he was carried to a boarding house, and then to a hospital where a doctor helped him recover.
>
> Hellstrom was well known for the songs he had written for striking workers. He had been a member of the Western Federation of Miners before joining the IWW. When he was released from the hospital, friends urged him to leave town, for his life had been threatened. Strikers secretly drove him to Salt Lake City, but the city fathers learned that he was there. Again the mining company thugs were out to get him, and in October the thugs murdered a hardware dealer and his young son. The following morning Hill was arrested and charged with murder.
>
> Company thugs and the city fathers paid witnesses to testify against Hill. The jury found him guilty and the judge sentenced him to be shot the next day.
>
> November 19th was the execution day. Hill walked, head high, to the wall, and was given permission to say his last words. "Workers, do not waste time mourning for me, ORGANIZE. I die like a rebel." Nine rifles went off at once and Hill went down.
>
> A song remains [eight lines of the Hayes/Robinson lyric are quoted from memory].
>
> Hill was forty years old; his freedom was a grave, in a wooden coffin.

There is no reason to think that Maata invented any of this. All through his memoir he tries to tell his story as he lived it, without embellishment; similarly, his chapter on the Wobbly bard is simply a summary of stories about Joe Hill that he had heard long ago. From the misspelling of Hillstrom to the concluding reference to Hill's burial in a wooden coffin (Hill of course was cremated and his ashes scattered), it is plain that Maata had not read much on the subject. Over the years, however, and probably mostly in conversation, he had *absorbed* a lot, and what he absorbed were not only solid facts but also rumors, reveries, and false memories.

His account of Hill is largely a dreamlike conflation of the murders of all three of the most celebrated IWW martyrs: Joe Hill, Frank Little, and Wesley Everest. Hill and Little both stayed at boardinghouses. It was Little who was "tied behind a car" and "dragged along the road," and it was Everest's body that was thrown, not exactly into a ditch, but into "a hole in the ground." Where Maata's hospital comes from is hard to say. His belief that company thugs and city fathers paid witnesses to lie in court was probably not a fantasy but a common (and fully justified) assumption in mining communities.

Especially remarkable is Maata's full-speed-ahead condensation of the Hill story; the twenty-three months between Hill's arrest and execution are covered here in a little over twenty-three words. The account of the execution, however, is dramatically magnified. That the IWW bard walked "head high" to his death echoes a Ralph Chaplin poem. Hill was not in fact permitted to say any last words; the passage quoted by Maata is from one of Hill's letters. Note, too, that in Maata's version the five-man firing-squad is almost doubled.

Maata's personal Joe Hill myth illustrates the psychoanalyst Géza Róheim's contention that myths should be considered "as having arisen from a dream which a person dreamed and then told to others, who retold it again, perhaps elaborated in accord with their own dreams" [1992, 149]. The very qualities that make John Maata's account unacceptable as history—conflation, distortion, condensation and magnification—are of course not only characteristic of dreams, but also of imaginative fiction, theater, and motion pictures.

However worthless it may be as a factual account, his chapter on Joe Hill is an extraordinary piece of folklore, a valuable psychological document of what are often called "tricks of memory," and a splendid miniature case-study in myth-formation.

As a plot-outline, moreover, John Maata's story is much better than most Hill-related novels, and could easily be worked up into a better-than-average play or movie.

Joe Hill

"WE CAN BE CANDID—BUT NOT IMPARTIAL!"
The prolific IWW cartoonist Charles E. Setzer (X13) exposes
the racism and hypocrisy of politicians and craft union
bureaucrats (*Industrial Worker*, 16 February 1945)

IWW button (1965)

222

VII
THE IWW & THE WHITE PROBLEM

1. ONE BIG UNION:
A CHALLENGE TO WHITE SUPREMACY

On Earth there is a single people to which all nations belong.
—**Amilcar Cabral**—

Joe Hill's songs and cartoons treat class issues with a straightforwardness so unequivocal and hard-hitting that it makes us blink. In the great struggle between the working class producers and the employing class parasites, there is never the slightest doubt about whose side he is on. Can the same be said for his approach to questions of race?

From day one the IWW started making history in race matters. In his opening call to order at the union's founding convention in 1905, Big Bill Haywood insisted that the existing so-called labor movement, the American Federation of Labor, did not truly represent the working class because many of its affiliates excluded Blacks and foreigners [*Proceedings* 1905, 1]. Delegate Lucy E. Parsons (of Black, Native American and Mexican ancestry), delivered two of the most inspired and forward-looking speeches of the entire gathering. In one, she predicted the sit-down strike ("staying in" rather than "going out") as "the strike of the future" and, in reference to the then-current revolution in Russia, emphasized world labor solidarity in the broadest terms:

> the red current that flows through the veins of all humanity is identical . . . [and] those who raise the red flag, it matters not where, whether on the sunny plains of China, or on the sunbeaten hills of Africa, or on the far-off snow-capped shores of the north, or in Russia or in America—they all belong to the human family and have an identity of interest. [*ibid.*, 170-171]

Even before the union's first anniversary, a Japanese daily published in Seattle praised it for welcoming "every nationality" into its membership [Brissenden 1957, 208]. Its second convention, in 1906, passed a strong resolution against lynching introduced by Roscoe T. Sims, the IWW's first important African American organizer [Foner 1974, 112n]. During the Fraser River Strike in

Canada, 1912, an IWW "manifesto" emphasized the union's policy of "doors wide open to *all* wage-workers," regardless of color [Laut 1912, 431]. The following year, Mary Ovington, a co-founder of the National Association for the Advancement of Colored People, declared that the IWW was the only organization in the U.S., aside from the NAACP itself, which "has stood with the Negro" and "attacks segregation" [Foner 1974, 107]. In *The Crisis* in 1919, W. E. B. Du Bois hailed the IWW because it "draws no color line" [Bird *et al.*, 1985, 139].

Du Bois's commendation is especially significant, because only a few years earlier, according to his 1962 *Autobiography*, he had regarded the IWW with mistrust, and felt that the 1912 Lawrence strikers, for example, "would not let a Negro work beside them" [305]. During that earlier period, Du Bois recalled, he never sang the songs of Joe Hill. It would be interesting to know which particular events and/or experiences in the intervening years led him to revise his opinion. The IWW's organization of thousands of Black longshoremen all along the East Coast starting in 1913, and the growing prominence of several Black organizers within the union—most notably Ben Fletcher and Charles Carter—may have been decisive factors in this regard. Du Bois, unlike such other Black radical intellectuals as Hubert Harrison and Claude MacKay, never developed close ties to the IWW, but the fact that he changed his mind about it is important.

The Messenger, a Socialist-oriented Black labor journal edited in New York by A. Philip Randolph and Chandler Owen, actively supported revolutionary industrial unionism; the July 1917 issue called the IWW "the only labor union that has never, in theory or practice, since its beginning twelve years ago, barred the workers of any race or nation from its membership" [Foner 1974, 50].

Radical attorney Clarence Darrow, noting that "most unions of the AF of L and the railroad brotherhoods barred Negroes," went on to point out that "until the IWW came into existence there was little the Black workers could do to improve their lot. But now the situation [is] different" [*ibid.*, 111].

Poet Kenneth Rexroth, who carried a red card in his Chicago years in the 1920s, emphasized in his autobiography the friendly relations that existed between Wobblies and the Black Nationalist Marcus Garvey movement. Rexroth says that he himself "used to soapbox quite a bit in association with Garveyites" and later with the more revolutionary-minded and explicitly anti-capitalist Afri-

Like many other Wobbly cartoonists, William Henkelman
liked to picture May Day as a joyous global festival
in which workers of all colors and languages turned out
to sing and dance to the music of world Revolution.

Multi-racial solidarity at work on the waterfront,
as shown by IWW organizer/cartoonist E. F. Doree
(*Industrial Pioneer*, October 1921)

can Blood Brotherhood" [268].[1]

In their 1931 study, *The Black Worker*, labor historians Sterling D. Spero and Abram L. Harris concluded that some 100,000 Blacks took out red cards at one time or another. Unfortunately, their estimate cannot be verified—yet another instance in which the federal government's theft and destruction of the union's records has made the historian's task much more difficult. But we do know that the IWW organized substantial numbers of Black workers throughout the country, and internationally as well. Black Wobblies were active from New York to California, and from New Orleans to Vancouver; a militant nucleus formed around the union's headquarters in Chicago; others took part in the Western and Midwestern harvest drives. The *Omaha World-Herald* noted in July 1916 that some "two hundred hoboes" had arrived in Council Bluffs, Iowa, among them "a score of Negroes." Most of them, the article said, were IWWs [Wagaman 1975, 302].

Among Black longshoremen in Philadelphia, Baltimore, and other eastern ports, and the Black timber workers of Louisiana and East Texas, IWW membership was especially large, frequently numbering in the thousands. Covington Hall's first-hand account of the IWW's integrated industrial unionism during the southern "Lumber Wars" of the 1910s—as depicted in his classic memoir, *Labor Struggles in the Deep South*—reveal some of the brightest moments of Black/white workingclass unity in U.S. history.[2] During the same decade, a Portuguese Wobbly named Big John Avila —later one of the 101 IWWs sentenced to long terms in Leavenworth—helped co-ordinate "a strike of about 1000 Portuguese Negro longshoremen" in Providence, Rhode Island [Gold 1972, 12].

Philip Foner, a historian in many ways highly critical of the IWW, nonetheless conceded that "the Wobblies united Black and white workers as never before in American history and maintained solidarity and equality regardless of race or color such as most labor organizations have yet to equal" [1974, 119].

The union's record in this regard exemplifies the unbeatable power and the glory of Wobbly-style an-injury-to-one-is-an-injury-to-all revolutionary industrial unionism. With his characteristic boldness, brevity and clarity, Big Bill Haywood spelled out the basic Wobbly strategy:

In order to have a healthy workers' movement in America, it is necessary to organize the huge mass of Negroes. They must be organized, whatever it costs, and brought into contact with the wide masses of worker-immigrants who haven't caught the stupid racial prejudices of native white workers. Meanwhile, educational work goes on, aimed at compelling the trade unions to open their doors to Negroes. . . . [McKay 1979, 32]

Such an approach meant a lot to the younger generation of African American radicals, whether or not they actually joined the IWW. Haywood Hall, a former member of the African Blood Brotherhood who as Harry Haywood became an important figure in the U.S. Communist Party, was deeply impressed by the IWW's point-of-production race politics, particularly as articulated by Bill Haywood himself. In his autobiography, *Black Bolshevik*, Harry Haywood recounted his days as a young African American student in Moscow in the 1920s, and recalled especially his visits with the ailing Wobbly refugee whose room at the Lux Hotel was a popular meeting-place for radicals from the U.S.:

For us Blacks, listening to Big Bill was like a course on the American labor movement. He was a bitter enemy of racism, which he saw as the mainstay of capitalist domination over the U.S. working class. . . . I'm sure for all us Black students, our meeting and friendship with this great man were among the most memorable experiences of our stay in Moscow. . . . Big Bill obviously understood from his own experience the truth of the Marxian maxim that in the U.S. "labor in the white skin can never be free as long as in the black it is branded." [Harry Haywood 1978, 172-174]

As an all-out, no-compromise Wobbly, Joe Hill unquestionably shared the union's stand for interracial workingclass solidarity and against white supremacy. In his song "Scissor Bill," satirizing the anti-union worker and his many ignorant prejudices, he devoted a stanza to Scissor's racist and xenophobic fear and hatred of Blacks, Chinese, Japanese, and other immigrants, including "the gol durn Swede." By including his own nationality in the list, Hill clearly meant to affirm his identification with the others. And in songs such as "What We Want":

Yes, we want every one that works
In one union grand,

and "There Is Power in a Union":

> *Come, all ye workers, from every land,*
> *Come join in the grand industrial band,*

we have no reason to doubt that Fellow Worker Hill meant exactly what he said.

We do well to recall, however, that the period 1902-1915—Hill's U.S. years—were among the most blatantly racist in the nation's history. Prestigious newspapers and popular magazines alike were full of racist jokes and cartoons as well as articles touting white supremacy, ridiculing the allegedly "inferior," and even defending lynching. Racist remarks by U.S. Presidents, Senators, and other "distinguished" Americans—novelists, businessmen, judges, churchmen, actors, athletes, and other celebrities—received wide circulation. "White racial superiority" was a central and defining element of the two-party system, vaudeville, popular music, best-selling fiction, sports, law enforcement, organized religion, mainstream AFL trade-unionism, and indeed, just about every aspect of what politicians and the emerging advertising industry liked to call "the American Way of Life."

U.S. society was, in short, thoroughly saturated with white supremacist myths and habits, and thoroughly segregated across racial lines. Bitter words penned by Frederick Douglass in 1852 were still true a half century later: "For revolting barbarity and shameless hypocrisy, America reigns without a rival" [1987, 288]. Textbooks still don't admit it, but the "red, white, and blue" in those years embodied and glorified a history of racist violence—from slavery to lynch-law to genocide—that Adolf Hitler found inspiring.

Could a young workingclass immigrant from Sweden have entirely escaped such all-pervasive racism?

---

1. The reliability of Rexroth's memoir has been questioned. (The title "An Autobiographical Novel" was in fact imposed by the publisher, who doubted the veracity of some of the narrative.) In a January 1992 phone call Philip Lamantia expressed the view that Rexroth's recollections suffered from confabulation rather than fabrication, and that—like many autobiographers—he tended to exaggerate his own role in events in which he in fact played a very small part. In conversations a few weeks apart in the spring 2001, Gary Snyder estimated that some twenty percent of the book was either made up or heavily embellished, and Lawrence Ferlinghetti assured me that perhaps as much as eighty percent was

solid fact. In areas that I have myself researched, such as the Dil Pickle Club and Bughouse Square, I have generally found Rexroth's reminiscences dependable.

2. Although Hall completed the manuscript of this book in 1951, the year before he died, disputes regarding its ownership and copyright prevented its appearance in book-form for almost half a century. Only in 2000 was it published in full for the first time, by Charles H. Kerr in Chicago, edited with an introduction and notes by David R. Roediger.

Doris Hall's woodcut for a 1947 Labor Calendar shows Joe Hill
with an unnamed African American. In the lower center,
the black and white guitar is probably meant to symbolize
America's most vital workingclass musical traditions.

Joe Hill's signature reproduced on a button
(Salt Lake City, 1990)

Joe Hill

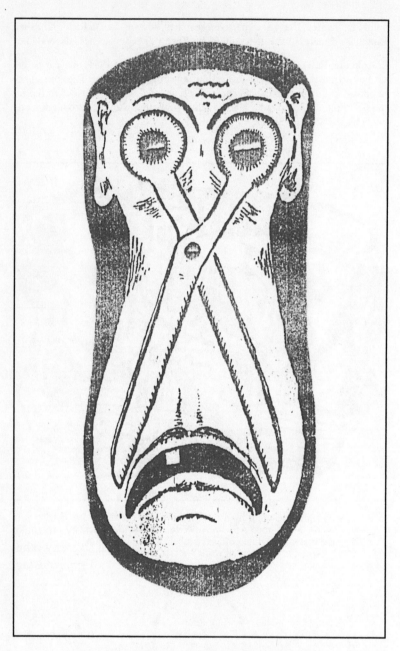

"Scissor Bill" as seen by IWW cartoonist Ern Hansen.
(*Industrial Worker*, 28 April 1923)

2. ANOTHER LOOK AT "SCISSOR BILL," OR, GOOD INTENTIONS ARE NOT ENOUGH

Hard are those questions!—answer harder still.
—Edward Young—

In view of the prevailing racist ideology and the degrading conditions of immigrant life in turn-of-the-century U.S., the simple fact that Joe Hill considered himself anti-racist—and in solidarity with all the oppressed—is itself extraordinary. It says a lot about the deep integrity of the man, about his fundamentally nonconformist spirit, and about the union that did so much to shape his life.

Alas, not even those heroic, full-time convention-shatterers, the Industrial Workers of the World, were able to vanquish *all* the conventions of their time. Racism, because of its *systemic* character—*i.e.*, because of the many and intricate ways it has been woven into the warp and woof of the entire repressive system—has proved especially insidious and difficult to overcome. Today, many of the most virulent racists deny being racist at all, while others— opponents of affirmative action, for example—hide their racism by calling it *anti*-racism. In Hill's time, with white supremacy openly championed in the nation's universities, press, and churches, and written into the constitutions of many AFL unions, the situation was very different, but surely no less difficult, for in the 1910s there truly was no precedent for what the IWW was trying to do.

The fact that the pre-IWW labor movement offered so few anti-racist models to draw on—the Haymarket anarchists, a part of the Knights of Labor, the New Orleans General Strike of 1892, and a handful of others—made it necessary for IWW members to make their own way on this complex terrain. Here as in so many other areas, Wobbly organizing was largely a matter of *improvising*: trying one thing, seeing how it went, and if it failed to produce the desired results, trying something else. The goal of a united working class—One Big Union of All Workers!—was constant, but everyone realized that the "ways and means" of reaching it depended on a bewildering array of variables.

In such situations, "intentions" and "plans" don't always count for much. Historian David Roediger, discussing the exasperatingly convoluted race politics of the great Deep South IWW organizer Covington Hall—one of the most successful in forging Black/white

unity—has shown how even the best-intentioned and most determined anti-racists can be severely limited by naive, mostly unconscious assumptions, as well as by pragmatic tactical compromises
hammered out in the course of particular struggles.

What Roediger has termed Hall's "curious mixture of egali-
tarianism and white blindspots" [Hall 2000, 20] seems to me to be
equally applicable to other IWW members who grappled with
problems of race—including Joe Hill himself. A closer look at the
lyrics of Hill's once-popular song "Scissor Bill," first published in
1913, is especially revelatory in this regard. There can be no doubt
that Hill intended this song to be a strong anti-racist statement—
particularly the second stanza, which ridicules Scissor for hating
racial and ethnic minorities. And yet, in this very stanza, Hill uses
precisely those abusive epithets that African Americans, Chinese,
and Japanese have always regarded as most offensive. The fact that
these objectionable words are quoted in the song as Scissor's rather
than the narrator's did not make them any less hurtful to African
American, Chinese or Japanese listeners. It is true that in those
years the same racist epithets routinely appeared in the daily
papers, the comics, and popular songs, but didn't working people
of color have the right to expect something better from the IWW?

Hill's lyrics make Scissor look bad, but they are far from
showing the IWW at its anti-racist best. It is impossible to believe
that Black or Asian workers ever sang this song. Indeed, in any
racially mixed gathering, the song could only have provoked embarrassment among singers and listeners alike.

The big question is: How did it happen that Wobblies, who
sincerely wanted Black and Asian workers to organize and be
active in the One Big Union, and in fact had already achieved some
important successes in that area, still considered it acceptable to
use racist language eight years after the founding of the union?

In Hill's case, every indication is that his intent in writing the
song was strictly satirical. He was seeking to portray a certain type
of hopelessly reactionary jerk—the bigoted, boss-loving, super-
patriotic, anti-workingclass worker—and Scissor's use of racist
terms seemed to fill out the image. Hill's use of racist language in
an overt attack on racism may appear to us as naive—and indeed,
he appears to have had not the slightest idea of just how "loaded"
those words were. I suspect, however, that for Hill the song was a
kind of experiment: an attempt to expose malicious stupidity in its
own maliciously stupid terms. In retrospect, it is easy to recognize

that the experiment failed. And insofar as the song was intended to let people of color know that the IWW despised white supremacy, it failed abysmally.

Granting that Hill in this instance was well-meaning but naive, what can be said for the *Little Red Song Book* editors, and the members of the IWW's General Executive Board, who authorized the reprinting of that song—racist terms and all—year after year, in edition after edition, well into the 1980s? During the seven decades in which "Scissor Bill" was featured in the Song Book, didn't any fellow workers point out that the song was, however unintentionally, insulting and injurious to racial minorities, and therefore to the entire working class?

Ironically, for a union with such a well-deserved reputation for anti-racism, Hill's dubious "Scissor Bill" was the only song in the *Little Red Song Book* to directly address the problem of racism. Not until the 1990s did the IWW *Song Book* include new songs that put some emphasis on anti-racism, or interracial workers' solidarity, or defeating white supremacy.

Despite its concentration on workers' education, the IWW provided very little education regarding race. One striking example of this obvious deficiency was the large library of the IWW's Work People's College, which I visited in 1964, when it was still largely intact. In many ways an excellent collection, it was well-stocked with the works of Marx, Engels, Labriola, Dietzgen, Kropotkin, Bakunin, Paul Lafargue, Rosa Luxemburg, Mary Marcy, Austin Lewis, Gene Debs, and scores of other socialists and anarchists. It included several volumes by Lenin and Trotsky, and perhaps as many as three dozen copies of Nikolai Bukharin's *Historical Materialism*, which was used as a textbook in one of Fred Thompson's classes in the 1930s. Works by and about Charles Darwin, Tom Paine, Adam Smith, and Robert Ingersoll were plentiful. There were also books by Charles Fourier, Théophile Gautier, Charles Dickens, Victor Hugo, Leo Tolstoy, Jack London, and Upton Sinclair; the complete works of the great Elizabethan and Romantic poets; and several sets of *The History of Labour in the United States* by John R. Commons and Associates. Scattered about were volumes on psychoanalysis, philosophy, geography, etymology, chemistry, accounting, the history of science, and numerous other topics.

Almost completely missing, however—apart from a few books on the Abolitionists—were books on African American history and literature. Also absent were books on contemporary China and Asian immigrants in the U.S. Truly, these were revealing omissions! The later history of the IWW might have been very different had its members spent more time reading Frederick Douglass, Martin R. Delaney, Paul Laurence Dunbar, Anna Julia Cooper, Jean Toomer, Claude McKay, Zora Neale Hurston, W. E. B. Du Bois, Sterling Brown, Langston Hughes, and the various works of the radical Chinese American novelist H. T. Tsiang.

The IWW's attitudes on race, and on the relation of race and class, were contradictory, full of loose ends, troubling ambiguities, and unresolved problems. Of course those problems were not the IWW's alone, and no other group can claim to have resolved them. What made the IWW distinct from other left and labor organizations, in race matters, was its passionate and unswerving focus on solidarity and equality. As one of the wisest, most far-seeing Wobblies—that man of mystery known as T-Bone Slim—once put it, in a memorable maxim: "Inequality and solidarity do not mix" [1992, 154].With that unbeatable one-two punch, the IWW early on established a record on race that has yet to be surpassed.

However, the fact that the Wobblies went further than anyone else in developing multi-racial workingclass solidarity does not mean that they had all the answers, or that every tactic they tried is worth trying again. Inevitably they had their share of missteps, bad breaks, wrong turns, and outright failures. Even Joe Hill, as it turns out, fell somewhat short of perfection in this regard. It just goes to show that the Man Who Never Died was only human after all, and capable of making mistakes like anyone else.

I like to think that Fellow Worker Hill would second David Roediger's suggestion that the best way to honor the IWW's anti-racist legacy is not by pretending that Wobblies "solved" the "race question," but rather by striving to transcend their limitations.

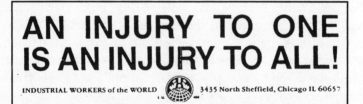

IWW bumper-sticker (1980s)

3. REDEEMING THE EARTH
FROM PRIVATE PROPERTY:
THE IWW & NATIVE AMERICANS

Unless we support one another
with our collective and united forces . . .
we will be driven away . . . and scattered
as autumnal leaves before the wind.
—Tecumseh—

American Socialists and Communists early on produced a copious literature on an impressive range of topics in such diverse fields as U.S. history, economics, politics, and culture. As is well known, they were especially prolific writers of books on revolutions and near-revolutions in Russia, Germany, China, and other countries.

On one important topic, however—the indigenous peoples of North America—they apparently had nothing to say. The numerous theoreticians and propagandists of the Socialist and Communist parties either ignored or trivialized the matter, except to point out that Indians had been rendered "obsolete" by the march of Progress, and were doomed to disappear. Rarely mentioned even in passing in their books, pamphlets, or articles, Native Americans were also overlooked in the party platforms.

This significant and disturbing silence, which undoubtedly reflects longstanding white anti-Indian prejudice, can also be traced to one of the many glaring flaws in the crude and over-schematized determinisms that have long dominated what is considered Marxism in this country. According to the "Marxism" perpetrated by the Socialist Party (largely derived from German social-democracy), and the Communist Party (which took its cues and miscues from Russian Bolshevism), certain "iron laws" of History, on the inexorable road to Progress, long ago rendered tribal (precapitalist) societies archaic, and doomed them to a speedy oblivion. Viewed from that simple-minded and cold-blooded perspective, Native Americans were "classified" as politically irrelevant.[1]

That this appallingly insensitive notion has nothing in common with Marx's own thinking will be obvious to those who know his work. Marx's deep respect and admiration for the Iroquois and other Native Americans is particularly evident throughout his last major text, the *Ethnological Notebooks*, which he wrote during

1880-82. Thirty years before his "disciples" in the 1910s were dismissing Native Americans as "backward" and "headed for extinction," Marx in his *Notebooks* argued that in important respects Native American cultures were vastly superior to the societies "poisoned by the pestilential breath of civilization" [Rosemont 1989].[2]

It was his would-be followers' wrongheaded, pseudo-scientific dogmatism in such matters that had led Marx, once upon a time, to declare that he himself was no Marxist.

To put it bluntly, the prevailing attitude of the U.S. Socialist and Communist parties toward the indigenous population was one of smug condescension and callous indifference.

In this regard, as in so many others, the Wobblies were a radically oppositional force. Their attitude toward the indigenous population was clear and consistent: sympathetic interest and revolutionary solidarity, combined with fervent denunciation of the brutal exploitation and persecution of Native Americans by U.S. capital and the capitalist state. In the One Big Union, the hand of fellowship was always extended to oppressed peoples everywhere.

The Haymarket anarchists may have been an influence here. In any event, their approach to what was then often called the "Indian Question" was practically the same as the IWW's a generation later. One of the Chicago Martyrs, August Spies, had actually lived for several months with the Chippewas in Canada. And Albert R. Parsons published a passionate defense of the Indians, and a no less passionate attack on their abhorrent mistreatment by the government, in his newspaper, the *Alarm* [Roediger 1986, 101-102). The genocidal war against Native Americans is further noted in the chapter on "Capitalism: Its Development in the United States," in Parsons's posthumously published book *Anarchism: Its Philosophy and Scientific Basis* (1887)—a book read by many Wobblies.

The impact of the Industrial Workers of the World on Native Americans is hard to gauge. As a labor union made up exclusively of wage-earners, the IWW did not presume to draw up a special program for the indigenous population, many of whom eked out a living in conditions closer to serfdom than to wage-slavery. Who knows how things might have turned out had the union heeded the urging of Covington Hall and others who wanted to open the membership to include sharecroppers and small farmers? That did not happen, however. A huge majority of Wobs were happy to admit unemployed, seasonal, and part-time workers, but feared that allowing *any* non-wage-earners to join would leave the union open to the dubious maneuvering of shopkeepers, landlords, professional gamblers, and all sorts of petit-bourgeoisie. As it turned out, sharecroppers and small farmers, openly inspired by the IWW, formed several organizations of their own—the Working Class Union, the Oklahoma Renters' League, and some years later, the Southern Tenant Farmers' Union—all of which included large numbers of Native Americans.

At least one notable incidence of IWW/Native American solidarity is on record, suggesting that there may well be others that have thus far escaped the notice of historians. In the aftermath of the 1913 Wheatland hop-pickers' strike in California, when Fellow Workers Richard Ford and Herman Suhr were framed for the murders openly committed by the local lawmen, the union urged workers not to work at the Durst ranch, where the violence had occurred. According to Mortimer Downing, the Native American community in the area actively supported the Wobblies' boycott [Weintraub 1947, 282].

Of course there were also Native American Wobblies, and it is puzzling that no one has taken time out to tell their story. At least one Native American helped organize the union in 1905: the heroic Lucy Parsons, tireless cross-country revolutionary lecturer, widow of Albert Parsons, and one of the best-known individuals at the founding convention. Although generally recognized as African American, Lucy Parsons's forebears also included Mexican Indians, and she is known to have identified herself as a descendant of the Aztecs. Along with her popular lectures on Anarchism and the IWW, she also frequently lectured on the "Indian Question."

The most celebrated Native American Wobbly was the indefatigable and fearless Frank Little, of Cherokee descent—widely regarded by fellow Wobs as the union's single greatest organizer. Little liked to boast to his fellow IWWs at the union's headquarters that he was the only real Red and the only true American among them. Murdered by Anaconda Mining Company thugs in Butte in 1917, Fellow Worker Little became one of the three most renowned IWW martyrs, along with Joe Hill and Wesley Everest.

Hardly remembered at all today, but unquestionably an important historic figure, was William Stanley, one of the IWW heroes of the Mexican Revolution. In his study of the Revolution in Baja California, Mexican historian Pablo L. Martinez identified him as a "Canadian Indian" [1960, 473]. Union sources indicate that prior to his departure for Mexico Fellow Worker Stanley was primarily active in the IWW local in Holtville, California. He played a prominent role in the early phase of the Baja Revolution, and even became something of a celebrity when he and a small band of fellow workers captured a train and took the town of Los Algodones on 21 February 1911. One of the most popular officers in the Magonista revolutionary army, General Stanley was killed in the Battle of Leroy Little's Ranch on April 8 and buried in Mexicali. He was highly praised in the *Industrial Worker* and saluted as "a red revolutionist through and through" [Weintraub 1947, 54].

Missourian Frank Ellis, like Frank Little of Cherokee ancestry, had helped organize the Amalgamated Meat Cutters and Butcher Workmen in Oklahoma City, but dissatisfaction with the AFL led him to the IWW. As a Wobbly organizer he traveled all over the country promoting the One Big Union, and established an IWW branch in Omaha. For his organizing efforts Ellis was often hunted by company gunmen and vigilantes, and he used to say that he had been in just about every jail from Texas to Minnesota. He is remembered today primarily as the chief instigator of the IWW-influenced Independent Union of All Workers (IUAW) in Austin, Minnesota, and as co-organizer of the historic Hormel strike in that town in 1933 [Engelman 1974, 489-90; Rachleff, in Lynd 1996, 53].

There was also the footloose IWW organizer/soapboxer known only as Lone Wolf, described by Ralph Chaplin as "a veteran of the Wheatland strike, half-Jewish, half-American Indian [who] always wore a wide Stetson hat. . . ." [1948, 174]. In the 1920s, Lone Wolf was a key figure in building up the Chicago IWW Branch. Henry McGuckin, in his *Memoirs of a Wobbly* (1987), remembers Lone Wolf with affection and admiration [6, 55-56].

If the IWW's influence on indigenous America remains unclear, there is no doubt whatsoever that Native American influence on the IWW was large, manysided, and ongoing. Fellow Workers Lucy Parsons, Frank Little, William Stanley, Frank Ellis, and Lone Wolf were living legends in their time, and their memorable contributions to the growth of the IWW were well known throughout the union.

The Native American impact on the IWW, however, was by no means restricted to the deeds of its American Indian members. As a later-generation Wobbly, Carlos Cortez—who is himself of Native American descent—noted in the *Industrial Worker* in the

1970s, we all have "something to learn from a culture that had no jails, insane asylums, or power-mad rulers" [Bennett, in Sorrell 2002, 56]. Abundant evidence in the IWW press and in Wobbly memoirs indicates that many members, from the union's very beginnings, shared an interest in the indigenous population that went far beyond the labor movement, politics and economics. More than a few clearly found themselves "passionally attracted"—to use Fourier's genial expression—by Native American art, mythology, and ways of life.

Young Bill Haywood, for example, frequented "Indian dances" and pow-wows out West, and never forgot how thrilled he was by the "hypnotic rhythm of the drums" and the accompanying "low crooning songs" [1929, 26]. A page and a half of his autobiography reproduces a moving account of the history of white/Indian relations related to him by Ox Sam, an elderly Paiute, and Haywood added this comment:

> There was wide historical meaning in the brief story that Ox Sam
> . . . told me. It began when the earliest settlers stole Manhattan
> Island. It continued across the continent. The ruling class with
> glass beads, bad whiskey, Bibles and rifles continued the massa-
> cre from Astor Place to Astoria. [*ibid.*, 29]

Abner Woodruff's pamphlet, *Evolution of American Agriculture*, published around 1915-16 by the IWW's Agricultural Industrial Union No 400, devoted an entire chapter to "Indian Agriculture," respectfully acknowledging not only the Native Americans' communal farming, but also their many historic contributions to agricultural improvement. Woodruff concludes with a ringing denunciation of white greed and rapacity:

> The history of the white man's dealings with the red man is a
> record of his cruelty, exploitation and dirty chicanery that bour-
> geois historians try hard to conceal, its last monumental infamy
> being the destruction of the buffalo during the seventies, by
> which act the Indians of the West were forced upon the reser-
> vation. . . .[21]

Among the illustrations in the pamphlet is "Dust" Wallin's handsome engraving of a Plains Indian wearing a feathered headdress. Titled "100% American," the image reflects a not-so-subtle attempt to "set the record straight" and also to deflate the nativist

"Dust" Wallin: "100% American,"from Abner E. Woodruff,
Evolution of American Agriculture (Chicago: IWW, *c.* 1915-16)

pretensions of racist and xenophobic patriots (see above).

In the same vein is a 1920s Wobbly cartoon by class-war prisoner Eugene Barnett (see page 242): An Indian in traditional costume accuses an obese flag-waving capitalist of spoiling the country, destroying the buffalo herds, and devastating the forests. The furious, spluttering, fat capitalist replies: "If you don't like this country, why don't you go back where you came from?"

Barnett's apoplectic capitalist reminds us that the prevailing employing class attitude toward Native Americans and IWW members was much the same. As David Mitchell pointed out in *1919: Red Mirage* (1970):

> The Wobblies were, in the deepest . . . sense, subversive; living affronts to a chain-store civilization and reach-me-down values;

spiritual successors to the Red Indians as number one public enemy and conscience-botherers. [12].

What the rapacious, land-grabbing, white bourgeoisie hated most about Indians—their communism, their indifference to money, their sense of wilderness as home, their entire value-system—were of course the very qualities Wobblies most admired. After Ralph Chaplin moved to Tacoma, Washington, he rapidly deepened his knowledge and appreciation of Native American life and lore. Much of his finest poetry was inspired by the history and legends of the tribes of the Northwest. Although this part of his work never reached a wide public, it was highly esteemed within the IWW. In his *Only the Drums Remembered* (1960), the Nisqually chief Leschi addresses the white man:

> *The Indian's wealth is in his Indian heart,*
> *Not in the Bank or on the auction mart. . . .*
> *You conquerors who cannot conquer Hate*
> *When will you learn that all men soon or late*
> *Need more than guns and gold to make them great*
> *Or spare them from a conquered people's fate?*

And Joe Hill? Here we draw a complete blank. We know as much about Hill's views on the "Indian Question" as we know about his opinion of Beethoven's *Fifth*, or *Don Quixote*, or the poetry of Li Po: that is, nothing at all. His only mention of Native Americans is a passing reference in his article "The People," published in the *Industrial Worker* in 1913, mentioning an "Indian regiment" during the period in which he and other IWW members took part in the Mexican Revolution in Baja California. Hill must have met many Indians during that period, but his few surviving letters do not mention them.

In the biographical introduction to his play, *The Man Who Never Died*, Barrie Stavis refers to a cartoon by Hill featuring "a cowboy on a humorous horse, lariat a-flying, chasing an Indian." It was drawn shortly before his execution on a copy of a short poem, "Bronco Buster Flynn," that Hill wrote for Elizabeth Gurley Flynn's young son [80]. This cartoon has evidently never been reproduced, and it has proved impossible to locate the original or even a photocopy. Stavis's description suggests that it portrays a comic stereotype. In the absence of the drawing itself, further commentary is superfluous.

One may fairly ask: How much did Wobblies in the years 1905-30 really know about Native American society and culture? I offer an admittedly tentative answer: They did not know enough —nor were they numerous enough—to be of much help to Native Americans in their struggles against the U.S. government and the ruthless oil, mining, lumber, and fishing industries. Almost certainly, however, they knew more about Indians and Indian ways of life than the members of any AFL union, more than the members of the Socialist and Communist parties, and *infinitely* more than the spiteful bureaucrats in charge of the U.S. Bureau of Indian Affairs in Washington, D.C.

Eugene Barnett: A cartoon from his book,
Nature's Woodland Bowers in Picture and Verse
(Walla Walla, 1927).

Wobblies were avid readers. Excellent books on Native American culture were readily available in those years—Frank Hamilton Cushing's *Zuni Folk Tales*, Natalie Curtis's *Book of the Indian*, George W. Cronyn's *Path on the Rainbow* (an anthology of Native American poetry)—and some IWW members probably read them. It can be said with certainty that many read Lewis Henry Morgan's *Ancient Society* (published in a low-priced edition by Charles H. Kerr and accessible at every IWW hall), which includes a fascinating 100-page section on the Iroquois, whom Morgan particularly admired (he was, in fact, initiated into the Seneca Hawk clan). I recall old Wobblies in Chicago in the 1960s insisting that whatever there was of democracy in the U.S. derived much less from European traditions than from the Iroquois.

The overall effect of the IWWs "Organization, Education, Emancipation" in the Native American community was undoubtedly greater than has been recognized by historians, but still much smaller than its impact on European immigrants and African Americans. The IWW never pretended to have all the solutions to all problems, and they certainly didn't claim to have all the answers to the "Indian Question." But they knew—as Bill Haywood expressed it in his introduction to the aforementioned Abner Woodruff pamphlet—that *no* solution to *any* major social problem was possible "until the Earth is redeemed from private ownership and the spirit of cooperation prevails. Use and occupancy will then be the only title to land and its products" [9].

That was the IWW way to a better world. Isn't it also the Native American way?

---

1. Pittenger 1993 surveys Socialist Party views on the "Indian Question." I have not found a comparable survey of Communist views.

2. A compilation of heavily annotated excerpts from the works of Lewis Henry Morgan, Henry Sumner Maine and other writers on "primitive" societies, Marx's *Ethnological Notebooks* were deliberately ignored—suppressed would not be too strong a word—by the international "Marxist" Establishment for ninety years. Published for the first time in 1972, it has yet to appear in a low-priced paperback edition. Mainstream "Marxists" continue to ignore it, just as they continue to ignore the struggles of Native Americans. See my "Karl Marx and the Iroquois" (Rosemont 1989).

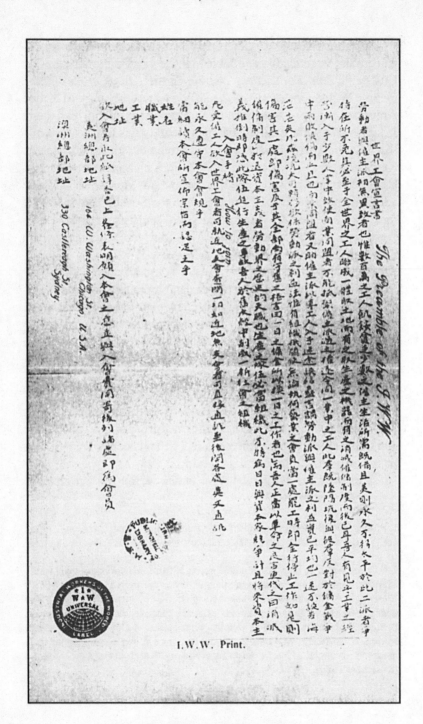

The IWW Preamble in Chinese

4. THE IMPORTANCE OF CHINESE COOKING IN THE HISTORY OF THE IWW

A word to those of you passing by—
Try coming to Cold Mountain sometime!
—Han-shan—

T o ascertain Hill's attitude toward particular social questions can be a daunting task, for we have so little to go on: his songs and cartoons, a handful of letters, a very few other scattered writings, occasional comments by relatives and friends. And that's it. Sometimes, however, the tiniest scrap of information can bring an unexpected illumination.

Strange as it may seem, for example, Hill's fondness for Chinese food, his skill in the use of chopsticks, and the fact that he was "well liked for . . . his marvelous Oriental cookery," as Wallace Stegner rather mockingly conceded, add a touch of concreteness to our otherwise hazy knowledge of his race politics [Chaplin 1923, 24; Stegner 1948, 21]. What makes such seemingly trivial details important—and even subversive—is the fact that the U.S. in the 1910s was rife with anti-Chinese "Yellow Peril" hysteria. Hatred of the Chinese was fomented not only by the usual culprits—employers, cops, churches, and the bourgeois press—but also by a large part of what passed for the "labor movement": *i.e.*, the American Federation of Labor. In the western states, and above all in California—where Hill spent at least four and probably more of his U.S. years—AFL unions carried on a massive and vicious anti-Chinese propaganda campaign. That this was related to the national AFL's overall commitment to white supremacy was spelled out in a characteristic but too-little-known statement by AFL President Samuel Gompers, rhetorically posing the question of how

> to prevent the Chinese, the Negritos, and the Malays coming to our country? How can we prevent the Chinese coolies . . . from swarm[ing] into the United States and engulf[ing] our people and our civilization? . . . Can we hope to close the flood-gates of immigration from the hordes of Chinese and the semi-savage races . . . [Lee 1999, 110-111]

There can be no doubt that AFL "Yellow Peril" propaganda

helped provoke some of the many lynchings of Chinese workers that occurred in those years.

A large part of this anti-Chinese propaganda consisted of racist caricatures in which everything Chinese was made to appear villainous, conspiratorial, evil, despicable, and dirty. "Chop suey" and eating with chopsticks were held up for especially scornful ridicule. Meanwhile, adding injury to insult, AFL unions vigorously promoted a boycott of Chinese restaurants.

In such a hate-filled climate, proclaiming one's passion for Chinese food and flaunting one's knack for using chopsticks would qualify as acts of dissidence and defiance. I am not trying to make too much of too little; I realize that Hill's simple gestures cannot be considered acts of great courage or revolutionary import, and do not tell us very much about his thinking. Nonetheless, such small, personal, "non-political" signs of nonconformism should not be altogether dismissed; surely they count for something in the broader scheme of things. In his own quiet way Joe Hill let it be known that he was friendly to the Chinese and therefore, at least to that extent, a foe of white supremacy. Moreover, the fact that his "Chinese dishes" were "well liked" suggests that his cookery was more than a personal matter, that it involved a certain amount of advocacy, and that his pro-Chinese sentiments were shared by his San Pedro friends and fellow workers, as one would expect of internationalist-minded members of the IWW.

Indeed, Hill's Far Eastern culinary preference seems to have been widely shared throughout the union. The evidence may not be overwhelming, but several sources suggest that a taste for Chinese food was something of a Wobbly trend during the 1910s and '20s.

In her autobiography, Elizabeth Gurley Flynn recalled going with strike organizers to a Chinese restaurant in Lowell, Massachusetts, in March or April 1912:

> It was decorated with new flags which we had never seen before, and signs in Chinese. It looked like a very special occasion. The smiling Chinese workers there told us that the Republic of China had been proclaimed by Dr Sun Yat-sen. . . . We rejoiced with them though we little knew the full significance of what was stirring in far-off Asia. But we were for freedom—everywhere—and their happiness looked good to us. They liked the IWW too. [1973 , 145]

Verily, Chinese workers were stirring, not only in far-off Asia

246

but also in the U.S. and Canada, especially in the northwest, and their activities were reported in the U.S. revolutionary press. To cite just a few typical examples: The December 1912 issue of the *International Socialist Review* reported that a Chinese-language "Socialist and Industrial-Unionist movement" in Vancouver was holding meetings at the local IWW hall [431]. And in March 1913, reporting on IWW activity in Hawaii in 1913, an *Industrial Worker* correspondent remarked with pleasure that "the Chinese are great advocates and users of sabotage" [6 Mar 1913].

That same year, as Covington Hall noted in his *Labor Struggles in the Deep South*, Chinese workers attended an IWW Marine Transport Workers Industrial Union 510 street meeting in New Orleans. Whether any of them took out red cards is not known, but according to Hall, "it is certain that they acted like 'inside Union men'" [1999, 101-2].

Recounting his own experience in the Wobblies just after World War I, Walter Rogers noted that in western Canada, *circa* 1920, when persecution of hoboes by "Mounties" was such that "few dared make jungle fires," IWW members chose to meet in Chinese restaurants instead. As Rogers tells it, several of these restaurants "served as [a kind of] information bureau for workers from all over the world. Great discussions on national and international affairs took place in them" [1945, 92].

In Mexicali, Mexico, during the last days of the 1911 Revolution in Baja California, in the wake of massive military defeat and under threat of further attack by Maderist troops (supported, Madero hoped, by the U.S. army), the town's hard-hit Magonista/IWW revolutionary forces formally disbanded. Before leaving, however, the thirty-five IWWs among them "ate their first full meal in several days at a Chinese restaurant in Calexico" [Blaisdell 1962, 176].

The files of the U.S. Bureau of Information—forerunner of the FBI—include an interesting report on IWW involvement in a Chinese restaurant workers' strike in New York shortly after the end of the First World War. In solidarity with the striking Chinese waiters, and in protest against the white scabs who had taken their places, a group of Wobblies entered the restaurant, ordered and ate their food, and then tossed a few sulfur "stink bombs" around the room and left without paying [Kornweibel 1998, 61].

In an unpublished autobiography, IWW organizer Thomas Bogard records that a few years later, while organizing for the

IWW's Agricultural Workers Industrial Union 110 in the wheat harvest, he and a friend rode a freight to Minot, North Dakota. "Getting up next morning," he wrote, "we went down and across the . . . tracks and had breakfast in the Chinese restaurant" [Bogard, 10].

Bill Haywood, in a statement on the IWW and race written for Claude McKay's book, *The Negroes in America* (1923), recalled a crucial episode in the prehistory of the Western Federation of Miners:

one of the most triumphant strikes which we carried out in the West was a strike in Rock Springs, Wyoming, in the 1880s, where more than half the workers were Chinese. [29]

He went on to emphasize that it was in fact the Chinese who proved to be the determining factor in the workers' victory. Later, in his 1929 autobiography—on the first page of the very chapter in which he describes how he became a radical and joined the WFM—Haywood considered it relevant to note that the first thing he did when he arrived in Silver City, Idaho (where that radical-ization occurred) was to go to a Chinese restaurant [56].

Meanwhile, in Chicago, the celebrated Wobbly soapboxer and Dil Pickle Club poet Eddie Guilbert was well known as a habitué of Chinese restaurants, to which he often brought the pet lion he called "Georges Sorel." In his autobiography, Kenneth Rexroth writes that Guilbert would always ask the "fellow worker waiter" to bring a platter of three raw T-bone steaks for the lion [140].[1]

Young Rexroth probably joined Guilbert for some of those dinners, and/or went to Chinatown to eat with other Wobblies. His long poem, "The Dragon and the Unicorn," begun in the 1940s but not published until 1952, invokes those 1920s nights:

> *Chicago. . . .*
> *Cold wind, deepening dark, miles*
> *Of railroad lights, 22nd*
> *And Wentworth. The old Chinese*
> *Restaurants now tourist joints.*
> *Gooey Sam[2] where we once roared*
> *And taught the waiters to say*
> *Fellow Worker. . . .*

Act II, Scene II of Upton Sinclair's IWW play, *Singing Jail-*

birds (1924) is set in "A Restaurant for Workingmen." The curtain opens, showing three men—Wobblies—seated at the counter. As the reader will surely have guessed by now, this is in fact a Chinese restaurant, and the Chinese proprietor/cook is an IWW sympathizer. When yet another Fellow Worker enters, the Wobs shout "Welcome to Chinatown!" A moment later, all of them, including the Chinese cook, start dancing and singing "Halleluhah, I'm a Bum" [36-39].

From coast to coast, and north and south of the U.S. border, IWWs evidently enjoyed hanging out in Chinese restaurants, or —like Joe Hill—cooking their own Chinese meals. I have no doubt that many Wobs also ate at Italian, Greek, Russian, Hungarian, Scottish, German, Indian, Swedish, Finnish, Armenian, and other restaurants, but they don't seem to have mentioned it much in their writings.

The question arises: Where and how did Hill learn the art of Chinese cooking? Hawaii and Canada, where large numbers of Chinese were active in the IWW, seem the most likely places, but beyond that, the field of speculation is endless.

The references to Canada in the preceding paragraphs bring to mind the legendary Chinese origin of the term "Wobbly," first recorded in 1914, and recapitulated by IWW editor and publicist Mortimer Downing in a letter to *The Nation* in 1923:

> Up in Vancouver, in 1911, we had a number of Chinese members, and one restaurant keeper would trust any member for meals. He could not pronounce the letter "w" but called it "wobble," and would ask: "You I Wobble Wobble?" and when the card was shown credit was unlimited. Thereafter the laughing term among us was "I Wobbly Wobbly". . . . [5 Sept]

Although this origin tale has found little acceptance from etymologists, folklorists, or historians, a good number of old Wobblies, including Carl Keller and Fred Thompson—as I can attest from my own experience—enjoyed telling it to youthful inquirers, and especially to young members of the union. For these old-timers, the legend clearly embodied two important characteristics of the IWW: multi-racial class solidarity, and humor. As Fellow Worker Downing commented in the above-quoted letter:

> Considering its origin, I rather like the nickname. It hints of a fine, practical internationalism, a human brotherhood based on

a community of interests and of understanding. [*ibid.*]

Interestingly, the strong anti-racist and internationalist implications of the Chinese cook legend were emphasized as early as 1914 by a California newspaper reporter, John D. Barry:

> If the name "Wobblies," now established in the slang of the IWW and pretty certain to make its way into our everyday vocabulary, could be definitely traced to the Chinese it would be seen to be related to the most attractive of the organization's qualities. The members cultivate a spirit that strives for a solidarity reaching even beyond the prejudices of race. In this regard it is remarkable. Only too often in the past has labor, crushed by capital, shown a similar cruelty to the labor of an alien people and a bitter and determined hostility. [Green 1993, 123-24]

In his splendid essay, "The Name *Wobbly* Holds Steady," Archie Green concludes that Mortimer Downing and Fred Thompson, as "IWW stalwarts,"

> helped circulate the Chinese cook anecdote out of their sense of justice rather than with a real belief that they actually might have established its historicity or linguistic veracity. [*ibid.*, 124]

Old-time Wobs, in other words, freely and joyfully passed on the legend to young recruits, not as "history," but as a kind of "tall tale" with a distinct anti-racist and international solidarity moral.

Despite the efforts of several generations of scholars to "disprove" or otherwise disqualify the legend, it retains a powerful symbolic resonance. As Archie Green has sagely observed:

> We shall find no evidence for the Chinese lingual tale, nor shall scholars drive it out of circulation. It remains too vivid a story, has circulated widely, and carries "the truth" of folktales long believed. [*ibid.*]

I would argue that the original success of the legend within the IWW reflected its challenge to the "Yellow Peril" hysteria of the time. I do not think it is purely accidental that the legendary originator of the IWW's favorite name for themselves is Chinese. Indeed, that a Chinese *cook* was selected for the honor—during the very period in which the AFL was actively urging its members and supporters to stay away from Chinese restaurants—seems to me to be strong evidence of the soundness of the IWW's revolutionary reflexes.

In the face of widespread anti-Chinese agitation, the IWW defended a thoroughgoing proletarian internationalism, denounced proponents of "Chinese exclusion," warmly welcomed Chinese workers into the union, and even held meetings in Chinese restaurants. Yet another indication of their complete rejection of white-supremacist "Yellow Peril" mythology was their promotion of a Chinese cook to a high place in the union's own revolutionary mythology.

Historian Robert Lee, in his excellent study, *Orientals* (1999), emphasizes that anti-Chinese racism was directly related to the consolidation of the American bourgeois family and, more generally, the consolidation of the whole system of capitalism in the West. Hoboes, and especially Wobblies, were not only alien to those repressive consolidations—they actively struggled *against* them.

The strongest evidence of Hill's solidarity with the Chinese thus lies above all in the fact that he was—as even his severest detractors have had to admit—a resolute, devoted, true-blue Wobbly.

---

1. Rexroth spells it Gilbert, but in the Jack Jones papers and Dil Pickle Club archives at The Newberry Library in Chicago, the name is more frequently spelled Guilbert.

2. Relying on memory, Rexroth spelled the name of this restaurant phonetically. No longer extant, Guey Sam's at 2205 South Wentworth Avenue was for many years one of the most popular eating-places in Chicago's Chinatown.

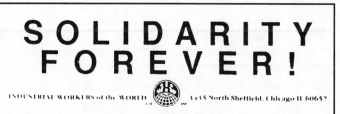

IWW bumper-sticker (1980s)

5. IN THE ABOLITIONIST TRADITION: WOBBLIES AGAINST WHITENESS

Poets who write of the "White Burden." Trash!
The White Man's Burden, Lord, is the burden of his cash!
—Wilfred Scawen Blunt—

B A. Botkin, archivist of American Folk Song at the Library of Congress, published an almost-1000-page *Treasury of American Folklore* in 1944. A wartime production, the book patriotically put the accent on the myth of U.S. "democracy" and "equality." With great embarrassment, however, Botkin had to concede "the essential viciousness of many of [America's] folk heroes, stories, and expressions, especially in their treatment of minorities—Indians, Negroes, Mexicans, Chinese, etc." [xxvi].

As an authentic American folk hero, Joe Hill is distinctive in many ways, and his IWW rejection of white supremacy tops the list.

A peculiar but suggestive phrase, used by the Salt Lake City police during their "interrogation" of Hill, helps us understand his and his fellow Wobblies' relation to that bizarre configuration of self-deception, hypocrisy, and terror that James Baldwin referred to as the "white problem."

On his first day in the Salt Lake County Jail, the police took Hill to an isolated cell upstairs, told him he had been charged with murder, and demanded that he confess. As Hill wrote later in his letter to the Utah Board of Pardons, "I did not know anything about any murder, and I told them so." Weak from loss of blood, Hill asked to be taken to a hospital. The police, however, continued to press him for a confession, assuring him that if he complied, they would take him to a hospital and *"treat him white"* [*Letters*, 65; italics added, FR].

When Hill again insisted that he knew "nothing about any murder," the police called him a liar, and from that point on he refused to answer their questions. It is reasonable to assume that he was treated the way poor and seemingly friendless "suspects" are usually treated by police in such circumstances: *i.e.*, that he was beaten and perhaps tortured by his "interrogators." In any case, as Hill put it, he "grew weaker and weaker," and for several days he was "hovering between life and death" [*Letters*, 64-65].

Subjected to such brutal interrogations, many innocent people have confessed to crimes they did not commit. Hill, however, absolutely refused to be a party to such flimflammery, even to save his life. And in revenge for his refusal to lie at their request, the police and the court in their turn refused to "treat him white."

Here, too, Joe Hill exemplified the Wobbly spirit. He identified himself as a Swede, worker, wage-slave, and above all as an IWW. Nowhere in his letters, songs, or poems—or in reminiscences of him by friends, or anecdotes about him by acquaintances—is there any indication that Hill ever thought of himself as "white."

Although Wobbly views of "whiteness" varied widely, the union as a whole vehemently rejected America's dominant "white mystique," and more or less systematically violated the rules of what a later generation of U.S. radicals called the "white power structure." Their strongly felt continuity with the old Abolitionist movement, their loudly proclaimed scorn for the "whites only" AFL unions and railroad brotherhoods, and of course their efforts to organize African Americans, Chinese, Japanese, Native Americans, Hawaiians, Mexicans and other people of color automatically situated the Wobblies outside the conformist parameters of "white society" and its weird racial mythologies. As outspoken outsiders and revolutionists with "nothing to lose but their chains," many Wobs were also articulate critics of whiteness and its discontents. T-Bone Slim, who could be considered Hill's heir as the union's leading writer and symbolic figure, zeroed in on the question with characteristically marvelous bluntness:

> Let us not lose sight of the fact that we are at grips with "the noble white man" that made agony both ingenious and scientific, and relegated life's possibilities to the select few and life's "garbage" to the many. [1992, 156]

To what extent Hill shared (or contributed to) this Wobbly critique of whiteness is not known, but we do know that he shared the union's identification with the Abolitionists. In one of his letters Hill compared the IWW organizer of his day with old John Brown. For each, the task was to emancipate the slaves, and more particularly, to inspire and help the slaves to emancipate themselves [*Letters*, 27].

As self-conscious successors of John Brown and the Abolitionist tradition, Hill and other Wobblies drew heavily on their forerunners' central themes and vocabulary. The third sentence of Bill

Haywood's opening address to the IWW's founding convention
defined the purpose of the new union as "the emancipation of the
working class from the slave bondage of capitalism" [*Proceedings*
1905, 1]. The words "slaves" and "slavery" figure in no less than
nine of Hill's songs:

> *Come slaves from every land.*
> *Come join this fighting band.*
>   ["The Girl Question"]

> *Arise, ye slaves of every nation,*
> *In One Union Grand.*
>   ["Workers of the World, Awaken!"]

> *For the workers we'll make upon this Earth a paradise*
> *When the slaves get wise and organize.*
>   ["What We Want"]

Appeals to "break your chains" and to "fight for your emancipation," along with derisive references to "the greedy master
class," also appear in many of Hill's lyrics.

Such Abolitionist-inspired imagery runs through the entire
Little Red Song Book. George G. Allen's "One Big Industrial
Union" (to the tune of "Marching Through Georgia") opens with
these lines:

> *Bring the good old red book, boys, we'll sing another song.*
> *Sing it to the wage slave who has not yet joined the throng.*

Here is the chorus of Richard Brazier's "The Workers of the World
are Now Awaking":

> *It's a union for true Liberty.*
> *It's a union for you and for me;*
> *It's the workers' own choice,*
> *It's for girls and boys,*
> *Who want freedom from wage slavery.*

And the chorus of E. S. Nelson's "Workingmen, Unite!" (to the
tune of "Red Wing"):

> *Shall we still be slaves and work for wages?*

It is outrageous—has been for ages;
This earth by right belongs to toilers,
And not to spoilers of liberty.

Wobbly-style Abolitionism was not only evident in the *Song Book*, but also in IWW newspapers, leaflets, poems, pamphlets, cartoons, stickers, campfire stories, and soapbox speeches. One of the most quoted of all Wobbly "one-liners" is Bill Haywood's aphorism: "For every dollar the parasite has and didn't work for, there's a slave who worked for a dollar he didn't get." The union's solidarity with Abolitionism was also affirmed in IWW trials. At the trial of Joseph Ettor and Arturo Giovannitti in connection with the most celebrated of all IWW strikes—the Lawrence textile strike of 1912—the defendants proudly invoked the names and revolutionary traditions of Wendell Phillips, William Lloyd Garrison, and John Brown [Ebert 1913, 135-136, 143]. Tributes to Abolitionists appear in poems by Giovannitti, Covington Hall, and other IWW poets. A book-length Wobbly history of anti-labor violence in the U.S. saluted the memory of Elijah Lovejoy, "the printer-abolitionist . . . murdered by a pro-slavery mob" in Alton, Illinois in November 1837 [Delaney and Rice, 1927, 52]. Justus Ebert, in the closing pages of his book, *The IWW in Theory and Practice*—one of the most frequently reprinted of all the union's publications—hails Lovejoy, Garrison, and John Brown for their inspiring idealism and revolutionary relevance:

Lovejoy's press was thrown into the river and he himself was afterward murdered. William Lloyd Garrison was dragged through Boston streets with a rope around his neck. John Brown was hanged. Yet his soul marches on, not only to the abolition of chattel slavery, but of wage-slavery, too; John Brown still lives, reincarnated in the abolitionists of modern times. Dreamers! Yes! . . . So were the abolitionists of chattel slavery. [n.d., 122]

It was not for nothing that Carl Sandburg once remarked that he "knew the Abolitionists better for having known the IWW" [Mitgang 1968, 94].

The Wobblies' songs and speeches about slaves uniting and rising up to vanquish their oppressors, about abolition and emancipation, and about creating an earthly paradise free of exploiting parasites, were not music to the ears of the "greedy master class." In the 1910s and early '20s, when the Civil War and Reconstruction were still vivid in the popular memory, the new "master class" (which, like the pre-Civil-War slave-owners, also happened to be white) recognized the winged words of the Wobblies as dangerous tocsins of revolt and revolution. Joe Hill and his friends may not have known much about African American history and culture, but their Abolitionist inclinations—and their unequivocal emphasis on organizing *all* workers, regardless of color—made their basic position stand out clearly. To the sons of private property and privilege, the IWW signified not only class war—war against capitalism—but also war against white supremacy.

In Hill's letter to the Board of Pardons, he put the cops' expression, "treat [you] white," in quotation marks, calling attention to that highly revealing phrase which he, as an immigrant who spent most of his time with fellow Wobblies, had probably never heard before. Those ironic quotation marks, his adamant refusal to comply with the cops' sleazy proposal, and his evident admiration for John Brown seem to me to confirm that Hill, like so many of his fellow workers, wanted no part of the "white game."

Indeed, for many Wobs, refusing to be "white" seems to have been practically synonymous with refusing to be a scissorbill. By upholding the great proletarian battle-cries—"Workers of the World, Unite!" and their own "An Injury to One Is an Injury to All!"—Wobblies were also refusing to think and act "white." And America's rulers, for their part, refused to "treat them white." Indeed, they treated Joe Hill the same way they treated John Brown. The latter, of course, had organized an armed insurrection, while Hill simply wrote songs for the IWW—but in both cases the slave power clearly felt threatened and chose to exact the maximum revenge.

In his statement written for Claude McKay's 1923 book, *The Negroes in America*, Bill Haywood wrote that the IWW "were workers 'outside the law,' and therefore attracted the sympathy of Negroes who represent a *race* 'outside the law'" [McKay 1979]. Certainly, in the history of the U.S. labor movement, no group was treated "less white" than the IWW. Wobs were arrested *en masse*, blacklisted, fire-hosed, beaten, framed up, kidnaped, deported, jailed by the thousands (and given long sentences), tarred and feathered, branded, tortured, murdered, and lynched. Their publications—as well as those of their fellow workers at the Charles H. Kerr Company—were repeatedly suppressed, denied access to the mail, seized and destroyed. Many IWW meeting-places, libraries, and bookstores were devastated by arson or wrecked by flag-waving company thugs.

The McCarthyite witch-hunt persecution of Communists and other leftists during the Cold War 1950s was a disgusting abomination, but it was nothing compared to the reign of blood and horror unleashed against the Wobblies some thirty-five years earlier.

In the face of that unprecedented government and hoodlum terror, many members of the IWW dropped out, abandoned the struggle, changed their names, fled to other lands. Some became alcoholics, or religious, or bureaucrats in AFL unions. A few went mad. But many held out and continued the fight against wage-slavery. One of them was Henry Pfaff.

"Born of footloose, semi-nomadic, nonconformist early proletarian stock," Pfaff came to the U.S. from Hungary in 1911 and lined up in the IWW during the Akron rubber strike two years later at the age of sixteen [Pfaff 1983, back cover; Bird *et al.*, 1985, 88]. In his eighties, still an active member, he told an interviewer that "the IWW saved my life. If I hadn't been swept up into it . . . I would have probably worked myself to death like a lot of others . . . " [Bird *et al.*, 92]. Inspired by the IWW vision of "how we could change America —from a profit-motivated society to a co-operative society," Fellow Worker Pfaff proclaimed himself The Opsimath and took up the writing of verses which were not, he insisted, intended as poetry, but rather as "a condensed and more agreeable method of presenting some random thoughts" from his "long and hectic life" [Pfaff 1983, Foreword]. And he added: "To entertain is not my desire, but to set seething minds on fire!"

One of his provocative verses sums up his own Wobbly view of being "white":

Call me red or call me brown.
Call me black or call me pink.
Call me yellow if you like;
But please, don't call me white.

AEROGRAM:—"HELP! HELP! WE'VE HIT SOMETHING."

Joe Hill: "Aerogram—'Help! Help! We've Hit Something.'"
Cartoon from *IWW Songs* (Los Angeles edition, 1912).
This appears to be Hill's first published cartoon.

6. RACE, CLASS, AND THE *TITANIC*: LOOKING AT A JOE HILL CARTOON

*What I want to do [is] to tear a hole in the net
in which humankind has caught itself, and not by preaching,
but by escaping from the meshes myself.*
—**Gustav Meyrink**—

Many IWW cartoons urged inter-racial workers' solidarity. May Day cartoons, for example, often showed the workers of the world united at last, and hence victorious in the global struggle against Capital. Others depicted workers of different colors and ethnicities winning strikes by sticking together. Still other cartoons were directed against white supremacy. Quite a few attacked the Ku Klux Klan, the American Legion, and other pious demagogues—politicians and preachers—whose white-supremacist ravings regularly included fulminations against the IWW. Ernest Riebe in his "Mr Block" strip, E. F. Doree, Ern Hansen, James Lynch, and William Henkelman are among the many artists who contributed anti-racist cartoons to the IWW press during its first three decades.

None of Joe Hill's cartoons take up race issues directly. Apart from the two saboteurs in his submarine cartoon (see page 166), whose features are concealed by their deep-sea diving-suits, all the people in his drawings appear to be white. One cartoon with possible racial overtones appeared in the Los Angeles edition of the *Little Red Song Book* in 1912, when Hill was working long-shore in the Los Angeles port of San Pedro (see facing page).

This cartoon is clearly based on the sinking of the *Titanic* earlier that same year. Everyone knows that the huge and "unsink-able" luxury liner had on board some of the wealthiest people in the world, but less well known (outside the Black community) is the fact that the ship's owners enforced a "whites only" passenger policy.[1] Inevitably, therefore, the disaster—major headline news for weeks—quickly became the target of grim jesting on the part of poor Blacks, and probably of other racial minorities, who saw it as a blow to the arrogance of white supremacy.

In a brilliant essay from 1968, titled "And Shine Swam On," Black poet Larry Neal quotes what he calls an African American urban "toast" called "The *Titanic*," which tells of a Black man who, swimming for his life, declines to save the ship's captain or his lily-white daughter, despite their offer of large rewards. The "toast," says Neal, "is part of the private mythology of Black America" [1989, 7]. Etheridge Knight's poem, "Dark Prophecy: I Sing of Shine," tells another version of the tale [1986, 49]. Such jokes about major news stories, especially when they involve celebrities, have a way of evolving into rumors, and often become part of folklore.[2] According to one rumor, heavyweight boxing champion Jack Johnson had applied for passage on the *Titanic* and was refused because of his race. The rumor appears to be without foundation, but it found its way into one of Leadbelly's blues:

> *Jack Johnson wanted to get on board;*
> *Captain Smith hollered, "I ain't haulin' no coal."*
> *Cryin', "Fare thee, Titanic, fare thee well!"*

> *Black man oughta shout for joy,*
> *Never lost a girl or either a boy.*
> *Cryin', "Fare thee, Titanic, fare thee well!"*
> [Roberts 1985, 134]

When Johnson was challenged by "Firefighter" Flynn—latest in a series of "Great White Hopes"—a writer for the Chicago *Defender*, the city's premier African American newspaper, ridiculed the contender as "the pugilistic *Titanic* of the Caucasian race" [*ibid.*].

(In the ninth round a state official stopped what he called John-son's "slaughter" of the hapless Flynn.)

Can Hill's cartoon be considered an example of what Marcus Garvey once called "thinking sympathetically Black"? [Clarke 1974, 314]. This seems plausible, especially in view of the fact that the IWW was engaged in major organizing efforts among Black workers at the time. But it is impossible to say yes with any certainty, for there is too much involved here that we don't know. However, the fact that a Wobbly cartoon should have such strong parallels with an unusual bit of African American folklore is striking indeed. At the very least, Hill's cartoon suggests that *Titanic* jokes entered the mythology of the downtrodden of all colors.

The ship in Hill's cartoon is labeled "M & M," short for the Merchants and Manufacturers' Association, a big Los Angeles businessmen's *bund*, organized to keep the public pacified and above all to keep labor unions out. Los Angeles in 1912 was a boomtown oozing with real-estate speculators, salesmen, devel-opers, boosters, schemers, con-men and fatuous frauds of all sorts, all under the ultra-authoritarian thumb of General Harrison Gray Otis, a flatulent multi-millionaire thug who also happened to be editor and publisher of the *Los Angeles Times*.

No run-of-the-mill labor hater, General Otis was an all-out stop-at-nothing union-buster. In editorials he referred to union workers variously as "rowdies," "trouble-breeders," and "scum." The M & M was Otis's creature, or rather his favorite instrument of war. According to journalist Louis Adamic,

> merchants, manufacturers and contractors were compelled to join it if they wanted to operate in Los Angeles. The greatest sin that a Los Angeles employer could commit was to hire a union worker. [1934, 204]

It was Otis who, as Mike Davis noted in his *City of Quartz* (1992), "militarized industrial relations in Los Angeles. Existing unions were locked out, picketing was virtually outlawed, and dissidents were terrorized" [25]. In a city already crawling with "private eyes," Otis had no difficulty maintaining a small army of snoopers, sluggers and "enforcers" to run "his" city just the way he wanted it. Largely thanks to the General, L.A. boasted some of the lowest wages and longest working hours in the country, and its repression of workers' efforts to organize was among the bloodiest and goriest in U.S. history. Indeed, the city's reputation for massive ruling-class violence against the working class, and especially against workingclass racial minorities, has persisted to our own time, as evidenced by the repression of the great Rebellion of 1992. It is no surprise that the National Association of Manufacturers—which in the 1930s gushingly admired the "labor policies" of Hitler's Germany and Hirohito's Japan—regarded Otis's Open Shop Los Angeles as a model worthy of emulation throughout the country.

Otis, whose militaristic mind-set amounted to an obsession—his home was an imitation medieval fortress, and he even had a small cannon mounted on the hood of his car—evidently perceived something of himself in Nietzsche's notion of the "Superman," which he probably learned about from one of his employees, Willard Huntington Wright, drug addict and racist, later well-known as the detective-story writer S. S. Van Dine [Loughery 1992]. In his more democratic moments, however, Otis seemed to enjoy the company of other wealthy and hate-filled crackpots, providing of course that their delusions of grandeur were compatible with his own. Among the ardent supporters of the M & M's Open Shop drive were numerous proponents of Anglo-Saxon racial purity, a provincial lily-white "Americanism," and other bizarre racist fantasies. (In 1907 the president of the University of Southern California published a book predicting that Los Angeles would become the world capital of white Aryan supremacy) [Davis 1992, 28].

Otis did not introduce white supremacy into Los Angeles—the city had long been notorious for lynchings and other forms of racist terror. But the "Generalissimo of the Open Shop" strengthened these white supremacist and other protofascist tendencies immeasurably. The M & M and the whole Otis oligarchy provided not only a "climate" in which the most reactionary elements in society were able to pullulate and prosper, but also a powerful social, political, and even military apparatus to shield those elements—to the point of letting them get away with murder.

After the General's death in 1917, his successor Harry Chandler continued the Otis traditions. As muckraker George Seldes summed it up in his excellent *Lords of the Press* in 1938:

Throughout the valleys where Chandler and his associates own and control California crops there is terrorism and the nearest approach to fascism in the United States. . . . There is child labor and even peonage. There is starvation in the midst of plenty. There is vigilantism, tarring and feathering, bloodshed and violence. There is also big money for the Chandler crowd. [75]

Such was life in sunny California under the dictatorship of the editor and publisher of the *L.A. Times*. (Elsewhere Seldes noted that Chandler was also, though perhaps less ostentatiously than Henry Ford and William Randolph Hearst, a supporter of Nazism.)

Wobbly poet Sam Slingsby published a sketch of Los Angeles, "In Movie Town," in the *One Big Union Monthly*:

> *In Movie Town the hokum's great,*
> *In Movie Town.*
> *In Movie Land, the hook holds bait,*
> *In Movie Land.*
> *The rents are high, they reach the sky,*
> *It costs to live, it busts to die*
> *In Movie Town.*
>
> *In Bunko Town the rebs are rare. . . .*
> *In Bunko Town they sell the air. . . .*
> *Don't whisper here of poetry,*
> *The arts are deader 'n hell, you see. . . .*
> *They act and strut, and blow and brag,*
> *Their paunches bulge, their eyelids sag. . . .*
> *They gorge and stink, they gulp and drink,*
> *They haste towards death, nor stop to think. . . .*
> [Dec 1920, 46]

As a young Louis Adamic learned from his IWW friends in San Pedro, L.A. under Otis and Chandler was "a nut town . . . a scab town . . . full of scissorbills [and] run by rich bastards who hate the Wobblies like poison" [1932, 210].

And this brings us back to Joe Hill, for as Mike Davis pointed out in his *City of Quartz*,

> Only IWW seamen and longshoremen defied the Merchants and Manufacturers Association's crusade to make the open shop complete. [1992, 31]

Fellow Worker Hill, a seaman and longshoreman active in Los Angeles, clearly took part in the struggle against Otis's bloody crusade, and that cartoon in the 1912 *Song Book* is one manifestation of his defiance. In the 1910s, moreover, Hill was also intimately involved in the affairs of the L.A.-based anarchist Mexican Liberal Party—the Magonistas, whose membership consisted mostly of Mexicans and Chicanos, but also included a good number of African Americans and Native Americans. His opposition to Otis and the M & M, therefore, was total—and wholeheartedly in the Wobbly spirit of "All for One and One for All!"

Viewed from that angle, it does not seem too far-fetched to suggest that Hill's 1912 cartoon was directed not only against the pretensions of the "Master Class," but also against the pretensions of the "Master Race."

1. More recently it has been established that the passengers in fact included an African-Caribbean family who, however, "passed" for Italian.

2. See Paul Oliver, *Songsters and Saints: Vocal Traditions on Race Records* (Cambridge: Cambridge University Press, 1984), 222-226.

Sam: "The White Terror."
(*One Big Union Monthly*, October 1919)

Carlos Cortez: Ben Fletcher poster (linocut, 1987)

7. JOE HILL & BEN FLETCHER

Rugged is the roadway to renown.
—Paul Laurence Dunbar—

Nothing is known about Hill's personal acquaintance with African Americans. He hoboed a lot, however, and hoboes tended to be highly egalitarian and anti-racist—'boes with red cards in their pockets even more so. The African American novelist George S. Schuyler, recalling his own experiences on the road in the mid- and late 1910s, noted that "there was no discrimination in the 'jungles' of the IWW. The writer has seen a white hobo, despised by society, share his last loaf with a Black fellow-hobo" [Foner 1974, 112].

William O. Douglas, who later became a U.S. Supreme Court Justice, "jungled up" and rode freights with Wobblies during his youth in the Pacific Northwest, and he never forgot the "kindness, compassion, [and] tenderness" of these "warm-hearted people." Among them, he said, "a hungry man was always welcome . . . not only was he offered food, but there he could feel that he was an equal with everyone" [1974, 77-78].

It was in a hobo "jungle" that a young Walter Rogers "learned that [in the IWW] there was no discrimination against Negroes, Mexicans, Chinese, or any other nationality" [1945, 86]. Interviewed in the 1980s, old-time Wobbly Joe Murphy recalled that the IWW frequently "offered free dues and free initiation to Negroes . . . because they had so little [money]. We did the same with the Chinese and Japanese" [Bird *et al.*, 51].

The very use of the term "jungle" for their impromptu cooperative encampments reveals the IWW hoboes' rejection of the values of the dominant order. Upper- and middle-class observers of workingclass life—not only hostile and uncomprehending "sociologists" but even such sympathetic souls as Upton Sinclair—used the term pejoratively to convey the horror of urban poverty, with its violence and squalor. The Wobbly hoboes' "jungle," intentionally disengaged from capitalist civilization and its discontents, was decidedly something else: a share-and-share-alike community that prefigured, in its small way, the equality and freedom of socialism.

This special IWW blend of solidarity, liberty, equality, fraternity, compassion, and big-hearted generosity is summed up neatly in Paul Walker's "A Wobbly Good and True" (to the tune of "Let the Rest of the World Go By"). It is the only IWW song I know of written by an African American Wobbly:

> *I was riding one day on a train far away,*
> *Wishing there was a Wobbly near,*
> *When it did just seem, like someone in a dream,*
> *Came a Wob with a hearty cheer. . . .*
>
> *With someone like you,*
> *A Wob good and true. . . .*
>
> *I don't know where you're from*
> *but I know you're true blue.*
> *Let us hope that some day*
> *All wage-slaves will say:*
> *"Hurrah for the OBU!"*[1]

Traveling Wobs generally made it a point to drop by the IWW hall in the places they visited, and often stayed around for a meeting or a "social." Surely Joe Hill, in the course of his transcontinental wanderings, met some Black Wobblies.

It also seems likely that he would have encountered Black fellow workers on the San Pedro waterfront, or in other ports, or among the volunteers who, like Hill, crossed the border to support the Mexican Revolution in Baja California. The hard facts may be missing, but probability is on our side.

Through the union's publications, Hill surely knew of at least one prominent African American Wobbly, Ben Fletcher, who, as a delegate to the 1913 convention in Chicago, played a significant role in the proceedings. Benjamin Harrison Fletcher was the central figure of the large and dynamic Philadelphia local of the IWW's Marine Transport Workers Industrial Union in the mid- and late 1910s, and also one of the 101 Wobs sentenced in 1918 to long terms at Leavenworth Penitentiary for, among other things,

> conspiracy to unlawfully and feloniously and by force to prevent, hinder, and delay the execution of certain laws of the United States concerned with the Government's preparation for and prosecution of the war. [Vorse 1935, 157]

(During the war, the IWW had demanded wage-increases at least roughly proportional to the profit-increases of the major industries.)

A loyal Wobbly till his death in 1949, Fellow Worker Fletcher was the best known of the union's Black organizers. And he remembered seeing Joe Hill in Philadelphia, "sometime before 1911."

This astounding revelation was quietly announced to the public in 1969 in a note on page 214, column 2 of Gibbs M. Smith's biography of Hill, and to the best of my knowledge has never been mentioned anywhere else. The source of the information is a 1966 letter from the IWW's in-house historian, Fred Thompson, who got it from Fellow Worker Jack Sheridan, who in turn got it direct from Ben Fletcher himself.

I knew Jack Sheridan quite well in the 1960s when I was active in the Chicago Branch of the IWW and editor of its magazine, *The Rebel Worker*. An old Dil Pickler, he was one of the "regulars" at Branch meetings, and the other old-timers considered him one of the union's best soapboxers. (It was Sheridan and Thompson who gave me my own first lessons in soapboxing at Bughouse Square in 1964.) I didn't always agree with Jack about everything, but I did find him to be scrupulously honest. If he told Thompson that Fletcher said he saw Hill, that's good enough for me.

Dick Brazier, for his part, vouched for Fellow Worker Fletcher's veracity. As he wrote to Thompson, the Fletcher/Hill meeting appeared "quite possible and plausible," for Fletcher was organizing longshoremen around that time, and besides, "Ben was not given to lying about things. If Ben told Jack Sheridan that he had met Joe Hill then Ben had met Joe Hill, without doubt" [7 Jan 1967].

Curiously, just before Thompson wrote to Brazier about Sheridan and the Fletcher/Hill meeting, Brazier had written Thompson noting that John Reed had told him that he (Reed) had met Hill—in Philadelphia in 1911 [21 Dec 1966]. In other words, Brazier was offering an interesting piece of supporting evidence even before Thompson had raised the question [Thompson to Tynne and Vaino Konga, 5 Jan 1967].

In yet another letter, and hinting at yet another dimension in the mystery of Hill's biography, Thompson noted that "Jack Sheridan recalls Fletcher 'speaking as though Hill had a Swedish girl friend in Philadelphia, whose name he recalls as something like Thelma Erickson" [to Sam and Esther Dolgoff, 6 Jan 1967].

But surely Fletcher must have told other fellow workers,

friends and acquaintances about seeing Joe Hill. Did any of them take notes of his recollections?

In 1948, during the IWW's dispute with the *New Republic* magazine, which had published a malevolent article on Hill by Wallace Stegner, many of those who had known Hill came forth to defend the honor of their old fellow worker. Did anyone ask Fellow Worker Fletcher to comment?

This is all we have in the way of facts: In the mid 1960s, in Chicago, Jack Sheridan told Fred Thompson that Ben Fletcher, during the late 1930s or early 40s in New York, told him that he (Fletcher) remembered seeing Joe Hill sometime around 1910-11, in Philadelphia. Beyond that, all we have in regard to this grand encounter between two legends-in-the-making—the man who became the IWW's most celebrated Black organizer and the man who would become the union's most famous bard and martyr—is conjecture. It makes us realize how much the history of the IWW remains a mystery.

---

1. The complete text of this song by Paul Walker is included in Ellington 1993 in Green, ed., 1993, 308.

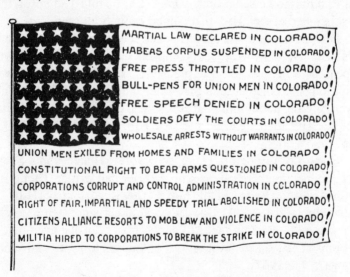

Though hardly known as a visual artist, "Big Bill" Haywood had a good eye for bold imagery. Dating from a pre-IWW Western Federation of Miners' strike, this "revised" flag signified the mine-owners, the corrupt state regime, and the U.S. army who, with violence and terror, had manifested their complete scorn for workers' rights and the Constitution. When this flag appeared as a poster, state authorities accused Haywood and the WFM of "desecrating" the national banner.

8. TOWARD THE NEW ABOLITIONISM:
GEORGE SELDES & RAY SPRIGLE

Who can tell or comprehend
the vast results for good or for evil
that are to follow the saying
of one little word.
—John Brown—

I shall conclude this digressive and admittedly speculative discussion of Hill, the IWW, and race with yet another Joe Hill "sighting" that historians seem to have missed. In his 1953 autobiography, *Tell the Truth and Run*, muckraking journalist George Seldes mentions having "roamed a day in Pittsburgh with Joe Hillstrom" [165]. Since none of Hill's biographers had mentioned his being in that city, I wrote Seldes for more information. To my barrage of questions he replied that he was introduced to Hill by his close friend Ray Sprigle, who was then city editor of the *Pittsburgh Post*, where Seldes worked as a reporter [letter to FR, 24 Mar 1985]. Sprigle and Hill, said Seldes, "addressed each other as old friends so I realized they had known each other before that day." The trio went for lunch at a saloon Sprigle liked, and it was Sprigle "who did all the talking" with Hill ("mostly about the Pittsburgh situation"), and Sprigle who picked up the tab [*ibid.*, 15 April 1985].

That evening all three attended "a big IWW labor union meeting" held in "a hall of considerable size" which Seldes could not recall with greater precision. At lunch, Hill had outlined a plan for the meeting. As Seldes wrote me:

> when we met Joe Hill he told us that when everyone sang his new song which ends with "You'll eat pie in the sky when you die" we and our friends were to shout as loud as we could: "And that's a lie!" and that is just what we did, and it was quite a sensation. [24 Mar 1985]

This occurred sometime before September 1912 [15 April 1985].

What makes Seldes' reminiscences so interesting in the present context is the fact that he himself, and particularly Sprigle, went on to make exceptionally important contributions to the civil rights movement and the struggle against white supremacy. Seldes's classics of investigative reporting—*Facts and Fascism* (1943), *One*

269

Thousand Americans (1947), and others—and his long-running weekly newsletter *In Fact* (1940-1950) contain a mass of material exposing the deadly shenanigans of the Ku Klux Klan and American fascists of the Father Coughlin and Elizabeth Dilling type. More importantly, he showed how the reactionary "master race" politics of such evidently demented people corresponded closely to the programs of much larger, wealthier and more "respectable" organizations such as the National Association of Manufacturers and the American Legion, as well as numerous and more or less "mainstream" religious, professional, and businessmen's groups. His exposé of the racist and anti-labor reign of terror fostered by *L.A. Times* editor/ publisher Harry Chandler in southern California is just one example of Seldes's admirable work in this regard.

In his race politics, Ray Sprigle went even further than Seldes. His 1938 series revealing Supreme Court Justice Hugo Black's membership in the Ku Klux Klan won him a Pulitzer Prize [Rees 1996, 57]. But his most notable achievement as a radical journalist was his first-hand study of racial segregation and discrimination south of the Mason-Dixon line. Originally a *Post-Gazette* series titled "I Was a Negro in the South for Thirty Days," it was later reissued in book-form as *In the Land of Jim Crow* (1949) [*ibid.*].

Working closely with the NAACP, Sprigle passed for Black in order to experience directly the injustices and indignities routinely endured by African Americans in their daily lives. This was something more than just another white appropriation of Black experience in the ignoble "blackface" tradition—indeed, it was something completely different. Rather, as a recent commentator in the anti-white-supremacist journal *Race Traitor* has argued, Sprigle's "daring stunt" embodied a profoundly radical questioning of racial ideology in the U.S., and "helped bring greater awareness to an issue that would soon become the focus of national attention" [*ibid.*, 58]. It is no wonder that young race rebels today—those who call for the complete abolition of this country's artificial racial barriers—have saluted Sprigle as a pioneer.

And there we have it: Two writers who "just happened" to have known Joe Hill when they were young, also "just happened" to become what the Klan's Imperious Buzzards would call "traitors to the white race," and in Sprigle's case, a direct forerunner of the most radical present-day critics of the whole miserabilist mystique of "whiteness." *Race Traitor*, the path-breaking "Journal of the New Abolitionism," edited by Noel Ignatiev and John Garvey, has for its motto: "Treason to whiteness is loyalty to humanity."

Apart from the above-quoted passages from Seldes' autobiography, neither of these two friends of the IWW poet appear to have discussed him elsewhere in print. It is pleasant to note, however, that Seldes, in his massive 1960 collection of *The Great Quotations* (1086 plus lvii pages) included two quotations by Joe Hill: one under the heading "Pie (in the sky)," and the other under "Organize." Significantly, the book marks Hill's first appearance in a mass-market collection that also includes the words of some of his great African American contemporaries, including Frederick Douglass, W. E. B. Du Bois, Langston Hughes, Claude McKay, and the man who introduced the IWW poet to millions around the world: Paul Robeson.

Carlos Cortez: Lucy Parsons poster
(linocut, 1986)

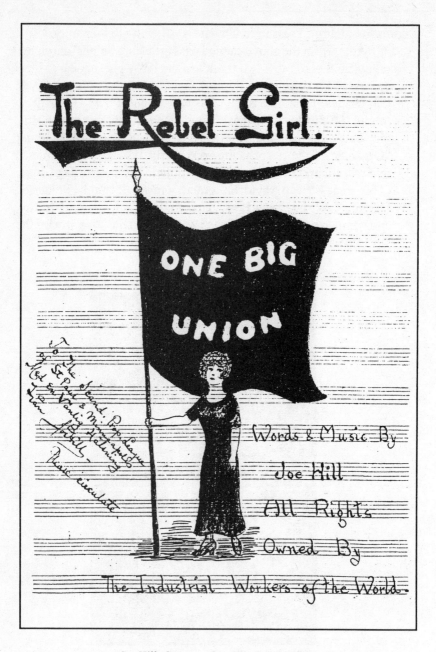

Joe Hill: Cover art for "The Rebel Girl,"
inscribed to the Scandinavian Propaganda League, 1915.

VIII
WOMEN WOBBLIES & WOBBLY FEMINISM

1. JOE HILL, *THE REBEL GIRL*, & REBEL WOMEN

Success is never so interesting as struggle.
—**Willa Cather**—

W as Joe Hill a feminist? It may be going too far to say so, but he was certainly moving in the right direction. Not only had he freed himself of most of the ideological baggage of male supremacy, he also actively supported IWW women's initiatives, urged that the union devote more time and energy to what he regarded as the urgent task of organizing women workers, and emphasized that the effort should be directed by women organizers. Few male Wobblies gave more sympathetic attention to questions of gender than the union's most renowned poet.

The first two decades of the twentieth century were years of extraordinary ferment among working women. Garment workers, telephone operators, bookbinders, textile mill workers, stage performers, hotel and restaurant workers, nurses, teachers, office workers, and store clerks were organizing and striking all across the country. The heyday of the IWW, from around 1910 through 1924, was also the most active period in the history of the Women's Trade Union League. Founded in Chicago in 1903, the WTUL held its first national conference two years later, and remained a dynamic presence in the U.S. labor movement well into the '20s. Although loosely associated with the American Federation of Labor, the WTUL was always far to the left of its "sponsor," and maintained an assertively autonomous existence. According to feminist historian Barbara Mayer Wertheimer, the AFL offered the WTUL little more than "polite encouragement and often found the League's program an embarrassment" [1977, 284]. The League, for example, strongly opposed the AFL-backed Alien Exclusion Act—the bill to ban Asians from the U.S. [*ibid.*]

Unlike the AFL, which permitted the great majority of its affiliates to exclude women from membership, and offered little or no aid to the relatively few unions which actively welcomed women, the IWW was serious about organizing women, and declared its intentions in that regard even before the union had begun to function. Indeed, women workers helped get the new union started. Of the 200-plus delegates and well-wishers who took part in the IWW's founding convention, only fifteen were women, but four of them were among the best known figures in the entire U.S. labor movement: Lucy E. Parsons, Mary "Mother" Jones, Emma F. Langdon, and Luella Twining.[1]

Parsons, one of the most celebrated labor agitators of her time, was also the editor and publisher of *The Life of Albert R. Parsons* (her martyred husband) and *Famous Speeches of the Eight Chicago Anarchists*—books read by practically every labor radical in the land in those years, and indeed, well into the 1930s. Parsons was also noted for her cross-country speaking tours, during which she addressed hundreds of large meetings of labor, anarchist, and free-thought organizations. At the IWW Founding Convention in 1905, she spoke frequently, sometimes at length, and always powerfully. Her speech at the June 29 afternoon session is regarded by many as the single finest address of the entire convention.

Mary Harris "Mother" Jones, in her sixties at the time of the Founding Convention, was one of the U.S. labor movement's most colorful and energetic organizers, renowned above all for her tireless efforts on behalf of the miners—from West Virginia and Pennsylania to Colorado and Utah. Although her association with the IWW lasted only six months, she remained active in the radical labor and socialist movements. A few years after the IWW's founding convention, she—like Joe Hill and other IWWs—took up the cause of the Mexican Revolution, especially the anarchist *Partido Liberal* of Ricardo Flores Magon [Thompson 1987].

Langdon, a printer by trade and a militant socialist, was a delegate of Denver Typographical Union No. 49. At the time of the IWW convention, her 463-page book, *The Cripple Creek Strike: A History of the Industrial Wars in Colorado, 1903-4-5*, had just appeared. Langdon herself, along with her friend Mother Jones, had played a courageous and even heroic role in the struggles described in her book. In a brief apology for the book's physical appearance and layout—which, by the way, needed no apology— she wrote:

> I have compiled the work, set the type, read the proofs, made the pictures from which many of the illustrations are made, folded the pages and while getting out the work have taken care of my work as usual, doing my own sewing, baking, washing and

ironing and other work that falls to the lot of woman. Outside of that I have worked at my trade sufficient to pay the greater part of the expense of halftones and press-work. . . . I have not slept the full number of hours necessary for rest. [1905, 249]

On the motion of Mother Jones, Langdon was appointed Assistant Secretary of the IWW Founding Convention [*Proceedings* 1905, 29].

Twining, from Pueblo, Colorado, was a delegate of the Federal Union of the American Labor Union. At the IWW convention she spoke several times from the floor, and presided over a session of the July 7 ratification meeting. A prominent suffragist, she was also active in the socialist movement, and in 1910 served as delegate to the International Congress of the Second International in Copenhagen.

Less well known than these, but also a committed revolutionist, was the delegate of the Industrial Workers Club in Chicago, Lillian Forberg, who took an active part in the convention debates, and served on the Literature and Press Committee.

Although women were only seven and a half percent of the IWW's founders, they were a forceful and articulate minority, and did much to get the new union off to the right start. Aware that women workers had been rejected by a large part of the AFL, the IWW also made it clear to all that women were welcome in the One Big Union. And in bright contrast to the many craft unions that permitted employers to pay women workers lower wages, the IWW from the very beginning upheld the principle of Equal Pay for Equal Work.

By 1912, according to Barbara Mayer Wertheimer, "the IWW had more women organizers and more women as public speakers and fund-raisers than any other labor union up to that time" [1977, 353]. In the Eastern textile towns, moreover, women made up a sizeable percentage of the membership of many IWW locals, in some cases a majority. In several major IWW strikes—mostly notably the New York shirtwaist strike of 1909, the "Bread and Roses" strike in Lawrence 1912, and the Paterson and Little Falls strikes the following year, the role of women IWWs was decisive. As Elizabeth Gurley Flynn wrote in *Solidarity* in 1915:

The IWW has been accused of putting the women in the front. The truth is, the IWW does not keep them in the back, and they go to the front. [31 July, 9]

Despite bitter opposition by AFL bureaucrats, the IWW and the Women's Trade Union League maintained friendly and cooperative relations for years. As early as 1906, when President Theodore Roosevelt denounced the IWW as "undesirable citizens" in a shameful attempt to influence the court in the Haywood/ Moyer/Pettibone case, the WTUL supported the IWW's defense campaign. Many thousands of "I am an Undesirable Citizen" buttons were sold by League members, at five cents each, on protest marches in New York, Chicago, and other cities. (All proceeds went to the Haywood *et al.* defense committee.)

The 1912 Lawrence Strike marked the closest cooperation between the IWW and the League. Working with the city's Central Labor Council, the WTUL opened a strike relief center—directed by WTUL co-founder Mary Kenney O'Sullivan—which distributed food and clothing to some eight thousand strikers. John Golden, however—president of the AFL United Textile Workers, which had scabbed through much of the strike—ordered the WTUL to shut down its relief station and to leave town. Under AFL pressure, the WTUL obeyed, but O'Sullivan resigned from the League and remained an active supporter of the strike [Wertheimer 1977, 360-61].

In Lawrence, women were always in the leadership of the strike, not only on the picketline, but in every phase of the struggle. Rose Cardullo, Josephine Liss, and Annie Welzenbach were elected by their fellow workers to the strike committee. A young woman picketer who wrote on her sign, "We Want Bread—and Roses, Too!" gave the strike its popular poetic nickname, which was soon worked up into a song by dime novelist and poet James Oppenheim. Another young striker, Annie LoPezzo, killed by a cop, became the IWW's first female martyr.

"Big Bill" Haywood expressed the greatest admiration for these women strikers and their union spirit. As he recalled years later in his autobiography:

The women strikers were as active and efficient as the men, and fought as well. One cold morning, after the strikers had been drenched on the bridge with the firehose of the mills, the women caught a policeman in the middle of the bridge and stripped off his uniform, pants and all. They were about to throw him in the icy river, when other policemen rushed in and saved him from the chilly ducking. [1929, 249]

In Lawrence 1912, as Haywood summed it up, "the women won the strike" [*ibid.*, 251].

Women Wobblies also made history west of the Mississippi. Lillian Forberg took part in an organizing drive among coal-miners in Kansas [Sellars 1998, 29]. Ethel Carpenter of Oklahoma, in a 1906 article for the *Industrial Worker*, was the first to stress the importance of organizing seasonal migratory workers in agriculture [*ibid.*, 20]. Laura Payne Emerson—poet, writer, organizer, soap-boxer—was a central figure in the IWW in San Diego, and became well known nationally for her courageous role in that city's Free Speech Fight in 1912 [Foner 1981, 135]. In Seattle, Billie Walden edited the *Industrial Worker* in 1920 [*IW*, 28 Apr 1923].

One of the IWW's most innovative and successful organizing campaigns of all time was Jane Street's unionization of the house-maids in Denver, 1916—a movement which soon spread to Salt Lake City, Duluth, Chicago, Cleveland, and Seattle. Out of this memorable struggle of workers considered "unorganizable" by the AFL came one of the all-too-rare woman-oriented IWW songs, "The Maids' Defiance," published in *Solidarity*:

> *We've answered all your doorbells and we've washed your dirty kids,*
> *For lo, these many weary years we've done as we were bid,*
> *But we're going to fight for freedom and for our rights we'll stand.*
> *And we're going to stick together in one big Union band.*
>
> *We've washed your dirty linen and we've cooked your daily foods;*
> *We've eaten in your kitchens, and we've stood your ugly moods.*
> *But now we've joined the Union and organized to stay,*
> *The cooks and maids and chauffeurs, in one grand array.*
>
> [6 May 1916]

At the age of seventeen, Milka Sablich—known as "Flaming Milka, the girl in the red dress"—played an important role in the IWW's Coal-Mine Workers Industrial Union No. 220, especially during the great Colorado coal strike of 1927, and made more than one speaking-tour for the union [Nelson 1993, 305-306, 310].

Minnie Abbot in Goldfield; Emma B. Little in Fresno; Marie Equi in Portland; Katie Phar in Spokane; Edith Frenette in Missoula; Rebecca August in Seattle; and Inez Rhoades in Seattle and other places: These are just a few of the many women who kept the banner of the One Big Union flying out West.

For the IWW, organizing women workers at the point of production was naturally a priority, but the union also took a larger view of the oppression of women in the capitalist patriarchy. As feminist historian Ann Schofield has noted:

> Wobblies had a sincere concern for working women that went beyond a pragmatic desire to organize them as workers. They addressed broader social issues such as prostitution and birth control, they wanted to organize the "feminine occupations" of domestics and telephone operators, and they urged male workers to recognize the importance of their wives to the class struggle. ... Wobblies, at least theoretically, did go one step further than any other labor organization in their view of women. The Rebel Girl, whether worker or wife of worker, was an activist in, rather than an auxiliary to, the One Big Union. In the words of Joe Hill, ". . . It's great to fight for Freedom with a Rebel Girl." [1983, 355]

Prostitution, a topic prudishly shunned by AFL unions, was recognized by the IWW as one of the many inevitable problems of capitalism, along with poverty, child labor, alcoholism, police brutality, air pollution, and war. As a problem particularly affecting women of the working class, prostitution was openly discussed in the union's periodical and pamphlet literature. In "The IWW Call to Women," published in *Solidarity* in 1915, Elizabeth Gurley Flynn wrote:

> Tragic indeed is the lot of the woman toiler! Her youth, her love, her home, her babies are "ground into dollars for parasites' pleasure."
>
> Hardly more attractive is the lot of the young girl toiler, who sells beautiful articles she is denied, who weaves delicate fabrics she never wears, who makes fine garments and shivers home in winter's snows with barely enough to cover her nakedness. Full of life and spirit, craving enjoyment, good clothes and youthful pleasures—is it any wonder that when resistance is weakened by hunger, many in despair sell their sex to secure what honest effort denies them; 350,000 prostitutes in the U.S.; 20,000 added

every year . . . is a staggering condemnation of our present society.

"Starvation or prostitution?"—how many girls last winter, with three million unemployed in the land, were compelled to face that question?

The IWW relies upon the organized power of labor to sweep away such nauseous conditions. . . . *Poverty,* the root of all crime and vice, must be destroyed and labor be free to enjoy the plenitude it creates. [31 July, 9]

The IWW's forthright and forward-looking attitude toward prostitution may account for the special treatment its women members were sometimes accorded by the police. During strikes, free-speech fights, or routine police raids, male IWWs who were placed under arrest were generally charged with vagrancy, disorderly conduct, or violation of some obscure (and frequently unconstitutional) ordinance, while women Wobblies in the same circumstances were often charged with prostitution. This did not mean that the arresting officers believed that these women were selling sexual favors; the charge was intended simply to humiliate and degrade them. In her early autobiography, *From Union Square to Rome* (1938), Dorothy Day recorded in some detail one of her own heartsickening experiences in this regard, from her youthful IWW days in Chicago.

In many IWW locals, wives of workingmen—whether they were wage-earners or not—were welcome to join, and many did. In 1908 Sophie Beldner argued in the *Industrial Union Bulletin* that

the married woman of the working class is no parasite or exploiter. She is a social producer. In order to sustain herself, she has to sell her labor power, either in the factory, directly to the capitalist, or at home, indirectly, by serving the wage slave, her husband, thus keeping him in working condition through cooking, washing and general housekeeping. . . . I think it should be encouraging for working men to see women enter their ranks and, shoulder to shoulder, fight for economic freedom. [Tax 1980, 130-1]

Covington Hall, in his *Labor Struggles in the Deep South*, relates a particularly impressive story in this regard. When the Louisiana- and East-Texas-based Brotherhood of Timber Workers voted to affiliate with the IWW, thus becoming the Southern District of the IWW's Forest and Lumber Workers Industrial Union,

> the men wanted their wives to have the right of membership. A motion to that effect was offered from the floor and seconded. It was thoroughly discussed, and finally agreed, that a house-wife, whether wife, mother, sister or daughter, would be allowed membership, her dues to be $1 a year. [1999,129]

To the question, "Does this mean that house women will have a full and equal vote with men on all matters pertaining to the union?" the unanimous answer was "Yes."

Hall goes on to note that "the part played by women in the 'Louisiana Lumber War' was a splendid one," and adds that "A woman, Fredonia Stevenson, was on our District Executive Committee, and many other women were in the forefront of the battle lines. Often they showed more courage than men" [*ibid.*].

Housewives also played a prominent part in the union's mass strikes on the East coast: Lawrence 1912 and Paterson 1913. In these strikes, as feminist historian Meredith Tax pointed out in her pioneering study, *The Rising of the Women* (1980), the IWW

> found new ways of connecting the workplace to the community . . . Housewives came out of the isolation of their kitchens and joined their husbands and working women in the fight for survival on the picket line. In doing so, they created new space for their own struggle as women, new bargaining power in the home, new political understanding for the future, as well as doubling the size and strength of the workingclass army. [162]

Indeed, in its recognition of housewives as part of the working class, and therefore welcome to union membership, the IWW made one of its greatest contributions to the organized labor movement. Significantly, America's best known theorist of housework as unpaid productive labor, maverick Communist Mary Inman—whose *In Women's Defense* (1935) became a radicalizing influence on the Women's Liberation movement in the 1970s—had been active in the IWW in Oklahoma in the 1910s [Gluck, in Buhle *et al.*, 1998, 363].

Wobblies were also vigorous supporters of women's reproductive rights. This was considered a taboo topic at the time; birth control literature was routinely confiscated and destroyed as "obscene" by misogynist postmasters. Birth control was also therefore very much a *free-speech* issue, which no doubt endeared it all the more to the "grand industrial band." AFL unions, heavily influenced by the Catholic church hierarchy, avoided the issue entirely.

IWW theory and practice did much to shape the early career of the woman who became America's best-known birth control advocate: Margaret Sanger, who in fact coined the phrase "birth control" in 1915. Sanger's close friends in the mid-1910s included Elizabeth Gurley Flynn, Big Bill Haywood, and the whole group around the *International Socialist Review* in Chicago. Active in the Lawrence and Paterson strikes, Sanger was frequently identified in the press as a member or "leader" of the IWW. The inaugural issue of her magazine, the *Woman Rebel*, included the IWW Preamble. Her pamphlets were enthusiastically promoted in the IWW press, and distributed by Wobbly organizers along with the union's own publications. Fellow Worker Bill Shatoff—organizer, noted Bughouse Square orator, and linotype operator—printed 100,000 copies of the first edition of Sanger's *Family Limitation*, which not only recommended and discussed various contraceptive methods, but also defended women's right to abortion. This pamphlet was circulated primarily through IWW locals [Sanger 1971, 117; Gordon 1977, 222].

Sanger's militant IWW orientation inevitably brought her into conflict with pro-capitalist feminists. In her magazine, *The Woman Rebel*, she insisted that

> We have no respect for the type of "modern" and "advanced" woman who becomes a willing and efficient slave of the present system, the woman who curries favors of capitalists and politicians in order to gain power and the cheap and fulsome praise of cheaper and more fulsome newspapers. [Gordon, 1977, 222]

In *Family Limitation*, she adopted the style of a soapboxer:

> The working class can use direct action by refusing to supply the market with children to be exploited, by refusing to populate the earth with slaves. [*ibid.*, 223]

Sanger later became quite conservative, but in those days she spoke, wrote and acted like a good Wobbly. Many other women Wobblies—including Marie Equi, Elizabeth Gurley Flynn, Georgia

Kotsch, Caroline Nelson, and Mary Marcy—were also active in birth control agitation.

In the IWW, birth control was no minor "side issue," but an integral part of the union's program, and was regularly a topic at street meetings and strike rallies. Gurley Flynn in her autobiography tells of an IWW women's meeting in Paterson during the 1913 silk strike, at which Bill Haywood, Carlo Tresca, and Flynn herself spoke. In the course of the meeting,

> Tresca made some remarks about shorter hours, people being less tired, more time to spend together and jokingly he said: "More babies." The women did not look amused. When Haywood interrupted and said: "No, Carlo, we believe in birth control—a few babies, well cared for!" they burst into laughter and applause. [1973, 166]

By affirming that housewives were part of the working class, analyzing prostitution from a proletarian standpoint, applying birth control to class struggle—and, more generally, demonstrating in many and diverse ways the inseparability of women's and workers' self-emancipation—women Wobblies showed that they were not only organizers and activists but also thinkers and theorists. Their contributions in this regard are rarely noted in histories of the union, but they appeared in abundance in the IWW's newspapers and magazines. Gurley Flynn's scattered IWW writings are full of noteworthy and stimulating insights, in bright contrast to her later hack work as a Communist Party official. Caroline Nelson, Lucy Parsons, Jane Street, Barbara Frankenthal, Mabel Kanka, and above all Mary Marcy also did much to expand Wobbly ideas in new directions.

Marcy was well known for her Marxist primer, *Shop Talks on Economics*, published by Charles H. Kerr and also by the IWW. The most widely read introductory work on the subject ever written by an American, it was translated into Chinese, Japanese, Finnish, Hungarian, Romanian, French, Italian, and Greek, and sold over two million copies [Carney 1923, 6]. It is still readable today, though it is hardly her best or most creative work. Described by Gene Debs as the "brainiest woman" on the U.S. Left, Marcy wrote brilliantly and extensively on a breathtaking range of subjects, including direct action, economics, birth control, education, problems of human expression, the relation of human beings to other animals, the need to defy prevailing (bourgeois) morality, the exceptional importance of play, and ways in which workers can struggle against war. For daring originality, imaginative sparkle, and revolutionary depth, no U.S. Marxist of her generation could compete with Mary Marcy [Marcy 1984, 5-14].

Women also contributed appreciably to the development of the Wobbly counterculture. Many classic Wobbly songs were written by women, including Ethel Comer ("Stand Up, Ye Workers"), Laura Payne Emerson ("The Industrial Workers of the World"), Rose Elizabeth Smith ("The Ninety and Nine"), and Vera Moller ("We Made Good Wobs Out There," which, by the way, was written in prison). Mary Gallagher's far-reaching IWW-connected project to collect, translate, and publish workers' songs from all countries will be examined in a later chapter.

Women Wobblies also wrote some of the finest IWW poetry: Matilda Robbins, Laura Payne Emerson, Mary Marcy, Vera Moller, Agnes Thecla Fair, Eva Curtis, Violet Kaminsky, Laura Tanne, and Sophie Fagin are among the most outstanding. Mary Marcy, Georgia Kotsch, and Mary Hope wrote notable IWW short stories. In 1910, even before she joined the IWW, Marcy had published a socialist novel, *Out of the Dump,* illustrated by Ralph Chaplin.

Women vocalists were important features of the entertainment at Wobbly May Days, "In November We Remember" gatherings, and other events. Jennie Woszczynska in Chicago in the 1910s and '20s, and Katie Phar in the Pacific Northwest from the 1910s through the '30s, were especially popular. Women were also active in the writing and production of IWW plays at Work People's College and elsewhere. Mary Marcy's satirical one-act drama, *A Free Union,* appeared in 1921. Some Wobbly theater groups went on tour [Altenbaugh 1990, 112].

Astonishingly, the single most outstanding figure in Wobbly theater—the great African Finnish singer, actor, and director Rosa Lemberg—has never been mentioned in any history of the union. And yet for some fifty years she was one of the best-loved entertainers in the Finnish-American community, and well known throughout the IWW.[2]

Born in 1875 of an Arab/Bantu mother and an English father in what is now Namibia in southwestern Africa, Rosa Emilia Clay was brought up by Finnish foster parents who were also Lutheran missionaries. In her teens she was taken to Finland and educated at a seminary. After graduating she became a teacher, and is today celebrated in Finland as the nation's "First Negro Teacher" [Erickson 1993, 26].

In 1904 she came to New York, became a socialist, and a few years later married a Finnish comrade, Lauri Lemberg—a printer, actor, and playwright. The couple moved to Ironwood, Michigan, and then to the west coast, where they split up after a few years. Exactly when Rosa Lemberg joined the IWW is not known, but by 1916 she was Drama Director of the Finnish Workers' Club in Butte, Montana, where she directed many plays, including one titled "The Lowell Strike," as well as a special program on the Everett Massacre (all proceeds going to the Defense Fund). Around 1919 she moved to Chicago where she remained, almost to the end of her life, a prime mover in the weekly cultural events at "Finn Hall"—as the local Wobs called it—at 2409 North Halsted, just a few doors down and across the street from the IWW's international headquarters.

As was true of all IWW entertainers at IWW events, Rosa Lemberg performed for her fellow workers for free, as a gesture of solidarity and a labor of love. To support herself and her two children, she worked nights as a seamstress, music teacher, teacher of the Finnish language, and domestic.

By all accounts she was a striking presence—her biographer recalls her as "a tall, dignified, quiet, dark individual of regal bearing, with a magnificent singing voice" [*ibid.*, 153]. Although best known as a singer, she was also an accomplished pianist, and directed as well as starred in numerous plays, operettas, and musical comedies at "Finn Hall" as well as at the Workers' Hall in nearby Waukegan. With her "rich, contralto voice" (sometimes described as soprano), she early became known as "The Nightingale," while her acting abilities led others to call her "the Finnish Sarah Bernhardt" and the "First Lady of the Finnish American Theater."

Sadly, she does not appear to have made any recordings. Those who were lucky enough to hear her sing seem to have found it an extraordinary experience. Jenny Lahti Velsek, one of the core militants of the Chicago IWW Branch for several decades, remembers Rosa Lemberg as "the most wonderful singer in the world" [FR interview].

Rosa Lemberg was still active in her seventies, in the 1950s, living on Wrightwood Avenue in the Lincoln Park area, not far from "Finn Hall." She died at a Finnish rest home in Covington, Michigan, in 1959 [Erickson 1993, 98].

All along the line, then—as organizers, activists, propagandists, theorists, creators, and entertainers—women Wobblies were "on the job." However, despite high hopes, the best intentions, and some notable successes, the IWW remained an overwhelmingly male organization, especially in the West, where a large majority of the members were migratory male workers. Women hoboes were by no means unknown, but they were far from numerous. Few of the IWW's women organizers were 'boes.

The "Woman Question" was a significant issue in the IWW, and in the entire U.S. Left, and Joe Hill had ideas of his own on the subject. In a letter dated 29 November 1914, and published in the Wob paper *Solidarity*, he wrote:

> The female workers are sadly neglected in the United States ... and consequently we have created a kind of one-legged, freak-ish animal of a union, and our dances and blowouts are kind of stale and unnatural on account of being too much of a "buck" affair; they are too lacking the life and inspiration which the women alone can produce. . . . I think it would be a very good idea to use our female organizers, Gurley Flynn, for instance, *exclusively* for the building up of a strong organization among the female workers. They are more exploited than the men, and John Bull is willing to testify to the fact that they are not lacking in militant and revolutionary spirit. [*Letters*, 16-17]

The last sentence refers to the window-smashing and other forms of direct action adopted by suffragists in England.

As it turned out, Hill's hope in Gurley Flynn as an organizer of women was misplaced. As her biographer Rosalyn Baxandall has noted:

> Flynn did not try to promote women to leadership positions within the IWW or to push the IWW to emphasize female issues. In fact, Flynn enjoyed her special token status. She liked being surrounded by admiring males and did not welcome competitors to her turf. [1987, 267]

Other women Wobblies, however—Lucy Parsons, Matilda Robbins, Mary Marcy, Agnes Inglis, Marie Equi, Georgia Kotsch, Emma B. Little, Theresa Klein, Jane Street, Mabel Kanka, Jessie Ashley, Helen Keller, and Sophie Cohen, to name a few—were more openly feminist, more concerned with specifically women's issues, and above all more devoted to the cause of organizing women. Surely they would have welcomed Fellow Worker Hill's encouraging words.

Of the union's top male organizers, Frank Little was the most vociferous supporter of Hill's proposals. In 1916 Little urged that the IWW greatly expand its efforts to organize women. He argued that the union needed more women organizers and agitators, as well as special literature for women. He also called for the establishment of an IWW women's bureau to develop new organizing strategies for women workers. No such bureau was formed, however, and the organization of women proceeded as haphazardly as before.

As in every large organization, the attitude of male Wobblies toward women, and toward the organization of women, varied widely. Some undoubtedly retained, to one degree or another, patriarchal notions of "woman's place," and were opposed or indifferent to the organization of female workers. Such retrograde views, however, rarely found expression in the IWW press. More common was the belief of many migratory workers that their homelessness and freedom from marital and family ties made them much more revolutionary than the "homeguards"—non-migratory workers with families. In this view, women were regarded as a potentially conservative force. The majority view, as suggested by the amount of space devoted to the subject in the union's publications, seems to have been a compromise: It was important to organize women workers, but it was not the highest priority.

More far-seeing Wobblies—Joe Hill, Frank Little, Bill Haywood, Ben H. Williams, and others—made the organization of women a high priority, and realized that a large influx of women would have constituted a qualitative transformation of the union's power and effectiveness.

On the "Woman Question," Hill as usual did not confine himself to letters to the editor. Many IWW lyrics refer only to men, and are otherwise afflicted with decidedly masculinist rhetoric, and even some of Hill's own songs reflect this narrow view. "There Is Power in a Union," for example, includes such lines as "There is pow'r in a band of workingmen," and "Come, do your share, like a man." Hill, however, more than most of the union's songwriters, made it clear that the IWW included "men and women side by side," as he put it in "Workers of the World, Awaken!" (1916). Earlier, in "Everybody's Joining It" (1912) he wrote:

> *Boys and girls in every land,*
> *All the workers hand in hand—*
> *Everybody's joining it now.*

And in his "What We Want" (1913) one of the union's main recruiting songs, women workers are even more prominent:

> *We want the sailor and the tailor and the lumberjacks,*
> *And all the cooks and laundry girls. . . .*
> *We want the tinner and the skinner and the chambermaid,*
> *And all the factory girls and clerks . . .*
> *In one union grand.*

Several of his songs—most notably "The Girl Question" and "The Rebel Girl"—focus on women, with the palpable aim of promoting women's self-organization via the IWW. "The Girl Question" (to the tune of the gospel song, "Tell Mother I'll Be There"), first published in the *Song Book* in 1913, tells the story of a young working woman who, having trouble making ends meet, is constantly advised to "get a beau/Some nice old man, you know." But then,

> *Next day while walking round she saw a sign inside a hall.*
> *It read: THE ONE BIG UNION WILL GIVE LIBERTY TO ALL.*
> *She said: I'll join that union, and I'll surely do my best,*
> *And now she's gaily singing with the rest:*
>
> *Oh, workers do unite!*
> *To crush the tyrant's might.*
> *The ONE BIG UNION BANNER IS UNFURLED.*
> *Come, slaves from every land.*
> *Come join this fighting band.*
> *It's named INDUSTRIAL WORKERS OF THE WORLD.*

"The Rebel Girl," for which Hill also composed the music, was written or at least completed in the Salt Lake City jail in 1915:

> *Yes, her hands may be hardened from labor,*
> *And her dress may not be very fine;*
> *But a heart in her bosom is beating*
> *That is true to her class and her kind.*
> *And the grafters in terror are trembling*
> *When her spite and defiance she'll hurl;*

For the only and thoroughbred lady
  Is the Rebel Girl.
We've had girls before, but we need some more
  In the Industrial Workers of the World.
For it's great to fight for freedom
  With a Rebel Girl.

Six of Hill's drawings portray women. Three—the callous Mrs Highbrow (see page 169), the fairylike "Job" temptress (page 195), and the burlesque queen (page 197)—could not have been of much help in the effort to unionize women. More promising is the woman flute-player (see page 305), whose obvious centrality in the three-piece band hints at Hill's belief that women should play active and leading roles; this drawing, however, is a Christmas card to his old childhood friend from Sweden, Charles Rudberg, and not the depiction of an IWW rally.

One of the cartoons "Suggested by Joe Hill" (reproduced here on page 187), illustrates the IWW view that prostitution was the result of an unjust social system, not of woman's "moral failure." As Hill put it in a song:

Who is to blame? You know his name:
It's the boss who pays starvation wages.
  ["The White Slave" (1913)]

The cartoon identifies the prostitute not as a "criminal" but as an exploited victim of capitalist society who "never had a chance." Together with the aging and ailing hobo, who is depicted trudging along the tracks, she is part of the proletarian "wretched of the Earth" hailed in "The Internationale."

Hill's most notable portrayals of woman are the designs he made for covers of the sheet music for his songs—for "The Rebel Girl," of which two versions have survived, and for "Workers of the World, Awaken!" The drawing on the copy of "Rebel Girl" sent to the Scandinavian Propaganda League in St Paul and Minneapolis (see page 272) shows a young woman in her early teens, holding high the scarlet banner of the One Big Union. This sketch of the rebel girl may well be based on a photograph of the well-known Katie Phar, the daughter of Wobbly parents, who at the age of ten had become "an ardent IWW" during the 1910 Spokane Free Speech fight.[3]

Celebrated as the "Songbird of the Wobblies," Phar was frequently mentioned in the IWW press, and was for many years one of the best known women in the union. Guy B. Askew's poem, "When the Crimson Flag Is Flying," published in the *Industrial Worker* (22 Mar 1930), carries the dedication: "To Fellow Worker Katie Phar." Years later, many old Wobblies retained fond memories of "Songbird" Katie. In an unpublished autobiography, Herb Edwards calls her "the most unforgettable" of the IWW's entertainers, and "without a doubt the most popular in the whole organization," at least out West [321]. Thomas Bogard recalled her at a union fund-raising meeting in the late 1910s: After Katie

> sang the famous lumberjack song, Big Bill [Haywood] picked little Katie up and hugged her and said . . . "Your songs have brought thousands of dollars to the defense of men and women who will make history." [Bogard n.d., 7]

Interviewed by Eugene Nelson in the 1970s, Joe Murphy also remembered her with real affection: "She was a little gal, only about four feet tall, but how she could sing!" [Nelson 1993, 56].

After Hill's arrest in Salt Lake City, he exchanged several letters with Phar, then in her mid-teens, and strongly encouraged her music studies. On 7 May 1915 he sent her an inscribed, hand-lettered and hand-illustrated copy of the words and music to "The Rebel Girl," now lost, and another (unnamed) song.

The letter Hill wrote to Phar on that occasion was published in badly mutilated form in Foner's *Letters of Joe Hill*.[4] Here it is in full:

> Dear Friend and Fellow Worker,
>
>   Yours received and am glad to note that you are getting along fine with your music lessons. Am sending you through the local Secretary two of my songs and would like to hear how you like them. One of the songs, "The Rebel Girl," was sung at several big meetings in Chicago and was making a big hit they are telling me.
>
>   I had the pleasure to shake hands with Gurley Flynn yesterday and she told me that she would be glad to see you when she comes to Spokane. If you would practice up on one of the songs you could help her a whole lot by singing it at her meeting in Spokane. "The Rebel Girl" would be best I think because Gurley Flynn is certainly some Rebel Girl and when you and her get together there will be "two of a kind," Ha, Ha.
>
>   Well, I hope you will help me to introduce the songs around Spokane, and lend them out to people who want to learn them

because Gurley Flynn is certainly some Rebel Girl and when you and her get together there will be "two of a kind," Ha, Ha.

Well, I hope you will help me to introduce the songs around Spokane, and lend them out to people who want to learn them because I am only writing two copies for each large city. I would like to make two copies for every Rebel in the U.S., but—it can't be done.

My case will come up this month some time and everything looks good.

As ever, Your Friend, Regards to All,

Joe Hill

I enclose a nice hair ribbon for you.

In another of Hill's letters to Phar he included a watercolor of a rose.

Many old-time IWWs maintained that Katie Phar was as much the inspirer of "The Rebel Girl" as Elizabeth Gurley Flynn, and Hill's artwork for the song, as well as the letter reprinted above, lend weight to their contention. However, as further proof that practically everything having to do with Joe Hill is a matter of controversy, Hill's friend Alexander MacKay—one of our most reliable sources of information—suggested that the song was in fact inspired by a woman named Agnes Fair, whom MacKay described as "the greatest rebel girl I ever encountered."

Who knows? Isn't it also possible—even likely—that Hill derived his inspiration for the song from more than one woman Wobbly?

We shall return later to the all-but-forgotten but fascinating Fellow Worker Fair. For now, let us conclude our discussion of Hill's artwork for "The Rebel Girl." The drawing on the copy sent to Elizabeth Gurley Flynn shows a somewhat older woman with a more lavish hairdo. Her face and hair are very different from those of the girl in the copy sent to the Scandinavian Propaganda League, but she does not resemble Gurley Flynn, whose photograph, however, is pasted elsewhere on the cover.[5] The drawing for "Workers of the World, Awaken!" (page 292) features a still older woman, more buxom and decidedly blond.

When the IWW printed sheet music for "The Rebel Girl," it was decided not to reproduce any of Hill's designs. Another Wobbly artist/cartoonist, Arthur Machia, drew a new cover (see page 291), which has been used in all subsequent reprints. Though clearly based on Hill's original, Machia's is a distinct improvement. In Hill's versions, in addition to their sentimental tinge, the woman seems isolated and small, dwarfed by the immense flag. In Machia's, the woman is slightly older, her expression resolute, the flag smaller, and the presence of two other figures—one a young boy waving his cap with joy—suggests that *this* "rebel girl" is at the forefront of a great strike demonstration or May Day parade.

Arthur (Arturo) Machia: Cover art for "The Rebel Girl" sheet music, as published by the IWW in 1915.

The printed version of "Workers of the World, Awaken!" retained Hill's lettering but discarded his drawing—or perhaps it would be more accurate to say that it discarded the drawing on the only *surviving* copy, which was sent to Gurley Flynn. As with "The Rebel Girl," other copies—now lost—may have had very different covers.

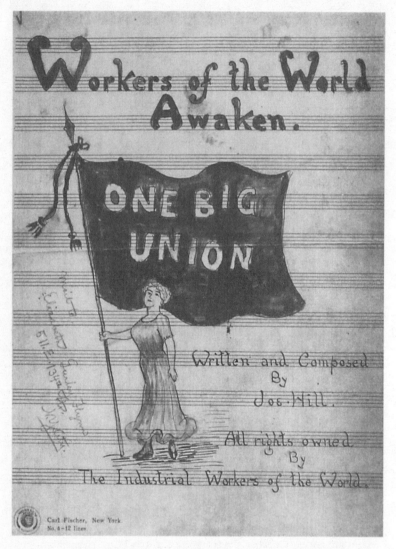

Joe Hill: Cover art for "Workers of the World, Awaken!"

Hill's lyrics to "The Rebel Girl" suffer from sentimentality far more than his sheet-music designs. We know he imagined the rebel girl as a true *fellow worker*, fighting alongside her male fellow workers. Part of the lyrics, however, reflect the then-common notion that women's role was largely to support the men: "She brings courage, pride and joy / To the fighting Rebel Boy."

Early on the song had its critics. Longtime agitator Mary Gallagher, a gifted songwriter in her own right, disdained the song not only as "poor music" and "poor poetry," but also because she regarded it as unrepresentative of the militant egalitarian spirit of the real rebel girls in the union—herself, for example [Green interview, 1959, 7].

Since the rise of the Women's Liberation movement in the late 1960s, the original lyrics have been considered outdated and inappropriate for strike meetings and demonstrations. It so happens, however, that Hazel Dickens, a traditional Appalachian singer active in the struggle for workers' and women's rights, has updated the song, replacing weak and ineffective passages with new words adapted to the needs of radical workingclass women today.[6] As Lori Elaine Taylor noted in the booklet accompanying the superb Smithsonian/Folkways album of Hill's songs, Hazel Dickens's update exemplifies the fact that these songs "live within an evolving tradition in which performers rewrite songs to reflect broad changes" [Taylor 1990, 21].

Such rewriting, moreover, was fully authorized by Joe Hill himself. As he put it in a letter in February 1915: "If Fellow Worker Ashleigh wants to change the 'Soupline Song' to make it fit the brand of soup they are dishing out in N.Y. he can hop right to it" [*Letters*, 27].[7]

In truth, the whole history of the IWW needs to be rewritten. More particularly, the activity of women workers in and around the union, and their interaction with their male fellow workers, needs to be explored more deeply. In a very real sense, the study of women Wobblies is only in its beginnings. So far, questions of gender have not received much attention from the union's historians. The relations between the sexes, and particularly how male Wobs treated women, are hardly frivolous matters, but they do not appear to have been taken very seriously by most researchers. For example: That some male IWW members regarded women as sex objects would seem to lie well within the bounds of possibility, but where are we to find reliable data on the subject?

Now and again an anecdote brings a little light. In 1937, recalling her early life with the Wobblies in the West ("adventurous, able-bodied, rollicking . . . men with muscles of iron") Elizabeth Gurley Flynn wrote:

At nineteen, I was as safe among them "as if you were in God's pocket," as one of them phrased it. Their attitude towards women was simple. There were "good women" like their mothers and "bad women" who fleeced them on pay day. But all who joined the IWW were necessarily good women and were treated accordingly. [11]

Some Wobs no doubt availed themselves of the services of prostitutes, and consensual, casual affairs were evidently quite common throughout the One Big Union. Nobody, however—to the best of our knowledge—bothered to document these practices at the time, or even to comment on them retrospectively. Famous for its songwriters, poets, organizers, soapboxers, cartoonists, pamphleteers, historians, and folklorists, the IWW somehow never got around to recruiting a sex-researcher.

Meanwhile, many fellow workers simply got married and, as far as anyone can tell, led long, happy, monogamous lives.

It so happened, however, that many nonconformist young women—and the young women who joined the IWW were nonconformists by definition—didn't want to marry, or raise families. Many, beyond a doubt, had to endure plenty of parental and social pressure to be "normal." Jenny Lahti Velsek, who lined up in the union in 1933, recalled her own bitter experience in this regard:

My mother and father wanted me to get married and have children. They liked to daydream about all the grandchildren they wanted me and my sisters to have for them. They thought I was strange because I wasn't very interested in getting married and having a family. I was more interested in books—Karl Marx, and psychology, and things like that—and in learning to play the accordion. [FR interview, 20 August 1994]

In regard to Wobbly sexuality, the "hard facts" at our disposal hover at zero, or slightly below. Although Wobblies tended to be far less puritanical than Socialists and Communists, they did not advertise the matter much in their publications. Despite IWW interest in psychoanalysis and birth control, the sexual life of workers—or what Wilhelm Reich called the "Sexual Revolution" —was almost untouched in the union's press. The most notable Wobbly contribution to the debate on sexual matters was the brave little book, *Women as Sex Vendors*, co-authored by Mary E. Marcy and her brother, Roscoe B. Tobias, and published by Charles H. Kerr in 1918. Noting that "the whole subject of sex is clothed in pretense," and that "few people speak frankly" about it, Marcy and Tobias developed a critique of the system of bourgeois marriage as a "respectable" form of prostitution, inseparable from the commodity economy. In the social upheavals of their time, and above all in the growing power of women at the point of production, they perceived anticipations of a new, non-exploitative society in which freer forms of sexuality—as of all forms of human expression— would flourish as never before.

As for the experiments in freer sexuality that were already under way, some Wobblies took part and others demurred. In her play, *A Free Union* (1921), Mary Marcy spoofed the cynical sort of "free love" touted by so much of the petit-bourgeois bohemian element. Some Wobs, meanwhile, were nudists. Probably the best known was Ray Corder—sign-painter, poet, cartoonist, class-war prisoner, and husband of longtime Wobbly agitator Minnie Corder. In the 1930s Ray Corder lived for several weeks in a nudist colony in New Jersey and worked on its journal, *The Nudist* [Minnie Corder, n.d., 313-315]. John Neuhaus, celebrated by Archie Green as the IWW's own folklorist, and incidentally a militant vegetarian and an ordained Unitarian minister, also championed the nudist cause [Modesto to Green, 23 Apr 1962]. At a Chicago IWW Branch "social" in 1963 Fred Thompson introduced me to an elderly Wobbly couple, Ed and Lillian Stattman, who told me they frequented a nudist colony in Indiana, often in the company of other Wobs. For the Stattmans, nudism—in its rejection of the repressive values of capitalist/christian society—was clearly related to IWWism, yet the topic does not appear to have been taken up in the *Industrial Worker*. The few Wobblies who wrote autobiographies generally avoided sexual matters as well, although the memoirs of Elizabeth Gurley Flynn and Minnie Corder (the latter's unpublished) do record marriages that were far from successful, and Fred Thompson's *Fellow Worker* includes an interesting discussion of young radicals' interest in Reichian theory.

Historian Philip Taft, who carried a red card and hoboed around a bit in his younger days, remarked in a 1978 interview that

the IWW "had more than the normal number of active male homo-
sexuals" [63], but never bothered to elaborate. At least a few Wobs
were openly gay—Charles Ashleigh and Philip Melman, for example, and Marie Equi among the women; others, such as Claude
McKay, were bisexual. Surely there were also those who kept their
homosexuality or bisexuality a secret among a small circle of
intimates. Here again the "known facts" are far too few to base
conclusions on. The IWW nonetheless qualifies as a significant
albeit modest forerunner of the Gay Liberation movement, for
unlike the Socialist, Communist, and Trotskyist parties, which had
overt or covert policies barring so-called "sex deviates" from the
ranks, the IWW had no such discriminatory restrictions: *All* wage-
earners were eligible to join, and that was that. Although "sexual
preference" was not specifically mentioned in the union's Constitution, as were color and creed, it was simply never an issue.

For the liberation of women, however, the Wobbly voice was
always loud and clear and unwavering. No other labor union, and
no other self-declared revolutionary organization went as far as the
IWW in the effort to free working women from the double bondage
of wage- and sex-slavery.

Wobbly feminism, a workingclass variant of socialist and/or
anarchist feminism, was never articulated into a detailed manifesto
or program, much less into a full-fledged movement. Like many
undeveloped projects, IWW writings on the "Woman Question"
retain their share of tensions, inconsistencies, and outright contradictions. Their basic emancipatory impulse, however, and their revolutionary direction, are unmistakable, and that is why the lives
and work of women Wobblies—and of the males who supported
them—continue to inspire us even today with their insight, audacity, courage, hope, and promise. Although the IWW was never
explicitly feminist, and the suffrage-oriented feminist movement
of those years was never close to the IWW, feminism and IWWism
nonetheless interacted and influenced each other in many ways.
Just as there were Wobbly-oriented feminists such as Crystal
Eastman, Mary Heaton Vorse, and Theodora Pollok, so too there
were feminist-oriented Wobblies, some of whom happened to be
male, such as Bill Haywood, Frank Little, and Joe Hill.

Hill is of particular interest in this connection precisely because of his near-mythic status. It is significant that the most
celebrated IWW member of all time is not renowned for the heroic
exploits, physical strength, or soldierly virtues of a mighty and

muscular "he-man," but rather as poet, artist, humorist, musician, writer and singer of songs. In short, just as he embodies the negation of the mystique of "whiteness," so too the archetypal Wobbly represents the antithesis of masculinist ideology.

Indeed, the IWW as a whole manifested a strong anti-patriarchal tendency. Despite the overly masculine rhetoric of its press, and other tactical shortcomings, the union always emphasized that the organized solidarity of the entire working class is the only effective means of abolishing slavery, domination, and all forms of inequality. More than any other largely male group of its size and its time—vastly more than the Socialist or Communist parties, or the American Federation of Labor—Wobblies were unequivocally on the side of the working women of the world in their struggle with the "master class."

Isn't it tellingly symbolic that the two foremost popularizers of Joe Hill have been an African American and a woman? Through their concert performances and recordings of the Hayes/Robinson "Joe Hill" song, Paul Robeson and Joan Baez have done more than anyone to "spread the word" about the living legacy of the Man Who Never Died. In matters of race and gender, the theory and practice of the IWW poet have proved to be more intriguingly nuanced than one might have expected from a self-described wharf-rat.

---

1. Several other women took part in one or more sessions of the IWW's founding convention: Mrs E. G. (or E. C.) Cogswell, Rosa Sullway, Julie Mechanic, Mary E. Breckon, Isora Forberg, Lily (and/or Libby) Levinson, Mrs Bohlman, Florence Basora, Joy Pollard, and Bessie A. Hanan.

2. In addition to printed sources on Lemberg, I have also drawn on the reminiscences of Jenny Lahti Velsek and the researches of Harry Siitonen.

3. A photograph of a somewhat older Katie Phar appears on page 4 of the 28th edition (July 1945) of the *Little Red Song Book.*

4. The version of Phar's letter published by Foner breaks off after the words "and when" in the sentence beginning, "The Rebel Girl would be best, I think."

5. The heavy red overlay on this cover design makes its reproduction almost impossible in black and white. In the photostatic version reproduced in Stavis 1955 (page 39) the photo of Flynn is invisible.

6. Hazel Dickens's rewritten "Rebel Girl" is featured on the Smithsonian/Folkways Joe Hill song album, now available as a CD.

7. Ashleigh's New York lyrics, titled "The Breadline Song," are included in Stavis 1960, 36.

"Dust" Wallin shows the relative strength of the organized
and the unorganized (*One Big Union Monthly*, November 1920).

An issue of the 1930s series of *One Big Union Monthly*
featured Taisto Luoma's drawing of women pickets.

2. THE STRANGE CASE OF AGNES THECLA FAIR

All revolutions are rooted in dreams.
—Grace Nichols—

Hill's friend Alexander MacKay was convinced that "most of Joe's songs were composed on the [San] Pedro waterfront." He even recalled him working on "The Rebel Girl" in San Pedro. "In fact," he added, "I think I inspired him to write 'Rebel Girl' by telling him about the greatest rebel girl I ever encountered—Agnes Fair" [27 Nov 1947].

Fellow Worker MacKay, a veteran of the San Diego Free Speech Fight of 1912 and one of that struggle's best chroniclers, was also, as the reader is surely aware by now, one of the most dependable informants on Joe Hill. When such a man declares that Agnes Fair was a great rebel, and that she inspired Hill's song, we have every reason to pay attention. Let us note in passing that the fact that "The Rebel Girl" is known to have been completed in the Salt Lake City jail does not preclude the possibility that an earlier version was written elsewhere.

When and where Hill in fact wrote "The Rebel Girl," and who inspired it, are relatively minor mysteries. The mystery of Agnes Fair, however, goes much deeper. The *Industrial Worker* for 17 July 1963 includes a letter from a young researcher who signed himself "Zapata Modesto," stating that he was nearing completion of a major study of the Wobbly bard, but still needed further information on a few of Hill's friends. One of the individuals he wanted to know more about was "Agnes Thecla Fair, who," he added, "committed suicide over Joe" [3].

The plot thickens!

Before examining this provocative assertion of "Zapata Modesto," let us first take up the question: Who was Agnes Fair? MacKay himself, who obviously held her in high esteem, seemed to know very little about her:

> In those days we didn't try to extract biographical material from the Wobs we encountered. If a guy or a gal, like Joe or Agnes, wanted to loosen up and spill some dope, good and well, otherwise we didn't pry into their antecedents. How in Hell were we to know that the world would some day want to feast on their heroic remains? The story of Agnes Fair was a tremendous epic, but no one thought anything much of it at the time. [letter to editor

of *Industrial Worker*, 27 Nov 1947]

Unfortunately, no one seems to have thought anything much about it later, either. None of the general histories of the IWW mention her. Her name appears only once in the five-thousand-plus listings in Dione Miles's monumental 1986 IWW bibliography. And like numerous other outstanding revolutionary women—Lucy Parsons, Martha Biegler, Laura P. Emerson, Mary E. Marcy, and Sarraine Berreitter, to name a few—Agnes Fair is not included in the multi-volume reference, *Notable American Women*.

That she has been so thoroughly ignored is surprising in view of the fact that Fair was significantly remembered in the autobiographical writings of Elizabeth Gurley Flynn. It is known that Fair played a notable role in the IWW's Spokane Free-Speech Fight of 1909-10 and that she was also a contributor to the influential *International Socialist Review*.

The Spokane Free-Speech Fight was a major event, and by all accounts one of the brightest moments in IWW history. It ended in a resounding victory for the union, and for the cause of free speech for all. Its many hundreds of participants included some of the IWW's most celebrated figures: James P. Thompson, George Speed, Elizabeth Gurley Flynn, Richard Brazier, and Walter Nef.

At one point in the fight, Fellow Worker Agnes Thecla Fair jumped on the box, started speaking, drew a big crowd, and after ten minutes was hauled off to jail by the cops. The same thing also happened to hundreds of other IWW members in the course of that four-month struggle. Only a few, however, wrote about their experiences, and Agnes Fair was one. The harrowing account of her arrest, "interrogation," humiliation, and near-rape by the Spokane police appeared in the Seattle *Workingman's Paper* in November 1911, under the title "Miss Fair's Letter." The text was also telegraphed to and published (slightly edited) in the December issue of the *International Socialist Review* in Chicago.

"I am now labeled by police as a DANGEROUS CHARACTER," her letter begins, and goes on to say

> My offense was mixing in the free speech fight. . . . They put me in a dark cell, and about ten, big burley brutes came in and began to question me about our union. I was so scared I could not talk. One said, "We'll make you talk." Another said, "She'll talk before we get through with her." Another said, "f--k her and

she'll talk." Just then one started to unbutton my waist, and I
went into spasms which I never recovered from until evening.

    I was hardly over the first when they brought in a man
disguised as a woman and put him in a cot next to me. I thought
it was a drunken woman until the officers went out. Then I felt a
large hand creeping over me. It's too horrible to put on paper. I
jumped out into an enclosure, screaming frantically and frothing
at the mouth. Had not two of our girls been arrested and brought
in just then I do not think I would ever come to.

    Even then they showed no disposition to treat me as human.
I never slept or ate the three days I was in there. The third day I
was so weak when the doctor called, and they would not have let
me out then only the doctor said . . . "She cannot stand it another
hour. . . ." [Later] fellow workers carried me on a stretcher
through the principal streets to my room.

Fair apologized to her readers for directly quoting the cops' foul
language ("I never heard anything so vile") but did not want to
falsify her account by using polite euphemisms. According to Philip
Foner, who reprinted her letter in his IWW free-speech fight
anthology, Fair's use of the "F-word" almost resulted in the banning of that issue of the *Workingman's Paper* from the mails [Foner
1981, 34].

    Elizabeth Gurley Flynn met Fair during the Spokane fight, and
was clearly impressed. In an autobiographical sketch published in
1937, Flynn recalled Agnes Fair as

an interesting woman character. . . . A slight, delicate woman,
very intense, she rushed frantically around on a self-appointed
mission—to convert the farmers. She was the first woman hobo
I met. . . . A little volume written in Alaska, called *Songs of the
Sourdoughs* was her means of livelihood. During hard times and
strikes her slogan was "Potatoes for the boys!" and she gathered
up huge quantities of food from her converts. She sensed the
strategic possibilities of a workers' and farmers' alliance. . . . She
died at Portland, Oregon, and was buried by that good samaritan
of the Pacific Coast, Dr Marie Equi [Flynn 1937, 26].

    Years later, in the account of the Spokane Free Speech Fight in
her full-length autobiography, Flynn offered another glimpse:

Agnes Thecla Fair . . . came from Alaska. . . . [She] went out
among the farmers to collect money and food for the Spokane

fighters. She met with a generous response. [1973, 108]

From these fragmentary recollections we infer that Fellow Worker Fair was a brave and well-respected member of the IWW (and perhaps of the Socialist Party as well)—an activist passionately devoted to the Cause, who, like Covington Hall, believed that farmers could become allies of the working class. Her Alaskan background is also suggestive; Wobblies and socialists were far from rare in the frozen north in those days. The fact that she was also a poet, and known as such, is particularly interesting in view of her hinted-at association with Hill. Rumor has it that Hill himself set foot in Alaska more than once.

Fair's book, actually titled *Sour Dough's Bible,* was published by the Trustee Printing Company in Seattle in 1910. How many were printed is not known, but today copies are much harder to find than first-folio Shakespeares. Though only fifty-seven pages long, it contains an impressive selection of poems, parables, maxims, and exhortations. Many, including the excerpts from "The Sermon on Chilkoot Pass" that are scattered throughout the volume, are written in an ironic and slangy Biblical style. There are poems dedicated to the Western Federation of Miners, one on the Moyer-Pettibone-Haywood trial, and several attacks on wage-slavery, religion, and middle-class conformity. A number of poems focus on women, including "To the Women of the Northland," "Daughters of Hi-Yu," and a tribute to Emma Goldman.

As the book's title implies, many of Fair's poems are directly related to Alaska: celebrations of northern wilderness, praise for sourdoughs and "Esquimaux," and—in a humorous vein—a "Sour Dough's Prayer" that prefigures T-Bone Slim's "Lumberjack's Prayer." Fair's prayer reads, in part:

Thy will be done in Fairbanks, as it is in Nome.
Give us this day a "poke" of [gold] "dust," that we may pay our
    debts; thereby make glad our debtors.
Lead us not into barren ground, but deliver the dust.

A distinctly radical Alaskan romanticism pervades much of her work. One poem calls for workers' revolution in the frozen north:

Alaskans take Alaska
    Before it is too late.
Alaska, young Alaska,

Will hoist another flag—
Freedom's only banner,
The brightest crimson rag.

Another poem, only three lines long but one of her best, is a little nugget of northern black humor:

When Father Time calls on some old Sour Dough,
And you would reach him where the wise ones go,
Telephone to 48 Below!

The *Sour Dough's Bible* was evidently put together in a hurry. Some of the poems were already several years old in 1910, but others were mere scraps of "works in progress." As for the arrangement of the texts, it could be described as whimsical, for it follows no chronological, thematic or other plan. Such rough, unpolished, "hodgepodge" qualities are not uncharacteristic of IWW poetic compilations.

It would be interesting to know what Fair wrote after 1910. Meanwhile, until some patient student takes the time to dig through the Alaskan and northwestern U.S. and Canadian radical press of those years, her *Bible* has to be considered a significant achievement, faults and all. As one of the few women worker-poets to actually publish a book in the first quarter of the twentieth century, Fair deserves greater recognition.

Did Joe Hill ever meet Agnes Fair? Perhaps—but no evidence of it has yet come to light.

This brings us back to "Zapata Modesto," the pen-name of a certain Barry Nichols who is something of a mystery himself. For several years in the early 1960s Nichols seems to have been obsessed with Hill, and determined to write his biography; he also had big plans for a "Joe Hill Film Project," and another scheme involving television. His correspondence with Fred Thompson, Archie Green and others indicates that he visited and interviewed (with a tape-recorder) a number of IWW old-timers who had known Hill. He published a couple of articles on Hill, but well before the decade was over he had dropped out of sight, and has not been heard of since. Nothing ever came of his ambitious Joe Hill projects. The present whereabouts of his extensive Hill-related correspondence, interviews and memorabilia is unknown. (If anybody out there *does* know the location of this material, I would very much appreciate hearing about it; please write c/o the publisher of this book.)

In his 1963 *Industrial Worker* letter, Nichols gave no source for his statement that Agnes Fair "committed suicide over Joe." The statement, moreover, is ambiguous: Did he mean that Hill and Fair were lovers, and that she killed herself because the relationship went sour? Or, as seems somewhat more plausible, that she took her life in despair after Hill's judicial murder? Neither Flynn's recollections nor Nichols's letter mentions the date or even the year of Fair's death. Helen Camp, in her biography of Flynn, says Fair "committed suicide in the Twenties"—*i.e.* five or more years after Hill's execution [1995, 17]. Until new information turns up, however, further speculation seems futile.

Indeed, the sole reason for taking Nichols's unsubstantiated assertion seriously is that the list of old-timers he claims to have interviewed includes such names as Alexander MacKay, Louis Moreau, and Sam Murray—genuine friends and fellow workers of the Wobbly bard. If and when those tape-recordings resurface, we might find a solution to the mystery of Agnes Fair—and to many other mysteries as well.

Meanwhile, someone with a genealogical bent would do well to trace her birth- and death-dates, and to determine whether Thecla is a middle-name or her maiden name. It is very uncommon; not one Thecla is listed in the Chicago phone book. An extraordinary, highly imaginative painter named Julia Thecla lived in Chicago from the 1920s till her death in 1973. Curiously, when asked about her background, she replied that she was "half Eskimo" [McKenna 1985, 5]. As she was evidently not of Native American ancestry, one wonders: Was her reply perhaps a kind of salute to an older cousin or aunt who happened to be an Alaskan Wobbly, long since disowned and unmentioned by Julia's embarrassed parents? Was Julia Thecla related to Agnes Thecla Fair? (Here, too, I urge anyone with information on the subject to write me c/o the publisher.)

Like Joe Hill who, after the firing squad ended his life, lived on as a many-faceted symbol of resistance and revolt, Agnes Fair also serves as a symbol—a symbol of the countless women Wobblies who, having fought the good fight and given their all in the cause of freedom, have been cruelly "disappeared" from History. What Alexander MacKay called the "tremendous epic" of Agnes Fair's life may never be recovered, and the question of whether she inspired or co-inspired "The Rebel Girl" may never be settled. Even so, the little that is known about her is enough to show that she was a remarkable revolutionary character, and to fan the flames of our hope that we may yet learn much more.

Joe Hill: "Merry Xmas and Then Some" (hand-drawn postcard
addressed to Charles Rudberg, 18 December 1914).

Carlos Cortez: May Day (linocut)

Joe Hill

PYRAMID OF THE CAPITALIST SYSTEM
(*International Socialist Review*, October 1911)
Based on earlier images extending back to the revolutionary
underground in Czarist Russia, the "Pyramid" was also
issued as an IWW poster and postcard.

IX

WOBBLIES VERSUS "SKY-PILOTS"

1. JOE HILL, THE IWW, & RELIGION

To divulge wizardries
As we know best. . . . our laughter more musical
Than angry churchbells, clanking the distance
—Sterling Brown—

Joe Hill, the IWW poet, also exemplifies the IWW Atheist. His surviving writings—songs, poems, articles, and letters— contain not a single sentence or even a phrase that could be construed as sympathetic to religion. As his friend Alexander MacKay put it, "Joe positively hated and despised anything that smelled of soup and salvation" [review of Stegner 1950]. For Hill, churches and their dogmas were at best something to make fun of—and at worst a deadly poisonous form of social oppression, to be exposed with the hardest-hitting revolutionary humor.

Hill was by no means the first, or anywhere near the first, IWW atheist. By the time Hill took out a red card, around 1910, unbelief was one of the union's oldest traditions.[1] Indeed, the IWW's antipathy to organized religion predated its existence as a union. Those who planned its founding convention in June 1905 tellingly neglected to invite a priest, minister, or rabbi to pronounce a blessing or benediction. By ignoring this ceremonial detail, which was already a standard part of the routine at many AFL union conventions, the IWW let it be known that its radical non-conformism was not confined to economics and politics, but extended to the spiritual realm as well.

The absence of religionists at the founding convention was no mere oversight. The prominent role in the proceedings played by the ex-Catholic-priest Thomas J. Hagerty—who was still jokingly called "Father" by many friends—left no doubt in this regard. Suspended from his "religious duties" by the Archbishop of Santa Fe in 1902, Hagerty contributed an article ridiculing "Christian Socialism" to the *International Socialist Review* in 1903, and broke completely with the Church the following year [Doherty 1962]. In the meantime he became well known in the labor movement for the uncompromisingly revolutionary and anti-parliamentary workers' program he developed in the pages of the American Railway Union paper, the *Voice of Labor*, which he edited, and in other influential publications. He was one of the six labor radicals who met in Chicago in November 1904 to discuss the possibilities of forming a new, all-inclusive and revolutionary labor organization, and one of the thirty or so who, at the follow-up meeting in the same city in January 1905, issued the call for the June "Industrial Union Congress" which founded the Industrial Workers of the World. As the leading theorist of revolutionary industrial unionism, co-author of the *Industrial Union Manifesto*, drafter of the famous industrial union chart (which Sam Gompers dubbed "Father Hagerty's Wheel of Fortune"), and principal author of the IWW Preamble, Hagerty had an impact on the IWW that was second to none.

Like Hagerty, the other founders of the IWW were experienced, no-nonsense workingclass revolutionists. Few if any of the other founding delegates had the former priest's inside knowledge of the corruption and anti-labor bias of America's religious establishment, but none appear to have had any illusions that the clergy were going to lend the new union a helping hand. The IWW's founders knew that America's churches had overwhelmingly supported chattel slavery, clamored for the deaths of the Haymarket anarchists, railed against labor's efforts to secure a shorter workday, justified child labor, and were not about to rally to the cause of revolutionary industrial unionism. They knew that the great majority of the clergy never dared to criticize capitalist exploitation, lynching, police brutality, or other forms of ruling-class violence, but had no trouble insisting that workers remain meek, obedient, and unorganized.

The founders of the IWW realized, in short, that the churches were solidly on the side of the bosses and the State.

Delegate Pat O'Neil from Arkansas, one of the most colorful of those founders—among other things, he had helped organize a sailors' union in Hong Kong in 1848—put it nicely in his speech at the new union's ratification meeting: "While they [the clergy] have been talking and praying about His kingdom on Earth as it is in heaven, *we* have had nineteen centuries of Christianity and jails" [*Proceedings* 1905, 593].

The IWW, of course, like all true revolutionary movements throughout history, radiated a certain "millennialist" fervor, and much of its poetry and declamation had a distinctly "prophetic" tone. In these qualities, as in so many others, Wobblies resembled their Abolitionist ancestors: William Lloyd Garrison, Wendell

Phillips, Frederick Douglass, Lydia Maria Child, Sojourner Truth, Elijah Lovejoy, and John Brown.

The fact that the founders of the IWW inherited something from the "Heaven-on-Earth-Now!" traditions of the more radical Protestant sects is not at all anomalous, given the important and recurring role such sects played in earlier U.S. history. The inheritance, in any event, turned out to be both large and lasting. Certainly it helped shield the IWW from the narrow and inhibiting rationalism that has always given most Marxist propaganda a drearily passionless and prosaic dullness. That such words as Poetry, Dream, Vision, Inspiration, and Imagination are as common in Wobbly discourse as they are rare in the vocabulary of most Marxists probably owes a lot to the fact that so many IWWs were brought up to revere and respect "The Word" and "The Gift of the Spirit" at least as much as Reason, Logic and $2 + 2 = 4$.

Wobbly "millennialism," it should be unnecessary to add, was always strictly secular, and indeed, openly atheist. Like enthusiasm and love, millennial fervor and prophecy are not the private property of the religious. The IWW's prophetic tone, moreover, is closer to William Blake's than to that of any fire-and-brimstone churchman:

> Every honest man is a Prophet; he utters his opinion both of private & public matters. Thus: If you go on So, the result is So. He never says, such a thing shall happen let you do what you will. A Prophet is a Seer, not an Arbitrary Dictator. [Blake 1966, 392]

The fact that the IWW has roots extending back to the Reformation and beyond—to the early Christian and not-so-Christian heresies—should not, however, be exaggerated. Its larger and more important roots lie in late-nineteenth and early twentieth-century social and industrial development, the Knights of Labor and the Haymarket anarchists, and in the class struggle experience of its own founding members. Specifically religious influence appears to have been negligible, even in minor matters. For every Wobbly soapboxer who learned the rudiments of public speaking in church there were probably a dozen who learned the art as hawkers or ballyhoos in carnivals and circuses.

Critics who, like Wallace Stegner, have misrepresented the IWW as a "militant church" [1950, vii], or Melvyn Dubofsky, who pretends that Wobs regarded the general strike with "the same ecstatic belief and fanaticism that anticipation of the Second Coming arouses among evangelical Christians" [1969, 166], advertise not only their ignorance but also their malice. Individual Wobblies, in many and varied ways, learned important lessons from the history of religions, but religion itself they left behind. A few may have looked back on it as a form of childhood naivete, but many more came to recognize it for what it was and is: a fundamentally authoritarian institution unswervingly in the service of the exploiting class.

Unlike many atheist, freethought, and anarchist groups, however, the IWW never made anti-religious propaganda a priority. The union's constitution explicitly stated that no one could be excluded from membership because of creed, and the IWW was in fact highly successful in its efforts to organize religious-minded workers. *Solidarity* noted in 1914 that the One Big Union included "followers of the carpenter of Nazareth, . . . followers of Mahomet, and . . . followers of Confucius" [Foner 1965, 131]. The union's speakers and publications consistently stressed two basic points: 1) Labor's struggle against Capital is the central issue, and 2) Solidarity, via revolutionary industrial unionism, is the only sure method by which workers can win. Religion, as such, was not a major topic of concern. As long as a member abided by the union's principles, it did not matter whether he/she was an Atheist or a Zoroastrian, or anything in between.

What *did* matter is that certain highly paid religionists, loyal to what Wobblies called "the Master Class," kept denouncing the union as un-Christian, ungodly, and evil incarnate. Many "Men of God" were hard to distinguish from company thugs or the KKK. Billy Sunday, America's best-publicized evangelist in the 1910s, was quoted as saying: "If I had my way with these ornery-eyed Socialists and IWWs I would stand them up before a firing squad" [Chaplin 1948, 302]. The motive behind such mindless raving was not, of course, to win sinners to the path of righteousness, but to discourage wage-slaves from joining the IWW and improving their working conditions. Whenever these mercenary anti-IWW preachers undertook one of their countless "crusades" against the union, usually in league with a gun-toting "employers' association," Wobblies responded with vigor and dispatch—but they emphasized that the issue was *unionism,* not religion.

During the famous Lawrence Strike of 1912, for example, the bosses, politicians and clergy combined under the banner "God and

Country" to stir up religious and patriotic sentiment against the union. The IWW responded in a leaflet written by Carlo Tresca:

> The masters and the upholders of the masters condemn the IWW in the name of God and country. These questions have no bearing on the IWW. We have never made an issue of religion in our union. . . . We unite to gain from our masters a better livelihood--- more bread. To gain this economic betterment we must be united, sustain the union, and help each other as brothers. Religion has nothing to do with these . . . activities. [Ebert 1913, 159]

With very rare exceptions, Wobbly criticism of religion avoided anything that smacked of theological disputation, Biblical exegesis, or the fine points of hermeneutics. Instead, it concentrated on the reactionary, anti-labor policies of the churches, as well as the hypocrisy, dishonesty, and greed of the clergy. The forces of capitalist "law'n'order," however, often found such criticism more offensive than blasphemy. When IWW soapboxer Art Boose, the "Old War Horse," declared that "the Bible shouters sell Jesus Christ over the counter like so much sugar," cops hauled him away and charged him with "profanity" [Holbrook 1946, 457].

Wobbly critics of religion were well aware that religion as such tends to be a conservative and inhibiting force, and that the larger purpose of workers' education is to free the workers' minds from repressive belief-systems. If the function of organized religion in capitalist society is "to keep the workers in a mental stupor and economic slavery," as Joseph Ettor said of the AFL-supported "Militia of Christ," the solution was obvious: *more consciousness* [1913, 20].

The problem was: How to combat religion without frightening away religious-minded workers before they had a chance to grasp what the IWW was all about?

The fact that the IWW was in a sense two groups in one—not only the One Big Union, by definition open to all wage-workers, regardless of their political or religious affiliation, but also a *revolutionary* organization, or rather: an *organization of revolutionists*—posed any number of tactical dilemmas, and sometimes led to seeming inconsistencies in policy. This helps explain why the "Religion Question," generally regarded as an inappropriate topic for discussion at the annual conventions, or in the union press, or even in the internal *General Organizational Bulletin*, nonetheless kept recurring in one guise or another. On the practical level the matter was left largely to the discretion of the union's editors, speakers, and pamphleteers. In the IWW, a union of readers and writers, this informality and openness kept the discussion as lively as it was unpredictable.

At Wobbly conventions, for example, religion—although semi-officially recognized as a "private matter," and never an "item on the agenda"—occasionally crept into the debates, willy-nilly. In his closing report to the 1914 convention, for example, Bill Haywood noted with pride that IWW members "are to a remarkable degree free from all religious superstitions" [Chaplin 1948, 167].

And if the *Industrial Worker* and the union's other publications customarily rejected articles ridiculing religious beliefs (just as they rejected articles *defending* such beliefs), they did feature exposés of the ruling-class nature of religious institutions, and regularly chronicled the hypocrisy and other misdeeds of the capitalist clergy. Now and then they even found space for open controversy on the subject, as in this contribution by George N. Falconer, who had been one of the speakers at Hill's Salt Lake funeral:

> Religion is no more a private matter than is politics. If religion is altogether good it is in no danger from discussion or criticism. If it in any way hinders mental or moral progress or tends to block the march of evolution, it should be scrapped like any other useless antique. . . . The big crime of today is the smug hypocrisy of self-deception. [*Industrial Worker*, 3 Feb 1917, 3].

IWW opinion on religion was far from unanimous. How many IWW members attended church is not known, but the number is probably larger than a reading of the Wobbly press might suggest. How long church-going members remained in the union would also be interesting to know. Now and then, moreover, in exceptional circumstances, tactical alliances between the IWW and religious or church-related groups did occur. When the union began its major interracial organizing drive among longshoremen in Philadelphia in 1913, it met with massive opposition from the bosses, the AFL, the Socialist Party, the local authorities, and the criminal element. The union's sole institutional support in the community was the African Methodist Episcopal Church, whose minister observed: "The IWW at least protects the colored man, which is more than I can say for the laws of this country" [Foner 1974, 113]. Unfortunately, the documents that would have made it possible to study these subjects in depth were long ago stolen and destroyed by the U.S. government.

If some Wobs were vociferously anti-religious, others preferred to avoid the topic entirely, and still others made it a point to stress the fact that the IWW welcomed workers of all faiths. Though not a church-goer himself, or even a "believer," Fred Thompson was highly critical of the union's more aggressive atheists, and at least a few other members agreed with him. Swedish-born lumberjack Pete Johnson, who joined the union around 1919 and lived most of his long life in Idaho, was one. As he told an interviewer in the 1970s, when he himself was in his mid-eighties:

> Like most Wobblies I didn't have much use for religion or preachers. Most always seemed to be on the side of the boss. But I never made fun of any man's religion [Russell 1979, 275].

Sam Dolgoff, recalling a discussion regarding church-affiliated sympathizers in New York in the 1930s, quotes Ben Fletcher as saying:

> What the hell do *you* care if they go to church if they beat up scabs after the services and practice solidarity on the job? Don't interfere. Give them a chance to learn from their own experience. [1986, 133]

The range of views was broad, but the balance leaned heavily on the anti-religious side. IWW branch libraries, as well as the union's Work People's College in Duluth, carried a large selection of openly atheist, freethought, and anti-religious literature by such authors as Tom Paine, Shelley, Clarence Darrow, Marx, Paul Lafargue, Robert Ingersoll, Friedrich Nietzsche, Mikhail Bakunin, Voltairine de Cleyre, and Emma Goldman. Upton Sinclair's *Profits of Religion* was a favorite of Wobbly soapboxers, as were the many pamphlets by former Episcopal bishop William Montgomery Brown—known as "Bad Bishop Brown"—whose motto was: "Banish Gods from Skies and Capitalists from Earth." Religious books, however, were noticeably absent—even books by such religious radicals as William Ellery Channing or Theodore Parker. If a copy of the Bible was usually available it was not for spiritual edification but rather to enable soapboxers and writers for the IWW press to check alleged "quotations from the Scriptures" used by religious union-busters and red-baiters.

Many Wobblies also contributed to atheist, humanist, and anti-religious periodicals—readily available at IWW halls and workers' bookstores—and frequently expressed themselves on religion-related matters at hobo colleges and other open forums.

Now and then writings by IWWs found their way into works of somewhat broader circulation. A big international symposium titled *Labor Speaks for Itself on Religion,* published by Macmillan in 1929, included an essay by James P. Thompson, at that time the IWW's national organizer, and one of its best known figures. Although most of the eleven contributions by U.S. labor officials are as mediocre as one would expect, the collection contains some surprisingly bold and critical essays: by James Maurer, the Socialist president of the Pennsylvania State Federation of Labor; A. Philip Randolph of the Brotherhood of Sleeping Car Porters; and A. J. Muste of Brookwood Labor College. Thompson's short piece, however, is far and away the most radical and forceful in the book. Titled "Religion Is the Negation of Truth," the essay concludes with a ringing challenge to the "old order" of "phantom-haunted" Capital:

> You ask what we of labor think of you? We are horrified—horrified at the unnecessary poverty and misery and slavery in the world, horrified at you and your savage Gods—and we are determined to drive all of you from your thrones. And when you have gone the truth will have a chance, and peace and love will come and bless the human race. [61]

Not without reason was Jim Thompson affectionately called "the rough-neck Isaiah of the American proletariat" [George 1918, 71], and for those who were lucky enough to hear him speak, the experience was unforgettable. His fiery eloquence, alas, like the articles in the *Industrial Worker* and pamphlets in the IWW branch libraries, reached relatively few workers. Fortunately, those who took up the cause of Wobbly education had other ways of "spreading the word"—ways of reaching workingfolk who had little time for books or lectures. And so it came to pass that the union's attack on what "Dublin Dan" Liston called "religious bunk" adopted the characteristically Wobbly weapons of humor, poetry and song—the weapons of Joe Hill.

Hill himself, in fact, played the major role in this development. He was the perfect man for the job. His contempt for the entire religious establishment is evident in his references to "sky-pilots," "long-haired preachers," "holy rollers," and "silly priests," and as a political prisoner in Salt Lake City he let it be known that he had no use for religious books, with their "moral uplift and angel food" ("I'd rather read old letters over again than waste time on that") [*Letters*, 56, 19].

His first song to appear in the IWW *Song Book*, "The Preacher and the Slave" (1911) was popular from the start, and in no time was sung all over the country. Often called "Long-haired Preachers" or "Pie in the Sky," it is surely the most widely sung anti-religious song in U.S. history. A parody of the hymn, "In the Sweet Bye and Bye," it was directed mainly at the Salvation Army (or *Starvation Army*, as Wobblies called it), but applies to all parasitical pulpiteers who preach abject submission to the workers and glibly advise them to wait for their reward in Heaven.

A wonderful book could be written about the diffusion and influence of this one song. Its lyrics—reprinted in full or excerpted in countless song collections—also turn up in numerous novels and autobiographies. Horace Cayton—co-author with St Clair Drake of *Black Metropolis*, the classic sociological study of African American Chicago—devotes a whole page of his memoir, *Long Old Road* (1963), to his initial encounter with the song. At the age of seventeen, Cayton wandered into an IWW road construction camp in Yakima, Washington during World War I and met a Wobbly called "Red," who invited the youngster to join them after work: "We sing around the fire at night." When Cayton asked "What do you sing?" the Wob replied: "I'll teach you one right now," and in no time the two were singing Hill's best known song. "That's great," Cayton cried when they were through. "I want to learn the words. It would be fun to sing in church. I don't like ministers much" [102]. And so Hill's lyrics led directly to further discussion—about religion, race prejudice, class struggle, the IWW, and revolution. Cayton concluded that this old Wobbly, Red, "was the first person who had ever really challenged my beliefs, and it shook me profoundly. . . . In a way he was my first real teacher" [106].

Carl Sandburg's daughter Helga, in her *Sweet Music: A Book of Family Reminiscences and Song* (1963) recalls her whole family singing "The Preacher and the Slave" during her midwestern childhood in the 1920s and '30s. The song, she notes, was "by a Wobbly songwriter, Swedish by birth, who was arrested and indicted and shot to the ground at Salt Lake City, Utah, in November of 1915. Up and down the nation they used his tune" [28].

A more recent memoir, Roxanne Dunbar Ortiz's powerful *Red Dirt: Growing Up Okie* (1997) also recalls the song in a family setting, from her own childhood in "dustbowl" Oklahoma in the 1940s. In her case, however, the song was an instrument of family disharmony: Dunbar Ortiz's father, Moyer Pettibone Haywood Dunbar, sang it in part to tease and torment her devout Baptist mother.

Radical journalist Harvey O'Connor, recalling his youthful days as a logger and IWW in the Pacific Northwest, quoted the song's first stanza and chorus in his *Revolution in Seattle: A Memoir* (1964), and again in *Harvey and Jessie: A Couple of Radicals* (1988), a joint autobiography prepared with his journalist wife, Jessie Lloyd O'Connor.

"The Preacher and the Slave" was only one of many of Hill's songs that lampooned religious authority head-on. Other masterpieces of Hill's Wobbly bluntness include "The Tramp," "Scissor Bill," "We Will Sing One Song," "John Golden and the Lawrence Strike," and "There Is Power in a Union" (to the tune of "There Is Power in the Blood"):

If you 've had "nuff" of "the blood of the lamb,"
Then join in the grand Industrial band.

In other songs, the criticism of religion may be less explicit, but it is still evident. For example, "Workers of the World, Awaken!":

Workers of the world, awaken!
Break your chains, demand your rights!
All the wealth you make is taken
By exploiting parasites.
Shall you kneel in deep submission
From your cradles to your graves?
Is the height of your ambition
To be good and willing slaves?

It was Joe Hill, more than any other individual, who gave this Wobbly-style atheism its most popular and enduring expression. His songs undoubtedly peeved the pious, and scandalized the sanctimonious, but they also freed the imaginations, warmed the hearts, and strengthened the resolve of wage-slaves everywhere.

Once Hill opened the sluice-gates, a veritable deluge of Wobbly anti-religious verse was unloosed on an unsuspecting world. Inevitably, some of it was doggerel, but much of it is proletarian poetry at its finest. Covington Hall's "The Curious Christians" scores the hypocrisy of the warmongers who pretend to believe in a religion of Love and Charity. Very much in the spirit of Blake, Shelley, and Swinburne, it is a Wobbly classic:

> *For "Jesus' sake" they shoot you dead,*
> *they fill you full of gas and lead;*
> *They starve your body, stunt your soul,*
> *Then pray to God to "make you whole."*
>
> *They preach "good will" and "peace" and "love,"*
> *The "Golden Rule," all else above;*
> *They teach Man's Brotherhood as true,*
> *Then turn their war dogs loose on you.*

Laura Payne Emerson compared her fellow IWWs with other historic figures who ran afoul of the religious authorities of their time:

> *As it was with Galileo*
> *And all thinkers of the past,*
> *So with these Industrial Workers,*
> *Tyrants' shackles hold them fast.*
>
> *How the masters dread you, hate you,*
> *Their uncompromising foe;*
> *For they see in you a menace,*
> *Threatening soon their overthrow.*

Arturo Giovannitti's fierce lyricism was merciless:

> *No holy fire of pentecost can force on me a savior's love.*
> *I fight alone and win or sink I need no one to make me free.*
> *I want no Jesus Christ to think he could ever die for me.*

The greed and hypocrisy of religionists are recurring themes of Agnes Thecla Fair's *Sour Dough's Bible:*

Religion and Poverty go hand in hand;
Proofs may be had by the score,
From the woman who sells her body,
To the beggar at your door. . . .

The teller who robbed your city bank,
And left his babes in a lurch,
Taking along another's wife,
Was the fellow who went to church.

Fellow Worker Fair also proposed some workingclass additions to the Biblical Commandments:

Verily, I say unto you, thou shalt not call the police or hire a bloodhound.

T-Bone Slim's "The Popular Wobbly" (to the tune of "They Go Wild, Simply Wild Over Me") sounded a note of uproarious humor:

Even God, he went wild over me.
This I found out as I knelt upon my knee.
Did he hear my humble yell?
No, he told me "go to hell."
He went wild, simply wild, over me.

With even blacker humor, John Kendrick's "Christians at War" (to the tune of "Onward Christian Soldiers") satirized the churches' support for militarism and war:

Onward, Christian soldiers! Blighting all you meet,
Trampling human freedom under pious feet. . . .
Trust in mock salvation, serve as pirates' tools;
History will say of you: "That pack of G--- d--- fools.

How is it that so few commentators have acknowledged the *Little Red Song Book* and other IWW publications as a treasure-trove of workingclass atheism?

Visual equivalents are much rarer. Of Hill's surviving cartoons, only one touches on religion: the postcard sketch of himself playing a piano at a San Pedro mission (see page 161). The caption reads: "I've Got a Mission in Life, Don't Ye Knauw?" The mocking tone is plain, but it's a long way from "The Preacher and the Slave."

Other IWW cartoonists, however—including Ernest Riebe, "Dust" Wallin, Jim Lynch, and the Russsian/Jewish artist known only as Sam—did take up the "religious problem" in their art.

The most famous example of IWW antireligious art is "The Pyramid of Capitalism," based on a similar image from the revolutionary underground of Czarist Russia (see page 306). It shows a many-tiered pyramid, with a large moneybag, the symbol of capitalism, on top. On the first tier beneath the bag are a king, prime minister, and president, labeled "We Rule You." Next are the clergy of various religions: "We Fool You," followed by soldiers: "We Shoot at You." Then we see the bourgeoisie at dinner, in formal attire and waving their wine-glasses: "We Eat for You." At the bottom, supporting all the rest, is the working class: "We Work for All. We Feed All." A few of the workers are bent and weary, but others are rising in revolt, and one has unfurled the red flag of workers' revolution.

Reproduced in color on the cover of the *International Socialist Review* for October 1911, this stunning image was for many years a popular IWW poster and a best-selling postcard at street meetings [Steelink n.d., 154]. As an illustration of the way the Wobblies viewed religion, it has never been surpassed.

In the entire history of the labor movement in the U.S., the IWW stands almost alone in its courageous opposition to capitalism's organized religions. Reporting on the IWW's seventh convention in 1912 for the *International Socialist Review*, delegate James P. Cannon observed:

> Here was an assemblage which, to a man, rejected the moral and ethical teachings of the existing order, and had formulated a creed of their own which begins with Solidarity and ends with Freedom. [Nov, 424]

Significantly, however, not one of the book-length histories of the union indexes "Atheism," and only one [Foner 1965] includes more than a passing mention of religion. In the U.S. today, even among the left—perhaps I should say: *especially* among the left—criticism of religion remains a major taboo.

With two or three exceptions, all of the several dozen old Wobblies I have had the pleasure of knowing over the years—folks who had lined up in the union in the 1910s or '20s—were not only irrepressible atheists but also avowed enemies of organized religion. Like Hill's, theirs was a practical, proletarian atheism—the kind that merrily tears away religion's masks of Power and Authority, undermines its paralyzing dogmas, and laughs at its gloom and terror. What Bill Haywood once called "the *idee-logical* stuff" counted for little in the Wobblies' struggle to vanquish the religionists' miserabilist mystifications. Their aim was never to insult people, or to hurt their feelings, but rather to *free the spirit*: to open workers' minds to wider horizons.

George N. Falconer once pointed out that "To prevent the workers, the slave class, from thinking, is the chief task of every ruling class" [1927, 5]. Such insights, which are common in the IWW press, show once again that distinctively Wobbly ways of carrying on the struggle were in many cases direct adaptations of nineteenth-century Abolitionist strategy. Frederick Douglass, in his classic 1855 autobiography, *My Bondage and My Freedom*, had observed that

> To make a contented slave, you must make a thoughtless one. It is necessary to darken his moral and mental vision, and, as far as possible, to annihilate his power of reason. He must be able to detect no inconsistencies in slavery. The man that takes his earnings must be able to convince him that he has a perfect right to do so. It must not depend upon mere force; the slave must know no Higher Law than his master's will. The whole relationship must not only demonstrate, to his mind, its necessity, but its absolute rightfulness [1987, 194].

As Wobblies saw it, the first revolutionary step was to inspire the wage-slaves to think, and to think *critically*, to expand their moral and mental vision, and thus to give them greater self-awareness, which in turn reinforced their confidence in their ability to liberate themselves and to transform the whole society. IWWs fully agreed in this regard with Rosa Luxemburg's argument that the revolutionist's "immediate task" is "the spiritual liberation of the proletariat from the tutelage of the bourgeoisie" [1970, 331]. In the Wobblies' guerrilla war against the sky-pilots, theory and polemic were never the main weapons. Instead, they relied on the union's tried-and-true arsenal of jokes, poems, soapbox parables, parodies, and songs above all. And this distinctively IWW strategy proved highly effective. No group in the nation's history contributed more to the proletariat's "spiritual liberation" than the IWW.

Warm, energetic, highly spiced, humorous, creative, and profoundly imbued with the spirit of workingclass solidarity, Wobbly atheism qualifies as the direct opposite of the cold, static, tasteless, laughless, mechanistic and mean-spirited atheism of the professional middle-class rationalist.

Now and then a fellow worker lost his way and succumbed to the scissorbillish temptation of church membership. Such was the sad fate of poor Ralph Chaplin who, in his last years, became a Catholic convert. I'll never forget my old friend O. N. Peterson, sitting behind his battered desk in the storefront Wobbly hall on Seattle's Yesler Way, recalling his and other fellow workers' consternation when they learned that the author of "Solidarity Forever" had lost his senses and "went holy on us!"

Such capitulations were relatively rare. Those who stuck with the IWW for decades usually stuck it out to the end. As Joe Hill's old friend Alexander MacKay put it in a letter to Upton Sinclair in 1953:

> In the sixty years since I stole away from that Presbyterian Sunday School in Scotland, I haven't encountered a speck of real evidence to counteract Marx's dictum that "Religion is the opium of the people." [25 July]

In another letter—this one to his fellow Scotsman, John Keracher, whose Charles H. Kerr pamphlet, *How the Gods Were Made*, was widely read by Wobblies—Fellow Worker MacKay reaffirmed that the struggle against religion is a fundamental part of the IWW program of agitation, education, and organization:

> Few people realize that all organized religions have their tap-roots in the current system of exploitation. If they could be made to realize it, it could make a lot of mischief for capitalism. [31 Aug 1957]

---

1. There is no consensus among historians or other students of the union regarding the IWW and religion. For views on the subject that are very different from mine, see Arnal 1979 and Winters 1985.

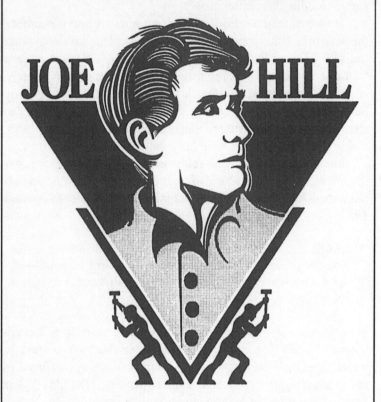

We Never Forget

JOE HILL

A Commemoration

Sugarhouse, Utah
November 19, 1915/1990

Cover of a brochure for the
Joe Hill Memorial Conference,
Salt Lake City, 1990.

2. THE MORMON INFLUENCE IN THE HILL CASE

Give a little more thought to the Quakers,
the Mormons, the Malthusians, and to Patagonia.
—Antonin Artaud—

The Joe Hill Defense Committee and its IWW, anarchist and socialist supporters held the Mormon Church as much to blame for Hill's frame-up as the Copper Bosses, the police, the court, Governor Spry, and other "authorities of the State of Utah." Later writers on the case have generally accepted this view. John Dos Passos, in his 1931 novel *Nineteen Nineteen*, was sarcastic about it:

> The angel Moroni didn't like labor organizers. . . . The angel Moroni moved the hearts of the Mormons to decide it was Joe Hill shot a grocer named Morrison. [456-457]

Decades later, Phil Ochs sang:

Oh, Utah justice can be had
But not for a union man.

Attempts to dissociate the Mormon hierarchy from the rest of the anti-IWW (and therefore anti-Hill) forces have been rare: a 1951 article by Vernon Jensen, and Gibbs Smith's 1969 biography are the most notable examples. Jensen and Smith, both of the Mormon faith, took pains to clear their church of complicity in Hill's judicial murder. To a far greater degree than most other researchers into the case, they examined its religious dimension, and some of their findings proved to be of the greatest interest. Jensen pointed out, for example, that the principal Utah officials involved in the Hill case were in fact not Mormons, including Judge Ritchie, District Attorney Leatherwood, and all three of the supreme court justices; half the jury was also non-Mormon [Jensen 1951, 365]. Smith, who complemented Jensen's data with observations and deductions of his own, made a clear and convincing argument that the Mormon Church *as an organization* was not involved in the Hill case "in any direct way," or as part of an "organized conspiracy" [Smith 1969, 130-131].

Smith acknowledged, however, that his and Jensen's findings were not enough to absolve the Mormon Church of all responsibility in the case. "Undeniably," Smith conceded, "there existed in Utah at that time an anti-IWW and Joe Hill sentiment which intensified during the months prior to Hill's execution" [*ibid.*, 129]. Insofar as the Mormon church was, in his words, "the single most powerful institution in Utah and clearly part of the state power structure" [*ibid.*, 130], it was obviously a contributor to that sentiment.

Having made these concessions, Smith's conclusions do not differ in substance from the view expressed by O. N. Hilton, Hill's appeals attorney, in his address at the Wobbly bard's Chicago funeral. The Utah authorities' hostility to Hill, Hilton pointed out, was not a matter of anyone's "direct influence," but it did reflect "the imponderable and undefined but always apparent and dominating fear of the Mormon Church" [Foner 1965, 99].

As Smith himself put it: "To say that there is no evidence of organized conspiracy against Hill is not to say that the people of Utah, and particularly Utah officials, can be held blameless in the handling of [Hill's] case." He goes on to acknowledge "indications" that "some Utah officials, whose special job it should have been to guarantee Hill justice since public opinion was against him, actually took steps to further aggravate that opinion" [Smith 1969, 131].

The evidence indicates that this was true not only of state officials, but also of Mormon church officials. The *Deseret Evening News*, official mouthpiece of the Mormon hierarchy, was unremittingly vicious and deceitful in its denunciation of Hill and the union to which he belonged. By helping to create a climate full of hatred for the IWW, the Mormon church hierarchy made Hill's legal murder easier.

Acute observers in Salt Lake City at the time were convinced that a "fair trial" for an IWW member was out of the question in Utah, at least partly because of the Mormon Church. Salt Lake City Episcopal Bishop Paul Jones pointed out the "well-known, but seldom mentioned" fact that "politics, finance, and organized religion form a powerful trinity in Utah which touches almost every question of public welfare" [Foner 1965a, 104].

The Defense Committee concurred:

We are confident that if the case of Joe Hill could be tried outside of the state of Utah, before unbiased judge and jury, that the jury would acquit him without even leaving their seats. This may sound like boasting, but the fellow workers from outside locals who witnessed the court trial and the hearing before the state Supreme Court know well that there is no case against Joe Hill. Some of the prosecution's testimony sounded so ridiculous that the spectators laughed outright and the judge threatened to clear the courtroom. [Rowan *et al.* 1915, 126].

In a letter to a friend, Virginia Snow Stephen asked

Do you believe there is justice for the poor working factory girl, or for the ill-paid person in other employment? If you knew and had seen right here in Salt Lake City what I have seen with my own eyes, you might change your view. [Smith 1969, 90]

Feminist Theodora Pollok was even more explicit. The IWW, she noted,

struck on a job for the Utah Construction Company, which is practically a financial subsidiary—and a very powerful one—of the Mormon Church, and thereafter had to fight for freedom of speech on the streets of Salt Lake. . . . Such then is the community from which Hillstrom's jury was chosen . . . and which decreed the death of Hillstrom. . . . [Foner 1965a, 73]

Pollok, furthermore, found that "Utah's ironbound conservatism and prejudice against [Hill's] labor affiliation was so great that otherwise stern disbelievers in capital punishment refused to ask commutation. . . ." [Smith 1969, 129]. In short, her own experience led her to the inexorable conclusion that the hostile "feeling" against the IWW was such that it "made a fair trial for Hillstrom ... impossible in Salt Lake" [*ibid.*].

In such cases, to remain silent is only to add to the prosecution's ferocity. If any prominent Mormon defended Hill, or denounced the murderous Axel Steele, or protested the University of Utah's firing of Virginia Snow Stephen for speaking out in Hill's favor, Smith doesn't mention it. Even more surprisingly, he ignores the considerable opposition to Hill's legal murder on the part of rank-and-file Mormons. Although Governor Spry never admitted it publicly, he complained privately to Mormon bishops that he was receiving petitions signed by the entire memberships of Mormon churches, as well as hundreds of protests from individual Mormons, demanding freedom or a new trial for the

IWW poet [Modesto 1962, 9].[1]

In his effort to demonstrate the Mormon Church's innocence in the Hill case, Smith would have done well to explore this groundswell of protest within the Church itself. Instead, and rather oddly, he argued that "perhaps the strongest indication that the Mormon church was not involved" is the fact that the 1948 review of the case by the "Friends of Joe Hill Committee," published in the *Industrial Worker*, made no mention of Mormon complicity [Smith 1969, 131]. This argument, however, is not tenable. Wobblies belonged to the *ad hoc* "Friends of Joe Hill," and probably even constituted a majority of its membership, but the "Friends" also included non-IWWs: socialists, anarchists, civil libertarians, trade-unionists, and liberals. The Committee, in short, was *not* the IWW and it did not pretend to speak for the IWW. The Committee statement, moreover, was drawn up exclusively to refute specific charges against Hill made by the Utah prosecution, as restated in 1948 by Wallace Stegner in his slanderous *New Republic* article. The question of Mormon Church complicity, therefore, was not germane.

The fact that the Committee statement makes no mention whatsoever of the Mormon church is probably at least in part attributable to Fred Thompson, an important force in the Committee, and a major contributor to the document. Unlike most Wobblies of his generation, Fellow Worker Thompson was decidedly "soft" on all matters pertaining to religion, and avoided controversy on the subject. Neither his 1971 pamphlet, *Joe Hill*, or the revised 1979 version, mention Mormon involvement in Hill's frame-up.

Other old-time Wobs, such as Richard Brazier, proved less willing to forgive and forget. In a 1967 letter to Thompson, Fellow Worker Brazier wrote:

> There can be no manner of doubt but that the Mormon Church played a major role in railroading Joe Hill to his death. And in this connection it might be well to note—and very few people have noted it—that the same Mormon Church played a major role in railroading 100 and more Wobblies to serve long, savage years of imprisonment in Leavenworth [in the Chicago Trial, 1918]. . . . In that trial the Special Prosecutor, hired by the Government, was the most savage and relentless one the Government could find. His being a Copper Trust lawyer, connected with the copper interests of Utah, should have been enough to disqualify him, but instead it only enhanced his value

as a Special Prosecutor. . . . Yes, Mr Nebeker was the ideal man for the Government's purposes. Nebeker was a high-ranking member of the Mormon Church, and no doubt had the full blessing of that Church. [18 July]

In any event, post-1948 articles on Hill in the Wobbly press (except those by Thompson), more often than not noted Mormon entanglement in the case. Fellow Worker Joe Murphy, in a 1980s interview, went so far as to say that "Joe Hill was killed organizing against the Mormon church in Utah construction" [Bird *et al*, 53].

Swedish historians have also been unrelenting. Ingvar Söderstrom, for example, considers the Mormon Church to have been "heavily involved" in the Hill case, albeit "from the back stage" [letter to FR, 5 Feb 2002].

Interestingly, in his surviving letters, Hill himself never mentions the Mormon church. His only reference to Mormons appears in Elizabeth Gurley Flynn's account of her brief visit with the poet in the Salt Lake county jail. As the two Wobblies said good-by to each other, Flynn was noticeably downcast. To cheer her up, Hill joked about an old man mowing the lawn outside: "He's lucky, Gurley. He's a Mormon and he's had two wives and I haven't even had one yet!" [1973, 193].

This light-hearted repartee, buoyant, almost flirtatious—with a touch of melancholy, perhaps, but not a trace of rancor—is a good illustration of Hill's character. It indicates, too, that the Wobbly bard, like the IWW itself, was not guilty of any narrow-minded anti-Mormon prejudice.

Indeed, Hill and his union scrupulously avoided bigotry in all its forms. IWWs were critical of the Mormon Church as they were critical of *all* organized religion, but not out of intolerance—not because they objected to this or that ceremony, or particular articles of faith. Their criticism—always focused on church hierarchies, never on individual believers—was based on the fact that all organized religions support the hellish horror called capitalism.

As they saw it, in Hill's words from "John Golden and the Lawrence Strike": "The preachers, cops and money-kings [are] working hand in hand."

---

1. Unfortunately, Modesto cites no source for this information.

Mary Lathrop: "Another One Who Was Framed:
Joe Hill, Executed by the state of Utah, November 19, 1915"
(mural, 1960).

3. AMMON HENNACY & THE SALT LAKE CITY
JOE HILL HOUSE OF HOSPITALITY

*Can you make a revolution without the help
of people who overreach themselves?
Indeed, does not a certain percentage
of light-mindedness enter as a constituent part
into all great human deeds?*
—Leon Trotsky—

For obvious reasons, religion-centered enterprises are rarely named for outspoken unbelievers, atheists, and blasphemers. Joe Hill, famous (or infamous, if you prefer) as a writer of fiercely anti-religious songs, would seem to be absolutely impervious to such inappropriate appropriation. And yet, for several years the Wobbly bard's good name was directly associated, in the eyes of a sizeable public, with the Roman Catholic Church.

While it lasted, the Joe Hill House of Hospitality in Salt Lake

City was recognized as one of the many "Catholic Worker Houses of Hospitality" scattered throughout the country. The Catholic Worker movement was informally organized—no membership cards, no dues—in New York in 1933, during the depths of the Depression. Its founders were Peter Maurin, a French oddball with quasi-mystical philosophical pretensions, and Dorothy Day, a former Chicago Socialist and IWW activist who, after a long emotional crisis, converted to Catholicism in 1927 [Day 1952].

As outlined in the *Catholic Worker* newspaper, Maurin's *Easy Essays*, and Day's many books, the movement's core principles include voluntary poverty, pacifism, nonviolent action, personalism (insistence on the individual's personal responsibility for creating a new society), and tax-refusal—*i.e.*, not paying taxes, a large portion of which are used for war purposes. The "Houses of Hospitality," however, have always been the focus of day-to-day CW activity. Their primary purpose is to feed, clothe, and shelter the homeless poor, but they also provide meeting-places for discussion, debate, and planning the next nonviolent guerrilla actions. Civil disobedience and trips to jail make up a large part of Catholic Worker history.

A majority of CW adherents have tended to think of themselves as Catholics to one degree or another, but an equally large or larger number have considered themselves anarchists, and a stubborn few have also identified themselves as atheists. Through the years the CW also attracted numerous against-the-stream artists and other wayward creators, including poet/novelist Emily Holmes Coleman, who had been Emma Goldman's secretary; Jamaican poet-novelist and one-time IWW member Claude McKay; and the great jazz pianist Mary Lou Williams.

Not too surprisingly, the movement immediately won, and has retained ever since, the distrust and/or outright hostility of the Catholic hierarchy, the FBI, local Red Squads, the political right and a large portion of the left, not to mention the great majority of church-going Catholics.

The CW story is in fact much more raucous, and infinitely less perfumed with the odor of sanctity, than its historians like to acknowledge. Dorothy Day brooked no opposition, and did her best to run a tight ship, but an endless succession of ideologues, heretics, provocateurs, dabblers in black magic, and more than a few completely deranged individuals kept climbing aboard anyway. To cite but one example of the "unorthodox" activities regularly carried on under CW auspices: Ed Sanders's then-notorious "little mag," *Fuck You: A Magazine of the Arts*—utterly inoffensive except for its silly title—was originally mimeographed at Catholic Worker headquarters in New York (until Day herself put a stop to it).

The name "Catholic Worker," however, has always conveyed the impression of a thoroughly respectable, official church affiliate, recognized by the Vatican. To this day many people think of it as a church-sanctioned lobbying group within the organized labor movement.

The Catholic reputation of the Joe Hill House of Hospitality thus turns out to be a misunderstanding, based in turn on the broader misunderstanding of the Catholic Worker movement. In truth, Joe Hill House had no formal connection with the Catholic Church, and received no support whatsoever from its hierarchy. The Catholic bishop in Salt Lake City expressly disavowed the project, refused to have anything to do with it, and let it be known that he and the rest of the Church hierarchy firmly believed in capitalism and the state, including militarism, the arms race, and the death penalty.

More surprisingly, Joe Hill House had very little to do with the Catholic Worker movement, either. In essence, the "Joe Hill," as most people called it for short, was basically a one-man operation, and the one man was Ammon Hennacy, also known as "the one-man revolution."

Brought up on an Ohio farm that had once belonged to two of John Brown's closest comrades (the Coppack brothers), Hennacy joined the Socialist Party and the IWW in the early 1910s, and took part in Joe Hill Defense activity in 1915 [Hennacy, 1970]. Two years later he was jailed for "conspiracy to resist the draft." In Atlanta Federal Prison he met Alexander Berkman and began to think of himself as an anarchist—or more specifically, as a "Tolstoyan anarchist Christian." In 1937 he met Dorothy Day at a Catholic Worker House of Hospitality in Milwaukee. Deeply impressed by the CW's pacifist opposition to World War II, he moved close to the movement in the late 1940s, joined a few years later and remained one of its most active and prominent figures through the early 1960s. He was a very close associate of Day's and for many years was her principal co-editor of the CW paper.

By the early '60s, however, friction had developed between Hennacy and others in the CW's upper echelons. Many of Day's acolytes resented his authority and influence in the movement. Some of the more dogmatic Catholics in the leadership, including Day herself, were particularly upset by what they regarded as his flippant criticism of church reactionaries. Worse yet, his relations with CW women seemed "at variance with church doctrine."

Hennacy's move to Salt Lake seems to have been his way of distancing himself from the New-York-based CW movement. Starting a new life in his late sixties, he returned to his Wobbly roots. Traditionally, CW "Houses of Hospitality" have been named after Catholic saints. "Joe Hill House" was anomalously, even heretically secular in this regard.[1]

Despite its worldly name, however, and Hennacy's estrangement from the CW movement, the "Joe Hill" exuded a strong Catholic atmosphere. Indeed, of all the houses of hospitality in the land, Joe Hill House was unquestionably the most ostentatiously Catholic. The heavy church emphasis was manifest in the large murals painted directly on the walls by Hennacy's girlfriend, Mary Lathrop. These gaudy paintings depicted the Holy Family, Joan of Arc, and in Hennacy's words, "something resembling a Russian icon." The centerpiece, however—Hennacy called it "the prominent feature of our House"—was a huge 12 x 15 foot mural of the execution of Joe Hill, together with Jesus on the cross (as Hennacy explained: "another One who was framed").

When Mary Lathrop helped Joe Hill House get started, she was a fairly recent Catholic convert. Her father had belonged to the Communist Party, and for a time she worked as a burlesque performer. Before moving to Salt Lake with Hennacy, she was very close to Dorothy Day, and had accompanied her on lengthy tours, as she did later with Hennacy. Anarchopacifist Karl Meyer, who took part in the CW movement in Chicago for many years, recalls Lathrop as "a wild character, very attractive, very pious. Many people thought she was a little crazy." And he added: "She was definitely not a great artist" [FR interview, 6 Nov 2000].

Indeed, no one—Hennacy excepted, perhaps—seems to have really liked Lathrop's painting of Hill and Jesus. Joan Thomas, a young CW activist who married Hennacy a few years later, conceded that the picture was not badly done, but found it "lacking in imagination" [Thomas 1974, 25]. Hennacy remarked that "The IWW wouldn't print this picture because it had Christ in it and the Catholic papers won't print it because Joe Hill is in it" [Hennacy 1970, 407]. Lathrop's Hill mural was destroyed long ago, but it remains one of the most bizarre artworks inspired by the Wobbly bard.

Hill's friend Alexander MacKay viewed the matter with characteristically barbed Wob humor:

> The mythical Jesus Christ rising to Heaven with the immortal soul of atheist Joe Hill is a spectacle to make the gods in High Olympus split their fat sides. I can still work up a chuckle when I think of Joe Hill up there on Cloud Number 75, gazing on that mural and on the general activities. . . .
>
> I suspect that [Joe] has added to his last wish another slogan: "Don't play around with my memory. Quit creating mythology around my memory. We don't need a Joe Hill cult, we need social action." [Modesto 1963, 7]

In fairness to Hennacy, a "Joe Hill cult" is not at all what he had in mind. His motives were strictly agitational and educational. He started by spotlighting a highly controversial topic that most Utahns had been all too willing to leave in the shade of confusion and deceit. In Salt Lake City, to name a public gathering place after Joe Hill—a convicted felon, after all, his obvious innocence notwithstanding—was of course a deliberate provocation. It disturbed people and made them ask questions, and that's just what Hennacy wanted, because he knew he had the answers.

Throughout his Salt Lake City years, he broadcast the truth about Joe Hill wherever he went. He spoke at the university, the local library, a Methodist church, a Unitarian church, four Mormon churches, and even to the Toastmasters Club. He spoke to interviewers from the Salt Lake dailies and the university paper, on local TV and radio station KSL. At the regular Friday night "radical meetings" at Joe Hill House, he repeatedly showed the half-hour Canadian Broadcasting Company film about Hill [1970, 418] and invited Bruce "Utah" Phillips and others to speak about Hill and to sing Hill's songs.

Not cultish mystification, but historical *clarification* was Hennacy's goal in reviving interest in Hill. He also wanted to stimulate local awareness that Hill was an important radical and poet, "the songwriter of the IWW." In a community where honest, disinterested information on Hill and the Hill case was almost impossible to find, the director of Joe Hill House made such information accessible to all at last.

Of Hennacy's numerous actions to make the truth about Joe

Hill better known in Salt Lake City, two stood out at the time and are still reverberating today. In 1965, the fiftieth anniversary of Hill's judicial murder, students Hennacy had influenced formed a Joe Hill Memorial Committee. Its main purpose was to erect a monument to Hill in Sugar House Park, former site of the prison in which the IWW poet was executed. The Committee organized a big meeting in the library auditorium, sponsored by the Friends of the Public Library and featuring talks by Hennacy and Bruce Phillips, after which Phillips and others sang Hill's songs.

Two years later Hennacy, Phillips, and others on the Committee brought out a 47-page mimeographed songbook titled *If I Were Free: A collection of songs sung every Friday night at the Joe Hill House*, under the imprint of the Utah Wobbly Press. The book included two introductions by Hennacy—a short sketch of Hill's life and another on Joe Hill House—along with four of Hill's songs as well as the Alfred Hayes/Earl Robinson lyric. The title-page noted that all proceeds from sales would go toward "the erection of a suitable monument to the undying memory of Joe Hill, poet and organizer for the Industrial Workers of the World, and murdered by the State of Utah, November 19, 1915."

Ammon Hennacy's tireless campaign to rehabilitate Joe Hill in Utah public opinion had a lasting impact, and it extended far beyond the boundaries of the state. Few people anywhere did more to make people aware of Joe Hill: aware of the life Hill lived, the ideals he upheld, the union he loved, the songs he wrote, why he was framed, why he was killed, and why he lives on in the hearts and minds of so many.

Somehow he also managed to find time to organize antiwar demonstrations, feed several dozen transients every day, commit civil disobedience in the service of many good causes, and confer with the many transcontinental hitchhikers passing through town, but his major mission in life seemed to be to make people *aware* of Joe Hill.

One may well wonder: What did Joe Hill do for Ammon Hennacy? Or to put it another way: How did Joe Hill affect *Hennacy's* awareness? To answer is not as easy as one might think. Hill was clearly an important inspiration, a real *force*, in Hennacy's life, especially during the Salt Lake years. He deeply admired Hill—talked a lot about him, lectured and wrote about him, reprinted his songs and often quoted them. But he never seems to have jotted down his most personal thoughts about the man. That Joe Hill occupied a very special place in his heart is plain, but Hennacy appears not to have taken the trouble to spell out the details.

The salient points are these: For nearly a decade, Ammon Hennacy lived *literally* "under the sign" of Joe Hill. And for Hennacy, that was a decade of profound change and liberation.

He started his House of Hospitality in Salt Lake City as a devout Catholic who attended mass daily. After a few years at the "Joe Hill," Hennacy not only left the Church, but denounced it with his characteristic obstreperousness. He added a new chapter to his autobiography, *The Book of Ammon* (revised edition, 1970), bluntly titled: "I Leave the Catholic Church."

No fondness interrupts this ferocious farewell. Hennacy's tone throughout the new chapter is scornful and sarcastic—in the old Wobbly manner. He renounces the "whole system" of Catholic theology; dismisses original sin, Papal infallibility, confession; and regards the Bible as folklore. But he does not stop there: He goes on to denounce the Church itself as a "reactionary organization," with its "emphasis upon pomp and wealth and prosperity while the world starves and wars go on." And then, with humor worthy of Joe Hill or T-Bone Slim, he defines Hell as "what the Christians have made of this Earth, in Christ's name."

Hennacy also emphasized his refusal to join any other church, "for they all support exploitation, and mostly they support war."

These are major changes in the life and thought of a man who for many years considered himself a loyal and militant communicant in the Roman Catholic Church. The hostility Hennacy had received from the local Church officialdom undoubtedly hastened his disillusionment, but Joe Hill and the Wobbly tradition surely played a role. Significantly, it was the *anti-religious* Hill that especially appealed to Hennacy. Even before he broke with Catholicism, he included Hill's "The Preacher and the Slave" in his autobiography—not just once, but twice (an abridged version on page 263, the complete text on 405). "Pie in the Sky" and "Preacher and the Slave" are both indexed.

Hennacy did not become an atheist; he retained plenty of what his IWW friends considered quirky beliefs. Fundamentally, in his mid-seventies he returned to the Tolstoyan Christian anarchism he had discovered as a Wobbly prisoner in the Atlanta Federal Prison during World War I. His "I Leave the Catholic Church" includes his new seven-point credo. Point One is: "To be an anarchist-pacifist and oppose as much as I can all war and violence, and the state which lives by these methods." He remained to the end a fervent advocate of nonviolent revolution.

Ammon Hennacy died as he lived—protesting statist violence. In January 1970 while picketing against capital punishment in Salt Lake City he had a heart attack, and passed away at the hospital. He was 79 [*Industrial Worker*, Feb 1970, 3]. As he had requested, his ashes were scattered (by Joan Thomas) around the Haymarket monument in Waldheim (now Forest Home) Cemetery, where a packet of Joe Hill's ashes had been scattered fifty-four years earlier [Thomas 1974, 224].

As a physical property "open to the public," Salt Lake City's Joe Hill House perished with its founder, but the spirit of the place lives on in Utah Phillips's heart-stirring song, "Good-bye, Joe Hill." Despite repeated efforts by the local labor movement and other Hill supporters, no monument to the IWW poet/martyr has been erected in Sugar House Park. Not that it makes much difference; as Jim Larkin said shortly before Hill's execution, "The man by his example has builded himself a monument that shall endure for all time."

1.Technically, the full name was Joe Hill House of Hospitality and St Joseph's Refuge, but only a handful of initiates seem to have known it

In this *Industrial Worker* linocut, Charles E. Setzer (X13) views capitalism's "boom and bust" mystique

Ralph Chaplin: Poster for the IWW Defense effort (*c.* 1918-19).
The drawing is adapted from an original by an Australian IWW
artist named Dino, whose name appears beneath
Chaplin's cartoonist pseudonym "Bingo."

X

COPS & WOBBLIES:
LAW, CRIME, PRISON, &
THE STRUGGLE FOR
WORKINGCLASS EMANCIPATION

1. HOW CRIMINALIZING THE IWW
HELPED GANGSTERIZE THE U.S.A.

The object of laws is either to multiply crimes,
or to allow them to be committed with impunity.
—D. A. F. de Sade—

Of the many bitter ironies that abound all through the Joe Hill case, the most striking is the cold-blooded, matter-of-fact way in which official representatives of "The Law" disregarded and broke the very laws they had sworn to uphold, in order to frame, convict and kill a man against whom they were unable to produce even the slightest real evidence. The prosecuting attorney who stopped slandering Hill and the IWW only when he felt called upon to bully a witness; the openly prejudiced judge who blandly suppressed vital defense testimony; the procession of perjurers known as "witnesses for the prosecution": Isn't it plain that *they* are the *real* criminals in the "Hill case"?

The Joe Hill trial, however, was by no means exceptional in this regard. This is one of the many bleak facts of life in class society: Once a poor person, and especially one with radical beliefs, is seized by the authorities—"the rapacious hell-hounds that growl in the kennel of justice," to quote Robert Burns—it is exceedingly difficult to make those hell-hounds let go. In his scathing review of the notorious 1887 trial of the Haymarket Anarchists, Illinois Governor John P. Altgeld referred to the court's "malicious ferocity," and those same words apply to the great majority of subsequent trials involving representatives of the radical labor movement [1986, 57]. The trials of IWW members Preston and Smith (1907), Ford and Suhr (1914), Haywood and a hundred other fellow workers (1918), and the Centralia victims (1920), are just a few of the most notorious of the many trials in which unprincipled, venomous judges and prosecuting attorneys, untroubled by mere lack of evidence, succeeded in convincing cleverly selected juries to convict honest workingclass radicals of the most unlikely crimes. In such cases, mere "evidence" and "due process" are not really relevant. As Charles Ashleigh noted in his autobiographical novel, *The Rambling Kid*: "A jury may think it's their patriotic duty to send all IWWs to jail, whether they're guilty or not" [1930, 266].

As demonstrated by the cases of Leonard Peltier, Mumia Abu-Jamal and many other radicals in more recent decades, the frame-up remains a central element in the U.S. injustice system today.

In Joe Hill's time as in ours, the cops and courts—in their cynicism and complacent hypocrisy—simply reflect the class-divided and white-supremacist social order they serve. The tiny minority who really benefit from the capitalist system have never accepted the blame for the immense and disastrous problems capitalism causes; it is easier to blame others—union-minded workers, for example, and especially revolutionaries. Capitalism is like the purse-snatcher who shouts "Stop, thief!" and points to some stranger in the distance to divert the crowd's attention from his own misdeeds. At every crisis, the directors and defenders of a system of thievery, robbery, murder, and terror have always found it expedient to accuse the critics of that system of thievery, robbery, murder, and terrorism.

This carefully calculated *misdirection*—as stage-magicians call it—is the basic ingredient of all capitalist propaganda. The propaganda helps stir up periodic Red Scares which make it easier to convict Wobblies and/or other radicals of crimes they didn't commit, and these convictions in turn appear to legitimize the propaganda ("The IWWs *must* be guilty, or they wouldn't be in jail, would they?").

In Hill's time propaganda for Capital was largely the jurisdiction of the daily newspapers and mass-market magazines, though clergymen, private detectives, scabherders, and college professors also played their part. Behind the scenes were powerful, often secret, organizations of businessmen or "citizens" (such as the Ku Klux Klan and the American Protective League), whose influence on the press, police and politicians was enormous. Church-going Christians, flag-waving patriots, xenophobes, champions of the "White Race," and other ill-assorted protofascist hoodlums: Such were the people who fabricated the myth that the IWW was, by definition, what Theodore Roosevelt called it—"a criminal organization"—and that its individual members therefore were all criminals [Taft 1972, 28] In front-page scare stories, outraged editorials, blood-curdling sermons, and a plethora of paranoid pamphlets, these anti-IWW zealots portrayed the most selflessly idealistic and altruistic union in U.S. history as a horde of fiendish felons.

From the mid-1910s through the late '20s, the persecution expanded. In 1919 a socialist paper friendly to the IWW, *The New Justice* of Los Angeles, noted that

> the reactionary press is indulging in a veritable debauch of invective and vituperation directed against the Industrial Workers of the World. There is scarcely any known disaster which it does not in some ingenious manner strive to blame upon the "wobblies" . . . It must be said in justice to the newspaper scribblers that they have not yet attempted to hold the "wobblies" responsible for earthquakes, floods or tidal waves. [Nov 1919, 1]

Discussing the way the IWW was treated in the U.S. press in those years, E. W. Latchem quipped, in the *One Big Union Monthly*: "Very rarely did a bit of truth get into print" [Aug 1920, 55].

Anti-IWW literature was not, however, produced only by journalistic hacks, befuddled Mr Blocks, hate groups, and deputized thugs. "Reputable" publishers also contributed heavily to the confusion. Emerson Hough's vile potboiler, *The Web: The Authorized History of the American Protective League*, was issued in 1919 by the Reilly and Lee Company in Chicago, publishers of L. Frank Baum's Wizard of Oz books. Hough's whole screed reads like a pep-talk to a lynch-mob:

> For months and years . . . the Industrial Workers of the World, as they call themselves, had been notorious for their anarchy and violence. Countless acts of ruthlessness had marked their career; millions and perhaps billions in property had been destroyed by them. . . . Nothing lacked in their record of lawlessness and terror, and they were inspired by a Hun-like frightfulness as well as a Hun-like cunning which for a time both excited and baffled the agents of the law in a dozen Western states. . . .
>
> When opposed, [the IWW] wrecked and burned and ruined, maimed, murdered. . . . They [were] guilty of almost everything a depraved mind could invent in the way of crime. [134-135, 139]

In truth, there is no evidence whatsoever of *any* IWWs, any-

where, at any time, engaging in such crimes. The wrecking, burning, maiming, and murdering were entirely on the other (capitalist)
side of the class line.

Former Seattle Mayor Ole Hanson's bulky *Americanism Versus Bolshevism*, issued by Doubleday, Page & Company of New
York in 1920, is filled such odious nonsense as this:

> The IWW hate all countries, but our country, being the freest
> country of all, is more hated and despised by them than all others
> combined. The IWW ridicule the Divine law as well as human
> law. They believe it necessary and right to destroy all existing
> things. Their doctrine is that whatever is, is wrong. . . .
>   They are against all government. They are against all mor-
> ality. They are against all progress. They are against all decency.
> . . . They plan to establish a rule of the unfit, of the untrained, of
> the ignorant, of the unable, of the cruel, of the disappointed, and
> of the failures. [237-39]

Such anti-IWW literature was piously presented to the public
as The Truth, but in reality it consisted entirely of lurid stories
made to order as circumstances required. Meanwhile, as news
editors filled their columns with "news" that was really *fiction*—
for the simple reason that its authors couldn't have cared less about
the facts—professional fiction-writers started including strong
doses of anti-IWW editorializing in their novels. The role of novels
in developing anti-IWW sentiment has been underestimated, and
merits a more detailed examination.

In many novels, the union is a very minor sub-theme, but pictured so hideously that the reader is not likely to forget it. For
example, in Edgar Rice Burroughs's *The Land that Time Forgot*
(published in the popular *Blue Book Magazine* in August 1918), a
deranged traitor announces to his shipmates on a submarine:

> I hate you. . . . I was kicked out of your shipyard at Santa
> Monica. I was kicked out of California. I am an IWW. I became
> a German agent—not because I love them, for I hate them
> too—but because I wanted to injure Americans, whom I hated
> more. [c. 1955, 51-52]

Zane Grey's *Desert of Wheat* (Harper, 1919), a jaundiced view
of Wobblies in the wartime grain harvest, was something of a best-
seller. IWW historian Fred Thompson summed it up in one word—

"poisonous"—and added that the book "helped send many Wobblies to jail" [1976 , 89]. Grey's flinthearted hatred of the union is evident on every page:

> The very first rule of the IWW [aims] to abolish capital. . . That's no labor union! . . . They're outlaws, thieves, blackmailers, pirates. . . . The IWW . . . is nothing less than rebellion. . . . They are against the war, and their method of making known their protest is by burning our grain, destroying our lumber, and blowing up freight-trains. . . . Western towns are seeking to deport these rebels. In the old days we can imagine more drastic measures would have been taken. The Westerners were handy with the rope and the gun in those days. . . . [8, 42)]

In *The Red Mesabi* by George Ryland Bailey (Boston: Houghton Mifflin, 1930), the heroine descends into a mine-shaft and finds that

> Strange markings decorated the heavy planking on all sides. The letters IWW glared at her from every angle. She sensed a sinister menace in this evidence of an organization which worked under cover, yet left so loud a trail in quiet places. It reminded her of the probable sensations of a ship captain upon viewing the ravages of rats within the darkness of his own hold. [261-262]

In these and many other bedtime horror stories for scissorbills and the panicky petit-bourgeoisie, the reader is hit hard with the glaring "message" that the IWW is dangerous, secretive, unmitigatedly wicked and yet mysteriously omnipresent, as if Frankenstein's monster, Captain Kidd, Svengali, Doc Holliday, Fantômas, the Purple Gang and a dozen others of the same ilk had all of a sudden banded together in One Big Union of All Evildoers.

The extreme fear and hatred of the IWW by the apologists for wage-slavery recall the fear and hatred of their Abolitionist precursors by pre-Civil-War slave-owners. Those whose "private property" consists entirely of what they have stolen from the labor of others do not want to hear or read about the evils of slavery or the virtues of freedom and equality, and do not want anyone else to hear or read about them, either. In their struggle against the slave-masters of their own time, Wobblies—who considered revolutionary industrial unionism to be the direct continuation of the crusade to abolish chattel slavery—were well aware that the legal and illegal persecution they suffered was basically an update of the cruel treatment meted out to their nineteenth-century Abolitionist forerunners. As James P. "Big Jim" Thompson said to the court during the notorious Chicago IWW trial of 1918:

> The people who are knocking the IWW are the same type who dragged William Lloyd Garrison through the streets of Boston with a halter, [and] who killed Lovejoy and threw his printing press into the Mississippi River. . . . [Haywood 1929, 320]

One novel of the 1920s that treated the IWW very differently from those mentioned above was Edith Summers Kelley's *The Devil's Hand*—a story about the multi-racial working population in California's Imperial Valley, with a sub-plot involving the mid-decade resurgence of IWW organizing among agricultural workers. In bright contrast to the books just quoted, Kelley's novel includes such striking passages as these, from a dinner-table conversation about the Ku Klux Klan:

> "I'll tell yuh, mister, who belongs to the Klan: It's storekeepers an' preachers an' lawyers an' undertakers an' real estate sharks an' the like, people that's livin' off the workers an' doin' good the way things is an' don't wanta see no change made."
> "The Klan is opposed to strikes and the IWW because it is opposed to every form of mob violence," said Mr McCumber, swallowing an angry lump in his throat.
> "Yep, that's what they holler, an' a course it has a mighty good sound. On'y thing wrong with it, it ain't true. What they really mean is that they're afraid the workers'll git together in dead earnest some day, an' they want to have a mob organized that'll be stronger than the workers' mob."
> "You have entirely the wrong idea, young man. When did business men, clergymen, lawyers and such people ever resort to mob violence in this country?"
> "When? On'y a few hundreds o' times this past few years. Like enough you haven't put much thought on it one way or t'other an' so you don't know that most mobs is mainly made up o' white-collared fellers. They're the ones that does the lynchin's an' tar and featherin' an' all sech." [200-201]

Later in the story, a Wobbly is given a stiff sentence for "criminal syndicalism":

"Ten years? In the penitentiary?"....
"Yes, that's what they give you these days for loving your neighbor as yourself." [244]

Are we to conclude that the existence of *The Devil's Hand* demonstrates the triumph of good old American "fair play"—that Kelley's thoughtful book obviously offset some of the damage wrought by the mindless and murderous ravings of Zane Grey and other believers in "the rope and the gun"? The answer is no, because Kelley's book was denied publication in the 1920s, and in fact appeared for the first time in 1974.

Edith Summers Kelley's earlier novel, *Weeds* (1923), had received favorable reviews, and though it was no best-seller at the time it has long since been considered a "major work of American fiction" and even a "masterpiece" [Kelley 1974, flyleaf]. *The Devil's Hand*, however, was effectively suppressed. Harcourt, Brace "didn't like it"; an authors' agent who read it wouldn't take it. Famous writers such as Upton Sinclair and Floyd Dell could get away with putting some friendly references to Wobblies in their books, but not a relative unknown like Kelley. The working rule in those years seemed to be that it was perfectly acceptable to include IWWs as characters in a novel—just so long as they were villains.

We should all be grateful to Edith Summers Kelley for this important object lesson, demonstrating that the books "respectable publishers" turn away can tell us as much or more about the "spirit of the times" as the books they actually publish.

Later anti-IWW novels have tended to be a bit more subtle than Zane Grey's, and some have even been passed off as at least slightly "sympathetic." Wallace Stegner's oft-reprinted *Preacher and the Slave* (later issued under other titles) is the best known example, and it has probably done more to distort the truth about Hill and the IWW than any other book—fiction or non-fiction.

A little further on the reader will have the opportunity to see what one of Joe Hill's friends had to say about Stegner's book. Here, in connection with the criminalization of the IWW, I want to take another look at the article Stegner wrote for *The New Republic* in 1948, two years before his anti-Joe-Hill novel appeared. In this article, "Joe Hill: The Wobblies' Troubadour," Stegner attempted to give the right-wing myth of the "criminal IWW" some semblance of sociological support. His "point" was not only simple but simple-minded: Inasmuch as the IWW was chiefly interested in organizing the poor, he argued, it inevitably "picked up among its membership a good proportion of people with police records" [21].

Need I add that Stegner provided not one bit of evidence to support this spurious "observation" which is really an accusation? As usual with Stegner's statements about the IWW, he is not only wrong here, but *dead* wrong. Far from inviting professional criminals into the ranks, the IWW was a powerful shield against them. In many AFL unions—in the building trades, for example, and the stage-hands, and the teamsters, and many others—corrupt leaders not only welcomed criminals into the membership, but often allowed them to take over entire locals. Nothing of the kind ever happened in the IWW. What could armed robbers, jackrollers, card-sharps, con-men, burglars, bootleggers, or pimps have in common with the struggle for revolutionary industrial unionism and the abolition of wage-slavery? In the IWW view, such men belonged not to the working class, but to an illicit petty capitalism—and indeed, the specialty of such crooks was preying on migrant workers, immigrants, and the unemployed.

Moreover, the IWW had no appeal for grafters, embezzlers, or "piecards" (bureaucrats who used union office as a meal-ticket). Locally and internationally, its treasuries were always nearly empty. The IWW was a low-dues union, and its elected officials, speakers and organizers were the lowest paid in the U.S. labor movement; their devotion to the union was a labor of love. Wobblies thought of themselves as fighters for the Revolution. Every member was expected to do all he or she could do, in Hill's words, to get

> *all the workers in the world to organize*
> *into a great big union grand.*

But they certainly weren't in it for the money.

In short, criminals found the IWW utterly repellent. They feared and hated it, and willingly cooperated with employer, police, and military efforts to destroy it. In those days as in ours, the worst crooks were among the most vociferous flag-wavers. (One particularly outspoken Red-hater in 1920s Chicago was Al Capone.)

Criminals were entirely right to hate the IWW, for as Bill Haywood remarked in his testimony before the U.S. Industrial Relations Commission, revolutionary industrial unionism would

> do away with crime and criminals. . . . Abolishing the wage
> system—abolishing private property—will remove ninety-five
> percent of the crime. [1915, 64]

Or as Joe Hill put it in "We Will Sing One Song," the IWW was
not only "the hope of the toiler and the slave," but also "the terror
of the grafter and the knave."

In the *International Socialist Review*, Walter T. Nef noted that
as IWW organizing made "gamblers, bootleggers and hold-up
men" unwelcome in the harvest fields, these "vultures" were quick
to be employed as gunmen, vigilantes, and deputies by the local
authorities in towns throughout the harvest belt [Sept 1916, 142-
143]. The tendency of criminals to become cops, and vice versa, is
well known and has a long history. The *Encyclopedia of Western
Gunfighters* is full of cattle-rustlers, counterfeiters, bank-, stage-,
and train-robbers, and other miscreants who, between murders and
other felonies, served as officers of the law [O'Neal, 1979].

In his *New Republic* article, Stegner's larger purpose was to
persuade readers that Hill was "probably guilty" of the crime for
which he was sent to his death. Stegner seems to have persuaded
himself that the Wobbly poet, surrounded as he was by "people
with police records"—*i.e.*, fellow working men and women in the
IWW—couldn't help be anything other than a stick-up man, and
that therefore he was "probably" a murderer as well. Unfortunately
for Stegner—quite apart from his highly dubious "reasoning" in
this regard—the absence of *any* evidence that the IWW membership included "a good proportion of people with police records"
suffices to discredit his lamentable hypothesis. As Ralph Chaplin
wrote at the time, in response to Stegner's allegations:

> The only Wobblies that I ever knew with police records got
> those same records for fighting for human rights—there was
> never anything in the IWW that appealed to criminals. . . . The
> gangster elements of those days were discouraged by the IWW
> at all points . . . . Anyone who attempts to recast Joe Hill into the
> role of a thug and hoodlum is sadly lacking in the facts of life.
> [1948a]

These remarks are excerpted from Chaplin's "Open Letter to the
New Republic," published in the *Industrial Worker* after the *New
Republic* suppressed it.

What is most remarkable about Stegner's 1948 attempt to re-convict Hill is the way he reproduces the mendacious procedures that characterized the 1914 prosecution. Once again, "burden of proof" is conveniently swept aside. Stegner made no effort to ascertain that the IWW had actually recruited people with criminal records; he obviously just thought it up and decided to put it in his article because it sounded good. That a person is legally innocent until *proved* guilty "beyond a reasonable doubt" has been of no more consequence to Hill's posthumous enemies than it was to Prosecutor Leatherwood and his clueless but obedient jury at the original trial. In Stegner's biased article—as in other, more recent attempts to convince us that the Wobbly bard was guilty—we are given no new information, no solid facts, nothing of substance: just bald assertion, hot air, confabulation, insinuation, and idle "the-way-I-heard-it" tittle-tattle that would never be accepted as "evidence" in any honest court. In labor/radical trials, however, such "inadmissible evidence," or even no evidence at all, is often the *only* evidence.

Several IWW members responded to Stegner's *New Republic* article, pointing out his many errors, inconsistencies, and misunderstandings, but to no avail. Clearly the novelist was not interested in learning the truth about Hill, and preferred instead to believe the Salt Lake City police reports, the Salt Lake City newspaper accounts, and various false witnesses of the Harry McClintock type, who were only too happy to confirm his erratic prejudices. Having declared Hill "probably guilty" at least three times —in two short defamatory articles and a letter to the editor— Stegner went on to prosecute the IWW poet yet again, in copious detail, in his 403-page novel.

In *The Preacher and the Slave* he restated practically all of his earlier mistakes and vagaries, and embellished them with new ones. Most of his charges have already been answered, and there is little point in examining the fictionalized version of his falsehoods in greater detail. It so happens, however, that one of Joe Hill's friends—Alexander MacKay—wrote an important critical review of Stegner's book. This review seems never to have been reprinted, and has even managed to escape the attention of most Hill scholars.[1] Because it appears to be the only detailed defense of Hill by someone who knew him well, and also because Fellow Worker MacKay's observations are of the greatest interest, it seems to me that this virtually unknown text warrants excerpting here at some length.

Describing Stegner's novel as "a long way from being a true conception of Joe or the Wobbly movement," MacKay goes on to say:

> I knew Joe Hill, and I'm here to testify that the Stegner portrait is quite unrecognizable, and in many respects is nothing but a gross libel, even in spots sheer vilification. . . . It is just a yarn based on odd scraps of hearsay. . . . Why pick on Joe Hill in an effort to destroy the constructive myth built on the power of his songs and martyrdom? Joe earned his mythology the hard way, which is a damned-sight more than can be said for much of the mythology of our capitalistic and theological heroes and saints.
>
> The book crawls with logical and chronological errors . . . indicative of much of the misinformation [Stegner] has collected on Joe Hill. Stegner frankly admits his ignorance of the IWW movement and his ambiguous knowledge of Joe Hill. . . . [He] was barely weaned when Joe Hill was alive, therefore he has to rely on hearsay, rumor and gossip, and even plain damn lies, out of which he has concocted a caricature. . . .
>
> Joe as a martyr sticks in Stegner's craw, he comes back to it again and again, but, after all, the word martyr is merely a synonym for *victim of the System.* . . . How can anyone doubt for a moment that Joe's membership card in the Wobblies cost him his life? There is surely nothing new in rebels losing their life or liberty on one excuse or another. It is notorious that a well known criminal would stand a better chance in a capitalistic court than a well known rebel.
>
> Suppose, for example, that a well known gangster was caught in the act of bumping off a buddy, or even a cop. The testimony is direct and ironclad, not dubious and circumstantial as in the case of Joe Hill. The gangster is found guilty, but at the last moment before execution the President of the United States and the representative of a foreign government both plead for a new trial or clemency. Under such circumstances do you think for a moment that the guilty gangster would be executed? Not on your tintype! No one believes any such thing. You know very well the machinery of the law would instantly go into reverse, and discover various loopholes. The upshot would be that the guy would be found guilty of *tax evasion*, and he would be asked to serve a few months in the County jail, or at worst, on the Rock, after which he could retire to his private island, and live happy ever after.
>
> Scan the whole legal history of the United States, and you will not find a single instance of a convicted murderer being

executed after a double-barreled plea from two governments, unless indeed he was a social rebel, and considered to be a menace to the unity of the System.

It must be admitted that the Wobblies were awful damn pests to the Lords of Copper and the minions of law and order in the State of Utah. The Patriarchate got the impression from the propaganda that swelled over the country that they had captured a powerful protagonist of the feared and hated IWW, in the person of Joseph Hillstrom. From that moment Joe Hill's goose was cooked, evidence or no evidence. . . . Martyrs are made when rebels are condemned and executed on flimsy evidence. . . . The record of history is plain and to the point. . . Cooked-up crimes and cooked-up evidence has been a powerful class weapon for the elimination of agitators. From Socrates to Sacco and Vanzetti the story always ends with long years of confinement, or a cup of hemlock, or the scaffold, or the firing squad. . . .

[Stegner] has confused the Wobblies with Murder, Inc., organized as a "militant church" [and] has Joe Hill masquerading as a half-Villon crossed with Wild Bill Hickock.

1.A clipping of the review is included in a file of letters from MacKay to Archie Green in the collection of Green's papers, now part of the Southern Folklife Collection in the Library of the University of North Carolina. MacKay's review (mentioned in his letter to Green, 11 June 1960) was clearly published, but I have not been able to identify what paper it appeared in, or its date.

Lisa Lyons: Independent Socialist Club button, 1968.
Others in the series featured John Brown, Eugene V. Debs,
Frederick Douglass, Big Bill Haywood, Harriet Tubman,
Malcolm X, and Emiliano Zapata.

2. WOBBLIES AS CRITICS OF THE "INJUSTICE SYSTEM"

Only the poor break laws—the rich evade them.
—T-Bone Slim—

To give the devil his due, we have to admit that capitalist society gave IWW members an unusual opportunity—one almost never offered to the rich and powerful: a chance to experience *from the inside* the way the U.S. criminal justice system really works. Regularly jailed for such crimes as vagrancy (having no money), "criminal syndicalism" (union organizing), and speaking in public without a permit (here, of course, the laws themselves were illegal, in flagrant violation of the Bill of Rights), Wobblies gained an extensive knowledge of law, law enforcement, criminology, courtroom procedure, and incarceration.

For most of them, this experience was highly educational, but none found it pleasurable, and none were eager to go back for more. Indeed, what they learned in America's police stations, courts and prisons not only confirmed their revolutionary hatred of capitalism and its institutions, but also deepened it. Fortunately for us, it also deepened their revolutionary critique of those repressive institutions.

Many IWW members read Clarence Darrow's classic pamphlet, *Crime and Criminals: An Address to the Prisoners at the Cook County Jail*, which was published by Charles H. Kerr in 1902 and frequently reprinted. And some surely studied more detailed treatises, such as John Peter Altgeld's *Our Penal Machinery and Its Victims* (1884). It was their personal experience as "insiders," however, that gave the union's "class war prisoners" a special insight into the "criminal justice" *system*, and its pivotal place in the larger system of injustice known as capitalism.

Joe Hill himself, in his letters, documents the rank injustice and foul play that made his own trial such a travesty. Four years before his arrest, his first text published in the *Industrial Worker* (27 August 1910) was a letter denouncing police brutality [reprinted in Smith 1969, 52-53]. Two of his letters written in the Salt Lake City jail explode the myth of "Equal Protection Under the Law," and emphasize the class nature of "justice." In one he points to the legal disadvantage of being poor and a rebel. Because Morrison was a person of some prominence, Hill noted, the police required a scapegoat, and

> the undersigned being, as they thought, a friendless tramp, a
> Swede, and worst of all, an IWW, had no right to live anyway,
> and was therefore selected to be "the goat." [*Letters*, 49]

In another letter, referring to a much-publicized case of the time, Hill commented wryly on the remarkable ability of the rich to avoid punishment for almost any crime:

> I see in the papers that Harry Thaw was declared 'sane' and will
> be free pretty soon. Isn't that nice? If I could afford to have one
> of them 'brainstorms' maybe they'd let me go too, but them
> brainstorms are luxuries that us wobblies have to do without.
> [*ibid.*, 40]

(Thaw, a millionaire, had murdered a man he accused of seducing his wife; declared "not guilty by reason of insanity," he spent several years in a high-class mental institution.)

As a good Wobbly, Hill was particularly interested in devising ways in which the workers' movement could protect itself from the injustice of capitalist law. In jail, as he wrote to Elizabeth Gurley Flynn, he spent much time

> trying to figure out some way to counteract the high-handed
> tactics used by the dispensers of "Justice." It is easy enough to
> see a remedy from an individual point of view, but when one
> looks at it as a class problem, then it becomes quite complex.
> [*Letters*, 30]

In later years, two of Hill's good friends from the San Pedro years, Sam Murray and Alexander MacKay, followed up Hill's suggestion that the whole matter of "law" be examined "as a class problem," and became particularly astute critics of the "injustice system" under capitalism. Fellow Worker Murray contributed a long, brilliant essay on capitalism and crime to the IWW magazine *Industrial Pioneer* in January 1926. Some of his observations are directly applicable to the Hill case, and could be considered "first principles" of an IWW critique of law and criminology:

> It is far safer to be a safe-blower, murderer or malefactor of any
> stripe than a worker with the spirit to refuse to be a snitch and to

have the courage to stand up for his rights and try to induce his fellow workers to do so. [22]

The frame-up is an established and highly developed art in American court and police circles. With the typical judge or district attorney the matter of finding the guilty party is secondary to that of securing a "subject" against whom they can frame up a conviction even though they have to use the perjured testimony of the denizens of the underworld who may have been brow-beaten into testifying because the police have something on them. All they want is a "record" with no commas misplaced and no technical error on the part of the court. It is safe to say that fully fifty per cent of the convicts are victims of a frame-up, the guilty party having escaped. [23-24]

It is a noticeable fact that there is little crime among the revolutionists either foreign or domestic, except the common "crime" of opposing a crime-breeding system. [24]

In another article in the September 1926 issue of the same magazine—a historical sketch of bootlegging in Mendocino County, California—Fellow Worker Murray offered some acute observations on the relation between crime and government:

Government, from the federal bureaucracies down to the dog-catchers, is nothing but a giant industry. An industry devoted to the collecting of taxes, imposing of fines, and taking of bribes. A government by a ring retaining their power by force of arms —that is, whenever the reptile press and the "moral" influence of molders of opinion fail to perform the job in a more satisfactory way. Of the people gainfully employed in this country, one in twelve are getting their living directly through this gigantic enterprise, besides those indirectly benefitting, such as lawyers, pensioners, bootleggers, and a host of retainers that hang on the fringe of public office. [10]

Fellow Worker MacKay, in a long three-part memoir of the 1912 San Diego Free Speech Fight, serialized in the *Industrial Worker* in 1947, also spelled out some Wobbly fundamentals.[1] Discussing the Bill of Rights and their guarantee of free speech, free assembly, etc., he concluded that

These lovely laws are legal fictions. . . . Capitalism is a woefully wicked parody on the Great American Promise when we have such just laws with so much shameless injustice, but it is the essence of a class society that laws for all cannot function equally for all. . . . The world cannot be made safe for Democracy as long as Capitalism rules the roost. [9 Aug, 4]

Many other Wobblies wrote about the "crime problem" and "law enforcement." Testifying before the U.S. Commission on Industrial Relations in 1915, Bill Haywood went straight to the crux of the matter:

Did you ever hear of a mine owner or a manufacturer being prosecuted for violation of a law? . . . The courts don't work that way. [9]

Fred Thompson, one of the most influential Wobs of the next generation (he joined the union in 1922), wrote frequently on the capitalist "injustice system," which he knew inside and out, having spent the years 1923-27 in San Quentin penitentiary for "criminal syndicalism." Like so many Wobblies, he knew how to pack a lot into a few words:

The prison population is about ninety-nine percent working class, so the labor movement should show concern for its locked-up fellow workers. The recurrent prison riots are unmistakable shrieks that the world outside should look at what goes on inside. [*Industrial Worker*, Sept 1984, 7]

As a former class-war prisoner, Thompson knew first-hand that prisons were not meant to "rehabilitate," but rather to intimidate, demoralize and destroy. Like most Wobs, he refused to give up, and explained why:

The fact that the lackeys of the upper crust threw me in the slammer is no reason to give up the fight to shove them out of the manger. [1993, 83]

Many of the classic works of IWW literature—including Justus Ebert's *The Trial of a New Society* (on the Giovannitti-Caruso Trial of 1912), Walker C. Smith's *The Everett Massacre* (1918), and Ralph Chaplin's *The Centralia Tragedy* (1920; revised 1924)—are carefully documented exposés of police- and court-supported ruling-class terror. All of the Wobbly autobiographies—including those by Haywood, Chaplin, Flynn, McGuckin, and Fred Thompson—discuss capitalist lawlessness. Covington Hall's memoir, *Labor Struggles in the Deep South*, shows how cops and courts aided and abetted the terrorist "Lumber Barons" in their war on the IWW's integrated unionism. Some articles from the IWW press of the 1910s, '20s and '30s anticipate recent scholarship on the social and ecological damage caused by "white collar" and "corporate" crime (as in the 1980s Savings and Loan debacle, the Exxon oil spill in Alaska in 1989, and a swarm of more recent scandals).

Wobblies have also been astute critics of prisons and the whole concept of imprisonment. As members of what is probably the single most incarcerated organization in U.S. history, they knew the subject well, and treated it in every genre from song and poem to essay and book. Sociologist Robert E. Park, in *The City* (1925), argued that the hobo's "only important contribution" to American culture was poetry. "It is an interesting fact," he went on to say, "that some of the best of this poetry has been produced in jail" —and he particularly emphasizes the "songs of protest . . . and hymns of the rebellious IWW" [160].

Prison literature has in fact always been a major revolutionary genre, and the IWW made major contributions to it. Among the best remembered are Ralph Chaplin's *Bars and Shadows* (1922),[2] written in Cook County Jail and Leavenworth Penitentiary, and Arturo Giovannitti's "The Walker" written in the Essex County Jail in Lawrence, Massachusetts jail during the famous textile strike, and published as the opening feature in the September 1912 issue of the *International Socialist Review*.[3] Another product of Cook County Jail, Harrison George's chorus to his song, "Remember" (to the tune of "Hold the Fort") is also a Wob prison classic:

> *In Chicago's darkened dungeons,*
>   *For the O. B. U.*
> *Remember you're outside for us,*
>   *While we're in here for you.*

Throughout history, imprisoned revolutionists have written outstanding works of world literature. Numerous short stories, novels, plays, theoretical treatises, and polemics have originated in cold, bleak cells. Letters, however, appear to be the primary prison genre. Rosa Luxemburg, Ernst Töller, Antonio Gramsci, James P. Cannon and other radicals authored entire books titled *Letters from Prison*. When Philip Foner published his collection of Joe Hill's letters, he could have given it the same title, for every one of the forty-five letters in the book was in fact written behind bars during the IWW poet's long travail with Utah law'n'order. Although Foner's volume was incomplete, Hill's non-prison letters total less than a dozen. As he wrote in January 1915, after being locked up nearly a year: "One thing this jail has made out of me is a good correspondent" [*Letters*, 19].

What Joe Hill, Sam Murray, Alexander MacKay, Bill Haywood, T-Bone Slim, Fred Thompson and other Wobblies had to say about law, police, crime, criminals, courts, and prison is of more than historical interest. Much of what they wrote on these subjects is as up-to-the-minute as today's headlines. Drawn from their own experience and unencumbered by legalistic jargon, their writings outline a devastatingly thorough critique of capitalist injustice. They emphasize the class bias of cops and courts; the constant, daily use of frame-up; the importance of "burden of proof" in trials; and more generally, the urgent need to defend at all times the ever-embattled rights of free speech and assembly. They also show that the injustice system is a complex problem that cannot be solved by mere "reform," but only by social revolution: that is, by abolishing the inherently criminal dictatorship of Capital, a.k.a. the profit system and wage-slavery.

These are all still burning issues here and now, and in every country of the world.

American society has changed in many ways since the heyday of the Wobblies, but the "official" approach to the problems of poverty, crime, and punishment is more callous, corrupt, and hypocritical than ever. The old Fourth-of-July bombast proclaiming the U.S. "the freest country in the world" was of course never true—indeed, was always as hollow as the Statue of Liberty. But it is significant that few even *pretend* that it's true any more. And how could they, when everyone knows that the U.S. has by far the largest prison population in the world?

A 1999 investigative report on "The Failure of the Death Penalty in Illinois" fully confirmed the IWW view. Whole sections read like a summary of Joe Hill's trial. The report, for example, calls capital punishment

> a system so riddled with faulty evidence, unscrupulous trial tactics and legal incompetence that justice has been forsaken. . . . Many defendants . . . have been given the ultimate punishment based on evidence that too often is inconclusive, and sometimes nearly nonexistent. They have been condemned to die in trials . . . rife with error. . . . [Armstrong and Mills]

It goes on to cite numerous examples of the same sort of prosecutor misconduct that characterized the Hill trial: falsification of evidence to make a defendant appear guilty, concealing evidence that points toward innocence, and deliberate misleading of juries.

This report, published in the arch-conservative *Chicago Tribune,* made it plain for all to see that the so-called "criminal justice system" in the U.S. is a disaster and a disgrace.

Alas, even today many U. S. citizens, particularly those who think of themselves as "white" and "middle class," believe that this country's police and judges are basically honest and law-abiding, that trials in U.S. courts are fair, that frame-ups are exceedingly rare, that the death penalty and imprisonment are "effective deterrents." This just goes to show that some people will believe anything. Some people, as Joe Hill put it in his "Mr Block" song, even believe they "may be President some day."

---

1. For this series, titled "Liberty and Justice in the U.S.A.: Memories of the San Diego Free Speech Fight of 1912" (*Industrial Worker*, July-August 1947), MacKay used the *nom de plume* "Johnnie Johns."

2. First published in 1922, *Bars and Shadows* appeared in two U.S. editions. In a postscript to the introduction in the revised and expanded 1923 edition, Scott Nearing noted that copies of the book had "gone to all parts of the world." Thanks to the initiative of the English feminist novelist Storm Jameson, a British edition was also published, by George Allen and Unwin.

3.. "The Walker" is also included in Giovannitti 1962. Other IWW prison poems include "The Girl Across the Way" by Richard Brazier (*Industrial Worker*, 12 January 1918); "Night in Prison," by Charles Ashleigh (*Liberator*, May 1918), "Leavenworth, 1919," by Mortimer Downing (*OBU Monthly*, May 1919); "Thoughts of a Dead-Living Soul," by Manuel Rey (*OBU Monthly*, August 1919); "The Cellmate," by Raymond Corder (*OBU Monthly*, November 1919); "What I Read in the Paper," by Card No. 41894 (*OBU Monthly*, July 1920); "Hypocrites," by Ammon Hennacy (*OBU Monthly*, November 1920); "The Bars Say: No!" by Edward E. Anderson (*Industrial Pioneer*, February 1921); "A Vision in Prison," by Vera Moller (*Industrial Worker*, 13 October 1923); and four poems written by Fred Thompson in the Yolo County Jail in Marysville, California (*Industrial Worker*, 24 November 1923).

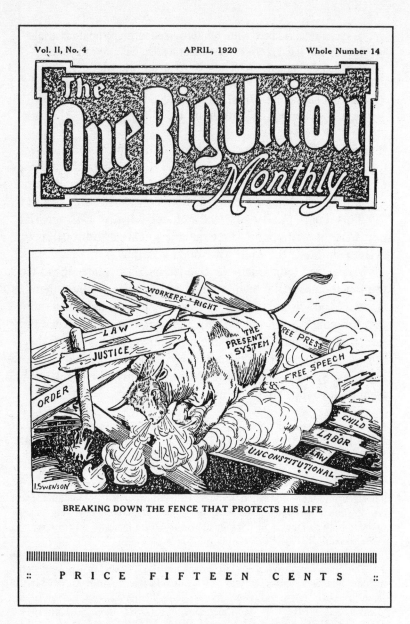

I. Swenson's play on the old "bull in the china shop" gag
shows "The Present System" (a.k.a. capitalism) destroying the
very institutions that have helped it remain in power.
(*One Big Union Monthly*, April 1920)

3. AXEL STEELE:
THE UNION-BUSTING THUG AS LAW ENFORCER

Government was intended to suppress injustice,
but its effect has been to embody and perpetuate it.
—William Godwin—

Inquirers into the background of Hill's frame-up have paid surprisingly little attention to the bloody career of a sinister character known as Axel Steele: gunman, thug, union-buster, and a prime example of what passed for "law enforcement" in Utah in the 1910s.

Steele was, in short, a hoodlum with "connections." Highly paid by the mine-owners and other corporations for his strikebreaking and violence against union organizers, he was also—at the same time—a duly appointed Deputy Sheriff. Thus he was allowed to commit the most nauseating crimes not only with impunity, but with the warm encouragement and support of the "better classes" and the State.

Steele's "type," alas, is far from rare; a long, miserable line of Klansmen, Pinkertons, blackshirts, American Legionnaires, White Citizens' Councils, stormtroopers, death squads, and neo-Nazi skinheads are all cut from the same shoddy cloth.

Utah police, like police in every other State and Territory, were old hands at persecuting the IWW. Steele, however, with the blessings of his corporate sponsors and Governor Spry, preferred the methods of State-protected organized crime. Brutal intimidation, armed assault, murder, mass arrests, deportation, and frame-up were his favorite ways of convincing Utah working people that the capitalist system was best. Steele and his gang had helped break the Western Federation of Miners' strike in Bingham, 1912, and during the IWW strike in Tucker the following year he directed the "removal" of 160 "agitators" (*i.e.*, union activists), transporting them by special train to the Provo jail [Smith 1969, 116-117]. The strikers, however, won their principal demands, and the prestige of the IWW soared throughout the area. The union's membership burgeoned, its literature was in great demand, and its street meetings, in Salt Lake City and elsewhere, attracted larger and larger crowds [Smith 1969, 117-120].

The rapid growth of the IWW in Utah was a direct threat to the occupational security of Axel Steele. We have no way of knowing whether his employers called him on the carpet for his obvious failure to exterminate the IWW. However, his next repressive effort involved a noticeable shift in tactics: It was more dramatic and more public, clearly calculated to make headlines. Above all, it was designed to present himself and his criminal cronies in a good light: as "true patriots" bravely challenging the IWW, which he and his press-agents depicted as a horde of traitorous un-American foreigners.

The stunt took place in August 1913, as Steele led an armed attack on a peaceful IWW street meeting in downtown Salt Lake City. As the assembled working men and women finished the last chorus of Joe Hill's "Mr Block" song, Steele (waving a U.S. flag) and his deputized plug-uglies charged the crowd, clubbing Wobblies and spectators alike with their revolvers. When the police showed up a few minutes later, they arrested the IWW speaker James F. Morgan,[1] who had been personally assaulted by Steele. Then the fire department dispersed what remained of the crowd by turning their fire hoses on them. No charges were filed against Deputy Sheriff Steele or any of his gang [Smith 1969, 119-120].

This was, in effect, a well-coordinated media event, and the Utah media loved it. Readily acknowledging that Steele was the aggressor, and that his attack violated the law, the press nonetheless unanimously took Steele's side against the IWW, which the Salt Lake *Tribune* (to cite but one example) called "a universal menace to the public peace, a standing threat against the good order of the community everywhere" [*ibid.*, 120].

Steele's repeated acts of violence against the labor movement made it easier for others to do the same. On 30 October 1915 an unarmed IWW street-speaker, A. J. Horton, was shot and killed by a Salt Lake City cop, H. P. Myton, for making "insulting remarks." This was murder in cold blood, in broad daylight, in front of hundreds of witnesses, but the cop was never brought to trial for the crime. Instead, he was acquitted of a lesser charge (Judge Ritchie presiding), and received hearty congratulations from his friends in the Elks Club [*ibid.*, 128]. Such was the climate of anti-IWW terrorism created by Steele and his bully-boys, aided and abetted by the *Deseret Evening News* and other papers.

A week before Hill's arrest, the IWW paper *Solidarity* called attention to the fact that "Axel Steele, the notorious scabherder" had been hired by the Utah Construction Company "to do its dirty work" [3 Jan 1914]. Did this "dirty work" involve, among other things, the frame-up of Joe Hill? In view of Steele's intimate association with the police and the real rulers of Utah (the copper bosses), as well as his long experience in frame-ups and his evident ability to manipulate the press, the possibility does not appear far-fetched. A brief notice in the June 1914 issue of the *International Socialist Review* is highly suggestive in this regard:

> The Utah Copper Company (alias the Mormon Church) are thirsting for revenge on the IWW. We have information that Axel Steele . . . has boasted in San Pedro saloons that the fact that Hill is a member of the IWW is enough to convict him with the jury they are getting ready for him. [763]

What was Axel Steele, hireling of the Utah Construction Company and Deputy Sheriff of Salt Lake City, doing in San Pedro— Joe Hill's old stomping ground? At this late date, it is probably impossible to find out. One suspects that, at the very least, he had a hand in the endless barrage of anti-IWW—and anti-Joe-Hill— tales of terror that filled the Salt Lake and Utah press for months.

The employing-class counteroffensive against the IWW was not, of course, confined to Utah. As Ed Rowan, Secretary of Salt Lake City IWW Local 69, noted in *Solidarity* a week before Hill's arrest:

> The moment the workers organize for material benefits on the job, not a stone is left unturned to use any means violent or otherwise to thwart them. . . . Profit is a serious proposition to tamper with. The masters never forgive or forget any action tending to reduce their bankrolls. Concerted action is now going on all over the country to imprison members of our organization. [3 Jan 1914]

Indeed, state and corporate terrorism against the working class in general and the IWW in particular—terrorism assisted by such groups as the KKK, the Burns and Pinkerton detective agencies and, after the war, the American Legion and the U.S. Army itself—raged for a large part of the next decade. The bleakest episodes in the union's history occurred in those years: the Everett Massacre (1916), the lynching of Frank Little (1917), the Centralia Tragedy and the murder of Wesley Everest (1919), the bloody raid on the San Pedro Wobbly hall in 1924, the Columbine Massacre of 1927.

Special unprecedentedly draconian laws were passed specifically aimed at destroying the IWW. Thousands of Wobs went to
prison for such spurious offenses as "criminal syndicalism" (which
often involved nothing more than passing out IWW newspapers or
leaflets) or "obstructing the war effort" (demanding better wages
and working conditions). In addition to the systematic anti-labor
Red Scare conducted by the U.S. Department of Justice and Military Intelligence, other agencies—including the Immigration Bureau, Post Office, and Forest Service—waged special anti-IWW
wars of their own. The whole ghastly campaign of terror against
the IWW has been told, and told very well, by William Preston, Jr.,
in his invaluable *Aliens and Dissenters* (1963).[2]

As government—local, state, and federal—criminalized the
IWW, government itself at all levels inevitably became more and
more criminal. The rise of large-scale organized crime, intimately
allied with urban political machines, business interests, and the
police, is a direct consequence of Capital's war on radical labor.
The traditional "glad-handing" varieties of corruption and graft
were replaced by a sort of "cowboy" version of proto-fascism,
characterized above all by massive and indiscriminate violence.
What was soon called "gangland-style" terror—very much on the
Axel Steele model—became part of the American Way of Life.
Kidnaping, torture, and murder were routine ways of dealing with
IWWs, and frequently applauded in the press, and by prominent
elected officials. Only once was the murder of IWWs denounced
on the floor of the U.S. Congress—by Jeannette Rankin of
Montana, in 1917. In the big Western mining towns, from Butte to
Bisbee, it was impossible to distinguish gun-toting hoodlums from
"constituted authorities," for as often as not they were one and the
same.

The attack on the IWW was thus a major defeat for all working
people, and a devastating blow to the little that remained of political democracy in the U.S. Criminalizing the IWW and terrorizing
the whole working class with a Red Scare made it all the easier for
gangs of real criminals to gain control of local governments and
business communities all over the country.

The gangsterization of daily life, and its relation to the bosses'
war on the Wobblies, are neatly encapsulated by Dashiell Hammett
in his first novel, *Red Harvest* (1929), which is in fact set in Butte,
Montana in the aftermath of a defeated IWW strike. (In the book
the town is called Personville, a.k.a. "Poisonville," but there is no

mistaking it for anyplace but Butte.) Introducing us to the "president and majority stockholder" of a big mining corporation who also happens to be president and majority stockholder of the First National Bank and owner of the city's only two newspapers, Hammett adds: "Along with these pieces of property he owned a United States senator, a couple of representatives, the governor, the mayor, and most of the state legislature" [Hammett 1972, 9]. After destroying the local IWW, however, this formerly omnipotent executive found himself sharing the power with people who were not exactly trustworthy:

> To beat the [IWW] miners he had to let his hired thugs run wild. When the fight was over he couldn't get rid of them. He had given his city to them and he wasn't strong enough to take it away from them. [The city] looked good to them and they took it over. They had won his strike for him and they took the city for their spoils. He couldn't openly break with them. They had too much on him. He was responsible for all they had done during the strike. [*ibid.*, 9-10]

Hammett's thumbnail digest of the process by which corporations and businessmen become criminals is particularly valuable because he himself, much to his later regret, had taken part in the events he describes. In the early summer of 1917 he was an operative of the notoriously anti-union Pinkerton detective agency, and as such, employed as a strikebreaker by the Anaconda Copper Company in Butte. His new employers were particularly eager to get rid of IWW organizer Frank Little; in Hammett's words, "An officer of Anaconda Copper offered me five thousand dollars to kill him" [Nolan 1983, 14; Johnson 1983, 20-21]. Shocked, Hammett refused the offer and by the end of June had enlisted in the army and was stationed at Camp Mead, Maryland—some 1500 miles from Butte.

On the night of 31 July 1917, Frank Little—one of the IWW's most effective and popular organizers—was kidnaped, beaten, tied up and dragged behind an automobile to a railroad trestle, where he was lynched. At least one of his murderers was known to the authorities, and indeed to a sizeable public, but neither he nor any officer of Anaconda Copper was ever arrested, much less brought to trial.

According to Hammett's friend in later years, Lillian Hellman, the assassination of Frank Little marked a major turning-point in Hammett's life. A rude awakening to the bloody reality of capitalism and its "justice system," it started the process which eventually led the former Pinkerton toward the radical left.[3]

Many years later, U.S. Supreme Court Justice William O. Douglas, who in his youth had known and admired many Wobblies, surveyed this grisly period in U.S. history in his autobiography:

> the logging companies, the mine owners, and the large ranches joined forces with the United States Army [which] in effect, displaced the courts [in dealing with the IWW]. . . . Our record as a nation against the IWWs was disgraceful. . . . For seven long terrible years the IWWs felt the full force of government persecution. [1974, 81-82]

As Douglas emphasizes, the logging companies, mine owners, and cattle ranchers, with their armies of gunmen and club-wielding thugs (euphemistically called "private detectives" and "sheriff's deputies"), were the arch-criminals in this national dishonor.

In the end, gangland persecution and government prosecution of the IWW helped make the nation safe for organized crime. In his 1930 book *Chicago Surrenders*, on gang terror in Chicago, reporter Edward Dean Sullivan—who, by the way, was no radical—showed how the gangsters' power and influence extended throughout the "respectable" (*i.e.*, employing class) community. He pointed out that

> no gang punk is more amenable to discipline from a gang mogul than are the corrupt judges, police officials, or politicians. . . . When they are in the graft they [too] are gangsters, no matter what they may protectively think of themselves. [237-238]

It thus appears that the Russian Marxist Nikolai Bukharin was more literally "on the mark" than even he may have realized when he wrote, in 1915, *à propos* the latest phase of world capitalism: "In our day the historic task [of the working class] . . . is to prepare a universal attack upon the ruling gangsters" [1982, 32].[4]

Quietly incorporated by the giant corporations, organized crime itself eventually became "respectable," and has long been a significant component of the dominant class. The gangsterization of capitalism in the U.S. and elsewhere didn't stop—it just changed its "image." Union-busting today is a thriving multibillion-dollar business, fully backed by government at all levels.

The old-time Wobblies warned us: A government that routinely convicts and imprisons the innocent, and simultaneously shields hired killers and other criminals, is a government on the side of crime—in a very real sense, it is a criminal government. As the IWW Preamble put it: "There can be no peace [and we can add: no justice] so long as hunger and want are found among millions of working people and the few, who make up the employing class, have all the good things of life."

1. Though ignored by historians, Morgan was one of the union's best organizers and speakers. The *Industrial Worker* (29 May 1913, 1) said that "Whenever he lights in a town the *IW* looks for several hundred increase in their bundle order." In Butte, the article added, Morgan sold—in three days—175 copies of the *Worker* along with "175 Song Books and 99 Ettor pamphlets."

2. On government repression of the IWW, see also Post 1923, Chaffee 1941, Fusfeld 1978, and McCormick 1997. In a more far-reaching study, Joel Kovel (1994) traces U.S. anti-communism and "Red Scares" back to the early white settlers' demonization of, and war against, Native Americans.

3. See Hellman, *Scoundrel Time* (Little, Brown, 1976): "I think I can date Hammett's belief that he was living in a corrupt society from Little's murder. . . . In time, he came to the conclusion that nothing less than a revolution could wipe out the corruption." Hellman's account of the actual murder of Little is, however, quite confused. In her statement that "Frank Little was lynched with three other men in what was known as the Everett Massacre," only the first four words are true.

4. This statement is excerpted from "Toward a Theory of the Imperialist State", written in 1915 during Bukharin's "semi-anarchist" phase.

Charles E. Setzer (X13): "For Whom the Bulls Toil" (linocut).
The cops' duty is to "serve and protect" capitalism;
clubbing workers is a big part of the job.

"Dust" Wallin: "The Ass in the Lion's Skin,
or 'All Dressed Up and No Place to Go.'"
This IWW view of U.S. Communism appeared in the
One Big Union Monthly (October, 1920).

XI

WOBBLIES VS. STALINISM

1. CONTRIBUTIONS TO A CRITIQUE
OF A COMICAL PARTY

Historically, the errors committed by a truly revolutionary movement
are infinitely more fruitful than the infallibility
of the cleverest Central Committee.
—**Rosa Luxemburg**—

The IWW was never impressed by the Communist Party's pretense to expertise in revolutionary theory—or in anything else, for that matter. After all, only a few years before the Party came into being many of the same gentlemen who formed it had been equally cocksure and belligerent spokesmen of the Socialist Party's right wing, or of the capitalist Democratic Party, imploring Wobblies to vote for Woodrow Wilson to keep the U.S. out of war. To IWWs, such flighty middle-class dilettantes were "experts" in nothing but party-line flip-flopping, and were incapable of inspiring even the slightest confidence in those who knew what the class war was all about.

Wobbly critiques of what many of them were already calling the "Comical" Party—I am thinking especially of George Williams's first-hand report on *The First Congress of the Red Trade Union International* (1921), and E. W. Latchem's open letter, *The IWW Reply to the Red Trade Union International* (1922)—are crucial documents in American labor and radical history, and should be carefully studied by everyone who seeks to understand the past hundred years of workingclass struggle in the U.S.

In the years 1917-21 the IWW was wholly sympathetic to the Bolshevik Revolution and its leading figures; indeed, the *Industrial Pioneer* ran a highly laudatory obit for Lenin in 1924, and as late as 1945 Lenin's birthday was a featured date on the union's official calendar. From around 1921 on, however, many Wobs were troubled by the increasingly statist character of the Revolution, and by the consequently diminished role of the workers' own organizations. As for the U.S. Communist Party, IWW members had a hard time taking it seriously. Despite repeated Communist efforts to "win over" the IWW to the Party's point of view, most Wobs never had any respect at all for America's so-called "Lenin-

ists." In the two pamphlets mentioned above, and in many other
IWW writings on the subject, the dubious theories and deplorable
practices of the U.S. "Bolsheviki" were subjected to a devastating
revolutionary criticism that the Party's subsequent and irredeemably squalid history has vindicated in all respects.

The Wobbly exposé of what a few years later would be known
as Stalinism tended to avoid gossip and *ad hominem* attacks, and
stuck to essentials: the Communists' massive ignorance of the U.S.
working class; the Party's naive and muddled misconception of
Marxism; its servile acceptance of each and every dictate from
Russian bureaucrats whose understanding of the U.S. workers'
movement was even more defective than its own; and, by no means
least, its obnoxious bullying arrogance and cynical disregard for
proletarian democracy. Much more than "style"is involved here,
but it is not without interest that the style of the IWW—as characterized by rank-and-file democracy ("We're *all* leaders!"), spontaneity, direct action, playfulness, songs, and humor—had virtually
nothing in common with that of the CP, with its overriding emphasis on the Central Committee, authority, obedience, total control,
and that holy-of-holies, the "Correct Line."

Fred Thompson in his autobiography (1993) quotes an unnamed friend who in 1920 observed that the Communist Party
"lived in the miasmata of their own effulgences" [76]. This is not
to deny that many CP members, especially among the rank and file
and local lower-level leadership, seriously thought of themselves
as proletarian revolutionists and did their best to act accordingly.
As with churches, AFL unions, and other top-down organizations,
the CP's rank and file was always more radical than the leadership,
and most Party members knew little of the chicanery of the "big
shots." With rare exceptions, the best didn't stay in the Party long.
Many could say, as a character in Chester Himes's *Lonely Crusade*
put it: "I never knew how much of a Communist I was until I was
expelled from the party" [1989, 378]. Not by accident, most of the
U.S. Communists' brightest successes occurred far from Party
headquarters in New York. I am thinking of the 1929 Gastonia,
North Carolina textile strike, for example, and the impressive
record of the Party's largely Black membership in Alabama
throughout the Depression years, as described by Robin D. G.
Kelley's illuminating *Hammer and Hoe* (1990). In his lightly
fictionalized memoir *Going Away* (1961), Clancy Sigal—who had
himself been active in the CP—remarked that

> the more the New York center of the Communist Party found itself in the cul-de-sac of its own formulations, the more frenzied its efforts to inform its membership with militant obedience. . . . It was a situation tailor-made for upper-class radicals who, above all, needed tight crises where they could justify abdicating their intelligences . . . to resolve all doubts and differences by opting for the crudest form of loyalty to "the working class": *i.e.*, the Party. [325]

From the IWW point of view, the CP turned out to be one of the worst things that ever happened to the U.S. labor movement. Unlike the AFL bureaucracy, however, Wobblies never succumbed to any form of right-wing anticommunism, and indeed always defended Communists against U.S. government persecution, and opposed anticommunist laws. As seasoned veterans in the workers' cause, moreover, Wobs knew the difference between the Party's hidebound elite and the broad rank and file. They were aware, too, that many thousands of one-time CPers eventually came to their senses and left the Party, but remained active in radical labor and other social struggles.

It was the Wobblies' own bitter experience with the Communist leadership—the self-styled "vanguard"—which led them to conclude that the Communist Party was not truly a workers' organization at all, but a hopelessly authoritarian middle-class political party, neo-byzantine in its hierarchical and bureaucratic structure, thoroughly dominated by a parasitical bourgeois intellectual elite, and therefore fundamentally *reformist* at best, and more often repressively reactionary, notwithstanding its occasionally shrill "revolutionary" rhetoric.

"Dust" Wallin's cartoon, "The Ass in the Lion's Skin, or 'All Dressed Up and No Place to Go,'" epitomizes the IWW view of the early Communist Party and its incoherent eclecticism. Published in the October 1920 issue of the *One Big Union Monthly*, it shows a small boy wearing adult clothes that are much too big for him: Liebknecht's hat, Lenin's coat, Trotsky's shoes and Haywood's pants. With an arm uplifted, he cries "Follow Me!" A pampered rich kid who, with delusions of grandeur, has proclaimed himself "vanguard" of the proletariat, but succeeded only in making himself look ridiculous: That is how the CP appeared to most Wobblies.

However, what may have started as comedy soon turned to

tragedy. The Party that decreed itself the "vanguard of the Revolution" became a bureaucratic machine determined at all costs to confine workingclass energies to the narrowest political channels. Vast subsidies from the USSR, along with donations from a sizeable corps of American multi-millionaire "fellow travelers," made it easy for the Party to pass for the dominant force on the U.S. Left, even as it slavishly accommodated itself to the propagandistic and electoral needs of Democratic Party fat-cats.[1]

The IWW's "disagreements" with the Communists have been noted in many studies, and sometimes described in detail, but the Wobblies have never received the credit they deserve as early, courageous, and thoroughgoing critics of Stalinism. *The Nation* and other credulous bastions of the U.S. liberal establishment continued to cherish the most absurd illusions about the Communist "miracle" decades after Wobs had recognized the CP as a political sect fundamentally inimical to the cause of workingclass self-emancipation.

Long before anyone else, for example—in fact, even before Stalinism as such existed—IWW members called attention to the infamously unprincipled and self-serving opportunism of William Z. Foster. A sectarian critic of the IWW in the 1910s, Foster led a tiny, short-lived, and utterly ineffectual group called the Syndicalist League of North America for a few years. An enthusiastic supporter of World War I and a patriotic buyer of U.S. war bonds, he eventually wormed his way into the favor of Sam Gompers and went on to become America's first and most sycophantic Stalinist. IWWs considered him one of the most pernicious figures in the history of the U.S. labor movement.

Communists, and especially Foster and the Fosterites, accused the IWW *ad nauseam* of "ignoring" or "shunning" the AFL unions. (CPers devoutly believed in Foster's pet notion of secretly "boring from within" such unions in order to "capture" them for Communist purposes.) The Communists' argument was deceptively simple: The revolutionists' duty was to be *with* the workers, and therefore *in* the AFL. In truth, of course, the overwhelming majority of U.S. workers were *outside* the racist, androcentric, xenophobic, anti-immigrant AFL unions, and among that immense unorganized mass the IWW was a real and dynamic force. It so happens, however, that Wobblies were *also* active in AFL unions, not to "capture" them, but to influence the membership in the direction of revolutionary industrial unionism and greater solidarity. As Fellow Worker Latchem noted in the aforementioned 1922 *Reply*:

> The militant minorities in the A. F. of L. consist, to a greater degree than is generally believed, of capable and active IWW members. They are not so concerned about advertising as they are about results. [9]

Many IWWs were in fact "doubleheaders"—that is, members of AFL (and later CIO) unions as well as the IWW. Some of the union's better known figures carried two cards, including Justus Ebert (Lithographers), J. T. "Red" Doran (Electrical Workers), Eugene Barnett (United Mine Workers), Donald M. Crocker (Typographical Union), and, among numerous Wobs in the various AFL seamen's and waterfront unions: Ben Fletcher, T-Bone Slim, Sam Murray, and possibly Joe Hill himself.

IWW agitation in AFL unions was well known, and not only to labor activists. Economist Carleton Parker, in his 1915 essay on "The Casual Laborer," noted that "many trade unionists in San Francisco were interested in the IWW, some going so far as to have cards in both organizations" [Parker 1920, 67-68]. Three years later, in another paper, Parker pointed out that "many" members of AFL unions "in the rough-handed trades, such as lumbering, stevedoring, and even shipbuilding," were known to also carry "the red cards of the IWW" [*ibid.*, 127].

The following year, 1919, in her firsthand account of an AFL-dominated "Free Tom Mooney Congress" in Chicago, Crystal Eastman noted that although "credentials from IWW unions . . . were not accepted" by the officials, it turned out that

> 38 out of the 40 Seattle delegates carried both cards; when excluded as representing IWW unions they offered their AF of L cards and were admitted. But they kept their red cards in their pockets and the IWW in their hearts. [1978, 304, 308]

Jean Spielman's sensational exposé, *The Stool Pigeon and the Open Shop Movement* (1923), is based largely on the files he obtained of confidential correspondence between union-busting detective agencies and the "management" of various industries. In one labor spy's report from 1920 the "operative" noted that "half of the officers of the different craft unions [in Minneapolis/St Paul] belonged to the IWW" [141].

When someone finally gets around to writing the story of the impact of these and thousands of other "two-card" Wobblies," the prevailing view of twentieth-century U.S. labor history will have to be radically revised.

The antagonism between Wobblies and Communists was by no means simply a war of words. Even as the Communist press slandered the IWW as "reactionary" and "counter-revolutionary," numerous Party members were secretly "infiltrating" the union with the express purpose of "liquidating" (*i.e.*, destroying) it. As one might expect, when such underhanded maneuvers were discovered, fistfights were often the result. In 1920, the Communist lie that IWW longshoremen in Philadelphia were loading arms to be used against the Soviets had a lot to do with the temporary suspension of the large Marine Transport Workers' local in that city. And in 1924, Communist Party skullduggery exacerbated the most catastrophic split in IWW history, a disaster from which the union never really recovered [Thompson 1976, 136-137].

Several former IWW members who later joined the CP, including William Z. Foster, George Hardy, Elizabeth Gurley Flynn, Len De Caux, and Art Shields, wrote lengthy memoirs designed to make the Party appear as the much-improved "successor" to the IWW. The same dubious picture is portrayed by historians sympathetic to the CP, most notably Philip Foner. Although these books are by no means devoid of interest, they are all warped by Stalinist assumptions and prejudices. All of them downplay IWW activity after 1918; ignore or deny Haywood's well-known disillusion with the way things had turned out in the USSR's "Workers' Paradise"; and maintain a discreet silence regarding the great majority of IWWs who rejected the Party, as well as those (James P. Cannon, Vera Buch Weisbord, Mary Inman, and others) who joined the Party but later resigned or were expelled. Needless to say, the Party's celebrity ex-Wob writers never mentioned the horrors of life in Stalin's Russia: the outlawing of workers' organizations and strikes, the bloody purges, show trials, mass executions, and forced labor camps. And not one ever acknowledged, much less condemned, the countless acts of violence perpetrated by Stalinists against more radical elements in the labor movement here in the U.S.

Indeed, the Communist Party's "goon squads," who rarely if ever had any trouble with the police, proved just as effective in eluding the attention of historians. However, despite the fact that the Party's rank and file barely knew of their existence, and that they are almost never mentioned in books on U.S. radicalism, these Stalinist hit-men were a brutal fact of life for independent and revolutionary-minded workers from the early 1920s well into the '40s.[2] In addition to their Party cards, these thugs carried black-jacks, clubs, knives, and guns, for their contribution to world labor unity consisted of beating up and sometimes murdering working-class revolutionists who dared to disagree with Stalin's constantly changing "political line."

It is interesting to note that the Communist Party, which meth-odically (and groundlessly) accused its revolutionary critics of being "social fascists" and "agents of Nazism," itself went on to support the infamous Hitler/Stalin pact of 1939.

The U.S.Stalinists' anti-worker violence—which also involved such related activities as breaking up meetings, burglarizing the apartments of expelled comrades, destroying opponents' publica-tions, and stealing mail—did a lot of damage to the labor move-ment, and fostered widespread demoralization throughout the working class, but it also had an unanticipated consequence of great interest: It brought Stalinism's revolutionary critics and oppo-nents together for mutual defense. Thus began one of the longest-lasting but least-written-about chapters in IWW history: its three-plus decades of good fellowship and cooperation with anarchists, Trotskyists, the Socialist Party, the Young People's Socialist League, the Proletarian Party, the Revolutionary Workers League (Oehlerites), and several other varieties of dissident communism. In addition to defending each other against Stalinist assaults, these groups regularly attended each others' socials, picnics, and picket-lines; spoke at each others' open forums; debated each other at such places as Bughouse Square and Jack MacBeth's Social Science Institute in Chicago; and jointly celebrated many a May Day over the years.

Relations with Trotskyists were particularly friendly, in large part because several of them—most notably James P. Cannon, Vincent R. Dunne, and Arne Swabeck—had been active in the IWW, and subsequently maintained comradely connections with many of their old fellow workers. When the first U.S. Trotskyist organization, the Communist League of America, held its founding meeting in Chicago in 1929, a large group of Wobblies formed part of the guard to ward off an expected CP attack [letter from Al Glotzer to FR, 22 Feb 1994, 2]. All through the early history of

U.S. Trotskyism, according to an old-timer in that movement, "the key" to its "organized self-defense" against Stalinist goons "was the rallying of many IWW militants or anarchists" [Gordon 1976, 52].

In New York from the late 1930s through much of the '40s the IWW shared a three-story office building with the Trotskyists (reorganized as the Socialist Workers Party) and the anarchist group around Carlo Tresca's paper, *Il Martello* (The Hammer). Here too mutual protection was the motive of this close coopera-tion. All three groups agreed that at lunch time and at the end of the day, or whenever any of them had to run an errand, they would leave in contingents of four or more—never as individuals—so as to be able to protect themselves from roving squads of blackjack-wielding Stalinists.[3]

This mutual protective alliance did not, of course, mean that Wobblies made any concessions to the Trotskyist program, or vice versa. Quite the contrary: Apart from defending each other from attacks by capitalist cops and CP thugs, and sometimes attending each other's affairs, they had little to do with each other. Here and there, however, individual friendships undoubtedly developed across organizational lines. In 1940s Cleveland, Fellow Worker Frank Tussey served as secretary of the local IWW Branch while his wife Jean carried on as an activist in the Socialist Workers Party. As late as the mid-1960s, in Duluth, a prominent SWP member and occasional candidate for office had a regular column in the English-language section of the IWW's Finnish-language daily *Industrialisti*.

Of all the dissident communist groups, as Fred Thompson noted in his autobiography, the IWW was undoubtedly closest to the Proletarian Party [1993, 74-78]. In this case the closeness was only incidentally related to self-defense, and in fact was largely social and personal, and almost certainly related to the fact that the PP, from the late 1920s to 1970, was the custodian of Charles H. Kerr's workingclass publishing house. Ironically, in matters of theory and program, the craft-union-oriented PP and the IWW were almost on different planets. The PP's quirky Marxism (which PPers considered very orthodox) emphasized the "proletarian epistemology" of Josef Dietzgen and the anthropology of Lewis Henry Morgan. Despite their differences, however, the two groups got along famously. PPers regularly made their meeting places available to Wobblies, and *vice versa,* in Chicago, Detroit, Flint, Cleveland and elsewhere, and they also conducted many joint rallies, debates, and social affairs. In Chicago, the most faithful co-organizers of annual Haymarket commemorations at Waldheim Cemetery, on May 1st and November 11th, were the IWW, the anarchist Free Society Group, and the Proletarian Party. Prior to the Second World War these memorial events, featuring speeches, poetry, music, and song, were often supported by the broader labor movement and drew sizeable crowds.

By and large, such joint programs were initiated by the IWW which, as a union rather than a political party, was considered better suited to the role of liaison. That other groups readily conceded it that role is itself significant. It shows that from the mid-1930s into the '60s, when the U.S. Left was dominated by the openly anti-revolutionary Communist Party, the IWW continued to serve, in its modest way, as a rallying-point for all forms of autonomous workingclass radicalism. Even in the tragically fragmented radical labor milieus of those trying and gloomy years, the IWW persevered as a unifying force.

In their absolute and unyielding antipathy to Stalinism, as in their ability and eagerness to interact amicably with labor radicals of other persuasions, Wobblies demonstrated how distant they were from what young radicals in the 1960s called the "Old Left." Significantly, the term "Old Left," always used abusively and in contrast to the rising "New" Left, was aimed above all at the Communist Party, *i.e.*, Stalinism, which for decades had been the most fashionable, influential, and lucrative brand of leftism in the U.S. Interestingly, too, although "Old Left" also included social-democrats and several varieties of Trotskyism, it most definitely did *not* include the Wobblies. In other words, the IWW was rightly perceived as *different*: Its disdain for dogma, its emphasis on crea-tivity, its openness to the new were the very qualities the early New Left cherished most. The roots of the New Left will long continue to be debated, but there can be no doubt that the IWW was one of its most dearly-loved ancestors.

---

1. Officially, the U.S. Communist Party always denied being subsidized by the USSR. On this subject I have drawn on a long discussion (6 December 1985) with James Allen, who for many years directed the Party's International Pub-lishers, a major recipient of undercover Moscow funding.

2. Most of the following information on Stalinist violence in the U.S. labor move-ment, and on the friendly relations between the IWW and other groups on the far left, is drawn from conversations and/or correspondence with old-time members of the IWW, the Trotskyist movement, the Socialist Party, the Revolutionary Workers League, and the Proletarian Party—including Carl Berreitter, Sam

Calander, Carl Cowl, Charles Curtiss, Ruth Dear, Sam Dolgoff, Rose and Joseph Giganti, Al Glotzer, Aldine Gunn, Walter Schonbrun, Arne Swabeck, Fred Thompson, Jean Tussey, Virgil Vogel, Vera and Albert Weisbord, Myra Tanner Weiss, George Weissman, and Al Wysocki. Several of these friends—Cowl, Curtiss, the Gigantis, Glotzer, Swabeck, and the Weisbords—had earlier belonged to the CP.

3. This story was related to me by George Weissman.

Charles E. Setzer (X13): "Don't Be a Screwball" (linocut).
A close cousin of Mr Block and Scissor Bill, X13's Screwball
specialized in doing the wrong thing. Although he turned up in
other cartoons, he never had a strip of his own.

2. THE COMMUNISTS & JOE HILL

Everything had become idiotic and comical
but I didn't feel like laughing.
—Gellu Naum—

Political groups, and especially left groups, seldom appropriate heroes who are widely and firmly associated with their opponents. The Communist Party's ill-starred attempt to adopt Joe Hill into the Communist pantheon adds up to a genuine historic curiosity.

The major effort to claim Hill for Communism dates from the 1930s. In the preceding decade, Party members managed to contribute only a few short passages on Hill to Party publications, most notably to November issues of *Labor Defender*, the official organ of the Communist-controlled International Labor Defense (ILD). Just how little the Wobbly bard loomed in Communist consciousness in those years may be gleaned from a couple of Party publications. *Poems for Workers*, No. 5 in "The Little Red Library" series, was published by the *Daily Worker* Publishing Company in Chicago in mid-decade. Edited by a certain Charles Phillips under the pseudonym Manuel Gomez,[1] the 55-page collection featured several poems by Carl Sandburg and Siegfried Sassoon, but not so much as a line by Joe Hill. Similarly, Anthony Bimba, in his 385-page *History of the American Working Class* (1927), chose to ignore that class's most celebrated poet/martyr.

In 1932, however, a Party pamphlet with the not-very-original title *Red Song Book* actually included one of Joe Hill's songs: "The Preacher and the Slave." If this was a conscious first step in a plan to "capture" Hill for the Party, the plan was, as today's book-reviewers are fond of saying, "deeply flawed": The lyrics were abridged, and the editors somehow neglected to credit Hill as the author. Thus the ambivalence that came to characterize the whole CP effort to co-opt Hill was discernible from the start.

Within months, however, the campaign was on in earnest. Mike Gold, a prominent and influential Communist journalist, complained—in the *Daily Worker*, no less—that the Communist movement lacked and needed to find "the Communist Joe Hill" [19 Oct 1933]. In fact, no Communist Joe Hills came forth; the sole nominee for the position—H. H. Lewis, the Missouri "Plowboy Poet"—was soon forgotten, and wound up as a Christian fundamentalist [Wixson 1994, 532n104]. Interestingly, Jack Conroy and his Communist-oriented "Rebel Poets" group (which for a time included Lewis), regarded Joe Hill—along with Covington Hall, Ralph Chaplin and Arturo Giovannitti—as their chief inspirers and guides. As an organized ferment, however, the early 1930s CP "worker-poets" movement was small, short-lived, and (with a few exceptions) mediocre. By mid-decade the Communist cultural commissars of the Popular Front were more interested in cultivating the collaboration of such best-selling liberals as Hemingway, Dreiser, and Erskine Caldwell. Although Conroy himself remained on the fringes of the Party for several years, he remained to the end of his life a steadfast admirer of the Wobblies and their "anarchic, independent spirit" [*ibid.*, 228].[2]

During the '30s, the usually very dull pages of Communist Party publications were sometimes brightened by poems and texts about Joe Hill, suggesting that more than a few Party members considered the IWW poet an object of real fascination. A few examples: Kenneth Patchen's poem, "Joe Hill Listens to the Praying," appeared in the *New Masses* in 1934, and was reprinted a year later in the International Publishers anthology, *Proletarian Literature in the United States*. That book also featured Alan Calmer's discussion of Hill in his article, "The Wobbly in American Literature," which in turn quoted excerpts from Alfred Hayes's "I Dreamed I Saw Joe Hill Again." And in 1936, Hayes's poem, now developed into a song by Earl Robinson, was published in the *Daily Worker*.

This Communist interest in Hill was closely related to the party's devotion to folk music. In the Depression years, many party intellectuals—Pete Seeger is undoubtedly the best known—were serious students of folk song, which they maintained was the true "people's music." All through the early years of the CIO, adaptations of folk lyrics were part of the entertainment at organizing rallies, picketlines, and other labor or party events. Almost none of these neo-folk songs, however, entered folk tradition. The contrast with the IWW in this regard is very striking. Wobbly interest in folk music was always rather secondary, yet many IWW songs and fragments of songs *did* enter the folk tradition and are still very much a part of it today. Indeed, as folklorist Richard Reuss noted years ago, the IWW "left more genuine folklore in its wake than any other labor or radical movement in this country" [1971, 262].

In the end, it was the Communists' own ignominious "Popular

Front" that pulled the rug out from under the efforts to "recruit" Joe Hill to their cause. Attempts to de-Wobblyize the foremost Wobbly of them all had proved utterly fruitless, and the concomitant effort to re-beatify him as some sort of proto-Stalinist never really clicked, either. However, all moves toward "a Communist Joe Hill" finally hit the skids when the Communist Party allied itself with "progressive" elements in the capitalist Democratic Party. As CP leaders quickly discovered, not one line in Hill's songs or letters could be used to bolster the Party's insipid mid-1930s slogan, "Communism is Twentieth-Century Americanism." Throughout the entire dreary Popular Front period and the ensuing jingoistic Second World War years, the Wobbly bard and his revolutionary songs were quietly dropped by the Communists, who had come to prefer safer and native-born heroes such as Thomas Jefferson, Abraham Lincoln, and Franklin D. Roosevelt. Hill was demoted to the status of distant (and not very relevant) ancestor, and revived only on particular occasions when the Party leadership sought to appear "left."

A truly quaint period-piece titled *Songs for America*—a words-and-music collection issued by the Communist Party's official Workers Library Publishers in 1939—documents the rapid decline of Joe Hill's prestige in Stalinist circles. Opening with a well-known Communist favorite, "The Star-Spangled Banner," the book includes not one song by Hill, or by any other Wobbly. Missing, too, is the Hayes/Robinson song. For the time being, the "comrades" seem to have stopped dreaming of Joe Hill, or at least stopped singing about him. However, as if to demonstrate the Party's intimate rapport with the mood of the U.S. proletariat, the book's editors were careful to make room for that ever-popular ballad, "Song of the Happy Soviet Youth."

Another Communist anthology published that same year, titled *Labor Songs*, did include Hill's "Preacher and the Slave," but with an incredible disclaimer explaining that it was "not intended as any reflection on religion or on honest ministers of the Gospel" [Nelson 1989, 157].

Glimmers of Communist interest in Hill lingered on in ensuing years. The Almanac Singers, for example, dedicated their 1941 album, *Talking Union*, to Hill's memory. Woody Guthrie, a CP "fellow traveler" who considered Hill a hero, dedicated a song to him (titled "Joseph Hillstrom") in 1946. The following year, in Cleveland, a group of local artists in and around the Party issued a "Labor Calendar" which featured an image of Hill by Doris Hall. In the 1950s and '60s, Philip Foner wrote extensively on Hill. Such interest, however, was strictly a sideline, a minor undercurrent, far from the mainstream of Party policy.

The 1948 publication of *The People's Songbook*, by far the best-circulated of the Communist Party song collections, shows the low status to which the IWW poet had fallen in Communist eyes. It contains no songs at all by Hill, and only one IWW song: an abridged and significantly altered version of Ralph Chaplin's "Solidarity Forever." The book does include the Hayes/Robinson song in a section titled "Songs that helped build America"—a rather arbitrary category for a song barely a dozen years old. The "Star-Spangled Banner" is also included (as one of the "World freedom songs"), but not "The Internationale."

The Party seems to have recognized at last what was obvious to just about everyone else: that Joe Hill wasn't one of them.

I agree with Archie Green's view that "One measure of Joe Hill's legacy is found in his acceptance by enemies of the IWW, past and present" [1997, 83]. But isn't the very notion of "a Communist Joe Hill" oxymoronic?

---

1. Phillips at various times also used the names Frank Seaman and Jesus Ramirez, and later, as a columnist for the *Wall Street Journal*, changed his name again to Charles Shipman. It is under this last name that his autobiography appeared; see Shipman (1993).

2. See, for example, Conroy's tribute to his old friend Fred Thompson in the *Industrial Worker* (July 1987, 6).

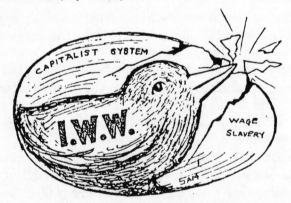

Like many IWW cartoons, Sam's depiction of
the "new" emerging from "the shell of the old"
is based on imagery from the natural world.
(*Industrial Pioneer*, August,1920)

XII

WOBBLIES & WILDERNESS

JOE HILL & THE IWW AS FORERUNNERS
OF EARTH FIRST! & ECO-SOCIALISM

I want to create wilderness out of empire.
—Gary Snyder—

Joe Hill is not commonly regarded as a man deeply interested in nature, but it was a recurring theme in his letters. "The thing the matter with the 'Underdog' today," he wrote to Elizabeth Gurley Flynn on 27 January 1915, "is that he has drifted too far away from nature" [*Letters*, 22]. The workers' separation from the natural world was in Hill's view a serious problem, and full of implications for the class struggle. As he explained in another letter, to Sam Murray:

> The animals, when in a natural state, are showing us the way. When they are hungry they will always try to get something to eat or else they will die in the attempt. That's natural; to starve to death is unnatural. [*ibid.*, 18]

In isolation, such arguments could perhaps be dismissed as examples of sensationalistic ballyhoo—the kind used by soapboxers to draw a crowd—or perhaps as mildly misanthropic witticisms. In Hill's case, however, passional attraction to nature, readiness to learn from it and even to follow its guidance, seem to have been vital components of his revolutionary *weltanschauung*. His core ideas were summed up in the IWW preamble, but he also seems to have had something of the sensibility of Henry David Thoreau and John Muir.

To recognize humankind's alienation from nature as an affliction, and especially life-threatening for wage-slaves, is hardly a commonplace even today, but it was rare indeed in the U.S. left of the 1910s. Hill's fleeting observations, scattered and undeveloped though they are, are a radical departure from the dominant modes of what passed for Marxism in the U.S. at that time. The mechanistic, nondialectical "Marxism" perpetrated by the Socialist Party and Socialist Labor Party, as of the later Communist Party, resembled explicitly capitalist ideology in regarding nature as a hostile force, and in glorifying humankind's efforts to "conquer" and exploit it. This bourgeois/Christian/European conception of nature was so entrenched throughout U.S. society that even radical critics of that society shared the same repressive values.

In his introduction to the 150th anniversary edition of the *Communist Manifesto* in 1998, Robin D. G. Kelley pointed out that the persistent image of Marx and Engels as hyper-urbanist, anthropocentric technocrats is "exaggerated if not outright wrong" [1998, vii], and refers us to the work of John Bellamy Foster and others who have painstakingly explicated the strong ecological dimension in Marx's and Engels's work. This dimension, however—like so much of the early Marx (the 1844 manuscripts) and the late Marx (the *Ethnological Notebooks*)—was altogether missing from the main currents of Marxism, especially in the U.S., where most "Marxism" has really been one variety or another of leftist positivism.

Of course there were heterodox thinkers who rejected the dominant ideology's arrogant and exploitative attitude toward the natural world. Poets, above all—Blake and Shelley in England, Burns in Scotland, Bryant, Thoreau, Whitman, and Lew Sarrett in the U.S.—had long dreamed of a more harmonious relationship between humankind and the Earth's other creatures, and poetry unquestionably did much to inspire the intellectual and activist currents that many decades later became known as radical ecology, deep ecology, and eco-socialism. Thoreau, whose writings provide a good working definition of that inherently anti-capitalist and anti-authoritarian outlook, was himself first and last a poet, and it is significant that John Muir—the single greatest inspiration not only for the early conservation movement, but also for the more recent and more radical Earth First! movement—cherished one book above all others: the *Complete Poems* of Robert Burns.

A more or less subterranean ecological tendency has existed even within Marxism, exemplified most notably in the work of such independent-minded thinkers as Rosa Luxemburg, Herbert Marcuse, and Amilcar Cabral—and it is interesting to note that all three of these non-mainstream Marxists were passionate readers of poetry. The influence of poets and poetry on the development of a revolutionary or Marxist ecology has rarely been acknowledged, much less studied, but there is every reason to believe that it has been immense. Wobblies, whose devotion to poetry is well known, also characteristically devoted far more attention to ecological concerns than the prosaic Socialist and Communist parties. Shelley, Burns, Blake, Thoreau, and Whitman were IWW favorites. Edward Bellamy's *Equality* and Peter Kropotkin's *Mutual Aid* were other quasi-ecological works well known to IWW members and, like the works of the aforementioned poets, readily available in the libraries of Wobbly halls across the continent.

Hints of the IWW's sympathetic approach to nature—their view that the natural world should be preserved for its own sake, and for its beauty, and not merely so that it can be exploited for production and profit—turn up as early as the union's founding convention in 1905. In the debate on which day of which month should be regarded as World Labor Day, for example, Delegate Schatzke of Denver said:

> I don't care whether you call it the first or the fifteenth of May, but I want it in this month when the trees commence to bloom and the flowers show their beauties and the Earth puts on its brightest colors. That month I want for the proletariat of the world. [*Proceedings* 1905, 197]

The intellectual sources of Joe Hill's interest in such matters remain unknown, but his early painting of a waterfall suggests that his love for wild nature dates back to his youth in Sweden. The poetry of Carl Michael Bellman may also have been a factor here. Hill's 1914-15 prison jottings, however, highlight the existence of a rudimentary radical ecological undercurrent in the IWW itself, and among the IWW-oriented Marxists around the *International Socialist Review*.

That the industrial workers of the "wild west" developed an attitude toward nature that diverged sharply from that of the bookish "Marxist" ideologues of New York and Boston was entirely in the order of things, for the IWW's migratory workers enjoyed a direct and prolonged experience of wilderness that was practically inconceivable for cloistered urban intellectuals. The IWWs out west were mostly outdoorsmen: loggers, construction workers, harvest stiffs. As Ralph Chaplin recalled in his autobiography, Frank Little, Vincent St John, "and other outstanding IWW members" had a real horror of the city's giant industries, with their smoke-belching factories and militaristic routine—"an atmosphere in which they just couldn't 'stay put'" [1948, 180].

Bill Haywood touched on the *unnaturalness* of cities in his testimony before the U.S. Industrial Relations Commission. "Do you suppose," Haywood asked, "under normal conditions, that there would be communities like New York or Chicago with great skyscrapers sticking up in the air?" And when Commissioner Weinstock asked him, "What would you do with the city of New York?" Haywood replied: "Tear it down, or leave it as a monument to the foolishness of the present day" [1915, 37-38].

This IWW anti-urbanism is also noted in Charles Ashleigh's 1930 novel, *Rambling Kid*, in which one of the characters is described as "a hobo and a Wobbly, one of the reckless rambling boys who despised the soft security and comfort of a dull-paced city existence" [Ashleigh, 109]. It was not, however, the city's "soft security and comfort" to which IWWs objected—Ashleigh's naivete here in fact reveals his own middle-class background—but rather the city's noise, stink, brutality, ugliness, misery, and lack of freedom. The essence of the hobo life, which Hill personified, was emphatically outdoors: fresh air, clear skies, unpolluted water, wide open spaces, an environment free of the city's regimentation and squalor. To the dangerous "amenities" of so-called civilization, many 'boes preferred the "jungle."

When a University of Chicago professor brought his economics class to the IWW hall—a not-uncommon practice in 1910s/20s Chicago—Fellow Worker "Spud" Murphy urged the "poor scissorbill" college kids to get out of the "slave-pen"city and see firsthand what real life was like:

> I'll tell ya, why don't you go out and grab a rattler and find out things for yourselves? Glom the belly of a drag and take out for the sticks on the lam. Ping a couple of clackers when you go broke and make a gut plunge on butch. Learn to feed the kitten cream when the Moonlight Monster is tight with his tin. Three months in the harvest fields and a thirty-day stretch in the hoosegow—that's the way to get smarted up. [Chaplin 1948, 180]

Certainly it was the way countless Wobblies "smarted up," which is doubtless why so many of them knew more about how the existing social order functions than most PhDs. Thanks to their frequent tours of inspection back and forth across the continent, these "road scholars"—as old-time hoboes often called themselves —had a close-up view of what capitalist industrialization was doing to the Earth. The IWW in the 1910s may not have had a sophisticated critique of ecological devastation, but they sensed the magnitude of the problem, as well as its causes and cure, far more than anyone else.

Wobblies pioneered, for example, in calling attention to the dangers of overpopulation. A smaller workforce, they argued, could more easily win higher wages and shorter hours, as well as better working and living conditions. Their promotion of birth control, alone among labor unions in the U.S., exemplified the Wobblies' ability to look at particular social issues in a larger context. The fact that their reasoning in this regard was neither specifically ecological nor feminist makes it all the more remarkable. Out of their *own* experience as rebel workers they reached conclusions that reinforce and extend the perspectives of ecologists and feminists.

Just as crucially, Wobblies early on decried the ruin of America's wild places. Indeed, the union recognized that its worst enemies, against whom they waged many of their fiercest battles, were precisely the Earth-raping, forest-destroying, air-and-water-polluting, wildlife-murdering lumber barons, railroad magnates, mining corporations, and big business farming conglomerates. At least from the 1910s on, and probably even earlier, the IWW press vociferously protested the destruction of the great forests by the lumber industry. An article in the *One Big Union Monthly* for October 1919 excoriated the "totally destructive" character of the then-prevailing methods of "reforestation," and noted that such mindless destruction could not occur under the system of workers' self-management proposed by the IWW [44-45]. The *Industrial Pioneer* for December 1925 demanded immediate "conservational action" to stop the lumber companies' "criminal and wholly unnecessary wastage" of forests: "Nothing but mute stumps over thousands of acres. . . . Where is it going to end?" An accompanying photograph of clearcut woodland is captioned: "A Forest Gone to Waste—Made Into *Chicago Tribune* Editorials" [15-17].

Covington Hall's *Labor Struggles in the Deep South* is required reading for everyone who wants to know the true story of the ecocidal industry that destroyed America's forests, and the organized workers who dared to challenge that industry.

At the 1918 Chicago IWW "conspiracy" trial the bitterly anti-labor prosecution took pains to portray the union as good-for-nothing malefactors, but now and then an unbiased witness let the truth be known. Joseph Davis of the U.S. Forestry Service testified that in 1917 he had hired 600 IWWs to fight forest fires in Montana. These Wobs, said Davis, were hired out of an IWW hall and they gave good service: "The best I have ever seen." And he added: "If it had not been for the IWW . . . the forests of Montana and northern Idaho wouldn't be there now" [George 1918, 124].

Many Wobs came to feel that wilderness was a part of their very being. Historians of conservation and environmentalism have ignored them—as they have ignored the IWW's heroic struggles against the lumber barons and mining corporations—but these wilderness Wobblies deserve to be better known. John Dennis, from Idaho, was one. After many long years of fighting the good fight at the point of production, Fellow Worker Dennis became "field consultant" for Harrison's *Flora of Idaho* and St John's *Flora of Eastern Washington.* "What they needed," he said, "was someone to show them where they could find various plants, and I knew the elevations and places where they grew" [*Industrial Worker*, May 1988, 5].

Numerous IWWs found the western landscape a powerful inspiration. Richard Brazier, in his 1960 interview with Archie Green, explained why there was so much creativity among Wobblies in the West in the 1910s:

> At that time, the west—it was a wide open country then, the wide open spaces really existed. There was plenty of room to move around, and . . . scenes of great grandeur and beauty, and there were journeys to be made that took you to all kinds of interesting sections of the country. And there was an atmosphere that seemed creative in its effect. I mean, even natives there seemed to be more creative than [people] in other places.
>
> It was so grand: the mountains around Seattle and Tacoma, and the roses of Portland, and the harvest fields around Spokane, . . . the lakes and the rivers, all on an immense and creative scale . . . . The grandeur and the scenery of the country that we were working in . . . had its effect on us. . . . And that's the feeling we all had. I think that's one of the reasons why we kept on moving as much as we did. [41-42]

Ralph Chaplin was another Wobbly who recognized that wilderness could never be reducible to "natural resources," and that it was obscene to think of forests in terms of "board feet." His early song, "The Commonwealth of Toil," remarked "the mighty gloom of cities" and invoked "our Mother Earth." In later years, deeply influenced by Native American mythology, the author of "Solidarity Forever" became an ardent defender of native peoples, of life in the wild, and of all wilderness,"untamed, unravished, beautiful and free." Scattered through his work are some powerful poems celebrating the Earth's natural diversity and the recovery of old-growth forests. *Only the Drums Remembered*, published as a pamphlet, honors the Nisqually chief Leschi who, early in the nineteenth century, led the Northwest Indians' struggle against the invading white settlers' army:

> *Some day our forests shall return again*
> *Back from our Mountain where they hide from men—*
> *That Indian Eden, called the Wilderness,*
> *That shames a soiled world with its loveliness.*
> *Grove after grove, tree after warrior tree,*
> *So shall they march unchallenged to the sea,*
> *Healing the death wounds that your greedy hands*
> *Have left upon the devastated lands*
> *With cool green leaves and patient, cleansing sands.*
> *Those cities, glowering where woods use to be,*
> *For one dark interval in untamed Space—*
> *Gone, and forgotten, leaving not a trace*
> *Either in Time or in Eternity.*

In a letter to Carlos Cortez dated 14 June 1961, Chaplin's widow Edith noted that Ralph regarded this poem as "his last will and testament."

Agnes Thecla Fair in her *Sour Dough's Bible* again and again hailed the awesome freedom and beauty of the Alaskan wilderness:

> *Give me the wilds, where the heart of man*
> *Is as bare as a babe just born*

and

> *Take me back to the Northland,*
> *Where the Yukon wends its way.*

And in one of her "Biblical" riffs she offered—in 1909!—a radical ecological critique of Capital:

And the Capitalist said by keeping the Workers divided, and we, the Capitalists uniting, we shall have dominion over the fish of the sea and operate canneries, and over the fowl of the air by bribing the game warden, and over the cattle of the east by monopolizing all water rights, and over every creeping thing that creepeth upon the earth, wherein we can make a profit.

Eugene Barnett has the distinction of being, to the best of our knowledge, the only Wobbly to devote an entire book to the wonders of the natural world. As one of the framed-up Centralia victims and therefore one of the union's best-remembered class-war prisoners, Barnett was a coal-miner well known throughout the left for his cartoons and poetry, and for his autobiography (serialized in the *Labor Defender*). Written and drawn in prison, his 56-page book, *Nature's Woodland Bowers in Picture and Verse* (1927), features full-page ink drawings of the Canada Lynx, Ruffed Grouse, Mountain Sheep, Black Bear, Wolf and other wild critters, interspersed with his poems and comments on the pictures. The opening lines of one of the poems indicate the tenor of the book:

> *There are pleasures in the woodlands and a fragrance in the air*
> *That a city cannot boast of anywhere.*

The drawings and texts demonstrate Fellow Worker Barnett's admiration for wildlife, his delight in the woods, and, among much else, his fervent opposition to capitalism in general and the use of steel traps in particular.

Jim Seymour, hobo poet and later a stalwart of Chicago's Bughouse Square, was another Wobbly whose life in the great outdoors seems to have changed his attitude toward the other creatures with whom we humans share this planet. A vegetarian, Fellow Worker Seymour left us this forceful maxim of animal rights: "Murder is murder, regardless of the number of feet possessed by the murdered creature" [1919, 13].

Like several other Wobblies, Hill's old friend Louis Moreau was for many years a wilderness guide. Perfectly at home in the wildest places, and wise in the ways of the woods, he knew the natural world and its animals, insects, trees, flowers, plants, and stones as deeply and intimately as any university-trained specialist, and probably much more so. From his remote outpost in Lone Pine, California, Moreau in his sixties and seventies was still leading climbers up Mount Whitney. In his modest home he kept a large collection of unusual pieces of rock and pebbles, which he was always happy to show visitors, pointing out their interesting details and peculiarities, but above all emphasizing their amazing beauty.

A hard-boiled proletarian revolutionist with an abiding appreciation of wild nature, Fellow Worker Moreau epitomized a synthesis of all that's best in libertarian socialism and the John Muir tradition of no-compromise conservation.

Was Joe Hill also one of the wilderness Wobblies?

Surprisingly, his love of nature hardly figures in his songs; only "Where the Fraser River Flows" even hints at it—and just barely, in the title. The place of nature in his surviving drawings is similarly slight: cacti and background mountains (or are they pyramids?) in his nostalgic sketch of Sam Murray in Mexico, and the fish and the eel (or is it a sea-snake?) in his IWW submarine cartoon.

In Hill's letters, however, the call of the wild sounds again and again. Writing to Murray on 15 September 1914, we find him fondly recalling a mutual acquaintance, "Knowles, the Nature Freak," advocate of the "simple life" [*Letters*, 13]. And on 22 March 1915, to Murray again, he wrote:

I note you have gone "back to nature" again and I must confess that it is making me a little homesick when you mention that "little cabin in the hills" stuff. You can talk about your dances, picnics, and blow outs, and it won't affect me, but the "little cabin" stuff always gets my goat. That's the only life I know. [*ibid.*, 32]

On the 6th of June he wrote yet again to Fellow Worker Murray: ". . . am glad to note that you are still sticking to your little 'cabin in the hills'" [*ibid.*, 34]. Hill, who at that point had been in jail for a year and a half, went on to say: "I would like to get a little of that close to nature stuff myself for a couple of months in order to regain a little vitality, and a little flesh on my rotting bones." (In California, where Murray lived, "hills" could well refer to mountains. Although none of Hill's friends seem to have mentioned him as a mountain-climber, it is easy to imagine him sauntering along in high rocky places.)

In a more speculative and critical vein, and pursuing the line of thought advanced in the letter quoted in the second sentence of this chapter, Hill wrote on 27 Jan 1915 to Elizabeth Gurley Flynn:

> The instinct that forces the animals of the jungle to make a bee line for the eats when hungry, has been chloroformed almost to death in the underdog by civilization, and any old thing that has a tendency to arouse the instinct would be beneficial to the revolutionary movement. [*ibid.*, 22]

Here, at the juncture of instinct theory and class struggle, the thought of the IWW bard coincides closely with that of his friends and fellow workers on the *International Socialist Review*. Consider this passage by *Review* editor Mary E. Marcy published almost the same week that Hill wrote the just-quoted letter to Fellow Worker Flynn: "All movements for the emancipation of the proletariat are based on the premise that the human animal seeks pleasure and avoids pain" [Feb 1915, 26-27].Contrasting this natural instinct with the self-defeating and unnatural "habit of taking orders, . . . of doing what one is told to do, of following a leader," Marcy concluded:

> All that encourages [people] to break the routine of their lives, . . . everything that jars them loose from the ruts of existence, that wrenches them away from their accustomed grind, is a thought stimulator, a stimulator to action. [*ibid.*]

That Marcy and Hill were indeed on the same wavelength is further indicated by one of Marcy's later articles, in which she wrote:

> Our natural instinct, when we are hungry, is to satisfy that hunger—and yet hundreds of thousands of starving men and women pass and repass, every day, wagonloads and trainloads of food which they do not touch. The *habit* of respecting Private Property in them has grown stronger than the old instinct to eat and to live. [Marcy 1984, 43-44]

No one knows whether Hill and Marcy ever met, or even whether they exchanged letters. It would seem likely that they corresponded— Marcy was a prolific letter-writer who made it a point to stay in touch with *Review* collaborators, and according to her friend Jack Carney, she always found time to write to her many fellow workers. Whether it was the lumberjack in his bunkhouse, the miner out in the wilds of Australia, the railroader, longshoreman, sailor or man counting the ties, the boy in the penitentiary, they all knew Mary Marcy. [1923, 8]

Alas, no Hill/Marcy letters seem to have survived. Hill, however, was surely familiar with Marcy's writings, for she was one of the most popular and influential Far Left writers of the time—Eugene Debs called her "one of the clearest minds and greatest souls in all our movement" [*ibid.*, 15]. The *Review*, moreover, was—as Paul F. Brissenden noted in his pioneering study of the IWW in 1919— "virtually an IWW organ" [399].

The most widely read revolutionary Marxist journal in Debsian socialist days, the *Review* gave considerable attention to the natural world. Along with features on "War and the Workers" by Vincent St John, "The Battle for Bread in Lawrence" by Mary Marcy, and "How to Make Work for the Unemployed" by Joe Hill, the *Review* published articles on "The Love Adventures of the Spider" and "The Ways of the Ant."

Hill may also have read, or at least browsed, at the San Pedro IWW hall, other nature-related Charles H. Kerr publications, such as *Germs of Mind in Plants* (1905), by Austrian biologist Raoul E. Francé, beautifully illustrated by Ralph Chaplin; the popular pamphlet, *Nature Talks on Economics* (1912) by Caroline Nelson, who also wrote for the *Review* as well as IWW publications; and J. Howard Moore's *Universal Kinship*, first published in 1905 and often reprinted—a book combining Darwinian evolution, elements of ecology, and a militant defense of animal rights. From 1905 on, these publications, along with scores of other titles on the Kerr Company list, were not only on sale at IWW halls and bookshops, but also energetically promoted in the union's newspapers and magazines.

In these old Charles H. Kerr Company works on the natural world, as in IWW writings on the same or related themes, there is much that—from today's standpoint—seems naive, confused, simplistic, and just plain wrong. Mary Marcy and her Kerr Company co-thinkers, like their Wobbly friends, had only a rudimentary, gut-level critique of technology and "Progress." It is true that they had no illusions regarding "labor-saving devices," and a few of them—Covington Hall, for one—openly exalted the "primitive."

Does Joe Hill's unflattering 1913 reference to automobiles as "stinkwagons" indicate that he shared Hall's neo-primitivist inclinations? Alas, we know too little about it even to hazard a guess.

We *do* know, however, that Hill's, Hall's, Marcy's and other Wobblies' knowledge of ecology was far from deep, marred by inconsistencies, and never fully integrated into their revolutionary program. As a union, moreover, the IWW necessarily reflected a wide range of opinion, and some members—those, for example, who later defected to the aggressively pro-technology and anti-nature Communist Party—clearly supported unlimited industrialization and gave little or no thought to wilderness preservation or other ecological matters.

What makes Hill's and Marcy's and the other Wobbly and Kerr Company writers' discussions of nature interesting and important, despite their many faults, is their seemingly instinctive *affirmation* of the wild—and their firm rejection of any world-view, "socialist" or otherwise, that had no place for it. They had the revolutionary vision and courage to reject a "Marxism" that viewed nature through the distorted spectacles of Capital. Unsophisticated though their writings often are, they were among the first to point the way toward workers' solidarity with wilderness and wildlife.

Hill's fugitive and cranky remarks on nature and instinct cannot be dismissed as merely idiosyncratic. Indeed, his workingclass critique—or, let us say, suggestions toward a critique—of humankind's alienation from the natural world corresponds to the bold efforts of the most original and creative group of revolutionary theorists in the U.S. at the time. Rejecting a pseudo-radical ideology in which the natural world was regarded as nothing more than an endless supply of commodities to be bought and sold, Hill and his co-thinkers dreamed dreams no U.S. Marxist ever dreamed before. In his modest way, the Wobbly troubadour helped develop, if not a Marxist ecology, at least a *nature-friendly* Marxism.

With their combination of revolutionary fervor, love for wild nature, and scorn for capitalist "development" (*i.e.*, destruction of wilderness), Joe Hill and others in the "rebel band of labor," along with their Kerr Company comrades, can truly be regarded as fore-runners of the Earth First! movement that emerged in the 1980s. Novelist Edward Abbey, whose *Monkey Wrench Gang* (1975) did much to spark Earth First! into action, was a longtime admirer of the IWW, and Utah Phillips went so far as to call EF! "the IWW of the environmentalist movement" [*Industrial Worker*, May 1988]. Indeed, Earth First!ers, with their watchword, "No Compromise in Defense of Mother Earth!," appropriated a large share of the Wobbly tradition, in style as well as substance: from nonviolent sabotage and "silent agitators" to a whole new school of rebel cartoons and songs. Earth First!'s *Li'l Green Song Book* is a splendid eco-radical offshoot of the Wobblies' most popular publication. One EF! song, Walkin' Jim Stoltz's "There Is Power in the Earth," is a rewrite of Hill's "There Is Power in a Union."

In a May 1988 interview in the *Industrial Worker*, EF! organizer Roger Featherstone noted some of the most crucial IWW/EF! affinities:

> A lot of people in the Earth First! movement admire the early history of the IWW. We admire the IWW spirit, sense of humor, art and music; its direct-action tactics; its unwillingness to buy into the political scene; its no-compromise attitude and, most importantly, its guts. I think the spirit of the Earth First! movement today would make Bill Haywood and Joe Hill smile and say "right on!"

Two or three weeks after that interview, Judi Bari, a California Earth First!er with experience in the labor movement, joined the IWW. As the principal organizer of a number of large EF! anti-clearcutting demonstrations—most notably the 1990 "Mississippi Summer in the Redwoods" protests in Mendocino County—Fellow Worker Bari convinced many lumber workers that their real interests lay not with the greedy, Earth-destroying lumber corporations, but rather with the supporters of forest preservation and workers' solidarity. Such talk, however, was not pleasing to the reigning powers in the lumber industry. When Bari was severely injured by a motion-triggered car-bomb, police and FBI immediately charged *her* with the crime of "transporting a bomb," and never made any attempt to seek Bari's would-be assassins.[1]

The struggle for workingclass emancipation and the struggle to save the Earth from destruction are in essence one and the same, and the enemy is Capitalism. Despite setbacks, frame-ups, massacres, and defeats of all sorts, these struggles go on, and must go on, as the Preamble puts it, "until the workers of the world organize as a class . . . and abolish the wage system."

In this regard, as in so many others, Joe Hill exemplifies the union as a whole. To a much greater degree than historians, and especially labor historians, have been willing to admit, the IWW embodied a critique not only of capitalism, but also of the *civilization*—or "civilinsanity," as T-Bone Slim called it—which Capital policed and polluted into its own hideous, repressive, life-threatening image. In their admirably romantic rejection of modernity, their love of wild nature, their emphasis on solidarity, poetry, humor and direct action, and also their long view of history and their refusal to quit, Joe Hill and the IWW prefigured and helped prepare a wide panorama of paradigm shifts in consciousness and culture.

In more ways than one, the old Wobblies were wiser than they knew.

---

1. On 11 June 2002 (twelve years after the car-bombing), a federal jury in Oakland, California, fully vindicated Bari and her EF!/IWW colleague Darryl Cherney, and found six FBI and Oakland police investigators liable for violating their First and Fourth Amendment rights. The EF! activists were awarded $4.4 million in compensatory and punitive damages. Bari died of breast cancer in 1997.

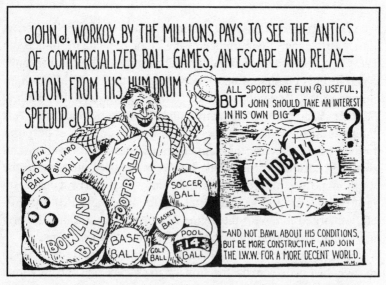

This cartoon by William Henkelman is a classic of Wobbly environmentalism (*Industrial Worker*, 9 April 1947)

XIII
JOE HILL, THE WOBBLIES,
& THE BEAT GENERATION

1. THE HIPPEST UNION IN THE WORLD

How funny it'll be, don't you see,
if this real New Spirit breaks loose!
—Jacques Vaché—

Joe Hill the outdoorsman, exemplar of the "simple life," and lover of wild nature—like Joe Hill the almost-feminist and Joe Hill the rejecter of the "white mystique"—has remained a perfect stranger to historians. Novelists, too (the exceptions are rarer than Yttrium) have persisted in making him conform to one-dimensional models— a good illustration of the old saying, "myths die hard." Many people want "their" Joe Hill to conform rigidly to whatever misinformation, pro or con, they happen to favor. New data is looked on as heretical and unwelcome because it challenges cherished opinions—*i.e.*, requires a little thinking, which is too much for some minds to bear. And in a sense they are right: New information can mean real trouble for petrified beliefs. In Hill's case, for example, once it is acknowledged that the Wobbly poet and cartoonist was also some kind of "Nature Freak," the long-fashionable Hill stereotypes—Hardhearted Hoodlum *versus* Anointed Super-Organizer—will dry up and blow away.

Our search for the "real" Joe Hill may be hopeless, but it does seem to help break down the old, stultifying myths.

As artist and songwriter, Hill himself specialized in breaking down the dominant economic, political, and religious mythologies of his time, and in doing so he "helped mold new values and hence a new culture" [Modesto 1963, 9]. Joe Hill's creative iconoclasm has indeed influenced an amazing range of rebels—individuals, groups and movements, and not only in the world of labor and far left politics, but also in the larger society.

His innovations in the realm of values and culture are insepara-ble from the new revolutionary *awareness* which was the collective invention of the IWW as a movement. Undeceived by capitalism's huge, non-stop propaganda machine, Hill and his fellow IWWs also saw through the mirages of craft unionism, reformist social-ism, left sectarianism, and other widespread "snares and delusions." Aware of the immensity of the problems before them, IWWs in the 1910s and '20s were also certain that they had the only workable solution, and that the practical realization of the great dream—the Revolution—was imminent. Alexander MacKay reflected on this sense of imminence in a letter he wrote to the Charles H. Kerr Company in Chicago in 1954. Noting that he still had some of the non-dividend-bearing shares the co-operative publishing firm had issued in its earlier years, Fellow Worker MacKay explained that

> At the time I bought this block of stock I had high hopes we would by this time be actually tasting the joys of the Co-Operative Commonwealth and that Charles H. Kerr & Company would be the official Administrative Publishing House, but things didn't move with the desired speed. . . . Honest to Allah, when I bought your stock certificate back in 1913 I REALLY thought the Revolution was just around the corner, and that the world had left its last war behind. Well, I was a better Wob than a prophet. [22 Sept]

This sense of revolutionary expectation, however, was an important factor in making the IWW what it was. The combination of awareness and certainty gave the Wobblies an all-abiding self-assurance, self-confidence, and camaraderie—their critics no doubt considered it a swagger—that distinguished them from just about everyone else in the labor movement or the left. As Senator Borah agonized:

> You cannot destroy the organization. . . It is something you cannot get at. You cannot reach it. You do not know where it is. It is not in writing. It is not in anything else. It is a simple understanding between men [sic], and they act upon it. . . [Kornbluh 1964, 255]

The *International Socialist Review* for December 1910 contains an article by Tom J. Lewis titled "Get Hip." Analyzing the ways and means by which "the workers can be hypnotized for such a long period of time" by reformist and opportunist illusions, the author urges his fellow wage-slaves to "beware" of the "apologists of capitalism" and "ambitious office-seekers," and to be aware of the urgent need for workers to think and act "for *ourselves*" [351]. Here, for the record, is Fellow Worker Lewis's short summary of what revolutionary socialists and Wobblies meant by being "hip" in 1910:

> Our only hope is revolution, so let us keep . . . to our duties; avoid bunko-peddlers, saviors, hero-worshipers, and leaders. Be our own guides and continually agitate, educate and organize on class, and not on craft lines. [352]

In other words: Get hip, not hypnotized!

Lewis's article seems to be the earliest appearance of the expression "get hip" in print. The *Random House Dictionary of American Slang*, edited by J. E. Lighter (1997, Vol. 2, H-O), lists no pre-1911 examples of "get hip," and only one use of "get hep."

The word *hip,* as David Dalby has shown, is of African origin, derived from the Wolof *hipi*—meaning "to open one's eyes, to be aware of what is going on." It was brought to North America in the late 1600s by enslaved Wolof speakers from what is now known as Senegal [Roediger 2002b, in Sakolsky 2002, 595]. Not until the 1940s—that is, some three and a half centuries later—did "hip" enter the so-called American "mainstream"—which, as the African American surrealist poet Jayne Cortez has argued, should really be called the "whitestream" [Cortez 2002 in *ibid.*, 278].

That the word *hip,* which for some of us is permanently and powerfully associated with the history of jazz—and particularly with such sublime geniuses as Charlie Parker, Thelonious Monk, Bud Powell, Max Roach, and Babs Gonzales—should turn up in the title of an article on revolutionary class-consciousness in an IWW-linked socialist magazine in 1910 (the very year, incidentally, that Joe Hill is thought to have lined up in the union) is one of those dizzyingly unexpected occurrences which make us realize that history is full of surprises.

Intriguingly, Lewis's article also contains a passage in which he mentions "listening to a sky-pilot orate about the 'sweet bye-and-bye,' while our internals are calling for something in the 'sweet now and now.'" Seven months later, the *Industrial Worker* for 6 July 1911 announced the publication of Hill's parody of the hymn, "In the Sweet Bye-and-Bye" in the new edition of the *Little Red Song Book.*

The question arises: Did Lewis's "Get Hip" inspire Hill to write his most popular song? Of course we have no way of knowing the answer.

It is likely, however, that Hill read the article. I say this not only because IWW members who enjoyed reading tended to read the *Review,* but also because the issue containing Lewis's article also contained substantial articles by Fellow Workers Elizabeth Gurley Flynn and William D. Haywood.

If I'm right, that Joe Hill *did* read Lewis's article, it means that *hip,* in the precise Wolof meaning of the word, was part of the Wobbly bard's vocabulary. And *that* is something to think about.

And so is this: At a certain moment in history, in the face of the entire "square" world (soon to be "represented" in the IWW press and the *Review* by Mr Block), the IWW not only exemplified hipness in all its fullness, but actually tried to get the whole working class to *be* hip.

The struggle continues!

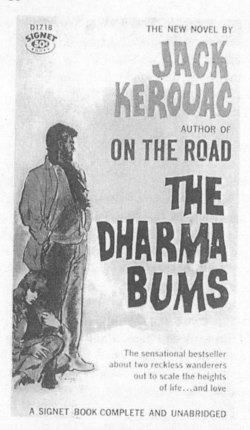

Jack Kerouac's 1958 novel inspired the 1960s
"rucksack revolution" and stimulated
interest in hobo culture.

2. FROM THE '29 DEPRESSION
THROUGH THE COLD WAR '50s

*In times when the levers of power are held by those
who have lost the will to act honestly,
it is those who have been excluded from the privileges
of our society, and left with only its horrors,
who forge new levers by which to return honesty to us.*
—Nelson Algren—

During the 1910s and '20s the IWW was very much a labor union, though its activities and influence extended far beyond traditional "labor" issues. What was it doing from the 1930s through the '50s?

Accurately predicted by the *Industrial Worker*, the Depression of '29 triggered a new phase in the class struggle, and the Wobblies, despite their drastically reduced membership, began a dramatically increased agitation that caught on like wildfire across the country. Shamefully ignored by most historians, the union's organizing activity during those hardest of hard times—coal-miners in Harlan, Kentucky; construction workers at Boulder Dam in California, and Cle Ellum, Washington; fruit-pickers in Yakima, Washington, and Watsonville, California—made headlines at the time, as did the IWW Unemployed Unions that flourished from coast to coast. The '30s also witnessed a notable resurgence of the IWW's Marine Transport Workers Industrial Union 510 in New York, Philadelphia, Baltimore, San Francisco, and along the Gulf Coast, while its Metal and Machinery Workers Industrial Union 440 organized several large and small foundries and factories in Cleveland, several of which remained IWW shops until 1950,when they became casualties of the Taft-Hartley "slave labor" law.

Most spectacular of all the Depression years' IWW organizing was the union's almost-successful effort to unionize auto workers in Detroit in 1932-33, a drive that ended with the defeat of the Murray Body strike. Wobbly influence, however, persisted in Detroit all through the decade. The IWW mini-leaflet, "Sit Down and Watch Your Pay Go Up," was a precipitating factor in the wave of sitdown strikes that swept the nation and marked the decade's revolutionary high point.

All too soon, alas, most of this IWW organizing was outma-neuvered by the Congress of Industrial Organizations (CIO). The sheer size of the CIO, not to mention the size of its bank account, led many naive and cynical workers to overlook its inherently undemocratic, conservative, and pro-capitalist character. In retrospect, it is easy to perceive that Wobbly savvy was more far-sighted than the opportunistic "realism" of the class-collaboration-ist labor bureaucracy. Practically alone among U.S. radicals of the '30s, Wobblies foretold the CIO's inevitable and rapid bureaucrati-zation and decay.[1]

The spontaneous mass upsurge of U.S. workers was a crucial revolutionary moment, but the moment was lost when the struggle was deflected into a form of industrial unionism that was not only explicitly non-revolutionary but also—via the "New Deal" and the National Labor Relations Board—directly linked to the capitalist state. For a few years, up to the Second World War "No-Strike Pledge," CIO unions won pay increases and other benefits for their members, but it was a long way from the abolition of wage-slavery. In the long run, Vincent St John was right on target when he wrote, in his pamphlet, *Industrial Unionism: The IWW* (*c.* 1913): "With-out revolutionary principles, industrial unionism is of little or no value to the workers."

Even in its decline, the IWW had all the right enemies: the capitalist class, the government, labor fakers, cops, organized crime, the Ku Klux Klan, fundamentalists, fascists, and Stalin-ists—but it was also widely respected, not only by the broad left, but also by rank-and-file members of the AFL and CIO, by defenders of civil rights and liberties, by pacifists and other anti-militarists, and by all those who were sincerely committed to the cause of liberty and justice for all. From the 1940s on, although its small size and aging membership prevented it from being the classwide organizing center it had been in the 1910s and '20s, the IWW continued to "hold the fort" as best it could. From New York to San Francisco, from Chicago to the Gulf Coast, Joe Hill's union was still a key reference-point for just about everyone actively involved in the revolutionary workers' movement.

As a union without clout, the IWW was clearly at low ebb, but class war veterans still looked up to it, sought its advice, and knew they could count on its support in their own struggles. And many newcomers to the labor movement were eager to learn its lessons and to follow in its footsteps. Many younger workers in AFL and CIO unions, repelled not only by the bureaucratic leadership of their locals but also by the sectarian in-fighting of various Commu-nist and Trotskyist caucuses, saw the IWW as a model, and tried hard to emulate it. Conscious identification with Wobbly-style unionism led some of them to form organizations of their own, independent of—but of course related to—the unions to which they belonged. Of the many quaint and curious (and mostly short-lived) IWW-influenced hybrids, one of the most interesting and certainly the oddest declared itself to be—of all things—a political party!

The United Labor Party of Akron, Ohio, was founded in 1946 by Burr McCloskey, a young worker in the rubber industry, and an old-timer, John C. Green, who had helped co-found the IWW in 1905 [Lynd 1973, 149]. Most of its members worked in rubber and steel. The ULP's platform emphasized demands most unions wouldn't dare to touch, such as collective ownership of basic industry, and militant opposition to racism, conscription, and the Korean War. The ULP also supported unemployed struggles, and even student struggles (against ROTC, for example). Its main day-to-day activity, in the words of ULP activist John Barbero, was the struggle "to introduce democracy on the job," and along the way its members broke many traditional leftist barriers and made a real effort "to get away from Marxist language" [ibid., 275].

Exemplifying how open-ended and free-wheeling a group it was, Marie Wagner, an old rubber worker and prominent ULP member, added a psychoanalytic dimension to the ULP program. As Barbero noted, this was a feature "no other left-wing party had: where Marx didn't fit, Freud did. . . . And every time a question came up, [Marie] would say, 'OK, what does Papa Freud have to say about this?'" [ibid., 274]

Like the IWW, ULPers had fights with management, white supremacists, union bureaucrats, the American Legion, and the Communist Party. "We were mavericks in the radical labor movement," said McCloskey. "We fought every battle there was to fight" [ibid., 162].

Co-founded by an IWW co-founder and inspired by Wobbly traditions, the ULP also maintained the friendliest relations with the IWW itself. During the 1948 "Friends of Joe Hill" protest against Wallace Stegner's scurrilous attack on Hill in the *New Republic*, the ULP sent the Friends a letter of wholehearted support which was published in the *Industrial Worker*. Among other things the letter announced a May Day celebration in Akron "in the Wobbly tradition with Joe Hill's songs" [1 May 1948, 4].

In the 1950s Burr McCloskey moved to Chicago where he became a "regular" at Bughouse Square, and the friend of many Wobblies. He also spoke at least once a year at Slim Brundage's forum, the College of Complexes, for the next forty-odd years. ULP member Ed Mann, a steelworker, later joined the IWW. Mann's autobiographical pamphlet, *We Are the Union*, edited by Alice and Staughton Lynd, concludes with a section titled "The Wobblies."

The Lynds' earlier book, *Rank and File: Personal Histories by Working-Class Organizers* (1973), has more on the ULP, including interviews with McCloskey, Barbero and Mann. In that book the editors pertinently observed that the ULP not only looked back to the IWW but also prefigured the radicalism of the Sixties:

> There is a good deal of kinship between the approach to action of Burr McCloskey and his friends, and that of the New Left of the 1960s. . . . Central both for McCloskey and the New Left, as for the IWW before them, was the notion that the best way to communicate an idea is to act it out. [149-150]

Other admirers of the IWW expressed their admiration in other ways. In 1945, when anarchist-oriented pacifist Dave Dellinger and his friends established a printing cooperative in Newark, New Jersey, it did not take them long to join the IWW and thus to make their printing office a Wobbly shop, complete with use of the IWW's union label. As Dellinger noted in his autobiography, this printing co-op, which later moved to the countryside, produced such publications as *Direct Action*, *Alternative*, and most importantly *Liberation*, one of the first and best New Left magazines, which stayed on the scene for more than twenty years [1993, 144-45, 147; Dellinger to Penelope Rosemont, 8 Dec 2000].

In the early 1960s, almost every card-carrying member of the Libertarian Tendency of the Young People's Socialist League (YPSL) also carried an IWW card. Few if any of them were active in the union, or entertained hopes for its revival. But they wanted to help keep it alive, and above all to identify themselves with it—to show other YPSLs, other leftists, and the world just which current of U.S. radicalism they loved best. Many used the salutation "Fellow Worker" in preference to the socialists' traditional "Comrade."

The YPSL, as the youth section of the Socialist Party, was an "umbrella" organization: Factions were welcome, and it had a full complement and more—from would be neo-Bolsheviki all the way to unabashed reformists, followers of Max Shachtman and Michael

Harrington, whose fondest hope was to "realign" the Democratic Party. Members of the Libertarian Tendency, sometimes called "Anarcho-Bolsheviks" or "Luxemburgists" (after Rosa Luxemburg), thought of themselves as libertarian Marxists; the Tendency was in fact the successor of the late 1940s Chicago-based Libertarian Socialist League, which also had a close connection to the IWW. Some YPSLs called the Libertarian Tendency the "Santa Claus Faction," because—so the joke went—most of its members had beards, wore funny clothes, and worked only one day a year.

Although the Tendency's revolutionary program was roundly outvoted at the 1962 YPSL convention in Kerhonkson, New York, most of its members went on to develop their subversive proclivities in other groups, especially the civil rights movement and SDS. My impression of them at the time was that they were by far the best-read young people on the U.S. left. It was from Libertarian Tendency YPSLs that I first learned of C. L. R. James, Herbert Marcuse, Raya Dunayevskaya, Grace Lee, James Boggs, Martin Glaberman, George Rawick, Cornelius Castoriadis, the Paris journal *Socialisme ou Barbarie* and London *Solidarity*.

The handful of old-timers who held the IWW together in those years welcomed these and many other sympathetic movements, groups and individuals who, in their various ways, wanted to help broadcast the Wobbly message. In the *Industrial Worker*, these oldsters wrote friendly articles on the movement to ban the bomb and to stop the testing of nuclear weapons; on the civil rights and anti-Vietnam-war movements; the Beat Generation, the New Left, and the "youth revolt" in the '60s; environmentalism, women's liberation, prisoners' rights, and other worthy causes.

Carl Solomon, to whom Allen Ginsberg dedicated *Howl*, once said that the youth revolt known as the "Beat Generation" rejected an America in which "freedom meant white supremacy and the suppression of every movement for human hope on the face of the planet" [Solomon 1966, 51]. The IWW was the direct opposite of that America. Even in the toughest times Wobblies remained implacable foes of white supremacy, and actively *encouraged* every movement for human hope.

---

1. Many Wobs and former Wobs did play important roles in the early period of the CIO. As Fred Thompson noted in 1984: "We had quite a few [IWWs] in the Detroit auto industry. . . . A large part of the personnel that built the UAW [United Auto Workers] were former members of the IWW. In fact, [Walter] Reuther used to come around [to the Wobbly hall] once in a while, his wife in particular, May—she was my student at summer courses" [Altenbaugh interview, 20 Oct 1984,18].

This 1920s ad lists twenty-one IWW periodicals in thirteen languages.

3. THE OLD WOBBLY:
KEEPER OF THE FLAMES OF DISCONTENT

Youth has no right to be humble.
The ideals it forms will be the highest it will ever have,
the insight the clearest, the ideas the most stimulating.
The best that it can hope to do is to conserve these resources,
and keep its flame of imagination and daring bright.
—Randolph Bourne—

In the 1950s and '60s, long after they had ceased to be a real power in the workplace, the Wobblies yet remained a strong revolutionary *moral* presence, an inspiration, and a living symbol of workingclass dissidence, revolt, and creativity. The union's extensive and many-sided influence was evident in the civil rights and anti-war movements; in groups such as the Student Peace Union, the Committee for Non-Violent Action, the Congress of Racial Equality, and the Student Nonviolent Coordinating Committee; in the far-flung folk-song revival; in the New Left, especially the Free Speech Movement in Berkeley, 1964 (in which Wobs young and old took an active part), and the Students for a Democratic Society in the years 1966-69; and in virtually every movement motivated by the desire for freedom, equality, and radical social change.

Some of this influence was purely historical, gleaned from recordings of Joe Hill's and other IWW songs, and books such as Ralph Chaplin's *Wobbly*, but much of it was also direct and personal, for many old Wobs were active in or around these movements: Henry McGuckin and Philip Melman in the San Francisco Bay Area; Fred and Aino Thompson, Carl Keller, and Jack and Ruth Sheridan in Chicago; Gilbert Mers in Houston; Herb Edwards in Seattle; Frank Cedervall in Cleveland; Nick and Fania Steelink in Tucson; Minnie Corder and Sam and Esther Dolgoff in New York—to name just a few.

Well into the 1960s, moreover, a handful of these glorious oldsters stubbornly maintained the decades-old Wobbly halls in Chicago, Seattle, Baltimore, Duluth, and a few other cities, waiting impatiently for young wage-slaves to wake up and rally to the Cause of workingclass emancipation.

Throughout the gloomy "Cold War" 1950s and early '60s, when cowardice and corruption were more than ever the rule in

U.S. politics, labor, and intellectual life, these aging Wobs actually dared to have *principles*, ideas, guts and—most amazing of all—an extraordinary *vision* of justice and freedom. As living, breathing negations of *The Man in the Gray Flannel Suit* and *The Ugly American* (best-selling books of the time), they became heroes and role-models. For young rebels of many persuasions, the "Old Wobbly"—a distinctly revolutionary variant of what Jack Kerouac called "The Vanishing American Hobo"—often assumed mythic proportions.

The old-timers who held down the old halls had in fact been hoboes in their day. Hopping freights, and on foot, they had traveled the length and breadth of the land, working at an incredible array of jobs, and agitating all along the way for One Big Union. Several of them had done hard time for "criminal syndicalism" (*i.e.*, urging workers to join the IWW). Few of these old-timers had ever finished grade school, but they had more to teach young people of my generation than most college professors.

In the early and mid-1960s I hitchhiked and rode freight trains around the country myself, and had the good fortune to meet quite a few of these grizzled veterans of the class struggle. I spent many days in those hallowed halls—the old Wobs were great talkers and they enjoyed regaling us youngsters, for hours on end, with stories of bright moments in IWW history. But what impressed me most about these ancient relics of Joe Hill's union is the extent to which they themselves embodied Hill's most characteristic virtues: humor, courage, audacity, integrity, imagination, and a way with words. They knew that the union had fallen on troubled times, but it never even occurred to them to give up.

I was nineteen in the Spring of '63 when I dropped by the Seattle IWW hall at 315 Yesler Way and talked for the first time with Fellow Worker O. N. Peterson, the longtime Branch secretary, who was, I would guess, in his mid- or late seventies. Astonished and delighted to find some "young blood" in the union, O. N.—as everybody called him—was clearly eager to boost my education in the ways of Wobblies. He was happy to share his vivid memories of the 1919 Seattle General Strike, and for good measure he tossed in a fascinating jumble of anecdotes about various other episodes of local Wobbly lore. These colorful ramblings were interspersed with brief but vituperative digressions on the gory history of capitalism, along with pungent criticism of the painfully long record of ineptitude and treachery on the part of the "official" labor movement.

And then suddenly O. N. switched to the present and said, in his inimitably rapidfire raspy voice:

> Let's face it, we're not organizing anybody here in Seattle. We're all too old. Once or twice a year somebody comes in and takes out a card, but for every new member two or three of the old duffers die, so the Branch just gets smaller all the time. I don't know how much longer we can hold out. But you want to know why I keep this hall open every day, year in, year out, all these years? It's because of Mr Capitalist Boss over there [pointing toward the Seattle business district], and because of the Comical [i.e., Communist] Party over there [pointing in another direction]. I don't want this hall to close because I don't want to give those bastards the satisfaction of saying, "Hah! We finally got rid of those goddamn Wobblies!"

Revolutionary tenacity, scornful laughter in the face of so-called "failure," the adamant refusal to play the existing order's game: These are all part of the "Old Wobbly" legacy.

Other old-timers upheld the legacy in ways of their own. As the One Big Union got smaller and smaller, many drifted away from what little remained of the organization as such—without, however, abandoning the revolutionary ideals of their youth or severing ties with their dues-paying fellow workers. Their attitude seemed to be: "Why sit around the old hall chewing the fat with a bunch of geezers as old as I am or older? Maybe there's some other way to bring working people together and get the word out." Lo and behold, several of the liveliest and most celebrated noncon-formist gathering-places in U.S. history were started and run by Old Wobblies.

Some were no doubt inspired by memories of the Wobbly hangouts of their own youth. Indeed, the story goes back to the union's fledgling years. The prototype of the IWW leisure-time lounge was probably the saloon Daniel A. Liston opened in Butte in 1910—one of the earliest Wobbly watering holes. Although many leading IWWs were teetotalers and the union generally discouraged the consumption of alcohol, in mining districts and other areas where heavy drinking was common, organizers clearly preferred that union members frequent a union-friendly saloon rather than those operated by businessmen linked to the mine-owners. As the author of several waggish ballads in the *Little Red*

Song Book, "Dublin Dan" Liston was an exceptionally popular figure in the union. Wobblies throughout the West knew "Dublin Dan's" at 348 South Main Street as a good place to meet fellow workers, to get filled in on the latest union news, and even fixed up with a place to stay [Calvert, 1985].

The Dil Pickle Club in Chicago, which flourished *circa* 1914 through the early '30s, was undoubtedly the most world-renowned of all IWW-connected hangouts. (The Dil, by the way, originally had two l's, but one was dropped—supposedly as a result of a trademark dispute—and the one-l spelling became standard.) The Club's early history is obscure, but it seems to have started as a kind of revolutionary labor forum [Fagin 1939]. According to some sources, its initial participants included Haywood, Gene Debs, Mother Jones, and Irish revolutionists Jim Larkin and Jack Carney. Persistent but unverifiable rumor attributes the club's name to Larkin [Brundage 1997, 90].

Later, in the famous Tooker Place barn and under the direction of Jack Jones—former member of the Western Federation of Miners, former Wobbly, and former husband of Elizabeth Gurley Flynn—the Pickle quickly metamorphosed into the wildest night-spot in the known universe, while maintaining the basic open forum structure. It offered light meals, but they didn't amount to much, and the drinks, during most of the Club's existence, were strictly non-alcoholic. (Jones was a teetotaler; only in the late '20s was he coerced into selling bootleg booze "under the counter.")

Few, however, ever went to the Pickle with food or drink in mind. Its main attraction was *talk*: fire-breathing lectures, maniacal and/or comical debates, delirious discussions, and poetry readings that were often as raucous as prize-fights. Always unpredictable and never dull, Jack Jones's joint epitomized a kind of home-brewed Dada. Dozens of other coffee-houses blossomed all over the Near North Side, but only the Pickle was always packed.

The most wide open of all "open forums," Chicago's Dil Pickle was at once a nonconformists' carnival, a hotbed of subversion, and a counter-institution of higher learning—a legend in its own time and a thousand legends since.

Legendary, too, is Chumley's, established in 1928 in Greenwich Village, and still going strong. Longtime Village photographer and historian Fred McDarrah has called it "the only restaurant in New York without an entrance sign" [McDarrah 1963, 52].

Its founder, a one-time covered-wagon driver named Leland

Stanford Chumley—Lee to his friends—was in the 1910s and '20s an organizer for the IWW's Hotel, Restaurant, and Domestic Workers Industrial Union, as well as a popular Wobbly pamphleteer and cartoonist. The *International Socialist Review* hailed him as "one of Chicago's best known revolutionary artists" [Dec 1915, inside front cover]. His most notable accomplishment as an artist is probably his limited edition set of twelve 15" by 18" original charcoal sketches of "Revolutionary Comrades," including Joe Hill, Mother Jones, Bill Haywood, Gene Debs, Jim Larkin, Karl Marx, and Rosa Luxemburg. Individual sketches were offered as a premium to *Review* subscribers. Chumley's sketch of Hill is one of the most frequently reproduced portraits of the IWW poet.

In New York in 1926, when Chumley rented the second-floor apartment at 86 Bedford Street, his main purpose, according to Terry Miller, another Village historian, was "to edit and publish a radical workers' journal and to hold secret meetings of the IWW" [1990, 203]. Two years later, however, Chumley also took over the ground floor, a former blacksmith's shop, and opened the restaurant/speak-easy that continues to bear his name.

From the start Chumley's was a hangout for writers as well as Wobblies. Chumley invited authors to decorate the walls with dustjackets of their books, and to this day faded jackets of books, many from the 1920s/30s, line the walls. Upton Sinclair, Floyd Dell, and John Do Passos were early "regulars," and Edna St Vincent Millay read her poetry there. Other frequenters of Chumley's include Eugene O'Neill, Orson Welles, James T. Farrell, Anaïs Nin, J. D. Salinger, Simone de Beauvoir, Dylan Thomas, and somewhat later, Lawrence Ferlinghetti, Gregory Corso, Ted Joans, Allen Ginsberg, and Jack Kerouac.

After Chumley died of a heart attack in 1935, his widow Henrietta ran the restaurant until her own death in 1960. The current owners, viewing themselves as custodians of an important historic monument, have resolved to maintain "Chumley's traditions."

Chicago's College of Complexes, also known as "The Playground for People Who Think," was yet another eat-drink-talk-and-change-the-world outsiders' outpost in the old Wobbly spirit. Its Founder and Janitor, Slim Brundage, joined the union in Aberdeen, Washington in 1919 and received organizer's credentials a week later. In 1922, after a few years of hoboing and organizing, he moved to Chicago where he became one of the mainstays at Bughouse Square, along with such other Wobs as Jimmy Rohn,

Sam Dolgoff, Jim Seymour, and Bert Weber. Like most of the city's soapboxers, he also hung out and even worked (as bouncer and waiter) at the Dil Pickle Club in its glory days. A little later he served as chief executive officer of the local Hobo College [Brundage 1997].

In short, Slim Brundage had all the requisite qualifications and more to start a disreputable educational institution of his own. The College of Complexes, which opened its doors in 1951, was widely recognized as the "successor" to the Pickle, but if anything Slim's place was even more radical than its predecessor, and friendlier to the IWW. Jack Sheridan was active in the College for a time, and other Wobblies—including Fred Thompson, Stanley McCauley, and Carlos Cortez—were College speakers. A memorial meeting for Ralph Chaplin "by some of the old Dil Picklers" was held at the College in 1960. Famed Pickle poet and former Wobbly Bert Weber read his poems there, and Tom Gannon, another former Wobbly and one of the heroes of Covington Hall's *Labor Struggles in the Deep South*, was a College stalwart for years.

One of the most interesting aspects of the College was its strong solidarity with the rising Beat Generation. Nostalgic old-timers considered Slim's joint a new and revised Pickle, but for a younger crowd it was simply the hippest place in town. By the late '50s the newspapers were calling it "Chicago's Number One Beatnik Bistro." When the cops' and media's anti-Beatnik crusade reached its peak around 1960-61, most local bars and coffee-houses made it a point to "discourage" alleged "Beatniks"; some places, under police pressure, stopped playing jazz. Slim Brundage, however, declared himself a member in good standing of the Beat Generation, multiplied Beat-related rants and readings at the College, and during the election year of 1960 even organized a satirical (and emphatically anarchist) Beatnik Party, which ran anti-Presidential and anti-Vice-Presidential anti-candidates in a well-publicized campaign whose main slogan was "Don't Get Out the Vote!"

As an Old Wobbly, outspoken champion of free speech, and publicist for the Beatnik Party, the Janitor naturally made a lot of enemies among the bureaucrats in power, and in May 1961 the College was forced to close by the Internal Revenue Service. While it lasted, however, it was the hangout of choice for diehard dissidents throughout the city. Novelist Jack Conroy, himself a College habitué, accurately described it as "a lively place—livelier than most," and added that Slim Brundage was "an ingenious sort of guy . . . the typical Wobbly type: good at talking and getting people to talk" [Brundage 1997, back cover].

Following the IRS crackdown, Brundage ran a once-a-week version of the College for several years at various venues, and then moved to Mexico; he died in California in 1961. College alumni and a crowd of newcomers have kept the once-a-week College going; it is currently meeting at the Lincoln Restaurant on Lincoln Avenue, and recently a Southside branch opened in Hyde Park.

In the brightest days of the College Brundage had opened a New York campus (it was there that the Beatnik Party held its nominating convention in 1960), but it too came into conflict with the bureaucrats. The Janitor had also entertained hopes of opening a College in San Francisco, but soon learned that it was impossible: anti-Beatnik prejudice was so great that no one would rent to him. Jack Langan, another old Wobbly and alumnus of the College's Chicago campus, had better luck, and in 1955 took over a place called The Place at 1546 Grant Avenue, in the heart of North Beach.

John Gibbons Langan, also known as "Teton Jack," has been a hobo, mountain man, wilderness guide, photographer, folksinger, poet, writer and songwriter [FR interview, Oct 2001]. At the age of six, when his father died, he went to live with a half-Sioux uncle on the reservation, and "grew up Indian." Philosophically, politically, and otherwise he has continued to think of himself as Native American, and he frequently uses his Oglala Sioux name, Pahizi Wawoyaka (Yellow-hair Storyteller). He joined the IWW in 1937—shortly after the police massacre of strikers at Republic Steel—and has also carried a card from the Newspaper Guild.

Active in the College of Complexes for several years in the early 1950s, Fellow Worker Langan carefully modeled his San Francisco establishment after the Chicago original. Like the College, the walls of The Place were painted black, and colored chalk was available to anyone who wished to write or draw on them. Like the College, which supplied regulars with "Schizo Certificates," signed by Brundage, The Place issued "Registered Blabbermouth" cards, signed by Blabbermaster Jack Langan. And like the College, the highlight of The Place was talk. At least one night a week was Blabbermouth Night, during which everyone was urged to speak out about anything, everything or nothing, ready or not.

The Place was already something of a historic site even before Langan showed up. In *The Dharma Bums*, Jack Kerouac called it "the favorite bar of the hepcats around the Beach"—meaning, of course, the North Beach "Beat" community [1958, 10]. And according to Kerouac's account, it was there that a group of then-little-known poets—Gary Snyder, Philip Lamantia, Allen Ginsberg, Kenneth Rexroth, Philip Whalen, and Kerouac himself —gathered on the evening of 13 October 1955 to talk, drink and get high before moving down the street to the Six Gallery to give the most famous poetry reading in the history of the Beat Generation. Rexroth proclaimed that reading the birth of the "San Francisco Renaissance."

The Place lasted a total of six years, and finally closed its doors in 1960. Like the neighborhoods in which Slim had his College, the area which once housed The Place has since been thoroughly gentrified. Fellow Worker Langan moved on long ago, and eventually settled in Jackson Hole, Wyoming. Now in his eighties, he is still that town's official IWW delegate.

While some Old Wobblies served the working class food and drink as well as food for thought, others ran bookshops. Here too the tradition goes back to the old days when the One Big Union was young. The IWW was always a union of big readers. Economist and University of Califrnia Professor Carleton D. Parker, who interviewed hundreds of Wobs in the 1910s, concluded that IWW members knew more about history, economics, biology, and popular science than any group of college students he had ever met [*Industrial Pioneer*, Oct 1921, 62].

Every Wobbly hall had IWW and other radical literature for sale—in addition to a library—and the union's storefront offices almost always doubled as well-stocked bookstores. Every big city where the IWW was active, and many smaller towns as well, also had at least one independent bookstore that was especially friendly to the IWW. These were often run by left-wingers in the Socialist Party, or ardent civil libertarians who admired the Wobblies' free-speech fights, or older IWW members who were no longer at the point of production. From New York to Los Angeles, these bookstores—many of them dealing only in used books—were popular places for Wobblies to meet, play chess, and talk.

The most celebrated of these unofficial Wobbly bookstore/hangouts was undoubtedly the Udells' Radical Bookshop in Chicago, but there were many more. In the Windy City alone Jerry

Nedwick, Harry Busck, Dan Horsley, and William Targ all ran bookstores notable for the special hospitality extended to customers with red cards. These booksellers, moreover, were all involved in the IWW/hobohemian nexus: They frequented the Dil Pickle, Bughouse Square, Hobo College, IWW socials, and the little theaters as well as each others' bookstores. In his autobiography, *Indecent Pleasures* (1975), Targ—who went on to become a big-time power-broker in the publishing industry in New York—reminisced about the old days in Chicago:

> My tiny bookshop on North Clark Street was almost a club; friends, including Bughouse speakers, wobblies, winos, convened there. We'd hold debates, hot arguments. Once in a while, someone would buy a book. [44]

Nathan Greist's bookstore at Seventh and Broadway in Los Angeles was an early IWW hangout in that city. A retired newspaperman who had once worked for Charles A. Dana on the *New York Sun*, Greist was also a lifelong left-wing socialist, and incidentally the model for the character named Kreis in Jack London's *Martin Eden* [Noel 1940, 39-40]. A few visits to the shop were all it took to convince Mortimer Downing to take out a red card, and in no time he became one of the best known West Coast Wobblies [Weintraub 1947, 281].

To this day Lawrence Ferlinghetti in San Francisco retains fond memories of Fellow Worker J. A. McDonald's bookstore at 48 Turk Street, near Market (the last of the shop's four locations). For forty years, starting in the late 1920s, McDonald's shop was a popular gathering-place for all shades of radicals in politics and the arts, but it stubbornly retained its Wobbly aura. McDonald's obit in the *San Francisco Chronicle* (he died in 1968 at the age of seventy-nine), describes him as "a lifelong radical," and notes that he "always spoke proudly" of his membership in the IWW [6 July, 23]. The obit adds that the crowded, labyrinthine shop "reminded customers of an Oriental bazaar." Ferlinghetti particularly recalls Mac's practice of posting short reviews of new books in his storefront window—reviews regularly cribbed by salaried reviewers for the Bay Area dailies [FR interview, 2 June 2001].

In our conversation on radical bookshops, Ferlinghetti also emphasized the anarchist/Wobbly roots and ongoing spirit of his own City Lights Bookshop, whose co-founder, Peter Martin, was the son of Carlo Tresca and Bina Flynn (Elizabeth Gurley's younger sister), and an anarchist himself. (When Martin later moved back to New York, he ran a bookstore there for several years.) Now a National Landmark, City Lights was one of the few bookstores in the entire country to carry the *Industrial Worker* during the Cold War '50s, and it was regularly listed in the paper under the rubric "Newsstands." Most bookstores and newsstands refused to stock the IWW's official organ out of hostility or fear. (In those years the IWW was on the U.S. Attorney General's list of "Subversive Organizations.") City Lights also sold the *Little Red Song Book* and other IWW publications, and years later held lively, well-attended, song-and-music-filled book-parties for Henry McGuckin's *Memoirs of a Wobbly* and the expanded edition of Joyce Kornbluh's *Rebel Voices*, both published by Charles H. Kerr.

Reciprocally, when the Chicago IWW Branch opened its storefront Solidarity Bookshop at 713 Armitage Avenue in the Fall of 1964, it stocked a large selection of City Lights books. Bob Kaufman's *Abomunist Manifesto*, the *Artaud Anthology*, and the *Journal for the Protection of All Beings* were among the most popular.

Solidarity, which "held the fort" for ten years, was in many ways the last of the old-time Wobbly bookshops: Its stock consisted mostly of pre-1940s books from the library of the union's long-defunct Work People's College in Duluth, the equally aged library of the Chicago IWW Branch, a hefty assortment of Charles H. Kerr books and pamphlets, and some 5000 Haldeman-Julius "Little Blue Books" purchased for six or seven dollars at a nearby resale store. However, with its selection of City Lights books, several shelves of books on surrealism, an array of mimeographed "little mags," numerous publications relating to the civil rights, anti-war, and ban-the-bomb movements, and hundreds of used comics, Solidarity Bookshop was also one of the first (perhaps *the* first?) of the "Movement" bookstores that flourished throughout the country in the late 1960s and '70s.

The bookshop was run largely by volunteers who also had full-time jobs elsewhere. A whole contingent worked days at the big downtown Post Office (where Richard Wright had worked decades before), and helped out evenings and/or weekends at Solidarity. Among them were three young African American women who went on to develop distinguished careers: Joan Smith as psychologist, Simone Collier as playwright, and Charlotte Carter as mystery writer. Another postal worker, Bernard Marszalek, learned the rudiments of the printing trade at Solidarity and is still active today in a "movement printshop" in Berkeley, California.

An important locus for radical activities in the community and a great place to pick up the finest in radical literature at bargain prices, Solidarity was also, and above all, a meeting-place for Wobblies and other incorrigible dreamers and dissidents, young and old. Within a few blocks were several other outposts of the revolutionary counterculture: the IWW hall at the intersection of Halsted, Lincoln, and Fullerton; the surrealists' Gallery Bugs Bunny at the corner of Mohawk and Eugenie; and the Regional Headquarters of the Students for a Democratic Society (SDS) on Larrabee Street. A single rickety old building at 333 North Avenue, just off Wells Street, housed the offices of the Chicago Area Draft Resisters (CADRE), the Charles H. Kerr Company, the Proletarian Party, and the Old Town School of Folk Music.

This chapter has focused on how individual Wobblies, and small groups of Wobblies, in their various ways, tried to keep something of the Wobbly spirit alive even as the union appeared to be doddering on its last legs. Now and then, however, something happened which, in effect, brought them together again.

Slim Brundage, like many old-time Wobblies, admired the Gandhian doctrine of *Satyagraha* and actively supported Martin Luther King's civil rights actions in the South and in Chicago. But like many old Wobblies he also believed in and practiced tactical flexibility. And so, in the late 1950s and early '60s, Brundage became the champion of Robert F. Williams, a young African American civil rights worker in Monroe, North Carolina, and author of the book *Negroes with Guns*.

A Black Nationalist, Williams not only "called for" Black armed self-defense against racist attack—he put it into practice when he and his friends fired back at an armed Ku Klux Klan attack, completely routing the hooded hoodlums, who thought they were attacking a defenseless meeting. This bold gesture of Black self-defense made headlines around the world, radicalized the civil rights movement overnight, and altered the course of U.S. history. In a letter that Williams published in his mimeographed newsletter, *The Crusader*, Brundage saluted him as "the most dynamic rebel in America today" [Brundage 1997, 27; Tyson 1999, 207].

The Founding Janitor of Chicago's College of Complexes was not, however, the only Old Wobbly to take up Williams's Cause. From a badly-lit room in the Fremont Hotel in the Skid Road district of Seattle came another communication that Williams deemed worthy of publication in *The Crusader* [16 Apr 1960, 4]. This time the encouraging words were in the shaky handwriting of Fellow Worker Guy B. Askew, a.k.a. Skidroad Slim, diehard anarchist Wobbly hobo who, many long years before, had fought under the sign of Joe Hill's "Good Old Wooden Shoe" as a militant in Agricultural Workers' Industrial Union 110.

In yet another issue of *The Crusader* [30 Apr 1960, 6], Williams published a third letter of solidarity from an Old Wobbly —this one from Tom Scribner, who was then living near Santa Cruz, California. A longtime lumber-worker (active in the IWW's Lumber Workers' Industrial Union 220 until around 1923), Scribner toward the end of his life put together a mimeographed collection of his writings titled *Lumberjack—with Appendix on Musical Saw*, for in addition to being an incorrigible proletarian revolutionist, he was also a highly accomplished and well-known saw-player [Leonard 1989, 35-37]. The life-size bronze sculpture of Fellow Worker Scribner playing his saw, in Scope Park, Santa Cruz, appears to be the only public statue of a Wobbly anywhere in the U.S.A. [*ibid.*, 36].

Widely separated geographically and probably unknown to each other, here were three old-timers who long, long ago had taken part in the IWW, acting once again in union.

As it happens, Robert F. Williams's revolutionary action was also written up in great detail, and with genuine enthusiasm, by *Industrial Worker* editor Chuck Doehrer, as a page-one feature (2 March 1959). In Williams's revolutionary program of Black armed self-defense, Wobblies all over the country instantly recognized a new stage in the class war, and did their best to support it and to get others to support it.

Retired or unemployed, down and out or running a forum or a bookshop, or just "holding the fort" or "looking for trouble," Old Wobblies everywhere were still "on the job."

Don't mourn, ORGANIZE.
JOE HILL
WAS HERE.
JOIN the IWW.

A "Silent Agitator" from Solidarity Bookshop (Chicago, 1965).

4. DISCOVERING THE IWW IN THE SIXTIES

The disinherited
must work out their own salvation
in their own way.
—Lucy E. Parsons—

Meeting old Wobblies face to face, seeing their soapboxing gestures, listening to their wild stories and hearing them argue and laugh: That was surely the best way to discover the One Big Union's incomparable legacy. But not everybody was so lucky. And yet, all through the Eisenhower/Kennedy/Johnson/Nixon years, despite the fact (or was it because of it?) that the IWW was practically invisible, young people found many ways of discovering it. Indeed, discovering the IWW seems to have been one of the most compelling spiritual needs of the time.

Think of it: In 1960 the union had only about a hundred dues-paying members. It was ignored in textbooks, slighted by historians, and pooh-poohed or ridiculed not only by the capitalist and trade-union press, but also by the left: from DeLeonists and Stalinists to social-democrats and Maoists. Amazingly, however, in the eyes of rebellious youngsters everywhere, the IWW's *reputation*—its aura of grandeur—was steadily rising. In an intellectual atmosphere heavy with lingering McCarthyism, the John Birch Society, corporate liberalism, and the lifeless dogmas of the traditional left, Joe Hill's union lived on, symbolically at least, as a life-renewing breath of fresh air.

Next to actually getting to know live old Wobblies, the best "open sesame" to the IWW's art and mystery was the union's own *Little Red Song Book.* Even in the bleak 1950s this pocket-size compendium was carried by a number of bookstores and record stores that also carried folksong materials, as well as by a few newsstands operated by IWW sympathizers. The folksong revival made a lot of people aware of the IWW. Many first learned about the union from folk-singers such as Joe Glazer, Pete Seeger, Cisco Houston, Dave Van Ronk, and young Bruce "Utah" Phillips. The last two actually took out red cards, and Phillips went so far as to keep his dues paid up, albeit sporadically; for some years now he has been a well-known "Old Wobbly" in his own right.

Other seekers in the Sixties found out about the IWW in song anthologies such as Carl Sandbug's *American Songbag* and Edith

Fowke's and Joe Glazer's *Songs of Work and Freedom*, or in critical studies of folk music and folklore.

William Preston, Jr's *Aliens and Dissenters* (1963) and Joyce Kornbluh's *Rebel Voices: An IWW Anthology* (1964), were major landmarks in the revival of interest in the union's history and culture. Focused on government repression during the First World War and its aftermath, Preston provided an invaluable historic context to a younger generation that had frequently encountered the heavy hand of the House Un-American Activities Committee (HUAC). Kornbluh's 419 large and lavishly illustrated pages of Wobbly theory, poetry, songs, fiction, humor, and cartoons convey much more of the *spirit* of the IWW than any of the formal histories. As Fred Thompson wrote in his introduction to the revised and expanded edition brought out by Charles H. Kerr in 1988:

> In this anthology Joyce Kornbluh captures, as few historians have been able to do, the zeal with which Wobblies battled for textile workers in Lawrence, steelworkers in McKees Rocks, lumberjacks and harvest hands, longshoremen and seamen, and incidentally free speech for themselves and others. [vii]

Many readers of *Rebel Voices* went on to read the IWW autobiographies—by "Big Bill" Haywood, Ralph Chaplin, Elizabeth Gurley Flynn—and found that Harvey O'Connor's *Revolution in Seattle* (1964), as well as memoirs by radicals as dissimilar as Louis Adamic, Horace Cayton, Ammon Hennacy, and Mary Heaton Vorse, were packed with valuable information on IWW history.

The Barrie Stavis/Frank Harmon compilation, *Songs of Joe Hill* (1960) and Philip Foner's collection of Joe Hill's letters (1965) also had their impact. Paul F. Brissenden's early and still useful *History of the IWW* (1919) was reissued in 1957.

A lot of college students first came across the union in sociological studies such as Nels Anderson's *The Hobo* (1923), or Harvey Zorbaugh's *The Gold Coast and the Slum* (1929). Histories of U.S. radicalism—Samuel Yellin's *American Labor Struggles* (1936), for example, and Charles Madison's *Critics and Crusaders* (1947)—attracted a growing readership as the "New Left" broke with the irredeemably capitalist Democratic Party.

Many students, I am sure, discovered the IWW while researching a seemingly unrelated topic. Scattered through America's periodical literature—in "little" as well as mass-market magazines and scholarly journals—are many hundreds of articles about, or at least touching on, the IWW, by writers as varied as Max Eastman, Randolph Bourne, Emma Goldman, Helen Keller, Eugene V. Debs, John Reed, Mary Heaton Vorse, Anna Louise Strong, Victor Yarros, Miriam Allen deFord, James P. Cannon, Ben Reitman, and Thorstein Veblen. These old articles have no doubt introduced many newcomers to the One Big Union.

Some found their way to the IWW through fiction. Probably the single most widely read IWW-related novel was John Dos Passos's 1930s trilogy about the 1910s and '20s, *U.S.A.*, reissued in paperback by the Washington Square Press in 1961 at sixty cents a volume. The first volume, *The 42nd Parallel*, features the character "Mac," a printer—one of the most effective and convincing novelistic portrayals of a Wobbly—as well as a powerful short sketch of Bill Haywood, and also evokes the 1912 Lawrence Strike. The second volume, *Nineteen Nineteen*, includes fine pen-portraits of Joe Hill and Wesley Everest along with vivid snippets on the Paterson Strike of 1913.

The union was treated with even greater respect and affection in Floyd Dell's books. *Mooncalf* (1920), *An Old Man's Folly* (1926), and the story "Hallelujah, I'm a Bum" in *Love in Greenwich Village* (1926), are especially rich in IWW content. Dell was out of fashion in the Sixties, which meant that you could find good clean copies of his books at almost any second-hand bookstore in the country for two bucks or less.

Ernest Poole's *The Harbor* (1915)—a great favorite among the Wobblies themselves—also served as a good introduction to the union. One of its highlights is a long, detailed account of a multiracial IWW strike meeting on the New York waterfront. This was probably based on what the author saw and heard at actual meetings, for Poole—who had many Wobbly friends—is known to have spent a lot of time at the union's Marine Transport Workers' hall.

Another Wobbly favorite was Jack London's *The Iron Heel* (1907), probably the single best-known work of IWW-related fiction, not only in the U.S. but worldwide. The book also includes a significant reference to "that struggling socialist publishing house in Chicago"—a.k.a. the Charles H. Kerr Company.

Much less well known is Olive Tilford Dargan's *Sons of the Stranger* (1947), written under the *nom de plume* of Fielding Burke. Focused on the struggles of the Western Federation of Miners and the early IWW, it is arguably the best novel about the radical labor movement of the early twentieth century. Although Dargan freely availed herself of the novelist's right to take liberties with chronology and geography, the story closely follows real events in the metal mining industry from the 1890s through the First World War. Of the many recognizable characters, Joe Hill alone retains his own name, but he appears only briefly and very sketchily. The portrayal of Bill Haywood, however (Robert Brennan in the novel), is exceedingly well done. Of particular interest is Dargan's attention to race matters: A Haitian-American soldier, sent to the area with an all-Black army regiment to crush the union, instead becomes a revolutionary; a hunted union organizer finds a safe hiding-place in a remote outpost of the Nez Percé Indians.

That *Sons of the Stranger* has never received the acclaim it merits can be attributed to the author's unflinching true-to-life depiction of the massive anti-labor violence on the part of the mining corporation bosses and their obedient minions, the forces of "Law'n'Order." Reviewing the book in the *Industrial Worker*, Fred Thompson proclaimed it "a novel that stands out over the bulk of current fiction" and "deserves to be widely read"; he urged IWW members not only to buy it and read it but also to pass it on to friends to advance the Cause [13 Dec 1947, 2].

Other novels in which the IWW is more or less honestly portrayed—albeit sometimes all too briefly—include Upton Sinclair's *Jimmie Higgins* (1919) and *Oil* (1926), Dashiell Hammett's *Red Harvest* (1929), Alexander Saxton's *The Great Midland* (1948), James Stevens's somewhat erratic *Big Jim Turner* (1948), Margaret Graham's *Swift Shift* (1951), James Jones's best-selling *From Here to Eternity* (1951), and Harvey Swados's *Standing Fast* (1970). Each one helped new readers to discover the IWW.

References to the IWW in Clancy Sigal's novelistic memoir *Going Away* (1961)—a kind of radical labor response to Kerouac's *On the Road*—are not exactly numerous, but their rhapsodic intensity mades up for their scarcity:

Coeur d'Alene has a romance all its own, different from Cripple Creek and Telluride. . . . the Western Miners Federation, the Industrial Workers of the World; it started here. . . . It was here that the westerner broke his head against the copper bosses' will—the country of Joe Hill and Haywood, of Moyer and Pettibone and of that great unsung Johnny Appleseed, Pat

Reynolds, Socrates to Haywood's Plato; the birthplace of
thousands of other Johnny Appleseeds who went up and out to
spread the gospel of One Big Union. Other men have their
Yorktowns and Little Big Horns and Gettysburgs. For me, and
my family, to rank with Haymarket and Lawrence there was
always Coeur d'Alene. . . . [120-121]

Even novels in which the IWW is presented in an equivocal or
unfavorable light are likely to have stimulated some readers to
learn more about it. Archie Binns's *The Timber Beast* (1944)—to
cite but one example—is basically a corny romance, and its leading
Wob character improbably becomes a contented capitalist in the
end. Anticipating the portrayal of Joe Hill as a criminal in Wallace
Stegner's later best-selling novel, Binns has one of his characters
remark that Hill "took what he needed. When he ran short of
money in Salt Lake, he shot him a grocer—and got caught" [143].
The book is sprinkled with IWW references, especially to Hill, and
even includes some misquoted lines from Hill's "The Preacher and
the Slave."

Occasionally, the union has even made its way into mass-
market fiction, though it is usually restricted to brief walk-on roles.
Fleeting as they are, however, I find these startling intrusions a
remarkable "sign of the times." In view of the U.S. government's
relentless and devastating efforts to destroy the IWW, and the
subsequent and ongoing efforts by the U.S. academic and journalistic intelligentsia to trivialize or deny the union's place in our
history, the fact that Wobblies keep making unscheduled appearances in unabashedly slick and commercial publications that
circulate in the many hundreds of thousands has to be considered
not only a joyful symbol of the IWW's refusal to die, but also a
good Wobbly joke at the bosses' expense.

On sale in bus stations and foodstores, mass-market paperbacks have undoubtedly reached a wider readership—and a vastly
larger *workingclass* readership—than most of the titles listed
above. Although there is no way to estimate their impact, it is
certain that many people first saw the words "Industrial Workers
of the World" or the name "Joe Hill" in these books. Historians, no
doubt regarding such books as "trash," have scrupulously avoided
them, and it is probably for the same reason that they tend not to be
listed in bibliographies. Like the IWW's own publications in the
old days, "cheap paperbacks" are much more likely to be read by
workers than by scholars, critics, and litterateurs.

The field is a large one, but even a hurried survey should be enough to demonstrate that it warrants further exploration.

Let us start with a spy thriller, one of the least likely genres in which to go looking for Wobblies. And yet here is Lawrence Block's *The Thief Who Couldn't Sleep* (1966) introducing a series character named Evan Tanner who, as we learn on page seven, is a member of the Industrial Workers of the World. He also belongs to the anarcho-syndicalist Confederación Nacional del Trabaja-dores de España (the Spanish CNT), and even the New York Libertarian League, an anarchist-communist group whose real-life members included such active Wobblies as Sam and Esther Dolgoff, Russell Blackwell, Richard Ellington, Jonathan Leake, and Walter Caughey. Fellow Worker Tanner, however, turns out to be a bit wayward in his commitment to the One Big Union, for it seems he also belongs to the Flat Earth Society of England, the Committee Allied Against Fluoridation, and any number of tiny ultra-nationalist and monarchist groups. In short, he is a devotee of what he regards as "lost causes." Nonetheless, he may well be the only character in mass-market fiction with a red card and his dues paid up.

The fact that real-life Wobs knew how sleazy real private detectives were may explain why so few IWW members turn up as characters in mystery stories. Dashiell Hammett's *Red Harvest* (1929) is of course the great exception. An earlier, little-known story by Hammett—"One Hour," published in *Black Mask* in 1924—involves two Wobblies working as printers in San Francisco. Decades later, the name of the Wobbly bard was invoked in *Indemnity Only* (1982), the debut novel of Sara Paretsky's ongoing series featuring Chicago female private eye V. I. Warshawski. Three pages before the end, a young woman who had spent the whole book hiding from cops and mobsters explains that she used the alias Jody Hill because "Joe Hill [was] always a big hero" in her labor union family.

Wobblies, and even Joe Hill himself, have also appeared in the world of science fiction. In Cyril M. Kornbluth's novel, *Not This August* (1955), a satire set ten years in the future, we meet a kid reading a comic book titled *Joe Hill: Hero of Labor*. A brief reference to "a man named Joe Hill" also appears in Poul Anderson's story, "The Last of the Deliverers" (1958). Mack Reynolds's science-fiction novel, *Of Godlike Power* (1966), later reissued as *Earth Unaware*, not only mentions the IWW, but also features a charming aside on soapboxing, and even a brief lecture on religion, in which the reader should have no trouble discerning the influence of a certain Wobbly songwriter:

At first [the Romans persecuted the Christians], but they made it the State religion after catching on to the fact that it was the perfect religion for a slave society. It promised pie in the sky when you died. Suffer on Earth, and you get your just desert after death. What could be a better creed to keep an exploited population quiet? [26]

The IWW "and its efforts to organize the One Big Union" are also mentioned in the same author's *Mercenary From Tomorrow* (1968). Reynolds's grandfather was a Wobbly, and he was an outspoken radical himself [Reynolds 1981]. After his death in 1983, fellow science-fiction writer Dean Ing was commissioned to complete several novels that Reynolds had left at "first-draft stage." Among them was a wacky dystopia titled *Deathwish World* (1986), featuring an IWW organizer in the starring role.

As the story opens, giant corporations based in the United States of the Americas control the world, and of course the World Government. A revolt to end corporate/consumerist slavery, organized by eighth-generation Wobblies together with the Black nationalist Anti-Racist League, finally defeats the government's trio of special forces: Mercenaries, Inc., the white supremacist Race Research Foundation, and the United Church. The book is full of fascinating allusions to people generally excluded from popular literature—Nat Turner, Geronimo, the Haymarket anarchists, Sacco and Vanzetti— and to such books as Cheikh Anta Diop's *The African Origin of Civilization*. Its single longest digression, taking up a full page, is devoted to Joe Hill, and includes three stanzas and the chorus of "The Preacher and the Slave."

Toward the end of the book a group called the Junior Wobblies appears suddenly, out of nowhere, and helps assure the IWW victory. Few readers realized that, once upon a time, there actually was a Junior Wobbly Union, organized in connection with the great Colorado coal strike in 1927. Made up mostly of the children of IWW parents, plus a few teenagers who had become radicalized on their own, the JWU had several locals in Colorado as well as in Chicago, New York, and other cities. There was even a Junior Wobbly song, written for the JWU by Fellow Worker Guy B. Askew (Skidroad Slim). One Junior Wob who went on to bigger things was Arthur Weinberg (known as "Art Hopkins" in JWU/ IWW circles), the biographer and anthologist of Clarence Darrow.

Very few labor historians, even those whose "specialty" is the IWW, have ever so much as mentioned the Junior Wobs, and yet here we find them in the distant future, saving the whole planet! This confirms an old hunch of mine, that what historians need above all is *more foresight!*

Mack Reynolds's *Deathwish World* is undoubtedly one of the oddest of all IWW-related novels,[1] but the *Illuminatus* trilogy by Robert Shea and Robert Anton Wilson (1975) surely wins the anti-academy award for sheer convoluted weirdness. Inspired largely by Ishmael Reed's riotous *Mumbo Jumbo*, this potpourri of psyche-delic schizo-occultist conspiracy fantasies is not what most people would call "IWW fiction," but the fact is that Wobblies, the Chicago Wobbly hall, and Joe Hill himself are—in all three volumes—basic foundation-stones as well as recurring reference-points in the whole anarcho-Lovecraftian manic-chaotic mix. There is even a mention of the IWW's Solidarity Bookshop, which both Shea and Wilson frequented in the late Sixties.

Surely real and imaginary Wobblies made other appearances in mass-market fiction. It would be nice if some research-team would make it their project to document them all. What is already obvious is that the IWW has resonated so profoundly in the pop-ular imagination that even the most assiduous and conscientious historians have been unable to keep track of its most far-reaching echoes.

Meanwhile, so-called "ordinary" folk—footloose workers, stu-dents, poets, the unemployable, misfits, and dreamers of all kinds —have proceeded to "discover" the IWW for themselves, willy-nilly and hit-or-miss. Songs, songbooks, concerts, records; history, sociology, biography, and fiction books: These are just a few of the uncountable ways in which people have stumbled upon the Wob-blies and thereby changed forever their way of looking at the past and at contemporary social reality.

The history of the many "discoveries" of the IWW is yet to be written, and will be hard to write, because the union is still con-stantly being discovered. The important point is this: From the late 1940s on, far from the sectarian in-fighting of the traditional left, and even farther from the "official" (pro-capitalist) labor move-ment, the IWW—though barely perceptible as a labor union—was nonetheless a *growing force*. In a society dominated by liars and their lies, young rebels recognized those old hoboes with their red cards as bearers of marvelous truths.

It is the height of irony that the IWW's emancipatory, counter-cultural, direct-action, forming-the-new-society-in-the-shell-of-the-old qualities found a secure place in the revolutionary imaginations of large numbers of young people at the very time that the IWW, as an organization, reached its lowest ebb. This wholly unantici-pated revival of interest seems to me analogous to the history of the Gnostics, those inspired radical heretics of the ancient Near East. Ruthlessly persecuted and exterminated by the Church in many a bloody battle, crusade, and inquisition, they nonetheless kept re-emerging—now here, now there, in one form or another—down through the centuries. Today, though still anathema to the ortho-dox, Gnostic teachings are studied with sympathy and appreciation by vastly more people than in the days when they were regarded as dreaded antagonists of the rising Christian hierarchy [Lacarriere, 1977].

What Hegel called "the cunning of history" is full of such strange and often cruel jokes. In the case of the IWW, however, the old Wobs enjoyed the last laugh. The paths to the rediscovery of Joe Hill's union were extraordinarily diverse and circuitous, but they helped a lot of people break out of the repressive Fifties into the revolutionary Sixties.

Not the least of these paths was *poetry*. For me, indeed, and for many of my friends—and I am sure for many others—poetry was vitally important in our introduction to the IWW. The union's historic and ongoing emphasis on poetry and song immediately impressed us as one of the decisive qualities that made it unique among labor and left organizations. And we were right: That the IWW produced and inspired more and better poetry than all other unions combined serves not only to distinguish it from all other unions, but also tells us a lot about the kind of world it was trying to build.

It was as poets that many of us came to discover the IWW, and the more we got to know the union, its history, art, and lore, the more we loved it. We found the IWW the same way we found surrealism, free jazz, certain films, S. P. Dinsmoor's "Garden of Eden," *The Hermetic Museum*, and the poetry of Sam Greenberg, Mina Loy, and Bob Kaufman: fortuitously but *necessarily*, because —without even knowing it—*we were searching for it*.

---

1. Authentic literary oddities have also emanated from the ranks of the IWW itself. Eugene Nelson's *Fantasia of a Revolutionary* (Infinite Possibilities Press, 1998), illustrated by Carlos Cortez, is a rambling tale of a present-day revolution in which scores of the great revolutionists of the past—including Flora Tristan, Mikhail Bakunin, Lucy Parsons, Emiliano Zapata, Buenaventura Durutti, and of course Joe Hill and other Wobblies—play an active part. See also Fellow Worker Nelson's collection of short stories, *Tales of Crapitalism* (Infinite Possibilities Press, 1999).

**PEOPLE IN HIGH PLACES READ BOOKS
PUBLISHED BY CHARLES H. KERR!**
Drawn by Mike Konopacki, this 1980s promotional
postcard highlights the affinities between
the IWW and Earth First!

5. THE KEROUAC CONNECTION

The IWW is composed largely of men who have ceased to care
for their jobs, who are rebels against business, and have
made up their minds to beat their way through life.
—**Ricardo Flores Magon**—

For me, for a lot of us, the search began with the haunting question: "Who am I?" and a deep, all-abiding refusal to adjust to the depressingly obtuse and bigoted 1950s version of the "American Way of Life"—which in turn led to another question: "What is to be done?"

In the fall of 1962, IWW General Secretary-Treasurer Walter H. Westman, an old "110 cat" (a member of Agricultural Workers Industrial Union No. 110) who had lost a leg jumping from a boxcar during one of the 1920s harvest drives, handed me my red card and said, "Welcome, Fellow Worker, into the Industrial Workers of the World." No recipient of the Nobel Prize has ever felt anything like the pride that swelled through me on that grand occasion.

Who was I, in 1962? How should *I* know? A "Marxist" acquaintance, somewhat older than I, pronounced me "insanely romantic." Classmates often asked me: "Why are you so frantic?" School administrators and at least one Professor of English told me I was "insolent." I already considered myself a surrealist (I wrote my first letter to André Breton a few weeks after I joined the IWW). In addition to the IWW, I was active in the Student Peace Union (SPU) and the Congress of Racial Equality (CORE). I was studying anthropology (with St Clair Drake) at Roosevelt University, a workingclass commuter school. On my own I also read a lot of books about Alchemy, Taoism, Zen, and the Seven Cities of Cibola, as well as everything I could find by Rosa Luxemburg and Clark Ashton Smith. My few prized possessions included a stack of *Bugs Bunny* comic books from the early '50s, a copy of Lautréamont's *Maldoror*, and some wonderful Thelonious Monk albums on the old Blue Note and Riverside labels.

At Roosevelt, several of us who had joined the IWW started a club, the R. U. Wobblies, which created quite a stir from the start. At its inception, a Maoist student sarcastically dubbed us the "Left Wing of the Beat Generation," and in no time all the campus Communists, Trotskyists, Social-Democrats, and Liberals (Roosevelt was a highly political school in those days) identified us the same way. For them, it was a term of derision and ridicule, but we found it rather charming. Indeed, coming from what we called the "square" left, it was quite a compliment!

The R. U. Wobblies later made headlines in the Chicago dailies when an invited speaker—Joffre Stewart, African American anarcho-pacifist, R. U. alumnus, and contributor to the *Industrial Worker*—burned a U.S. flag in the course of his talk. (During the 1960 Presidential elections Stewart had been the anti-candidate for anti-vice-president on Chicago's Beatnik Party ticket.) At that point, the label "Left Wing of the Beat Generation" outgrew the boundaries of Roosevelt U. and began to be applied to us by the entire Chicago-area left.

In any event, the name stuck. Years later, people I did not even know would stop me on the street and say, "Hey, I remember you! You were part of the Left Wing of the Beat Generation!"

At that time, none of us knew of the Tom Lewis article in the 1910 *International Socialist Review*. In retrospect, I find it both funny and weird that we, who regarded ourselves along with our Black Nationalist friends as the hippest people on the left, should have found our way to the *only* radical labor organization in U.S. history which has ever urged working people to "get hip."

Even then, however, we wondered: Were there *real* connections, aside from our young and unknown selves, between the IWW and the Beat Generation? We had no trouble finding correspondences galore, relating to hitchhiking and hoboing; a disdain for commercialism, conformity, and cops; rejection of the work-ethic, white supremacy, authoritarianism, and militarism; respect for wilderness and wildlife; and of course, an emphasis on poetry and freedom.

Connections, however—direct, concrete, *physical* links— proved elusive, hard to track down, and harder to confirm. In 1962, for example, we did not know that Slim Brundage, who ran the College of Complexes—Chicago's principal Beat gathering-place—and who also "managed" the 1960 Beatnik Party campaign, had been a Wobbly "way back when." (His College, in any case, had not been much of a meeting-place for *us*: Slim's place not only served liquor but also checked ID's, and most of the R.U. Wobblies were under 21.)

We knew, however, that at least *some* connections between Wobs and Beats must have existed, because significant mentions of the IWW had appeared in the works of several Beat writers.

Jack Kerouac, for example.

To backtrack a little: I first encountered the IWW in October 1959, in the just-published fifty-cent Signet paperback edition of *The Dharma Bums*. I was in study hall at high school, pretending to read a textbook, but I was infinitely more interested in what Kerouac had to say. The story involves hopping freights, hitchhiking, sex, poetry, jazz, Zen Buddhism, mountain-climbing, and other ways of getting high. I found it all very appealing. Less than a year later, not quite seventeen, I hitchhiked West, spent a few days in the Beat community in Venice, nearly two months in San Francisco's North Beach, and several days wandering in California's High Sierras.

The hero of *The Dharma Bums* is a mountain-climbing Zen poet named Japhy Ryder, whose interests include Native American mythology, John Muir, and ecology as well as "old-fashioned IWW anarchism" and "old worker songs" [Kerouac 1958, 9-10]. The narrator, who is clearly Kerouac himself, is fascinated by Ryder's "anarchistic ideas about how Americans don't know how to live," imprisoned as they are "in a system of work, produce, consume, work, produce, consume" [*ibid.*, 14, 78]. Critical of this repressed and repressive "America where nobody has any fun or believes in anything, especially freedom," Ryder is "always sympathetic to freedom movements . . . like anarchism in the Northwest, the old-time heroes of [the] Everett Massacre and all" [*ibid.*, 31].

The Dharma Bums is, in fact, basically a book about freedom and the obstacles to freedom. Strictly speaking, the "bums" celebrated in the title are really more like hoboes—but that's a mere detail (many a 'bo sang "Hallelujah, I'm a Bum"). In any event, the ideal of freedom defended throughout the book is an irrefragably hobo freedom, neatly summed up in one of Kerouac's maxims: "Better to sleep in an uncomfortable bed free, than sleep in a comfortable bed unfree" [*ibid.*, 123].

It didn't take me long to find out that "Japhy Ryder" was in reality the poet Gary Snyder, whose poems and texts I enjoyed in *Chicago Review*, *Evergreen Review* and other, even more obscure reviews. I had hoped to meet him in San Francisco, but Shig Murao at City Lights told me he was still in Kyoto.

It took much longer, however, to verify Snyder's interest in the IWW. The "bios" in such books as Seymour Krim's *The Beats* and Don Allen's *New American Poetry* didn't mention it. With the poet himself far away in Japan, we didn't know how to pursue the matter. Meanwhile, the "Left Wing of the Beat Generation" at Roosevelt U. got involved in a protracted free-speech fight (a modest forerunner of the huge struggle at the University of California at Berkeley a year later)—as well as other agitations. In those feverish times, the scholarly quest for Wobbly/Beat connections was not uppermost in our thoughts.

Today, thanks to several decades' accumulation of interviews, biographies, and reminiscences, the Kerouac/Snyder/IWW/Beat connections are now much clearer.

In 1978, discussing *The Dharma Bums*, Snyder told an interviewer:

> I think Jack saw me, in a funny way, as being [an] archetypal twentieth-century American of the west, of the anarchist, libertarian, IWW tradition, of a tradition of working outdoors and fitting in already with his fascination with the hobo, railroad bum, working man. [Gifford and Lee, 1978, 202]

A little further on in the same interview, he zeroes in on the import of that fascination:

> In harking back to the American hobo, Jack was harking back to one of the few models—myths—of freedom and freshness and mobility and detachment, detachment from the world of scrambling for power and prestige—that was available to us at that time. [*ibid.*, 213]

Kerouac's admiration for the hobo, as a near-mythic figure, was sincere, profound, and enduring. In this predilection he may well have been influenced by his father Leo, who, as a linotype operator and member of Lowell Typographical Union No. 310, was for many years a tramp printer, working for brief periods in printing offices all over the East Coast. At times Jack even liked to think of himself as a hobo, "but only of sorts," and he finally conceded that he was never "a real hobo" [1960, 173]. His essay, "The Vanishing American Hobo," hails the migrant worker as ancient inspirational precursor and contemporary poet-hero survivor [*ibid.*]. Unfortunately, Kerouac's very real enthusiasm for the subject was marred by sentimentality and stereotype ("the hobo lives in a Disneyland"!) and, even more lamentably, by sheer ignorance, as when he bestowed the honorable title of hobo on

Teddy Roosevelt, of all people—a sworn enemy of hoboes, whose defamation of the Wobs as "undesirable citizens" was clearly meant as a "go ahead" signal to lynch-mobs and company thugs.

The fact remains that Kerouac, more than any writer of his generation, exalted the hobo as an exemplar of freedom, and urged young people everywhere to respect and emulate hobo ways and wisdom. His naivete notwithstanding, the author of *The Dharma Bums* and *Desolation Angels* (in which he again invokes the IWW and the Everett Massacre) stood solidly on the side of the 'boes. Subtly, indirectly—almost unwittingly—Jack Kerouac, "Apostle of the Beat Generation," hastened young America's rediscovery of the IWW.

Sadly but predictably, Kerouac's biographers and commentators have played down—in most cases, never acknowledged—the IWW, anarchist, and other labor elements in his work. Oddly enough, the first important scholarly study of Kerouac—and the only one published during his lifetime—was Frederick Feied's small book, *No Pie in the Sky: The Hobo as American Cultural Hero* (1964), which focused primarily on these elements; its title, of course, was borrowed from Joe Hill's most popular song. Most subsequent criticism has maintained the dominant image of an apolitical or even reactionary Kerouac. The publication of his *Atop an Underwood: Early Stories and Other Writings* (2000) challenges the conventional wisdom in this regard, for it includes such stories as "The Birth of a Socialist," and other texts reflecting the youthful Kerouac's far-left inclinations. Particularly interesting, and related to his later interest in hoboes, is the short note on a plan the young writer himself called "Kerouac's Socialism," centered around a two- or three-hour working day:

> Shorter hours will provide the laborer with a new desire to live, not to be a productive animal, but to have time to be a man, to have time to enjoy the rights of man in the use of his divine intellect. . . . [2000, 85]

An IWW "Silent Agitator"

429

6. GARY SNYDER:
COLD MOUNTAIN WOBBLY

What do you suppose will satisfy the soul
except to walk free and own no superior?
—Walt Whitman—

The R. U. Wobblies' hunch proved right: There *was* a solid and direct connection between the IWW and the Beat movement, and his name was Gary Snyder. One of the major poets of our time, an important influence on Kerouac and many other writers, and a resounding voice for all that is best in bioregionalism and deep ecology, the author of *Mountains and Rivers Without End* remains the strongest link between the hippest labor union in U.S. history and the most vibrant poetic ferment of the mid-twentieth century.

From Snyder's childhood on, the IWW has been a living presence. Asked for the "formative influences" on his life and work as a poet, the first person he mentioned was his grandfather, "a Wobbly, dues-paying member of the Industrial Workers of the World—that was from back in his days as a logger" [Cook 1971, 32]. Henry Snyder, who had soapboxed for the union on Seattle's Skid Road, died when Gary was only seven, but he left his grandson some powerful memories. He recalls, for example, that his grandfather was "very musical" and played a transverse silver flute. In the "strongest memory" of all, "grandfather was sitting in his big black chair and he looked at me—I was six—and said, very sternly: 'Boy, read Marx!'" [FR interview, 16 May 2001].

As in many other households in the Pacific Northwest, Wob history and lore loomed large at the Snyder place. "The old IWW mythology," Gary told interviewer Bruce Cook, "became very important to me as I grew up" [1971, 32]. Joe Hill, for example,

> was one of the names I heard, when my father and his friends got to talking. I heard a lot of talk about the Wobblies, about Centralia, about the Everett Massacre. My father was fourteen at the time of the Everett Massacre. [FR interview, *op cit.*]

Gary recalls buying his first *Little Red Song Book*:

> I was around seventeen or eighteen, and I went to the IWW

office in Seattle. It wasn't on Yesler Way at that time. I forget what street it was on. Anyway, I went in and bought a copy of the *Song Book* and a couple other IWW pamphlets. I've had the *Song Book* ever since. [*ibid.*]

Friends from his early college years recall that Snyder often spoke of the Wobblies, and knew "a large repertoire of labor and Wobbly songs, which he sang with great vigor while whacking away at his guitar" [Halper 1991, 15, 31].

Asked whether others in the Beat milieu knew about Joe Hill or his songs, he replied:

Well, we all sang that song, "I Dreamed I Saw Joe Hill Last Night." Even at Reed College, which was pretty Stalinist in those days [1947-51], everybody knew that one. But hardly anyone knew Joe Hill's own songs. I used to talk about the Wobblies a lot, and sang Joe Hill's songs, but I ran into very few people who knew what I was talking about. But everybody knew "I Dreamed I Saw Joe Hill Last Night." [FR interview, *op cit.*]

By that time, if not earlier, the IWW had become a crucial part of the poet's identity. Meeting with Diggers in San Francisco shortly after his return from a long sojourn in Japan in the mid-1960s, Snyder—still in his thirties—identified *himself* as an "old Wobbly" [Halper 1991, 461]! Among the first to join the IWW Poets' Union that younger Bay Area Wobs had formed, Fellow Worker Snyder was issued red card No. X323420.

The union's lore had long since entered into his poetry, as in his warm salute to Fellow Workers

> *Felix Baran*
> *Hugo Gerlot*
> *Gustav Johnson*
> *John Looney*
> *Abraham Rabinowitz*
> *Shot down on the steamer Verona*
> *For the shingle-weavers of Everett*
> *the Everett Massacre November 5 1916*
> . . .
>
> *"Thousands of boys shot and beat up*
> *For wanting a good bed, good pay,*
> *decent food, in the woods—"*

No one knew what it meant:
"Soldiers of Discontent."
[1992, 38]

Another poem evokes the Seattle IWW hall:

"Forming the New Society
*   Within the shell of the Old"*
The motto in the Wobbly hall
Some old Finns and Swedes playing cards
Fourth and Yesler in Seattle
[in Allen 1960, 316]

(Almost certainly one of those old Swedes was my friend O.N.)

In other poems of Snyder's we find such now almost arcane words as "scissorbills" and "gypos" and others drawn from the bottomless wellspring of old Wobbly slang.

Snyder's 1961 manifesto, "Buddhist Anarchism," originally published in the first issue of the *Journal for the Protection of All Beings* and later revised and retitled "Buddhism and the Coming Revolution" (1969), is one of the earliest, most adventurous, and most playful efforts to mix IWW perspectives together with ideas from radically "other" traditions—in this case, Far Eastern philosophy—to form a new dialectical synthesis. More successful in radicalizing Buddhists than in drawing Wobblies toward the Eightfold Noble Path, Snyder's manifesto has had its greatest impact on activists in the antiwar, animal rights, anti-nuclear, ecology, gay, and feminist movements. A bold reaffirmation of Beat priorities, deeply suffused with the Wobbly spirit, its aim is the realization of a "true community." In Snyder's view, this means

> supporting any cultural and economic revolution that moves clearly toward a free, international, classless world. It means using such means as civil disobedience, outspoken criticism, protest, pacifism, voluntary poverty, and even gentle violence if it comes to a matter of restraining some impetuous redneck. It means affirming the widest possible spectrum of non-harmful individual behavior—defending the right of individuals to smoke hemp, eat peyote, be polygynous, polyandrous or homosexual. Worlds of behavior and custom long banned by the Judaeo-Capitalist-Christian-Marxist West. . . . Working on one's own responsibility, but willing to work within a group. "Forming the new society within the shell of the old"—the IWW slogan.

In a 1959 essay Jack Kerouac identified a heterogeneous throng of characters—real and imaginary—as sources, forerunners, and prefigurations of the short-lived, diffuse, disorderly, but always effervescent collective commotion that remains known as the Beat Generation. One of his strongest short pieces, "Origins of the Beat Generation" attempted to identify the historic as well as the mythic roots of that movement. Among the anticipatory co-conspirators named by Kerouac are George Herriman's Krazy Kat ("with the irrational brick"), The Shadow, the Marx Brothers, W. C. Fields, Popeye the Sailor, Humphrey Bogart, "dear old Basil Rathbone," and bebop magicians Charlie Parker, Dizzy Gillespie, and Babs Gonzales. By way of Gary Snyder, hero of *The Dharma Bums*, this merry band of ancestors welcomed yet another recalcitrant dreamer and doer from the not-too-distant past: the "Old Wobbly," a distinct social type: the definitive embodiment of the hobo as poet, genius, and Inspiring Wonder Worker.

It is pleasant to note that Gary Snyder, grandson of a good Wobbly, went on to learn Chinese, and that he translated the great ancient Chinese poet Han-shan ("Cold Mountain," his name taken from the place he lived). Described in *The Dharma Bums* as "a Chinese scholar who got sick of the big city and the world and took off to hide in the mountains," Han-shan is a lot like an "Old Wobbly" himself. In a short preface to his Han-shan translations, Snyder explains that Han-shan and his pal the "Zen lunatic" Shih-te became "great favorites with Zen painters of later days. . . . They became Immortals and you sometimes run into them today in . . . the hobo jungles and logging camps of America" [1992, 22]. Kerouac dedicated *The Dharma Bums* to Han-shan.

With a nod to Joe Hill, I want to record here that it was Gary Snyder who taught Kerouac how to eat with chopsticks (Kerouac 1958, 16).

And what does Snyder think of the IWW today?

> I think the IWW is more relevant today than ever, because of globalization. All these anti-globalization demonstrations are great and I'm all for them, but there's another aspect to the question that's even more important: *labor*. Globalization will proceed and do its worst until workers start organizing globally, across national boundaries. Only a global labor movement can check global capitalism, and that's what the IWW is all about. [FR interview, *op. cit.*]

IWW Joe Hill postcard (1915)

XIV
WOBBLY POETICS IN THEORY & PRACTICE

1. THE IWW PASSION FOR POETRY

Does the reading of poetry train us to insurrection?
—**William Ellery Channing**—

L ong after the IWW had ceased to be a major force "at the point of production," its reputation as "the singing union" persisted—and remains intact today. What a telltale commentary on the stagnation and decay of the official U.S. labor movement that no other union during the past hundred years has come even close to challenging the IWW's supremacy as labor's songsters and poets!

The IWW's penchant for song attracted journalistic and even a bit of academic attention early on. Hill himself was pleased, as he remarked in June 1914 to a reporter from the *Salt Lake Tribune*, that his songs had been "adopted by the revolutionary forces, such as the IWW and the Socialist organizations" [Smith 1969, 40]. Quite a few Wobbly songs—Joe Hill's above all, but also Chaplin's "Solidarity Forever" and a few others, as well as some of T-Bone Slim's—have been widely anthologized, and at least a few have been the object of scholarly examination.

Early criticism of Hill's songs consisted mostly of three- or four-line comments by fellow workers and comrades from other left groups. One of the first comments, which reached a length of seven lines, was Upton Sinclair's prefatory note to "The Preacher and the Slave" in his big social protest anthology, *The Cry for Justice*, published in September 1915, while Hill was still alive. The book, which marks the IWW poet's first appearance in cloth covers, had an immense readership. For decades copies were on hand at every Socialist Party and IWW library, as well as in numerous trade-union libraries and even many public libraries. Because Sinclair was a very popular author, not just among radicals but also among the broad public—and also because the book had an introduction by Jack London—*The Cry for Justice* had a large general sale and was reprinted many times. In short, the book brought Joe Hill and a sample of his work to the attention of many tens of thousands of new readers.

Sinclair's prefatory note, however, was disappointingly churlish and snooty. He introduced Hill's song as a

> sample of many parodies upon Christian hymns which are pub-
> lished by the Industrial Workers of the World, and sung by the
> migratory workers of the Far West in their camping-places, known
> as "jungles." While this selection and the one following [a rhymed
> parable by Henry M. Tichenor of the Socialist *Rip-Saw*] can hardly
> be classed as literature, they have their interest as social docu-
> ments. It was Napoleon who said that if he could write a country's
> songs, he would not care who wrote its laws. [1915, 707]

This strange comment tells us more about Sinclair than about
Hill. By denying the Wobbly bard a place in literature (in a book
subtitled *An Anthology of the Literature of Social Protest*), and
then citing Napoleon—erroneously, by the way[1]—on the power of
song, Sinclair revealed two of his principal personality traits: ambivalence and confusion. The same traits characterized his politics as
well: A social-democrat who supported U.S. involvement in the
First World War, Sinclair was also—before and after the war—a
supporter and friend of the Wobblies. Consistent in his inconsis-
tency, the cautious "slowcialist" who waved the flag for Woodrow
Wilson's imperialist war but somehow could not repress his admiration for the revolutionary IWW, was also the anthologist who refused to acknowledge any intercourse between High Culture and
Low, but secretly found Joe Hill's songs appealing anyway.

By and large, Wobblies liked Sinclair, and read his books with
appreciation, especially his great non-fiction studies: *The Brass
Check* (on journalism) and *The Goose Step* (on education). Some
Wobs, however, were quite critical of his fiction. C. E. Setzer,
a.k.a. X13, one of the union's wildest cartoonists, left us a little
classic of Sinclair criticism in the form of a knockout one-liner. In
conversation with critic Edmund Wilson during the IWW's 1931-
32 Construction Workers strike at Boulder Dam, Fellow Worker
Setzer (one of the strike organizers) mentioned to Wilson that

> reading Sinclair's novels is like eating a half-ripe melon: the social
> thesis spoils the story and the simple-minded stories spoil them as
> pamphlets. [Wilson 1982, 115-116]

Too harsh? Too flippant? Perhaps—but think of it as a good Wobbly's payback for Sinclair's ungracious comment on Hill.

Other early Hill criticism tended to be unambivalently friendly, but even briefer than Sinclair's. Saluting Hill as "a free spirit" and "the inimitable songster and poet of the IWW" in *Solidarity* (17 July 1915), Elizabeth Gurley Flynn set the tone:

> Joe Hill writes songs that sing, that lilt and laugh and sparkle, that kindle the fires of revolt in the most crushed spirit and quicken the desires for fuller life in the most humble slave. . . . He has crystalized the organization's spirit into imperishable forms, songs of the people—folk songs.

Just after Hill's judicial murder, writing in Emma Goldman's *Mother Earth*, W. S. Van Valkenburgh described the IWW poet as "a genius in the rough," and "a poet [whose] verse stirred his fellows like the gale an aspen leaf."
Ralph Chaplin found Hill's lyrics

> as coarse as homespun and as fine as silk; full of lilting laughter and keen-edged satire; full of fine rage and finer tenderness; simple, forceful and sublime . . . songs of and for the worker. [1926, 189]

Noting that these songs "have gained a wider audience than any similar songs written in any language," Chaplin concluded that Hill was "about as close to being the poet laureate of labor as any poet the working class movement has yet produced" [1923, 26, 23].

Harold Roland Johnson, in a two-fifths-of-a-page *Industrial Pioneer* article on "Joe Hill, Song Writer," affirmed that Hill's poems and songs "are known everywhere that social protest has arisen in group expression," but also recognized that much of his work was far from extraordinary. "Some, however," he went on to say, "reveal such rare expression of true gift and talent that they are assured working class permanence," and he singled out "Workers of the World, Awaken!" for special praise [June 1924, 44].

For James P. Cannon, an IWW organizer and speaker who later became the central figure of U.S. Trotskyism, Hill's songs combined "shrewd common sense with a vision of the future society where workers are not legally murdered behind tall stone walls" [1992, 472]. J. Louis Engdahl, the Communist editor of the *Labor Defender*, merely added an alliterative touch when he noted in that magazine that Hill's lyrics can be found "on the lips of labor in every land" [Nov 1929, 224].

Paul F. Brissenden did not comment on Hill's songs in his 1919

book, *The IWW: A Study in American Syndicalism*—the first scholarly history of the union—but the fact that his eleven-page
selection of IWW songs included five songs by Hill, and that no
other songwriter was represented by more than a single song, is
itself a strong statement. That the volume was published by Columbia University Press further indicates that the IWW poet was
steadily becoming known to an ever-broader public.

Significant, too, was Carl Sandburg's note on Hill in his popular
and oft-reprinted *American Songbag* (1927). Introducing "The
Preacher and the Slave," the author of the *Chicago Poems* described Hill as the IWW's

> star song writer and . . . the only outstanding producer of lyrics
> widely sung in the militant cohorts of the labor movement in
> America. Jails and jungles from the Lawrence, Massachusetts,
> woolen mills to the Wheatland, California, hop fields, have heard
> the rhymes and melodies started by Joe Hill. [222]

A few years later, in an article on "Poesy in the Jungles" in H.
L. Mencken's popular magazine, the *American Mercury*, George
Milburn proclaimed Hill "the most ingenious of [the] hobo parodists" [May 1930, 85]. In his *Hobo's Hornbook*, published that
same year, Milburn proclaimed Hill "the hobo's poet laureate."

Numerous all-too-similar remarks can be found in IWW, Socialist Party, anarchist, Communist, and other left newspapers and
magazines. These telegram-like notations do not add up to a large
or exciting body of criticism, but they nonetheless served as
models for the great bulk of subsequent writing on Hill as songwriter. One is struck by the dearth of ideas in most of these later
critical remarks on Hill's songs, not to mention the dearth of
imagination. Alan Calmer's survey of "The Wobbly in American
Literature," in the International Publishers anthology, *Proletarian
Literature in the United States* (1935), includes three paragraphs
on Hill that are little more than a digest of earlier writers' comments [342-343]. Calmer's brief sketch, in turn, reads like an
abstract of the later critical evaluations of Hill by Barrie Stavis and
Philip Foner.

Most recent criticism has done little more than refine the term-
inology. The interesting study, *Music and Social Movements:
Mobilizing Traditions in the Twentieth Century* (1998) by Ron
Eyerman and Andrew Jamison, includes a wealth of useful infor-

mation, and concludes that Hill "changed, or at least added something important to, American culture" [60]. However, when the authors describe Hill as "perhaps the most active articulator of the IWW's cognitive praxis," and explain that his songs sought "to educate and empower at one and the same time," they cannot be said to have told us anything that was not already well known when our grandparents were young [58-59].

Isn't there something just a tad ridiculous in the fact that critical commentary on Joe Hill's hilarious, wild, exuberant songs should be notable chiefly for its unrelieved sameness?

With a few very important exceptions, Wobbly song in general has not fared much better. The literature on the IWW is vast, but surprisingly little of it is devoted to songs. New critical approaches to the songs are even rarer. Much important source material meanwhile remains unpublished: Fred Thompson's copious files, and Dick Brazier's correspondence and interviews are full of invaluable insights on Wobbly songs and songwriters, as are the colorful stories ad-libbed by Utah Phillips during his many concerts over the years, but few critics or historians have made much use of this material.

The most penetrating, original, and prolific writer on the subject is unquestionably laborlorist Archie Green, whose own collection of interviews, correspondence, field notes, and documents—now part of the Southern Folklife Collection at the University of North Carolina in Chapel Hill—teems with treasures of the Wobbly counterculture. Green's innovative explorations of IWW songs, including such little-known lyrics as "Kitten in the Wheat" and "The Dehorn's Nose," are models of their kind: sympathetic—indeed, enthusiastic, truly appreciative of workers' creativity—but also searching, and full of questions. Proving a preconceived theory is the least of his concerns; he is always far more interested in probing complexities and puzzling over contradictions. In contrast to the work of most "labor historians," whose knowledge of working life is almost entirely gleaned from books written by non-workers, Green's monumental research has been greatly enhanced by his personal on-the-job experience as shipwright and carpenter, and by his long friendship and extensive correspondence with many old Wobblies. And to a far greater degree than most writers on the IWW, Green is fascinated by words and wordplay, and genuinely loves poetry, music, and song. Especially illuminating are the provocative ways he has related Wobbly culture to earlier labor traditions—and beyond those, to world literature, mythology and folklore—as well as to the very different traditions of other unions: AFL, CIO, and independent.

All too few researchers, however, have followed Archie Green's admirable lead. When one considers the richness of IWW songs, their role in shaping the union and documenting its history, and their lasting impact on five generations of singers and listeners, the critical literature on the subject seems pitifully sparse.

The lack of a readily available and complete-as-possible *corpus* of Wobbly songs has surely been an inhibiting factor in this regard. Back in the 1940s John Neuhaus—the brilliant self-taught Wobbly folklorist whose life's work is told in a splendid article by Archie Green—undertook to assemble a *Big Red Song Book*: a compilation of all the songs that have appeared, at one time or another, in the many editions of the *Little Red Song Book*. Such a collection would mark a big step forward for the study of IWW songs. Neuhaus's dream, alas, is still a project for the future.

One should keep in mind, however, that only a relatively small fraction of Wobbly songs ever made it into the *Song Book*. Hundreds more—probably thousands—linger on in the fragile and too-rarely-perused pages of old IWW periodicals. Many songs known to have been sung never seem to have reached print at all, and have survived only in oral tradition or manuscript.

If scholarship in the field of Wobbly songs is still in its beginnings, the study of Wobbly poetry has hardly even reached the starting point. Excluded from practically all anthologies—Marcus Graham's *Anthology of Revolutionary Poetry* and Joyce Kornbluh's *Rebel Voices* are the notable exceptions—IWW poets are also conspicuously unmentioned in histories, reference-works, and critical assessments of U.S. poetry. Of the several hundred card-carrying IWW poets, book-length studies have been devoted to exactly none; only a handful have received even the limited recognition conferred by a short article. Non-existent, too, are discussions of the influence of Wobbly poets on other, allegedly "more important" poets.

In this book I have concentrated on the IWW in the U.S., and have discussed its presence in other lands only in those instances in which Joe Hill is known to have ventured beyond the U.S. borders. The IWW, however, as its name implies, was truly a world movement. Few indeed are the countries in which it did not exert an influence. Its activity in Australia proved especially strong and long-lasting, and the Fellow Workers "down under" produced an impressive body of original IWW poetry and song, very little of which is known in the States. From the admittedly small sampling I have seen, the work of the Australian Wobblies—Guido Barrachi, Lesbia Harford, Harry Hooton, Mick Sawtell, and others—seems to be more daringly "experimental" than that of their U.S. counterparts, and in any event surely deserves a wider readership.[2]

In the 1940s the *Industrial Worker* published poems by German-born John Olday, who lived for extended periods in England and Australia. A veteran of the anarcho-syndicalist dockworkers' movement in Hamburg and a noted fighter in the anti-Nazi resistance, he was also active in the Surrealist Group in London during and after the Second World War. In 1945 Olday was jailed for anti-militarist agitation. Two of his "Poems from Prison" appeared in the Wobbly weekly of 1 September 1945 along with a letter of introduction from Simon Watson Taylor, editor of the English surrealist journal *Free Unions*. Like Joe Hill, Ralph Chaplin, Ernest Riebe, and in later years Carlos Cortez, Olday was not only a poet but also a cartoonist; his antiwar cartoon collection, *The March to Death*, was issued by Freedom Press in London in 1943. In the just-cited issue of the *Industrial Worker*, editor Pat Read hailed Olday as "one of the greatest cartoonists of the world labor movement," and concluded: "Proud to reproduce his cartoons, the *Industrial Worker* is equally proud to reprint his poems."

At various times the IWW has also been a significant force in Canada, Mexico, Chile, and South Africa. Did Canadian, Mexican, Chilean, and South African Wobblies write poetry? One of my favorite books as a teenager—Langston Hughes's 1961 paperback anthology, *An African Treasury*—includes a delightful little poem by a poet named I.W.W. Citashe. I have always wondered how this poet happened to have those particular initials. Hughes's note explains only that Citashe was deceased, that he was of the Xhosa tribe and wrote largely in that language, and that he had lived at Uitenhage, Cape Province.

Even in the U.S. itself the international dimension of the IWW was hard to miss. Every one of the union's foreign-language periodicals—and there were dozens of them—published songs and poems, many of them original. Typically, the various histories of the union tell us nothing about them. Henry Bengston's memoirs include a three-line mention of the Swedish IWW poet, Signe Aurell, who worked as a laundress in Minneapolis [1999, 160]. She came to the U.S. around 1914 and returned to Sweden six years later. In 1919 she published a collection of her poetry, *Irrbloss* (Will-o'-the-Wisp). One of Aurell's poems is a tribute to Joe Hill, and she also translated several of his songs into Swedish. According to Bengston's book, she was still alive in the late 1960s. Why is the name of this obviously interesting and important character missing from books on Joe Hill and the Wobblies?

The union's prolific foreign-language activity serves to remind us that the IWW, far more than most intellectual/poetic/artistic currents of the time, was a *multilingual* movement, and that its members were more aware of new developments in other cultures than most U.S. workers or intellectuals. Many Wobblies were themselves multilingual. IWW National Organizer Joseph Ettor, of Italian parentage, was fluent in Italian, English, Polish, Hungarian, and Yiddish [Dubofsky 1969, 236]. Carlos Cortez's father Alfredo Cortez, a Mexican-born Native American whose activity in the union began in 1916, was fluent in Spanish, English, Italian, Portuguese, and German [Bennet, in Sorell 2002, 51n6].

Directly related to the Wobbly preference for vernacular forms of expression, this multilingualism also helps explain the IWW's acceptance of many diverse styles in poetry and art. Despite the prevalence of a kind of "roughneck" realism in the union's visual art, the more adventurously creative Wobblies played and experimented with many varieties of "modern" art and literature. When Archie Green asked several IWW old-timers to name their favorite labor fiction, most headed the list with Dos Passos's trilogy *U.S.A.*, a novel inspired by the extravagantly modernist "Unanimism" of Jules Romains, far from the puerile dogmas of the Communist Party's "proletarian literature."

As has often been remarked, the funny thing about so-called "proletarian" literature" is that it was rarely written and almost never read by proletarians. Today, even university professors are beginning to recognize what working people have known since they were in fourth grade: that the long-despised "noir" writers of "paperback originals" were incomparably more adept at conveying the total corruption of bourgeois society, including the horror, misery, and degradation—in a word, the reality—of workingclass life, than the hopelessly tiresome propagandists promoted by the *Daily Worker*. No matter how hard Communist publicists pushed the Party's "socialist realist" novels, millions of workers obviously preferred to read Fredric Brown, David Goodis, Helen McCloy, Day Keene, Gil Brewer, Helen Nielsen, Howard Schoenfeld, and others whose unpretentious volumes could be had for two-bits in dime-stores, drugstores, and bus-stations everywhere.

The IWW's writers and poets were as far from the Communists' imagination-stifling ideological rigidity as they were from the sensationalistic sex-and-violence commercialism that marred so much of the work of the lurid paperback pulpsters. At its best, IWW literature, and especially IWW poetry, seethes with dark imagination, critical audacity, excitement, and enthusiasm, with large doses of wild humor, and headlong wonders at every turn. A literature written *and* read by working people, it has also influenced a broad range of middle- and even upper-class intellectuals, including innovators in the so-called avant-garde. Here was an unprecedented, incredibly rich ferment of working-class countercultural creativity thriving in at least two dozen languages, most of it published in widely-circulated weekly IWW newspapers and monthly magazines. If America's educational system were not so abjectly class-biased—so thoroughly under the thumb of capitalist/miserabilist ideology—the works of Joe Hill, T-Bone Slim, Mary Marcy, Jim Seymour, Laura Tanne, and other Wobblies would be a cherished part of the curriculum of every grade school, high school, and college in the land.

Instead, what is probably the largest movement of worker-poets in history—and certainly in U.S. history—has been virtually blotted out from the public record. Such suppression, however, hardly comes as a surprise. As William Blake warned us as long ago as 1798: "Nothing can be more contemptible than to suppose Public Records to be true" [1966, 392]. In the present instance the suppression is particularly glaring because the very fact that hundreds of IWW members were poets already tells us so much. In addition to upsetting strongly held suppositions about working people and the ways in which they prefer to spend their leisure time, the sheer quantity of poetry-writing IWWs also emphasizes how incredibly *different* the One Big Union was from other unions.

For a man to declare himself a poet during the early years of the twentieth century was a real act of defiance. By 1905, the IWW's Year One, the repulsive petit-bourgeois stereotype of "The Poet" was already well-established throughout the media. In popular fiction, vaudeville, light opera, the Sunday funny papers, and even in the news itself, "poets" were constantly portrayed as effeminate, elitist, pretentious snobs, bursting with affectation, hot air and conceit. Typically, in these mean-spirited, philistine portrayals, the poor "poet" was the recipient of a swift kick in the pants, a black eye, or other rough comeuppance. Women poets were ridiculed as well—as pompous, inane, unattractive, obese, bejeweled, and utterly bourgeois. Has the popular conception of what it is to be a poet ever sunk lower?

And yet, in Wobbly halls all across this land, one could find lumberjacks, longshoremen, hard-rock miners, weavers, machinists, barge-captains, waitresses, dishwashers, house-painters, ship-builders, and apple-pickers with red cards in their pockets and pencils in hand, writing poems and, what's more, getting them published in the best-circulated labor periodicals of their time.

In other words, Wobblies not only challenged the stereotype, but also did much to change it. By the mid-1910s, when Joe Hill became known as "the IWW poet," the term was reappearing once again as a title of honor and respect.

These IWWs were not only writers of poetry, but also avid *readers*. Besides reading and rereading books at the union's branch libraries, Wobs were also constant frequenters of public libraries and bookstores. Of Fellow Worker James Kelly Cole it was said that

> The library almost became his home. . . . The poets of all times he
> knew well, and much of their works he was ever ready to recite in
> a manner that they themselves would have been proud to hear.
> [Cole 1910, 10]

For Ralph Chaplin, reading *Leaves of Grass*—which his friend Charles H. Kerr had recommended as "rebel poetry of the highest order"—was a "revelation" that marked a major turning-point in his life [1948, 98]. Mila Tupper Maynard's book, *Walt Whitman: The Poet of the Wider Selfhood*, published by Kerr in 1903, did much to introduce Whitman's work to workingclass and radical readers. Kerr himself appears to have been radicalized in the 1880s largely by reading Shelley, whose poetry he regarded as "unsurpassed in beauty" [Ruff 1997, 18-19].[3] When and where T-Bone Slim discovered the work of Robert Burns is not known, but he readily acknowledged his admiration for the great Scottish bard [1992, 43].

"Big Bill" Haywood is not generally thought of as a man who cared for poetry, much less as a poet, but those who knew him best knew otherwise. Steeped in the works of Shakespeare and Milton years before the founding of the IWW, he remained an ardent reader of poetry for the rest of his life, and wrote poems himself —in his Idaho prison cell, in Greenwich Village's Washington Square, in Chicago's Cook County Jail. Vigorous, colorful, imaginative language is the hallmark of the many articles Haywood contributed to IWW publications and the *International Socialist Review*. One of the most compelling orators of his time, he frequently addressed crowds numbered in the tens of thousands (at least once, in Chicago's Riverview Park, the number was almost eighty thousand). Many of his speeches ring with Whitmanesque fervor. During the 1913 Paterson strike, for example, when word reached the IWW that striking miners in Johannesburg had been deported, Haywood wrote his greeting to the workers of the world:

You, O Men of Africa, Greeting!
Greeting to you who are on the high seas.
You who have been exiled.
You who are on strike. . . .

You who are white, black, brown, red or yellow of skin.
You who have been denied the sunlight of life.
You who have been denied knowledge.
You who have been denied love.

You who are wage-slaves in the mart.
You whose drops of blood turn the wheels of all
    industries. . . .
You who have made all invention possible.
You who feed, and clothe, and shelter, and succor
    the peoples of the world. . . .
You must feel that an injury to the least is an injury
    to all your class. . . .
You, O Men and Women and Children of Labor, you can end
    forever the wrongs your class has endured. . . .
Think, Organize, Act Together.
Industrial Freedom Will Come to All.

No wonder Hutchins Hapgood considered Haywood "essentially a poet" [1939, 293]. Max Eastman, too, noted that Haywood was "more at home in figurative than analytic language" [1948, 449].

Ralph Chaplin and Arturo Giovannitti were also among the IWW's most popular platform speakers. They were in constant demand not only within the union itself, but also by many other groups, and their talks usually included recitals of one or more of their poems. Friends of James P. Cannon marveled at the ease with which he could recite long poems by Shelley and Swinburne from memory, years after he had learned them as an IWW organizer in the 1910s [FR interview with Rose and Joseph Giganti, 1985]. Fred Thompson's favorites were Shelley and Robert Burns, but he also knew the poems of many others by heart. When I asked him about Voltairine de Cleyre, Thompson said he found her poems too "pessimistic," and then spontaneously recited several stanzas of her "Toast of Despair."

In 1965 I helped organize a Chicago IWW Branch Fiftieth Anniversary Joe Hill Memorial Meeting in Chicago at a folk-music club called Poor Richard's on Sedgwick Avenue. One of the features of the evening was a recitation of Ralph Chaplin's antiwar poem, "Red Feast," by Jack Sheridan, a prominent member of the Branch. Like most of the crowd, I expected that Fellow Worker Sheridan, who was himself a poet, would quietly read the text from a book. No one was prepared for his electrifying performance. Reciting from memory in a booming voice punctuated by powerful gestures, he had everyone in the hall on the edge of their seats. I have been to many poetry readings since—some of them very moving—but I have never heard anyone read with more dramatic force than Jack Sheridan.

Later I learned that he had recited "The Red Feast" (and other poems) many times, on many occasions: at IWW events, at the old Dil Pickle Club, and other venues. As Fred Thompson once put it, Sheridan's recitation "always brings down the house." Fellow Worker Sheridan was, in short, like Chaplin and Giovannitti, a highly skilled Wobbly reciter. None of us realized it then, but he was probably the last of the union's old-time reciters. In the 1910s and '20s there were many. It was a noble calling. Good reciters of poetry were highly valued in the movement: around the campfires, at "socials" in the halls, at street-meetings, strike rallies, and open forums. And the fact that good reciters were so much in demand also shows that there were plenty of eager listeners.

It is often said that "the audience for poetry is small," but for many thousands of Wobblies, poetry was a passion.

1. Bartlett's *Familiar Quotations* (Little, Brown, 1953, 290b), attributes the words to Andrew Fletcher of Saltoun (1655-1716).

2. The best and most thorough study of the IWW in Australia is Burgmann 1995, but see also Fry, ed., 1965, Walker 1972, and Harris 1970.

3. In a letter to Penelope Rosemont dated 26 May 1986, Charles H. Kerr's daughter, Katharine Kerr Moore, wrote: "My parents enjoyed Walt Whitman, the Brownings, Smollet and Fielding, Byron, Shelley, and Keats," as well as "the New England poets," including Emerson and Bryant. The family favorites, she added, were Shakespeare and Dickens.

2. REVOLUTIONARY
WORKINGCLASS ROMANTICISM

A poet must be more useful than any other citizen of his tribe.
—Isidore Ducasse, Comte de Lautréamont—

D uring the IWW's first quarter-century, a vibrant awareness of poetry, and of poetry's imperatives, seems to have pervaded the entire union. So widespread was the Wobs' zeal for the poetic art that a gossipy contributor to a mass-circulation magazine sneered, with smug cynicism, that "practically every Wobbly imagined that he [*sic*] was a heaven-endowed poet." Such was the high-nosed opinion of one Samuel Putnam, a bourgeois aesthete and hack journalist who happened to know quite a few IWWs in those years, and who for some reason even carried a red card himself for a time [1933, 64].

It was not by accident, in any case, that several of the IWW's leading poets were also among its best known spokespersons. Joe Hill seems to have been content writing his songs, drawing an occasional cartoon, and taking care of the day-to-day chores as secretary of the San Pedro local, but not all Wob poets were so self-effacing. Ralph Chaplin, Arturo Giovannitti, and Covington Hall were active as organizers, strike coordinators, and editors of IWW papers. Chaplin edited *Solidarity* in Cleveland, and later the *Industrial Worker* in Chicago; Giovannitti edited the Italian-language *Il Proletario* in New York; and Hall edited *The Lumberjack*, and later *The Voice of the People*, in New Orleans and elsewhere.

Another well known Wobbly poet, Richard Brazier served as secretary of the joint IWW locals in Spokane, helped organize the Agricultural Workers Organization—which soon became the largest of the IWW's constituent industrial unions—and also served on the IWW General Executive Board. Laura Payne Emerson played an important role in the San Diego Free Speech Fight of 1912. Matilda Robbins was active in the IWW strikes in Little Falls and Akron in 1913, and later in the Sacco-Vanzetti defense.

Mary Marcy wrote one of the most widely read IWW pamphlets, the much-translated *Shop Talks on Economics*, as well as many other pamphlets and countless articles in the Wobbly press, the *International Socialist Review*, and other publications. Jane Street unionized the housemaids in Denver in 1916. Charles Ash-

leigh, whose poetry appeared not only in the IWW press but also in many other publications, from *The Little Review* to the *Liberator*, took part in important organizing drives and served as the union's publicist during the Everett defense. Mortimer Downing was also a union publicist, especially active in defense work. Henry George Weiss's *The Shame of California and Other Poems* was issued by the General Defense Committee *circa* 1924 as propaganda in the struggle against "criminal syndicalism" laws. Donald Crocker edited the *Industrial Worker* for a time around 1920, and Henry Van Dorn edited the IWW magazine *Industrial Pioneer* later in the decade.

Never before or since have so many practicing poets held so many positions of responsibility in a U.S. labor organization.

Even the union's pamphlet literature often reflected a poetic spirit. Nils H. Hanson, for example, in a pamphlet titled *The Onward Sweep of the Machine Process*, invoked the IWW revolution as "the time about which poets all through the ages have dreamed" [8]. And Justus Ebert, in one of the most frequently reprinted IWW publications, *The IWW in Theory and Practice*, responded affirmatively to the "realist" charge that IWWs are dreamers: "Dreamers! Yes! . . . For what is it to dream, if not to achieve?" [124]. To critics who doubted the "practicality" of the IWW program, Joseph Ettor, in his pamphlet, *Industrial Unionism: The Road to Freedom*, retorted with the insouciance of an Oscar Wilde: "It is said that our ideas are impractical. That is true. From the standpoint of old institutions, interests and their beneficiaries, the new is always impractical" [5].

Such provocative and lyrical digressions, uncommon in propaganda—particularly in labor movement propaganda—suggest how far the IWW was from any sort of rationalist ideology, and how much importance its pamphleteers attributed to audacity and imagination. IWWs read Voltaire as well as other rationalists and anti-romantics, but clearly they preferred the poets and dreamers. In essentials, their outlook had deep affinities with the writings of the great romantics and pre-romantics, and most especially with Blake, the young Wordsworth, and Shelley.

Linking the Chicago-based revolutionary industrial union movement to three of England's most illustrious poets will no doubt strike some as impertinent or worse, but that's just too bad, for the link happens to be very real. At a time when bourgeois professors on both sides of the Atlantic were busy concocting a sickeningly domesticated, depoliticized, drawing-room version of romanticism, the IWW—and its poets first and foremost—reaffirmed romanticism's original revolutionary impulse and situated it in the service of workingclass self-emancipation.

Every so often one hears the complaint that someone or other is "romanticizing" the IWW. I have been accused of romanticizing it myself, and the redundancy of the charge always makes me laugh. Romanticizing the IWW would be like pouring a glass of water into the ocean. The truth is that the IWW is way beyond romanticizing, for the entire union was wildly and unabashedly romantic from its very first day. No group in U.S. history ever set out with nobler aims or higher hopes, and no group achieved so much, or left such a grand legacy, in the face of such terrible opposition. Despite repeated efforts by historians, journalists, propagandists, memoirists, and novelists to *de*romanticize the IWW—to demean its aspirations, degrade its accomplishments, and deny its contemporary relevance—the union's marvelous dreams, and the heroism of its struggle to realize those dreams, remain ineffaceable and glorious. The Wobblies were romantic through and through; and what's more, they knew it themselves, and their legacy is, in the best sense of the word, a defiantly romantic legacy.

Indeed, unlikely as it may seem, this rough-and-tumble organization of unskilled migratory workers—the self-proclaimed "rebel band of labor"—turned out to be one of the last major upheavals of the international romantic movement. "Revolutionary industrial unionism" perfectly describes the IWW's basic social-economic program, but the union's cultural dimension, especially as manifest in its poetry and song, could more accurately be called *revolutionary workingclass romanticism.*

Historians have insufficiently emphasized the fact that the IWW, especially the large hobo contingent which provided so many of the union's poets and thinkers, was not simply *anti*-capitalist, but also shared certain *pre*capitalist values. By and large these were the same precapitalist values championed by the early romantics: freedom, beauty, generosity, and a heightened sense of *life*—life as adventure, exaltation, self-fulfillment, and enchantment. Wobblies fully shared the early romantics' rejection of bourgeois acquisitiveness, the mechanization and compartmentalization of every aspect of life, the reification of human relationships and the consequent bureaucratization and destruction of real human

Joe Hill

community. Some Wobs, most notably Bill Haywood, Covington Hall, and T-Bone Slim, went on to question the whole debilitating myth of Progress, and to revalorize the "primitive."

In short, the IWW's economic critique of capitalist society was enhanced by a powerful poetic critique that was largely inspired by the romantic poets. Wobblies hated capitalism not only because it is exploitative, authoritarian, and unjust, but also because it is ugly, foul-smelling, noisy, stultifying, cretinizing, completely incompatible with the "good life" as dreamed by poets through the ages, and therefore irremediably *wrong*. Unalterably opposed to capitalist rationalization of misery and injustice, the IWW did not favor irrationalism, but a higher reason. That the imagination is

in truth . . . but another name for
clearest insight, amplitude of mind,
And reason in her most exalted mood

as Wordsworth put it in his *Prelude*, was second nature to many Wobblies, practicing poets or not.

To replace the oppressive order based on wage-slavery, the accumulation of capital, and the fetishism of commodities the IWW imagined and proposed a radically new community based on solidarity, mutual aid, and the ideal of One Big Union. Although they saw the "new society" taking shape primarily in on-the-job agitation, in the organization of industrial unions, and in strikes, it was also prefigured in the migratory workers' own highly mobile and always libertarian community, in which capitalist competition was replaced by proletarian creativity and cooperation. Like the older romanticism, the IWW workingclass version included a strong "utopian" element. There was nothing "reactionary" in this, however—as some myopic "Marxists" feared—for the aim was not to return to the past, but rather to nurture certain still-living elements of the precapitalist past that had managed to survive amidst the ruins of the capitalist present.

Untrammeled nonconformism and innovative experiments in living characterized the IWW/hobohemian community. Wobblies prided themselves on being "rebels" against all forms of capitalist misery, and were far more consistent than most Marxists in following Marx's dictum that "Communists support every revolutionary movement against the existing order of things." According to Richard Brazier, the basic aim of IWW poetry and song was to arouse workers from apathy and complacency, and above all to "exalt the spirit of rebellion" [1968, 97]. Against scissorbillish conformity and respect for bourgeois "norms," hoboes not only tolerated "difference" but even welcomed eccentricity. No one could call the IWW's strikes or free-speech fights "undisciplined," and yet "discipline" as such was rarely emphasized in the union's literature. In this regard (as in so many others), the IWW was practically the opposite of the Communist Party, in which "discipline" was glorified and "individualism" was considered one of the worst counter-revolutionary deviations. In the One Big Union, the flamboyant expression of one's individuality and the collective struggle for proletarian revolution were not considered disharmonious. In their practice of poetry, humor counted for a lot.

Indeed, humor was central to the Wobblies' floating community, as it had been to so many earlier romantics. Every IWW member was expected to be an organizer, but many also enjoyed *dis*-organizing the existing (exploitative) social set-up, and for that purpose, humor was the perfect weapon. By pulling the rug out from under rulingclass pretenses, Wobbly humor reinforced working-class self-reliance, provoked inspiration, and stimulated new forms of action. IWW soapboxers, the finest stand-up comedians of their day, had whole crowds laughing at the appalling silliness of the capitalist system.

The "singing union," in other words, was also very much the "laughing union." The IWW gave the U.S. working class its funniest songs, cartoons, and plays, as well as an inexhaustible geyser of first-rate class-war jokes that are still told today, in infinite variations, in workplaces all over the world. And with the one and only T-Bone Slim, American labor found its all-time greatest humorist:

> Once again speech is free, but you must not mention anything. [1992, 154]

> *Tear gas*: The most effective agent used by employers to persuade their employees that the interests of Capital and Labor are identical. [*ibid.*, 155]

> The shorter workday requires no extended remarks. Just go out later and come in earlier—no labor board or other lumber is required. [*ibid.*, 156]

> I'm telling you that if we trust the boss to look after our interest, our interest will suffer. [*ibid.*, 159]

In the struggle to form the new society in the shell of the old, the Wobbly poet was both creator and destroyer. Overturning the old society's prosaic, degraded, stultified, and repressive language was naturally a priority. To the Wobbly poets, poetry was *agitation*, first and last: Its aim was to *move*—to thrill and excite, to inspire dreams as well as action. The best IWW poetry has nothing in common with the brutal language of commerce and power, or with the stunted, sectarian, sermonizing rhetoric of the traditional left—both of which are as far from real life as a presidential proclamation or TV news. Instead, the best of the Wobbly poets offered their fellow workers a language full of habit-breaking insights, illusion-toppling images, Luciferian laughter, riotous metaphors to stir the mind and quicken the spirit: a language of endlessly creative slang. Joe Hill, jongleur of the jungles, who created or popularized such classic expressions as scissorbill, Mr Block, Starvation Army, Weary Willie, shark (employment agent), and pie in the sky—was the IWW's original master of the art.

The very existence of workers' slang, as the surrealist poet Benjamin Péret was perhaps the first to observe,

> reveals first an unconscious need for poetry which is no longer satisfied by the language of the other classes, and second, an elementary and latent hostility toward those classes. . . . From the slang of the disinherited, new words constantly arise, [words which hasten] the development of a [new] poetic language. [1943, 13]

Romantic inspiration and insurgency were keynotes not only of the union's poetry and song, but also of its artwork, cartoons, theater, and soapboxing. Against the classical values of authority, obedience, normality, order, balance, propriety, and maturity, the Wobbly arts resound with their romantic negations: freedom, revolt, passion, wildness, urgency, defiance, and the genius of youth.

Among the IWW poets who exemplified the union's own workingclass version of romanticism were Richard Brazier, Ralph Chaplin, James Kelly Cole, Laura Payne Emerson, Agnes Thecla Fair, J. Waldo Fawcett, Arturo Giovannitti, Covington Hall, Mary E. Marcy, Vera Moller, Joseph O'Carroll, T-Bone Slim, Jim Seymour, Laura Tanne, and in later years, Carlo Cortez and Utah Phillips. Romantic, too—and frenetically so—were the poets who clustered around Chicago's Dil Pickle Club, most of whom were Wobs or sympathetic ex-Wobs: the cosmopolitan G. G. Florine (also known as "Om," the High Factotum of the "Bearers of Cosmic Light"),[1] the half-mad Eddie Guilbert, the Byronic Lionel Moise (pronounced Mo-eese), who is said to have taught Hemingway how to write,[2] and Bertie (Bertram Lewis) Weber, the Pickle's Poet Laureate. In the face of the bourgeois order's stifling imbecility, these daredevil workingclass wordsmiths invented and played with new forms of insolence and refusal. Following the imperative to "get hip," their rowdy, blue-collar poetic praxis allowed romanticism to run wild again—this time in an urbanized industrial context. "After all," as was pointed out long ago, "the hipster is a romantic concept." Thus spake poet John Hoffman, himself a hipster—indeed, the original "angelheaded hipster" invoked in *Howl*.[3]

The epitome of the romantic Wobbly hipster, of course, was Joe Hill himself. In his prison cell, awaiting execution, he wrote: "I have lived like an artist and I shall die like an artist" [*Letters*, 50]. In another letter he put it differently, but no less romantically: "I have lived like a rebel and I shall die like a rebel" [*ibid*., 83]. Artist, rebel: Were they not the same for the IWW's troubadour of discontent? For Hill, living "like an artist" and "like a rebel" signified going where he wanted, doing as he pleased, calling no man master, living outdoors, pursuing his dreams, reading poetry, writing poetry, writing songs, composing music, drawing, painting, and fighting for the Revolution: "to advance Freedom's Banner a little closer to its goal" [*Letters*, 59].

With Joe Hill as prototype, Wobbly romanticism flourished well into the 1920s and even beyond. Despite all the constraints imposed by a repressive social system—on the working class in general, and on revolutionary workers in particular—Wobbly romantic poets carried on the "bardic responsibility" exemplified generations earlier by Blake and Shelley. In the prophetic bardic tradition, Hill and other IWW poets, songwriters, and artists excoriated the parasitical rulers of the capitalist Babylon, rallied the rebellious proletariat 'round the banner of One Big Union, shared their poetic visions of a new and classless society, and boosted workers' self-awareness as builders of that free society.

Because so many IWW lyrics and images are humorous, parodic, and satirical, few critics have grasped the essential truth that Fellow Worker Hill and other Wobbly poets and artists were communicators of authentic visionary experience, and consequently not only "entertainers" and "educators," but also and above all bearers of great *moral* power.

Artist and rebel, a hip Prometheus with a red card: Joe Hill remains to this day the definitive exemplar of revolutionary workingclass romanticism.

1. Chaplin 1948 calls him J. J. Florine, but documents in the Dil Pickle Archives at The Newberry Library consistently refer to him as G. G.

2. Probably the strongest evidence in this regard is Moise's poem, "The Workin' Stiff," published in the *Industrial Worker* in 1910 [Green 1993, 147]. The twelve-stanza tale about a migratory worker is notable for its use of (mostly) mono-syllabic hobo slang. The opening lines are: "On the road he's a cat, and a bloody fink. And a scissor-bill to boot."

3. Dead at twenty-five, Hoffman was a major (though seldom credited) formative influence on the Beat ferment of the 1950s. My information about him, including the quotation, is from an interview with Philip Lamantia (12 January 1992).

Invitation to a 1920s Dil Pickle Club Halloween Party.
Wobblies figured prominently in Pickle activities.
By Arturo Machia.

3. WHAT JOE HILL TAUGHT CARL SANDBURG

Beyond the symbol's extractions,
we transform our verse into those creatures
we admire, protesting: "Here am I!"
—Robert Stock—

For most people, Carl Sandburg is a veritable model of the old-fashioned, mild-mannered, utterly inoffensive poet. The fury and ridicule his work provoked in the 1910s is practically incomprehensible today. Other poets, most notably Amy Lowell and Ezra Pound, were also drawn into the poetic controversy of the time, but their classical backgrounds shielded them from the worst. It was Sandburg who really drew the enemy fire. Throughout the decade and well into the '20s, the harshest attacks on the new American poetry were focused on the author of *Chicago Poems*.

It is still widely but wrongly believed that the hostility toward the new poetry—and toward Sandburg in particular—had mostly to do with "form." In truth, "free verse" and even "Imagism," shibboleths of the day, were decidedly secondary matters. The philistines' war on Sandburg centered emphatically on *content*: his "brutal" subject matter and his use of "coarse" language (*i.e.*, slang), which the self-appointed guardians of America's Poetic Tradition considered inappropriate and even intolerable.

In that long-drawn-out literary war, Sandburg of course emerged as hands-down winner. Those who had hailed him as a bold innovator in the mid-1910s—Harriet Monroe, Floyd Dell, and a few others—were fully vindicated. The man blamed for destroying American poetry was increasingly recognized as the very one who had in fact renewed it, and even made it popular. The "bad boy" of the 1910s was honored at last as the "founding father" of the new poetry.

In his panoramic history of U. S. poetry published in 1929, Alfred Kreymborg insisted that Sandburg's *Chicago Poems* "had more to do with the new American poetry than the work of any other man since Whitman" [386]. Recalling the "violent sensation" experienced by many readers when some of those poems first appeared in *Poetry* magazine in 1914, Kreymborg went so far as to credit Sandburg with making Chicago—more or less single-handedly—"the literary capital of the nation" for a decade or more [385].

Forty-odd years later, Kenneth Rexroth reaffirmed Sandburg's landmark status: "If the modern movement in poetry [in the U.S.] has a definite beginning it is either the publication of Carl Sandburg's *Chicago Poems* or the first Imagist anthology, *Des Imagistes*" [1971, 32-33].

The very features most despised by anti-Sandburg critics in the 1910s naturally came to be the most celebrated. As Harry Golden once summed it up:

> Sandburg was the first American poet able to use and exploit slang in his diction. He was the first poet to incorporate concrete political and social images into his poems; both radical innovations. [1961, 85]

These impressive and sweeping claims have been repeated so often, and by so many, that they are generally taken for granted. But are they true?

To speak plainly: These "firsts" cannot be attributed to Sandburg unless we agree that the only poets who count are those who are *academically accepted* as poets.

Many poets, however, are not now and never have been academically accepted—Joe Hill is a good example—and the fact is, many of these academically unacceptable poets, like Hill, used slang to good effect, and also incorporated "concrete political and social images" into their poetry, several years before the publication of *Chicago Poems*.

Followed through with critical and imaginative rigor, the questions, "Who is a poet, and who isn't, and who decides?" lead us straight to a critique of the whole society, and point the way to its transformation. Like those common everyday questions that every wage-earner gets around to asking sooner or later—such as "Why do most people have to work but some don't?" and "What are bosses for?" and "Who needs cops?"—merely to *ask* them takes you more than half way to the answer.

Or try these: Are *you* a poet? And if not, *why* not?

This brings us to the consideration of one of the weirdest curiosities in Academia: the ludicrous "holy of holies" known as The Canon. The term is in fact ecclesiastical in origin—signifying the "sacred writings" recognized by the church—but it also has strong military connotations: In French, the same word, *canon*, also means "cannon, gun; barrel (of a gun)." To rephrase the famous saying of Mao Ze-dong, "The Canon is something that power comes out of." The very concept is not only authoritarian, but phallocentric.

Applied to poetry, The Canon means:

This Is the Official List of Those Who Have Been Accepted!
All Others Keep Out!
No Help Wanted! No Vacancies!
Violators Will Be Towed Away at Owner's Expense!

As many critics of The Canon have pointed out, it tends to exclude women, African Americans, ethnic minorities, working people, and revolutionists. In American poetry The Canon consists overwhelmingly of long-deceased, prosperous, well-educated, native-born, white, Christian, politically conservative males. Would it surprise you to learn that a lot of them also happen to be insufferable bores? A second-generation Swede who had been to college and found a nice sinecure at the *Chicago Daily News*, Carl Sandburg was—a bit begrudgingly, perhaps, and not without a struggle—eventually admitted into this highly exclusive old-boys club. His early socialism may have been a handicap, but he made up for it by his fervent support for World Wars I and II, and his adulatory biography of Lincoln.

Joe Hill, however, never had a chance. His only "plus," canonically speaking, is being a dead male. Otherwise, his *resumé* is all wrong: limited formal education, immigrant, wage-slave, atheist, hobo, Wobbly, convicted felon, jailbird. Obviously he is not even close to being "white" enough or "American" enough (or, for that matter, domesticated enough) to qualify. Besides, his songs convey a rather negative view of the owners and managers of industry, the business community, the military and other branches of government: the very people who provide the billions of dollars upon which our institutions of higher learning depend. The many-sided, radical *otherness* that makes Joe Hill so appealing to rebel poets and all manner of dissident dreamers also excludes him from the New World Order's Literary Canon.

Defenders of The Canon would object that Hill's poetry is aesthetically unsatisfying and therefore does not qualify as Literature with the capital L. We may note in passing that these same criticisms were made generations ago—by equally belligerent defenders of very different canons—of such poets as Shakespeare, Blake, Whitman and, not so terribly long ago, of Carl Sandburg himself. The Canon does leave a little room for what are usually designated "minor" literary genres. Even in the pretentious, hyper-jargonistic, profit-oriented, superstar Literature Departments of our time, a place in the curriculum is reserved for certain "folk" and other so-called "subliterary" texts. "Tom O'Bedlam's Song" and other anonymous religious and secular lyrics from the Middle Ages through the Elizabethan era are included in many a textbook.

The bestowers of literary status, however, won't even allow the Wobbly bard into the "minor leagues." Hill's problem here seems to have been bad timing: Had he simply taken the precaution to be born four or five hundred years earlier, his works would not only be required reading in graduate study programs, but would also be available in thoroughly annotated variorum editions in fine hand-tooled leather bindings.

That Joe Hill preceded Sandburg in the effective poetic use of slang, and in the use of a certain kind of radical social imagery, is far from astonishing. Hill was, after all, a migratory worker who wrote songs for workers about class struggle. More is involved here, however, than a question of priority. I would go so far as to suggest that Joe Hill's songs are a significant albeit heretofore unremarked *influence* on Sandburg's *Chicago Poems*.

In making this suggestion, I am not in any way attempting to diminish Sandburg's great achievement, or trying to boost Hill's poetic reputation at Sandburg's expense. On the contrary, it seems to me that it is precisely because he had the courage and imagination to embrace such forbidden revolutionary and workingclass influences that Sandburg discovered his own profoundest originality, strength, and depth as a poet. We have here a stunning example of a phenomenon all too rare: "the intellectual . . . listening to his own people speak their own language." The quoted words are from a discussion by the Guyanese poet Jan Carew of changes in language that occurred during the 1970s/80s revolution in Grenada. Revolutionary periods, Carew points out, promote a sudden receptivity to the "flow" of creative expression *from below*—an opening of the floodgates of long-suppressed social and individual inspiration. And when this happens, says Carew,

> *writers create language:* writers who are listening to the echoes of the speech of the people constantly [and] who are distilling those echoes into a creative form . . . [are in fact] creating a language. [Searle 1984, 242]

These reflections by a contemporary Caribbean poet seem to me to be a perfect description of Carl Sandburg's relationship to the revolutionary IWW in the U.S. of the 1910s. Many poets, writers and intellectuals heard hobo songs, and Joe Hill's songs, and Wobbly soapboxers—but how many really *listened*? Sandburg was the first—yes, and for many years the only one—to transmute those uproarious songs, and the provocative patterns of Wobbly speech, into a distinctive poetic language of his own.

All this seems so obvious to me, and so easily demonstrated, that I confess my amazement that it has not been universally recognized from the beginning. I am convinced, moreover, that Sandburg himself would heartily concur with this interpretation, and that if he did not specifically mention it himself, it is only because he, too, considered it obvious.

The facts speak for themselves. The natural starting-point is Sandburg's early poetry. His 1904-05 volumes—*In Reckless Ecstasy*, *The Plaint of a Rose*, and *Incidentals*—mostly inspired by his "deeply beloved teacher," Lombard College economics professor Philip Green Wright [Jordan-Smith 1960, 182; Sandburg 1952, 141]—were conventional, a half-step from trite, with scarcely a hint of the raw power, beauty, and simplicity of the *Chicago Poems* ten years later. The intervening years were drastic and decisive: Sandburg joined the Socialist Party, hoboed around the country, and met many IWWs. Sometime around 1907 he moved to Chicago where he met many more IWWs and soon began his long and intimate association with the left-wing IWW-oriented socialists at the Charles H. Kerr Company. Between 1908, when Kerr published Sandburg's pamphlet *You and Your Job* in the "Pocket Library of Socialism" series, and 1917, Sandburg was among the most prolific contributors to the *International Socialist Review*. His occasional column titled "Looking 'em Over," as well as long articles, "short takes" and poems (including some of the *Chicago Poems*) appeared regularly in its pages, usually signed with his own name but sometimes with his initials or under such pseudonyms as "Jack Phillips," "Live Wire," or "Militant." Also recognizably his were a few unsigned articles; these mostly appeared in issues that already included one or more of his texts under a byline.

Sandburg's collaboration on the *Review* was most intense during 1915 and '16, two years in which the magazine was practically inseparable from the IWW. To that period belong the fiercest, most uncompromisingly revolutionary articles he ever wrote. In one, for example, he charged that Standard Oil's John D. Rockefeller, Jr. was a "chip off the old block": *i.e.*, a liar, thief, pirate, and murderer. In his *Review* writings the author of *Chicago Poems* (published in book form in 1916) often sounded very much like a Wobbly. Here is a brief sample, on capitalist "justice":

> Courts are run by judges. Nearly all judges sit in close some way to the big money men. When judges decide cases in court they look at things the way the big money men want them to look. Labor gets the dirty end of the stick. . . .
>
> When strikes are on, in many places, the regular government goes out of business, a new government of soldiers, detectives and strikebreakers is set up. They call it "martial law."
>
> What they do to strikers with this martial law government is a dripping, bleeding crime and shame. To call it "civilization" makes any decent man let out one loud, bitter horse-laugh. [Oct 1915, 199-200]

Sandburg made no secret of his fondness for the IWW and Joe Hill. As early as 1907 he wrote admiringly of Big Bill Haywood: "a Whitmanic type—raw, strong, canny, and yet with the flavor of romance that we want in our heroes" [Mitgang 1968, 51]. Even after he broke with the Kerr group and his IWW friends over the war, and began his long career as a fussbudget liberal, he retained his respect—and something more than respect—for the Wobs, and Gene Debs, and others of the "extreme Left." In 1917, when Amy Lowell criticized some of his *Chicago Poems* as IWW propaganda, Sandburg replied that

> the aim was rather the presentation of motives and character than the furtherance of IWW theories. Of course, I honestly prefer the theories of the IWW to those of its opponents, and some of my honest preferences may have crept into the book, as you suggest. . . . [Mitgang 1968, 117-118]

In the *International Socialist Review* for January 1917, Sandburg—writing as "Militant"—included Hill along with the Haymarket anarchists in a list of radical labor frame-up victims [403]. And in the March issue he cited Hill together with Margaret Sanger, Ford and Suhr, and Matt Schmidt as "souls of sacrifice" who have been "held within the walls of American bastilles" because they took risks for the working class. "Without these and their kind," he asked, "how far would the working class get?" [549]

In October of the same year, Sandburg's *Daily News* interview with the indicted Bill Haywood—accused of participation in "10,000 separate and distinct crimes"—was described by Ralph Chaplin as "a fair job of presenting our side of the case to the public" [1948, 230]. Fairness toward the IWW was practically unheard-of in the daily papers once the U.S. had entered the war.

Two years later, in October 1919, Sandburg wrote to Romain Rolland in France: "I am an IWW but I don't carry a red card" [Mitgang 1968, 169].

It is not well-remembered today that Sandburg was not only a writer and reader of poetry, but also a tireless singer of songs: folk songs, work songs, hobo songs, Wobbly songs, Joe Hill's songs. Year after year he sang, accompanying himself on a guitar, all over the country. By 1927 he estimated that he had sung to student audiences at two-thirds of the state universities of the country. At the University of California the audience numbered three thousand.

His *American Songbag* (1927) was one of the first major compilations of such lyrics (with music). Its 500-plus large pages include two of Joe Hill's songs—"The Preacher and the Slave" and "The Tramp"—along with an appreciative biographical paragraph on the IWW's "star song writer."

In the 1960s Sandburg's daughter Helga recalled that she used to sing Hill's songs as a child [1963, 28].

Joe Hill also put in an appearance in Sandburg's book-length poem, *The People, Yes* in 1936:

"Don't mourn for me but organize," said the Utah IWW before a firing squad executed sentence of death on him, his last words running "Let her go!" [42]

Sandburg's admiration for the Wobblies seems to have been at least somewhat reciprocal. During the trial of the 100-plus indicted IWW members in Chicago in 1918, according to Ralph Chaplin, many of the defendants "brought books along to lighten the tedium of prolonged litigation" [1948, 243]. Thoreau's *Civil Disobedience* was one title that appears to have made the rounds. Another was Sandburg's *Chicago Poems* [*ibid.*].

Joe Hill

CAPITALISM COMMITTING SUICIDE

This photomontage cartoon by Sam appeared in the
One Big Union Monthly for July 1919.

4. SUGGESTIONS FOR THE FUTURE:
WOBBLIES & THE "AVANT-GARDE"

This is the age of the new dimension,
dare, seek, seek further, dare more,
here is the alchemist's key
—H. D. (Hilda Doolittle)—

S ocial revolution was "in the air" in the U.S. during the 1910s
and early '20s, but cultural revolution proved far more successful. The IWW was a prime mover in both.

The search for the new—in poetry, art, politics, and life itself
—involved a radically *negative* view of the existing order: a profound break not only with the Protestant work-ethic and other puritanical values, but also with all forms of middle-class propriety.
For many artists and intellectuals, Joe Hill's union was an
important factor in hastening that break. As historian Henry F. May
observed in *The End of American Innocence* (1959):

> Nobody took a harsher view of conventional moralism than the
> Industrial Workers of the World. . . . Their hard migratory
> existence . . . confirmed the Wobblies in their proud and sweeping
> rejections. Not only the political institutions of the possessing
> class, but their ideas as well were to be thrown on the ash heap,
> from patriotism to pussyfooting legalism to religion. [177-178]

Like many artists, Wobblies had no use for the smug, hypocritical conceits of standard U.S. Christianity, liberalism, or even
"progressivism." And like all true poets, they aimed at nothing less
than the creation of an entirely new and non-repressive civilization.
Challenging the dominant social order from top to bottom, the
IWW naturally was interested in, and generally sympathetic to,
creative individuals who in varying degrees shared their
revolutionary outlook.

Oddly enough, aside from the Paterson Strike Pageant of 1913,
the many links between Wobblies and the various literary/artistic
currents of those years do not appear to have attracted the interest
of historians. At the time, however, such links were an important
part of everyday life for workers and intellectuals alike. In an
article titled "Art and Unrest" in Alfred Stieglitz's *Camera Work*
in April 1913, Hutchins Hapgood pointed out that "Post-

Joe Hill

Impressionism is as disturbing in one field as the IWW is in another" [Abrahams 1986, 165]. An erudite anarchist liberal gadabout whose friends included IWW members as well as contemporary artists, Hapgood was well aware—unlike most of today's scholars —that these "fields" were not so far apart, and touched or even merged at many points. Like revolutionary industrial unionism, the IWW's revolutionary workingclass romanticism was not a monolithic, all-encompassing, and dogmatic theory, but rather a constellation of inspirations, impulses, and insights. The fact that so many IWWs were late-blooming romantics did not prevent them from interacting with the whole gamut of neo- and post-romantic cultural rebellion, from Post-Impressionism and the Harlem Renaissance to Dada and the Dil Pickle Club. And the appearance of enthusiastic notices of "Joe Hill, the IWW Poet" in such far-from-proletarian publications as *Survey*, *Mother Earth*, and *The Little Review* would seem to indicate that many rebels from the so-called "upper" classes were ready to listen to what the Wobblies had to say.

In New York, for example, Bill Haywood is known to have "dropped in occasionally" at Stieglitz's celebrated gallery 291 —the most up-to-the-minute avant-garde gallery in the U.S. at the time, and best-remembered today as the principal showplace of the work of Georgia O'Keeffe [*ibid.*, 166]. Haywood also frequented Mabel Dodge's Greenwich Village salon, where he may have met such other attendees as painter/poet Francis Picabia, soon to be notorious as a co-founder of the international Dada movement, Imagist poet Amy Lowell, modern American painters Charles Demuth and Marsden Hartley, feminist novelist Mary Austin, who was also an insightful student and translator of Native American poetry, and A. A. Brill, foremost popularizer of Freudian psycho-analysis in the U.S. [Golin, 1988, 116-117; Green, 1988, 56-60].

Wobblies and the artistic avant-garde also rubbed shoulders in other New York venues: "evenings" at the apartment of William and Margaret Sanger; lectures at the anarchists' Ferrer Modern School; informal lunches at Polly Holladay's café on MacDougal Street; planning sessions at Mary Heaton Vorse's Tenth Street studio; and the editorial meetings of the independent socialist magazine, *The Masses*, and its successor, *The Liberator*. At the *Masses/Liberator* gatherings, visiting IWWs were likely to meet Max Eastman and his brilliant sister Crystal, Floyd Dell, painters

464

John Sloan and Stuart Davis, cartoonist Art Young, and poets as different as John Reed, Claude McKay, Dadaist Elsa von Freytag-Loringhoven, and Arturo Giovannitti.

IWW members, writers, artists, and intellectuals of all kinds also came together in less formal situations—at parties, for instance. George Andreytchine's friendship with silent-film comedian Charlie Chaplin (no relation to Wobbly Ralph Chaplin) started at a party in New York *circa* 1919-20. A Turkish-born, Paris-educated Bulgarian, Andreytchine came to the U.S. in the 1910s at the age of nineteen. A profile of him in the *International Socialist Review* describes him as "a disciple of Tolstoy, Thoreau, and William Lloyd Garrison" [Sept 1916, 170]. He speedily evolved into a Wobbly, and became editor of the IWW's Bulgarian-language paper, *Rabotnjcheska Mysl* (Workers' Thought) in Chicago. One of the 101 Wobblies sentenced to long terms at Leavenworth in the infamous 1918 Chicago trial, he was out on bond, pending appeal, when he met Chaplin at a Greenwich Village party. In his 1964 autobiography, Chaplin described their meeting:

> [Andreytchine] was playing charades, and as I watched him Dudley Field Malone [the host] whispered, "He hasn't a chance of winning his appeal."
>
> George, with a tablecloth wrapped around him, was imitating Sarah Bernhardt. We laughed, but underneath many were thinking, as I was thinking, that he must go back to the penitentiary for eighteen more years.
>
> It was a strange hectic evening and as I was leaving George called after me: "What's the hurry, Charlie? Why going home so early?" I drew him aside. It was difficult to know what to say. "Is there anything I can do?" I whispered. He waved his hand as if to sweep the thought aside, then gripped my hand and said emotionally, "Don't worry about me, Charlie. I'll be all right." [1966, 269]

As it turned out, Andreytchine jumped bond and fled to the young Soviet Union. When Chaplin met him again in Berlin a year or so later, the former Wobbly had become an important functionary in the Bolshevik government [*ibid.*, 301-302]. A few years later he joined Trotsky's Left Opposition and seems to have disappeared in Stalin's purges of the 1930s [Naville 1979, 12].

Andreytchine was not, by the way, the only IWW member to

meet the most popular and creative motion picture star of the day. Chaplin himself noted in his autobiography that he met (at another New York party) Fellow Worker Claude McKay, "the Jamaican poet and longshoreman" [1966, 307]. And in Hollywood some years later, Fellow Worker Joe Murphy met Chaplin, who immediately asked him how the Centralia prisoners were doing, and proceeded to help Murphy raise some five hundred dollars for the defense fund [Nelson 1993, 315-316].[1]

Whether IWW members attended the 1913 Armory Show—America's first large exhibition of Post-Impressionist, Fauvist, and Cubist paintings and sculpture—cannot be verified by hard evidence, but in view of the aforementioned associations it would seem likely that at least some Wobblies stopped by for a look. In any event, many of the Greenwich Village writers, poets and artists who organized and/or promoted the Armory Show—including John Reed, Mabel Dodge, John Sloan, and Walter Lippmann—also worked closely with Bill Haywood, Elizabeth Gurley Flynn, and other Wobblies in organizing the famous Paterson Pageant at Madison Square Garden later that same year, in connection with the big IWW silkworkers' strike in New Jersey. The pageant, performed by the strikers themselves, combined theater, song, soapbox oratory, and picketline protest in an unprecedented way. Its effect on the audience was extraordinary, and even critics were deeply impressed—Hutchins Hapgood, for example:

> In two weeks' time this pageant was organized—and yet more than a thousand strikers came to New York, presented in an orderly, systematic, truthful, and moving way the salient features in the history of the great strike. . . . The art of it was unconscious, and especially lay in the suggestions for the future. People interested in the possibilities of a vital and popular art . . . would learn much from it. In this way it foreshadowed much more than it realized. . . . [1939, 351]

And Randolph Bourne:

> Who that saw the Paterson Strike Pageant in 1913 can ever forget that thrilling evening when an entire labor community dramatized its wrongs in one supreme outburst of group-emotion? Crude and rather terrifying, it stamped into one's mind the idea that a new social art was in the American world, something genuinely and excitingly new. [1977, 519]

Fred Thompson often complained that more has been written about the unsuccessful Paterson strike than about any other aspect of the union's history. Out of respect for my old friend I shall not prolong the discussion of that strike here, except to note that the pageant marked the high point in the association of the IWW and the cultural avant-garde in New York.

In Chicago—which H. L. Mencken and many others considered the nation's major literary center in those years, and which was also the nation's hobo capital and the home of the IWW's international headquarters—Wobblies and the more adventurous young writers and artists mingled to a far greater extent than in New York or anywhere else. It would be no exaggeration to say that nearly every one of the well-known personalities of the "Chicago Renaissance" knew at least a few card-carrying Wobs, and the union itself—a bold, young challenge to the capitalist system—loomed large in the city's cultural and intellectual life. It was while "living on the outskirts of Chicago's hobohemia" that George Milburn came to the romantic realization that 'boes were the modern era's counterpart of the medieval troubadours and jongleurs [1930, 90-91]. With a population overwhelmingly immigrant and working-class, the city where the IWW was founded also turned out to be the city in which the Wobbly counterculture penetrated most deeply and enduringly.[2]

For many workers as well as radical intellectuals, one major attraction in Chicago was the Charles H. Kerr Company and its *International Socialist Review*. Revolutionists from all over the world visited the Kerr Company offices, including James Connolly from Ireland, Sen Katayama from Japan, and Alexandra Kollontai from the Bolshevik underground of Czarist Russia.

Under Mary Marcy's editorship, the *Review* in the 1910s was unlike any other socialist publication in the country: more revolutionary, more workingclass, closer to the IWW, and open to an incredible range of new ideas. The *Review* published not only the finest Marxian Socialist theorists in the U.S.—Austin Lewis, Louis B. Boudin, Hubert Harrison, Louis Fraina, and Marcy herself—but also much of the best IWW theory. Evidently, when the One Big Union's heavyweight thinkers—Bill Haywood, Vincent St John, Covington Hall, Elizabeth Gurley Flynn, J. A. MacDonald, Walter Nef, Caroline Nelson, and others—had something too long for *Solidarity* or the *Industrial Worker*, they sent it to the *International*

Socialist Review.

As a measure of its distance from other socialist periodicals, the *Review* also published writings by anarchists. Along with declarations by anarchist groups in Japan and revolutionary Mexico, the *Review* ran articles by Emile Pouget, William C. Owen, and George Barrett, as well as book reviews by Lillian Udell, including a review of Emma Goldman's book on the modern theater. Further evidence of the magazine's non-sectarianism is visible in its display ads for Lucy Parsons's books and Margaret Anderson's *Little Review.*

On the cultural plane, the *Review* was not as flashy as the New York *Masses*, which no doubt accounts for the fact that several books have been devoted to the latter, but—so far—not one to the *Review*. The *Review* did in fact publish many interesting articles on radical culture—on the ideas of Raymond Duncan (Isadora's brother), sculpture, socialist cartoons, and contemporary literature. It also published many of Jack London's best stories, and poems by Eunice Tietjens, James Oppenheim, and Carl Sandburg, as well as by Joe Hill, Arturo Giovannitti, Ralph Chaplin, Covington Hall and other IWWs. And in at least one of the arts—photography—the *Review* was far ahead of the *Masses* and all other radical publications. Its coverage of strikes, free-speech fights, and workers' demonstrations featured the best photos by the best radical photographers in the country.

Not far from the Charles H. Kerr Company and IWW headquarters were a number of workers' gathering-places noted for their exceptional conviviality. Bill Haywood, Vincent St John, Ralph Chaplin, Lucy Parsons, Jim Larkin, and other Wobblies and Comrades often spent their evenings at the Radical Book Shop at 817½ North Clark Street, a storefront in the North Side Turner Hall building. The bookshop—a great Chicago landmark, as Chaplin called it in his autobiography—was started in 1914 by a former Unitarian minister named Howard Udell and his wife Lillian, who considered themselves "philosophical anarchists" [1948, 170-171]. The chief backer of the project was Charles H. Kerr, who supplied the shop with a large quantity of books and pamphlets on consignment.

The Radical Book Shop was, in Ralph Chaplin's words, "a hangout for radicals of all shades of red and black, as well as for the Near North Side intelligentsia" [*ibid.*]. Its "regulars" included such poets, writers, and artists as Sherwood Anderson, Eunice Tietjens, Carl Sandburg, Margaret Anderson, Stanislaus Szukalski, Mark Turbyfill, Edgar Lee Masters, G. G. Florine, and a very young Kenneth Rexroth. In addition to carrying the complete line of Charles H. Kerr and IWW publications, the Radical Bookshop seems to have been the only place in Chicago to stock the latest publications of the Russian futurists, German dadaists, and French surrealists [Rexroth 1966, 140]. The shop also doubled as a "little theater," the Studio Players, in which many IWWs took part.

Chicago was also the home of that outpost of outlandishness known as the Dil Pickle Club, run by that rascally ex-Wobbly Jack Jones. Often called "the indoor Bughouse Square," the Pickle specialized in controversy—and the hotter the better. Speakers' topics included local and national political scandals, Dadaism, psychoanalysis, women's rights, the erotic element in religion, modern art, birth control, current philosophy, pornographic literature, the new physics, the contemporary novel, homosexuality, the educational system, the Russian Revolution, the Chinese Revolution, and the need for revolution right here in the U.S.A. [3]

Among the hundreds who spoke there were Lucy Parsons, Clarence Darrow, Mary MacLane, Ben Hecht, African-American Wobblies R. T. Sims and Robert Hardoen, "General" Jacob Coxey (of Coxey's Army), "Captain" Streeter (Chicago's most celebrated squatter), German "sexologist" Magnus Hirschfield, Gandhian agitator Taraknath Das, "Council Communist" Paul Mattick, and F. M. Wilkesbarr, also known as "The Sirfessor," an eccentric veteran of London's Hyde Park, who considered himself an Individualist Syndicalist. Many poets read there, including Max Bodenheim, Emanuel Carnevali, Jun Fujita, Helen Hoyt, Alfred Kreymborg, Carl Sandburg, and H. T. Tsiang. And it was a major hangout for Anarchists, Feminists, Single-Taxers, Socialists, Communists, and Wobblies.

In his autobiography, Ralph Chaplin remarked that Big Bill Haywood "detested" Jack Jones and Ben Reitman—the Pickle's two major figures—but many Wobblies were also active Picklers, including Chaplin himself, Edward "Triphammer" Johnson, Mary E. Marcy, Jimmy Rohn, John Loughman, Nina Spies, Slim Brundage, and Jack Sheridan. The club's Music Director was Wobbly composer Rudolph von Liebich. Among the full-time Picklers— those closely associated with the Club over a long period—poets

Bertie Weber and Eddie Guilbert were also Wobblies (Weber's "A.F. of L. Sympathy" had appeared in the *Little Red Song Book*), and possibly G. G. Florine as well, though all three were probably behind in their dues.

The relation of these full-time "Pickle poets" to such Wobbly bards as Ralph Chaplin and Arturo Giovannitti is not unlike that of the so-called "minor" French romantics—Gérard de Nerval, Petrus Borel, Xavier Forneret, Philothée O'Neddy, and others—to Victor Hugo and Théophile Gautier. The Picklers' works tend to be much smaller in quantity but also much more "extreme" or experimental in form and content, just as they themselves, in their public manifestations, were inclined toward exaggerated forms of inspired misbehavior, bad taste, frivolity, and scandal. In their wackier moments, the Picklers not only recalled the romantic escapades of a distant Parisian past, but also anticipated such later subversive developments as guerrilla theater, happenings, graffiti art, billboard revision, and untold other forms of cultural/political mischief and monkey-wrenching.

In contrast to Chicago's havens of literary gentility—the Cliff Dwellers, for example, or the less elitist but equally conventional Schlogl's—the Dil Pickle chose to be unrespectable to the *n*th degree. All through its riotous and much-troubled existence (the story of Jack Jones's difficulties with the police could fill a fat book), the Club remained—until it was forced to shut down in 1933 or '34—the principal Chicago forum for the most outrageous expressions of cultural and political nonconformity.

An intriguing (and Dil-Pickle-related) example of the complex reciprocal correspondences between cultural avant-gardists and Wobblies was highlighted in the September 1916 issue of the *International Socialist Review*, which included a poem by Eunice Tietjens titled "Cormorants." Tietjens was one of the most interesting figures of the Chicago Renaissance—part of *The Little Review* from the start, and of *Poetry* magazine as well. She was also a mountain-climber, active in John Muir's Sierra Club, and one of the first U.S. poets whose basic outlook was decisively shaped by the art and poetry of China and Japan, which she visited in 1914; she was, for example, interested in Zen [Tietjens 1938]. "Cormorants," which portrays the gloomy existence of domesticated (enslaved) aquatic birds, was in fact one of the "impressions" from her voyage to the Far East, and later appeared in her book, *Profiles from China*. In its *Review* appearance, the poem was preceded by a note, almost certainly by Mary Marcy:

> A bunch of "wobblies" read this one night in a place called the Dil
> Pickle, on the North Side of Chicago. They decided that all scabs,
> strikebreakers, detectives, spies and spotters are human
> cormorants, who "grow lousy like their lords." [169]

As it happens, the substance of Tietjens's poem was also a
staple soapbox fable—Archie Green has traced it back as far as
1902, when California Socialist Gaylord Wilshire (for whom
Wilshire Boulevard in Los Angeles is named) published a 12-page
pamphlet version titled *Hop Lee and the Pelican* [Green 1996, 60].
A different version, featuring cormorants, was favored by Fred
Thompson, who says he first heard it from James P. Thompson in
Seattle in the 1920s, and a decade later from John Keracher of the
Proletarian Party during a strike in Cleveland. Three of Fred
Thompson's versions have appeared in print [*ibid.*]

That an avant-garde poet's narration in free verse of a parable
heard in China should correspond so closely to a theme familiar to
revolutionary soapboxers is a coincidence worth thinking about.
For Tietjens as for the Wobblies, of course, the tale was a strong
protest against exploitation, degradation, and servitude.

As the foregoing short survey indicates, the IWW in the 1910s
and '20s was clearly at the crossroads of many vital currents of
thought and action. That the One Big Union brought together all
manner of groups and tendencies in the revolutionary workers'
movement is remarkable enough, but it did not stop there—Wobblies also affected, and were affected by, some of the most exciting
and far-reaching trends in poetry, art, music and theater.

Such creative exchanges and mutual aid are well-documented
in the Wobbly press. IWW newspapers and magazines of course
continued to publish much traditional rhymed verse; Chaplin,
Dublin Dan, Dick Brazier, and Vera Moller were among the
union's favorite poets. But Wobbly publications also remained
refreshingly receptive to the new and daring and different. Their
hobo and workingclass readership admired the wildly imaginative
texts of Jim Seymour, Laura Tanne, and—wildest of all—T-Bone
Slim, who was, significantly, the most popular Wobbly writer after
Joe Hill. The innovative IWW cartoonist Sam—last name
unknown—was one of the first U.S. artists to make use of
photomontage, a technique much favored by the Dadaists of

Germany. Two other Wobbly cartoonists, Ern Hanson and C. E. Setzer (a.k.a. X13), were considered eccentric in their own time, but would today qualify as front-ranking "outsider artists."

Some IWW members were cultural conservatives, and decried their fellow workers' tolerance for what pseudo-Marxist ideologists probably considered "bohemian deviationism." One unusually narrow-minded member was the little-known Henry George Weiss. A dogmatic defender (and practitioner) of doggerel for doggerel's sake, Weiss bitterly opposed what he termed "experimental" poetry and new verse forms. Not too surprisingly he eventually defected to the Communist Party and wrote for the *New Masses* and *Daily Worker*. To pay his bills, however, this born-again "Leninist" contributed to such bourgeois pulps as *Weird Tales* and *Amazing Stories* [Wixson 1994, 257]. Ironically, Weiss's science-fantasy tales—to which he probably attributed no importance whatsoever—are almost certainly his best work.

How much the IWW influenced the cultural avant-garde, or vice versa, in New York or Chicago or anywhere else, is of course impossible to measure. The fact that the union and Joe Hill himself live on in the work of such poets as Ralph Chaplin, Covington Hall, Carl Sandburg, Kenneth Patchen, Kenneth Rexroth, Woody Guthrie, Gary Snyder, Phil Ochs, Meridel LeSueur, Carlos Cortez, Utah Phillips, and Joseph Jablonski suggests that the IWW's impact has been greatest, as one might expect, in the very art that the Wobblies themselves esteemed most highly.

The union's impact on other poets and writers, and on the other arts, and on particular artists, is harder to gauge, but that doesn't mean that the impact wasn't real. Although specifically IWW themes in their works are rare, we know that poets and writers as varied as Lola Ridge, James Oppenheim, John Reed, Hi Simons, Jack Conroy, and Edna St Vincent Millay at one time or another came under the Wobbly spell, as did such painters as John Sloan and others of the "Ashcan School" and its offshoots. In most cases, the IWW influence was probably sidelong and diffuse—a question of sensibility, of "latent" rather than "manifest" content: discernible, if at all, not in clearly thought-out ideas and even less in programmatic politics, but rather in half-conscious, recalcitrant moods, tempers, or impulses, and hard to relate to a given "work."

Consider, for example, Marcel Duchamp. In a rarely cited interview in the *New York Tribune* for 24 October 1915—that is, right in the midst of the world war—this artist who is generally considered apolitical affirmed his admiration for "the attitude of combating invasion with folded arms." It is possible that Duchamp had heard of "the power of folded arms" from anarcho-syndicalists in France, but in New York in 1915 that was pure, unvarnished Wobbly talk. Thus the enigmatic Duchamp, who is increasingly regarded as the most influential artist of the twentieth century, at least on one occasion spoke like a true Wobbly. Was the painter of the "Nude Descending a Staircase" and "The Bride Stripped Bare by Her Bachelors, Even" reading *Solidarity* or the *International Socialist Review*?

Painter/photographer Man Ray was, with Duchamp, one of the principals of New York Dada in the years 1917-1921, and shortly afterward became the first American to join the Surrealist Group in Paris. Did his rapidly evolving art and ideas during the 1910s owe something to the rapidly evolving IWW in the same period? Man Ray's commentators (and his own autobiography) are silent on the matter, but it is known that the artist regarded himself as an "out-and-out anarchist" at the time. He was active in the New York Ferrer Center, which included several Wobblies, and was well-acquainted with at least one of them: Bill Shatoff. His other artist/writer friends included many who had close ties to the union —among them John Sloan, Adolf Wolff, and Max Eastman. He collaborated on the journal, *The Modern School*, and contributed cartoon covers to Emma Goldman's anarchist *Mother Earth*. The one-shot Dada magazine *TNT*, which he co-edited with Adolf Wolff and Adon Lacroix in 1919, was—as he later told Arturo Schwarz—explicitly "a tirade . . . against the exploiters of workers" [Schwarz 1977, 49].

As he remarked in his *Self-Portrait* (1963), Man Ray in his youth was an admirer of Thoreau, and he hoped "some day to liberate [himself] from the restraints of civilization" [31]. He was an enthusiastic and active player in several revolutions in the arts, and to the end remained faithful to his anarchist ideals. It is hard to believe that he was not in some way "under the influence" of the Industrial Workers of the World.

Jackson Pollock is another interesting example. As a child in the desert around Phoenix, Arizona, he noticed the letters "IWW" scrawled on walls and fences all along the railroad tracks, and asked his father what they signified [Naifeh and Smith 1989, 56].

Pollock's father Roy was, if not a dues-paying Wob, at the very least a vigorous supporter, and it is known that he harangued his five sons about the union, and about the U.S. government's shameful attempts to suppress it at the behest of the capitalists. (Of the five boys, two became union organizers, one joined the Communist Party, and the other two became painters.) How did Jackson Pollock's childhood impressions of the Wobblies affect his outlook, his life, his art? Did the union that put "direct action" into the language contribute something to the creative ferment that came to be called "action painting"?

Also worth looking into in this regard is the life of 1950s jazz musician Art Pepper, who was not only the son of a militant Wobbly, but even grew up in Joe Hill's old stomping-ground, San Pedro—still a stronghold for the "Grand Industrial Band" during young Pepper's childhood. Pepper senior, like Hill, was an unabashed "wharf-rat," and according to family legend he once shipped a boatload of guns and ammo to Pancho Villa during the Mexican Revolution [Pepper 1979, 24]. What did the old man's two-fisted tales of class war mean to a rebellious kid who was crazy about Black music? Did the Wobbly emphasis on individual and group creativity, spontaneity, and solidarity—as manifested, for example, in the union's celebrated "flying squadrons"—help propel young Pepper toward active involvement, during the Cold War, in the collective improvisation of bebop and post-bebop jazz? Isn't there a vital, passional link between the IWW's dream of organizing a divided working class so that it could express itself through One Big Union, and the rebellious artist's quest to transform the individual "divided self" by expressing the total human personality?

Bursting with ifs and maybes, such troubling questions tend to be answered with shrugs and "Who knows?" But the analogies persist and will not go away. And everyone knows that the many attempts to abolish capitalism without liberating the mind and spirit have led only to disaster—*i.e.*, to more and more barbarous forms of capitalism. In their cultural politics and their political culture Wobblies shared, to an impressive degree, the larger, deeper, dialectical view of their young contemporaries in the surrealist movement. As André Breton put it in 1935: "'Transform the world,' said Marx; 'change life,' said Rimbaud. These two watchwords are for us but one" [Breton 1962, 285].

IWW interaction with various "avant-gardists" in the arts was in any case far more extensive and enduring than historians have admitted, and seems to have affected not only the direct participants but also their children. In the ongoing struggle to build a new revolutionary workers' movement worthy of the name, a good study of the sons and daughters of old Wobblies might prove to be a real boon. Pending further research, all we can say is that the IWW was not only a much larger part of the mix than has generally been acknowledged, but was often at the very center of the action.

Henry May was right: The One Big Union, and particularly the author of "Mr Block" and "Everybody's Joining It," was a powerful presence in the cultural and intellectual life of those years:

> The harsh, tough, skeptical songs of Joe Hill convey most clearly the nature of the IWW's appeal to well-brought-up intellectuals of radical sympathies. Here, if anywhere, was a clear breach with timidity, moralism, and the whole manner and content of the standard American culture. [1959, 178]

---

1. Although fictionalized, Nelson's book is drawn from his extensive interviews with Murphy.

2. On Chicago as the center of the IWW counterculture, see my introductions to Brundage 1987 and Beck 2000.

3. I have compiled this short list of Dil Pickle lecture topics from handbills in the Jack Jones/Dil Pickle Club papers at The Newberry Library, and from the lecture notices in the *Chicago Daily News.*

"Silent Agitator"

SONGS

Of The Workers

The Latest

I. W. W. SONG BOOK

General Defense Edition

CONTAINS sixty-four pages of satirical, humorous and inspiring
songs of labor. Parodies on the well
known popular airs. Wherever the
English language is spoken, there
will be found countless numbers of
workers singing these real rebel songs

PRICES

Single Copies Ten Cents
$5.00 a Hundred

Address

I. W. W. Publishing Bureau

1001 W. Madison St., Chicago, Ill.

Advertisement for IWW Song Book

476

5. THE POWER OF SONG:
THE LITTLE RED SONG BOOK,
ITS FRIENDS & ENEMIES

It is but a short step from the empirical discovery
of psychic release by singing, to the notion that
song itself is of magical curative power.
—Mary Hunter Austin—

In "normal" times, most writers, artists, and other intellectuals tend to ignore the working class and its struggles—except, perhaps, to pity or belittle them. The fact that during the 1910s and early '20s a large part of the "avant-garde" intelligentsia—painters, poets, playwrights, musicians—openly admired the IWW and considered themselves its supporters and allies, tells us something of the extraordinary temper of those revolutionary times, just as it also says something about the special character of the IWW. For the first time in U.S. history, a sizeable number of "avant-gardists" in the arts identified themselves with a truly revolutionary workingclass movement—and not to "lead" it, much less profit from it (as was so often the case during the "Popular Front" '30s), but rather to *learn from it*, and even, in their modest way, to help it along.

Those who sincerely wanted to know more about the rising of the working class, and its aspirations, naturally explored the literature of the IWW and attended the union's open-air meetings. In their quest to discover what the revolutionary working class wanted, and what the IWW was all about, many found the IWW's songs the best of all possible introductions.

Wobbly songs are unashamedly and indeed proudly meant to be *songs for workers*. They are not, however, the silly and sentimental sort of songs that intellectuals commonly and condescendingly expect working people to like. The purpose of Wobbly songs is not to soothe or divert, or to provoke nostalgic tears, but rather—as the *Song Book*'s front cover states boldly: *To Fan the Flames of Discontent.* An ad in a 1912 IWW pamphlet described them further:

> Songs that strip capitalism bare; show the shams of civilization; mock at the masters' morals; scorn the smug respectability of the satisfied class; and drown in one glad burst of passion the profit patriotism of the Plunderbund. [*On the Firing Line*, 47].

Not too surprisingly, people who did not want the flames of discontent fanned tended not to like these songs. If rebel intellectuals such as John Reed, Floyd Dell, and Mary Heaton Vorse learned to love them, the great majority of their social class feared and hated the same songs. Even today, you won't find groups of billionaires, bosses, cops, politicians, prison guards, stockbrokers or strikebreakers singing the songs of Joe Hill and his colleagues.

Indeed, the *Little Red Song Book* has had a lot of enemies. It was often introduced as State's Evidence in trials of IWW members, to show juries how un-Christian, un-American, and just plain awful the IWW really was. By reading aloud isolated passages and concealing the fact that the songs are mostly comic parodies, prosecuting attorneys used the U.S. labor movement's all-time best-seller to send many good union organizers to jail.

A thick and stupid book titled *Americanism Versus Bolshevism*, by Ole Hanson, "Former Mayor of Seattle," appeared in 1920 and was well-promoted by businessmen's organizations and the American Legion. It contains some "extracts" of IWW songs, including two stanzas and the chorus of "The Preacher and the Slave," with these introductory words by the former mayor:

> The IWW publish and sing songs filled with sacrilege and hatred, songs reeking of the mire, glorifying crime, encouraging revolt, debauching the hearer, and ridiculing God and good, and all that is sweet and dear to true men and women everywhere. [235]

Decades later, the *Song Book* was still the object of bitter hatred in some circles. Rev. David Noebel's *Rhythm, Riots and Revolution*, published by a certain "Christian Crusade" in Tulsa, Oklahoma, in 1966, is a paranoid exposé purporting to show how the pop music industry was taken over by the international Communist conspiracy, with the help of such "notorious Communist agents" as (I'm not kidding—it's in the book!) Bob Dylan and the Beatles. Two pages of this nutty farrago are devoted to the "vicious" songs of Joe Hill, who is identified as a "forerunner" of the sinister subversive plot to capture the "young people of America" [Noebel, 1966, 162-164].[1]

The fact that prosecuting attorneys, former mayors, and right-wing religious crackpots hate IWW songs will surprise no one. But even scholars, from whom one might expect a more balanced view, or at least a glimmer of historic perspective, sometimes seem to be unable to control their condescension—or loathing—when it comes to Wobbly songs. In a once-influential book on "protest" songs, critic John Greenway superciliously decreed that only two of Joe Hill's songs "have any permanent value," and deemed almost all the rest "contemptible" [1953, 197]. Of the other songs in the *Little Red Song Book*, this then-respected authority found all but three or four to be nothing but "bombast," "poor taste," "hack work" and "doggerel" [*ibid.*]. Professor Wallace Stegner squeezed his own "critique" of Hill's songs into one syllable: "crude."

Even people who genuinely regard themselves as lovers of poetry have been known to dismiss the IWW's songs as simplistic, coarse, inelegant, or barbaric. In their classificatory zeal to assign Wobbly songs a position several notches lower than "real" poetry, whatever that is, they lose sight of what poetry is all about.

Such objections to IWW songs reflect a conspicuous class bias, a patronizing incomprehension of the audience for whom these songs were intended, and an overweening insensitivity to the power of song. Haters of Wobbly lyrics forget too easily that, from Shakespeare to Maxine Hong Kingston, simplicity, "ordinary" language, and slang—the "language of the streets"—have been regarded as the life-blood of poetry and good writing. During the heyday of the IWW, for example, Chicago Renaissance poets and other rebel modernists had no gripe with the "crude" lingo of workingstiffs; what repelled them was pretentious middle-class verbosity, unwieldy Latinisms, artificially "flowery" phrases, and soporific clichés: everything that Jacques Vaché would have called "pohetic." Ironically, the very songs poor Greenway mistook for "doggerel" actually offered a foretaste of the "rugged" rhythms and "vulgar speech" that Harriet Monroe signaled as decisively "revivifying" factors in the U.S. poetry of those years [1967, 36-37].

Those who dismiss or disparage IWW songs reveal their ignorance of the origin and function of these songs. For the Wobblies, as for the vastly larger folk tradition, aesthetics was not the major motive underlying creative activity. What was important in songs, in their view, was information, participation, and the reinforcement of group solidarity. Many IWW songs were essentially summaries of the IWW Preamble, or IWW pamphlets, or articles from the *Industrial Worker*. Others were proverbs, anecdotes, jokes, and fables set to music. Rhyme and rhythm made memorization easier.

Unlike what is called "popular" song today, the Wobbly song tradition made no distinction between singer and audience. Singing was something one did together with other Fellow Workers. Some songs were reserved primarily for what could be termed "ritual" uses. Even today, "Solidarity Forever" is most often sung as strike rallies, meetings, conventions, or funerals are brought to an end. "Hold the Fort," a British song adopted by the IWW, was generally associated with strike-support and defense campaigns, just as "The Red Flag" and "The International" were favorites on May Day parades. "Hallelujah, I'm a Bum," "Mr Block," "The Tramp," and T-Bone Slim's songs were especially popular around camp-fires in hobo jungles. During mass arrests, tense strike situations, and free-speech fights, singing the union's songs boosted the singers' courage and strengthened their resolve.

In "the singing union," what counted above all was "spreading the word" about the IWW. Far from being the consequence of "hack work" or any sort of literary affectation—as was true of so many commercially contrived pseudo-folksongs, not to mention rock lyrics, in later years—the simplicity of the IWW's songs was largely a matter of practical necessity. As Utah Phillips has explained, one of the main functions of Wobbly songs was

> to help people define their problems and to suggest what the solutions might be. A lot of working folks came from other countries and couldn't speak very much English and didn't have a chance to go to school here. If the songs were going to communicate, they had to be simple. [Bird *et al.*, 25]

That these songs *did* communicate was demonstrated time and again during IWW strikes and free-speech fights, as documented in numerous on-the-spot reports by participants and observers. In her autobiography, *Footnote to Folly*, Mary Heaton Vorse left us a vivid eye- and earwitness account of the Lawrence Strike of 1912. What impressed her most of all was the fact that the strikers

> were confident, gay, released, and they sang. They were always marching and singing. The gray tired crowds ebbing and flowing perpetually into the mills had waked and opened their mouths to sing, the different nationalities all speaking one language when they sang together. . . . [1935, 6]

Vorse goes on to note that short speeches by Haywood, Elizabeth Gurley Flynn, and others were followed by more singing:

> It was as though a spur of flame had gone through this audience, something stirring and powerful, a feeling which has made the liberation of people possible; something beautiful and strong had swept through the people and welded them together, singing. . . .

The workers sang everywhere: at the picketline, at the soup kitchens, at the relief stations, at the strike meetings. Always there was singing. [*ibid.*, 9, 12]

Over a decade later, in 1923, police broke up a big IWW dock-workers' strike in San Pedro, California—herding the strikers onto trains and sending them to various southern California jails. Louis Adamic, then a young journalist, was at the scene:

> While the strike was thus being broken, the Wobblies—rough, strong men; native-born and foreigners—sang their songs. They sang in the prison stockade in San Pedro, on the way to the trains, in the trains, and finally in jail.
>
> "God!" another young newspaper man remarked to me. "One feels like singing with them. They got guts!" [Adamic 1932, 235]

Perhaps the finest description of the transformative quality—or the *spiritual force*—of Wobbly songs is that of B. Traven in his novel, *The Cotton-Pickers* (*Der Wobbly* in the original German):

> They had never heard the song before but with the instinct of the burdened they felt that this was *their* song. . . . They didn't know what the IWW was, what a labor organization meant, what class distinctions were. But the singing they heard went straight to their hearts. The words were as the breath of life to them, and the song welded them together as into a block of steel. A first dim awareness of the immense power and strength of the working people united in a common purpose was awakened in them. [1969, 38]

The effect of these songs can be gauged, too, by the *Song Book*'s phenomenal sales year after year, edition after edition, printing after printing. In the mid-1910s, the usual print-run was 50,000 copies; by 1917 it was up to 100,000. And most editions went through several printings.

Singing these songs, as Vorse and Traven indicate, was an *education*: morally, intellectually, and politically. Singing these songs provoked thought, stimulated the imagination, stirred the spirit of revolt. Singing these songs was often the first big step in the learning process by which deceived and disheartened wage-slaves, who had long cowered in ignorance, fear, and silence, became clear-thinking, brave and outspoken fighters for workingclass freedom.

In short, singing these songs was instrumental in making Wobblies. Fania Steelink, who immigrated to the U.S. from Russia in 1907 and joined the IWW a few years later, told an interviewer in the 1970s that what initially attracted her to the union was, precisely, its "beautiful songs" [Bird *et al.*, 1985, 170]. She went on to emphasize that "It wasn't only Joe Hill. Plain ordinary people produced those songs. That should be a hope, because they came from the heart of the people." As with so many other working men and women, Fania Steelink found that IWW songs awakened a desire for more poetry, more knowledge. "Even though I was very discouraged by conditions here [in the U.S.]," she explained, "I began to read Emerson and Walt Whitman" after hearing those songs.

---

1. Noebel's other heavily-footnoted fulminations include a 26-page pamphlet, *Communism, Hypnotism and the Beatles*, and the 352-page *Rhythm, Riots and Revolution: An Analysis of the Communist Use of Music* (1966).

Douglas Robson: Cover art for "The Advancing Proletaire"
(International Songs Publishers, Chicago, 1917-18)

6. "THE WHOLE WORLD IS LISTENING": MARY GALLAGHER & INTERNATIONAL SONG PUBLISHERS

Something was about to happen. Something big.
Something clean and new and strong, and it had
something to do with the music.
—**Frank London Brown**—

That Joe Hill and other Wobblies wrote labor's best songs and made startlingly effective use of them is common knowledge. Few people, however, including most historians of the union, seem to be aware that IWWs also studied the history of song, researched and translated labor songs from other lands, and even approached the matter theoretically. The "Song Question" was early on a topic of debate in the IWW press, and numerous letters and articles on the subject continued to appear in later years as well. Joe Hill himself touched on it in his letters—quoted elsewhere in these pages—as did other Wobbly songwriters, including Covington Hall, Ralph Chaplin, and Dick Brazier.

Of the many IWW-connected song-research projects, the most ambitious and influential was Mary Gallagher's International Song Publishers, headquartered at the Clarion Book Shop at 204 North Clark Street in Chicago, a few blocks from Bughouse Square.

Best known for her tireless efforts for the IWW's General Defense Committee, Gallagher had been a Socialist since 1908, when she heard Eugene Debs speak. On the same occasion she also heard "The Marseillaise," her first experience of radical labor song. "From then on," she told Archie Green in a 1959 interview, "everything fell into place in my life" [7].

In 1917, when she was running a boarding house for Wobblies in Chicago, a young Scotsman named Douglas Robson, who was preparing a theatrical extravaganza for the IWW, came to board there. A former coal-miner, Robson was a poet, singer, songwriter, vaudeville actor, artist, a student of Shakespeare, and an authority on Robert Burns. With their shared passion for song, music, and workers' revolution, the two Wobblies immediately became fast friends, and in no time Gallagher introduced Robson to two other friends of hers: the English-born musician-composer Rudolf von Liebich (the pianist at Joe Hill's Chicago funeral), who had a doctorate in music from the University of London, and Franz Beidel, a well-known German bandleader and music teacher.

With the spontaneity and enthusiasm characteristic of Wobblies, this remarkable quartet set about the herculean task of collecting workers' songs and folksongs from all over the world. As songs came in, rough translations were made by fellow workers who were native speakers, and then put into better English by Gallagher and/or Robson. Von Liebich and Beidel tracked down the original music. When the songs were perfected, Robson sang them at IWW as well as AFL union meetings.

This was no academic or antiquarian project; Gallagher and her friends sought to assemble a living body of song "in the service of the Revolution," including new and original material. Indeed, Gallagher and Robson contributed songs of their own, and Von Liebich original compositions.

"The songs became so popular," Gallagher wrote Archie Green in 1961, "that I ventured to publish them" [10 Apr]. Thus the informal foursome evolved into the International Music Publishers. Their first publication, "Funeral Song of a Russian Revolutionist" (in English and German), sold four thousand copies. The second, which included two songs—"An Ancient Jewish Lullaby" and the "Child Laborers' Spring Song" (with lyrics by Mary Gallagher) —sold two thousand, as did the third, "The Advancing Proletaire," an instant Wobbly favorite (to be played and sung "not too fast but with fire and vigor"), featuring lyrics by Robson and music by Von Liebich.

On the backs of the International Song Publishers' sheet music Gallagher and her fellow workers set forth their views on the role of song in social change. Taking a historical approach, they noted that

> the great and memorable music of the world [was created by] workers singing at their tasks as they tilled the soil or gathered around the hearth when their labor was done. In the days when each worker owned his shop, when the tailor or cobbler produced an article of clothing for his neighbor, he could sing as he watched his work completed under his eyes. [Later, however, under capitalism,] when the worker lost the ownership of his tools, he lost his joy spirit also. In the modern factory of today, there is no joy in feeding small bits of material into a machine. . . .[*Ancient Jewish Lullaby*, 4]

The dialectic of history, however, is full of surprises:

> Under the monotonous hum of the motor-driven machinery is growing an heroic chorus . . . [and a] new song arises: "When we take our hands from these machines and their wheels stop, then you know our power; when we fold our mighty arms, then you feel our strength." This is the new hymn of the workers that is stirring the world and the whole world is listening to this song and the whole world is startled by its sound.
>
> The International Song Publishers are sending out to the world this new music of the awakened workers. [*ibid.*]

Gallagher and her associates also related their research, as well as their own creativity, to the broad field of contemporary art:

> Each epoch in the world's history gives forth its own art expression. We are told that the day of the Folk Song is past, that in a complex civilization such as we have in America, no true folk song can be produced; that America never has had true folk song..... [However,] as our civilization becomes more complex our art must express that complexity. The proletariat, working in the modern industries, constitutes the majority of the people. Shall not the [workers'] activities . . . influence the art of their time as they become more and more conscious of their social status?
>
> [The new song] must be the song of Internationalism. All over the world there is the cry for greater democracy. . . . Only the artists who have their fingers on the heartbeats of that struggling mass will write the songs, paint the pictures, and play the music that will endure. It is the mission of the International Song Publishers to fulfill that trust. Now is the day of "The Advancing Proletaire"! [*Advancing Proletaire*, 4]

The International Song Publishers' miniature manifestoes are further proof that Wobblies, who have been portrayed so frequently as well-meaning but naive and semi-literate bumpkins, were in truth exceptionally knowledgeable and articulate, and that—in bright contrast to so many would-be radicals of their time and ours—they also *knew what they were doing*.

The new revolutionary song heralded by Mary Gallagher and her co-workers calls to mind the new song the freed slaves in the American South started creating even before the Civil War was over, as described by W. E. B. Du Bois in a resplendent passage of his classic work, *Black Reconstruction*. Much of what Du Bois wrote in this regard also applies to the IWW's songs, for they too were songs of "wild appeal," songs in which "old and new melodies in word and in thought" are woven together, and above all songs that "throbbed and thundered on the world's ears with a message" too rarely heard and heeded: the message of equality and freedom [Du Bois 1970, 124].

A comparative study of African American and IWW songs would be of the greatest interest. Many IWW lyrics, such as Hill's "Workers of the World, Awaken!," "We Have Fed You All for a Thousand Years" by "An Unknown Proletarian," and John Brill's "Dump the Bosses off Your Back," resonate with themes explored by Sterling Stuckey in his resplendent discussion of slave songs and spirituals in *Going Through the Storm* (1994). Other Wobbly songs, especially the more satirical ones—with their workingclass humor, candor, irreverence, and imagination—have strong affinities with the blues. Hill's "Preacher and the Slave," for example, has much the same spirit as Joe McCoy's "Preacher Blues":

Now some folks say a preacher won't steal,
But he'll do more stealing than I get regular meals.

Similarly, T-Bone Slim's "The Popular Wobbly" shares the ironic mood and wit of Lonnie Johnson's "Hard Times Ain't Gone Nowhere":

Peoples raving 'bout hard times, tell me what it's all about.
Hard times don't worry me, I was broke when they started out.

Peoples raving 'bout hard times, I don't know why they should.
If some people was like me, they didn't have no money when times
*   was good.*

Indeed, as a reading of Paul Garon's indispensable *Blues and the Poetic Spirit* (1996) makes clear, blues as a major form of Black workingclass poetry—poetry which is "emphatically materialist" and "uncompromisingly atheistic" [148]—parallels IWW songs in many and profound ways. As Garon himself puts it:

There is, in the blues, a strong and unmistakable desire for freedom from toil. Instead of the conservative motto "A fair day's wage for a fair day's work," the blues singers inscribe on their banner the revolutionary watchword: "Abolition of the wage system". . . . For alienated labor is recognized [by blues-singers] as one of the most destructive forces in society today. . . . And it is in [the blues-

singer's] poetic activity that alienated labor finds its most definitive negation and supersession. [138-139]

Were Mary Gallagher and her associates aware that the period
in which IWW song-creation reached its apogee was also the
heyday of Ma Rainey, Blind Lemon Jefferson, Charlie Patton and
many other blues people long since regarded as classics? Many
Wobs were of course familiar with the blues, and the thousands of
Black members very likely included several practitioners of the art.
However, the intermingling of African American and IWW song
and music traditions did not go very far. The project undertaken by
Gallagher *et al.*, sympathetic to the whole range of workingclass
songs, might have provided an ideal meeting-place, had it endured.
Alas, conditions proved inhospitable to such dreams. It was the
declared intention of Mary Gallagher and her fellow worker poets
and musicians to bring out a new song every month, at ten cents
each ("our songs are written for love and not for profit"), but the
whole project collapsed shortly after the U.S. entered the World
War. By 1919, International Song Publishers was history—yet
another casualty of the anti-IWW terror carried out by the U.S.
government under the direction of the capitalist class.

Ralph Chaplin: "Somebody Spoiled the Feast"
(*Solidarity*, 18 August 1917)

7. THE ART OF SOAPBOXING, OR STORYTELLING IN THE SERVICE OF THE REVOLUTION

The wind breathes, the instinct howls,
the idea expresses itself.
—Villiers de l'Isle-Adam—

In the Wobbly emphasis on the practice of poetry and the pursuit of knowledge, songs remained paramount. But they also had many other ways to light up workingclass imaginations. At IWW strike rallies, "socials," street-meetings, picnics, and other gatherings, singing songs, listening to poetry, and watching plays were always supplemented by soapboxing and storytelling. Practitioners of the last-named arts usually managed to combine serious expositions of economic theory and the recital of fables, anecdotes, tall tales, riddles, and jokes. Dialogues—two-person skits that communicated a lot of information in a minute or two—were also popular. Sam Lesher's "Shut Up," which appeared in the April 1924 issue of the *Industrial Pioneer*, is a Wob classic:

What did you tell that man just now?
I told him to hurry.
What right have you to tell him to hurry?
I pay him to hurry.
How much do you pay him?
Four dollars a day.
Where do you get the money?
I sell products.
Who makes the products?
He does.
How many products does he make in a day?
Ten dollars worth.
Then instead of you paying him, he pays you $6 a day
    to stand around and tell him to hurry.
Well, but I own the machines.
How did you get the machines?
I sold products and bought them.
Who made the products?
Shut up, he might hear you.

In those pre-radio and pre-television years, IWW events were a kind of class-war variant of what Vachel Lindsay—a poet many Wobblies admired—called the "Higher Vaudeville." In the One Big Union, education and entertainment were practically synonymous.

Unlike books, newspapers, and leaflets, soapboxers gave people a chance to see and hear real live agitators, and even to ask them questions. Soapboxing was always a direct, intimate, face-to-face encounter—the opposite of the depersonalized and over-rehearsed phoniness of TV "talk shows."

What the Wobbly soapboxers said, and the stories their story-tellers told, are much less well documented than the songs they sang, but enough has survived to give us a good general picture. By all accounts, the union's soapboxers were dynamic, creative, and highly skilled; even competitors from other organizations conceded that they were the best in the field. They had to be, for in street-meetings, their first task was to draw a crowd—and then to hold it for a half-hour or more before the cops came to bust things up.

Wobbly soapboxers were regarded as "characters." Many of them would today be considered "performance artists." They culti-vated their individual eccentricities as assiduously as any stage or silent-film comedian. "Every speaker," as Richard Brazier put it in his 1960 interview with Archie Green, "had his own way of acting on the soapbox" [36]. Brazier went on to reminisce about George Swazey, a soapboxer Joe Hill called "the human phonograph" in one of his letters. According to Brazier, Swazey

> had one of the most peculiar approaches to getting a crowd's attention I ever saw. George had a pet duck that he used to take to the soapbox under his arm. And when George wanted to emphasize a point that he was making, like "It's time you ought to organize, you fellow workers here, standing there just gaping, get down there and join the union!"—he'd squeeze the duck, you know, and the duck would go "quack, quack, quack." George would say, "Even the duck knows enough to say yes to that" . . . And every time he wanted to emphasize a particular point, he'd squeeze the duck, and the duck would "quack, quack, quack". . . [By then,] the crowd was enormous. [*ibid.*]

For a time in the 1910s Swazey lived in England, trying to build up the IWW's British Section. Bonar Thompson, a longtime speak-er at London's Hyde Park, recalled him as "a good speaker, with a racy style and a sprightly personality; and he beat me at taking collections and selling literature. . ." [1934, 149]. Thompson goes on to record an interesting example of what was always the soap-boxers' chief occupational hazard—police harassment:

Swazey was arrested once, at Leeds, for inciting the unemployed to steal. "There are dummies in a shop-window in Briggate wearing good clothes—warm overcoats, thick boots. Yet you stand shivering in rags!" he told a meeting of unemployed. He was taken before the magistrate, who remarked as Swazey appeared in the dock, "Anybody can see you're guilty," and fined him—after a trial lasting less than five minutes—the sum of thirty shillings. We in London had the utmost difficulty in raising the money to pay the fine. Yet we had no doubt about our ability to overturn the capitalist system. [*ibid.*]

In the interview with Archie Green quoted above, Dick Brazier recalled another soapboxer, Jack Phelan, known as "the silver-tongued boy orator of the Wobblies," and one of the IWWs who, like Hill, took part in the Baja Revolution:

He'd get on the soapbox, and he'd open an umbrella over his head, and put his hand over his head, and then he'd start yelling at the top of his voice: "Help! Help! I'm being robbed!" And they'd come a-running, the crowd, and he'd say "I'm still being robbed!" And when he had a crowd, he'd say "I'm being robbed by the master class! They're all wet!" Then he'd start up into his spiel. [39]

Hubert Henry Harrison has been called "the foremost Afro-American intellect of his time," "one of America's greatest minds," and "the Father of Harlem radicalism." He is also increasingly rec-ognized as a major influence on Claude McKay and other writers and artists of the Harlem Renaissance. An original thinker and political activist, a prolific writer and newspaper editor, an impor-tant educator and critic, he was also—throughout his adult years —an indefatigable soapboxer. Indeed, Hubert Harrison was widely hailed as one of the finest soapboxers of all time.

In his excellent *Hubert Harrison Reader* (2001), Jeffrey B. Perry summarizes Harrison's achievements as an "ozone orator":

Harrison's outdoor lectures pioneered the tradition of militant street-corner oratory in Harlem. As a soapbox orator he was brilliant and unrivaled. He had a charismatic presence, a wide-ranging intellect, a remarkable memory, impeccable diction, and exceptional mastery of language. Factual and interactive, he utilized humor, irony, and a biting sarcasm. With his popular indoor and outdoor style he paved the way for those who followed—including A. Philip Randolph, Marcus Garvey, and, much later, Malcolm X. [5]

Non-Black listeners also recognized Harrison's power on the box. Novelist Henry Miller idolized him during his own youthful socialist days in New York, and years later admiringly recalled how Harrison's soapboxing skills enabled him to "demolish any opponent" [*ibid.*, 1].

Harrison, who was born and raised in St Croix in the Danish West Indies, emigrated to New York in 1900 while still in his teens. Active at first in the freethought movement, by 1911 he was the most prominent Black member of the Socialist Party in New York. His participation in the IWW began around 1912, by way of the Socialist Party's left wing. A contributor to the *International Socialist Review*, he also defended Bill Haywood from attacks by the Party's AFL-oriented right wing. A few months later, Harrison —along with such well-known IWW speakers as Haywood, Elizabeth Gurley Flynn, Carlo Tresca, and Patrick Quinlan—was addressing huge crowds from the IWW platform during the 1913 Paterson silk strike.[2]

Although Harrison's active involvement in the IWW did not last long, he continued to defend revolutionary industrial unionism in later years, not only on the soapbox, but also in *The Voice*, the African American weekly he edited. In the summer of 1917, for example, he strongly advocated

the twentieth-century type of unionism [which] says: "To leave a single worker out is to leave something for the boss to use against us. Therefore we must organize in One Big Union of *all* the working class." This is the type of unionism which organized, in 1911, 18,000 white and 14,000 Black timber workers in Louisiana. This is the IWW type of unionism. . . . [*ibid.*, 81]

One of the most popular and influential IWW soapboxers was J. T. "Red" Doran, a "chart-talk" or "chalk-talk" artist. As he spoke to the crowd, Fellow Worker Doran kept drawing pictures or diagrams on a portable blackboard, erasing them and drawing new ones as the talk progressed. His lectures have been described as "worthy of a good university" [Conlin 1969, 186]. Thanks to a fluke of history, one of his long spiels has survived. As one of the hundred-plus Wobblies charged with "conspiracy" in the 1918 Chicago trial, Doran was persuaded to re-enact a chalk-talk in the courtroom, and did so. Full of class-conscious humor and easy lessons in economics and history, the talk is featured in a pamphlet titled *Evidence and Cross-Examination of J. T. (Red) Doran in the Case of the U.S.A. vs. Wm. D. Haywood et al.*, published that same year by the union's General Defense Committee.

Soapboxers have rarely received much recognition, but the women among them have been especially ignored by historians. Elizabeth Gurley Flynn, the best known IWW woman speaker, did her share of soapboxing, but she is remembered primarily as a platform orator. One notable woman streetcorner soapboxer was Russian-born Minnie F. Corder, who joined the IWW in 1919 and remained one of the union's stalwarts till the end. Even during her last difficult years in the 1980s at New York's Florence Nightingale Nursing Home she continued, in her nineties, to agitate and organize—for better food and better living conditions.

Minnie Corder, too, spoke from the platform now and then, at least once together with Big Bill Haywood. But Fellow Worker Corder's strong voice was heard above all from a soapbox on the busy sidewalks of poor workingclass neighborhoods on New York's Lower East Side and elsewhere on the East Coast. As her "trademark," she always concluded her spiel with the famous lines from Shelley's *Mask of Anarchy*:

> *Rise like lions after slumber*
> *In unvanquishable number,*
> *Shake your chains to earth like dew*
> *Which in sleep had fallen on you—*
> *Ye are many—they are few.*

Swazey, Phelan, Harrison, Doran, Corder, and hundreds of other soapboxers are the IWW's unsung heroes. Their medium was the spoken word, and few left more than the faintest traces in the printed record; of the five discussed here, only Harrison was as much a writer as a speaker. Many of them were poets in their own way—creative monologists with a gift for improvisation, metaphor, and novel figures of speech. Not many soapboxers were noted as singers, but their impact on audiences was often similar to that of song. When workers listen to IWW speakers, as Mary Heaton Vorse observed in Lawrence 1912,

> they are going to school. Their minds are being opened. They are learning history and economics translated into the terms of their own lives. Many of them suddenly find hitherto unsuspected powers. Men and women, until now dumb, get upon platforms and speak with fire and with the eloquence of sincerity to their fellow workers. Others write articles and leaflets. New forms of demonstration are invented, and the workers set off singing the songs they themselves have made up. . . . Like new blood these new talents flow through the masses of the workers. [12]

---

1. Years later, this Wobbly dialogue was made into an oft-reprinted comic strip by the noted United Electrical Workers cartoonist Fred Wright.

With its focus on the soapboxer's opposition to slavery,
this 1920s drawing from the *Industrial Pioneer*
relates the IWW to the older Abolitionist movement.

8. THE FUTURIST SOCIETY OF AMERICA

One must tear happiness from the days to come.
—Vladimir Mayakovsky—

A lthough the word "Futurist" was bandied about in news reports, reviews, and spoofs of the 1913 Armory Show, no authentically Futurist paintings were in fact included in the exhibit. Not until May 1915 were works by the Italian Futurists exhibited in the U.S., at the Pacific-Panama Exposition in San Francisco.

As early as 1911, however—two years *before* the Armory Show and only two years *after* the publication of F. T. Marinetti's *Manifesto of Futurism* in Italy—the French-born American writer André Tridon started a Futurist agitation in New York.

Born near Paris in 1877, Tridon was educated at the Sorbonne and the University of Heidelberg. After moving to the U.S. in 1903, he made his living as a freelance writer, contributing articles, essays, and reviews to a great number of newspapers and magazines. By 1910, or perhaps even earlier, he considered himself something of a socialist. He served as secretary for the original *Masses*, contributed photographs to the *International Socialist Review*, and became a frequent contributor to the New York daily *Socialist Call* as well as *The New Review*, "A Weekly Review of International Socialism." He was also a frequent lecturer at the anarchist Ferrer "Modern School" [Avrich 1980, 133].

Exactly when and how he first encountered Futurism is not known, but a full-page interview with him in the Sunday magazine section of the *New York Herald* for 24 December 1911, identified him as the "archpriest of Futurism in America." In this interview, Tridon emphasized what he regarded as Futurism's nonconformist and revolutionary goals:

> Futurism believes in making the present an attribute of the future rather than of the past. . . . To forget convention as convention. . . To knock convention—which is only the past crystallized into habit—out of painting and writing and talking and everything we do. [8]

Tridon's Futurism was undoubtedly inspired by Marinetti's Italian original, but the disciple's revisions of the doctrine were extensive and drastic. Simply and quietly he dropped the maestro's obsessions with violence, war, speed, noise, and brutality, along with his extreme glorification of technology and hatred of nature. While Marinetti's Futurism led him and the Italian Futurist group to become vigorous supporters of Mussolini (Marinetti himself held high office in the fascist government), Tridon's Futurism stressed freedom, transformation, introspection, life, and Hegel's "becoming."

Interestingly, too, Tridon recognized Futurist elements in popular culture, with what appears to be a left-handed tip of his hat to *Krazy Kat* cartoonist George Herriman:

> Nature is never still, therefore in art movement is as important as form. The newspaper cartoonist who by lines indicates the progress of a brick through the air is a crude Futurist. . . . [*ibid.*]

Did others rally to Tridon's Futurist banner? It seems likely, but nobody seems to know. There were painters in the U.S. in the 1910s who imbibed at least some of the fundamental tenets of Futurism—Joseph Stella and Max Weber in New York, and Manierre Dawson in Chicago—but they do not appear to have linked up with Tridon. The *New York Sun* for 25 February 1912 described Tridon as the "Organizer of the Futurist Society of America," but no other documentation has been found to prove that such a Society ever existed [Hand 1981, 339].

Paul Jordan-Smith's novel of pre-World-War-I Chicago radicalism and bohemia, *Cables of Cobweb* (1923), devotes many pages to a Futurist group centered in Rogers Park (a suburb in those days), three blocks from Lake Michigan. Closer to the Tridonian model than to the Marinettist original, this midwestern U.S. Futurism focused above all on social reform of the sort usually considered crackpot. "The Futurists," we are told, "aim to work out a great synthesis of the sciences"; their program included "complete emancipation in food, sex, religion, science, philosophy, clothes, medicine, housing, morals, art and education" [223, 217]. The novel describes them as puritanical and confused; its leading figure is said to have been "no more able to think an impure thought than to express a logical one" [224].

More than a novel "based on fact," *Cables of Cobweb* is truly a *roman à clef*—Joe Hill's friend Alexander MacKay appears as one of the characters (but not as a Futurist). In an autobiography written nearly forty years later, Jordan-Smith indicates that the Futurists in the novel were largely inspired by a crank reformer and heavyweight wrestler named Parker H. Sercombe, head of a community known as the Spencer-Whitman Center, and editor of its magazine, *Tomorrow*. (Very briefly, Carl Sandburg was co-editor.) Did the Tomorrowites call themselves Futurists? Were they in touch with Tridon? The answer is: We know nothing about it. However, if the Rogers Park Futurist Group really did exist, it seems odd that no one besides Jordan-Smith has ever mentioned it.

Tridon, in any case, alone or with others, continued to defend Futurism as a movement which held that art had to pass into life:

> Futurism . . . wishes to see and reproduce living life, everlastingly changing, and to watch today the growth of the germ from which tomorrow will spring up. [*New York Sun*, 25 Feb 1912]

To my mind, the second half of the just-quoted sentence sounds a lot like "forming the new society in the shell of the old." Unfortunately, we do not know when Tridon joined the IWW. Join it he did, however, and in the early months of 1913 the *Industrial Worker* and *Solidarity* ran articles of his—not, however, on Futurism, but on "the new unionism": syndicalism in Europe and the IWW in the U.S. In June of that year Fellow Worker Tridon's articles on the subject—revised, expanded, and supplemented by other articles— were published by B. W. Huebsch as a 200-page volume titled *The New Unionism*. The section on the IWW is by far the largest in the book, and in his preface to the second edition (February 1914), Tridon acknowledged the direct collaboration and other assistance he had received from many IWWs—Justus Ebert, Joseph Ettor, Arturo Giovannitti, William D. Haywood, Vincent St John, Walker C. Smith, William E. Trautmann, and Ben H. Williams.

Heavily promoted in the IWW press, *The New Unionism* was the first popular presentation of the history, philosophy, and practice of the new labor organizations throughout the world which put the accent on workers' *self*-emancipation: *i.e.*, the principle that the proletarian revolution must be made not by "leaders" or political parties, but by the workers themselves in workers' organizations.

And where, one might ask, was Futurism in all this? It is hard to say. Neither Tridon's 1911 interview nor his 1912 article on Futurism mentioned the IWW, and his articles in the IWW press did not mention Futurism. His articles in *The New Review* for 1913 —such as "Charpentier, Musical Anarch and Labor Agitator," or

"The Truth About the Irish Players," or even his interesting sketch of Bill Haywood during the Paterson strike—cannot be said to reflect a Futurist spirit.

Did Tridon insist on keeping his two revolutionary causes distinct and separate? Or did he drop Futurism for the IWW? Or did the Futurist Society of America go underground? The questions are easy to ask, but in the present state of our knowledge they cannot be answered with any certainty.

Based on what we know of Tridon's writings, however, as well as his later career, it seems clear that—like many other intellectuals, and especially Greenwich Villagers—the man was above all else a petit-bourgeois dilettante. He was a competent journalist, a popularizer and modifier of other people's ideas—not an original thinker or a creative artist. Hopelessly eclectic throughout his successive enthusiasms, his writings rarely rise above a snobbish sort of superficiality. He was a rebel with too many causes, and none of his grandiose projects seem to have had much effect.

In the later 1910s Tridon took up yet another new hobby—psychoanalysis—and published several books on the subject, including *Psychoanalysis: Its History, Theory and Practice* (1919) and *Psychoanalysis and Behavior* (1920). Although worthy of note as early works on the subject in English, they are nothing more than slapdash surveys and, as Sal Salerno (1989) has pointed out in regard to *The New Unionism*, "riddled with inaccuracies" [53]. Clarence P. Oberndorf, in his *History of Psychoanalysis in America* (1953), sums up Tridon as "typical of [the] flagrant invasion of psychotherapeutics without preparation" [175]. Like his unauthorized and greatly abridged translation of Freud's *Interpretation of Dreams*—published under the title *Dream Psychology: Psychoanalysis for Beginners* (1921)—Tridon's own attempts to contribute something to psychoanalytic literature were, at best, flashes in the pan, and are no longer of any interest to anyone except as oddities.

The two and a half matter-of-fact lines on Futurism in his *Psychoanalysis: Its History, etc.* indicate that his former passion for the topic had long since evaporated [143]. In retrospect, Tridon's Futurism appears as a project that never quite got off the ground. Futurism in the U.S. had a self-proclaimed Organizer, but it does *not* seem to have had an organization. If the "Futurist Society of America" ever actually *did* anything, it has yet to be brought to public attention. The impact of Tridon's Futurism on the larger society remains a mystery.

Within the IWW, however, the effect of Tridon's Futurism can be measured accurately: It was nil, or less. Not one Wobbly appears to have taken up the Futurist cause. The sole reference to Futurism that I have found in the IWW press is a satirical one: In the *Industrial Worker* for 22 May 1913, Ernest Riebe's "Mr Block" comic strip is replaced by a blank square with a rule around it, with the "Mr Block" title above it, and the following caption underneath:

> As our artist failed to send his drawing in time for this issue we reproduce herewith a futurist drawing of Mr Block's mind when he is deeply pondering on the labor problem.

The fact that the "Organizer of the Futurist Society of America" carried a red card in the Industrial Workers of the World is not without its charm, but the fact that nothing came of it tends to reduce it to the level of a "Believe-It-Or-Not" type of bizarre anecdote. The truth is that Futurism, even in Tridon's new and improved variety, with Marinetti's reactionary elements removed, had nothing to offer the Wobblies. In terms of making the present an attribute of the future and knocking convention out of everything we do, the IWW was so far ahead of the Futurists that it made Futurism itself look *passé*.

As Joe Hill put it: "I don't know anything about the future, but am prepared for anything" [*Letters*, 36].

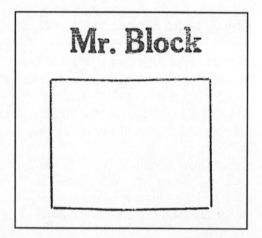

One week, when Ernest Riebe's "Mr Block" strip didn't arrive in time, the *Industrial Worker* substituted this "futurist drawing of Mr Block's mind when he is deeply pondering on the labor problem." (*Industrial Worker*, 22 May 1913)

9. REVOLUTIONARY REWRITING
& INFRAPOLITICS:
NEW SONGS & COMICS
IN THE SHELL OF THE OLD

Innovative imaginative work is born of a profound necessity
to transform legacies that we neglect at our peril.
—Wilson Harris—

Ralph Chaplin, in his 1923 biographical sketch of the Wobbly poet/martyr, noted that "It was in the IWW that [Hill] found his fullest and freest expression" [25]. Expression was always vital for the Wobblies: the collective expression of a class, and the individual expression of those who make up that class. Direct action, strikes, free-speech fights, poetry, soapboxing, song and solidarity formed one big continuum in the One Big Union. As Fellow Worker Sophie Cohen, a veteran of the union's 1913 Paterson Strike, suggested in a 1970s interview, the union itself became a "medium of expression," not only for those who joined it, but for all who entered its sphere of influence [Bird *et al.*, 68].

Expression is first and last about language, and in class society language is always in trouble. Indeed, wherever inequality exists, language itself is at war. The words aimed and fired at working people, and especially immigrant working people, by those who presume to be their superiors, are words designed to bewilder and bully, confuse and control. In its spoken form, the language of bosses, supervisors, teachers, preachers, cops, judges, jailers, government bureaucrats, and "officialdom" of all sorts consists largely of commands ("Do only what I tell you to do"); prohibitions, which are also commands ("Don't take that leaflet"); threats, which usually embody commands ("If you take that leaflet, you're fired"); and finally, ideological platitudes that completely contradict the rest ("This is the freest country in the world").

In its printed forms, this language is no less authoritarian, but far more convoluted. Textbooks, religious tracts, newsstand magazines and the daily papers—to say nothing of legal documents and company rulebooks—reflect the values, mores, and point of view of the dominant class, and consequently exacerbate the working population's feelings of inferiority and insecurity.

In speech as well as writing, those who do the world's work

have always found secret, "underground" ways to turn the boss's words around, and to make these words serve their own ends. Jokes, too, are part of the class war; puns and punchlines can be powerful weapons. In practically every workplace you will find workers making fun of the company name, and the boss's name, and rephrasing the pronouncements of company bigshots in such a way as to elicit the laughter of fellow workers.

This workingclass wordplay—flipping phrases backward and forward and mixing them up—was a staple of Wobbly soapboxers. Sometimes a simple turned-around phrase did more to jolt the listeners' brains than an entire speech. In the 1920s, when the demagogic evangelist Aimee Semple MacPherson drew huge crowds with her absurd slogan, "Millions now living will never die," a soapboxer in Pershing Square in her own home base of Los Angeles pointed out that "Millions now living are already dead!" The follow-up spiel on how capitalism kills the worker's mind and spirit long before his heart stops beating really gave *his* audience something to think about.

Rewriting is a strategy used, in uncountable ways, by all the oppressed—chattel slaves, wage-workers, colonized peoples, immigrants, women, children, prisoners, sexual minorities, so-called "criminals" and the "mentally ill"—against the language of power. In other words, it is a strategy used especially by outcasts.

As immigrant, workingstiff, hobo, Wobbly, and writer in a second language, Joe Hill was quintuply an outcast in U.S. capitalist society. And rewriting—significantly altering a pre-existing text and thereby transforming its meanings and impact—is a good one-word description of one of Hill's principal methods of song composition. Most of what are known as "Joe Hill's songs" are in fact his radical rewritings of old hymns and pop tunes. Their very real originality lies in the changes he made in the originals. Sometimes, as in Max Ernst's collages, Gherasim Luca's cubomanias, and Penelope Rosemont's landscapades and prehensilhouettes, the act of rearrangement suffices to create an entirely new work. Hill's "Everybody's Joining It" includes whole lines of Irving Berlin's "Everybody's Doin' It," but the Wobbly context makes it a very different song. In most of Hill's lyrics, however, nearly every word of the original is replaced by another.

Here, for example, are the first and last stanzas, plus chorus, of Sanford Fillmore Bennett's hymn, "In the Sweet Bye and Bye":

There's a land that is fairer than day
and by faith we can see it afar,
For the Father waits over the wave
To prepare us a dwelling place there.

Chorus:
In the sweet bye and bye
We shall meet on that beautiful shore.
In the sweet bye and bye,
We shall meet on that beautiful shore.

To our bountiful Father above
We will offer a tribute of praise
For the glorious gift of his love
And the blessings that hallow our days.

And here are the equivalent elements of Hill's parody:

Long-haired preachers come out every night,
Try to tell you what's wrong and what's right;
But when asked how 'bout something to eat
They will answer in voices so sweet:

Chorus:
You will eat, bye and bye,
In that glorious land above the sky;
Work and pray, live on hay,
You'll get pie in the sky when you die.

Workingmen of all countries, unite,
Side by side we for freedom will fight;
When the world and its wealth we have gained,
To the grafters we'll sing this refrain:

Final chorus:
You will eat, bye and bye,
When you've learned how to cook and to fry.
Chop some wood, 'twill do you good,
And you'll eat in the sweet bye and bye.

Note that Hill found almost nothing of the insipid original worth retaining, and that his chorus keeps only the phrase "bye and bye." What is parodied here is not Bennett's pitifully weak verse—itself almost a parody of saccharine sentimentality—but rather the dim-witted, superstitious, and submissive spirit that permeates the old hymn. In contrast, Hill's lyrics satirize the whole "work and pray" ideology: capitalist callousness in general, and the phony piety of the clergy in particular. From start to finish, Hill replaces Bennett's neurotic and patriarchal idealism with his own clear-sighted IWW focus on the concrete, the materialistic, the here and now. His concluding stanza, and the closing chorus, drive home the Wobbly message that workers' solidarity is the only way to create a good life for all right here on Earth.

As this typical example of his "rewriting" shows, Hill's rewritten songs, unlike their religious and commercial models, were not meant to console and/or distract, but rather to alert and arouse. In opposition to capitalist culture, in which "entertainment" tends to be the artificial sweetener of an inherently distasteful and indigestible system—and is in fact specifically designed to deaden awareness and stifle the free play of the imagination—Hill's songs and poems provoke critical reflection, expand consciousness, and spark liberating, imaginative thought. As such, they are a creative/destructive assault on the deadly myths that help hold the whole white-supremacist/capitalist/miserabilist nightmare together. In their wild, creative improvisations, Hill, T-Bone Slim and other Wobbly poets and artists counted optimistically on what Ralph Ellison once called "the unexpectedness of the American experience" [Ellison 1995, 401]. The demand for freedom and equality silences, if only for a moment, the order-givers' commands, decrees, warnings, threats, and lies—that is to say, the repressive language of the billionaire-owned media—and in effect reduces and ultimately wrecks the credibility of the established "order." In such moments, new worlds are born.

The same impulse underlies the revolutionary rewriting of the capitalist comics page. Hill's cartoons, and all Wobbly cartoons, let us know that the fundamental problems of life are not fickle girlfriends, nagging wives, lazy husbands, unruly children, obnoxious neighbors, demanding pets, and bad luck at the race-track or poker-table—but rather stupid jobs, low pay, the insane relations of production, and the systemic brutality, injustice, and inequality that sustains the whole mess. To paraphrase a passage from James Baldwin's *The Fire Next Time*, the power of Capital is threatened whenever a worker refuses to accept the capitalists' definitions.

Always and everywhere, demystification is the first principle of revolutionary rewriting. Hill and his fellow IWW cartoonists, by challenging the dishonest, distorted images of working people in the bourgeois media, helped undermine the repressive ideology that legitimizes such hurtful images. In Wobbly cartoons, capitalism itself is regarded as a sick joke, and the laughs are always at the system's expense. The joyful mayhem in many IWW songs and cartoons is as good as anything in Ring Lardner, the Marx Brothers, Smokey Stover, Daffy Duck—and can also boast an extra added attraction: *revolutionary class-consciousness*!

Exposing the irrationality of existing property relations and the whole grim comedy of the profit system, Hill's songs—and his cartoons as well—spotlighted the "lower depths" of social reality, helped working men and women realize their collective strength, and thus served as prime vehicles of workingclass self-definition.

In this often painful process of self-definition, language is the key. The Swedish immigrant Hill was well aware of the conflict between "standard English" and the everyday language of the working class. He knew that the English language, as employed by the media, schools and courts, and even the ruling-class version of "popular" literature, was an instrument of class rule. In our own time, "standard" English is more than ever the language of capitalism, imperialism, militarism, church and state—the language of exploitation and manipulation.

Hill's letters show that he was quite capable of using "standard" English when necessary, as when writing to the Utah Board of Pardons, but that he felt much more at home in the informal language of his fellow workers. The best of his songs are defiantly slangy, simple and forceful, full of the spice of life. Nowhere do we find Hill or other Wobblies "talking down" to workers, as is so often the case in Socialist and Communist Party literature. Hill and his fellow Wobbly songwriters wrote in plain workers' language because it was *their own* language, and because they realized how urgent it was for working people to speak and read and write their own language openly and confidently, without worrying too much about the rules of grammar and syntax, or the fads and fashions of literary style.

This, too, is one of the tasks of revolutionary rewriting: to release the pent-up creative energies of those who, from childhood on, are humiliated and reviled by all sorts of "authorities" for "not knowing how to speak English correctly."

Thus Joe Hill and the IWW devised their own ways to tell

"Their Own Story." As the Trinidadian Marxist C. L. R. James remarked in another but related context (the writing and rewriting of Caribbean history), such an effort has

> constantly to bear in mind how we came into being, where we have reached, who we are and what we are. . . . We are not dealing with abstractions. . . . We are dealing with concrete matters that penetrate into the very immediate necessities of our social existence....[The aim is] to stimulate the imagination . . . to create a wider and deeper reality beyond the thin scraps of . . . recorded history. [1969, 46]

With their demystifying defiance, savage humor, free invective, and easygoing indifference to so-called "good" grammar, Hill's contributions to the *Little Red Song Book* were radically *outside* the parameters of linguistic propriety maintained by the propertied class. Adding insult to injury, his lyrics were also *not for sale*. Not least of the many admirable qualities of Joe Hill's songs—and other IWW songs—is that they are absolutely unsuited for use in advertising. When Hill decommercialized a pop song by rewriting it and making it revolutionary, he in effect made it impossible for the song to be used for any publicitary purposes other than advancing the cause of abolishing of wage-slavery in general, and building up the IWW in particular.

Hill's experience in this regard contrasts sharply to that of the great majority of later writers of "protest songs." Consider, for example, the case of Woody Guthrie, who has sometimes been considered a kind of latter-day Hill. Guthrie's most popular song, "This Land Is Your Land," was not only repeatedly recorded by such non- and anti-radicals as Bing Crosby, Paul Anka, Connie Francis, Jay and the Americans, and the Mormon Tabernacle Choir, but also used in the 1960s in TV commercials for Budweiser beer, the Ford Motor Company, United Airlines, and later as the official campaign song for the pro-capitalist George McGovern in his unsuccessful bid for the Presidency [Hampton 1986, 141-142; Garman 2000, 164].

That Guthrie was sincere in his own variety of radicalism there is no reason to question. Joe Hill, however, was much more than a songwriter with left sympathies—he was an all-out revolutionary who wrote and rewrote songs explicitly "to fan the flames of discontent." Decades later, Hill's songs are still so definitively anti-capitalist and anti-statist that they simply cannot be used to promote the buying and selling of commodities or candidates or anything else.

As a revolutionary rewriter in a second language, Hill and his work naturally invite comparison with the writings of numerous other immigrants—and also with the natives of many lands whose language differs sharply from that of their rulers. Hill has been likened to writers such as Jack London and Woody Guthrie, and of course there are parallels and convergences that make such comparisons plausible. His bilingualism, however, in addition to his varied working life, also allies him to very different writers: to the Polish-born Joseph Conrad, for example, and to Jack Kerouac, who spoke nothing but a French-Canadian dialect (*joual*) during his early years. Even more obvious are Hill's affinities with the radical Yiddish-speaking worker-poets of New York's Lower East Side—Moshe Nadir, Reuben Iceland, H. Leivick—who, like Hill himself, yearned for the day "When the grand red flag is flying in the Workers' Commonwealth."

Today, Hill's strongest affinities seem to me to be with the radical Calypsonians and Reggae bands of the Caribbean, the Aboriginal poets of Australia, and, in the U.S., the African American "Black Arts" movement and its successors, as well as like-minded currents among Native Americans, Asian Americans, Chicanos, Puerto Ricans, and others. As living exemplars of the desperate struggle to liberate language and all of humankind, these insurgent currents—whether they know it or not—are continuing the great work of the Man Who Never Died. And that helps explain why the best criticism of Joe Hill—the criticism that does most to illuminate his work, to *situate* it, and to heighten our awareness of its resonance—is often to be found not in writings about Hill *per se*, but in the writings of Third World critics writing about Third World poets. I know of no better short exposition of Joe Hill's historic and cultural importance than these four sentences about the famous Trinidadian Calypsonian Francisco Slinger, "The Mighty Sparrow," written by his fellow Trinidadian, C. L. R. James:

> He handles the language, and [writes] with great poetic and powerful effect the language and rhythms of the population. His English is composed of sharp, pointed . . . expressions. His work should be [more widely available], and critics should talk about it, but they don't. *His* language has given English an extra dimension. [Searle 1984, 247]

The following reflections by the Guyanese poet/critic Jan Carew, on the role of songs in the Grenada Revolution, are also fully applicable to the work of the Wobbly bard:

> Language does not grow unless elements from the bottom erupt out and enter into it. It is constantly fed by the experience of working people at all levels. They pour new words, new images into the language. When you shut that off you have a dead language. [*ibid.*, 242]

Above all else, the project of the revolutionary workingclass rewriter consists of interruption and disruption: changing the subject, redefining the terms, reversing priorities, and otherwise, as the Earth First! slogan puts it, "subverting the dominant paradigm," thereby turning the patriarchal/bourgeois/authoritarian view of the world upside-down and inside-out. Such subversion, exceeding the narrow framework of the "practical" and mundane, extends to the sphere of desire, emotion, our sense of beauty. Listen to these lines "To a Fair Libertarian," by Wobbly poet Jim Seymour:

> *Though moonbeams romp through softest shadows there,*
> *I write no tuneful sonnets to your hair;*
> *Nor pencil lyrics simply that your eyes*
> *Recall the peaceful stars of tropic skies;*
> *Nor shall your cheeks be subject of an ode*
> *Because therein the roses make abode;*
> *No verse about the goblet of your lip*
> *Whence I, a god, the honeyed nectar sip;*
> *To greater beauty far I write instead—*
> *A paean to a gem of priceless worth;*
> *To that which wakes the sleep from his bed*
> *Of matted thorns upon a blood-soaked earth:*
> *I write but to the brilliance of your mind*
> *That to the heights of freedom leads the blind.*[1]

In fourteen jaunty lines, a hobo who was also one of the union's noted soapboxers has merrily toppled several centuries' worth of shopworn sexist conceits, preferring to celebrate the deeper beauty of intellectual insight and revolutionary audacity rather than the gaudy, superficial "good looks" of the cosmetic ads.

As Fellow Worker Seymour's frolicsome sonnet shows, revolutionary rewriting is also a form of *playing*: arranging and rearranging for the sheer subversive fun of it. Proletarian revolution is not, of course, simply a matter of play, but *without* the play element it tends to be nothing more than a change of masters.

As a form of play, and thus somewhat beyond the clutches of the "serious," rewriting is only one of numerous kinds of social struggle that are not ordinarily considered "political," even by specialists in politics, radical or otherwise. Ranging from workplace restroom graffiti and clowning on the job to property-damaging pranks and outright sabotage, such hidden or disguised manifestations of revolt—which anthropologist James C. Scott (1990) has called "infrapolitics"—have rarely been recognized for what they are: guerrilla skirmishes in the class war. Sociologists might classify such gestures as "the result of a breakdown in communications," but the police term is "malicious mischief," and employers have been only too ready to prosecute perpetrators of infrapolitics to the full extent of the law.

Revealingly, old-line Socialists and Communists—not to mention trade-union officials—have all through the years been just as confused and upset by these clandestine proletarian protests as the bosses, and in their ideological haze have done little more than churn out the old reliable accusations: "irresponsible," "individualistic," and "ultraleft." The old-time Wobblies, however, saw things differently. As their own adventures in rewriting demonstrate, they not only recognized infrapolitics for what it was—they were receptive to it, adapted it to their own open-ended strategies, and went on to develop it creatively in many novel ways.

The concept of infrapolitics, as Robin D. G. Kelley pointed out in his important book *Race Rebels: Culture, Politics, and the Black Working Class* (1994) "illuminate how power operates, and how seemingly innocuous, individualistic acts of survival and resistance shape politics, workplace struggles, and the social order generally" [9]. Rejecting the deplorable tendency of so many would-be Marxists "to dichotomize people's lives," Kelley goes on to formulate what deserves to be known as the fundamental axiom of the infrapolitical, that "Politics is not separate from lived experience or the imaginary world of what is possible" [*ibid.*]. The fact that such crippling separation was intrinsic to the "Old Left," but *not* to the IWW, is yet one more and very important reason why working people today need to learn more about the old-time Wobblies.

Further study of the impact of the infrapolitical on everyday life and in broader cultural change should help us understand why the IWW never ballyhooed the inherently undialectical and anti-Marxist notion of "proletarian culture" (often shortened to "proletcult") promoted at various times by proto-Stalinist and Stalinist Communists. In this area, too, the Wobblies' unpretentious Marxism proved to be vastly superior to the more fashionably "orthodox" varieties. IWWs recognized that with the abolition of wage-slavery, the proletariat thereby ceases to be a proletariat, and that talk of a "proletarian culture" without a proletariat was foolish and misleading. The Wobbly view of the question was basically the same as that of Marx himself, and of such otherwise very different Marxists as Friedrich Engels, William Morris, Antonio Labriola, Herman Gorter, Rosa Luxemburg, V. I. Lenin, and Leon Trotsky. As the last-named wrote in his influential book *Literature and Revolution* (1927):

> The proletariat acquires power for the purpose of doing away forever with class culture and to make way for human culture.... There is no real analogy between the historical development of the bourgeoisie and of the working class. . . . [Workers' revolution] is a means of clearing the road, and of laying the foundations of a society without classes and of a culture based upon solidarity. [186, 194]

In the meantime, Trotsky pointed out, much of what passed itself off as "proletarian" art was in truth pseudo-proletarian, populist, reactionary—and "second-rate art" [*ibid.*, 204-205].

This is a crucial point: The IWW—more concerned with "cultural" issues than any workers' organization in U.S. history—rejected the ahistorical goal of a "proletarian culture." While "clearing the road" for a truly *human* culture, Wobblies instead sought to develop a *revolutionary* culture or, to use the more recent term: a *counter*culture. For one of the major tasks of every revolution, as the great African revolutionary Amilcar Cabral pointed out in the 1960s, is "to destroy the negative influence of the culture of the enemy," and simultaneously to discover "new ways of seeing reality" [1979, 239, 60]. Discrediting the ruling ideologies and their figureheads, along with the entire military/prison/industrial/cultural/media complex that holds the *status quo* together, is the first prerequisite of a new, emancipatory culture. In this struggle against inherited habits, senile ideas, mercenary (often misnamed "philanthropic") institutions, and false consciousness, the most effective weapons in the proletarian arsenal have always been humor, dream, and poetic thought.

As to the culture of the new, free society, predictions are out of order here, except to note that such categories as "worker," "poet" and "artist" will be superseded, for the necessary labor will be equitably shared, and all forms of creativity and play will be open to everyone. For the rest, the best advice—in the spirit of Heraclitus and Ralph Ellison—is to expect the unexpected. As Bill Haywood pointed out:

> When we stop fighting each other—for wages of existence on one hand, and for unnecessary luxury on the other—then perhaps we shall all be human beings and surprise ourselves with the beautiful things we do and make on this Earth. [Golin 1988, 121]

Had Haywood been reading Friedrich Schiller's *Letters on the Aesthetic Education of Man*? That is something we may never know, but it is a fact that the passage I have just quoted admirably expresses the German Romantic poet's concept of a "lovelier necessity" beyond the realms of power and law, in which the "creative impulse" develops a new "joyous realm of play," freeing us all "from everything that may be called constraint, whether physical or moral" [Schiller 1965, 135-136]. In Wobbly discourse, the abolition of wage-slavery, or the drudgery known as work, automatically implies the advent of *free play*: an idea central also to the great visionary utopians, Fourier and Bellamy.

Some Wobblies, moreover, definitely *were* reading Schiller. Haywood's good friend Mary Marcy even cited the poet/philosopher in an article on "Work and Play" in the *International Socialist Review*. Envisioning the day when the workers of the world would "throw off the burden of work at the sound of the whistle at five o'clock . . . and revert to [our] original nature and *play*," Marcy goes on to complete Marx's argument that capitalism had turned human beings into machines by quoting Schiller's observation that "man is only fully human when he is at play" [Nov 1916, 297]. Far from the humdrum, moralistic and Chatauqua-like notions of workers' education that prevailed in the Socialist Party at the time, Marcy's insights also illuminate the IWW's remarkable ability "to mix music and song and dancing with new ideas and books and lectures."

Marcy's orientation toward play also brings to mind her great contemporary, Neva Boyd, who at Jane Addams's Hull House developed a theory and practice of play as a decisive element in education and therapy [Boyd 1971]. Boyd's ideas later became the basis of the improvisational theater of her student, Viola Spolin, who in turn inspired such celebrated comedy groups as the

Compass Players and Second City. For Boyd and Spolin, as for Marcy, play involved nothing less than a fundamental transformation in the relations between people, and a liberation of their creative imaginations. And isn't that also what social revolution is all about?

Here the IWW's revolutionary workingclass romanticism not only rejoins Schiller, Blake, Shelley, and Emily Brontë, but also anticipates the surrealist revolution and the triumph of the Pleasure Principle. Philip Sansom, an English anarcho-syndicalist and class-war prisoner who also took part in the activities of the Surrealist Group in London in the 1940s, posed the question from a slightly different angle:

> If the freeing of the body of the worker through his own efforts does not involve also a freeing of his mind and spirit, it leaves his essential self to be controlled by somebody else. [Sansom 1987, 278][2]

Rewriting, itself a form of play, not only shows the way, but also helps establish free territories of the imagination here and now, outside the mental prison of commodity fetishism and the wage system. By breaking up the hegemony of the "official" discourse, revolutionary rewriting and other countercultural infrapolitical games are also big steps toward the creation of a new and non-repressive language, and hence, toward a desirable future.[3] What else but poetry, after all—poetry as "the supreme *disalienation* of humanity with its language," as the surrealist poet Philip Lamantia has described it—could really make revolutionary change thinkable? [Rosemont 1997a, 206].

1. This poem, originally published in the IWW press, is reprinted here from Nelson 1993, 286-287.

2. Sansom is probably best known for his excellent pamphlet, *Syndicalism: The Workers' Next Step* (Sansom 1951). He also edited the Anarcho-Syndicalist Committee's newspaper, *The Syndicalist* (1952-53), which included a "Scissor Bill" comic strip by a cartoonist named "Dan." Sansom was himself a noted artist who collaborated on the surrealist journal *Free Unions*, helped run E. L. T Mesens's London Gallery, and contributed excellent cartoons to *Freedom* and other anarchist publications.

3. The concept of "free territories of the imagination," and the revolutionary significance of play and games, are explored in greater detail in Rosemont 1997a and Sakolsky 2002.

10. COLLECTIVE CREATION:
PLAYERS OF THE WORLD, UNITE!

The distinct virtue of genius
is the recognition of genius in everyone else.
—Harry Hooton—

Joe Hill's song based on Ernest Riebe's "Mr Block" comic; Riebe's single-panel cartoon of Hill's song, "Everybody's Joining It"; Hill's rewriting of Richard Brazier's "good cream ... on high above"; Brazier's later (and anonymous) addition of a concluding stanza to Hill's "The Tramp"; Hazel Dickens's rewriting of "The Rebel Girl"; Arthur Machia's redrawing of Hill's "Rebel Girl" art; the cartoons "Suggested by Joe Hill" and drawn by others: These very different examples of collaborative effort spotlight an important point: that the IWW counterculture was not only, and by its very nature, a *collective* creation, but also that its creators went about their work quite consciously, unaffectedly, and above all playfully.

Carefree collective goofing is in fact almost a synonym for improvisation. The inseparability of theory and practice in this lively form of intervention in the public sphere was superbly formulated by no less a dialectician than Marx himself—Groucho, to be precise:

> If they don't laugh, take it out and try another [line]. If it gets a laugh, leave it in. If you keep talking long enough, you say something funny. [Chandler 1979, 560]

From Hill's brother Paul, and from fellow workers who had known Hill in San Pedro, Ralph Chaplin learned something of the Wobbly bard's method of song-creation:

> He would strum out well known tunes lightly with his nimble fingers, improvising new words as he went along. Everyone within hearing distance would come under the spell of the humor of his parodies and his infectious smile as he worked them out a verse at a time. The idea of saving these little skits or writing them down never seemed to have entered Joe Hill's head. He just dashed them off on the spur of the moment and then proceeded to forget them. [Chaplin 1923, 24].

"Improvising new words" and "dashed off on the spur of the moment" are the operative expressions here, and they tell us a lot about how Hill's songs came to be. And if we assume that those "within hearing distance" who came under the poet's spell were not simply listeners but played an *active* role in the proceedings, then Hill himself can be said to epitomize Wobbly-style collective creation. There is in fact other evidence to support this supposition. Incidentally, Chaplin's account also makes it clear that many of Hill's songs, as spontaneous inventions of the moment, went unrecorded, and are irretrievably lost. Evanescence is one of the characteristics of play.

The enlightening testimony of another of Hill's song-writing fellow workers superbly documents the One Big Union's participatory poetics. Reminiscing about the early days of the *Little Red Song Book* in a 1968 letter to Fred Thompson, Richard Brazier shared a memory of hearing some fellow workers in a Wobbly hall out west quoting verses from the hymn, "Nearer My God to Me," and transposing them with others of their own invention:

> One chap would say this should be the last line in that song—
> "Nearer no god to me, he and I just don't agree." Then someone
> else would chime in with "Nearer my beer's to me, than God will
> ever be." I asked them, "What is this?" They told me "It's a song
> we heard and we are trying to make it sound right." Well, I know
> Wobblies get that way sometimes, only the one they used most was
> "Hallelujah, I'm a Bum." [28 May, 5]

Hill's "Nearer My Job to Thee" was not published until 1913 or '14. Had he too overheard fellow workers improvising new lyrics to the old hymn, "trying to make it sound right"? Or is this simply a case of great proletarian minds running in similar channels? That particular puzzle will probably never be solved. However, according to Hill's old friend Alexander MacKay, collective creativity definitely had a part in Hill's own *modus operandi*:

> . . . he enjoyed giving his verses a workout on any of us Wobs that
> were hanging around. One could say with considerable justice that
> the songs were communal productions, because Joe always got tips
> and suggestions from whatever Wobs were in the neighborhood.
> [Smith 1969, 20]

Some years later, MacKay took up the topic again in greater detail:

My most vivid memory of Joe was in the act of composition.
Picking out the tune was easy, but composing the song was a
Herculean task. Words did not flow easily from Joe. Every line
was a tough chore, and mostly a co-operative effort.

Here's the way a song was actually knocked out. Joe and a few
of us would be sitting around the dock, outside Joe's tarpaper
shack. We would be working over a mulligan and shooting the
bull. Joe would invariably be crabbing about conditions on the
waterfront. Suddenly he'd perk up and make a dash for the shack.
In a minute or so we'd hear the plunk-plunk of a guitar. In a little
while he'd come out and give us a rehearsal of a line or two of his
latest rhyming achievement. For his pains his reward was a slather
of devastating criticism, which generally he took in good part. If,
by some chance, he received an accolade of praise, he beamed all
over.

No one pretends that the works of Joe Hill are polished literary
masterpieces to be ranked with Shelley and Keats, but many a good
Wob had a hand in the production of raw material, hence they
evolved right out of the guts of the working class, and these songs
continue to hit the slave right in the solar plexus. [review of
Stegner 1950]

Fellow Worker MacKay's first-hand description of Joe Hill in
the act of song-creation confirms and amplifies what Chaplin had
heard, but seems to contradict Edward Mattson who, as we have
seen, marveled at Hill's ability to improvise lyrics as he played.

Can this discrepancy be attributed simply to the probability that
Hill, like other writers and singers, sometimes had "off" days?
Perhaps, but I think the explanation lies elsewhere: in the difference between inventing a new song and entertaining friends with
old ones. The fact that Mattson heard Hill sing a song and then
sing it again with entirely new lyrics does not mean that Hill was
improvising each and every word as he went along. It is far more
likely that he had memorized many stanzas for certain songs, and
sang only a few at each rendition, and now and then inserting new
words or lines by way of additional variation. This is also the procedure in most of today's improv comedy.

MacKay's vivid account is reminiscent of Giambattista Vico's
"discovery of the true Homer" in his *La Scienza Nuova* (The New
Science, 1730), according to which the epic works attributed to the

ancient Greek poet were not the product of an individual genius, but of a broad collectivity consisting of countless authors over a period of many generations. In effect, as one of Vico's earliest English-language commentators—Robert Flint, of the University of Edinburgh—noted in 1884, "The true Homer is . . . affirmed to be the Greek people itself, in its ideal and heroic character, relating its own history in national poetry" [174]. Would it be going too far to suggest, in the spirit of Vico, that the true author of "Joe Hill's songs" was the Industrial Workers of the World, or indeed, the revolutionary working class, relating its own history in its own way?

Until relatively recent times, collective creation was widespread and socially approved. Like the earliest art painted on the walls of caves, the great gothic cathedrals of the Middle Ages were collective to the point of anonymity. Many celebrated painters of the Italian Renaissance had assistants whose job it was to paint in backgrounds, or clouds, or particular small details: hands, for example, or the folds in clothing. Collaborative poetry has flourished in Japan for a thousand years, and the nation's finest poets, including the incomparable Basho, were among its most frequent and enthusiastic practitioners.

In more recent times, however, especially in Europe and the U.S., as a specifically *bourgeois* individualism came to dominate the arts, collective creation has been associated with protest and rebellion. From the 1910s on, its prime exemplars have been African American jazz musicians, modern dancers, and the Surrealist Movement. That the Wobbly poets were as committed to collective creation as the pioneers of jazz, modern dance, and surrealism shows once again, from another angle, how incredibly far the IWW diverged—spiritually as well as politically—from the business-unionism-as-usual of the AFL and the mainstream left. Despite their markedly dissimilar experiences of life, and following their own separate paths, Joe Hill, "King" Oliver, Isadora Duncan, and André Breton reached the same general conclusion: that the crisis of modern culture required collective creative action, and that the best way to go about it was by *playing*.

Their agreement on this crucial point is surely a "sign of the times," but it should not be taken to imply that any one of them suggested the idea to the others. There is nothing to indicate that Wobbly collective creation was derived from jazz, modern dance, or surrealism. The impact of jazz on the IWW, and vice versa, remains elusive, and probably was not very extensive. The Black Wobblies we know about do not appear to have been musicians; jazz musicians of the period do not appear to have joined the IWW; and non-Black Wobs do not appear to have pronounced themselves to any extent on the subject of Black music.[1] For a union that urged the workers to "get hip," the IWW's musical preferences were rather on the square side: traditional hymns and the latest hits from tin pan alley. All the same, it would be interesting to know how bluesmen Blind Joe Hill and Joe Hill Louis got their names.

The influence of modern dance on the IWW is also hard to assess. Many of the New York radical intellectuals who were close to the IWW in the 1910s—Mary Heaton Vorse, Floyd Dell, John Sloan and Alexander Berkman, among others—were also close friends and ardent admirers of Isadora Duncan. The great dancer's outspoken support for international workingclass solidarity and revolution ("I am a revolutionist. All artists are revolutionists") cannot have been ignored by IWWs, especially since Duncan was repeatedly denounced as "un-American" in the bourgeois press. Interestingly, too, Duncan always insisted that her revolution in dance was inspired not by dance-masters, but by poets—and they were the same poets most admired by Wobblies: Blake, Shelley, Byron, and Whitman. Clearly inspired by Duncan and her free dance are the images of joyous young dancing women, barefoot and clad in diaphanous Greek tunics, featured in many IWW May Day cartoons, and often on the covers of Wobbly magazines.

That some IWW members were acquainted with Duncan, or at least saw her dance, seems likely, for she is known to have given several free dance concerts for working people in New York, and probably elsewhere. One young Wobbly who saw her perform, and who counted the experience as an important moment in her life, was Vera Buch (later Vera Buch Weisbord), best known for her important role in the Gastonia Textile Strike.

We also know of at least one modern dance recital performed under Wobbly auspices. The *Labor Defender*, an IWW paper published in New York (not to be confused with the later Communist Party magazine of the same name), announced a November 1918 benefit for IWW class-war prisoners at the Finnish Socialist Party hall. For the featured entertainment, the announcement stated that pupils of Elizabeth Stuyvesant will "interpret the Russian Revolution" in a "Dance of Defiance" [15 Nov].

These points of contact between dancers and Wobblies are significant and interesting, and may have had a powerful influence on certain individuals. Their effect on the union as a whole, however, was small.

As for surrealism, the first surrealist work, properly so called— *The Magnetic Fields*, by André Breton and Philippe Soupault —appeared in 1919, long after collective creation was an accomplished fact in the One Big Union. Wobbly songsters and cartoonists offered readers of the IWW press strong doses of delirious imagery, black humor, and other manifestations of the Marvelous, but they took their inspiration straight from daily life in the U.S.A.

Other approaches to collective creation were also "in the air" during the first quarter of the century, and were certainly familiar to many IWW members. Earlier I mentioned Neva Boyd's important theories regarding collective play. Much better known examples include the early silent films, Percy MacKaye's public pageants, and the burgeoning "Little Theater" movement. (Wobbly theater flourished for years in Chicago, San Francisco, Cleveland, and at Work People's College in Duluth.) Less well known, but even closer to the IWW in spirit, was the radical theory of "tribal poetics" set forth by the feminist novelist Mary Hunter Austin.

Though not a joiner herself, Austin in fact had close ties to the Wobblies, at least in the mid-1910s. She was, for example, a friend and admirer of Elizabeth Gurley Flynn. The admiration was mutual: Flynn wrote to Austin years later, in 1930, that her novel *A Woman of Genius* had been an important inspiration to her in her youth, after her separation from her husband, Jack Jones [Porter 1985, 318-319]. Austin also knew Bill Haywood, as well as Margaret Sanger in her IWW days, and in 1913 she took part in support work for the Paterson silk strike [1932, 327]. Her many other radical friends included Charlotte Perkins Gilman, Ethel Duffy Turner, Ida Tarbell, W. E. B. Du Bois, Emma Goldman, Mother Jones, Isadora Duncan, and Paul Robeson.

Like many other experimenters with new ideas, Austin had more than a few contradictions. As Richard Drinnon observed in a chapter about her in his excellent book *Facing West* (1990), she "never liberated herself completely from the religious and secular prohibitions and repressions of her youth" [230]. Despite her wayward ways she managed, for example, to sustain a friendship of sorts with—of all people!—the notorious Indian-hater (and Wobbly-hater) Theodore Roosevelt. However, Drinnon argues, unlike the great majority of the historians, anthropologists, writers, and other intellectuals of her time, Austin

> took the trouble to enter Indian lives, found therein the reverse of "primitive" simplicity, gave way to their rhythmic utterances, and thereby experienced a true rebirth in the spirit of the land. With her rare openness to visionary experience she brought to the West more than conventionally blinding assumptions and attitudes. [231]

It was Austin's ambitious project to expand and deepen the consciousness of the "new" by reviving interest in certain "ancient ways." In her view, the rapidly evolving sensibility of the early twentieth century—as exemplified by the "new woman" and the "new unionism" of the IWW—could become the basis of a radically new, free, and creative society if it went on to develop a new awareness of traditional Native American values concerning tribal solidarity, the human relation to Nature, the land, and the landscape. What motivated her above all was a sudden intuition of the ways in which Native Americans, through poetry and dance, wholeheartedly identified themselves with the land they lived on. This "divination," as Richard Drinnon called it,

> lifted her to the distinguished company of Thomas Morton, George Catlin, and the few others who sensed that the "frontier" continent they had invaded possessed its own cherished rhythms [230].

Austin pointed out that European poetry too had once been tribal, but that the rise of class society had allowed "the communally affective uses of poetry [to pass] out of the hands of the tribe" into the control of a dominant class [1970, 22]. The aim, then, was to renew the democratic, collective, and participatory character of poetry. Not too surprisingly, her chosen instrument to bring about this new awareness—in effect a sweeping transformation of social values—was poetry itself.

Inspired by an intense, first-hand, and, as it turned out, lifelong study of Native American culture, Austin began to develop her theory of "tribal poetics" in the early 1900s, and gave her first lecture on the subject during the winter of 1904-05. She outlined her views briefly in 1918 in her introduction to George W. Cronyn's pioneering anthology of Native American poetry, *The Path on the Rainbow*, and in much greater detail in the introduction to her own anthology, *The American Rhythm*, in 1923, which she revised in 1930. Convinced that what she called "Amerindian" poetry would eventually become the basis of a new American poetry, she scandalized her contemporaries by pointing out the obvious truth that American Indian poetry was, and always had been, "free verse." Austin's theories and translations were in fact an influence on the "free verse" movement in this country, which she hailed with enthusiasm. As "old habits of work and society" are radically changed, she argued, "a new rhythmic basis of poetic expression is not only to be looked for, but is to be welcomed" [1930, 9]. Among the poets she especially liked were Vachel Lindsay, Carl Sandburg, Lew Sarett, Amy Lowell, and Edgar Lee Masters.

Insisting on the "original communal" character of poetry, she emphasized—in a passage resounding with Wobbly implications— the Native American conception of "poetry as a means of raising the plane of group consciousness" [*ibid.*, 36]. Once the "communally affective uses of poetry" are liberated from the stifling control of a ruling elite and people begin to discover the "rhythmic sense" and its "inestimable treasures of swinging thought" within themselves, poetry becomes the basis for a social transformation as marvelous and comprehensive as the utopia of Fourier [*ibid.*, 7]. For Austin, the experience of poetry involved nothing less than ecstasy, in which everything comes "alive together with a pulsing light of consciousness" [1932, 371]. Guided by her own poetic experiences as well as her study of Native American (especially Paiute) philosophy, with its emphasis on "wholeness" and what she called "the sweetness of ultimate reality," Austin looked ahead to a free global society in which mind and body, spirit and matter, humankind and the Earth will exist in real creative harmony [*ibid.*, 198].

Interestingly, Austin further urged that "an intelligent use of jazz" would also benefit the new poetry, particularly in the "unharnessing of traditional inhibitions of response, indispensable to the formation of a democratic society" [1930, 168-169]. Witnessing the Corn Dance of the Rio Grande Pueblos was enough to make her realize "how it was that Aristotle came to treat of Poetry as comprising several arts which we now think of as distinct from it" [*ibid.,* 46]. She was interested in "the relation of gesture to poetry," and in the *physical* effects of poetry: the ways in which "the autonomic centers are aroused and the collective consciousness set in motion" [*ibid.,* 47]. In an Appendix to *The American Rhythm* she noted that the Greek word for *labor* is derived from the same root as *orgy*; that the latter word "originally applied only to ecstatic states entered into by rhythmic movements"; and that the same root word relation also exists in many Native American languages [*ibid.,* 169]. Invoking olden times when songs were danced and dances were sung, she argued that "The long divided Muses of poetry, music, and dance must come together again" [1918, xxviii].

In her overall perspective, and especially in her eagerness to transcend the artificial and class-based separation of poetry from the other arts, and from life, Austin had much in common with the surrealists, whose revolution began with the insight that poetry has nothing to do with literature, and that poetry today has much to learn from the primordial peoples of the Earth. The surrealists' insistence on the unification of the arts under the guidance of poetry found support not only in Hegel and Lautréamont, but also and above all in the indigenous cultures of Africa and the Americas. "Music and poetry," André Breton wrote in 1945, "have everything to lose by not recognizing a common origin in song" [2000, Part 2: 351].

Austin, hailed by critic Edward Wagenknecht as "the foremost sybil of our time" [1952, 230] was among the first in the U.S. to discuss shamanism and "tribal-mindedness" in connection with the practice of poetry and changing the world. Although such themes were passionately pursued by surrealists as early as the 1920s, they were practically unheard of in this country until the '60s.

How many Wobblies read Mary Austin is anybody's guess. Predisposed in favor of Native Americans, whom they tended to regard as the "original communists" as well as present-day allies in the struggle against capitalism, many IWWs were deeply attracted by American Indian culture. This was especially true of the union's large hobo contingent, among whom the spirit of "tribal-mindedness" was by no means uncommon. The fact that Austin's radical conception of poetry was brusquely condemned in the capitalist press would also have signaled to many Wobs that her ideas must have real merit.

At this point in time, however, all we know for sure is that the coincidence between Mary Austin's theory and Wobbly poetic practice is striking and suggestive. Both envisioned the collective creation of a radically new society in which what Austin called the "urge toward communality" and what the IWW called a new human solidarity would replace the alienated, exploitative, corrupt, militaristic, and thoroughly anti-poetic social order based on the dictatorship of Capital.

Both recognized, too, that with the abolition of classes, poetry will truly come into its own. Everyday life and the Marvelous, freedom and enchantment, dream and reality will no longer be regarded as contradictory. Austin's dream of humankind's "reconciliation with the Allness" will be recognized as the flipside of the Wobblies' cry: All for One and One for All!

In such a society, the possibilities of life would be limitless, for as Fellow Worker J. A. MacDonald put it in the *International Socialist Review* in February 1916: "Who can set limits to the possibilities of an awakened working class?" [464]

---

1. At least a few Wobs are known to have been jazz enthusiasts. Gilbert Mers, for one, was an ardent fan of Louis Armstrong. And Slim Brundage regularly featured Big Bill Broonzy and other blues-singers at his College of Complexes.

In the 1910s, playing games like this was one way to learn the ABC's of Marxism.

The Charles H. Kerr Company's popular Socialist Playing Cards
featured Ralph Chaplin's comic drawings and Mary Marcy's
witty anticapitalist rhymes.

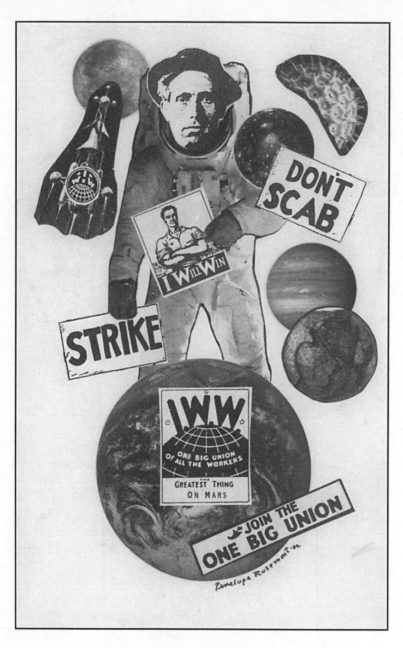

Penelope Rosemont: "Joe Hill Heading Out for Mars"
(collage, 2002)

522

XV
THE IWW COUNTERCULTURE
& VERNACULAR SURREALISM

1. SURREALISM, WOBBLY STYLE

Poetry is the greatest force on Earth.
—**Saint-Pol-Roux**—

W hen André Breton and his friends formed the world's first Surrealist Group in 1920s Paris, they were much less concerned with constituting a new "avant-garde" —and eventually disavowed that military term altogether—than in *recovering* something ancient and (in Western civilization) long lost: the sense of *poetry* as life's *fundamental experience*. This experience or state of mind, which immeasurably exceeds the boundaries of what infatuates of reason and common sense consider the "real," they called *surrealism*. They found evidence of it in the greatest poets—including Shakespeare, Blake, Novalis, Emily Brontë, Hugo, Saint-Pol-Roux, Lautréamont—and in painters from Bosch and Uccello and Dürer to Seurat and Van Gogh and Picasso. Significantly, at a time when most "Marxists" condescendingly disdained "popular culture" as a cesspool of bourgeois propaganda, surrealists also hailed the surrealist evidence in screwball comedies, horror films, animated cartoons, jazz, pulp fiction, and the comics—as well as in the work that later became known as "outsider art." The Surrealist Movement, which early on identified itself with the cause of proletarian revolution—as it has continued to do ever since—has always recognized these manifestations of *vernacular* surrealism as sure signs that the artificial barriers between poetry and the proletariat are being assaulted from both sides [Rosemont 1980].

Among the Wobblies, too, as we have seen, the assault on those barriers was being carried out with remarkable energy. A small but strong undercurrent of vernacular surrealism percolated in the union from the 1910s and continued into the Forties. The IWWs who immersed themselves in those troubled waters did so out of some inner necessity which, alas, they chose not to explicate for our benefit. In this they resemble their more-or-less contemporaries, the great and creative African American blues-singers—Charlie Patton, Peetie Wheatstraw, Memphis Minnie,

523

Robert Johnson, Yank Rachell and others—who, as Paul Garon has shown in his *Blues and the Poetic Spirit* and other writings, also discovered vernacular surrealism on their own, and made use of it for their own purposes.

What is truly impressive is the degree to which Wobblies and blues people, in their various ways and without even knowing it, helped advance the cause of the revolution that surrealists have always dreamed about. Surrealist revolution—the realization of poetry in everyday life—was in fact never conceived as the exclusive project of a small group of poets, but rather as a world-historic process, closely allied to the abolition of wage-slavery, leading to the creation of a non-repressive civilization.

The fact that working people have made significant contributions to what is commonly supposed to be an "avant-garde" movement illuminates one of the many ways in which surrealism differs *qualitatively* from all other currents in the arts. Unlike Futurism, Fauvism, Cubism, Abstract-Expressionism and other transient "schools of art," surrealism has existed as long as humankind. It is emphatically *not* an ideology, and it goes far beyond "art." As an organized movement, surrealism has had many theorists, but surrealism is by no means a theory. Indeed, it is not even an *ism* in the sense of "doctrine or system," but rather in the sense of "condition of being" or "activity or qualities characteristic of"; its linguistic analogues are not Confucianism or Marxism, much less Futurism or Fauvism, but such non-ideological isms as somnambulism and ventriloquism. Historically, however, surrealists have always affirmed their affinities with rebellious currents of thought and action, from Gnosticism and alchemy to romanticism and anarchism: currents that defy narrow definition, and have ways of reappearing when and where they are least expected.

In the IWW, the bold protagonists of revolutionary working-class romanticism raised the *question* of poetry with greater urgency than it had ever been raised before in the labor and radical movements, or, for that matter, has ever been raised since—in the U.S., at any rate. In recognizing the *necessity of poetry* in revolutionary workers' struggle, the IWW also made it a part of daily life. Most of the union's poets, however, in their self-identification with the romantic tradition, were content to take their places as modest followers of that tradition. The impulse behind their poetry—as well as its themes—were audacious and revolutionary, but the results were often hampered by old romantic conventions. A lot of Wob poems are full of annoying and archaic poeticisms: *o'er*, *ye*, *ne'er*, *oft*, *'tis*, and many more. Many of the union's poets freely borrowed meters, rhymes, images, and sometimes whole phrases from the models they most admired. Shelley, Byron, Poe, Swinburne, and even Robert Service were imitated again and again. On the soapbox or at Wob picnics such defects scarcely mattered, but they are hard to miss on the printed page.

Journalist/critic Samuel Putnam's sour contention that the IWW's poets (with the sole exception of his friend Charles Ashleigh) produced nothing but "sentimental and unartistic sloppiness" tells us more about Putnam's own pseudo-aristocratic crankiness than it does about Wobbly poetry [1933, 64]. It is nonetheless true that a lot of verse published in the IWW press was poor stuff—"written by the yard," as Fred Thompson used to say. (Putnam's own effusions, by the way, were no better.) Now and then Wobbly editors pleaded with their fellow worker poets to raise their standards, and above all to cease and desist sending in inferior work.

It is hardly remarkable, however, that many Wobblies wrote bad verse, for many famous poets who are considered among history's finest also wrote bad poems on their bad days. What *is* remarkable is that so many Wobblies wrote poetry at all, and that the poetry they wrote was so widely read and appreciated throughout the union, and even had its effect on the "avant-garde" of the time. Viewed in its own particular context, as the product of a largely immigrant workingclass community consciously struggling to understand an incoherent social order, and to make a social revolution, a lot of Wobbly poetry is powerful and moving, and retains our interest today. Although it rarely attains the heights of Shakespeare, Blake, Shelley, or Bob Kaufman, much of it is surely as good as the work of poets long held in high esteem but now read mostly by antiquarians and other specialists: Longfellow, Whittier, James Russell Lowell. And even the poorest IWW rhymes are stronger and more inspiring than the so-called "popular" bourgeois poetry of the past century, from Edgar Guest to Rod McKuen.

As this enumeration of now-unread authors suggests, tastes and trends in poetry seem to be subject to change without notice. Who knows—perhaps the rappers and hip-hoppers will yet spur a rediscovery of the Wobblies' rebel rhymes from yesteryear.

What makes so much IWW poetry still readable today are, no

buts about it, the unique Wobbly touches: the hobo slang and the IWW's own contributions to it, the emphasis on revolt, wry asides on current events, references to IWW strikes, musings about sabotage, jabs at the boss or Sam Gompers, the contagious spirit of solidarity—a whole kit-bag full of extra- and anti-literary devices.

Such distinctively Wobbly touches are especially abundant in Joe Hill's songs, and probably have contributed appreciably to their continued popularity. Hill was the "IWW poet" not merely because he happened to have a red card, but because so many of his songs seem to epitomize the whole union, and/or made such appealing use of characteristically Wobbly words and phrases. Of his twenty-four labor songs, eleven specifically mention the Industrial Workers of the World, or the IWW, or the One Big Union.

As for surrealism, there is every reason to think that Fellow Worker Hill would have responded to it in much the same spirit as Nelson Algren, who said in 1975: "I don't really know what surrealism is. But I recognize it when I see it, and I like it" [interview 1975, 50]. Hill's sister Ester recalled that, even in his teens, Joel Hägglund was "a dreamer" whose playful and offbeat imagination made him "a special personality among his more realistic brothers and sisters" [Takman 1956, 25]. As the opinion of one who had known him intimately for years, this praise of Hill for his rejection of "realism" is particularly persuasive.

It is a fact that many of Joe Hill's best known songs—"Casey Jones," "Mr Block," "Stung Right," and his raucous paean to sabotage, "Ta-Ra-Ra-Boom-De-Ay"—remind us more of the vaudevillean rowdiness of Jaroslav Hasek's *Good Soldier Svejk* and Tex Avery's *Bad Luck Blackie* than they do of, say, the soberly naturalistic novels of Theodore Dreiser or the films of Sergei Eisenstein. Strictly speaking, these songs may not be "surrealist," but their wacky characters, phantasmagorian slapstick, and no-holds-barred black humor are well beyond the grasp of any sort of "realist" aesthetic, and their incompatibility with such bureaucratic monstrosities as "proletcult" and so-called "socialist realism" is nothing less than absolute. Hill's 1914 appeal in *Solidarity,* that the union pay "a little more attention to . . . original song, and original stunts and pictures," prefigures the chief aim of the Wobblies' revolutionary counterculture: to enable individual workers as well as the working class as a whole to discover their own originality [*Letters*, 17]. To fellow Wobbly poets, songwriters, and artists, Hill's legacy was loud and clear: *humor and imagination all the way!*

"Such stuff as dreams are made of" also turn up in Hill's other writings. One of his three known non-IWW songs, "Come and Take a Ride in My Aeroplane," contains the lines:

> *The man in the moon you will meet face to face,*
> *We'll take a trip to Venus, to Jupiter, and to Mars.*

Some years later, on 30 September 1915, Hill—who expected to go before the firing squad the next day—continued his interplanetary flights of fancy in a letter to Ben H. Williams, editor of *Solidarity*:

> Tomorrow I expect to take a trip to the planet Mars, and if so, will immediately commence to organize the Mars canal workers into the IWW, and we will sing the good old songs so loud that the learned star-gazers on Earth will once and for all get positive proofs that the planet Mars really is inhabited. [*Letters*, 60]

Hill, however—thanks to the agitation of the Joe Hill Defense Committee—received a stay of execution, and his letter to Fellow Worker Williams was published in *Solidarity*. On November 10—nine days before Hill was actually put to death—Fellow Worker C. L. Lambert, secretary of IWW Local 71 in Sacramento, notified Utah Governor Spry that he had

> forwarded credentials to Joseph Hillstrom today, so that he can go to work officially on the mission he has planned as an Organizer of the Canal Construction Workers on the Planet Mars. [Modesto 1963, 6]

Forty-five years later, when "Sputnik" sparked widespread interest in the "space race," Fellow Worker Al Grundstrom told an interviewer that any astronauts who landed on Mars would find "that they were preceded by Wobbly organizer Joe Hill" [*ibid.*]. (Grundstrom also told the interviewer that he had known Hill in San Pedro.)

Hill's Martian IWW organizing fantasy, Fellow Worker Lambert's readiness not only to participate in it, but even to add an element of "reality" to it by sending Martian Canal Construction Workers' Industrial Union organizer's credentials to Hill, and Fellow Worker Grundstrom's reviving the game in the "Space Age" demonstrate that, in the Wobblies, poetic playfulness added a fourth dimension to workingclass solidarity.

At their best, Joe Hill's songs are so enticing, vivid, powerful, funny, idealistic, earthy, on the button, and full of surprises that any attempt to criticize them would seem beside the point: One might just as well criticize "Humpty Dumpty" or "The Old Woman Who Lived in a Shoe." Hill's songs, moreover, prove beyond any shadow of a doubt that his sense of poetry was strong and sure. His "Workers of the World, Awaken!" is one of the most beautiful songs of the U.S. labor movement; his "Last Will"—

> *And let the merry breezes blow*
> *My dust to where some flowers grow.*
> *Perhaps some fading flower then*
> *Would come to life and bloom again*

—is right up there with Blake's *Songs of Innocence.* That Hill did not often ascend to the heights on his poetic quest—that he generally preferred such lighter, down-to-earth, more popular forms as parody, satire, and exhortation, is really nothing against him. In the language of the streets, workplace, and hobo jungle, he penned his horror and hatred of present-day misery, but also his dreams and visions of a marvelous future, and the very simplicity of his words and rhythms make that future seem all the more possible. As Sterling Brown wrote of Robert Burns, Hill gave the world a "poetry which springs from life itself . . . intense, vivid, honest, and singable" [Brown 1956, 64]. Hill was not only a workingclass poet, and an IWW poet, but also a *popular* poet, whose lyrics have been continuously in print, repeatedly recorded, and widely sung in many languages all over the world for nearly a hundred years. What Joe Hill wrote was so admirable, and has endured so well, that it would be absurd to reproach him for not writing something else.

The following five chapters, however, are focused on the minority of IWW poets who, each in his or her distinctive ways, ventured further on poetry's perilous, dark and humid path. For the poets discussed here, the *poetic experience* was clearly higher and deeper and a thousand times more intense than it was and is for the great majority. For them, poetry was neither vocation nor pastime, and much more than a "contribution to the Cause." Rather, it was an *all-absorbing passion*, and in a very real sense embodied the Cause itself. These are the Wobbly poets who—to one degree or another—heard and heeded the *surrealist voice*.

Ralph Chaplin: "The Fungus *Pilobolus*."
(From Raoul Francé. *The Germs of Mind in Plants*.
Chicago: Charles H. Kerr, 1905).

2. RALPH CHAPLIN:
BROTHER OF THE WILD WIND

This morning, all the leaves
are satinlike,
the rain soft and cool,
and the songs of yesterday
come back to haunt us.
—Francis Vielé-Griffin—

R alph Chaplin's associations with surrealism were infinitesimal and fleeting, but the magnitude of his role in the development of Wobbly poetics more than justify a brief examination of his work in a surrealist light. No other IWW poet, with the possible exception of Arturo Giovannitti, enjoyed greater prestige as a lyric poet, not only within the IWW but also outside it, especially in the "poetry world," and even among critics.

Chaplin was also a leading Wobbly songwriter, pamphleteer, artist, cartoonist, letterer, cover-designer, organizer, editor, soapboxer, and platform speaker. He illustrated the Charles H. Kerr Company's colorful deck of "Socialist Playing Cards," for which Mary Marcy wrote humorous couplets; drew posters for the Mexican Revolution; and designed most of the union's early "stickerettes" (a.k.a. "silent agitators"). Millions of these small stickers printed on gummed stock, featuring slogans provided by Bill Haywood, were posted on windows, fences, boxcars, factory walls, lamp-posts, farm equipment and countless other surfaces where wage-slaves would be sure to see them.

Fellow Worker Chaplin was, in short, a veritable Wobbly "Renaissance Man," but in the 1910s and '20s he was celebrated above all as a poet.

Long before Joe Hill ran afoul of Utah "law'n'order," Chaplin regarded the Wobbly bard as hero, idol, and role-model, even though his own poems embodied a lyricism that his hero seems never to have attempted. He was Hill's first biographer, the author of two of the best known poems dedicated to Hill and several articles about him, and he also devoted a full chapter of his auto-biography to Hill. With the exception of Fred Thompson, no individual Wobbly wrote more about Hill, and it seems fair to conclude that few Wobs were more influenced by Hill. As a songwriter, moreover, Chaplin was—at least prior to the advent of T-Bone Slim around 1920—perhaps the second most popular in the union, not only for his "Solidarity Forever," but also for "Paint 'er Red," "The Commonwealth of Toil," "The Sabo-Tabby Kitten"(a sabotage ballad),"All Hell Can't Stop Us!," "Up From Your Knees," "Hey! Polly" (an attack on politicians), and his "May Day Song," set to music by Rudolph von Liebich.

Chaplin's reputation as a lyric poet depended on two early books: *When the Leaves Come Out* (1914) and *Bars and Shadows* (1922). According to Mary Marcy, the title-poem of the first collection was by far the most popular poem ever to appear in the *International Socialist Review*, and the privately printed book brought Chaplin instant recognition. Praise for his second volume —his prison poems, with an introduction by Scott Nearing—was even greater, and made him something of a celebrity, not only throughout the labor movement, but also in intellectual circles. It is for these poems written in Cook County Jail and Leavenworth Penitentiary—the unforgettable "Mourn Not the Dead," "The Bars

Say No!" and a few others—that Chaplin is generally remembered as a poet today.

It so happens that Chaplin also wrote some very different poems, and collected some of them in another volume, *Somewhat Barbaric*, published in Seattle in 1944. In "Snowfall in Xanadu," "Rebuilding Atlantis," several of the poems in "Lilac Interlude" and in the concluding section, "Altar to Chaos," Chaplin's revolutionary workingclass romantic imagination soared beyond his usual themes, and lighted in wonderlands of magic and myth. One of the best of his prison poems, "The Warrior Wind," foreshadowed the dense imagery, largely drawn from the natural world, of these remarkable "other" poems:

> *The wind alone, of all the gods of old,*
> *Men could not chain.*
> *O wild wind, brother to my wrath and pain,*
> *Like you, within a restless heart I hold*
> *A hurricane.*

It is in the unreprinted and never-cited "other" poems of *Some-what Barbaric* that the faint gleams of Fellow Worker Chaplin's surrealism quietly appear, sometimes so subtly as to seem almost "between the lines," as in this whispered declaration of love:

> *You are the song the summer thrush is singing. . . .*
> *You are the trillium open for an hour*

or this bold chant on the same theme:

> *Love is fierce and unashamed,*
> *Love has never yet been tamed. . . .*
> *Love is such a lawless thing.*
> *Love is like a hawk's gray wing*

or this five-word picture of a daisy:

> *Part snowflake and part flame*

or this, from "Rosa Mystica":

> *. . . unseen except to lovers dreaming. . . .*
> *The flower that shrinks from everything save silence*

or this gnomic verse in the guise of a nursery rhyme:

Where the color comes from,
Where the color goes,
Wisdom never figured out;
Only music knows!
          ["Red Poppy"]

It is not by accident that most of these poems were inspired by flowers, for after his release as a class-war prisoner from Leavenworth Penitentiary, Fellow Worker Chaplin became an ardent flower gardener. In the 1920s, with his friend and neighbor E. J. Costello, director of the Federated Press (a labor news service) and active in the IWW's General Defense Committee, Chaplin organized a huge lilac festival in the Chicago suburb of Lombard, where he lived for many years. Complete with giant Maypole and dancing in the streets, the festival, attended by over twenty thousand out-of-town visitors, was a grand success, and became an annual event. To this day the Lombard Lilac Festival, initiated by the author of "Solidarity Forever" and "Paint 'er Red," is one of the biggest and most popular "happenings" in the Windy City's western suburbs [Chaplin 1948, 363].

Chaplin's flower poems, radiant with a kind of *hermetic transparence*, are not, of course, "class war" poems. However, as celebrations of natural harmony—the harmony of the parts and the whole—and of the mutual aid of Nature and humankind, they are truly poems of solidarity and freedom. I find in them something of the sparkle and warmth of the poetry by Chaplin's contemporary, the American-born and anarchist-inclined French Symbolist poet, Francis Vielé-Griffin, whose work was so deeply admired by André Breton.

Such "surrealist" passages, however, are all too rare in Chaplin's work. The "sturdy Wobbly poet," as Carl Sandburg called him [Mitgang 1968, 510], was too conscious of literary "craft" to really let himself go, and yet too much of a poet to let himself be completely tied up in tradition. Sometimes, under the conflicting pressure of his few certainties and many doubts, poetry erupted. In his best moments, and in spite of himself, Chaplin was almost surrealist—or, more accurately, almost a *pre*surrealist. Alas, they were only moments!

3. ARTURO GIOVANNITTI:
AGAINST SILENCE, DEATH & FEAR

The impossible is easy to reach
Who knows the way out of the labyrinth
These are not rhetorical questions
—Philip Lamantia—

Helen Keller, in her introduction to Arturo Giovannitti's first book of poems, *Arrows in the Gale* (1914), called him "a better poet than has come out of the privileged classes of America in our day," and also pointed out that he was "a poet quite unlike any other" [137, 136].[1] She went on, however, to liken his poetry to that of Virgil, Dante, Shakespeare, Shelley, and the prophecies of Isaiah. The truth is, Giovannitti had far stronger affinities with such modern poets as Guillaume Apollinaire, Vladimir Mayakovsky, and Federico Garcia Lorca, although he differed from them as much as they differed from each other.

Whether Giovannitti ever pronounced himself on the matter of his particular poetic inspirations I do not know, but it is beyond question that poetry—or poesy, as he liked to call it—was central to his life. In his "Credo" he saluted the "foremost of the Seven Sisters, Poesy, first cry and last breath, laughter and rattle, mistress and teacher of all human ecstasies" [86]. It is obvious that he read hugely and voraciously, and that he helped himself freely from an incredible array of sources. A characteristic Giovannitti "line," which often runs to ten or fifteen lines, is an amazing wizard's brew of the most disparate poetic ingredients: a dash of Walt Whitman, echoes of "The Ode to the West Wind," thick slices of the Old Testament, hints of fairy tales, snippets of soapbox oratory, Elizabethan dramatic "asides," fragments of conversation, ancient myths, and vaudevillean one-liners. And of course this elegant and magical mix is seasoned and stirred with the poet's own very special and supremely romantic fervor along with an equally unique and all-encompassing humor.

In nine words, Giovannitti is a staggeringly unconventional poet who defies classification.

To defy classification, however, is already to veer close to surrealism. And of the American poets of his generation who practiced surrealism without knowing it, very few—perhaps only Samuel Greenberg, Mina Loy, and T-Bone Slim—practiced it with greater zeal than Giovannitti. If Ralph Chaplin can be said to have *touched* surrealism with a ten-foot pole that he might have borrowed from Francis Vielé-Griffin, then—by way of contrast—we could say that Giovannitti went *swimming* in it, and deep-sea diving, and we could add that he made many friends among the myriad wondrous creatures that he met in its depths. Giovannitti's relation to surrealism in the U.S. can in fact be stated with some precision, for it is fully comparable to the relation of such vertiginously against-the-current figures as Petrus Borel, Xavier Forneret, and Villiers de l'Isle-Adam to surrealism in France: that is, he is not simply an "influence," or even a "formative" influence, but rather a *guiding example*, and a *moral force*. The only contemporary U.S. poets I know who have persistently championed Giovannitti's genius, and openly declare themselves his fervent admirers, have long been active participants in the Surrealist Movement: Philip Lamantia and Joseph Jablonski.

Giovannitti's poetry is invariably disquieting, weird, passionate, clairvoyant, and bristling with paradox, and at times can also be nightmarish, carnivalesque, hysterical, erotic, feverish, lugubrious, bittersweet, delirious, ferocious, and magnificently *dry*. Not infrequently, a poem only three or four pages long will encompass many moods. "Spring at the Bronx Zoo" opens with a calm, reflective description of the flowers ("the self-made narcissus and the business-like dandelion") and fledglings ("tawny ducklings and cignets scratch through the silt of the pond") of an April morning at the zoo. A little later in the poem, growing nostalgic about "this last sanctuary of the lost world of my childhood," he parenthetically poses questions that remind us of Lewis Carroll:

Are there left any worlds outside of children's books and young
    love,
And when shall we ever be wise if animals no longer speak?

But then, arriving at "the cage of the big birds"—the raptors, "starsighted, cruel, admired and unloved"—he brusquely shifts into a black humor worthy of Sade's *120 Days of Sodom*, as he wishes he could feed these birds of prey

. . . the brains of our politicians,
The dried kidneys of our patricians,
And the cowardly tongues of my senseless remorses. [11]

His use of ordinary speech and clichés is often jarring. Here he is describing a group of old men entering a room:

*They came in from nowhere, like the thunder, like death, like the
presentiment of a senseless joy, like the wild urge to sing. . . . [82]*

Each phrase beginning with *like* is unimpressive by itself, but their
cumulative effect is disturbingly eerie.

Many IWW poets, echoing the first word of the "Internationale," have made good use of the verb "Arise!" None, however,
have done so with greater power than Giovannitti in "When the
Cock Crows" (dedicated "To the memory of Frank Little, hanged
at Midnight"):

Arise, and against every hand jeweled with the rubies of murder,
Against every mouth that sneers at the tears of mercy,
Against every foul smell of the earth,
Against every hand that a footstool raised over your head,
Against every word that was written before this was said,
Against every happiness that never knew sorrow,
And every glory that never knew love and sweat,
Against silence and death, and fear,
Arise with a mighty roar!
Arise and declare your war. [28-29]

In this same poem, dedicated to one of the great IWW martyrs,
Giovannitti also salutes another:

*you, Joe Hill, twice my germane in the rage of the song and the
    fray*

Giovannitti's hammer-wielding irony and his tornado-like
laughter are always unsparing, and their violence is often apoca-
lyptic. "The Day of War," "The Nuptials of Death," and "The
Cage" are among the most harrowing poems in the English
language. Even poems much "lighter" in tone—such as "To the
English Language"—are fundamentally *unsettling*:

. . . You and I are enemies, but we have a habit of truces
And often feast and get drunk together, at the same table
*   with the flesh of the same quarry from the gourd*
*   of the same song.*

Like two rival hunters after the chase. [110]

All of his poems glisten with audacity, risk and even reckless-
ness—a sense of *life* as an adventure on the outermost limits of the

unexpected and the impossible. For Arturo Giovannitti, everything
that happens in the world is a question, and poetry is the surest way
of finding the answer. In "The Closed Window," for example, he
passes a shuttered room "near Grant's tomb," and wonders

What does it mourn in the dark . . . ?
An old love, an old faith, an old dread of the great towers
*   that chime. . . .*
What is hid there? . . .
Unheeded love letters, blood-tainted records of glories
*   or crimes. . . .*
Or belated inventions, ruins of deeds unaccomplished,
Poems that were never read, writs of great wisdoms
*   demolished*
By the sudden surge of new fads?
Perhaps the cult of a failure, perhaps a masterpiece,
A misery that dreads the light, a triumph that woos the
*   peace*
Of an ever even twilight.

Whatever there is in that room, I would love to sleep
*   there tonight.* [114]

---

1. Page numbers refer to *The Complete Poems of Arturo Giovannitti.*

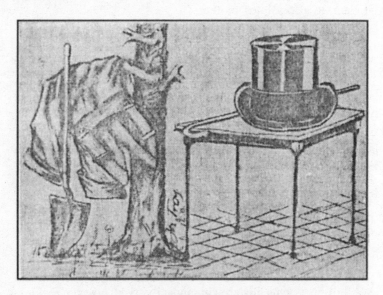

Joe Troy: "Between These Two Classes a Struggle
Must Go On" (*Industrial Worker*, 1940s)

4. LAURA TANNE:
RUNNING ON SWIFT FEET
OUT OF THE DARKNESS

The war against the imagination is the only war that matters.
—Diane di Prima—

Laura Tanne was a gloriously original presence in IWW poetry, and by any standard qualifies as one of the union's finest creative voices. Her wild, wondrous, spellbinding imagery and her blisteringly bitter proletarian black humor distinguish her from all other American poets of her time—in or out of the One Big Union.

Sadly, nothing seems to be known about this truly extraordinary poet. Compared to Laura Tanne, the biographical data on Joe Hill is immense. I have not found her name in any of the books on the IWW, or in Wobbly memoirs. None of the old-timers I have interviewed or corresponded with remembered her at all. A query of mine about Tanne in the *Industrial Worker* years ago elicited no response. In view of the consistently high quality of her poetry, the wall of silence around her seems as outrageous as it is inexplicable.

Fred Thompson provided the only small clue. Although he never met her, the name seemed to ring a vague bell and he was fairly sure she was Finnish. Inasmuch as Finns were one of the largest ethnic groups in the IWW this "hunch" did not prove to be a big help, but it's a start. An exhaustive search of the Finnish-language IWW periodicals may yet turn up something on Laura Tanne, and if any readers of this book wish to undertake such a task I hope they will let me know about it.

Meanwhile, apart from her poems, what is known about Laura Tanne stands just about at zero. Arturo Giovannitti's reputation as a Wobbly was extensive and long-lasting, despite the fact that his actual membership in the union was comparatively brief. In Tanne's case, it cannot be said with absolute certainty that she was *ever* a member, though she probably was. In one of her poems she refers to "our *men*—Wobblies," and in another, she alludes to Joe Hill's best-loved song, invoking the "incorrigible masses" who

*. . . scoff at queens
in democratic jeans
For they've lost all fears*

of gods and peers
With heads held high
They want their pie
on Earth. . . .

Whether she joined or not, however, is of little importance. Many participants in the IWW were non-members—either because they were retirees, or immigrants worried about deportation, or wives and mothers with kids to care for, or because they derived their income from small businesses, or for other reasons. If the history of the IWW was limited to the achievements of members whose dues were paid up, the books on the subject would be much thinner.

Tanne, in any event, participated actively in the IWW culture through her poetry. Between 1924 and 1927 she published twenty-three poems in the IWW magazine *Industrial Pioneer*, and there may well be others in the pages of *Industrial Solidarity* and the *Industrial Worker*. In 1930 she also published poems and a short story in W. E. B. Du Bois's magazine, *The Crisis*. She does not appear to have published any books, or even to have been represented in any of the "left" anthologies.

Fortunately, IWW editors were far-sighted enough to publish her poetry. The day will come when people will say: "Those Wobblies knew more about poetry than we thought—after all, they were the first to publish Laura Tanne!"

In the creation of scandalous, eye-opening, *surrealist* images, Tanne surpassed all other IWW poets. Indeed, she had very little competition in this regard, in or outside the IWW. Compared to her, in the matter of imagery, most of America's "avant-garde" poetry in those years seems tame. Admirably free of literary "posing," her improbable adjectives and unexpected verbs injected flashes of lightning into ordinary speech. Often the result is a simple, irresistible beauty, as when she lets us see

moonrays scrawl across the sky
   ("Vigil")

or describes a waitress:

I saw a shower
Of blossoms fall
From her orchard

Of smiles
   ("Economics")

During a strike in the Northwest woods, we suddenly run into

a wall of knitted wind and ice
   ("Strike")

Elsewhere she shows us

steel towns
 which have no sun-yellow handkerchief
for the wind to blow into
   ("Gary Rides Swiftly")

   Still other images reveal Tanne's highflying humor, as when she pictures

[a] factory where sausages form a skyline of profit
   ("Version")

or informs us that

A bundle of wind will blow God's underwear
All over the blue grass
   ("The Loot")

   A third of her poems are devoted to the theme of "women's work." Characteristically, Tanne's marvelous mix of feminism, black humor, and the Wobbly "point of production" perspective had explosive results. These poems are not merely devoid of sentimentality, they are studies in the grotesque, and absolutely merciless. Here are the opening lines of "Waitress":

It's funny—
I can't seem to remember anything
Except 50-cent checks and customers
Who give a smile
On the silver plattie of their belly-full good nature.
I can't seem to remember anything
Except omelettes and torrents of sweat and dishwashers

And a few lines from "Restaurant":

The rats scurry over the dishes.
The cockroaches play tag in the bread jar.
Nice designs of grime embroider the greasy soup.
And inside the liquid
Scraps of meat and potatoes float questioningly:
"Why did that chemist commit suicide?"

Tanne refuses, however, to give in to despair. Even in the smallest actions of workers in the poorest jobs she was able to perceive a new society taking shape. In a poem titled "?" she tells of shop girls

. . . running to the movies. . . .
Giggling, gaudy, gum-chewing, rouge-lipped. . . .
sending thought-webs
of kisses in the dark for the cinema hero. . . .

but later in the same poem, she shows us how these same shop-girls

With sleepy pale lights in their night-before eyes,
With lingering patches of powder-snow on their cheeks,
. . . seriously calculate chances of winning
A fight against a 10 per cent cut in wages

"Boss," Tanne's best, bitterest, and blackest poem—and a triumph of Wobbly surrealist feminism—is not only a poem of woman's work, but also of revenge. Here it is in its entirety:

He is a decaying pumpkin in a rosy field.
Of redwood is the elegant office
And round and yellow his senile head.
Prim and straight I sit taking dictation.
My hair lies in dark, peaceful folds,
My fingernails cut in pink foreignness
*   to grime.*
"Yes, sir." "No, sir." inhabit my speech.
But yet I am one of the masses
A black vicious beetle
Which will someday inject
The black cancer of class war

Into the rosy field of the office
To suck and destroy the essence of
  decrepit pumpkins.

Part of the impact of "Boss" lies in the juxtaposition of the "He" and the "I." A couple of other first-person allusions in her poems tell us a little something about Laura Tanne herself. Until some lucky and/or diligent researcher discovers more information about her, these modest snippets are the closest thing we have to a self-portrait:

My thoughts are smoky and grimy,
They are garbed in red and black;
They speak blasphemy and feel a strange, fine hate.
  ("Growth")

I too have become an Incorrigible—
A vagabond-thief of yellow mornings
Running on swift feet out of the darkness
  ("Vagabonds")

Walt Whitman, in the 1855 preface to his *Leaves of Grass*, called for poems "to cheer up slaves and horrify despots." Alas, such poems are still needed today by the wage-slaves of the world. As Laura Tanne herself put it in "Two Who Ride Forward":

Little red sprigs of hope
Spring from their words.

"Silent Agitator"

A sketch of Covington Hall by B. W. Lauderdale (1915)

SONGS OF LOVE AND REBELLION
By COVINGTON HALL

Being a collection of his finest Revolutionary, Love and Miscellaneous Poems. Paper. 50c a volume. Special discounts to Locals, Speakers, News Agents in lot orders,

Address COVINGTON HALL, 520 Poydras Street, New Orleans, La.

An advertisement in the *International Socialist Review.*

5. COVINGTON HALL:
VISIONING THE UNSEEN FROM THE SEEN

One must desire to dream and know how to dream.
—Charles Baudelaire—

Clarence John Laughlin, the great New Orleans photographer often identified himself as an *extreme romantic*, but he also enjoyed pointing out how in certain cases (his own, for example) extreme romanticism tended to evolve into surrealism, or at least into something "very close" to surrealism. Laughlin's townsman and contemporary, the IWW poet Covington Hall, is another fascinating example of this evolution.

Even by Wobbly standards Covington Hall was a certifiable eccentric. He was an anarchist (of sorts) who found much to admire in Lenin; a vigorous opponent of white supremacy who was also something of a Southern nationalist; a Bible-reading atheist whose insatiable curiosity led him to study ancient mythology, Confucianism, Buddhism, and a variety of "Christian" heresies. His close friend Oscar Ameringer, the "Mark Twain of American Socialism," once described him as "the best-dressed, handsomest young man" in early twentieth-century New Orleans. That Hall was a Dandy should not surprise us, for Dandyism was one of the "excesses" of Romanticism, and Covington Hall more than any other Wobbly embodied the whole gamut of Romantic excess. His passion for dreams and dreaming was boundless, his interest in madness serious and sympathetic, and he was very much at home in the visionary world. His proletarian credentials were impeccable, but his obsession with Vision—that is, with being a *seer*— and his related interest in developing the possibilities of the "mad" fairy tale situate him closer to the German romantic Novalis and the surrealist Leonora Carrington than to any "proletarian" writer of the Mike Gold type. In an *Industrial Worker* article titled "Where No Vision Is, The People Perish," Hall argued that

> All revolutions have and must center around some great ideal, some sublime, heart-stirring conception of the"world as it ought to be," and . . . the American working class will not accomplish anything so long as it cannot dream higher than the Socialist Party's ideal of "ten dollars a day for four hours a day." [Winters 1985, 77]

Fellow Worker Hall, moreover, openly admired the "primitive" and disdained the bourgeois ideology of "Progress." Few Wobs were more strident in their ridicule and rejection of the hypocritical mores of "Western Civilization." For Hall, poetry and social transformation were one and indivisible; his lifelong revolutionary labor activism reflected an untiring devotion to what David Roediger has called Hall's "Luciferian spirit of rebellion" [Hall 1985, 11].

Even Hall's IWWism was eccentric and excessive. From its very first day the union was adamantly restricted to *wage-earners only*. Hall, however—like Agnes Thecla Fair, E. F. Doree, and a few others—fought long and hard (and unsuccessfully) to open the ranks to poor farmers and sharecroppers. At once a Marxist (of sorts) and an ardent "decentralist," at least for a time he advocated armed struggle and considered himself far to the left of Vincent St John and Bill Haywood.

Hall's many-faceted career—as IWW poet, organizer, speaker, publicist, editor, educator, humorist, and historian—has attracted considerable scholarly attention in recent decades. Most of this literature has focused on Hall's anti-racism, and more particularly on his crucial role in developing the IWW's integrated industrial unionism among waterfront workers in New Orleans and timber workers in Louisiana and East Texas. Hall's own *Labor Struggles in the Deep South*, published by Charles H. Kerr in 1999 with an introduction and notes by Roediger, is an unusual combination of personal memoir and straight narrative history, and one of the most informative accounts of the IWW's efforts to build workers' solidarity across racial lines.

More than most Wobblies, Hall was also active in other organizations, and their diversity is impressive. He was a publicist for the farmers' Non-Partisan League in North Dakota; taught at the socialist Commonwealth College in Arkansas as well as at the IWW's Work People's College in Minnesota; lectured at the Stelton, New Jersey, anarchist forum; lived for a time at the New Llano Cooperative utopian community in Louisiana; and was a revered friend and mentor of H. L. Mitchell and other members of the Southern Tenant Farmers' Union [FR interview with Mitchell, 1988].

Above all, however, Covington Hall—also known as Covami, Covy, Uncle Covami, and Covington Ami—considered himself a poet. He published four books of his poems between 1915 and 1946, and *hundreds* of other poems appeared in the IWW press, the

International Socialist Review, and other publications.

The very title of the journal Hall edited in 1915-16—*Rebellion: Made Up of Dreams and Dynamite*—conveys a sense of this flamboyant poet-agitator's devil-may-care sense of humor, as well as his determination to pursue, no matter what, the dialectical resolution of the existing social order's most paralyzing contradictions. Hall's *Rebellion*, a free-wheeling concoction of poetry, industrial unionism, revolutionary criticism, romantic insolence, and all manner of miscellaneous subversion, is one of the most passionately *personal* periodicals in the history of U.S. radicalism.

Hall took the view that the unity of revery and revolt, and of poetry and direct action, are fundamentally inseparable from the unity of theory and practice. An unequivocal champion of individual and class revolt and social revolution, he was no less unstinting in his support for the revolution of the mind and spirit.

David Roediger, who is not only the most indefatigable reinterpreter of Hall's life and work, but also the most insightful, has illuminated the interconnectedness of the various elements in Hall's polymorphous dialectic. In his introduction to Hall's *Dreams & Dynamite: Selected Poems*, published in the Charles H. Kerr "Poets of Revolt Series" in 1985, he emphasizes Hall's "profound appreciation for the wisdom and artistry of 'primitive' peoples," and argues that his poetic

> explosion of the distinction between the developed and the undeveloped, the 'civilized' and the 'uncivilized,' doubtless contributed to his further musings on the line between sanity and insanity as well as the distinctions between fantasy and reality and between heaven and hell. [9]

Hall recognized dreaming, by day and by night, as an important and radical *activity*. That grand watchword of the Greek surrealist poet Nicolas Calas—"The dream, too, must have its Bastille Day!" —sums up a good part of Hall's politics. Indeed, he seems to have felt most at home "when the real is in eclipse" [Hall 1946, 105]—that is, "in the magic realm of Dreamland" [*ibid.*, 97]. His confidence in the capacity of the workers of the world to "dream this planet once more Paradise" was total [*ibid.*, 100]. Hall was so convinced of the revolutionary urgency of dreams that he insisted on sharing his awareness with his fellow workers throughout the land. And so we find the former editor of *Rebellion* defending his heterodox views on the subject *theoretically and polemically* in the IWW press. His "In Defense of Dreaming," published in *Industrial Solidarity* in 1925, is almost a manifesto:

> In their secret heart of hearts all men and women are always dreaming, are always visioning things that are not but should be, and this we must do or perish. . . . It is out of this faculty, out of this power to dream, to imagine beyond things as they are . . . that man has developed the power to overcome adverse environments and has created the thoughts that brought a sense of the good, the beautiful and true into our lives, and from whence has arisen all we have of culture. . . .
>
> The "practical" man is ever the worshiper of "business as usual," undesirous of change, a friend of priesthoods and an enemy of prophets. . . . Not until [people] begin to dream of better bread and higher liberty do they become "dangerous citizens" and a hopeful sign. . . .
>
> It was by this very . . . power to dream, to think beyond the known to the unknown, to vision the unseen from the seen, that were born the sciences, . . . music and poetry, sculpture and painting and architecture. . . . It was all but a dream once. . . . All of our achievements were but dreams once, and many things that are dreams today will be realities tomorrow. . . .
>
> Man dreams, and he does not dream in vain. [1999, 224-226]

Hall's defense is broad enough to encompass "dreaming" in the most expansive sense of the word—from Blake's "What is now proved was once only imagin'd" to Martin Luther King's "I have a dream"—but the solid core of his argument remains the *oneiric faculty* itself: the vital psychological *and physical* need of human beings to dream. At the same time, as Eugene Debs perceived, Hall's poetry blazed with a "marvelous awakening power," for his dream-drenched lyrics are also, of course, incitements to action.

The practice of poetry, for Hall, meant nothing less than under-standing what the hermetists called "the language of birds," and the ability, as he phrased it, "to hear the heart of things" [1915, 42]. In a world dominated by the deadening prose of business and misery, poetry was his favorite way of dreaming while awake. He read and adored the poets: the Elizabethans, the pre-Romantics, Blake, Burns, Wordsworth, Coleridge, Shelley, Byron, Keats, Swinburne, William Morris, the Pre-Raphaelites—and surely dozens more. He may have read and adored too much, for he obviously had trouble freeing himself of the immense burden of his predecessors' influence. For all his excesses, Covington Hall strangely remained the prisoner of conventional Victorian verse-forms. He may have felt, as doubtless other IWW poets felt, that metrical forms good enough for the greatest poets of all time were good enough for him. The sad fact is that all but a handful of his many poems suffer from musty, jingle-jangle meters, an embarrassingly derivative imagery, and tired, overworked rhymes. His occasional attempts at free verse tend to be ponderous and prosaic. According to Fred Thompson, who knew him well, Hall himself conceded that most of his poems were "doggerel designed to put a point across" [Stodder, *op cit.*, 6].

This was of course a problem shared by many Wob poets. One of the hazards of being a poet *and* a proletarian *and* a union organizer *and* a revolutionist—all at the same time—is that one's poems tend to be written in fugitive moments and in conditions that at the very least can be called challenging. When we realize that Hall's poems had to be dashed off in those all-too-rare minutes in which he wasn't organizing, soapboxing, taking part in a strike, fleeing company gunmen, writing leaflets and editorials, answering urgent letters from IWW headquarters, or struggling to "make a living," the wonder is *not* that many of his poems aren't very good, but that *some* of them are so very fine.

The exceptions, in any case, though few in number, suffice to assure Hall a high place among the best of the Wobbly poets. In these vivid, energetic poems—especially "Us the Hoboes and Dreamers" and "The Madman's Boast," but also "The Strike," ""A Fair Trial'" (on the execution of Joe Hill), "A Hymn to Hate," "All Night Long," the poems to Lucifer, and a few others—the imaginative substance is so alluring and unrestrained that it triumphs over the sing-song meters.

"Us the Hoboes and Dreamers" is Hall's greatest hymn to Revolt and Revolution. I do not know whether Hall ever read Lautréamont, but the Uruguayan-born French poet's great battle-cry, "Poetry must be made by all!" seems to me to be as present in this poem as the "Internationale" and the IWW Preamble. "Us the Hoboes and Dreamers" is a lyric of sweeping negation that is also an impassioned affirmation of Freedom and the Marvelous—very much in the spirit of Bakunin's famous observation that "the urge to destroy is also a creative urge." Although the poem does not appear to have been set to music, it is hard to imagine a better marching song for an aroused Southern working class:

*We shall laugh to scorn your power that now holds the South in
    awe,*
We shall trample on your customs and shall spit upon your law;
*We shall come up from our shanties to your burdened banquet
    hall—*
We shall turn your wine to wormwood, your honey into gall.

*We shall batter down your prisons, we shall set your chain-gangs
    free,*
*We shall drive you from the mountainside, the valley, plain and
    sea.*

*We shall outrage all your temples, we shall blaspheme all your
    gods—*
We shall turn your Slavepen over as the plowman turns the clods!

In his introduction to *Dreams and Dynamite*, Roediger points out
that this song

is written in the future tense, emphasizing the fact that, in his finest
works, Hall's commitment to revolt embraced an imaginative conception not only of the past but also of what *shall be*. [Hall 1985,
-11]

"The Madman's Boast" is a cry of anguish but also of defiance.
Like Hall's Swiftian "Factful Fables"—short, world-turned-upside-
down fairy tales of capitalism's limitless follies—"The Madman's
Boast" is an acrid laugh at the bourgeois notion of the "rational"
even as it celebrates the broad creative possibilities of "irrational"
knowledge:

*What know you of madness, you whose minds have never gone
    astray,*
You whose souls have never ventured 'yond their barriers of clay?
You who know no other kingdom save this profit-wasted earth,
Where you fear the fevered thinking that great ideas bring to birth!

I who walk this floor of diamonds, with my head among the stars,
*While you dream your keepers hold me chained behind your
    prison bars!*
I who hear immortal music, soft, strange rhapsodies divine,
*Played for me by master demons when the moons of madness
    shine!*

I who dwell with Love and Laughter, who the face of Joy behold,
And who never yet have worshiped at the cloven feet of Gold! . . .

You! 'tis you who are the madman! You whose eyes are on the
ground,
Kneeling with Ahriman's angels, with the gyves of custom bound!
You who never knew the ecstasy and never felt the pain
Of the souls who roam the empire of the man you call insane.
[1999, 238-239]

These high-intensity poems, which to my eye show every sign of having been written at white-hot speed in veritable "fits" of inspiration—or a state of trance—are far and away the best he ever wrote, and surely, along with his dream-manifesto, constitute his strongest *surrealist evidence*. More particularly, these two poems offer us precious glimpses of what Hall proclaimed, in a poem dedicated to Oscar Ameringer, the "Republic of Imagination": a free society in which dream and reason, subjective and objective, work and play are no longer perceived as opposites. The concept corresponds closely to what Hall's older French contemporary, Saint-Pol-Roux—a poet regarded by André Breton and his surrealist comrades as their only living precursor—designated *The Repoetic*. This was a poet's radical response to Plato's authoritarian *Republic*. In the ancient Greek philosopher's projected state, all poets are banned; in *The Repoetic*, however, *all* are poets!

Thousands of miles apart but almost simultaneously, two very different poets and utopian dreamers shared a vision of the new society that each in his own way was helping to form in the shell of the old. In this regard, I think both would agree with Clarence John Laughlin that "the quality of the human imagination" is always what matters most.

Bumper-sticker, 1990

Mike Konopacki: T-Bone Slim postcard (1992)

7. T-BONE SLIM:
BRINGING THE SUBLIME & THE RIDICULOUS
INTO A COMPROMISING PROXIMITY

Whoever has the Key of our Art can unlock all gates.
—Eiranaeus Philalethes—

The most surrealist Wobbly of them all, beyond question, was the footloose rebel genius who called himself T-Bone Slim. Ralph Chaplin had a few surrealist moments; Giovannitti, Tanne, and Hall had many more—but T-Bone Slim was the living, breathing personification of *surrealism itself* [Rosemont 1992].[1] When someone gets around to recording the history of vernacular surrealism in the U.S.A., few writers will loom larger in its pages than this inspired hobo poet and specialist in revolt.

T-Bone Slim was also a major contributor to the development of the IWW's revolutionary counterculture. His songs, poetry, humor, ideas, and "attitude" did much to shape the One Big Union's second generation, from the late 1910s through the Great Depression to the start of World War II. Many brilliant and colorful Wobs broadened, deepened, or otherwise enhanced the union's already far-reaching perspectives in those years, but it is hard to think of any individual whose overall and enduring impact was greater than his.

Almost nothing is known of his background or "personal life." In this as in much else he resembles Joe Hill. In fact, no other Wobbly writer seems to me to have more affinities with Hill than T-Bone Slim. Both, for example, were Scandinavian. T-Bone was of Finnish descent, born in the early 1880s in the large Finnish community in Ashtabula, Ohio. His "real" name was Matt Valentine Huhta, but he never seems to have used it as a writer, and very few Wobs knew that Matt Huhta was T-Bone Slim. According to a letter from his sister Ida in the files of the New York City Medical Examiner's Office, T-Bone also used the name Joseph Hilgor.

Like Hill, too, T-Bone was "a dyed-in-the-wool hobo"—as Chicago Wob old-timer Charlie Velsek put it—whose "songs in the IWW Song Book pretty much describe his life style." Exactly when he lined up in the IWW is not known, but his red card had the number 198308. He worked in construction, in the harvest fields, as lumber camp cook—Guy B. Askew said he made "the finest and tastiest Swedish hotcakes of any chef in the U.S.A." And "when he wasn't working on some job," Askew added, "he was a damn good bum on the Main Stem. . . ." In his later years T-Bone was a barge-captain on the Hudson River in New York. A "doubleheader" or "two-card" Wobbly, he was a member not only of the IWW but also of the AFL-affiliated Barge Captains' Union.

Also like Hill, to quote Askew once more, T-Bone was "strictly rank and file." Neither organizer nor soapboxer, he does not appear to have attended any IWW conventions, and did his best to avoid the limelight. In what could pass verbatim for a recollection of Hill by one of his friends, Sam Dolgoff recalled T-Bone as "a modest, quiet guy" who "spoke very little, and never about himself."

As one of the foremost "workingclass writers of his time," as his *Industrial Worker* obituary phrased it in 1942, T-Bone Slim enjoyed a renown that reached far beyond the ranks of the IWW. For twenty years his column was the most popular feature in the union's weekly. He wrote two IWW pamphlets, collaborated extensively on the Wobbly magazines, and was second only to Joe Hill as the union's best-loved songwriter. To this day several of his boisterous hobo lyrics—"The Popular Wobbly," "Mysteries of a Hobo's Life," and "I'm Too Old to Be a Scab"—are among the most frequently sung of all Wobbly songs. For years, just about every 'bo in America knew "The Popular Wobbly" by heart:

> Oh the "bull" he went wild over me,
> And he held his gun where everyone could see.
> He was breathing rather hard when he saw my union
>   card—
> He went wild, simply wild over me. . . .

> Oh the jailer went wild over me
> And he locked me up and threw away the key.
> It seems to be the rage so they keep me in a cage.
> They go wild, simply wild over me.

> They go wild, simply wild over me—
> I'm referring to the bed-bug and the flea.
> They disturb my slumber deep and I murmur in my
>   sleep,
> They go wild, simply wild, over me.

Other T-Bone Slim songs were popular once upon a time, such as "I Wanna Free Miss Liberty":

> While the moon was softly shining

On my cot, as I lay pining. . . .
Came a drowsy feeling o'er me—
And Joe Hill stood there before me—
I seemed to hear this joyous fighter say:

I came to free Miss Liberty, from the bonds of slavery;
From mock Democracy; from inequality;
I want to feel no Iron Heel shall disgrace our peaceful shore;
That all 'he world may do away with war. . . .

and "Gesundheit, Mr Wob":

There are two famous men,
They're always on the job.
One is Mr Scissorbill,
The other is Mr Wob.

Although his poems are less well remembered, his roguish "Lumberjack's Prayer" ("And if thou havest custard pies, I like, dear Lord, the largest size") remains a Wobbly favorite. Printed on wallet-size card-stock in deliberate imitation of a "holy card," and sold for a dime, this was a popular item at IWW street meetings.

To T-Bone Slim we also owe many of U.S. radicalism's snappiest and most effective aphorisms and epigrams:

Half a loaf is better than no loafing at all. [1992, 153]

Charity: Throwing a life-preserver into a drowned man's coffin. [*ibid.*, 155]

Doesn't the very word *worker* presuppose that there are some who do no work? [*ibid.*, 154]

Wherever you find injustice, the proper form of politeness is attack. [*ibid.*, 153]

All through the 1920s, '30s, and '40s these and dozens of other examples of T-Bone Slim's Wobbly witticism and criticism were widely quoted on the job and in the jungles, and copied onto the walls of boxcars from coast to coast.

His admirers included many radicals who were otherwise critical of the IWW. Jack Conroy, Harvey O'Connor, Upton Sinclair and Meridel LeSueur, are just a few of those who refused to let sectarian differences interfere with their appreciation of T-Bone's manic verbal magic and topsy-turvy humor. Indeed, his work received considerable attention even outside the labor and radical movements. H. L. Mencken was so impressed by his linguistic innovations that he gave him a significant mention in *The American Language*. Journalist Lee Taylor was pleased to inform the readers of the Denver *Rocky Mountain News* that T-Bone's writing had "the force of Hemingway and the sting of Swift." George Milburn included two of his songs in *The Hobo's Hornbook.*

No question about it: T-Bone Slim was not only the IWW's greatest "man of letters" and America's premier hobo poet, but also one of the nation's outstanding humorists, and for that matter, one of our most daringly original writers. As Noam Chomsky has remarked: "It is a rare pleasure to read wise comment on important matters, put so simply and directly. T-Bone Slim has a lot to tell us and does it well."[2] Were it not for the deeply ingrained prejudice against authors who also happen to be workers, hoboes, and revolutionaries, the works of T-Bone Slim would long ago have been made available in "The Library of America" or at least as a Penguin Classic.

What most distinguishes T-Bone Slim from his fellow IWW writers, from other writers on the Left, and from just about all other American writers of his time, is—beyond all doubt—his *absolute surrealism*. With T-Bone, poetry is something more than a "means of expression"—it is an *activity of mind*. Others had surrealist moments, but T-Bone went all the way. A large part of his writing is as authentically surrealist as anything that appeared in *La Révolution surréaliste*. Indeed, André Breton's 1922 description of the results of his and Philippe Soupault's first experiments with automatic writing applies, down to the last detail, to the writings of T-Bone Slim. In Breton's words, these first *surrealist* texts properly so called were notable above all for their "high degree of *immediate absurdity*" as well as their

> extraordinary verve, much emotion, a considerable assortment of images of a quality such as we should never have been able to attain in the normal way of writing, a very special sense of the picturesque, and, here and there, a few pieces of out-and-out buffoonery. [2000, Book 2:163]

Wordplay, untrammeled, extravagant, and in endless variety, runs all through T-Bone Slim's writing, and gives many of his texts their distinctive tang. His word-magic is every bit as powerful as Lewis Carroll's or Marcel Duchamp's, and like theirs, resonates with echoes and premonitions of "phonetic cabala." A tireless inventor of fantastic neologisms, he renamed a famous West Coast gold-rush metropolis *Saphroncisco*, poked holes in the pretensions of the *silksockracy*, and scorned so-called "oil magnates" as a mere *oleogarchy*. During the '29 Depression he suggested that President Hoover's much-ballyhooed slogan, "Prosperity Is Just Around the Corner," was in truth a matter of *porousperity* (*i.e.*, "full of holes"), or perhaps a case of *perhapsperity*, probably perpetrated by *Perhapsbyterians*.

For T-Bone Slim, capitalist newspapers were *nutspapers*, and one of the most reactionary, Hearst's *Herald-Examiner*, he dubbed the *Haroil-Eczema*. Hearst's top editor and publicist, Arthur Brisbane—one of the big names in U.S. journalism in the 1920s and '30s—was a frequent target of T-Bone's satirical spitballs. His term *brisbanalities*, signifying the Hearst spokesman's insipid patriotic and anti-radical editorializing, was picked up by Mencken and other non- and anti-Hearst writers, and was a part of everyday American speech for years.

Most of these examples of T-Bone's verbal prankishness—neologisms, puns, turns of phrase—do manage to communicate a recognizable Wobbly message, albeit in an offbeat and roundabout fashion. In other texts, however—and they tend to be his best—concrete irrationality and word alchemy clearly hold the floor. "Electricity," for example, opens with these magnificently hermetic reflections:

> Juice is stranger than friction.
> A friendly stranger is half as strange as a strange friend.
> The world's champion friend has 198 friends—two, former friends, are no more.
> China has 440,000,000 opportunities for a man looking for friends. [1992, 80]

In "31,680 Hotcakes Per Mile," he computes the cost and number of pancakes required to lay a carpet of them from San Francisco to Los Angeles:

> In $2,600,000 there are 260,000,000 pennies, and—hotcakes selling three for a cent—it will buy 780,000,000 Aunt Jemima's pancakes. My! What a carpet we'll have!
> A mile having 5,280 feet would require 10,560 hotcakes, single file—or do you want 'em three abreast? All right, all right—three abreast. That's 31,680 hotcakes per mile. Five hundred times 31,680 hotcakes equals 15,840,000 hotcakes, and that is how many cakes it takes to lay a carpet three cakes wide from Frisco to L.A. [1992, 105]

As sophisticated readers will have guessed by now, much of T-Bone Slim's writing qualifies as first-class *poetic nonsense*. Without any warning he tosses out screwball proverbs such as "Mazuma is the rutabaga of boll-weevil," or invites us to ponder hysterical extravanzas like "The Passing Show," which begins:

> Soupposing some soupernatural souperintendent souperciliously soupprest soup! [*ibid*, 79]

and goes on with the same balmy "soupposition" for twenty-five lines. At the end he wonders whether this sort of thing could be called a "cussword puzzle."

He seems to have been incapable of writing anything boring, and his love for the unpredictable kept everyone on the go. In his 607-word novel, "Mr Hammond Deggs," the hero, heroine, and villain are all killed off in a few funny, dark and stormy paragraphs, and only the author and his readers get to "live happily ever after."

In reading T-Bone Slim, much of what may appear at first glance to be "only" nonsense turns out sooner or later to be revolutionary humor at its hottest and blackest. Savor this sample from "49,000,000 Jobs":

> Are we afraid of being fired? There are at least 49,000,000 jobs I can get should I become "fired" from this one. There are 2,000,000 bosses waiting with power to hire me as soon as I am at liberty.
>
> If every boss hires me once I'll be well along in years by the time the last foreman invites me to "see the timekeeper."
>
> If I get fired twice per day I'll be 2,739 years old when the last pair of bosses requests my resignation. By that time quite a few bosses will have been fired and I start all over again. [1992, 45]

Or this lesson in "T-Bone Economics":

> In this capitalist society of ours, you have to do the strangest things. If you want to eat a piece of pie you take a coal scoop and swing it eighty-eight times over your shoulder full of coal, and the pie is yours. By looking at you, not a living creature could guess you were ordering a piece of pie. They'll swear up and down you were shoveling coal and stick to it. You could show them the pie-crusts and they'd still insist you were shoveling coal—I'd hate to have them on a jury. [*Industrial Worker*, 28 Feb 1933]

"Get Your Tickets Now" features the stupendous news that the

IWW has

> engaged bier-side seats for the wake arranged for capitalism. . . .
> Date not yet set. Watch for announcement. . . . An unobstructed
> view of the casket and its contents. Bring your friends. . . . Come
> early and stay as long as you like. . . . The first show of its kind. .
> . . Refreshments will be served. Dancing to follow. [1992, 74]

André Breton, reflecting in 1942 on the possibility that "pure
psychic automatism" might intuit aspects of the future, quoted a
passage from his "Letter to Seers," written in 1925:

> There are people who pretend that the [1914-18] war taught them
> something; they are, all the same, less well off than I, who know
> what the year 1939 has in reserve for me. [2000, Part 2: 321]

In effect, the "Letter to Seers" foretold the Second World War
fourteen years in advance.

A remarkably similar instance of precognition occurs in a text
by T-Bone Slim, written in 1941 and titled, "Preparing for War in
1960":

> Official spokesmen close to hindquarters intimate that if the folks
> don't get busy right now and produce boy-children, the politicians
> won't be able to rig up a war in 1960-65.[1992, 150]

Did anyone else, anywhere, foretell the U.S. war in Vietnam with
greater accuracy?

Never a mere question of "style," what I have called T-Bone
Slim's "absolute surrealism" went to *the very heart of the matter*
of poetry and revolution. The "unfettered imagination"—Hegel's
definition of the essence of that "universal art" known as poetry—
was always T-Bone Slim's true medium. He attributed his hot and
dreamy use of language to the "fact" that he wrote "using a cross
between a Chinese and a Hebrew grammar," and defined humor
not only as "the carefree manhandling of extremes," but also as a
way of "bringing the sublime and the ridiculous into a
compromising proximity" [*ibid.*, 31-32]

In the 1940s, Australian poet and IWW member Harry Hooton
argued that

> Absolute rationalism has failed, but there is no need for despair.
> We can approach our problems from a healthier angle—we can *live*
> through our problems, we can fight through them and surpass
> them. Or we can *ignore* them. Surrealism is trying to do some of
> these things . . . But one thing is sure—if we continue trying to

solve them logically, they will infect us still more with their decay. [Hooton 1990, 68][3]

T-Bone Slim's perspective was much the same. More than any other IWW writer, he grasped the fundamental surrealist principle that the "logical" and the "rational" are not enough, and can never be enough; that reason without imagination is only a form of unreason, and inevitably leads to misery and disaster; that poetry and other forms of imaginative activity are not only important but *essential*, and of the greatest urgency in the re-creation of a truly livable world.

The key to T-Bone Slim's vernacular surrealism, as to all surrealism, is *freedom*. A concept that tends to fade and wither in the language of governments and political parties, freedom was always first in Wobbly theory and practice, as it has continued to be throughout the history of the international surrealist movement. "Since Bakunin," Walter Benjamin observed in 1929, "Europe has lacked a radical concept of freedom. The Surrealists have one" [1978, 189]. At the beginning of World War II, Ralph Chaplin wondered: "Who, anywhere in the world, [is] concerned about freedom the way the Wobblies used to be concerned about it?" [1948, 418]

True revolutions always seek to realize the dream of freedom, and poetry always lights the way, because true poetry is always about dreams of freedom. André Breton's lifelong insistence that "Human emancipation remains the only cause worth serving" is still as fresh as the future. "Freedom," after all, in the words of T-Bone Slim, "is what makes life worth fighting for." And that is why great things can yet be expected from the marvelous dialectical encounters of IWW surrealism and surrealist IWWism—in our work and our play as in our dreams and our struggles for a better world.

---

1. Unless otherwise specified, all statements by and about T-Bone Slim in this chapter are from this same source.

2. This statement has appeared in recent catalogs of the Charles H. Kerr Publishing Company. Chomsky has also quoted T-Bone Slim in his books and speeches.

3. Harry Hooton is increasingly recognized as one of twentieth-century Australia's finest poets. In the 1940s, he contributed poems to the *Industrial Worker* (6 June and 30 June 1947), and at least one article: "The IWW in Australia" (17 November 1947). In the 1950s he collaborated on the surrealist/jazz-oriented Beat magazine *Climax*, published in New Orleans.

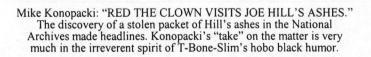

Mike Konopacki: "RED THE CLOWN VISITS JOE HILL'S ASHES."
The discovery of a stolen packet of Hill's ashes in the National
Archives made headlines. Konopacki's "take" on the matter is very
much in the irreverent spirit of T-Bone-Slim's hobo black humor.

XVI
"YOURS FOR A CHANGE"

1. ON THE ROAD TO CHICAGO

Chicago, Chicago, that is the town for me.
Drop me off on the lakefront,
that's where I'll be contented to be.
—Little Brother Montgomery—

Chronicling the life of a "Man Who Never Died" poses unusual difficulties from the start, but ending it is inevitably and hopelessly arbitrary. This chapter and the next examine a few details of the Hill story not otherwise covered here or elsewhere in the literature. A concluding chapter reflects on the meaning(s) of Hill's multiple legacies for our time and the future.

When Hill was waylaid and set up for framing by the authorities of the state of Utah, he was en route to Chicago. None of his friends seem to have recorded why Fellow Worker Hill, in the winter of 1913-14 chose to abandon the balmy warmth of southern California for a very cold Windy City in the heartland. Later commentators on Hill have also declined to speculate on the matter, as have the great brooders on Chicago, from Carl Sandburg and Floyd Dell to Nelson Algren and Studs Terkel.

Chicago, of course, was the home of the IWW's international headquarters, selected as such by the delegates to the union's founding convention. Other cities—Joliet, Denver, Milwaukee, and Washington, D.C.—were nominated for the honor, but the great majority of delegates (few of whom, by the way, were Chicagoans) clearly favored the sprawling industrial metropolis on the shores of Lake Michigan. As Delegate J. W. Saunders, of the Scandinavian Painters, Decorators and Paper Hangers Union, put it:

> Chicago is the proper place. It is the place where all can come. Read French history and you will find that Paris is always the center of the revolutionary spirit. We want Chicago as the headquarters because it is going to be the center of the economic revolution. . . . Chicago is centrally located. . . . It is the industrial center of the United States. [*Proceedings* 1905, 550]

Chicago's pivotal position in the revolutionary movement was a recurring theme in the IWW press, even in later years. In response to a reader's query, "Why does everyone from Jack London down predict that Chicago will be a central point in the social revolution?," the editor of the *Industrial Pioneer* replied:

> In every respect Chicago is the key place in all our modern American industry. . . . Who holds Chicago district holds the key to the advance of the American proletariat. [Oct 1921, 54]

Hill himself had lived in Chicago for some two and a half months in 1903. According to Ralph Chaplin, citing his interview with "John Holland," Hill "evidently didn't like New York so well and so [he] . . . came to Chicago where he tried to find his vision in a big machine shop" [1926, 189]. He left the shop after two weeks, but remained in the city eight weeks more working odd jobs [Chaplin 1923, 24].

Even then, two years before the IWW was formed, lucid observers recognized Chicago as "the heart of the radical labor movement in America" [Hapgood 1939, 186]. It is unlikely, however, that Hill in 1903 had much interest in the radical labor movement, although his unhappy job experiences, and what he doubtless saw of the misery of immigrant life in this country, were certainly propelling him in that direction.

However, apart from the few meager facts noted above, Joe Hill's ten weeks in Chicago in 1903 are a blank slate. Did he make any friends in the city, or run into old ones? Did he look at paintings at the Art Institute, or find his way to the open-air market on Maxwell Street? These are all good questions—and there are lots more where those came from—but the answers are way beyond reach: Hill's Chicago days are a complete mystery.

And when Ralph Chaplin informs us that a decade later, in 1913, Hill left San Pedro for Chicago, "for what purpose no one knows"—we have another mystery [1923, 25].

But it is not hard to think of reasons why Hill might have wanted to move to a large city, at least for a time—and what better city for a Wobbly than Chicago? At the age of thirty-four, he may well have yearned for just a little more of an intellectual life than San Pedro afforded: a big library, used bookstores, the company of other artists, writers, and musicians. And he probably heard from 'boes passing through that Chicago had grown into the wildest, most exuberantly creative city in the land. In the first three decades of the twentieth century, the city attracted an enormous number of geniuses of all kinds, including such imaginative writers as Mary MacLane, L. Frank Baum, Theodore Dreiser, Floyd Dell, Emanuel Carnevali, Lawrence Lipton, Sherwood Anderson, and Richard Wright. Years later Lipton described the migration to Baghdad-by-the-Lake that was already well on its way by 1913, when youngsters from all over

> were only waiting for a chance to light out for the big city. "I'll see you in Chicago—one of these days" was always their wistful good-by, and some of them made it. They would show up one morning at the door of my Near North Side studio with a knapsack or a battered old wicker handbag containing a change of shirt and socks. Some were boys, some were girls—they never came in pairs—and they had the furtive, conspiratorial air of refugees. They had come to join the ranks of the young rebels who were the *real* "flaming youth" of the twenties, but whose story was not being told in the newspapers. [Lipton 1959, 282]

The newcomers were not all boys and girls; they were youngsters of all ages on the road to adventure, seeking more light, more life, and freedom above all. Some were attracted to the city by the new poetry, and the new tremors running through all the arts. Others wanted to take part in the lively discussions and debates at the bustling cafés, tea-rooms, free-speech forums, and Bughouse Square. Many joined the "movement" and some became well-known soapboxers, organizers, or pamphleteers. There were those who came to Chicago to go to school, or to study with a particular artist, or to get a job at the *Daily News*, or to write the Great American Novel. And there were also those who, in their modest ways, came simply to do what they could to make the Earth a little better for the working class, and who, in their spare time, enjoyed drawing cartoons, writing songs, and playing the fiddle or piano.

It is easy to imagine the IWW poet among them.

Alas, when Joe Hill finally reached Chicago, it was in a coffin. But what a crowd he had to welcome him! An attendance of two hundred is regarded as a large funeral; over a thousand is considered immense. The thirty thousand who turned out for the funeral of Joe Hill set a record for labor/radical funerals that has never been topped.

The Utah copper bosses prevented Joe Hill from coming to Chicago, but the working people of Chicago came out for Joe Hill.

2. THE LATER YEARS OF JOE HILL'S FRIENDS

Each step is new . . .
But on I travel, with no end in view.
—Jones Very—

A few of the Wobblies whose friendship with Joe Hill is well-documented lived to ripe old ages, and their longevity proved to be a real boon for us all: Who else could have answered, with any authority, a younger generation's questions about the IWW poet? In the dusk of their hard lives, Fellow Workers Alexander MacKay, William Chance, Sam Murray, and Louis Moreau on many occasions took time out from the daily scuffle to defend their old friend from calumny, to clarify misunderstandings and rectify historians' errors, and more generally, to share their memories, criticisms, and reflections with young fellow workers, interviewers, correspondents, and all manner of busybodies and scholars. As the years rolled by, it became clear that these old-timers—whom the reader has met again and again throughout this book—made significant contributions to our knowledge of Hill, his life, his work, and his character. Without them, our basic knowledge of the Wobbly troubadour would be substantially smaller, and our conception of his character and personality—our sense of him as a person—would also be much reduced.

This foursome, who maintained fairly close ties with each other, constituted a distinct albeit informal grouping within the IWW, although I cannot recall that anyone has ever made a note of it. That there were many such groupings in the IWW, as in any group with any life in it, is indicated in the memoirs by Chaplin, Haywood, McGuckin, and others, as well as in numerous oral histories. Workingclass analogues to the many middle-class artistic and intellectual circles and cénacles—the Godwin/Shelley group, the Pre-Raphaelite Brotherhood, the so-called "Ashcan School"— such informal associations played a role in the IWW out of proportion to their numerical strength. Historians of the union, obviously more comfortable dealing with individual personalities and well-defined factions, have neglected these loose formations, and therefore missed a crucial element in the dynamics of the Wobbly counterculture.

The "Hill group"—although none of its members probably ever thought of themselves as part of such an entity—is particularly notable in that it outlasted all other such groups in the union.

The Wobbly bard was murdered by the authorities of the state of Utah in November 1915. This quartet of his friends lived on into the 1960s and '70s. What were Joe Hill's old buddies doing in their later years? It should be noted right off that all of them have proved to be elusive characters, rather like Hill himself. Not one of the four seems to have been the subject of a biographical sketch. By and large, historians have preferred not to notice them at all. They are mentioned and even cited in some of the literature on Hill—notably in Gibbs Smith's biography and Fred Thompson's pamphlet—but solely as informants about Hill, not as significant individuals of interest in their own right.

Even so boisterously "public" a fellow as Alexander MacKay has remained as hard to find as a hermit.

In his first novel, *Cables of Cobweb*, Paul Jordan-Smith describes the young, pre-World-War-One MacKay as a boxcar-riding 'bo who, like many 'boes, was also something of a dandy:

> genial, good looking, with a fine sense of humor . . . by turns, a street urchin, a revolutionist proposing to overthrow the government, and a critic of letters—recommending Flaubert, Stendhal and Oscar Wilde, or excoriating Emerson and Rudyard Kipling. [Flaunting] a gorgeous tie in the colors of the peacock [he called himself] a labor agitator [and was] now en route to some radical headquarters in Chicago. At twenty-five, he had more experience than most men have at fifty. [1923, 127]

Forty-odd years later Fellow Worker MacKay may have given up freight trains as his preferred mode of transportation, but he remained to the last a confirmed humorist, literary critic, and labor agitator, and stayed in touch with that "radical headquarters."

MacKay, who knew Hill in San Pedro in the 1910s, seems to have spent most if not all of his later years under that same warm California sun and smog—in Los Angeles, San Luis Obispo, and finally in San Jose. Other old-timers interviewed by UCLA history student Hyman Weintraub in the late 1940s remembered MacKay chiefly as an important California IWW organizer; unfortunately Weintraub never seems to have gotten around to interviewing him. Incidentally, Weintraub spelled the old Wob's name phonetically as "Mekiah" [1947, 275], indicating that MacKay held fast to the Scottish pronunciation, in which the latter half of his surname rhymes with "high" rather than "day."

In addition to organizing for the One Big Union, Fellow Worker MacKay had many other irons in the fires of discontent. Like other old California Wobblies, some of whom had been Bellamyists in the 1890s, he worked for Upton Sinclair's EPIC (End Poverty in California) campaign in 1939.[1] His friendship with Sinclair seems to have gone back a long way, and the letters MacKay wrote him, spanning the years 1934-1963, are our chief source of information on the old Wob's later years.

In the 1930s, MacKay hosted a radio show and wrote articles for the local papers. In a 1939 letter, Sinclair refers to him as a "journalist and radio commentator, known throughout this state" [13 Oct 1939]. In the 1940s and '50s, he collaborated on the atheist/freethought journal *Progressive World*, and in 1947, under the name "Johnnie Johns," his series on the San Diego Free Speech Fight of 1912, in which he been an active participant, appeared in the *Industrial Worker*.

Toward the end of the '30s, or early in the '40s, MacKay and his wife Marie ran a health-food store that lasted twenty years.[2] During that period, as he remarked to Sinclair, he made a serious study of the science of nutrition—a science severely retarded, in his view, by the profit system. In the '50s he worried that fallout from atom-bomb testing would ruin the Earth's atmosphere. On the lighter side, he took up photography as a hobby (Does anyone know what happened to the pictures he took?), and amused himself by documenting the "colossal errors and inaccuracies" of the *Encyclopædia Britannica*. To the end, however, MacKay's main activities were strictly in line with Wobbly priorities: keeping "the Red Flag flying" [to Sinclair, 4 Apr 1940] and "kicking Capitalism in the guts" [*ibid.*, 3 June 1945]. He died in 1966.

Archie Green, who met him only once but went on to exchange a few letters with him in the 1960s, recalls MacKay as "a man of real substance," given to "serious reflection," and with "nothing of the blowhard or braggart about him" [FR telephone interview, April 2001].

In the 1910s, for several months, or perhaps even a year or more, William Chance shared a shack with Joe Hill in San Pedro, and later visited him in jail in Salt Lake City. In those years Fellow Worker Chance was, as he wrote in a letter to an old IWW friend, Minnie F. Corder, "a roughneck foot-loose Wobbly" [letter, n.d.]. Fellow Worker Corder, for her part, remembered Chance as "a quiet and orderly person but very efficient," and wholeheartedly devoted to the IWW [letter to Fred Thompson, 26 Aug 81].

During the late 1910s, all through the raids and the 1918 federal trial, Chance worked at the union's international headquarters in Chicago. Around 1920 he served as secretary of the New York IWW's General Recruiting Union. Mostly, however, he lived in California. While working at a hamburger joint on the San Francisco beach in the mid-1920s, he met his wife-to-be, a woman named Rose. The Chances lived much of their later life in Banning, California, and Santa Rosa. They were together forty years, until Rose's death in the 1970s; his own came not long afterward.

Neither writer nor speaker, Fellow Worker Chance was a solid, dependable, rank-and-file militant Wobbly—the type who could always be counted on for tough assignments, in good times and bad. The fact that he was not one of the union's big "names" did not, however, prevent him from making a big contribution to IWW history. This did not happen during his long years on the West Coast, but during his relatively short stint in Chicago. As Fred Thompson summed it up in a 1981 letter, it was Bill Chance who convinced the IWW "to move into the block that later became famous as 1001 West Madison" [to Minnie Corder, 27 Aug 1981]. Moving into a new space might not seem like a major achievement, but in fact its impact on the union was immense.

When Chance came to Chicago, the IWW was still on Washington Street, in the old business district. General Secretary-Treasurer Haywood and others had long desired to establish a strong IWW presence in the heavily populated migratory worker, flophouse, and jobshark district on West Madison Street, the city's skid road, but nothing came of it until Fellow Worker Chance secured a small office at 1001. It did not take long for the union to acquire, bit by bit, the greater part of the block. In addition to making full use of this extensive office-space and large meeting-rooms, the IWW set up a massive first-floor printing operation which, for years, printed nearly all of the union's numerous periodicals, books, pamphlets, and "silent agitator" stickers. The move to skid road was thus an important factor in the great Wobbly resurgence of 1918-1924, which brought in many tens of thousands of new members. While it lasted, the Wobbly hall at 1001 West Madison was the largest and most productive beehive of revolutionary agitation in the entire country. (In 1981, the building was still standing, with a bar on the first floor and a flophouse upstairs. The whole area has long since succumbed to gentrification.)

Modest and unassuming, Fellow Worker Chance never got much recognition for instigating the move that made such a difference for the union. Like his old friend Hill, he was happy to do his part, and abjured the limelight. A letter he wrote to Minnie Corder, undated but probably *circa* early or mid-1970s, conveys a sense of the kind of guy he was. At eighty, and aware that his time was short, he regretted that "we will leave the world in a hell of a mess," but went on to add that it would always be in a hell of a mess "until the ideals expressed in the IWW Preamble be[come] universal," especially the part about the workers of the world organizing as a class to "Abolish the Wage System."

Sam Murray and Hill were fellow workers and friends in southern California, and went off together to Baja to take part in the Mexican Revolution: "a little pleasure . . . that few rebels have had the privilege of having," as Hill put it in a letter to him [*Letters*, 57]. The Wobbly bard's eight surviving letters to Murray, all written in his Salt Lake City cell, are remarkable not only for their exceptional warmth and camaraderie, but also because they are some of his longest and most informative, with revealing reflections on animals, nature, and revolutionary thought, as well as their Mexican sojourn. Regrettably, Murray's letters to Hill are all lost. For that matter, very little information of any kind has turned up on Murray, which is surprising, because he was an important and well-liked figure in the union.

Of the foursome discussed in this chapter, Fellow Worker Murray was by far the oldest. He was thirty-five when the IWW was formed in 1905; if not a founding member, he lined up soon after. He appears to have worked both as seaman and shipbuilder, and like many Wobblies, may have been a jack-of-lots-of-other-trades as well. He was a fine writer, and although he gave the world no full-length book or even a pamphlet, his many scattered articles and essays in the IWW press are among the best in the union's history. Clearly at ease in the heady atmosphere of Marxist economics and critical theory, Fellow Worker Murray was probably, like MacKay, a shareholder in the Charles H. Kerr Company,[3] and in any case was surely one of the IWW's most strikingly original thinkers. His "Industrial Unionism Triumphant!" in the internal *General Office Bulletin* (March 1925) is a clear and effective re-affirmation of IWW perspectives, refuting a whole gamut of ideological criticism. His series of articles in the *Industrial Pioneer* in 1925-26—on agriculture, bootlegging in Mendocino County, the building industry, the city of Detroit, the partnership of capitalism and crime, and other topics—reflect his careful study of the shifts and innovations on the industrial front, and qualify as worthy updates of Marx's *Capital*.

In the course of Ethel Duffy Turner's interview with him at the Veterans' Home in Yountville, California in 1955, Murray fondly invoked Joe Hill's "warm, agreeable and yet quiet disposition"—a description that seems equally applicable to Murray himself. Turner found him "lively, sharp and high-spirited," and, at the age of eighty-five, still "proud to call himself a Wobbly and a rebel" [Turner 1981].

Louis Moreau, who knew Joe Hill in British Columbia during the Fraser River Strike of 1912, was a member of the union's General Executive Board a half century later. My friend Richard Ellington, a New York anarchist who became a fixture of the San Francisco Bay Area IWW branches from the early 1960s on, told me in the '80s that he regarded Moreau as one of the "sharpest" and most uncompromisingly radical of the many old-timers he had met in the union—and he had met quite a few.[4]

Aside from a few core facts—that he was a lifelong uncompromising Wobbly, first-class organizer, friend of Frank Little's, mountaineer, and wilderness guide who lived in Lone Pine, California, and was often called "Frenchy"—biographical data on Moreau is next door to non-existent. He did not think of himself as a writer, but many of his GEB reports and letters to the editor of the *Industrial Worker* pack a real polemical punch, and tell us a lot about him, his outlook and ideas. Like Hill's other pals, Moreau was clearly a man of the highest caliber, intellectually and morally as well as politically, but his self-assurance and stubbornness may have set him apart just a little. In contrast to the serene MacKay, the taciturn Chance, and the high-spirited Murray, Fellow Worker Moreau appears rather cranky and sarcastic: a journeyman wisecracker always ready for a few rounds of verbal fisticuffs.

Writing from his cabin in Lone Pine in 1961, Moreau considered it "laughable" for the *Industrial Worker* to waste space printing lengthy anarchist critiques of the Cuban Revolution when, right here in the U.S., "we have about 65 million scissorbill workers to work on" [29 Mar 1961]. The following year he wrote to his fellow GEB members: "I have been on this mud ball a long time but I have never seen such hypocrisy, greed, and cruelty as I have seen in the last two decades," and proceeded to stress the urgency of putting several full-time Wobbly organizers in the field [GEB Report, 8 Nov 1962]. A year and a half later, the *Industrial Worker* ran another of his letters under the heading: "Time for Action Is Running Out." Pointing out that "all present governments are a form of fascism, call them what you will," and noting further that U.S. wage-slaves are "more thoroughly brainwashed than ever" and "in a hell of a fix," Moreau concluded with yet another of his Wobbly-style jeremiads: "If we don't heed the warning and organize—not tomorrow, but today—we're really going to suffer for our stupidity" [17 June 1964].

Louis Moreau died in the summer of 1969, an irreconcilable rebel worker to his last breath.

There is something depressing in the fact that so little is known about Joe Hill's friends. And the fact that so much *more* is known about the misguided witnesses for the prosecution who testified against Hill, and even about the prejudiced jurors who convicted him, is nothing less than creepy. I for one am convinced that the more we can learn about "Frenchy" Moreau and the other friends and fellow workers who not only stood by the Wobbly bard, but also devoted the rest of their lives defending the very cause he died for—*workingclass emancipation*—the better we shall understand Joe Hill, the IWW, and their many and varied legacies for our time.

---

1. Information on the connections between Bellamyists, Wobblies and Upton Sinclair's EPIC campaign was relayed to me in the course of a long telephone interview with Stan Weir, 8 Feb 1987.

2. Sigal 1961 mentions visiting an unnamed old Wobbly friend who was then running a health food store in California. Between the wars, wrote Sigal, "he used to edit a lumberworkers' journal up in Canada" [1963, 74]. Was this Joe Hill's old friend, or were other old Wobs also running health food stores?

3. The name Samuel Murray appears under the heading "Stockholders' Addresses Wanted" in the *International Socialist Review* (May 1912, 800). Other Wobblies who were also Charles H. Kerr Company shareholders include George Markstall (Lucy Parsons's companion during the last several decades of her life), Ralph Chaplin, John Neuhaus, and Fred Thompson, who served as President of the cooperative's Board of Directors in the 1980s.

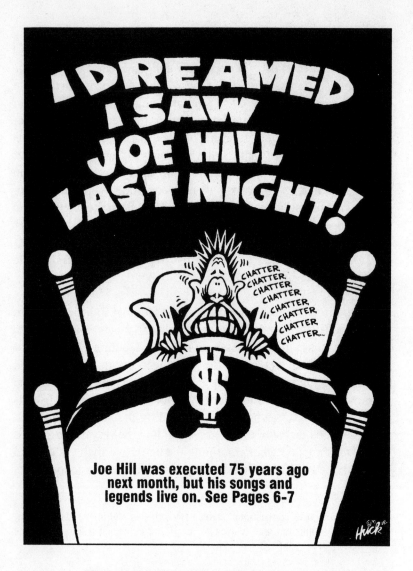

This cartoon by Gary Huck was featured on the cover
of *UE News*, official organ of the United Electrical
Workers Union, 5 October 1990.

CONCLUSION

ALL THE GOOD THINGS OF LIFE

The law of creation is the constitutive law of all reality.
—**Hoene Wronski**—

Open just about any newspaper and you'll find references to "the late President So-and-So" or "the late Chairman of the Board of Such-and-Such." No one, however, from the nineteenth of November 1915 on, has ever referred to "the late Joe Hill." To do so would sound as ridiculous as referring to "the late Spinoza," or "the late Mary Wollstonecraft," or "the late Thelonious Monk." The truth is, the Man Who Never Died is still very much alive and kicking, and seems to have no intention of giving up the ghost, now or ever. Joe Hill was the most famous Wobbly of them all when the authorities of the State of Utah had him shot, and he remains the most famous Wobbly of them all today.

"What kind of a man is this whose death is celebrated with songs of revolt and who has at his bier more mourners than any prince or potentate?" Thus a journalist wondered aloud in his coverage of Joe Hill's Chicago funeral on Thanksgiving Day 1915.

Over the years, many others have asked the same and similar questions. What was it that set Joe Hill apart? What made him unique? How did a kid from a small town in Sweden grow up to become the most famous Wobbly of them all?

To date, no one has been able to pinpoint the "secret" of Joe Hill's enduring—and indeed, steadily expanding—popularity, perhaps because there is no "secret." His IWW friends, who loved and admired him, nonetheless agreed that he was, in many ways, an ordinary Joe—unpretentious, devoid of personal ambition, allergic to the limelight, just one of the guys. That "ordinariness" was, of course, one of his strengths as a songwriter, and it has continued to be a strong element in the long-lingering legends that have clustered around him and made the troubadour of discontent a folk hero, a recurring character in fiction, an icon of the popular imagination.

Hill's songs made him popular in the union, and in the larger radical milieu, but he was never a "public" figure like Haywood, Ettor, Flynn and so many others. When we compare Hill's accomplishments in his various fields of endeavor with those of other notable Wobblies, he does not appear at the head of the class. Judged by the quality and quantity of their work, Ralph Chaplin, Covington Hall, Arturo Giovannitti, and Laura Payne Emerson are just as deserving of the title "IWW Poet." Chaplin, T-Bone Slim, John Brill, and "Dublin Dan" Liston wrote songs that are as good or better than his, and Fellow Workers Ernest Riebe, "Dust" Wallin, Chaplin, Ern Hanson, Jim Lynch and William Henkelman were certainly more gifted cartoonists. "Father" Hagerty, Bill Haywood, Vincent St John, Justus Ebert, and many others contributed much more to shaping the union's ideas and ideals. Hill's role as an agitator was far from outstanding, and if he soapboxed, no one seems to have been impressed enough to write it up. He was only one of many thousands of IWW frame-up victims and class-war prisoners, and neither the first nor the last of the Wobbly martyrs. And yet his fame soared far beyond all others.

Of course, part of what makes Joe Hill so special is that he was *all* of these: poet *and* songwriter *and* cartoonist *and* man of ideas *and* frame-up victim *and* class-war prisoner *and* martyr—not to mention immigrant, hobo, musician, composer, master of the art of Chinese cookery, and volunteer soldier in the service of the Mexican Revolution. Modest to a fault, he was an IWW Joe-of-all-trades, a specialist in nothing except being a Wobbly. He was one of those strange characters who turn up now and then in the course of history—people who, without necessarily blazing with luminosity themselves, somehow become *conductors of light* for others.

Active on many fronts, footloose and fearless, the softspoken and well-liked rebel songster was increasingly recognized, in and around the union, as the quintessential Wobbly—the embodiment of the Preamble and building the new society in the shell of the old. Everybody knows that the IWW from the very beginning overflowed with the stuff that legends are made of—One Big Union of All Workers, Dump the Bosses Off Your Back, Industrial Freedom, the Thousand-mile Picketline, Bread and Roses, Songs to Fan the Flames of Discontent, Solidarity Forever, The Power of Folded Arms, the Good Old Wooden Shoe, Direct Action Gets the Goods, Sit Down and Watch Your Pay Go Up, and All for One and One for All!

Keeping aloft the unsullied red and black banner of freedom, equality, and solidarity, the IWW bravely shouted "No!" to the shameless butchery, selfishness and hypocrisy that defined the first half of the "American Century." The Wobblies were too few in number to win, but the beauty and justice of their Cause, along with their courage, tenacity, and generosity, assured them a moral victory that inspired a new generation in the Sixties, as it will continue to inspire future generations until wage-slavery is abolished at last. Wobblies spawned legends galore because they defied the impossible, fought the good fight against staggering odds, and never conceded defeat. How could they give up when they knew they were right?

To this day Joe Hill personifies these legends as well as the deeper truths behind them.

Hill's reputation, then, is made up of what an old TV commercial used to call "a special combination of ingredients"—an odd blend of fact and legend. And as new facts are brought to light, or given new emphasis—his solidarity with wild nature, his strong views on the urgency of organizing women, his rejection of the "white mystique," his friendly feelings toward the Chinese, his meeting with Ben Fletcher, his participation in the Mexican Revolution—they will inevitably collide and merge with the old legends, and help a number of new legends start on their way.

At the 1990 Joe Hill Conference in Salt Lake City, Lori Elaine Taylor discussed the shifting conceptions of Hill along with the even more troubling questions of the "real" Hill and conflicting proprietary claims to his legacy. Focusing on several generations of singers of Hill's songs, and songs and poems about Hill, she discovered not only a man who never died, but also a man almost uninterruptedly in a state of being reborn. No two of these many Joe Hills, she argues—citing the various models depicted by Ralph Chaplin, Earl Robinson, Woody Guthrie, Billy Bragg, and others—are exactly the same. Invoking a "continually recontextualized" Joe Hill, Taylor welcomes this pluralism:

> Who owns the past? I do. I own Joe Hill. You do, too. We may not be his legal heirs, but we control what he means to us. . . . When we hear the past in the teller's words, we hear the tellers as much as the tale. . . . We are not obligated to serve the past at the expense of the present. It is in the new contexts, created by the teller and the listener, that we find meaning in Joe Hill and his words. [Green 1993, 34]

The often subtle distinctions between different writers' or songsters' versions of Hill have not, however, altered the broad lines of the legend as it lives in popular consciousness. The "Communist" Hill, like the later "Hippie" model, were mere mirages of the moment, and faded away. Is anyone surprised that the tried-and-true Wobbly Joe Hill has proved to be made of stronger stuff, and the only one accepted in the ranks of the Immortals? Not only did he never die, he is clearly here to stay.

In his *Vision of the Last Judgement*, William Blake commented on the perplexing process of mythic condensation by which an individual comes to signify the collective. "At a distance," he wrote, surely referring to a distance in time, "Multitudes of Men in Harmony" can "appear as One Man" [Blake 1966, 607]. If Joe Hill was all things to all Wobblies—the very *image* of itself that the union liked to present to the world—the broader public increasingly looked upon him as *The* Wobbly, as many of their forebears once regarded William Ellery Channing as *The* Unitarian, and William Lloyd Garrison as *The* Abolitionist.

In all essentials, this image of the IWW troubadour persists to this day. For if Joe Hill is still a subject of disputation for some, he is a larger-than-life inspiration for many, many more. His songs are sung wherever working people rise against slavery, wherever kids say no to arbitrary authority, wherever freedom is "in the wind." His prison letters are classics of coolness and defiance in the face of massive injustice. His Wobbly turns of phrase—"pie in the sky," "wooden medal," "Don't mourn, organize!"—keep turning up anywhere and everywhere.

Next to Blake's limpid insight I add this observation by Novalis: "Every person who consists of several persons is a person raised to a higher power—or a genius" [1960, 70]. The rapidity with which Hill's songs went 'round the world, with no high-powered advertising or celebrity promotion, and their persistent popularity throughout the past century, are proof enough of his genius. It is essential, however, to keep in mind that what raised Hill "to a higher power" was not some mystical force, or even his own super-human effort, but rather *the revolutionary movement of the working class*—or, to be precise: the Industrial Workers of the World. As T-Bone Slim once said, "A man is only great as a writer if his readers are great. Never was, is, or will be a writer greater than his readers."

To put it bluntly: Joe Hill did much to make the IWW what it was, but it is far more important to realize that it was the IWW that made Joe Hill *who he is*: a world-renowned rebel worker of near-mythic proportions. It is an extraordinary phenomenon: The Wobbly bard, a penurious wage-slave, is probably known to more people today than ninety-nine percent of history's kings, queens, emperors, and prime ministers. And he is easily ten thousand times better remembered than any of the multi-millionaire slave-drivers the Wobblies fought against, or the journalists who systematically slandered the union, or the judges who railroaded him and thousands of his fellow workers to jail for the crime of trying to make the world a better, freer, healthier, and happier place.

In his legendary role of Wobbly *in excelsis*, Hill is truly and significantly a symbol of *the revolutionary rank and file*. His characteristic virtues—imagination, simplicity, directness, creativity, humor, and bravery—are *not* the virtues of "leadership," but of the working men and women "furthest down." And that's Joe Hill, the Wobbly prototype: the individual revolutionary workingstiff "raised to a higher power." The Man Who Never Died may be "hard to get hold of," biographically speaking, but somehow he is *always there*, a constant reminder of what the class struggle is really all about. Feminist Theodora Pollok called him "a man of unusually exemplary life." As such, he became a "role model"— and even what psychoanalysts call an "ego ideal"—for several generations of younger Wobs, for other labor radicals, and for recalcitrant working people generally. Few historic figures equal Joe Hill as a real and persistent *presence* in the consciousness of the labor movement and the working class.

In recent years, however, Fellow Worker Hill has become a more and more disturbing and even *haunting* presence, and the reason why should not be hard to guess: The very qualities we most admire in the troubadour of discontent are those that are most obviously lacking in the labor unions of our own time. The so-called organized labor movement today is—let's face it—ludicrously disorganized, not at all representative of the laboring population, and, local exceptions aside, definitely not moving. Its mottoes seem to be "Solidarity? Forget It!" and "Don't organize, mourn!" Its archaic and bureaucratic structure makes it virtually impossible to practice the principle, "An injury to one is an injury to all." Its servile dependence on capitalist party politics paralyzes initiative from below, and leads only to one defeat after another. Anti-democratic to the core, its officials are far more afraid of the members of their own unions than of their drinking buddies—the bosses, the bosses' lawyers, and the bosses' politicians. Vapid, uninspired, cynical, ignorant, cowardly, weak, flabby, senile, and dull: That's the "labor movement" we've got today—the direct linear descendant of what President Carter once called, in a revealing slip, the AFL-CIA.

The "House of Labor" is in terrible shape, but of course it is not alone. In U.S. politics and culture, too, a complacent scissorbillist miserabilism has ruled the roost for years. A few contented dot-com billionaires and "developers" notwithstanding, Late Capitalism is a depressing mess all around. Ecological devastation, pollution, racism, xenophobia, homophobia, misogyny, genetic engineering, state terrorism, police brutality, the prison-industrial-military-media complex, the ghoulish pharmaceutical/medical establishment, white-collar crime, homelessness: All these problems and many more have gone from bad to worse, with no let-up in sight.

The question is posed: What are we going to do about it?

Today the old bourgeois and Stalinist clichés about the IWW's "incorrect policies" and other "mistakes" sound emptier than ever. Who but incurable dogmatists could believe such claptrap? The time has come to affirm that most of the IWW's so-called "failures" were in actuality its greatest triumphs, and that the alleged "successes" of its competitors have turned to dust. To reread the harshest criticisms directed against the One Big Union by its political enemies (from the left as well as right and middle) is truly to savor the sweetest tributes to its glory. All that the Old Left—social-democratic, Stalinist, "Progressive," Trotskyist, etc. —liked least about the Wobblies reappears now in an entirely new light and is increasingly recognized as the union's most important legacy to revolutionaries in our own time.

Among the IWW's most notorious "weaknesses" that can now more accurately be recognized as strengths, and essential building-blocks for a new revolutionary movement—are these:

* its uncompromising insistence on *abolishing wage-slavery*, and, as evidenced in part by its use of that particular expression, its self-conscious continuity with the older Abolitionist tradition;

* its focus on organizing the *workers furthest down*: the un-skilled, immigrants, people of color, women, unemployed, the dis-abled, and the homeless;

* the *nomadism* of a large portion of its membership;

* its relentless non-sectarianism and *uncompromising practice of solidarity*, and hence its refusal to divide the struggle ("An injury to one is an injury to all");

* its open acceptance of different points of view, and its stubborn *refusal to succumb to a rigid one-size-fits-all ideology*;

* its emphasis on *nonviolent direct action* and other forms of *rank-and-file initiative*, along with its principled *non-participation in the sham of electoral politics*;

* its strategic concentration on the *point of production and the streets* as the key areas for the creation of revolutionary situations;

* its recognition that *song, poetry, art, and theater* are not "secondary" but *defining elements of revolutionary struggle*;

* its impassioned awareness that the ongoing "romantic" and "utopian" project of *building the new society in the shell of the old*—so derided by authoritarian and mechanistic-minded leftists of all stripes—is not a substitute for, or "alternative" to, proletarian revolution, but the only effective way of realizing it;

* and finally, its *refusal* (critics are wont to call it "inability") *to establish stable (or "permanent") institutions*.

This last point—the alleged "failure" of the IWW most harped upon by opponents of all ages and sizes—not only reveals the union at its brightest and far-seeing best, but also highlights its up-to the-minute revolutionary actuality. One need not look hard or long to see that the stable, "permanent" institutions of this society, far from being emancipatory or in any way desirable, are on the contrary the sources of our worst woes. The state, military apparatus, churches, business, police, prisons, political parties, Boy Scouts, television, and organized crime are "stable" to a degree, but are they doing anybody except the billionaire capitalists any good?

I take it as a given that, if humankind's age-old dreams of freedom are to be realized, the "stable institutions" of this society of *un*freedom have got to go.

Did the Wobs 'way back sense that institutional "stability" inevitably means hierarchy, bureaucracy, stagnation, and repression? Certainly it is a fact that, with a couple of notable exceptions (Philadelphia longshoremen, Cleveland metal workers), the IWW did not build long-lasting job-connected institutions. Indeed, in its most vital and active years, the union tended to lead a rather precarious existence, with a rapidly fluctuating membership. New branches kept appearing and older ones surrendered their charters, but stability was nowhere to be found.

In part, of course, this lack of stability can be blamed on state and corporate violence. Instability, however, was characteristic of

577

the IWW before such repression became a major factor in the life of the union, and remained characteristic after the worst repression was over. It would appear, therefore, that indifference to the development of "permanent" institutions reflects essential elements of the Wobbly sensibility: anti-authoritarianism, romanticism, mobility, creativity, and spontaneity. The IWW was not only countercultural but also vehemently counter-institutional.

As exemplified by their strikes and free-speech fights, the Wobbly conception of revolution was never a question of "stable institutions," but rather of "festivals of the oppressed": collective play-by-play negations of the existing social structure which at the same time open windows on a new society. Organizing not only the unorganized but above all those the AFL considered "unorganizable," Wobblies excelled in the fine art of *rising to the occasion*, redefining the "possible" in terms of the revolutionary imagination. Work experience was essential, but the play factor was no less decisive. In the IWW, the "informal work group" that many post-vanguardist Marxist theorists have perceived as the true nucleus of a new society was always also an informal *play* group, and its activity was by no means limited to the workplace. With their inexhaustible bag of tricks full of do-it-yourself direct actions, Wobs improvised new situations—on the job, of course, but also in the streets and even in jail: *revolutionary* situations in which the Old Order, if only for a day or a week, gave way to working people's dreams and desires.

This strong counter-institutional tendency was reinforced by the union's radically and self-consciously *unfinished* character—yet another feature the IWW shared with revolutionary currents in poetry and the arts, from romanticism to surrealism, just as it also served to distinguish Wobblies all the more from the AFL and the many left political parties. That the IWW regarded itself as still "in the works," far from "finished" and indeed, barely more than a rough sketch, was noted by many commentators in and outside the union. As Justus Ebert insisted in his pamphlet, *The IWW in Theory and Practice*, for decades one of the union's best-selling pieces of literature,

The IWW . . . is germinal, rather than full-grown. It is a beginning, rather than a completed article. It is raw, rather than refined. [n.d.,124]

At a time when some impatient ideologues were pretending that the
IWW was over and done with, Floyd Dell, in the *Liberator* for
June 1919, pointed out that it was just getting started:

> The IWW is not a fixed institution, not a finished project. . . . It is
> the still-evolving embodiment of certain terrifically significant
> forces, which have not yet made their full concussion upon society.
> [55]

Mary Marcy, reviewing that year's IWW Convention in the July
issue of the same magazine, declared the union to be

> not a fixed and static thing, but an organization in the swift process
> of growing and becoming. . . . [12]

Such open-ended views in turn fit in well with the union's
renowned genius for improvisation, as epitomized in a few words
by Frank Little in the course of one of his talks to Butte, Montana
miners in 1919. "We [in the IWW] have no set rules to go by," said
Little, but in strikes, for example, we aim to win by "any means
necessary" [Gutfeld 1969, 185].

That Little defined the IWW with a phrase later made famous
by Malcolm X shows not only that great revolutionists often think
the same thoughts, but also that the IWW was a forerunner—
symbolically if not physically—of just about every subsequent
emancipatory movement in this country. And that helps explain
why today, when the "organized left" is almost universally
recognized as rigid, boring, and dead, the IWW—as inspiration and
heritage—is still vibrant, exciting, and alive.

What I am arguing here is not particularly new, and I am far
from alone in arguing it. In recent years an impressive number of
labor activists, radical environmentalists, socialists, anarchists,
feminists, pacifists, poets, puppeteers, novelists, artists, musicians,
cartoonists and historians have concluded—notwithstanding many
differences among them—that of all revolutionary and labor
organizations in U.S. history, the IWW is the single most important
inspiration and model—or at least one of the top two or three—for
a new revolutionary movement in our time.[1]

In the end, it is always up to the working class to turn things
around, to make the changes that make life better. Other sectors of
the population often have the motivation, the will, and a gift for
mass consciousness-expansion in regard to particular urgent prob-

lems, and such autonomous allies, frequently ignored or disparaged by the old left, are in fact crucial to the success of any decisive social transformation. Only the working class, however, has the collective power and the sheer numbers to really overturn the deadly system known as capitalism. If the wage-slaves don't make the revolution, it won't happen.

And that is why it is so urgent for all wage-workers to do what they can to help build a new labor movement in this country. It won't be easy, and it won't be accomplished overnight, but somebody's got to do it, and now's the time.

In fact, it has already begun. The "official" labor movement may be moribund, but widespread discontent is discernible everywhere—even in the ranks of many of the most ossified old-line craft and pseudo-industrial unions. And the largely unorganized working class, as a class—however confused and demoralized certain sectors of it may be—has never ceased to wage class war in its own unorganized ways. From the Los Angeles Rebellion of 1992 through the 1999 anti-WTO demonstration in Seattle and its many escalating sequels, working men, women, and children have been in the forefront of resistance to the ever-greedier and more oppressive capitalism known as globalization. Many new forms of struggle, as well as important new alliances, have emerged in this period, both *within* the existing unions, and outside them, in a wide variety of new groupings.[2]

One especially heartening sign of this new spirit in the labor movement, which could also be seen as a resurgence of the old Wobbly spirit, is the rhymed cry heard on many recent workers' demonstrations across the country:

An injury to one is an injury to all!
Free Mumia Abu-Jamal!

Indeed, there is no better antidote for the confusion and demoralization of unorganized workers, or for the zombie-like lethargy of the allegedly organized, than a good dose of Joe Hill's pure, no-artificial-ingredients, accept-no-substitutes IWWism. Hands-on experience of striking on the job and other forms of workers' direct action tends to give even the most timid wage-slaves a new self-confidence along with a vivid sense of the potential power of class-wide action. The practice of workers' solidarity irresistibly works wonders.

By prescribing Joe Hill's Wobbly-style boldness, audacity, creativity, and humor as a remedy for the ills of the labor movement today, I do not mean to imply that the IWW is or was infallible—far from it. Like all groups, the One Big Union had its share of internal problems: notably, acrimonious factionalism (not all, by any means, provoked by Communist infiltrators), programmatic inconsistencies, and tactical goofs (the 1924 decision to automatically expel jailed members who sought pardons did much to tear the union apart). When we compare it, however, to its bureaucratic, authoritarian, and reformist competitors—the AFL as well as the Socialist, Socialist Labor, and Communist parties—the IWW was clearly superior in all respects. Unlike the sectarian, self-serving, opportunistic, and anti-proletarian blunders and betrayals of these competing groups, the Wobblies' mistakes were those of honest workingclass revolutionists engaged in real class struggles in the face of massive terror on the part of the capitalist class and the State. Tactical errors made by workers themselves in the heat of battle have to be judged very differently from the devious maneuvers of Central Committees whose policies reflect the selfish and narrow needs of a trade union or political party bureaucracy rather than the long-range needs of the working class.

Much to its credit, the IWW always tried—and tried mightily —to resolve its conflicts and contradictions in open democratic debate, mass struggle, workingclass self-activity, collective creation, and also with *laughter*: the laughter of an oppressed but rising class well aware of the fact that its own bitterest and most painful mistakes are often its best teachers. The importance of the Wobblies' sense of *humor*, intimately allied to the sense of poetry, can scarcely be exaggerated. Wobblies laughed at capitalism and capitalists, at their competitors and critics, but they also had the rare ability to laugh *at themselves*—to recognize their own weaknesses, deficiencies, missteps, and follies. The Wobs' creation of such outrageous "characters" as Mr Block, Scissor Bill, and Screwball— proletarian equivalents of Charles Dickens's Gradgrind, Alfred Jarry's boorish Ubu Roi, and Villiers de l'Isle-Adam's invidious petit-bourgeois Tribulat Bonhomet—highlights the fact that Wobbly Marxism, unlike other Marxisms, is not just a critique of bourgeois society and its relations of production, but also a merciless *and humorous* workingclass critique of the working class itself.

Critical humor is the essence of the very term "Wobbly" which, whatever its origins, was the IWW's vaunted name for themselves from around 1913 on. Such a singularly irrational nickname, as David Roediger has pointed out, already sets the union dramatically apart from every other group on the left:

> How do we account for a group of radicals adopting a label which implied uncertain movement, even slipping and sliding? . . . Part of this riddle's answer lies in the [IWW's] readiness to embrace the swaggering and rambling aspects of the word *wobbly*. In their name, IWW members also accepted notions of uncertainty, indeterminance, and even the craziness of the modern world in a manner abhorrent to "scientific socialists."
>
> To be a Wobbly involved tremendous uncertainty—state-sponsored victimization and vigilante- based repression. Other left organizations experienced fluctuating fortunes, but consoled themselves as having mastered the laws of societal evolution and the science of revolution. Such groups could not "own up" to their own internal wobbles. Instead, as weaknesses became apparent, they intensified serious self-characterization and grand theory. Wobblies understood the heritage of direct action. . . . No polemical line could rival everyday deeds against injustice. . . . T-Bone Slim's song "The Popular Wobbly" is the perfect example of the importance of defiant laughter amidst disaster.
>
> [For] IWW members . . . necessary struggle superseded visions of inevitable victory. Workers who wrote "Nut-house News" skits could direct black humor and sardonic wit against society's lunacy, as well as against socialist rationality. Enjoying their name, Wobblies flaunted it . . .. Accepted in 1913, *Wobbly* continues to ring proudly, the sole effervescent self-referential name on the left. [Green 1993, 131-132]

Only Wobblies could have produced a grossly satirical version of their own favorite publication. *The Bosses' Songbook: Songs to Stifle the Flames of Discontent* was not in fact issued by the union, but was compiled by two IWW members, Richard Ellington and Dave Van Ronk, and sold primarily through IWW Branches. Its lyrics included "Which Side Are We On?," "The Twelve Days of Marxmas," "The Good Old Party Line," and "This Land Is Their Land." Thirty-six pages of nose-thumbing irreverence, ribaldry, and bad taste, the pamphlet also featured original cartoons in the same spirit, among them the first published work by the now-well-known artist Trina Robbins [Ellington 1959].

The IWW's distinctively proletarian and revolutionary self-critical sense of humor—wholly antithetical to the sinister and spirit-crushing "self-criticism" promoted by Stalinists in the 1920s and '30s—is a particularly vital need of those who are trying to accomplish difficult tasks, and world revolution has proved to be rather more difficult than Fellow Worker Hill and his friends anticipated. Inasmuch as the only alternative is a steadily worsening barbarism, we have no choice but to struggle on. Without humor, however, even the best-intentioned revolutionary movement quickly degenerates into its own worst enemy. In the spirit of Joe Hill and T-Bone Slim, I would suggest that a revolutionary movement without a sense of humor is a contradiction in terms.

I would argue further that a direct and causal relationship exists between the Wobblies' emphasis on humor and poetry, and the fact that the IWW, mistakes and all, remains far and away this country's finest model of unionism, workers' democracy, and revolutionary organization. And the fact that Joe Hill, poet and humorist, is the single best known model of a "Wobbly true-blue," lends considerable substance to this argument.

The time, space, and energy the IWW devoted to poetry and song still occasions wry smiles from critics, but the importance of these outpourings of the revolutionary workingclass imagination in the life and legacies of the union remains inestimable. Rare indeed are issues of IWW newspapers or magazines without at least one song or poem. Many old-time Wobs counted the *Little Red Song Book* as their most cherished possession. Agnes Inglis, in a 1948 letter bemoaning Wallace Stegner's malignant article on Hill in the *New Republic*, asked plaintively: "What had Joe Hill done?" and answered her own rhetorical query: "He surely did something. He set folks to singing" [to Fred Thompson, 18 Apr 1948]. The fact that once upon a time the U.S. labor movement *sang*, and by singing gave the ruling class some of its biggest scares ever, is not the least of the IWW's historic achievements. As Judi Bari put it, "Only great movements that mark turning-points in history inspire great music" [Sakolsky 1995, 173].

The *Little Red Song Book* can be read as a tribute to, and update of, the songs of the IWW's predecessors, and/or as an *open sesame* to rebel songsters of later years. Peter Linebaugh and Marcus Rediker, in their superb book *The Many-Headed Hydra: Sailors, Slaves, Commoners and the Hidden History of the Revolutionary Atlantic* (2000), note that "The movement to abolish slavery sang its way to freedom" [300], reminding us once more how closely Wobblies followed in the footsteps of their Abolitionist antecedents, for the

IWW was itself an abolitionist movement, a revolutionary movement, a multiracial movement, and a singing movement.

In the 1960s the Student Non-Violent Coordinating Committee
(SNCC) songbook, *We Shall Overcome*, featured a very slightly
rewritten civil-rights version of T-Bone Slim's "Popular Wobbly"
[Carawan 1963, 15-16]. The interplay between the IWW and the
Black Freedom Struggle of that decade has not yet been the subject
of detailed exploration, but I would wager that such a study will
uncover far more incidents of mutual aid and influence than
anyone has heretofore suspected.

Consider this powerful declaration: "Our music is our mightiest
weapon. It is the tool with which the burden of oppression can be
lifted from the backs of our people." It is inconceivable that such
a statement could have been made by a spokesperson for the
Socialist Party, the Communist Party, or any of the Trotskyist or
Maoist groups, or even the New Left of the 1960s, but it *does* have
a distinctly IWW ring to it. In fact, the words are those of
trumpeter Lester Bowie of the great "free jazz" group, the Art
Ensemble of Chicago [n.d., *c.* 1968]. I have not found that Joe Hill
or the Wobblies influenced the Art Ensemble or any other members of the Association for the Advancement of Creative Musicians
(AACM)—in whose mimeographed journal Bowie's statement
appeared—but the spiritual affinity between Bowie's moving
words and IWW pronouncements on poetry and song indicate that
the creative utopianism of the subversive imagination, like music
itself, knows no limits.

To dream of hearing Joe Hill's songs sung in free jazz is not in
fact so far-fetched. The range of music in which IWW lyrics have
already made their appearance is impressive: from old hymns and
spirituals to tin-pan-alley hits, folk-songs, and the wild Ani DiFran-
co/Utah Phillips collaborations to the "classical" compositions of
Fellow Worker Rudolf von Liebich. And of course there are Paul
Robeson's recordings of the Hayes/Robinson "Joe Hill" song. In
any event, all signs suggest that lots more is "in the wind." A punk
band named Sons of Emma, out of Oakland, California, has recently released a CD, *Red Lies and Black Rhymes* (Broken Rekids,
2002), which includes the song "Service Sector," with these lines:

Sing a song for Joe Hill,
He sang to his death for you.

As if in direct response to the Sons of Emma, Fred Alpi—a Swedish-born French rock'n'roller, as he is described on the *info-groupes.com* website—has written and recorded a "Chanson pour Joe Hill" (Song for Joe Hill), with this rousing chorus:

> *You can kill a singer*
> *But you can't kill songs.*
> *No bullet in the world*
> *Could kill Joe Hill.*[3]

Since 1999, Alpi's trio has played in the subways, streets, and workingclass cabarets all over Europe (and more recently Quebec, on a "Love and Anarchy" tour). That a "Song for Joe Hill" is part of the group's repertoire is proof not only that the troubadour of direct action continues to appeal to the young, but also that that appeal disregards barriers of language and nation.

Hill was no youngster when the Utah authorities took his life—he was thirty-six—but he embodied and retains youth's essential qualities: boldness, imagination, candor, defiance, and pluck. The passing of a century has not aged him a bit. Alive as you and me, Hill and his story have never been the "property" of historians, antiquarians, or other academicians. Instead, he and his legends have always belonged to working people, poets, songsters, musicians, artists, the dispossessed, the disaffiliated, and above all the young and the young at heart. Ancient as the jongleurs, goliards, and other rebel vagabonds of long ago, he is yet younger than the day after tomorrow. Significantly, in this regard, the name, image, humor, songs, and sayings of Joe Hill are rarely invoked today in a mood of nostalgia or sentimentalism, but rather in *struggle*—on demonstrations, picketlines, disruptions, and newer forms of protest, resistance, and revolt.

The work of Ron Sakolsky is particularly engaging in this connection, for his aim is not so much to examine history, as such, but rather to explore the many radical "underground" cultural/political continuities here and now. He has been especially intrigued by the many ways in which old-time Wobbly tactics, generally dismissed by academics and traditional leftists as "ancient history," keep resurfacing as state-of-the-art subversive activities. His anthology, *Sounding Off! Music as Subversion/Resistance/Revolution*, co-edited by Fred Wei-Han Ho (1995), discusses the use of song in the Earth First! movement and the IWW, and the creation of new

EF! songs in the Wob tradition, written and recorded by EF!ers who are also, like Sakolsky himself, latter-day members of the IWW. His later collection, *Seizing the Airwaves: A Free Radio Handbook*, co-edited by IWW member Stephen Dunifer (1998), identifies the IWW's celebrated free-speech fights of yesteryear as the principal precursor and model of today's rapidly growing independent micropower radio movement (sometimes called "pirate" radio), which has evolved into a major component in the worldwide struggle against globalization, and indeed, against all forms of oppression.[4]

Viewing current radicalism through the One Big Union looking-glass can be an illuminating experience. Jeff Ferrell, whose earlier work includes important studies of Covington Hall, the Brotherhood of Timber Workers, and the IWW in Louisiana in the 1910s, has recently [2002] published a book in which the specter of the old-time Wobbly counterculture once again looms large. Focused on the reappropriation and transformation of the "public sphere" by the disenfranchised "undesirable citizens" of our time, Ferrell regards the IWW as the ancestor and inspirer of a broad spectrum of contemporary youth revolt—from the punk scene, graffiti art, and other forms of creative vandalism, to the gender-bending circle-a skateboarders and the new urban squatters.

The reappearance of venerable Wobbly strategies and tactics in new guises and unforeseen situations is also, of course, a stimulus to look again, and more deeply, into the maze of history. Introducing the 1998 sesquicentennial edition of the *Communist Manifesto*, Robin D. G. Kelley urged that

> If we want to understand how the Marxist tradition deals with racism and colonialism, with forms of alienation that cannot be understood simply in terms of social relations of production, with the vicious brutality of global white supremacy and its consequences for *all* of us, then we need to look at *other* Marxist traditions. . . . [1998, x]

Kelley's long list of these "other" traditions that radicals today urgently need to re-examine and learn from is headed by "the strikes and free-speech fights of the Industrial Workers of the World" [*ibid.*, x-xi]. In *Yo Mama's Disfunktional: Fighting the Culture Wars in Urban America* (1997), Kelley—responding to some ex-new-leftists' neoconservative "second thoughts"—takes up the question of the relations between organized labor and "identity politics":

> How might people build class solidarity without suppressing or
> ignoring differences? How can we build on differences—by which
> I mean different kinds of oppressions as well as different
> identities—rather than in spite of them? One way to conceive of
> alliances across race and gender is as a set of "affiliations," of
> building unity by supporting and perhaps even participating in
> other peoples' struggles for social justice. Basically, that old-
> fashioned IWW slogan, "An injury to one is an injury to all!"
> [1997, 122]

As Paul Buhle has noted in his *Taking Care of Business:
Samuel Gompers, George Meany, Lane Kirkland and the Tragedy
of American Labor* (1999), "models of solidarity" for a new labor
movement "inevitably return" to the IWW [252].

Similarly, in their book *Empire* (2000)—a critique of the new
global empire—Michael Hardt and Antonio Negri have nothing but
the highest praise for what they call the "perpetual movement of
the Wobblies . . . erecting a new society in the shell of the old,
without establishing fixed and stable structures of rule" [207]. In
their view, the old Wobblies' "organizational mobility and ethnic-
linguistic hybridity," along with their remarkable ability, in the
process of organizing working people "from below," to stimulate
"utopian thought and revolutionary knowledge" [412], mark the
IWW as an ideal prototype for the contemporary counter-
globalization movement.

Historically, Wobbly humor, poetry, songs and cartoons not
only inspired working people to see that a "better world" was possible—they also reinforced the moral courage to struggle to make
that better world real. Although the union's countercultural focus
has long been the object of a condescending sentimentality, and is
often regarded as quaint and outmoded, it seems to me to be just
the opposite: not merely forward-looking but truly prophetic. Most
assuredly it is not the "romantic" and "utopian" IWW which is out-
of-date today, but rather its so-called "realistic," "rational" and
anti-utopian critics and competitors.

On the key question, "how to make the Revolution," all that the
many varieties of mainstream Marxism have left us—as my old
friend Eugenio F. Granell once put it—is an "encyclopedia of ignorance" [1979]. The orthodox, bureaucratic, pragmatic, utilitarian,
and boring forms of social radicalism—with their closed systems,

finished programs, party lines, and lifeless publications—really belong to capitalism, and simply cannot articulate the emancipatory desires and aspirations of the contemporary working class.

In other words, the prosaic and humorless left, old and not-so-new, has been left behind by the dialectic of the historic process, and the revolutionary *imagination* has rightly risen to the fore. Joe Hill and the IWW, meanwhile, far from being relics of a dead past, have turned out to be what the German romantic philosopher Franz von Baader called "representatives of the future" [Baader 1976, 4].

Wobblies have not been commonly thought of as dialecticians, and references to Hegel in the union's publications are few and far between. The IWW Preamble, however, and the *Little Red Song Book*, could be considered some of the finest commentaries ever written on one of Hegel's central themes: the "dialectic of Master and Slave," which inspired a young Karl Marx to develop his critique of Capital and Labor.

Whether Joe Hill himself ever dipped into the *Phenomenology of Mind* is something we shall probably never know; J. B. Baillie's translation appeared in London in 1910, and a copy could easily have found its way to one of the hundreds of IWW libraries. What really matters is that Hill's life and songs, as well as the always-evolving legends about him, reverberate with a veritable three-ring circus of antinomies: dream and action, poetry and revolution, work and play, solitude and solidarity, realism and romanticism, passion and serenity, melancholy and humor, tragedy and hope, death and immortality, silence and song. These themes recur again and again in the *Song Book* and the union's cartoons. "The power of Spirit," according to Hegel, "is only as great as its expression" [Miller's translation, 6].

Like Hegel, too, Joe Hill and the entire IWW were aware that they were living in "a birth-time and a period of transition to a new era" [*ibid.*]. For the Wobblies, the abolition of the wage system opened the way to nothing less than the re-creation of the world. Their boundless confidence in workingclass imagination and creativity made them all the more willing to take risks, to challenge unjust laws, to organize the so-called "unorganizable," and to take on all of the most pressing problems of the day.

And today? Does anyone really believe that we can find effective solutions to the pressing problems of *our* time—not only the persistent and agonizing problem of wage-slavery but also the problems of "whiteness," misogyny, homophobia, homelessness,

Leaflet promoting the *Little Red Song Book*
(Chicago, early 1960s).

and ecocide—with anything *less* than the freest and most revolutionary imagination and creativity?

The reason why Joe Hill and the old-time Wobblies are still so popular among young radicals, and so profound an influence on so many contemporary social movements—from Justice for Janitors to micropower radio, from anti-globalization to animal rights, from Earth First! to feminism, from gay liberation to Critical Mass, and all the various new abolitionisms: from the group around the journal *Race Traitor* to the movement to abolish prisons—is because the Wobblies' dreams of a better world, and the means they imagined and improvised to realize those dreams, have never ceased to touch the hearts and minds of those who value freedom above all, and who are now daring to dream revolutionary dreams of their own.

For in building a new revolutionary movement today, as always, freedom and dreams are the essentials.[5] Describing Hill's character, Sam Murray, who was one of those who knew him best, emphasized "the love that Joe always had for freedom and the untamable spirit that refuses to surrender it" [1923, 53]. More than anything else, that love of freedom and that untamable spirit—the spirit of poetry, dream, and the Marvelous—are what the U.S. labor movement, and U.S. radicalism as a whole, need today.

1. Among those who have pronounced themselves in this spirit recently—in print, or in public addresses, or in open discussions—are Gale Ahrens, Paul and Mari Jo Buhle, Noam Chomsky, Mike Davis, Dave Dellinger, Roxanne Dunbar Ortiz, Lorenzo Komboa Ervin, Jeff Ferrell, Paul Garon, Dan Georgakas, Linda Gordon, Archie Green, Robert Green, Herbert Hill, Noel Ignatiev, Joseph Jablonski, Robin D. G. Kelley, Joel Kovel, Staughton Lynd, Peter Rachleff, David Roediger, Ron Sakolsky, Salvatore Salerno, Gary Snyder, Meredith Tax, and Howard Zinn.

2. See Lynd 1992, Rachleff 1993, Kelley 1997, and Roediger 1994 and 2002.

3. My translation (FR).

4. Sakolsky's newest anthology, *Surrealist Subversions: Rants, Writings and Images by the Surrealist Movement in the United States* (2002), also includes much material on the IWW, including texts on Covington Hall and T-Bone Slim.

5. Robin D. G. Kelley's splendid *Freedom Dreams: The Black Radical Imagination* (2002), which appeared as I was putting the finishing touches on this book, adds immeasurably to the perspectives advanced here.

Bumper-sticker, 1990

Robert Green: Ink drawng,1990

ENVOI

T he following poem erupted in a fit of automatic writing in the early fall of 1965. In November I added a few lines, gave it a title, and intended to read it at a Joe Hill Memorial organized by the Chicago IWW Branch at a club called Poor Richard's in Old Town. The program, however, ran longer than expected, and the poem remained unread. It was issued as a broadside in 1990, with the drawing by Robert Green that is reproduced above.

I regard this wild call across the years, written in a kind of trance, as a suitably *sur-objective* conclusion to this book. As the poet Jones Very once put it, "I value these verses, not because they are *mine*, but because they are *not*."

JOE HILL: A LONG-DISTANCE CALL

The desert sand a veinless sky
weeping thorns of sleepless water
Slowly but suddenly a roof
which is not even barking
collapses in the white eyes of a dog
looking out

from behind the corner
of its teeth

But no ghostly girl blinks her hands

Joe Hill Joe Hill your hat is full of stones
Magic stones piano stones dream stones fire stones
They are too small to see
They are very far away
beyond all first fruits
beyond all second thoughts
beyond all last chances
out there
where all windows are broken like flies
where all rooms are grayer than spoons
where all nights are blotched with scorpions
Yet somehow somewhere
there is an orange

Joe Hill they started killing you the day you were born
They tightened their whistles around your neck
They stole all the things
they never would have let you have
You watched you listened you drifted you dreamed
You spat in the face of their facelessness
You felt the touch of an unseen sun
of a life more real than real estate
The eye and its double
doubled you
and played back your own true voice
for the first time
once and for all

You sang an algebra aching with rage
The laughter you breathed was blacker than tea
and a million times hotter than hope
You sparked a defiance so vast so light
that the streets of the city
ran away with the stars

These passenger pigeons are confused in their flight

through fog choked up with glaciers of news
Someone is waving a fork in the dawn
No doubt a carnival is opening
a thousand miles away

Joe Hill Joe Hill I have found you at last
in ships that have grown back into trees
in desperate pedestrians' white hair
in diagrams of impossible machines
in the red breath of escaped gorillas
in charts of seismographic tremors
in the taste of strange medicines
in old photographs of cave men
in the numbers of disconnected telephones
in maps of secret Catalonias
deep in the Himalayas

Joe Hill your restlessness is our best bet
Joe Hill your solitude is our call of the wild
Joe Hill your extravagance is our jump for joy
Felonious freedom's indivisible dream
multiplied by lovers armed and dangerous
and always
on the loose

Meanwhile orchestras bleed like bees
A ghostly girl wrings her eyes

How many spokes are there
in the wheel of the wind

Chicago, November 1965

Carlos Cortez: Joe Hill poster (linocut, 1979)

ACKNOWLEDGMENTS

One reason why this book turned out to be as long as it is—four or five times longer than I intended—is that a couple hundred people, in many and varied ways, kept offering good ideas and information, and in effect helped me write it.

My single biggest debt is to the Wobblies I met in the early 1960s—Guy B. Askew, Carlos Cortez, Esther and Sam Dolgoff, Patricia and Richard Ellington, Fanny and Carl Keller, James "Bozo" Kodl, Philip Melman, Alex Murto, O. N. Peterson, George Roby, Ruth and Jack Sheridan, Lillian and Ed Stattman, Aino and Fred Thompson, Jenny Lahti and Charles Velsek, Walter Westman, Abraham Wuori, and others I encountered later—most notably Archie Brown, Minnie Corder, Fred Hansen, Gilbert Mers, Art Nurse, Henry Pfaff, Utah Phillips, Anna Matson and John Shuskie, Harry Siitonen, and Nick Steelink. All but a few of these Fellow Workers were "well on in years" when we met, but many of them proved to be grand *raconteurs*, eager to communicate to a younger generation their Wobbly adventures in the days of yore. They were some of the best teachers I ever had, and I am grateful to them all. Of these old-timers, I came to know Fred Thompson best, and the countless discussions I had with him on IWW history, individual Wobs, and the union's lore and literature echo throughout these pages.

What I owe to previous biographers of Joe Hill, starting with Ralph Chaplin, is amply documented in the text and notes.

Thanks to my parents, Sally Kaye and Henry P. Rosemont—both lifelong labor activists—I early on became aware of organized labor: I was on picketlines before I could walk, and the first song I learned was "You can't scare me, I'm stickin' to the union." My mother, a jazz accordionist/vocalist who in her late teens had been the Chicago Theater's "Boop-boop-a-doo Girl," taught me the importance of music, song, and other forms of creativity, not only in the labor movement but in all of life. My father, who directed the longest and most important strike in the history of Chicago Typographical Union No. 16 (the 1947-49 newspaper strike), gave me an "inside" view of labor history and culture that has greatly deepened my appreciation of Joe Hill and the IWW—especially regarding the creative role of workers' clubs, hangouts, and all manner of informal associations in and beyond the workplace.

The material used in this study was gathered over a period of many years, much of it long before this particular book was begun. I have drawn heavily on interviews and correspondence related to my earlier books and essays on IWW history—on T-Bone Slim, Slim Brundage, Wobbly cartoons, etc.—and my ongoing research on Bughouse Square and the Dil Pickle Club. The many friends and acquaintances who shared memories, answered questions, clarified details, recommended books, supplied me with odds and ends pertaining to Joe Hill or the IWW, looked up obscure references, copied rare documents or pages on microfilm, taped songs, showed me old photographs, letters, and clippings, put me in touch with other researchers, offered encouraging words, and/or in dozens of other ways assisted in making the book a reality include: Gertrude Abercrombie, Irving Abrams, Gale Ahrens, Nelson Algren, Mike Alewitz, Federico Arcos, Paul Avrich, James Barrett, Jennifer Bean, Clif Bennett, Carl Berreitter, Jan Boudart, Slim Brundage, Paul Buhle, Harry Busck, Sam Calander, Harry Chase, Peter Cole, Polly Connelly, Jack Conroy, Joan Smith Cooper, Carl Cowl, Charles Curtiss, Ruth Dear, Dave Dellinger, Leon M. Despres, Diane di Prima, George Esenwein, Tor Faegre, Lawrence Ferlinghetti, Beth and Paul Garon, Dan Georgakas, Rose and Joseph Giganti, Frank Girard, Martin Glaberman, Al Glotzer, Eugenio F. Granell, Archie Green, Sarah Gruber, Aldine Gunn, Clark "Bucky" Halker, Kenan Heise, Toby Higbie, Herbert Hill, Frances Horn, Gary Huck, M. Virginia Hyvarinen, Noel Ignatiev, Joseph Jablonski, Paige and Michael James, Ella Jenkins, Ted Joans, Steve Kellerman, Robin D. G. Kelley, Mike Konopacki, Joel Kovel, Maynard Krasne, Philip Lamantia, Jack Langan, Meridel LeSueur, Peter Linebaugh, Frank Lovell, Mary Low, Michael Lōwy, J. Anthony Lukas, Lisa Lyons, Bernard Marszalek, Ilse Mattick, Burr McCloskey, Karl Meyer, Jack Micheline, Katherine Kerr Moore, Grandizo Munis, Pierre Naville, Sheila Nopper, Henry Oettinger, Anne Olson, Lisa Oppenheim, Jeffrey B. Perry, Nancy Joyce Peters, Martin Ptacek, Charles Radcliffe, Ralph Rieder, David Riehle, Trina Robbins, David Roediger, Gérard Rosenthal, John Ross, Ron Sakolsky, Salvatore Salerno, Stephen Sapolsky, Walter Schonbrun, Pete Seeger, George Seldes, John Sillito, Bruce E. Sloan, Gibbs Smith, Tamara L. Smith, Gary Snyder, Vicki Starr, Wallace Stegner, Joffre Stewart, Arne Swabeck, William Targ, Studs Terkel, Joan Thomas, Geraldine Udell, Jorge Valadas, Ngo Van, Michael Vandelaar, Virgil Vogel, Theo Waldinger, Lila and Arthur Weinberg, Stan Weir, David

Wieck, Vera Buch and Albert Weisbord, Myra Tanner Weiss, George Weissman, Francis Wright, and Al Wysocki.

Special thanks to those who read and commented on one or more chapters as this book began to take shape: Gale Ahrens, Jen Besemer, Alex Dodge, Paul Garon, Archie Green, Robin D. G. Kelley, Lisa Oppenheim, David Roediger, Constance Rosemont, Salvatore Salerno, John Sillito, and most especially to Tamara L. Smith, who not only read the entire typescript and made scores of valuable suggestions, but also straightened out any number of technical problems.

Librarians helped a lot on this project. I am especially grateful to Julie Herrada and Ed Weber of the Labadie Collection, at the University of Michigan Library in Ann Arbor; Rachel Canada of the Southern Folklife Collection in the Wilson Library at the University of North Carolina in Chapel Hill, which houses the Archie Green Collection; Dione Miles and William LeFevre, at the Walter Reuther Library, Wayne State University, Detroit, where the IWW's archives are deposited; Mark Rosenzweig, of the Reference Study for Marxist Studies in New York; Dorothy Swanson, Tamiment Library, New York University; Archie Motley, Jr., at the Chicago Historical Society; Diana Haskell, Special Collections, The Newberry Library, Chicago; Russell Maylone, Special Collections, Northwestern University Library, Evanston; Martha Quinn, Evanston Public Library; Ellen M. Engspeth, Director of Archives and Special Collections at North Park University, Chicago; Dennis Cooper, Loyola University Library, Chicago; Thomas Carey, of the San Francisco History Center at the city's Main Library; and the staffs of the Stanford University Library in California; the Library of the University of California at Los Angeles; the Lilly Library at Indiana University in Bloomington; and the Beni Memorial Library in Ann Arbor.

As is true of practically everyone involved in the study of labor history in the Midwest, I have benefitted from the thoughtful aid of William Adelman, Les Orear, Lynn Orear, and Mollie West of the Illinois Labor History Society, Chicago.

Thanks to Ingvar Söderstrom, Hans Haste, Bruno Jacobs, and the staff of the Joe Hill Museum in Gävle for their generous assistance in researching the Swedish side of the Hill story.

And thanks most of all to Penelope, by way of our old friend Eiranaeus Philalethes.

All for One and One for All!

Mike Alewitz: Portable Joe Hill Mural (1990)

BIBLIOGRAPHY

I. Books, pamphlets, articles, dissertations and unpublished manuscripts (except letters)

Note: An asterisk (*) at the end of a reference indicates that the item includes one or more songs or poems by Joe Hill.

Abrahams, Edward. 1988. *The Lyrical Left: Randolph Bourne, Alfred Stieglitz and the Origins of Cultural Radicalism in America.* Charlottesville: University Press of Virginia.

Abrams, Irving. 1989. *Haymarket Heritage: Memoirs of Irving S. Abrams.* Edited by Phyllis Boanes and Dave Roediger, with an introduction by Joseph Jacobs. Chicago: Published for the Illinois Labor History Society by the Charles H. Kerr Company.

The ACTWU Songbook. n.d., c. 1982. New York: Amalgamated Clothing and Textile Workers Union.*

Adamic, Louis. 1932. *Laughing in the Jungle.* New York: Harper & Brothers.

—. 1935. *Dynamite: The Story of Class Violence in America.* New York: Viking Press.

Adelman, William J. 1986. *Haymarket Revisited.* Revised edition. Chicago: Illinois Labor History Society.

Ahrens, Gale. 2002. "Abolish All Prisons! Stop the Genocide!" In Sakolsky 2002, 265.

Algren, Nelson. 1961. *Chicago: City on the Make.* Sausalito: Contact Editions.

Allen, Donald M. 1960. *The New American Poetry.* New York: Grove Press.

Allsop, Kenneth. 1967. *Hard Travelin': The Hobo & His History.* New York: New American Library.*

Altenbaugh, Richard J. 1990. *Education Through Struggle: The American Labor Colleges of the 1920s and 1930s.* Philadelphia: Temple University Press.

Altgeld, John Peter. 1986 (1893). *Reasons for Pardoning the Haymarket Anarchists.* Introduction by Leon M. Despres. Chicago: Charles H. Kerr.

Anderson, Evert. 1964. "Joe Hill, IWW Rebel, Is Honored in Sweden." *Industrial Worker,* 20 May.

—. 1969. "Ture Nerman" (obit). *Industrial Worker,* December

—. 1970. "New Joe Hill Song Book for Sweden." *Industrial Worker,* January.

Anderson, Margaret. 1953. *The* Little Review *Anthology.* New York: Horizon Press.

Anderson, Nels. 1923. *The Hobo: The Sociology of the Homeless Man.* Chicago: University of Chicago Press.*

"And Now a Joe Hill Opera." 1970. *Industrial Worker,* November. 8.

Arcos, Federico. 1971. "Joe Hill," in *Ford Facts,* official organ of Local 200, United Auto Workers. Detroit, 23 December.

Armstrong, Ken, and Maurice Prossley. 1999. "Trial and Error: How Prosecutors Sacrifice Justice to Win." Serialized in the *Chicago Tribune,* January.

—. 1999a. and Steve Mills."The Failure of the Death Penalty in Illinois." Serialized in the *Chicago Tribune,* November.

Arnal, Oscar L. 1979. "A New Society Within the Shell of the Old: The Millenarianism of the Wobblies." *Sciences religieuses/Studies in Religion* 8/1, 67-81.

Ashbaugh, Carolyn. 1976. *Lucy Parsons: American Revolutionary.* Chicago: Charles H. Kerr.

Ashleigh, Charles. 1914. "The Floater." *International Socialist Review,* July.
—. 1915. "Reflections on Joe Hill's Reprieve." *Solidarity,* 9 October.
—. 1930. *The Rambling Kid.* London: Faber & Faber.*
Austin, Mary. 1918. Introduction to Cronyn 1962 (1918).
—. 1932. *Earth Horizon: An Autobiography.* New York: Literary Guild.
—. 1970 (1930). *The American Rhythm: Studies & Re-expressions of Amerindian Songs.* New York: Cooper Square.
—. 1985 (1912). *A Woman of Genius.* Afterword by Nancy Porter. Old Westbury: The Feminist Press.
Avrich, Paul. 1980. *The Modern School Movement: Anarchism & Education in the U. S.* Princeton: Princeton University Press.
—. 1988. *Anarchist Portraits.* Princeton: Princeton University Press.
Baader, Franz von. 1976. *Les Enseignements secrets de Martines de Pasqually.* Paris: Robert Dumas.
Bailey, George Ryland. 1930. *The Red Mesabi.* Boston: Houghton Mifflin.
Baldwin, James. 1961. *Nobody Knows My Name.* New York: Dell.
—.1963. *The Fire Next Time.* New York: Dell.
—.1972. *No Name in the Street.* New York: Dell.
Barker Tom. 1965. *Tom Barker and the IWW.* Recorded, edited & introduced by E. C. Fry. Canberra: Australian Society for the Study of Labour History.
Barnett, Eugene. 1927. *Nature's Woodland Bowers, in Picture and Verse.* Walla Walla: WSP Press.
Baxandall, Rosalyn Fraad. 1987. *Words on Fire: Life & Writing of Elizabeth Gurley Flynn.* New Brunswick: Rutgers University Press.
Beck, Frank O. 2000 (1956). *Hobohemia: Emma Goldman, Lucy Parsons, Ben Reitman & Other Agitators & Outsiders in 1920s/30s Chicago.* Edited & Introduced by Franklin Rosemont. Chicago: Charles H. Kerr.
Bengston, Henry. 1999. *On the Left in America.* Edited and introduced by Michael Brook. Carbondale: Southern Illinois University Press.*
Bennett, Scott H. 2002. "Workers/Draftees of the World, Unite!: Carlos A. Cortez Reccloud Koyokuikatl, Soapbox Rebel, WWII CO & IWW Artist/Bard." In Sorell 2002.
Bier, Jesse. 1968. *The Rise & Fall of American Humor.* New York: Holt, Rinehart.
Bimba, Anthony, 1927. *The History of the Working Class.* New York: International.
Binns, Archie. 1944. *The Timber Beast.* New York: Scribners.*
Bird, Stewart, Deborah Shaffer and Dan Georgakas, eds. 1985. *Solidarity Forever: An Oral History of the Industrial Workers of the World.* Chicago: Lake View Press, 1985.*
"Birth of a Song Hit." 1938. *One Big Union Monthly.* March, 28, 51.
Blair, Walter. 1978. *America's Humor: From Poor Richard to Doonesbury.* With Hamlin Hill. New York: Oxford University Press.
Blaisdell, Lowell L. 1962. *The Desert Revolution: Baja California, 1911.* Westport: Greenwood Press.
Blake, William. 1966. *The Complete Writings of William Blake.* Edited by Geoffrey Keynes. London: Oxford University Press.
Blechman, Max, ed. 1999. *Revolutionary Romanticism.* San Francisco: City Lights.
Block, Lawrence. 1984 (1966). *The Thief Who Couldn't Sleep.* New York: Jove.
Bock, Gisela. 1976. *Die Andere Arbeiterbewegung in den USA von 1909-922: Die IWW.* Munich: Trikont Verlag.
Bogard, Thomas. n.d. *Memoirs.* Unpublished autobiographical typescript; original in the Bogard file in the Archie Green papers, Southern Folklife Collection,

Wilson Library, University of North Carolina at Chapel Hill; photocopy in author's possession.

Bogorad, Miriam, *et al*, eds. 1939. *Songs for America*. New York: Workers Library.

Boggs, Grace Lee. 1998. *Living for Change: An Autobiography*. Minneapolis: University of Minnesota Press.

"Bookseller McDonald Dies at 79." 1968. *San Francisco Chronicle*, 6 July.

Botkin, B. A., ed. 1944. *A Treasury of American Folklore*. New York: Crown.

Bourne, Randolph. 1977. *The Radical Will: Randolph Bourne, Selected Writings, 1911-1918*. New York: Urizen.

Bowie, Lester. n.d., c. 1968. "A Word from the Desk." *The New Regime: Association for the Advancement of Creative Musicians*. Chicago: AACM.

Boyd, Neva Leona. 1971. *Play and Game Theory in Group Work: A Collection of Papers*. Edited by Paul Simon. Chicago: Jane Addams Graduate School of Social Work, University of Illinois.

Brazier, Richard. 1966. "The Mass IWW Trial of 1918: A Retrospect." *Labor History* 7:2 (Spring), 178-192.

—. 1968. "The Story of the IWW's Little Red Song Book." *Labor History* 9:1 (Winter), 91-105.

Brennan, Frederick Hazlitt. 1931. *Pie in the Sky*. New York: Century Co.*

Breton, André. 1962. *Manifestes du Surréalisme*. Paris: Jean-Jacques Pauvert.

—, ed. 1966 (1939). *Anthologie de l'humour noir*. Paris: Jean-Jacque Pauvert.

—. 2000 (1978). *What Is Surrealism? Selected Writings*. Edited & introduced by Franklin Rosemont. New York: Pathfinder Press.

Brissenden, Paul F. 1937. "CIO vs. AFL." *The American Scholar* No. 2 (Spring), 180-194.

—. 1957 (1920). *The IWW: A Study of American Syndicalism*. New York: Russell & Russell.*

—. 1971 (1913). *The Launching of the Industrial Workers of the World*. New York: Haskell House.

Brown, Geoff. 1974. Introduction to *The Industrial Syndicalist* (reprint edition). Nottingham, U.K.: Spokesman Books.

Brown, Milton W. 1963. *The Story of the Armory Show*. New York: Joseph H. Hirshorn Foundation.

Brown. Sterling. 1956. "Robert Burns," in *The Reader's Companion to World Literature*. New York: Mentor, 64-65.

—. 1969 (1937). *Negro Poetry and Drama* and *The Negro in American Fiction* (one volume edition). New York: Atheneum.

Brundage, Slim. 1997. *From Bughouse Square to the Beat Generation: Selected Ravings of Slim Brundage, Founder & Janitor of the College of Complexes*. Edited & introduced by Franklin Rosemont. Chicago: Charles H. Kerr.

Bruns, Roger A. 1987. *The Damnedest Radical: The Life and World of Ben Reitman, Chicago's Celebrated Social Reformer, Hobo King, and Whorehouse Physician*. Urbana: University of Illinois Press.

Buhle, Mari Jo, Paul Buhle, and Dan Georgakas, eds. 1998. *Encyclopedia of the American Left*. New York: Oxford University Press. Revised, expanded edition of a reference-work originally published by Garland in New York, 1990.

Buhle, Paul. 1985. "Great Moments in Agitpop: The Kerr Company's Rad-Lit Revival," *Voice Literary Supplement*, September, 24-25.

—. 1987. *Marxism in the U.S.* London: Verso.

—. 1999. *Taking Care of Business: Samuel Gompers, George Meany, Lane Kirkland, and the Tragedy of American Labor*. New York: Monthly Review

Press.

Bukharin, N. I. 1982. *Selected Writings on the State and the Transition to Socialism*. Edited by Richard B. Day. New York: M. E. Sharpe.

Burgmann, Verity. 1995. *Revolutionary Industrial Unionism: The IWW in Australia*. Cambridge, UK: Cambridge University Press.

Burke, Fielding [pseudonym of Olive Tilford Dargan]. 1947. *Sons of the Stranger*. New York: Longman's Green.

Burroughs, Edgar Rice. n.d., c. 1955 (1918). *The Land that Time Forgot*. New York: Ace.

Byington, Robert H. 1978. *Working Americans: Contemporary Approaches to Occupational Folklife*. Los Angeles: California Folklore Society.

Cabral, Amilcar. 1979. *Unity and Struggle: Speeches & Writings*. New York: Monthly Review Press.

Calmer, Alan. 1935 (1934). "The Wobbly in American Literature." In Hicks 1935.

"Calumny on Joe Hill Refuted: Analysis of Trial Record by Committee of Friends Gives Answer to Professor Stegner's *New Republic* Article on Hill's Character." 1948. *Industrial Worker*, 13 November.

Calvert, Jerry W. 1985. "Butte's Wobbly Poet" [on Dublin Dan Liston], in *The Speculator* 2:1, Winter, 35-40.

—. 1988. *The Gibralter: Socialism & Labor in Butte, Montana, 1895-1920*. Helena: Montana Historical Society.

Camp, Helen C. 1995. *Iron in Her Soul: Elizabeth Gurley Flynn and the American Left*. Pullman: Washington State University Press.

Cannon, James P. 1912. "The Seventh IWW Convention." *International Socialist Review*, November, 424.

—. 1956. *The IWW: The Great Anticipation*. New York: Pioneer Publishers.

—. 1992. *James P. Cannon and the Early Years of American Communism 1920-1928*. New York: Prometheus Research Library.

Carawan, Guy and Candie Carawan, eds. 1963. *We Shall Overcome! Songs of the Southern Freedom Movement*. New York: Oak Publications.

Card No. X22063. 1937. "Current Lessons from the Experience of Labor." *One Big Union Monthly*, June. 16-20.

Carew, Jan. 1984. "Carribean Writers Speak," in Searle, 1984, 239-244.

Carnevali, Emanuel. 1967. *The Autobiography of Emanuel Carnevali*. New York: Horizon Press.

Carney, Jack. 1922. *Mary E. Marcy, 1877-1922*. Chicago: Charles H. Kerr.

Carpenter, Mecca Reitman. 1999. *No Regrets: Dr Ben Reitman and the Women Who Loved Him*. Lexington: South Side Press.

Castillo, Richard Griswold del. 1970. "The Discredited Revolution: The Magonista Capture of Tijuana in 1911." *Journal of San Diego History*. Fall, 256-273.

Cayton, Horace R. 1970. *Long Old Road: An Autobiography*. Seattle: University of Washington Press.*

Chafee Jr, Zechariah. *Free Speech in the U.S.* Cambridge: Harvard University Press.

Chandler, Charlotte. 1979. *Hello, I Must Be Going: Groucho and His Friends*. New York: Penguin.

Chapman, Robert L., ed. 1987. *American Slang*. New York: Harper & Row.

Chaplin, Ralph. 1916. "Joe Hill's Funeral." *International Socialist Review*, January, 400-405.

—. 1922. *Bars & Shadows: The Prison Poems*. New York: Leonard Press.

—. 1923. "Joe Hill: A Biography." *Industrial Pioneer*, November, 23-26.

—. 1924. *The Centralia Conspiracy*. Chicago: General Defense Committee.

—. 1926. "Joe Hill." *The Labor Defender*. New York: November, 189-190.

---. 1944. *Somewhat Barbaric: A Selection of Poems, Lyrics & Sonnets*. Seattle: Dogwood Press.

—. 1948. *Wobbly: The Rough-and-Tumble Story of an American Radical*. Chicago: University of Chicago Press.

—. 1948a. "An Open Letter to the *New Republic*." *Industrial Worker*, 31 January 1948, 2.

—. 1960. *Only the Drums Remembered*. Tacoma: Washington State Historical Society.

Chaplin, Charles. 1966. *My Autobiography*. New York: Pocket Books.

The Charles H. Kerr Company Archives, 1885-1985: A Century of Socialist & Labor Publishing. 1985. Chicago: Beasley Books, in association with the Charles H. Kerr Publishing Company.

Child, George B. 1915. "For Joe Hill."*International Socialist Review*, June, 754.

Churchill, Allen. 1959. *The Improper Bohemians*. New York: E. P. Dutton & Co.

Clarke, John Henrik, ed. 1974. *Marcus Garvey & the Vision of Africa*. New York: Vintage.

Cochran, David. 1991. "The Charles H. Kerr Company: Books to Change the World," in Sanford Berman and James P. Danky, eds., *Alternative Library Literature, 1990-91: A Biennial Anthology*. Jefferson: MacFarland & Co.

Cole, James Kelly. 1909. *Poems and Writings*. Chicago: IWW.

Conlin, Joseph R. 1969. *Big Bill Haywood and the Radical Union Movement*. Syracuse: Syracuse University Press.

—. 1974. *Bread & Roses Too, Studies of the Wobblies*. Westport: Greenwood Press.

—. 1981. *At the Point of Production: The Local History of the IWW*. Westport: Greenwood Press.

Cook, Bruce. 1971. *The Beat Generation*. New York: Scribner's.

Cooper, Wayne. 1987. *Claude McKay: Rebel Sojourner in the Harlem Renaissance*. Baton Rouge: Louisiana State University Press.

Corder, Minnie F. 1978. *You'll Never Go Hungry: An Autobiography."* Unpublished typescript in author's possession.

Corder, Raymond. 1937. "Industrial Unionism in the IWW: The Job Branch." *One Big Union Monthly*, July, 9-11.

Cortez, Carlos. 1965. "My Dust to Where Some Flowers Go." *Industrial Worker*. November.

—.1971. "Movie Review: Joe Hill."*Industrial Worker*, August.

—.1985. *"Wobbly": 80 Years of Rebel Art*. Chicago: Gato Negro Press.

—.1990. *Crystal-Gazing the Amber Fluid & Other Wobbly Poems*. Introduction by Eugene Nelson. Chicago: Charles H. Kerr.

—.1997. *Where Are the Voices? & Other Wobbly Poems*. Introduction by Archie Green. Chicago: Charles H. Kerr, 1997.

—, ed. 2002. *Viva Posada! A Salute to the Great Printmaker of the Mexican Revolution*. Chicago: Charles H. Kerr.

Cortez, Jayne. 2002 (1990). "Mainstream Statement." In Sakolsky 2002, 278.

Cox, Gary. 1970. "Joe Hill Day: Nov. 19th, Salt Lake City," *Industrial Worker*, January, 11.

Cronyn, George W. 1962 (1918). *American Indian Poetry: An Anthology of Songs and Chants*. Introduction by Mary Austin. New York: Liveright.

Dargan, Olive Tilford—See Burke, Fielding.

Darrow, Clarence. 2000. *Crime & Criminals: Address to the Prisoners in the Cook County Jail & Other Writings on Crime & Punishment*. Chicago: Charles H. Kerr.

Davis, Mike. 1992 (1990). *City of Quartz: Excavating the Future in Los Angeles.* New York: Vintage Books.

Davis, Jerome. 1929. *Labor Speaks for Itself on Religion: A Symposium.* New York: Macmillan.

Day, Dorothy. 1938. *From Union Square to Rome.* Silver Spring: Preservation of the Faith Press.

—. 1952. *The Long Loneliness.* New York: Harper & Row.

Debs, Eugene V. 1905. *Craft Unionism.* Chicago: IWW.

—. 1910 (1908). *Debs: His Life, Writings & Speeches.* Third ed. Introduction by Mary E. Marcy. Chicago: Charles H. Kerr.

—. 1972. *Eugene V. Debs Speaks.* New York: Edited by Jean Y. Tussey. Pathfinder Press.

—. 1990. *Letters of Eugene V. Debs. 1913-1919.* Edited by J. Robert Constantine. Urbana: University of Illinois.

—. 1990a. *Letters of Eugene V. Debs. 1919-1926.* Edited by J. Robert Constantine. Urbana: University of Illinois.

—. 2000 (1927). *Walls & Bars.* Introduction by David Dellinger. Chicago: Charles H. Kerr.

De Caux, Len. 1970. *Labor Radical, From the Wobblies to CIO—A Personal History.* Introduction by Staughton Lynd. Boston: Beacon.

—.1978. *The Living Spirit of the Wobblies.* New York: International.*

De Cleyre, Voltairine. 1990. *Written in Red: Selected Poems.* Introduction by Franklin Rosemont. Chicago: Charles H. Kerr.

Delaney, Ed, and M. T. Rice. 1927. *The Bloodstained Trail: A History of Militant Labor in the U.S.* Seattle: *Industrial Worker.*

Dell, Floyd. 1926. *An Old Man's Folly.* New York: George H. Doran Co.

—. 1926. *Love in Greenwich Village.* New York: George H. Doran Co.

—. 1933. *Homecoming: An Autobiography.* New York: Farrar & Rinehart.

Dellinger, David. 1993. *From Yale to Jail: The Life Story of a Moral Dissenter.* Marion, SD: Rose Hill Books.

DeShazo, Peter, and Robert J. Halstead. 1974. *Los Wobblies del Sur: The Industrial Workers of the World in Chile and Mexico.* Thesis. Madison: University of Wisconsin.

Di Pietro, Robert J., and Edward Ifkovic, eds. 1983. *Ethnic Perspectives in American Literature.* New York: Modern Language Association.

Doherty, Robert E. 1962. *Thomas J. Hagerty , the Church & Socialism.* Ithaca: NY State School of Industrial & Labor Relations.

Dolgoff, Sam. 1980. *The American Labor Movement: A New Beginning.* Champaign: Resurgence.

—. 1986. *Fragments: A Memoir: Personal Recollections Drawn from a Lifetime of Struggle in the Cause of Anarchism.* Cambridge, UK: Refract.

Donner, Frank. 1990. *Protectors of Privilege: Red Squads and Police Repression in Urban America.* Berkeley: University of California Press.

Doran, J. T. (Red). 1918. *Evidence & Cross-Examination of J.T. (Red) Doran in the Case of U.S.A. vs. Wm. D. Haywood.* Chicago: General Defense Committee.

Dos Passos, John. 1961. *U.S.A.* A trilogy including *The 42nd Parallel* (1930), *Nineteen Nineteen* (1931), and *The Big Money* (1936). New York: Washington Square Press.

Douglas, William O. 1974. *Go East Young Man: The Early Years.* New York: Random House.

Douglass, Frederick. 1987 (1855). *My Bondage and My Freedom.* Urbana: University of Illinois Press.

Dowell, Eldridge F. 1939. *History of Criminal Syndicalism Legislation.* Baltimore: Johns Hopkins University Press.

Dreyfus, Philip J. 1997. "The IWW and the Limits of Inter-Ethnic Organizing: Reds, Whites and Greeks in Gray's Harbor, Washington,1912." *Labor History* 38:4, 450-470.

Drinnon, Richard. 1997 (1980). *Facing West: The Metaphysics of Indian-Hating & Empire Building.* Norman: University of Oklahoma Press.

Dubofsky, Melvyn. 1966. Review of Foner's *Case of Joe Hill* and *Letters of Joe Hill. Labor History* 7:3. Fall. 354-358.

— 1969.*We Shall Be All: A History of the IWW.* New York: Quadrangle.*

—.1974. *We Shall Be All: A History of the IWW.* Revised paperback second edition.*

—.1987. *"Big Bill" Haywood.* Manchester: Manchester University Press.

Du Bois, W. E. B. 1970 (1935). *Black Reconstruction in America.* New York: Atheneum.

Dunbar-Ortiz, Roxanne. 1997. *Red Dirt: Growing Up Okie.* New York: Verso.

Eastman, Crystal. 1978. *On Women and Revolution.* Edited by Blanche Wiesen Cook. New York: Oxford.

Eastman, Max. 1936. *The Enjoyment of Laughter.* New York: Simon & Schuster.

—. 1948. *The Enjoyment of Living.* New York: Harper.

Ebert, Justus. n.d., c. 1919. *The IWW in Theory and Practice.* Chicago: IWW.

—. n.d., c. 1912-13. *The Trial of a New Society.* Cleveland: IWW Publishing Bureau.

Edwards, Herb (Hagbart M. Edvartsen). n.d., c. 1960s/70s. *A Norwegian Wobbly in America's Northwest: An Autobiography.* Unpublished typescript; copy in author's possession.

Ellington, Richard 1993. "Fellow Worker Guy Askew: A Reminiscence." In Archie Green 1993, 303-315.

—, and Dave Van Ronk, eds. 1959. *The Bosses' Songbook: Songs to Stifle the Flames of Discontent.* New York: Richard Ellington.

Emerson, Laura Payne. 1911. "A Visit to Mexico." *Solidarity* (Cleveland), No. 76, 2.

Engelmann, Larry D. 1974. "'We Were the Poor People': The Hormel Strike of 1933." *Labor History* 15:4 (Fall), 510.

Erdman, David V. 1969. *Blake: Prophet Against Empire: A Poet's Interpretation of the History of His Own Times.* New York: Anchor.

Erickson, Eva H. 1993. *The Rosa Lemberg Story.* Superior: Tyomies Society.

Eskin, Sam. 1972. "Harry K. McClintock (Haywire Mac)." Liner notes for Folkways album No. FD 5272. New York: Folkways Records.

Ettor, Joseph J. n.d., c. 1912. *Industrial Unionism: The Road to Freedom.* Chicago: IWW.

Evans, Les, ed. 1976. *James P. Cannon as We Knew Him.* New York: Pathfinder Press.

"The Execution of the IWW Poet." 1915. *Survey,* 27 November, 200.

Eyerman, Ron, and Andrew Jamison. 1998. *Music and Social Movements: Mobilizing Traditions in the Twentieth Century.* Cambridge, UK: Cambridge University Press.

Fagin, Sophia. 1939. *Public Forums in Chicago,* M.A. Thesis, Department of Sociology, University of Chicago.

Fair, Agnes Thecla. 1909. "Special Telegram to the *Review*." *International Socialist Review,* December, 558.

—. 1910. *The Sour Dough's Bible.* Seattle: Trustee Printing Company.

Falconer, George N. 1927. "The Slavery of Words." *The Proletarian,* September,

5-7.

Feied, Frederick.1964. *No Pie in the Sky: The Hobo as Cultural Hero.* New York: Citadel Press.

Ferrell, Jeff. 2001. *Tearing Down the Streets: Adventures in Urban Anarchy.* New York: Palgrave.

Flint, Robert. 1884. *Vico.* London: Blackwood.

Flynn, Elizabeth Gurley. 1915. "The IWW Call to Women." *Solidarity* (Cleveland), 31 July, 9.

—. 1937. "I Have No Regrets: A Chapter from American Labor History," in *The Woman Today*, April, 11, 26.

—. 1955. *I Speak My Own Piece: Autobiography of "The Rebel Girl."* New York: Masses & Mainstream.

—. 1973. *The Rebel Girl: An Autobiography. My First Life—1906-1926.* New York: International Publishers.

—. 1977. *Memories of the Industrial Workers of the World.* New York: American Institute of Marxist Studies.

—. 1997. *Direct Action & Sabotage.* With other texts by Walker C. Smith and William E. Trautman. Edited and introduced by Salvatore Salerno. Chicago: Charles H. Kerr.

Foner, Philip S. 1965. *History of the Labor Movement in the U.S.: The Industrial Workers of the World 1905-1917.* New York: International.

—. 1965a. *The Case of Joe Hill.* New York: International*.

—. [1965.] *Letters of Joe Hill.* Compiled by Philip Foner. New York: Oak.* NOTE: As specified in "A Note on the Notes," this volume is simply cited as *Letters*, without date, throughout this book.

—. 1975. *American Labor Songs of the Nineteenth Century.* Urbana: University of Illinois Press.

—. 1976. *Organized Labor and the Black Worker, 1619-1973.* New York: International.

—. 1981, ed. *Fellow Workers and Friends: IWW Free-Speech Fights as Told by Participants.* Westport: Greenwood Press.

—. 1984. *First Facts of American Labor.* New York: Holmes & Meier.

—. 1989, and Ronald L. Lewis. *Black Workers: A Documentary History from Colonial Times to the Present.* Philadelphia: Temple University Press.

Foot, Paul. 1984. *Red Shelley.* London: Bookmarks.

Foreman, Dave. 1987. *Ecodefense: A Field Guide to Monkeywrenching.* Tucson: Ned Ludd.

—. 1991. *Confessions of an Eco-Warrior.* New York: Harmony Books.

Fowke, Edith. 1960. With Joe Glazer. *Songs of Work and Freedom.* Garden City: Doubleday.*

Fox, Stephen. 1985. *The American Conservation Movement: John Muir and His Legacy.* Madison: University of Wisconsin Press.

Franklin, H. Bruce. 1982 (1978). *Prison Literature in America: The Victim as Criminal and Artist.* Westport: Lawrence Hill.

Freeman, Joseph. 1938. *An American Testament.* London: Victor Gollancz Ltd.

Freud, Sigmund. 1960. *Jokes and their Relationship to the Unconscious.* New York: Norton.

Friedman, Samuel H., ed. 1935. *Rebel Song Book.* New York: Rand School Press.*

Friends of Joe Hill Committee. 1948. "Joe Hill: IWW Martyr." *New Republic,* 15 November. 18-20.

Fusfeld, Daniel R. 1992 (1980). *The Rise & Repression of Radical Labor* in the United States: 1877-1918. Chicago: Charles H. Kerr.

Galarza, Ernesto. 1971. *Barrio Boy*. Notre Dame: University of Notre Dame Press.

Gallagher, Dorothy. 1989. *All the Right Enemies: The Life & Murder of Carlo Tresca*. New York: Penguin.

Gambs, John S. 1966 (1932). *The Decline of the IWW*. New York: Russell & Russell.

Garman, Bryan K. 2000. *A Race of Singers: Whitman's Working-Class Hero from Guthrie to Springsteen*. Chapel Hill: University of North Carolina Press.

Garon, Paul. 1970. "Blues and the Poetry of Revolt." *Arsenal/Surrealist Subversion* 1. Chicago: Black Swan Press, 24-30.

——. 1996 (1975). *Blues and the Poetic Spirit*. San Francisco: City Lights.

——. 1992, and Beth Garon. *Woman With Guitar: Memphis Minnie's Blues*. New York: DaCapo.

Gentry, Curt. 1967. *Frame-Up: The Incredible Case of Tom Mooney & Warren Billings*. New York: W. W. Norton.

Georgakas, Dan. 1975. *Detroit: I Do Mind Dying*. With Marvin Surkin. New York: St Martin's.

George, Harrison. 1918. *The IWW Trial: The Story of the Greatest Trial in Labor's History by One of the Participants*. Chicago: IWW.

Gerhard, Peter. 1946. "The Socialist Invasion of Baja California, 1911." *Pacific Historical Review*, September, 295-304.

Gibson, Morgan. 1986. *Revolutionary Rexroth: Poet of East-West Wisdom*. Hamden: Archon Press.

Giffin, Frederick. 1988. *The Tongue of Angels: The Mary Marcy Reader*. Selinsgrove: Susquehanna University Press.

Gifford, Barry. 1978. *Jack's Book: An Oral Biography of Jack Kerouac*. With Lawrence Lee. New York: St Martins Press.

Ginsberg, Allen. 1963. *Reality Sandwiches*. San Francisco: City Lights.

Giovannitti, Arturo. 1962. *Collected Poems*. Chicago: E. Clemente & Sons.

Girard, Frank, and Ben Perry. 1991. *The Socialist Labor Party: 1876-1991*. Philadelphia: Livra Books.

Glazer, Joe. 1997. "Power of the Union." *International Musician*. September, 8.

——. 2001. *Labor's Troubadour*. Urbana: University of Illinois Press.*

Gold, Mike. 1972. *Mike Gold: A Literary Anthology*. Edited & introduced by Michael Folsom. New York: International.

Golden, Harry. 1961. *Carl Sandburg*. Greenwich: Fawcett Publications.

Goldman, Emma. 1934. *Living My Life*. New York: Garden City.

Golin, Steve. 1988. *The Fragile Bridge: The Paterson Silk Strike—1913*. Philadelphia: Temple University Press.

Gomez, Manuel (pseudonym of Charles Shipman). n. d. (c. 1925). *Poems for Workers: An Anthology*. Chicago: *Daily Worker* Publishing Company.

Gordon, Linda. 1976. *Woman's Body, Woman's Right: A Social History of Birth Control in America*. New York: Penguin.

Gordon, Sam. 1976. "Reminiscences," in Evans 1976, 51-8

Graham, John. 1990. *"Yours for the Revolution": The* Appeal to Reason, *1895-1922*. Lincoln: University of Nebraska Press.

Graham, Marcus, ed. 1929. *An Anthology of Revolutionary Poetry*. New York: Active Press.*

Graham, Margaret. 1951. *Swing Shift*. New York: Citadel.

Graham, Maryemma, and Amritjit Singh, eds. 1986. *Conversations with Ralph Ellison*. Jackson: University of Mississippi Press.

Granell, Eugenio F. 1979. "A Living Vision of the Revolution," in Mary Low and Juan Brea: *Red Spanish Notebook: The First Six Months of the Revolution and the Civil War*. San Francisco: City Lights.

ı, Archie. 1960. "John Neuhaus: Wobbly Folklorist." *Journal of American Folklore* 73: 189-217.

—.1965. "American Labor Lore: Its Meaning and Uses." *Industrial Relations* 4. Urbana: University of Illinois.

—.1972. *Only a Miner.* Urbana: University of Illinois Press.

—.1978. "Industrial Lore: A Bibliographic-Semantic Query," in Robert H. Byington, ed. *Working Americans: Contemporary Approaches to Occupational Folklore.* Los Angeles: California Folklore Society.

—. 1983. "Afterword," in Reuss 1983.

—. 1989. "Working with Laborlore." *Labor's Heritage,* 1 July, 66-75.

—. 1993. *Wobblies, Pile Butts, and Other Heroes: Laborlore Explorations.* Urbana: University of Illinois Press.

—, ed. 1993a. *Songs About Work: Essays in Occupational Culture for Richard A. Reuss.* Bloomington: Indiana University Press.

—.1996. *Calf's Head & Union Tale.* Urbana: University of Illinois Press.

—.1997. "Carlos Cortez and Wobbly Artistry." Introduction to Cortez 1997.

Green, James R. 1978. *Grass-Roots Socialism: Radical Movements in the Southwest 1895-1943.* Baton Rouge: Louisiana State University.

Green, Martin. 1989. *New York 1913: The Armory Show & the Paterson Strike Pageant.* New York: Macmillian.

Greenberg, Martin H. 1981. *Fantastic Lives: Autobiographical Essays by Notable Science Fiction Writers.* Carbondale: Southern Illinois University Press.

Greenway, John. 1953. *American Folksongs of Protest.* New York: A. S. Barnes & Co.*

Grey, Zane. 1919. *The Desert of Wheat.* New York: Grosset & Dunlap.

Gutfeld, Arnon. 1969. "The Murder of Frank Little: Radical Labor Agitation in Butte, Montana, 1917." *Labor History* 10:2, Spring.

Hagerty, Thomas J. 1902. "How I Became a Socialist," in *The Comrade,* II:1, October, 6-7.

—. 1903. "Socialism Versus Fads "*International Socialist Review.* February, 449-453.

Hahn, Emily. 1967. *Romantic Rebels: An Informal History of Bohemianism in America.* Boston: Houghton Mifflin Co.

Halker, Clark D. 1991. *For Democracy, Workers, and God: Labor Song-Poems and Labor Protest, 1865-95.* Urbana: University of Illinois Press.

Hall, Covington. 1915. *Songs of Love and Rebellion.* New Orleans: John J. Weihing.

—.1946. *Battle Hymns of Toil.* Oklahoma City: General Welfare Reporter.

—.1985. *Dreams & Dynamite: Selected Poems.* Edited & introduced by Dave Roediger. Chicago: Charles H. Kerr.

—.1999. *Labor Struggles in the Deep South & Other Writings.* Edited & introduced by David R. Roediger. Chicago: Charles H. Kerr.

Halper, Jon. 1991. *Gary Snyder: Dimensions of a Life.* San Francisco: Sierra Club Books.

Hamalian, Linda. 1991. *A Life of Kenneth Rexroth.* New York: W. W. Norton.

Hammett, Dashiell. 1972 (1929). *Red Harvest.* New York: Vintage.

Hampton, Wade. 1986. *Guerrilla Minstrels: John Lennon, Joe Hill, Woody Guthrie, Bob Dylan.* Knoxville: University of Tennessee Press.

Hand, John Oliver. 1981. "Futurism in America: 1909-14." *Art Journal,* Winter, 337-342,

Hansen, Harry. 1923. *Midwest Portraits.* New York: Harcourt, Brace & Co.

Hanson, Nils H. n.d., c. 1910s. *The Onward Sweep of the Machine Process.* Chicago: IWW Publishing Bureau.

Hanson, Ole. 1920. *Americanism versus Bolshevism.* New York: Doubleday, Page & Co.

Hanson, Rob E., ed., n.d. c. 1985. *The Great Bisbee IWW Deportation of July 12, 1917.* Bigfork, Mt: Signature Press.

Hapgood, Hutchins. 1939. *A Victorian in the Modern World.* New York: Harcourt, Brace & Co.

Hardt, Michael, and Antonio Negri. 2000. *Empire.* Cambridge: Harvard University Press.

Hardy, George. 1956. *Those Stormy Years.* London: Lawrence & Wishart.*

Harris, Joe. 1970. *The Bitter Fight: A Pictorial History of the Australian Labor Movement.* Brisbane: University of Queensland Press.

Harris, Wilson. 1967. *Tradition, the Writer & Society: Critical Essays.* London: New Beacon.

Harrison, Hubert. 2001. *A Hubert Harrison Reader.* Edited & introduced by Jeffrey B. Perry. Middletown: Wesleyan University Press.

Haywood, Harry. 1978. *Black Bolshevik: Autobiography of an Afro-American Communist.* Chicago: Liberator Press.

Haywood, William D. 1910. *Industrial Socialism.* With Frank Bohn. Chicago: Charles H. Kerr.

—. n.d. (1915). *Testimony of William D. Haywood Before the Industrial Relations Committee.* Chicago: IWW Publishing Bureau.

—. 1915. "Sentenced to Be Shot—Act Quick!" *International Socialist Review,* August, 110.

—. 1923. Statement on the U.S. labor movement, the IWW and the Negro worker, in Claude McKay 1923.

—. 1929. *Bill Haywood's Book.* New York: International.

Hegel, G. W. F. 1981 (1977). *Phenomenology of Spirit.* Translated by A. V. Miller. New York: Oxford University Press.

Heise, Kenan. 1998. *Chaos, Creativity, and Culture: A Sampling of Chicago in the Twentieth Century.* Salt Lake City: Gibbs Smith.

—. *Songbird of the Wobblies.* Unpublished play about Katie Phar and Joe Hill. Typescript in author's possession.*

Hellman, Lillian. 1976. *Scoundrel Time.* New York: Little, Brown.

Hennacy, Ammon. 1970. *The Book of Ammon.* Revised edition. Introduction by Steve Allen. Salt Lake City: The Author.*

—, ed. 1967. *If I Were Free: A collection of songs sung every Friday night at the Joe Hill House.* With Utah Phillips *et al.* Salt Lake City: Utah Wobbly Press.*

Henry, W. G. 1912. "Bingham Canyon." *International Socialist Review,* October, 340-343.

Herrada, Julie. 1999."Agnes Inglis: Anarchist Librarian." With Tom Hyry. *Progressive Librarian/Special Supplement to No. 16.* Fall, 7-10.

Herreshoff, David. 1967. *American Disciples of Marx: From the Age of Jackson to the Progressive Era.* Detroit: Wayne State University Press.

Hicks, Granville, *et al.,* eds. 1935. *Proletarian Literature in the U.S.* New York: International.

Higbie, Tobias. 2000. *Indispensable Outcasts: Seasonal Labor and Community in the Middle West.* Doctoral Dissertation. Urbana: University of Illinois.

Hill, Joe. 1906. "The Catastrophe in San Francisco—A Resident of Gävle Tells the Story." In Gibbs Smith 1969, 49-51.

—. 1910. "Another Victim of the Uniformed Thugs," *Industrial Worker.* 27 August.

—. 1913. "The People." *Industrial Worker,* March 6. Reprinted in Kornbluh, *Rebel Voices.*

—. 1914. "How to Make Work for the Unemployed." *International Socialist Review*, December. Reprinted in Kornbluh, *Rebel Voices.*

—. 1915. "A Few Reasons Why I Demand a New Trial." In Gibbs Smith, *Joe Hill*, 264-268.

—. 1915a. "To the People of Utah." *International Socialist Review*, October, 222-223. (Excerpts from the preceding text.)

—. 1915b. *The Rebel Girl.* Sheet music. Chicago: IWW.

—. 1915c. *Workers of the World, Awaken!* Sheet music. Chicago: IWW.

—. 1915d. *Don't Take My Papa Away from Me: Song-Picture from the War.* Sheet music. Chicago: IWW.

—. 1923. "The Last Letters of Joe Hill." Introduced by Sam Murray. *Industrial Pioneer,* December.

—. 1960 (1955). *Songs of Joe Hill.* Edited by Barrie Stavis and Frank Harmon. New York: Oak Publications.

—. 1965. *Letters of Joe Hill.* Compiled by Philip Foner. New York: Oak Publications.

—. 1969 (1915). Letter to E. W. Vanderleith. In Gibbs Smith, *Joe Hill*, 132.

—. 1969. "A Joe Hill song checklist compiled by Archie Green," including the complete texts of Hill's labor songs. In Gibbs Smith, *Joe Hill*, 231-260.

—. 1984. (1911-14). Four postcards to Charles Rudberg, introduced by Philip Mason. *Labor History* 25:4 (Fall), 553-557.

Hille, Waldemar, ed. 1948. *The People's Song Book.* New York: Boni & Gaer.

Hilton, Orrin N. 1915. "On the Hill Case." *International Socialist Review*, September, 171-172.

—. 1915. "The IWW scare in Salt Lake City." *Sunset Magazine*, November, 854-855.

—. 1915. "A Challenge: An Open Letter to the Board of Pardons of the State of Utah." *International Socialist Review,* December, 328

Himes, Chester. 1989 (1947). *Lonely Crusade.* New York: Thunder's Mouth Press.

Hokanson, Nels. "Swedes and the IWW," in *The Swedish Pioneer* XXIII:1, January 1972, 25-36.

Holbrook, Stewart. 1946. "The Last of the Wobblies" [on Art Boose]. *American Mercury*, April, 462-468.

—. 1957. *Dreamers of the American Dream.* New York: Doubleday.

Hooton, Harry. 1945. "The IWW in Australia." *Industrial Worker,* Chicago, 17 November.

—. 1990. *Harry Hooton: Poet of the 21st Century. Collected Poems.* Australia: Collins/Angus & Robertson.

Horn, Maurice, ed. 1976. *The World Encyclopedia of Comics.* New York: Chelsea House.

Hough, Emerson. 1919. *The Web.* Chicago: Reilly & Lee.

Hughes, Langston, ed. 1961. *An African Treasury.* New York: Pyramid Books.

Ignatiev, Noel. 1995. *How the Irish Became White.* New York: Routledge.

—, and John Garvey, eds. 1996. *Race Traitor* (anthology). New York: Routledge.

Inman, Mary. 1935. *In Woman's Defense.* Los Angeles: Committee to Organize the Advancement of Women.

"IWW Fights Slander: Friends of Joe Hill Picket *New Republic*." 1948. *Industrial Worker,* 20 April, 1, 4.

IWW:s Sångbok. Stockholm: IWW. (Swedish edition of the Little Red Song Book).*

IWW Songs—To Fan the Flames of Discontent. Various editions. Chicago: IWW.*

Jablonski, Joseph. 1982. "Millennial Soundings: Chiliasts, Cathari, and Mystical

Feminism in the American Grain." *Free Spirits: Annals of the Insurgent Imagination*. San Francisco: City Lights.

—. 1989. "The War on Leisure." Introduction to Paul Lafargue, *The Right to Be Lazy*. Chicago: Charles H. Kerr.

James, C. L. R. 1969. "The West Indian Intellectual." Introduction to a new edition of J. J. Thomas, *Froudacity: West Indian Fables Explained*. London: New Beacon Books.

—. 1984. "Caribbean Writers Speak," in Chris Searle 1984, 246-248.

—. 1994. *C. L. R. James & Revolutionary Marxism: Selected Writings, 1939-1949*. Edited by Scott McLemee and Paul Le Blanc. Atlantic Highlands: Humanities Press.

Jensen, Vernon H. 1951. "The Legend of Joe Hill." *Industrial & Labor Relations Review* 4:1 (April), 356-366.

Johnson, Harold R. 1924. "Joe Hill, Song Writer."*Industrial Pioneer*, June, 44.

Jones, James. 1951. *From Here to Eternity*. New York: Scribner's.

"Joe Hill." 1915. *International Socialist Review*, December, 329-330.

"Joe Hill's Ashes Discovered." 1988. *Industrial Worker*, June, 5.

"Joe Hill's Ashes to be Reclaimed." 1988. *Industrial Worker*, July, 1.

"Joe Hill's Character Assailed." *Industrial Worker*, 17 January 1948, 1.

"Joe Hill's Sister Hopes Youth Today Spreads His Ideas." 1956. *Industrial Worker*, 23 January, 2.

Johnson, Diane. 1983. *Dashiell Hammett: A Life*. New York: Random House.

Johnson, Oakley C. 1974. *Marxism in United States History: Before the Russian Revolution, 1876-1917*. New York: Humanities Press.*

Johnson, Stancil E. D. 1975. *Frisbee: A Practitioner's Manual & Definitive Treatise*. New York: Workman.

Jones, Mary Harris. 1996 (1925). *The Autobiography of Mother Jones*. Chicago: Charles H. Kerr.

Jordan-Smith, Paul. 1923. *Cables of Cobweb*. New York: Lieber & Lewis.

—. 1960. *The Road I Came*. Caldwell: Caxton Printers.

Jungmarker, Gunnar. 1946. *Oskar Anderson (OA): 1877-1906*. Stockholm: Sveriges Allmanna Konstforenings Publikation LV.

Katz, Bernard, ed. 1969. *The Social Implications of Early Negro Music in the U.S.* New York: Arno Press.

Keller, Helen. 1967. *Helen Keller: Her Socialist Years. Writings and Speeches*. Edited by Philip S. Foner. New York: International.

Kelley, Robin D. G. 1990. *Hammer and Hoe: Alabama Communists During the Great Depression*. Chapel Hill: University of North Carolina Press.

—. 1993. "Lucy Parsons." In Darlene Clark Hine, ed., *Black Women in America: An Historical Encyclopedia*. Brooklyn: Carlson. 909-910.

—. 1994. *Race Rebels: Culture, Politics, and the Black Working Class*. New York: The Free Press.

—. 1997. *Yo' Mama's Disfunktional: Fighting the Culture Wars in Urban America*. Boston: Beacon Press.

—. 1998. "Introduction." In Marx and Engels, *Communist Manifesto*, 150th Anniversary Edition. Chicago: Charles H. Kerr.

—. 2002. *Freedom Dreams: The Black Revolutionary Imagination*. Boston: Beacon Press, 2002.

Kelley, Edith Summers. 1974. *The Devil's Hand*. Carbondale: Southern Illinois University Press.

Keracher, John. 1955. *The Head-Fixing Industry*. Chicago: Charles H. Kerr.

Kerouac, Jack. 1958. *The Dharma Bums*. New York: Viking.

—. 1959. "The Origins of the Beat Generation." *Playboy* 6:6, 31-32, 42, 79.

Reprinted in Parkinson, ed., 1961, 68-76.

—. 1966. *Desolation Angels.* New York: Bantam.

—. 1960. *Lonesome Traveler.* New York: Grove.

—. 1999. *Atop an Underwood.* New York: Penguin.

Kerr, Charles H., ed. 1901. *Socialist Songs With Music.* Chicago: Charles H. Kerr.

—. 1910. "Mexico, Our Capitalists' Slave Colony." *International Socialist Review,* December, 364.

Kiesler, Frederick J. 1942. "Some Testimonial Drawings of Dream-Images." *VVV No. 1..*27-32.

Klemanski, John S., and Alan DiGaetano. 1982. "Wobblies and Autoworkers: The Industrial Workers of the World in Detroit." *Detroit in Perspective,* Spring, 22-39.

Knight, Etheridge. 1988. *The Essential Etheridge Knight.* Pittsburgh: University of Pittsburgh Press.

Kokk, Enn, ed. 1973. *Joe Hills Sånger.* Stockholm: Bokförlaget Prisma.*

Kornbluh, Joyce L., ed. 1998 (1988, 1964). *Rebel Voices: An IWW Anthology.* Revised/expanded edition. Chicago: Charles H. Kerr.*

Kornbluth, Cyril N. 1955. *Not This August.* Garden City: Doubleday.

Kornweibel, Jr., Theodore. 1998. *Seeing Red: Federal Campaigns Against Black Militancy, 1919-1925.* Bloomington: Indiana University Press.

Kovel, Joel. 1994. *Red-Hunting in the Promised Land: Anticommunism and the Making of America.* New York: Basic Books.

—. 2002. *The Enemy of Nature: The End of Capitalism or the End of the World.* New York: Zed.

Kramer. Dale. 1966. *Chicago Renaissance: The Literary Life in the Midwest, 1900-1930.* New York: Appleton-Century.

Kreymborg, Alfred.1925. *Troubadour: An Autobiography.* New York: Boni and Liveright.

—. 1929. *Our Singing Strength: An Outline of American Poetry 1620-1930.* New York: Coward-McCann.

Lacarriere, Jacques. 1977. *The Gnostics.* New York: E. P. Dutton.

Lafargue, Paul. 1989 (1883). *The Right to Be Lazy.* Introduction by Joseph Jablonski; bio-bibliographical essay by Fred Thompson. Chicago: Charles H. Kerr.

Lang, Lucy Robins. 1948. *Tomorrow Is Beautiful.* New York: Macmillan.

Langdon, Emma F. 1904-05. *The Cripple Creek Strike: A History of Industrial Wars in Colorado 1903-4-5, Being a Complete and Concise History of the Efforts of Organized Capital to Crush Unionism.* Denver: The Great Western Publishing Co.

Larkin, Jim. 1915. "Murder Most Foul." *International Socialist Review,* December, 330-331.

Latchem, E. W. 1920. "The Modern Agricultural Slave." *One Big Union Monthly,* August, 54-56.

—, et al. 1922. *The IWW Reply to The Red Trade Union International.* Chicago: IWW.

Laut, Agnes. 1912. "Revolution Yawns!." *International Socialist Review,* November, 426-431.

Lee, Robert. 1999. *Orientals: Asian Americans in Popular Culture.* Philadelphia: Temple University Press.

Leier, Mark. 1990. *Where the Fraser River Flows, The IWW in British Columbia.* Vancouver: New Star Books.*

Leonard, Jim "Superstar," and Janet E. Graebner. 1989. *Scratch My Back: A Pictorial History of the Musical Saw and How to Play It.* Santa Ana (CA):

Kaleidoscope Press.

Lesher, Sam. 1924. "Shut Up." *Industrial Pioneer*, April.

Lewis, Austin. n.d. *Proletarian & Petit-Bourgeois*. Chicago: IWW Publishing Bureau.

—. 1911. *The Militant Proletariat*. Chicago: Charles H. Kerr.

Lewis, Tom J. 1910. "Get Hip." *International Socialist Review*, December, 351-352.

Lieberman, Robbie. 1986. "People's Songs: American Communism and the Politics of Culture." *Radical History Review*, September, 63-78.

Lighter, J. E., ed. 1997. *Random House Dictionary of American Slang*. New York: Random House.

Linebaugh, Peter, and Marcus Rediker. 2000. *The Many-Headed Hydra: Sailors, Slaves, Commoners, and the Hidden History of the Revolutionary Atlantic*. Boston: Beacon Press.

Lipton, Lawrence. 1959. *The Holy Barbarians*. New York: Julian Messner, Inc.

Little Red Song Book—See *IWW Songs: To Fan the Flames of Discontent*

Loughery, John. 1992. *Alias S. S. Van Dine. The Man Who Created Philo Vance*. New York: Scribner's.

Lovell, Jr., John. 1939. "The Social Implications of the Negro Spiritual," in Katz 1969.

Löwy, Michael, and Robert Sayre. 2001. *Romanticism Against the Tide of Modernity*. Durham: Duke University Press.

Lynd, Staughton. 1966. *Nonviolence in America: A Documentary History*. Indianapolis: Bobbs-Merrill.

—, and Alice Lynd, eds. 1973. *Rank & File: Personal Histories by Working-Class Organizers*. Boston: Beacon Press.

—, ed.1996. *"We are All Leaders": The Alternative Unionism of the Early 1930s*. Urbana: University of Illinois Press.

—.1992. *Solidarity Unionism: Rebuilding the Labor Movement from Below*. With cartoons by Mike Konopacki. Chicago: Charles H. Kerr.

Maass, Alan.1986. "The Little Red Book House: The Charles H. Kerr Publishing Company of Chicago." (Chicago) *Reader*, 17 October.

Maata, John. 1985. *My Father's Heritage*. New York Mills: Parta Printers.

MacDonald, J. A. 1916. "Homes for Yourself or Your Boss?" *International Socialist Review*, February, 462-464.

—. 1925. *Unemployment & the Machine*. Chicago: IWW.

Macdonald, Dwight. 1960. *Parodies: An Anthology from Chaucer to Beerbohm —and After*. New York: Random House.

MacKay, Alexander, writing as "Johnnie Johns." 1947. "The San Diego Free Speech Fight of 1912." Serialized in the *Industrial Worker*, July-August.

—. n.d., 1950. Review of Wallace Stegner's *The Preacher and the Slave*. Publication data unknown. Copy in the MacKay file in the Archie Green papers, Southern Folklife Collection, Wilson Library, University of North Carolina at Chapel Hill.

Magon, Ricardo Flores. 1977. *Land and Liberty: Anarchist Influences in the Mexican Revolution*. Edited by David Poole. Sanday: Cienfuegos Press.

Maitron, Jean. 1983. *Le Mouvement anarchiste en France. II: De 1914 a nos jours*. Paris: Maspero.

Mann, Ed. n.d., c. 1980s. *We Are the Union: The Story of Ed Mann*. Edited by Alice & Staughton Lynd. Niles, OH: Solidarity USA.

Manners, Jane. 2001. "Joe Hill Goes to College." *The Nation*, 2 July.

Man Ray. 1963. *Self-Portrait*. Boston: Little, Brown.

Marcy, Mary. 1910. *Out of the Dump*. Illustrated by Ralph Chaplin. Chicago:

Charles H. Kerr.

—. 1910a. "Introduction" to Debs 1910.

—. 1911. *Shop Talks on Economics*. Chicago: Charles H. Kerr. Also published by the IWW.

—. 1916. "Work & Play." *International Socialist Review*. November, 297.

—. 1917. *Stories of the Cave People*. Chicago: Charles H. Kerr.

—. and Roscoe B. Tobias.1918. *Women as Sex Vendors*. Chicago: Charles H. Kerr.

—. 1919. "The IWW Convention," in *The Liberator,* July, 10-12.

—. 1919a. *Industrial Autocracy*. Chicago: Charles H. Kerr.

—. 1921. *A Free Union: A One-Act Drama of "Free Love."* Chicago: Charles H. Kerr.

—. 1922. *Rhymes of Early Jungle Folk*. Woodcuts by Wharton H. Esherick. Chicago: Charles H. Kerr.

—. 1984. *You Have No Country: Workers' Struggle Against War*. Edited and introduced by Franklin Rosemont. Chicago: Charles H. Kerr.

Markholt, Ottilie. 1998. *Maritime Solidarity: Pacific Coast Unionism 1929-1938*. Tacoma: Pacific Coast Maritime History Committee.

Martin, Tony. 1983. *Literary Garveyism: Garvey, Black Arts & the Harlem Renaissance*. Dover, MA: Majority Press.

Martinez, Pablo L. 1960. *A History of Lower California*. Translated by Ethel Duffy Turner. Mexico: Editorial Baja California.

Marx, Karl, and Frederick Engels. 1998 (1848). *The Communist Manifesto*. 150th Anniversary Edition. Introduction by Robin D. G. Kelley. Chicago: Charles H. Kerr.

—. 1972. *The Ethnological Notebooks*. Edited and introduced by Lawrence Krader. Assen: Van Gorcum & Co.

Mason, Philip. 1984. "Joe Hill—Cartoonist." *Labor History* 25:4 (Fall), 553-557.

Matera, Lia. 1997. *Star Witness*. New York: Pocket Star Books.

Mattson, Edward. 1941. "Joe Hill." *Signalen* (publication of the Miners' Union in Sweden).

May, Henry F. 1959. *The End of American Innocence: A Study of the First Years of Our Own Time, 1912-1917*. New York: Knopf.

Maynard, Mila Tupper. 1903. *Walt Whitman: The Poet of the Wider Selfhood*. Chicago: Charles H. Kerr.

Mayoux, Jehan. 1968. "Avant-Propos." In Grandizo Munis and Benjamin Péret, *Les Syndicats contre la révolution*. Paris: Eric Losfeld.

—. 1979. *La Liberté une et divisible: Textes critiques et politiques. Oeuvres complètes V*. Ussel: Editions Peralta.

McCormick, Charles. 1997. *Seeing Reds: Federal Surveillance of Radicals in the Pittsburgh Mill District, 1917-1921*. Pittsburgh: University of Pittsburgh Press.

McDarrah, Fred W. 1963. *Greenwich Village*. New York: Corinth Books.

McDermott, John. 1971. *Joe Hill*. New York: Grosset & Dunlap. (A novel based on the Bo Widerberg film.)*

McGuckin, Henry E. 1987. *Memoirs of a Wobbly*. Chicago: Charles H. Kerr. *

McKay, Claude. 1965. *Home to Harlem*. New York: Pocket Books.

—.1970. *A Long Way from Home: An Autobiography*. Introduction by St Clair Drake. New York: Harcourt Brace.

—.1979 (1923). *The Negroes in America*. London: Kennikat Press.

McKenna, Maureen A. 1985. "Julia Thecla: Painter of Magic Worlds and Magic Visions." Springfield: *The Living Museum*, 47:1 (Winter), 2-6.

Mellen, Joan. 1972. "*Sacco and Vanzetti* and *Joe Hill*." *Film Quarterly* 25, Spring

48-53.

Mers, Gilbert. 1988. *Working the Waterfront: The Ups and Downs of a Rebel Longshoreman*. Austin: University of Texas Press.

Milburn, George. 1930. "Poesy in the Jungles." *American Mercury*. May, 80-86.

—. 1930a. *The Hobo's Hornbook*. New York: Ives Washburn.

Miles, Dione. 1986. *Something in Common—An IWW Bibliography*. Detroit: Wayne State University Press.

Miller, Terry. 1990. *Greenwich Village and How It Got That Way*. New York: Crown.

Mills, C. Wright, ed. 1962. *The Marxists*. New York: Dell.

Mitchell, David. 1970. *1919: Red Mirage*. New York: Macmillan.

Mitchell, H. L. 1987 . *Roll the Union On! A Pictorial History of the Southern Tenant Farmers Union*. Chicago: Charles H. Kerr.

—. 1988. "The IWW & the Southern Tenant Farmers' Union: An Interview with H. L. Mitchell." Interview by Franklin Rosemont. *Industrial Worker*, April.

Mitgang, Herbert, ed. 1968. *The Letters of Carl Sandburg*. New York: Harcourt, Brace.

Modesto, Zapata (pseudonym of Barry Arlen Nichols). 1962. "The Death of Joe Hill." *Mainstream*, September. 3-16.

—. 1963. "Joe Hill: Some Notes on a American Culture Hero." *Wobbly* (mimeographed publication of the Berkeley, California IWW Branch).

—. 1963a. "Joe Hill Biographer Needs More Material." *Industrial Worker*, 17 July.

Monoldi, Peo. 1937. "The Construction Worker." *One Big Union Monthly*, July, 3-6.

Monroe, Harriet. 1967 (1932). *Poets & Their Art*. Freeport: Books for Libraries Press.

Moore, J. Howard. 1916. *The Universal Kinship*. Chicago: Charles H. Kerr.

More Truth About the IWW. 1918. Chicago: IWW.

Moreau, Louis. "Readers' Soap Box." *Industrial Worker*, 29 March 1961, 2.

—. "Time for Action Is Running Out." *Industrial Worker*, 17 June 1964, 2.

Morgan, Elizabeth. 1997. *Socialist and Labor Songs of the 1930s*. Introduction by Utah Phillips. Chicago: Charles H. Kerr.*

Morris, James O. 1950. "The Joe Hill Case." Thesis. In the Labadie Collection, University of Michigan Library, Ann Arbor.

—, and Philip S. Foner. "Philip Foner and the Writing of *The Joe Hill Case*: An Exchange." *Labor History* 12:1 (Winter), 81-114.

Munson, Gorham. 1985. *The Awakening Twenties: A Memoir-History of a Literary Period*. Baton Rouge: Louisiana State University Press.

Murray, R. Emmet. 1989. *The Lexicon of Labor*. New York: New Press.

Murray, Morgan. 1962 (1951). *Skid Road: An Informal Portrait of Seattle*. New York: Viking Press.

Murray, Sam. 1923. Introduction to "The Last Letters of Joe Hill." *Industrial Pioneer*, December, 53-54, 56.

—.1925. "Industrial Unionism Triumphant." *General Office Bulletin*, March.

—.1925a. "The Passing of a Building Trades Boss." *Industrial Pioneer*, April, 26-28.

—.1925b. "Detroit: Mother of 12,000,000 Fords." *Industrial Pioneer*, October, 28-31.

—.1926. "Crime, Salesmanship, and Such Things."*Industrial Pioneer*, January, 21-25.

—.1926a. "Some Observations on the Building Industry." *Industrial Pioneer*, July, 30-34.

—.1926b. "Mendocino: Where Volstead Made Two Grapevines Grow Where None Ever Grew Before." *Industrial Pioneer*, September, 9-11.

Naifeh, Steven, and G. W. Smith. 1989. *Jackson Pollock: An American Saga*. New York: Clarkson Potter.

Naville, Pierre. 1979 (1962). *Trotsky Vivant*. Paris, Maurice Nadeau.

Neal, Larry. 1989. *Visions of a Liberated Future: Black Arts Movement Writings*. New York: Thunder's Mouth Press.

Nef, Walter T. 1916. "Job Control in the Harvest Fields." *International Socialist Review*, September, 141-143.

Nelson, Bruce C. 1985. *Culture and Conspiracy: A Social History of Chicago Anarchism 1870-1900*. Dekalb: Dissertation, Northern Illinois University.

—. 1988. *Beyond the Martyrs: A Social History of Chicago's Anarchists 1870-1900*. Condensed version of the preceding title. New Brunswick: Rutgers University Press.

Nelson, Caroline. 1912. *Nature Talks on Economics*. Chicago: Charles H. Kerr.

Nelson, Cary. 1989. *Repression & Recovery: Modern American Poetry & the Politics of Cultural Memory, 1910-1945*. Madison: University of Wisconsin Press.

Nelson, Eugene. 1993. *Break Their Haughty Power: Joe Murphy in the Heyday of the Wobblies—A Biographical Novel*. San Francisco: Ism Press.

—. 1998. *Fantasia of a Revolutionary*. Illustrated by Carlos Cortez. Haleiwa, HI: Infinite Possibilities Press.

Nerman, Ture. 1979. *Joe Hill: Mördare eller Martyr?* Stockholm: Pogo Press.*

Neubauer, John. 1980. *Novalis*. Boston: Twayne.

Neufeld, Maurice, ed. 1978. "Portrait of the Labor Historian as Boy and Young Man: Excerpts from the Interviews of Philip Taft by Margaret Honig." *Labor History*, 19:1 (Winter). 39-71.

The New Justice. 1970. (1919-1920). Westport: Greenwood.

Noebel, David A. 1965. *Communism, Hypnotism and the Beatles*. Tulsa: Christian Crusade Publications.

—. 1966. *Rhythm, Riots and Revolution*. Tulsa: Christian Crusade Publications.

—. 1974. *The Marxist Minstrels: A Handbook on Communist Subversion of Music*. Tulsa: American Christian College Press.

Noel, Joseph. 1940. *Footloose in Arcadia: A Personal Record of Jack London, George Sterling, Ambrose Bierce*. New York: Carrick & Evans.

Nolan, William F. 1983. *Hammett: A Life at the Edge*. New York: Congdon & Weed, Inc.

North, Joseph, ed. 1980. *New Masses: An Anthology of the Rebel Thirties*. New York: International.

Norwood, Stephen H. 1990. *Labor's Flaming Youth: Telephone Operators and Worker Militancy. 1878-1923*. Urbana: University of Illinois Press.

Novalis (Friderich von Hardenburg). 1960. *Hymns to the Night and Other Selected Writings*. Translated and introduced by Charles E. Passage. Indianapolis: Bobbs-Merrill.

Oberndorf, Clarence. 1953. *A History of Psychoanalysis in America*. New York: Harper & Row.

O'Brien, Charles M. n.d., c. 1950s. Unpublished autobiography in the Archives of the Proletarian Party, Labadie Collection, University of Michigan Library, Ann Arbor.

O'Brien, Frederick. 1921. *Mystic Isles of the South Seas*. New York: The Century Company.

O'Connor, Harvey. 1964. *Revolution in Seattle*. New York: Monthly Review Press.*

—. 1988, and Jessie Lloyd O'Connor, with Susan M. Bowler. *A Couple of Radicals.* Foreword by Dave Roediger. Philadelphia: Temple University Press.*

Olay, Maximiliano. n.d., c. 1941. *Mirando al Mundo.* Preface by Rudolf Rocker. No place of publication: Impresos Americalee.

O'Neal, Bill. 1979. *Encyclopedia of Western Gunfighters.* Norman: University of Oklahoma Press.

On the Firing Line. n.d., c. 1912. Spokane: *Industrial Worker.*

Palkkaorjain Lauluja [IWW Songs in Finnish]. 1925. Duluth: Workers Socialist Publishing Company.

Paretsky, Sara. 1990 (1982). *Indemnity Only.* New York: Dell.

Park, Robert E., and Ernest W. Burgess. 1967 (1925). *The City.* Chicago: University of Chicago Press.

Parker, Carleton. 1920. *The Casual Laborer and Other Essays.* New York: Harcourt, Brace.*

Parkinson, Thomas. 1961. *A Casebook on the Beat.* New York: Thomas Y. Crowell Co.

Parnack, Jack. "My Experience at the College." *Industrial Worker,* 15 October 1927.

Parry, Albert. 1960. *Garrets and Pretenders: A History of Bohemianism in America* New York: Dover.

Patai, Daphne, ed. 1988. *Looking Backward, 1988-1888: Essays on Edward Bellamy.* Amherst: University of Massachusetts Press.

Pepper, Art. 1979. *Straight Life: The Story of Art Pepper.* With Laurie Pepper. New York: Schirmer.

Péret, Benjamin. 1943. *La Parole est à Péret.* New York: Editions Surréalistes.

Perlman, Selig. 1935. With Philip Taft. *History of Labor in the U.S. 1896-1932.* New York: Macmillan.

Perry, Grover H. n.d., c. 1910s. *The Revolutionary IWW.* Chicago: IWW Publishing Bureau.

Petaja, Emil. 1968. *The Time Twister.* New York: Dell.

Peters, Nancy Joyce, and Lawrence Ferlinghetti. 1980. *Literary San Francisco: A Pictorial History, from the Beginnings to the Present Day.* San Francisco: City Lights Books and Harper & Row.

Peterson, Joyce Shaw.1993. "Matilda Robbins: A Woman's Life in the Labor Movement, 1900-1920." *Labor History* 34:1 (Winter), 33-56.

Pfaff, Henry J. 1983. *Didactic Verses.* Buffalo: Henry J. Pfaff.

Phillips, Utah. 1984. "Utah Phillips Sings the Songs and Tells the Stories of the Industrial Workers of the World." 12-page insert in the LP, *We Have Fed You All for a Thousand Years.* Introduction by Fred Thompson. Philo Records.

"Picketing of *New Republic* for Hill Slander Continues." Industrial *Worker,* 17 April 1948. 1.

Pittenger, Mark. 1993. *American Socialists & Evolutionary Thought, 1870-1920.* Madison: University of Wisconsin Press.

Poole, Ernest. 1915. *The Harbor.* New York: Macmillan.

—. 1940. *The Bridge: My Own Story.* New York: Macmillan.

Porter, Nancy. 1985. "Afterword" to Mary Austin 1985, 295-321.

Portis, Larry. 1985. *IWW et syndicalisme révolutionaire aux Etats-Unis.* Paris: Spartacus.

Post, Louis F. 1923. *The Deportations Delirium of Nineteen-Twenty.* Chicago: Charles H. Kerr.

Powers, Joe, and Mark Rogovin, eds. 1994. *The Day Will Come: Stories of the Haymarket Martyrs and the Men and Women Buried Alongside the*

Monument. Chicago: Published for the Illinois Labor History Society by the Charles H. Kerr. Company.

Preamble and Constitution of the IWW. Various editions. Chicago: IWW.

Preston Jr., William.1963. *Aliens & Dissenters, Federal Suppression of Radicals 1903-1933.* New York: Harper Torchbooks.

—.1971. "Shall This Be All? U.S. Historians versus William D. Haywood *et al.*" *Labor History*12:3 (Summer), 435-453. Review of books on the IWW by Conlin, Dubofsky, Renshaw, and Gibbs Smith.

Proceedings 1905. *The Founding Convention of the IWW.* New York: New York Labor News. Reprinted 1969 by Merit Publishers, New York.

Putnam, Samuel. 1933. "Red Days in Chicago." *American Mercury*, 30:117 September.

Rachleff, Peter. 1993. *Hard-Pressed in the Heartland: The Hormel Strike and the Future of American Labor.* Boston: South End.

—. 1996. "Organizing 'Wall to Wall': The Independent Union of All Workers, 1933-37," in Staughton Lynd, ed. 1996.

Rammel, Hal. 1990. *Nowhere in America: The Big Rock Candy Mountain and Other Comic Utopias.* Urbana: University of Illinois Press.

Read, Pat (under the pseudonym "Con Dogan"). 1937. "Songs of the Struggle." *One Big Union Monthly,* July.

The Rebel Worker. 1964-67. Journal of the Chicago Branch of the IWW. Seven issues.

Reed, John. 1972. *The Education of John Reed.* New York: International.

Rees, Richard. 1996. "Ray Sprigle, Pioneer." *Race Traitor* 6 (Summer).

Reitman, Ben, ed. 1937. *Sister of the Road: The Autobiography of Box-Car Bertha.* New York: Macaulay.

Renshaw, Patrick. 1968. *The Wobblies, The Story of Syndicalism in the U.S.* Garden City: Doubleday, Anchor.

Reuss, Richard A. 1971."The Roots of American Left-Wing Interest in Folksong." *Labor History* 12:9 (Spring), 259-279.

—. 1983. *Songs of American Labor, Industrialization, and the Urban Work Experience: A Discography.* Ann Arbor: Program on Working Culture, University of Michigan.

Reynolds, Mack. 1966. *Of Godlike Power* (later reissued as *Earth Unaware*). New York: Belmont.

—. 1968. *Mercenary from Tomorrow.* New York: Ace.

—. 1981. "Science Fiction and Socioeconomics." In Greenberg, ed., 1981.

—. 1986. *Deathwish World.* With Dean Ing. New York: Baen Books.*

Rexroth, Kenneth. 1952. *The Dragon and the Unicorn.* Norfolk: New Directions.

—. 1966. *The Collected Shorter Poems of Kenneth Rexroth.* New York: New Directions.

—. 1971. *American Poetry in the Twentieth Century.* New York: Herder & Herder.

—. 1991. *An Autobiographical Novel.* New York: New Directions, 1991. Revised & expanded edition; originally published in 1977 by Whittet Books, Weybridge, Surrey, U.K.

Richards, Sam. 1993. "The Joe Hill Legend in Britain," in Archie Green 1993.

Riebe, Ernest. 1984 (1913). *Mr Block: Twenty-four IWW Cartoons.* Introduction by Franklin Rosemont. Chicago: Charles H. Kerr.*

Robbins, Bob. 1925. "Those Processional Blues." *Industrial Pioneer*, April, 25.

Robbins, Matilda. 1962. "Baja Revolution 1911: The Desert Revolution" (review of Blaisdell 1962). *Industrial Worker,* June.

Roberts, Randy. 1983. *Papa Jack: Jack Johnson and the Era of White Hopes.*

New York: Free Press.

Robeson, Paul. 1988 (1958). *Here I Stand*. New introduction by Sterling Stuckey. Boston: Beacon Press.

Rocker, Rudolf. 1989 (1938/1947). *Anarcho-Syndicalism*. Preface by Noam Chomsky. London: Pluto Press.

Roediger, David. 1982. "Covington Hall: The Republic of Imagination." *Free Spirits: Annals of the Insurgent Imagination*. San Francisco: City Lights.

—. and Franklin Rosemont, eds. 1986. *Haymarket Scrapbook* Chicago: Charles H. Kerr.

—. 1986a."100 Years Young: The Charles H. Kerr Company," in *Canadian Dimension* (Fall).

—. 1988. "An Injury to One: IWW Organizing in the Deep South." *Industrial Worker*, April.

—. 1989, ed. *Our Own Time: A History of American Labor and the Working Day*. With Philip Foner. London & New York: Verso.

—. 1990, ed. *In the Shell of the Old: Essays on Workers' Self-Organization. A Salute to George Rawick*. With Don Fitz. Chicago: Charles H. Kerr.

—. 1994. *Towards the Abolition of Whiteness: Essays on Race, Politics, and Working Class History*. London: Verso.

—.1994a. "A Working-Class Jokester" [on T-Bone Slim]. *Against the Current*, March-April, 44.

—. 2002. *Colored White: Transcending America's Racial Past*. Berkeley: University of California Press.

—. 2002a. "A Long Journey to the Hip Hop Nation." In Sakolsky 2002, 595.

Rogers, Walter. 1945. *John Donar: Common Man: For the Little Shots of American Labor*. With Elizabeth Rogers. New Orleans: Victory Library.

—. 1972. *Big Wheels Rolled in Texas: 1940 through Pearl Harbor*. With Elizabeth Rogers. New Orleans: Victory Library.

Róheim, Géza. 1992. *Fire in the Dragon & Other Psychoanalytic Essays on Folklore*. Princeton, NJ: Princeton University Press.

Rosemont, Franklin, ed. 1978. *What Is Surrealism? Selected Writings of André Breton*. New York: Monad Press; new edition, New York: Pathfinder, 2000.

—, ed. 1984.*You Have No Country! Workers Struggle Against War: Selected Writings of Mary E. Marcy*. Chicago: Charles H. Kerr.

—, ed. 1984. *Mr Block: Twenty-Four IWW Cartoons* by Ernest Riebe. Chicago: Charles H. Kerr.

—, and Dave Roediger, eds. 1986. *Haymarket Scrapbook*. Chicago: Charles H. Kerr, 1986.

—. 1987. "Labor Cartoons," in Gary Huck and Mike Konopacki, *Bye! American: The Labor Cartoons of Huck and Konopacki*. Chicago: Charles H. Kerr.

—. 1988. "Bellamy's Radicalism Reclaimed," in Daphne Patai, ed., 1988, 147-209.

—. 1988a. "Ralph Chaplin: Wobbly Poet." *Industrial Worker*, May.

—. 1988b. "A Short Treatise on Wobbly Cartoons," in Kornbluh, ed., 1988; new edition, 1998.

—. 1989. "Karl Marx and the Iroquois: A Study of the *Ethnological Notebooks*," in *Arsenal/Surrealist Subversion 4*. Chicago: Black Swan Press, 201-213. Reissued as a pamphlet, without notes, by Red Balloon (New York, 1992).

—, ed. 1990. *Apparitions of Things to Come: Edward Bellamys Tales of Mystery & Imagination*. Chicago: Charles H. Kerr.

—, ed. 1990. *Written in Red: Selected Poems of Voltairine de Cleyre*. Chicago: Charles H. Kerr.

—, ed. 1992. *Juice Is Stranger Than Friction: Selected Writings of T-Bone Slim*.

Chicago: Charles H. Kerr.
—. 1994. "John Muir," in Mari Jo Buhle *et al*, eds., *The American Radical*. New York: Routledge.
—, ed. 1994 (1981). *Isadora Speaks: Writings & Speeches of Isadora Duncan*. Revised and expanded, Chicago: Charles H. Kerr.
—, ed. 1997. *From Bughouse Square to the Beat Generation: Selected Ravings of Slim Brundage*. Chicago: Charles H. Kerr.
—, Penelope Rosemont and Paul Garon, eds. 1997a. *The Forecast Is Hot! Tracts & Other Collective Declarations of the Surrealist Movement in the United States, 1966-1976*. Chicago: Black Swan Press.
—. 1998 (1990). "IWW Cartoons," in Mari Jo Buhle *et al*, eds., 1998, 359-362.
—. 1998. "Joe Hill,"in the preceding volume, 310-313.
—. 1998. "Radical Environmentalism," in the preceding volume, 660-666.
—. 1998. "T-Bone Slim," in the preceding volume, 816.
—. 1998. "Walter T. Nef," in the preceding volume, 542.
—, ed. 1998. *Surrealism: Revolution Against Whiteness* (special issue of the anti-white-supremacist journal *Race Traitor*, 1998.
—. 2000. "Introduction" to Frank O. Beck: *Hobohemia: Emma Goldman, Lucy Parsons, Ben Reitman & Other Agitators & Outsiders in 1920s/30s Chicago*. Chicago: Charles H. Kerr.
Rourke, Constance. n.d. (1931). *American Humor: A Study of the National Character*. New York: Doubleday Anchor.
Rowan, Ed, *et al*. 1915. "Save Joe Hill." *International Socialist Review*, August. 126.
Ruff, Allen. 1997. *"We Called Each Other Comrade": Charles H. Kerr & Company, Radical Publishers*. Urbana, University of Illinois Press.
Russell, Bert. 1979. *Swiftwater People*. Harrison, ID: Lacon Publishers.*
Russo, Pasquale, 1923. *Tony, the Immigrant*. Chicago: Pasquale Russo.*
Sagebrush, Johnny, *et al*. 1986. *The Li'l Green Songbook*. Tucson: Ned Ludd.
St John, Vincent. 1908. "The Economic Argument for Industrial Unionism." *International Socialist Review*, September, 172-179.
—. 1910. "The Brotherhood of Capital and Labor: Its Effect on Labor." *International Socialist Review*, January, 587-593.
—. 1912. "The Fight for Free Speech at San Diego." *International Socialist Review*, April, 649.
—. n.d., c. 1913. *Industrial Unionism: The IWW*. Chicago: IWW.
—. n.d., c. 1914. *Why the American Federation of Labor Cannot Become an Industrial Union*. Chicago: IWW.
—. 1914. "The Working Class and War." *International Socialist Review*, August, 117-118.
—. 1919 (1913). *The IWW: Its History, Structure, and Methods*. Revised edition. Chicago: IWW.
Sakolsky, Ron. 1990. "Culture from the Bottom Up: The Traveling Wobbly Art Show," in Roediger 1990.
—, and Fred Wei-han Ho. 1995. *Sounding Off! Music as Subversion/Resistance/Revolution*. New York: Autonomedia.
—, and Stephen Dunifer. 1998. *Seizing the Airwaves: A Free Radio Handbook*. San Francisco: AK Press.
—, ed. 2002. *Surrealist Subversions: Rants, Writings & Images by the Surrealist Movement in the United States*. New York: Autonomedia.
Salerno, Salvatore. 1986. "The Impact of Haymarket on the Founding of the IWW: The Anarchism of Thomas J. Hagerty," in Roediger and Rosemont, eds., 1986, 189-191.

—. 1989. *Red November, Black November: Culture and Community in the Industrial Workers of the World*. Albany: State University of New York Press.

—. "Soapboxing the Airwaves," in Sakolsky 1998.

Sandburg, Carl. 1927. *The American Songbag*. New York: Harcourt, Brace & Co.*

—. 1936. *The People, Yes*. New York: Harcourt, Brace & Co.

—. 1952 *Always the Young Strangers*. New York: Harcourt, Brace.

Sandburg, Helga. 1963. *Sweet Music*. New York: Dial Press.*

Sandos, James A. 1992. *Rebellion in the Borderlands: Anarchism and the Plan of San Diego, 1904-1923*. Norman: University of Oklahoma Press.

Sånger av Joe Hill. 1915. Swedish edition off the Little Red Song Book.* Stockholm: IWW.

Sanger, Margaret. 1971. *Margaret Sanger: An Autobiography*. New York: Dover.

Sansom, Philip. 1951. *Syndicalism: The Workers' Next Step*. London: Freedom Press.

—. 1987. "Surprise, Surprise! A Curate's Egg!" (on Surrealism in England). *The Raven 3* (November), 267-79.

Saxton, Alexander.1948. *The Great Midland*. New York: Appleton-Century-Crofts.

Schiller, Friedrich. 1910. *Essays Aesthetical and Philosophical*. London: George Bell & Sons.

—. 1971. *Letters on the Aesthetic Education of Man*. New York: Ungar.

Schofield, Ann. 1983. "Rebel Girls and Union Maids: The Woman Question in the Journals of the AFL and IWW, 1905-1920." *Feminist Studies* 9:2 (Summer), 335-358.

Schulze, David. 1990. "The Industrial Workers of the World and the Unemployed in Edmonton and Calgary in the Depression of 1913-1915." *Labour/Le Travail* 25 (Spring), 47-75.

Schwarz, Arturo. 1977. *Man Ray: The Rigour of Imagination*. New York: Rizzoli.

Scott, Jack. 1975. *Plunderbund & Proletariat: A History of the IWW in British Columbia*. Vancouver: New Star Books.*

Scott, James C. 1985. *Weapons of the Weak: Everyday Forms of Peasant Resistance*. New Haven: Yale University Press.

—. 1990. *Domination and the Arts of Resistance: Hidden Transcripts*. New Haven: Yale University Press.

Scribner, Tom. 1976. *Lumberjack, with Appendix on Musical Saw*. Mimeographed. Third edition. No publishing data given.

Searle, Chris. 1984. *Words Unchained: Language & Revolution in Grenada*. London: Zed Books.

Seeger, Pete. 1954. "'The Man Who Never Died'" (review of Barrie Stavis's play). *Sing Out!* 6-7 (Fall), 22-23.

—. 1985. *Carry It On! A History in Song and Picture of America's Working Men and Women*. With Bob Reiser. New York: Simon & Schuster.*

Seldes, George. 1935. *Freedom of the Press*. Indianapolis: Bobbs-Merrill.

—. 1941. *Lords Of the Press*. New York: Blue Ribbon Books.

—. 1943. *Facts and Fascism*. New York: In Fact, Inc.

—. 1947. *One Thousand Americans*. New York: Boni & Gaer.

—. 1953. *Tell the Truth and Run*. New York: Greenberg.

—. 1967 (1960). *The Great Quotations*. New York: Pocket Books.

Sellars, Nigel Anthony. 1998. *Oil, Wheat & Wobblies: The IWW in Oklahoma 1905-1930*. Norman: University of Oklahoma Press.

Seymour, Jim. 1919. "R-R-R-Raw Food!" *The New Justice* 1:13, 15 August, 13.

Shea, Robert, and Robert Anton Wilson. 1975. *Illuminatus* (a trilogy). New York:

Dell.

Shelley, Percy Bysshe. 1961. *The Complete Poetical Works*. New York: Oxford University Press.

Shields, Art. 1983. *My Shaping Up Years*. New York: International.

Shipman, Charles. 1993. *It Had to Be Revolution: Memoirs of an American Radical*. Ithaca: Cornell University Press.

Sigal, Clancy. 1963 (1961). *Going Away: A Report, A Memoir*. New York: Popular Library.

Sillito, John R. 1981. "Women and the Socialist Party in Utah, 1900-1920." *Utah Historical Quarterly*, Vol. 49 (Summer), 220-238.

Sinclair, Upton. 1915. *The Cry for Justice*. New York: Upton Sinclair.*

—. 1924. *Singing Jailbirds: A Drama in Four Acts*. Pasadena: The Author.*

—. 1927. *Oil!* New York: Grosset & Dunlop.

—. 1970. *Jimmie Higgins*. Lexington: University of Kentucky Press.

Skandinavisk IWW Sang Bok. n.d., c. 1920s/30s. Seattle: Skaninaviska Propaganda Gruppen. Songs in Swedish, Norwegian and Danish.*

Skårdal, Dorothy Burton. 1983. "Scandinavian-American Literature," in Di Pietro 1983, 232-265.

Smith, Alson J. 1953. *Chicago's Left Bank*. Chicago: Henry Regnery Company.

Smith, Gibbs M. 1984 (1969). *Joe Hill*. Salt Lake City: Gibbs M. Smith, Inc.

Smith, Todd. 1988. "I Dreamed Joe Hill Was Playin' Rock and Roll." *Labor Notes,* June 1988, 2.

Smith, Walker C., n. d., c. 1916. *The Everett Massacre: A History of the Class Struggle in the Lumber Industry*. Chicago: IWW Publishing Bureau.

Snyder, Gary. 1961. "Buddhist Anarchism." *Journal for the Protection of All Beings*. San Francisco: City Lights. Revised and retitled "Buddhism and the Coming Revolution" in Snyder's collection, *Earth House Hold* (New Directions, 1969).

—. 1980. *The Real Work: Interviews & Talks—1964-1979*. New York: New Directions.

—.1992. *No Nature: New & Selected Poems*. New York: Pantheon.

Söderström, Ingvar. 1970. *Joe Hill: Diktare och Agitator*. Stockholm: Bokförlaget Prisma.* Reissued in a new, expanded edition, 2002.

Solomon, Carl. 1966. *Mishaps, Perhaps*. San Francisco: City Lights.

Sorell, Victor Alejandro, ed. 2002. *Carlos Cortez Koyokuikatl: Soapbox Artist and Poet*. Chicago: Mexican Fine Arts Center Museum.

Souchy, Augustin. 1920. *Anarkist maertyrena i Chicago*. Stockholm.

—. 1992. *Beware Anarchist! A Life for Freedom*. Edited by Sam Dolgoff & Richard Ellington; translated & introduced by Theo Waldinger. Chicago: Charles H. Kerr.*

Spargo, John. 1913. *Syndicalism, Industrial Unionism & Socialism*. New York: B. W. Huebsch.

Spencer, Fanny Bixby 1920. *The Jazz of Patriotism*. Long Beach: George W. Moyle.

Spero, Sterling D., and Abram L. Harris.1969 (1931). *The Black Worker*. New York: Atheneum.

Spielman, Jean E. 1923. *The Stool Pigeon and the Open Shop Movement*. Minneapolis: The American Publishing Company.

Stansell, Christine. 2000. *American Moderns: Bohemian New York and the Creation of a New Culture*. New York: Holt.

Starrett, Vincent. 1965. *Born in a Bookshop: Chapters from the Chicago Renascence*. Norman: University of Oklahoma Press.

Stavis, Barrie. 1954. *The Man Who Never Died: a Play about Joe Hill*. New York:

Haven Press.*

—. 1955. *The Songs of Joe Hill.* With Frank Harmon. New York: People's Artists. Reissued 1960 by Oak Publications.*

—. 1964. "Joe Hill: Poet: Organizer." Part I. *Folk Music,* June, 3-4, 38-50.*

—. 1964. "Joe Hill: Poet: Organizer." Part II. *Folk Music,* August, 27-29, 38-50.*

Steelink, Nicolas. n.d., c. 1970s. *Journey into Dreamland: An Autobiography.* Unpublished typescript; copy in author's possession.

Stegner, Wallace. 1947. "'I Dreamed I Saw Joe Hill Last Night.'" *Pacific Spectator,* Spring 1947, 184-189.

—. 1948. "Joe Hill: The Wobblies' Troubadour." *The New Republic,* 5 January, 20-24, 38.

—. 1950. *The Preacher and the Slave.* Boston: Houghton Mifflin Co.*

Stevens, James. 1975. *Big Jim Turner.* Albuquerque: University of New Mexico Press.

Stevenson, Elizabeth. 1998. *Babbits and Bohemians: From the Great War to the Great Depression.* New Brunswick: Transaction.

Stodder, James. n.d., c. 1970s. "Covington Hall, Life & Values," introduction to Hall's *My Life in the Louisiana Class Struggle* (excerpts from *Labor Struggles in the Deep South*).

Stuckey, Sterling.1987. *Slave Culture: Nationalist Theory & the Foundations of Black America.* New York: Oxford University Press.

—. 1994. *Going Through the Storm: The Influence of African American Art in History.* New York: Oxford University Press.

Sullivan, Edward Dean. 1930. *Chicago Surrenders.* New York: Vanguard Press.

Swados, Harvey. 1970. *Standing Fast.* Garden City: Doubleday.

Swankey, Ben. 1977. *"Work and Wages"! A Documentary Account of the Life & Times of Arthur H. (Slim) Evans.* With Jean Evans Sheils. Vancouver: Trade Union Research Bureau.*

Taft, Philip. 1972. "A Note on 'General' Mosby." *Labor History* 13:4 (Fall), 552-554.

Takman, John. 1956. "Joe Hill's Sister: An Interview." *Masses & Mainstream,* March, 4-30.

Targ, William. 1975. *Indecent Pleasures: The Life and Colorful Times of William Targ.* New York: Macmillan.

Tax, Meredith. 1980. *The Rising of the Women.* New York: Monthly Review Press.

Taylor, Lawrence D. 1999. "The Magonista Revolt in Baja California: Capitalist Conspiracy or Rebellion de los Pobres?" *Journal of San Diego History* 45:1 (Winter).

Taylor, Lori Elaine. 1990. *Don't Mourn—Organize! Songs of Labor Songwriter Joe Hill,* booklet accompanying the Smithsonian/Folkways recording of the same title (SF40026, recorded 29 January 1990).*

—. 1993. "Joe Hill Incorporated: We Own Our Own Past," in Archie Green 1993.

T-Bone Slim. 1933. "T-Bone Economics." *Industrial Worker,* 28 February.

—. 1992. *Juice Is Stranger Than Friction: Selected Writings.* Edited and introduced by Franklin Rosemont. Chicago: Charles H. Kerr.

Terkel, Studs. 1970. *Hard Times.* New York: Pantheon.

—. 1977. *Talking to Myself: A Memoir of My Times.* New York: Pantheon.

—. 1986. *Chicago.* New York: Pantheon.

Thomas, Joan. 1974. *The Years of Grief & Laughter.* Phoenix: Hennacy Press.

Thompson, Bonar. 1934. *Hyde Park Orator.* New York: G.P. Putnam's Sons.

Thompson, E. P. 1993. *Witness Against the Beast: William Blake and the Moral*

Law. New York: The New Press.

Thompson, Fred W. 1930-1932. "The IWW Tells Its Own Story." Serialized in *Industrial Solidarity* from 21 December 1930 through 2 August 1932. *Note:* In this book I have cited *not* the printed version, but the original typescript (copy in author's possession).

—. n. d., c. 1930s. "Marxism and Union Policies." Unpublished typescript; copy in author's possession.

—.1955. *The IWW: Its First Fifty Years*. Chicago: IWW. Reissued 1976 with new material, under the title *The IWW: Its First Seventy Years*.

—.1965. Review of Frederick Feied's *No Pie in the Sky*. *Industrial Worker*, May.

—.1966. "Why Joe Hill Wrote His 'Casey Jones.'" *Industrial Worker*, February.

—.1969. *World Labor Needs a Union*. Chicago: IWW.

—. 1969a. "Another 'Labor Historian' Writes a Book About the Wobblies—So What Else is New?" [review of Melvyn. Dubofsky's *We Shall Be All*]. *Industrial Worker*, November.

—.1970. "More Books on Joe Hill and the Wobblies" [on Gibbs Smith's biography and others]. *Industrial Worker,* May.

—.1971. *Joe Hill*. San Diego: IWW.

—.1971a. "Was Joe Hill Guilty?" (on James Morris's views as expressed in *Labor History*). *Industrial Worker*, March.

—.1979. *Joe Hill: Wobbly Songwriter*. Revised, expanded edition of the 1971 title. With Dean Nolan. Chicago: IWW.

—.1976. *The IWW: Its First Seventy Years*, with an update by Patrick Murfin Chicago: IWW.

—.1984. Interview by Harry Doakes in "Just Folkies: Songs the Wobblies Taught Us." (Chicago) *Reader*, 31 August, Section 1, 6.

—.1984a. "Joe Hill Revisited." *Industrial Worker*, September.

—.1987. "Notes on 'The Most Dangerous Woman in America,'" in *The Autobiography of Mother Jones*. Chicago: Charles H. Kerr.

—.1988. Introduction to Kornbluh 1988.

—.1989. "Paul Lafargue, Life & Leisure," in Lafargue's *The Right to Be Lazy*. Chicago: Charles H. Kerr.

—.1998. *Fellow Worker: The Life of Fred Thompson*, edited and introduced by Dave Roediger. Chicago: Charles H Kerr.

Thompson, James P. 1929. "Religion Is the Negation of Truth," in Jerome Davis 1929.

—. 1930. "Revolutionary Class Union." *Twenty-Five Years of Industrial Unionism*. Chicago: IWW, 3-12.

Tietjens, Eunice. 1916. "Cormorants." *International Socialist Review*, September, 169.

—. 1938. *The World at My Shoulder*. New York: Macmillan.

Toomer, Jean. 1931. *Essentials*. Chicago: Private Edition.

Traven, B. 1969. *The Cotton-Pickers*. New York: Hill & Wang.

Tridon, André. 1911. "The New Cult of Futurism Is Here" (interview). *New York Sun*, magazine section, 24 December.

—.1912. "The Futurists, Latest Comers in the World of Art." *New York Sun*, 25 February.

—.1915 (1914). *The New Unionism*. New York: B. W. Huebsch.

Tripp, Anne Huber. 1987. *The IWW and the Paterson Silk Strike of 1913*. Urbana: University of Illinois Press.

Trotsky, Leon. 1960 (1924). *Literature & Revolution*. Translated by Rose Strunsky. Ann Arbor: University of Michigan Press.

The Truth About the IWW Prisoners. n.d., c. 1921. New York: American Civil

Liberties Union.

"Trying to Railroad a Rebel." 1914. *International Socialist Review*, August, 126.

Turner, Ethel Duffy. 1981. *Revolution in Baja California: Ricardo Flores Magon's High Noon*. Edited and annotated by Rey Devis. Detroit: Blaine Etheridge.

Turner, John Kenneth. 1910. *Barbarous Mexico*. Chicago: Charles H. Kerr.

—.1911. "The Mexican Revolution." *The Pacific Monthly*, June, 609-625.

Twenty-Five Years of Industrial Unionism. 1930. Chicago: IWW.

Tyson, Timothy. 1999. *Radio Free Dixie: Robert F. Williams & the Roots of Black Power*. Chapel Hill: University of North Carolina Press.

Vaché, Jacques. 1970 (1919). *Lettres de guerre*. Paris: Eric Losfeld.

Vanderveer, George F. 1918. *Opening Statement of Geo. F. Vanderveer in the case of the U.S.A. vs. William D. Haywood, et al*. Chicago: IWW Publishing Bureau.

Van Valkenburgh, W. S. 1915. "The Murder of Joseph Hillstrom." New York: *Mother Earth*. December. 326-328.

Varney, Harold Lord. "The Story of the IWW." Serialized in the *One Big Union Monthly*, 1919-20.

Vorse, Mary Heaton. 1935. *A Footnote to Folly*. New York: Farrar & Rinehart.

Wagaman, David G. 1975. "The Industrial Workers of the World in Nebraska, 1914-1920." *Nebraska History*, 295-337.

Wagenknect, Edward. 1952. *Cavalcade of the American Novel*. New York: Henry Holt & Co.

Walker, Bertha. 1972. *Solidarity Forever!* Melbourne: National Press.

Walker, Charles Rumford. 1937. *American City: A Rank-and-File History*. New York: Farrar & Rinehart.

Waring John. 1916. "Questioned the Executioners." *International Socialist Review*, January, 405.

Watson, Patrick. 1973. *Fasanella's City*. New York: Alfred A. Knopf.

Weintraub, Hyman. 1947. "The IWW in California." Thesis, in the library of the University of California at Los Angeles.

Weisberger, Bernard A. 1967. "Here Come the Wobblies!" *American Heritage* 18-4,.June, 30-35, 87-93.

Weisbord, Vera Buch. 1977. *A Radical Life*. Bloomington: Indiana University Press.

Weiss, Henry George. n.d., c. 1924. *The Shame of California and Other Poems*. Chicago: General Defense Committee.

Werstein, Irving. 1969. *Pie in the Sky: An American Struggle—The Wobblies and Their Times*. New York: Delacorte Press.*

Wertheimer, Barbara Mayer. 1977. *We Were There: The Story of Working Women in America*. New York: Pantheon.

Whitehead, Fred, and Verle Muhrer. eds. 1992. *Freethought on the American Frontier*. Buffalo: Prometheus Books.*

Whitman, Walt. 1967 (1945). *The Portable Walt Whitman*. New York: Viking.

Wieck, David Thoreau.1992. *Woman from Spillertown: A Memoir of Agnes Burns Wieck*. Carbondale: Southern Illinois University Press.

Wilkesbarr, Frederick M. 1927. *The Gospel According to Malfew Seklew*. Chicago: The Author.

Williams, Ben H. n.d., c. 1912. *Eleven Blind Leaders, or "Practical Socialism" and "Revolutionary Tactics."* New Castle, PA: IWW Publishing Bureau.

—. n.d., c. 1960. *Saga of the One Big Union*. Unpublished manuscript, copy in author's possession.

Williams, George. 1921. *The First Congress of the Red Trade Union International at Moscow, 1921.* Chicago: IWW.

Wilson, Edmund. 1980. *The Thirties.* Edited by Leon Edel. New York: Washington Square Press.

Wilson, James. 1908. "The Value of Music in IWW Meetings." *Industrial Union Bulletin,* 24 October, 1.

Winters Jr, Donald E. 1985. *The Soul of the Wobblies.* Westport: Greenwood Press.*

Wixson, Douglas. 1994. *Worker-Writer in America: Jack Conroy and the Tradition of Midwestern Literary Radicalism, 1898-1990.* Urbana: University of Illinois Press.

"The Wobblies March Again." 1948. *Time,* 19 April, 26.

Wohlforth, Tim. 1968. *The Struggle for Marxism in the United States.* New York: Bulletin Publications.

Woodruff, Abner E. n.d., c. 1910s. *Evolution of American Agriculture.* Chicago: Agricultural Workers' Industrial Union.

Workers Music League. 1932. *Red Song Book.* New York: Workers Library.*

Yelensky, Boris. 1951. "Twenty-Five Years of 'Free Society' Activity in Chicago," in *The World Scene From the Libertarian Point of View.* Chicago: Free Society Group.

Young, Art. 1928. *On My Way.* New York: Horace Liveright.

Young, Henry. 1981. *Haywire Mac & The Big Rock Candy Mountain.* Temple, TX: Stillhouse Hollow Publishers.

Zaniello, Tom. 1996. *Working Stiffs, Union Maids, Reds, and Riffraff: An Organized Guide to Films About the Labor Movement.* Ithaca: ILR Press.

Zanjani, Sally, and Guy Louis Rocha. 1986. *The Ignoble Conspiracy: Radicalism on Trial in Nevada.* Reno: University of Nevada Press.

Zorbaugh, Harvey W. 1929. *The Gold Coast and the Slum.* Chicago: University of Chicago Press.

II. Letters

Letters to Archie Green from Richard Brazier, Mary Gallagher, Alexander MacKay, Barry Nichols (Zapata Modesto), and Fred Thompson are in the Archie Green Collection in the Southern Folklife Collection of the Wilson Library at the University of North Carolina in Chapel Hill.

Fred Thompson's correspondence with John Beffel, Richard Brazier, William Chance, Minnie Corder, Archie Green, Aubrey Haan, Ammon Hennacy, Agnes Inglis, Tynne and Vaino Konga, Louis Moreau, Barry Nichols, Carl Person, and Gibbs Smith is part of the Fred Thompson Collection in the Walter Reuther Library at Wayne State University in Detroit, which also houses the IWW Archives.

Augustin Souchy's letters to the IWW are also in the IWW Archives at Wayne State.

A letter to Carlos Cortez from Ralph Chaplin's widow is in Cortez's possession.

A letter from Frances Horn to Philip Mason, regarding Hill's friend Charles Rudberg, is included in the IWW Archives at Wayne State.

Alexander MacKay's letters are widely scattered. The largest collection (fifty-eight letters and a telegram to Upton Sinclair, dating from 1934 through 1963), is in the Lilly Library. His correspondence with Archie Green is included in the Archie Green Collection at the University of North Carolina in Chapel Hill. The IWW Archives at Wayne State contain three letters from MacKay (1947-48). Two 1957 letters to John Keracher are included in the Proletarian Party

Archives in the Labadie Collection at the University of Michigan, and his 1954 letter to the Charles H. Kerr Company is part of the Charles H. Kerr Publishing Company Archives in The Newberry Library, Chicago.

The IWW Archives at Wayne State also include: an important exchange of letters between William Chance and Minnie Corder, as well as letters from Louis Moreau and Harry McClintock, addressed to the *Industrial Worker*.

Letters to Franklin and/or Penelope Rosemont from Guy B. Askew, Slim Brundage, Jack Conroy, Minnie Corder, Dave Dellinger, Esther and Sam Dolgoff, Al Glotzer, Archie Green, Hans Haste, Frances Horn, Meridel LeSueur, Gilbert Mers, Katherine Kerr Moore, O. N. Peterson, Henry Pfaff, George Seldes, Ruth Sheridan, Bruce E. Sloan, Ingvar Söderstrom, Fred Thompson, and Jenny Lahti Velsek are in the author's possession.

III. Interviews

Richard J. Altenbaugh. Interview with Fred Thompson. 1984. Transcript in author's possession.

Archie Green. Interview with Richard Brazier. 1960. Tape-recording and transcript in the Archie Green Collection at the University of North Carolina..

Archie Green: Interview with Mary Gallagher. Notes in the Archie Green Collection.

Franklin Rosemont: Interviews with Gertrude Abercrombie, Nelson Algren, James Allen, Carl Berreitter, Harry Busck, Sam Calander, Harry Chase, Carlos Cortez, Carl Cowl, Ruth Dear, Sam Dolgoff, Richard Ellington, Lawrence Ferlinghetti, Ruth and Joseph Giganti, Al Glotzer, Archie Green, Sarah Gruber, Ted Joans, Ella Jenkins, Carl Keller, James "Bozo" Kodl, Philip Lamantia, Jack Langan, Burr McCloskey, Karl Meyer, Jack Micheline, H. L. Mitchell, Art Nurse, O. N. Peterson, Utah Phillips, Ralph W. Rieder, Trina Robbins, Walter Schonbrun, Harry Siitonen, Gary Snyder, Lillian and Ed Stattman, Wallace Stegner, Joffre Stewart, William Targ, Studs Terkel, Fred Thompson, Geraldine Udell, Jenny Lahti Velsek, Virgil Vogel, Stan Weir, Vera Buch and Albert Weisbord, George Weissman, and Al Wysocki. Recordings, transcripts, and/or notes in author's possession.

IV. Films and Videos

"*The Man Who Never Died*." c. 1960-1963. Canadian Broadcasting Company; made for TV.*

"Joe Hill." 1971. Bo Widerberg, director. In Swedish, with English subtitles.*

"The Wobblies." 1979. Stewart Bird and Deborah Shaffer, directors.*

"The Return of Joe Hill." 1990. Eric Scholl, director. Chicago.*

"Joe Hill." 1998. Ken Verdoia, director. Salt Lake City: KUED TV. *

V. Recordings

Joan Baez. 1970. *Woodstock*. Cotillion SD 3-500.

Joe Glazer. 1954. *The Songs of Joe Hill*. Folkways FA 2039.*

—. 1977. *Songs of the Wobblies*. Collector Records 1927.*

Harry McClintock. *Haywire Mac*. Folkways FD5272.*

Utah Phillips. 1981. *We Have Fed You All a Thousand Years*. Philo 1076.*

Joe Hill

—. 1984. *Rebel Voices: Songs of the IWW*. Flying Fish/Rounder Records.*
—. *Making Speech Free*. Philadelphia IWW.*
—, and Ani DiFranco. 1996. *The Past Didn't Go Anywhere*. Righteous Babe.*
—, and Ani DiFranco. 1999. *Fellow Workers*. Righteous Babe.*
Paul Robeson. 1990. *Freedom Songs*. Topic Records TOP 62.
Earl Robinson.1970. *Strange, Unusual Evening: A Musical Tribute to the Life & Work of Walter Reuther*. Santa Barbara: UAW Western Region Six.
Various Artists. 1990. *Don't Mourn, Organize: Songs of Labor Songwriter Joe Hill*. Smithsonian/Folkways.*

The Struggle Continues

INDEX

Joe Hill

Blake, William, 25, 34, 309, 317, 380, 443, 453, 457, 510, 515, 528, 546, 574
Bliss, Philip, 105
Block, Lawrence, 420
Block, Mr (comic strip by Ernest Riebe), 57, 62n, 185-186, 258, 396, 498, 511
Blues, 1, 259, 486-487, 515, 523-524
Bobo (IWW member), 80, 86
Bodenheim, Max, 141, 469
Bogard, Thomas, 247, 289
Boggs, James, 401
Boni, Albert, 62
Boose, Arthur, 205, 311
Borah, Sen. William, 401
Borel, Petrus, 470, 534
Bosch, Hieronymus, 523
Botkin, B. A., 252
Boudin, Louis B., 467
Bourne, Randolph, 417, 466
Bowen, George C., 63
Bowie, Lester, 584
Boyd, Neva, 509, 516
Boykin, David, 172
Bragg, Billy, 152, 153, 154, 573
Braznier, Richard, 5, 32, 37, 41, 53, 54, 55, 60, 63, 66, 72, 153, 174, 191, 192, 202, 213, 214, 215, 216, 217, 254, 267, 300, 326, 384, 439, 447, 450, 452, 471, 483, 490, 511, 512
Brennan, Frederick Hazlitt, 192
Brennan, Robert, 418
Breton, André, 28, 178, 218, 425, 474, 514, 516, 519, 528, 532, 549, 554, 557
Brewer, Gil, 442
Briggs, Cyril, 20
Brill, A. A., 464,
Brill, John, 486, 572
Brisbane, Arthur,
Brissenden, Paul, 389, 416, 437
Brontë, Emily, 510, 523
Brown, Frederic, 442
Brown, Gösta, 122
Brown, John, 199, 253, 255, 256, 309, 330
Brown, Sterling, 65, 234, 528
Brown, William Montgomery, 313
Browning, Elizabeth Barrett, 65
Brundage, Myron "Slim," 399, 407, 408, 409, 413, 426, 469
Bryant, W. C., 380
Buch, Vera, 515—see Weisbord, Vera Buch.
Bughouse Square, 25, 154, 267, 281, 371, 286, 399, 407, 411, 469
Bugs Bunny, 425
Buhle, Paul, 19, 20, 587, 590n1,
Bukharin, Nikolai, 233, 362
Burke, Fielding—See Dargan, Olive Tilford
Burns, Robert, 25, 129, 181, 199, 337, 380, 381, 444, 445, 483, 528, 546
Burroughs, Edgar Rice, 340
Busck, Harry, 411
Byron, Lord George Gordon, 515, 525

Cabral, Amilcar, 380, 508
Calamity Jane, 143
Calas, Nicolas, 545
Caldwell, Erskine, 376
Calmer, Alan, 200, 376, 438
Camp, Helen, 304

Cannon, James P., 217, 319, 354, 370, 371, 417, 437, 445
Capone, Alphonse, 344
Cardullo, Rose, 276
Carew, Jan, 458, 505
Carnevali, Emmanuel, 469, 562
Carney, Jack, 388, 406
Carpenter, Ethel, 277
Carrington, Leonora, 543
Carroll, Lewis, 534, 554
Carter, Charles, 224
Carter, Charlotte, 412
Carter, Pres. Jimmy, 576
Castoriadis, Cornelius, 401
Catlin, George, 517
Caughey, Walter, 420
Cayton, Horace, 315, 416
Cedervall, Frank, 403
Centralia Conspiracy, 15, 359, 386, 466
Chance, William, 43, 86, 217, 563, 565, 566-567
Chandler, Harry, 86, 261, 262, 270
Channing, William Ellery, 313, 574
Chaplin, Charlie, 168, 465
Chaplin, Edith, 385
Chaplin, Ralph, 19, 36il, 39-43, 45-47, 53, 66, 70, 74, 75, 79, 86, 95, 118, 131, 136il, 140, 152, 153, 155il, 157, 158, 165, 175, 177il, 179, 197, 201, 203, 217, 221, 238, 241, 283, 321, 336il, 345, 352, 353, 376, 378, 381, 284, 389, 403, 408, 416, 437, 441, 444, 446, 447, 452, 461, 465, 466, 468, 470, 471, 472, 483, 487il, 499, 511, 521il, 529, 529il, 530, 531, 532, 534, 551, 558, 561, 563, 572, 573
Charpentier, Gustave, 496
Chellman, John, 74
Child, George B., 72, 125, 126, 137
Child, Lydia Maria, 309
China, Chinese, and IWW, 47, 96, 97, 186, 223, 227, 234, 235, 244il, 245-251, 252, 253, 265, 282, 433, 469, 470, 471, 555, 573
Chomsky, Noam, 554, 590n1
Chopin, Franz, 147
Christ, Jesus, 199, 311, 331, 332
Chumley, L. Stanford, 42il, 152, 158, 203, 406, 407
Citashe, I.W.W., 441
City Lights Bookstore, 411-412, 427
CNT, 26
Cohen, Sophie, 285, 499
Cole, James Kelly, 65, 444, 452
Coleman, Emily Holmes, 329
Coleridge, Samuel T., 546
College of Complexes, 400, 407-409, 413, 520n
Collier, Simone, 412
Comer, Ethel, 283
Committee for Non-Violent Action (CNVA), 493
Commons, John R., 233
Communist Party, 14, 19-21, 24, 26-27, 28-29, 31, 32, 35n5, 67, 102, 200, 204, 210n2, 227, 235-236, 242, 243n1, 280, 282, 294, 297, 331, 364il, 365-374, 375-478, 379, 381, 390, 398, 399, 437, 442, 451, 472, 474, 503, 515, 581, 584
Confederación Nacional del Trabajadores (CNT), 26
Congress of Racial Equality (CORE), 403, 425
Conlin, Joseph, 17

Index

Connolly, James, 467
Conrad, Joseph, 505
Conroy, Jack, 376, 408, 472, 553
Cook, Bruce, 430
Cook, George W., 40
Cooper, Anna Julia, 234
Cooper, Wayne, 67
Corder, Minnie, 295, 403, 492, 565, 567
Corder, Raymond, 295
CORE, 425
Coria, Pedro, 78
Corso, Gregory, 407
Cortez, Alfredo, 442
Cortez, Carlos, 3, 18,150, 152, 157, 238, 264*il*, 271*il*, 305*il*, 385, 408, 423n, 441, 442, 452, 472, 594*il*
Cortez, Jayne, 395
Costello, E. J., 531
Coughlin, Father, 270
Coxey, Jacob, 49, 469
Crevel, René, 141
Crocker, Donald M., 369, 448
Cronyn, George W., 243, 518
Crosby, Bing, 504
Cuban Revolution (1959), 568
Curtis, Eva, 283
Curtis, Joseph A., 121
Curtis, Natalie, 243
Cushing, Frank Hamilton, 243

Dada, 31, 406, 464, 469, 473
Dahl, Ester, 49-52, 119, 167, 183, 206, 213
Dalby, David, 395
Dana, Charles A., 411
Dante, 533
Dargan, Olive Tilford, 417
Darrow, Clarence, 224, 313, 349, 422, 469
Darwin, Charles, 233
Das, Taraknath, 469
Davis, Joseph, 384
Davis, Mike, 260, 262, 590n1
Davis, Stuart, 464
Dawson, Manierre, 495
Day, Dorothy, 279, 329, 330, 331
De Caux, Len, 370
de Cleyre, Voltairine, 65, 67, 313, 445
Debs, Eugene V., 2, 8, 101, 128, 233, 282, 389, 406, 407, 417, 460, 483, 546
deFord, Miriam Allen, 417
Dehorn Squad, 152
Delaney, Martin R., 234
DeLeon, Daniel, 15, 35n, 54, 109, 581
Dell, Floyd, 34, 54, 343, 407, 417, 455, 464, 478, 515, 560, 562, 579
Dellinger, Dave, 400, 590n1
Demuth, Charles, 464
Dennis, John, 384
Diaz, Porfirio, 77, 78, 79
Dickens, Charles, 233, 446, 581
Dickens, Hazel, 152, 293, 511
Dietzgen, Joseph, 233, 372
DiFranco, Ani, 152, 584
Dil Pickle Club, 25, 248, 267, 406, 408, 411, 446, 452, 454, 464, 469, 470
Dilling, Elizabeth, 270
Dinsmoor, S. P., 423
Diop, Chiekh Anta, 421

Dirks, Rudolf, 163
Dodge, Mabel, 464, 466, 564
Doehrer, Chuck, 414
Dolgoff, Esther, 403, 420
Dolgoff, Sam, 54, 313, 403, 420, 552
Doran, J. T. (Red), 19, 206, 369, 491-492
Doree, Edward F., 14, 131, 225*il*, 258, 544
Dorgan, Thomas A. "Tad," 163
Dos Passos, John, 203, 323, 407, 417, 442
Douglas, William O., 265, 362
Douglass, Frederick, 228, 234, 271, 309, 230
Dowell, E. F., 111
Downing, Hardy, 105
Downing, Mortimer, 86, 237, 249, 250, 411, 448
Drake, Hamid, 172
Drake, St Clair, 315, 425
Dreiser, Theodore, 376, 526, 562
Drinnon, Richard, 516, 517
Du Bois, W. E. B., 224, 234, 271, 485, 516, 538
Dubofsky, Melvyn, 13, 14, 15, 77, 114, 211, 213, 218, 309
Ducasse, Isidore (Comte de Lautréamont), 145, 195, 425, 519, 523
Duchamp, Marcel, 141, 472, 473, 554
Dunayevskaya, Raya, 401
Dunbar, Paul Laurence, 234
Dunbar, Robin, 202
Dunbar-Ortiz, Roxanne, 316, 590n1
Duncan, Isadora, 468, 514, 515, 516
Duncan, Raymond, 468
Dunifer, Stephen, 586
Dunne, Vincent R., 217, 371
Dürer, Albrecht, 523
Dylan, Bob, 153, 478

Earth First!, 379, 380, 390, 391, 424*il*, 506, 585, 588
Eastman, Crystal, 296, 369, 464
Eastman, Max, 64, 172, 417, 445, 464, 473
Ebert, Justus, 19, 26, 104, 255, 352, 369, 448, 496, 572, 578
Edwards, Herb, 217, 403
Eisenstein, Sergei, 526
Ekberg, Anita, 73
Ellington, Duke, 183
Ellington, Richard, 420, 568, 582
Ellis, Clifford B., 206
Ellis, Frank, 238
Ellison, Ralph, 502, 509
Emerson, Laura Payne, 66, 80, 277, 283, 300, 317, 447, 452, 572
Emerson, Ralph Waldo, 482, 564
Engdahl, J. Louis, 437
Engels, Friedrich, 23, 233, 380, 508
Engle, Phil, 126
Equi, Marie, 278, 281, 285, 296, 301
Ernst, Max, 500
Ervin, Lorenzo Komboa, 590n1
Eselius brothers, 74
Eskin, Sam, 95
Ettor, Joe, 26, 89, 205, 214, 217, 255, 311, 442, 448, 496, 571
Everest, Wesley, 147, 202, 221, 237, 359, 417
Everett Massacre, 284, 359, 430, 431, 448
Eyerman, Ron, 438

Faegre, Tor, 178

Index

Index

Index

Index

About PM Press

PM Press was founded at the end of 2007 by a small collection of folks with decades of publishing, media, and organizing experience. PM Press co-conspirators have published and distributed hundreds of books, pamphlets, CDs, and DVDs. Members of PM have founded enduring book fairs, spearheaded victorious tenant organizing campaigns, and worked closely with bookstores, academic conferences, and even rock bands to deliver political and challenging ideas to all walks of life. We're old enough to know what we're doing and young enough to know what's at stake.

Contact us for direct ordering and questions about all PM Press releases, as well as manuscript submissions, review copy requests, foreign rights sales, author interviews, to book an author for an event, and to have PM Press attend your bookfair:

PM Press ✦ PO Box 23912 ✦ Oakland, CA 94623
510-658-3906 ✦ info@pmpress.org

Buy books and stay on top of what we are doing at:

www.pmpress.org

 # About Between the Lines

Founded in 1977, Between the Lines publishes books that support social change and justice. Our goal is not private gain, nor are we owned by a faceless conglomerate. We are cooperatively run by our employees and a small band of volunteers who share a tenacious belief in books, authors, and ideas that break new ground.

Between the Lines books present new ideas and challenge readers to rethink the world around them. Our authors offer analysis of historical events and contemporary issues not often found in the mainstream. We specialize in informative, non-fiction books on politics and public policy, social issues, history, international development, gender and sexuality, critical race issues, culture, adult and popular education, labour and work, environment, technology, and media.

"Who is your leader?"

We create high-quality books that promote equitable social change, and we reflect our mission in the way our organization is structured. BTI has no bosses, no owners. It's the product of what some would likely describe as "sixties idealism"—what we call political principles. Our small office staff and Editorial Committee make decisions—from what to publish to how to run the place—by consensus. Our Editorial Committee includes a number of original and long-time members, as well as several younger academics and community activists eager to carry on the publishing work started by the generation before them.

www.btlbooks.com